THE WEST

Key Eras in the Transformation of the West

Map 1   Roman Empire at Its Greatest Extent, ca. 117 c.e.
Western civilization has undergone many transformations throughout its history. When the Roman Empire was at its greatest extent, the basic intellectual, religious, political, and geographic outlines of what we call the West today were drawn.

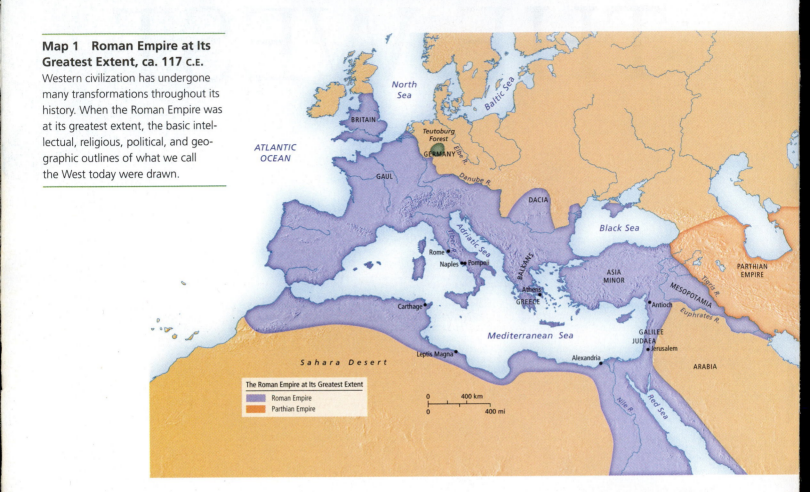

The Roman Empire at Its Greatest Extent
- Roman Empire
- Parthian Empire

0   400 km
0   400 mi

Map 2   Carolingian Empire
During the Carolingian Empire, Europe experienced greater political cohesion, as the Carolingian armies successfully reunified most of the western European territories of the ancient Roman Empire, distinguishing it from the Byzantine Empire in the east.

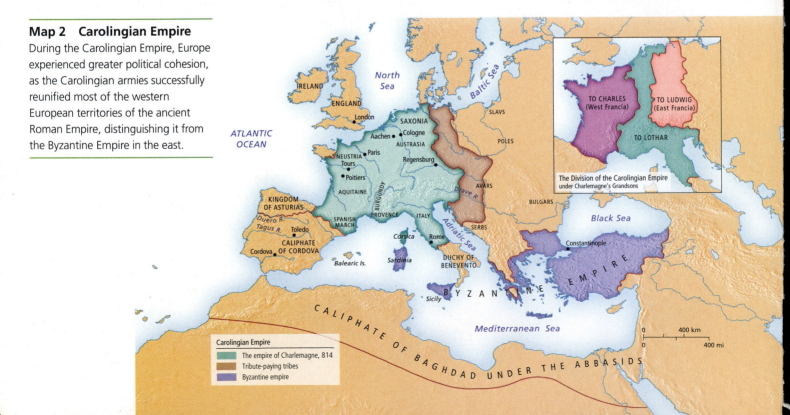

The Division of the Carolingian Empire under Charlemagne's Grandsons

Carolingian Empire
- The empire of Charlemagne, 814
- Tribute-paying tribes
- Byzantine empire

0   400 km
0   400 mi

Map 3   Europe After the Congress of Vienna, 1815

The major European powers re-drew the map of Europe with the Congress of Vienna in 1815 after the defeat of Napoleon. This map shows the dismantlement of the massive empire France had acquired under his leadership.

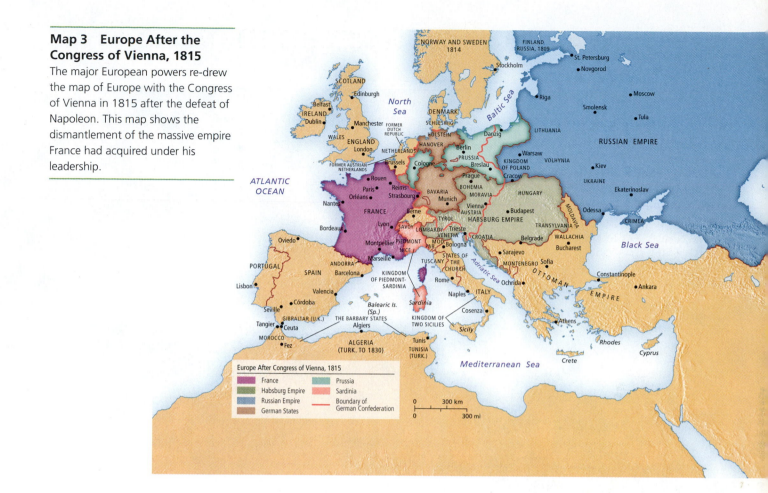

Europe After Congress of Vienna, 1815

- France
- Habsburg Empire
- Russian Empire
- German States
- Prussia
- Sardinia
- Boundary of German Confederation

Map 4   Europe After World War I

The map of Europe changed dramatically after World War I with the collapse of the old authoritarian empires and the creation of independent nation-states in eastern Europe. What neither Map 3 nor Map 4 can show, however, is the expansion of "the West" beyond European borders to embrace cultures on other continents, including Australia, Africa, and North America.

Europe and the Middle East After World War I

- To Great Britain
- To France
- To Italy
- To Rumania
- To Denmark
- To Yugoslavia (Serbia and Montenegro)
- To Belgium
- To Greece
- Became independent
- 1914 boundaries
- New boundaries

THE WEST

Encounters & Transformations

Second Edition

VOLUME A: TO 1550

Brian Levack
University of Texas at Austin

Edward Muir
Northwestern University

Meredith Veldman
Louisiana State University

Michael Maas
Rice University

PEARSON

Longman

New York   San Francisco   Boston
London   Toronto   Sydney   Tokyo   Singapore   Madrid
Mexico City   Munich   Paris   Cape Town   Hong Kong   Montreal

Senior Acquisitions Editor: Janet Lanphier
Senior Development Editor: David B. Kear
Executive Marketing Manager: Sue Westmoreland
Supplements Editor: Kristi Olson
Media Editor: Melissa Edwards
Production Manager: Donna DeBenedictis
Project Coordination, Text Design, and Electronic Page Makeup:
    Elm Street Publishing Services, Inc.
Cover Designer/Manager: John Callahan
Cover and Frontispiece Art: Meeting of peasants and tradesmen. Illustration of Aristotle's
    Politics, translated into French by Nicolas Oresme. 15th century. Ms Fr. 22500, F01. 174 v.
    Location: Bibliothèque Nationale, Paris, France. Photo Credit: Shark/Art Resouce, NY.
Cartography: Maps.com
Photo Researcher: Photosearch, Inc.
Manufacturing Buyer: Roy L. Pickering, Jr.
Printer and Binder: Quebecor World Versailles
Cover Printer: Coral Graphic Services, Inc.

Library of Congress Cataloging-in-Publication Data

The West : encounters & transformations / Brian Levack . . . [et al.].
    2nd ed.
        p. cm.
    Includes bibliographical references and index.
    ISBN 0-321-36404-X
    1. Civilization, Western—History—Textbooks.   I. Levack, Brian P.

CB245.W456 2007
909'.09821—dc22

2005032587

Please visit us at http://www.ablongman.com/levack2e

ISBN 0-321-36404-X (single-volume edition)
ISBN 0-321-36405-8 (volume I)
ISBN 0-321-38413-X (volume II)
ISBN 0-321-38414-8 (volume A)
ISBN 0-321-38415-6 (volume B)
ISBN 0-321-36403-1 (volume C)

1 2 3 4 5 6 7 8 9 10—QWV—09 08 07 06

Brief Contents

Detailed Contents

11 The Italian Renaissance and Beyond: The Politics of Culture 342

The Cradle of the Renaissance: The Italian City-States 344

Documents

Maps

Features

Chronologies

Preface

We wrote this textbook to answer questions about the identity of the civilization in which we live. Journalists, politicians, and scholars often refer to our civilization, its political ideologies, its economic systems, and its cultures as "Western" without fully considering what that label means and why it might be appropriate. The classification of our civilization as Western has become particularly problematic in the age of globalization. The creation of international markets, the rapid dissemination of ideas on a global scale, and the transmission of popular culture from one country to another often make it difficult to distinguish what is Western from what is not. *The West: Encounters & Transformations* offers students a history of Western civilization in which these issues of Western identity are given prominence. Our goal is neither to idealize nor to indict that civilization but to describe its main characteristics in different historical periods.

The West: Encounters & Transformations gives careful consideration to two basic questions. The first is, how did the definition of the West change over time? In what ways did its boundaries shift and how did the distinguishing characteristics of its cultures change? The second question is, by what means did the West—and the idea of the West—develop? We argue that the West is the product of a series of cultural encounters that occurred both outside and within its geographical boundaries. We explore these encounters and the transformations they produced by detailing the political, social, religious, and cultural history of the regions that have been, at one time or another, a part of the West.

Defining the West

What is the West? How did it come into being? How has it developed throughout history? Many textbooks take for granted which regions or peoples of the globe constitute the West. They treat the history of the West as a somewhat expanded version of European history. While not disputing the centrality of Europe to any definition of the West, we contend that the West is not only a geographical realm with ever-shifting boundaries but also a cultural realm, an area of cultural influence extending beyond the geographical and political boundaries of Europe. We so strongly believe in this notion that we have written the essay "What Is the West?" to encourage students to think about their understanding of Western civilization and to guide their understanding of each chapter. Many of the features of what we call Western civilization originated in regions that are not geographically part of Europe (such as northern Africa and the Middle East), while ever since the fifteenth century various social, ethnic, and political groups from non-European regions (such as North and South America, eastern Russia, Australia, New Zealand, and South Africa) have identified themselves, in one way or another, with the West. Throughout the text, we devote considerable attention to the boundaries of the West and show how borderlines between cultures have been created, especially in eastern and southeastern Europe.

Considered as a geographical and cultural realm, "the West" is a term of recent origin, and the civilization to which it refers did not become clearly defined until the eleventh century, especially during the Crusades, when western European Christians developed a distinct cultural identity. Before that time we can only talk about the powerful forces that created the West, especially the dynamic interaction of the civilizations of western Europe, the Byzantine Empire, and the Muslim world.

Over the centuries Western civilization has acquired many salient characteristics. These include two of the world's great legal systems (civil law and common law), three of the world's monotheistic religions (Judaism, Christianity, and Islam), certain political and social philosophies, forms of political organization (such as the modern bureaucratic state and democracy), methods of scientific inquiry, systems of economic organization (such as industrial capitalism), and distinctive styles of art, architecture, and music. At times one or more of these characteristics has served as a primary source of Western identity: Christianity in the Middle Ages, science and rationalism during the Enlightenment, industrialization in the nineteenth and twentieth centuries, and a defense of individual liberty and democracy in the late twentieth century. These sources of Western identity, however, have always been challenged and contested, both when they were coming into prominence and when they appeared to be most triumphant. Western culture has never been monolithic, and even today references to the West imply a wide range of meanings.

Cultural Encounters

The definition of the West is closely related to the central theme of our book, which is the process of cultural encounters. Throughout *The West: Encounters & Transformations,* we examine the West as a product of a series of cultural encounters both outside the West and within it. We show that the West originated and developed through a continuous process of inclusion and exclusion resulting from a series of encounters among and within different groups. These encounters can be described in a general sense as external, internal, or ideological.

External Encounters

External encounters took place between peoples of different civilizations. Before the emergence of the West as a clearly defined entity, external encounters occurred between such diverse peoples as Greeks and Phoenicians, Macedonians and Egyptians, and Romans and Celts. After the eleventh century, external encounters between Western and non-Western peoples occurred mainly during periods of European exploration, expansion, and imperialism. In the sixteenth and seventeenth centuries, for example, a series of external encounters took place between Europeans on the one hand and Africans, Asians, and the indigenous people of the Americas on the other. Two chapters of *The West: Encounters & Transformations* (Chapters 12 and 17) and a large section of a third (Chapter 23) explore these external encounters in depth and discuss how they affected Western and non-Western civilizations alike.

Internal Encounters

Our discussion of encounters also includes similar interactions between different social groups *within* Western countries. These internal encounters often took place between dominant and subordinate groups, such as between lords and peasants, rulers and subjects, men and women, factory owners and workers, masters and slaves. Encounters between those who were educated and those who were illiterate, which recur frequently throughout Western history, also fall into this category. Encounters just as often took place between different religious and political groups, such as between Christians and Jews, Catholics and Protestants, and royal absolutists and republicans.

Ideological Encounters

Ideological encounters involve interaction between comprehensive systems of thought, most notably religious doctrines, political philosophies, and scientific theories about the nature of the world. These ideological conflicts usually arose out of internal encounters, when various groups within Western societies subscribed to different theories of government or rival religious faiths. The encounters between Christianity and polytheism in the early Middle Ages, between liberalism and conservatism in the nineteenth century, and between fascism and communism in the twentieth century were ideological encounters. Some ideological encounters had an external dimension, such as when the forces of Islam and Christianity came into conflict during the Crusades and when the Cold War developed between Soviet communism and Western democracy in the second half of the twentieth century.

* * *

The West: Encounters & Transformations illuminates the variety of these encounters and clarifies their effects. By their very nature encounters are interactive, but they have taken different forms: they have been violent or peaceful, coercive or cooperative. Some have resulted in the imposition of Western ideas on areas outside the geographical boundaries of the West or the perpetuation of the dominant culture within Western societies. More often than not, however, encounters have resulted in a more reciprocal process of exchange in which both Western and non-Western cultures or the values of both dominant and subordinate groups have undergone significant transformation. Our book not only identifies these encounters but also discusses their significance by returning periodically to the issue of Western identity.

Coverage

The West: Encounters & Transformations offers both balanced coverage of political, social, and culture history and a broader coverage of the West and the world.

Balanced Coverage

Our goal throughout the text has been to provide balanced coverage of political, social, and cultural history and to include significant coverage of religious and military history as well. Political history defines the basic structure of the book, and some chapters, such as those on the Hellenistic world, the age of confessional divisions, absolutism and state building, the French Revolution, and the coming of mass politics, include sustained political narratives. Because we understand the West to be a cultural as well as a geographical realm, we give a prominent position to cultural history. Thus we include rich sections on Hellenistic philosophy and literature, the cultural environment of the Italian Renaissance, the creation of a new political culture at the time of the French Revolution, and the atmosphere of cultural despair and desire that prevailed in Europe after World War I. We also devote special attention to religious history, including the history of Islam as well as that of Christianity and Judaism. Unlike many other textbooks, our coverage of religion continues into the modern period.

The West: Encounters & Transformations also provides extensive coverage of the history of women and gender. Wherever possible the history of women is integrated into the broader social, cultural, and political history of the period. But there are also separate sections on women in our chapters on classical Greece, the Renaissance, the Reformation, the Enlightenment, the Industrial Revolution, World War I, World War II, and the postwar era.

The West and the World

Our book provides broad geographical coverage. Because the West is the product of a series of encounters, the external areas with which the West interacted are of major importance. Three chapters deal specifically with the West and the world.

- Chapter 12, "The West and the World: The Significance of Global Encounters, 1450–1650"
- Chapter 17, "The West and the World: Empire, Trade, and War, 1650–1815"
- Chapter 23, "The West and the World: Cultural Crisis and the New Imperialism, 1870–1914"

These chapters present substantial material on sub-Saharan Africa, Latin America, the Middle East, India, and East Asia. Our text is also distinctive in its coverage of eastern Europe and the Muslim world, areas that have often been considered outside the boundaries of the West. These regions were arenas within which significant cultural encounters took place. Finally we include material on the United States and Australia, both of which have become part of the West. We recognize that most American college and university students have the opportunity to study American history as a separate subject, but treatment of the United States as a Western nation provides a different perspective from that usually given in courses on American history. For example, this book treats America's revolution as one of four Atlantic revolutions, its national unification in the nineteenth century as part of a broader western European development, its pattern of industrialization as related to that of Britain, and its central role in the Cold War as part of an ideological encounter that was global in scope.

Organization

The chronological and thematic organization of our book conforms in its broad outline to the way in which Western civilization courses are generally taught. We have limited the number of chapters to twenty-eight, in an effort to make the book more compatible with the traditional American semester calendar and to solve the frequent complaint that there is not enough time to cover all the material in the course. However, our organization differs from other books in some significant ways:

- Chapter 2, which covers the period from ca. 1600 to 550 B.C.E., is the first in a Western civilization textbook to examine the International Bronze Age and its aftermath as a period important in its own right because it saw the creation of expansionist, multi-ethnic empires linked by trade and diplomacy.
- In Chapter 4 the Roman Republic, in keeping with contemporary scholarship, has been incorporated into a discussion of the Hellenistic world, dethroned slightly to emphasize how it was one of many competing Mediterranean civilizations.
- Chapter 12 covers the first period of European expansion, from 1450 to 1650. It examines the new European encounters with the civilizations of sub-Saharan Africa, the Americas, and East Asia. By paying careful attention to the characteristics of these civilizations before the arrival of the Europeans, we show how this encounter affected indigenous peoples as well as Europeans.
- Chapter 16 is devoted entirely to the Scientific Revolution of the seventeenth century in order to emphasize the central importance of this development in the creation of Western identity.
- Chapter 17, which covers the second period of European expansion, from 1650 to 1815, studies the growth of European empires, the beginning of global warfare, and encounters between Europeans and the peoples of Asia and Africa. It treats the Atlantic revolutions of the late eighteenth and early nineteenth centuries, including

the American Revolution, as episodes in the history of European empires rather than as revolts inspired mainly by national sentiment.

- Chapter 26 not only offers a comprehensive examination of World War II, but also explores the moral fissure in the history of the West created, in very different ways, by the Holocaust and the aerial bombings of civilian centers that culminated in the use of the atomic bomb in August 1945.
- Chapter 28, "The West in the Contemporary Era: New Encounters and Transformations," includes an extended discussion of the emergence of European Islamic communities and the resulting transformations in both European and Islamic identities.

What's New in this Edition?

In preparing the second edition of *The West: Encounters & Transformations* we have focused on two goals: to make the textbook more teachable and to strengthen our emphasis on the encounters that have transformed the West.

Organization

We have reduced the number of chapters from twenty-nine to twenty-eight, in order to make the book even more compatible with the typical fifteen-week semester. In a number of chapters, moreover, we have made significant rearrangements of material:

- In Chapter 3, we have discussed the Persian Empire before beginning our study of Hebrew and Greek civilizations to emphasize the argument that the latter two civilizations emerged in a political world dominated by Persia.
- Chapters 6 through 9, which deal with the period from about 300 to 1300 C.E., have been rearranged along more thematic, less chronological lines. We have adopted this strategy to emphasize the importance of the interactions among different religious communities during a period that was crucial to the development of Christianity and Islam.
- Chapter 17, "The West and the World: Empire, Trade, and War, 1650–1815," which appeared as Chapter 19 in the first edition, has been placed earlier in the book because it is concerned mainly with eighteenth-century developments. It now precedes the discussion of eighteenth-century society and culture.
- In Chapter 22, "The Coming of Mass Politics: Industrialization, Emancipation, and Instability, 1870–1914," we have replaced the "nation-by-nation" narrative with a thematic approach that more effectively conveys the processes by which European elites sought both to capitalize on and control the new forces of popular nationalism.
- Our treatment of both the Holocaust and the decision to use atomic bombs against Japan, which appeared as a separate chapter in the first edition, is now embedded in Chapter 26, "World War II." This volume still includes a far more extensive and in-depth exploration of these developments than any other Western civilization textbook.
- New sections on "Postwar Nationalism, Westernization, and the Islamic Challenge" in Chapter 25, and "Islam, Terrorism, and European Identity" in Chapter 28 are the most striking examples of our decision to give more coverage to Islam throughout the book.

New Feature: "Encounters & Transformations"

We have introduced a new feature, "Encounters & Transformations," in about half the chapters. These essays reinforce the main theme of the book by giving specific examples of the ways in which cultural encounters changed the perception and identity of the West.

Features and Pedagogical Aids

In writing this textbook we have endeavored to keep both the student reader and the classroom instructor in mind at all times. The text includes the following features and pedagogical aids, all of which are intended to support the themes of the book.

What Is the West?

MANY OF THE PEOPLE WHO INFLUENCE PUBLIC OPINION—POLITI-cians, teachers, clergy, journalists, and television commentators—refer to "Western values," "the West," and "Western civilization." They often use these terms as if they do not require explanation. But what *do* these terms mean? The West has always been an arena within which different cultures, religions, values, and philosophies have interacted, and any definition of the West will inevitably arouse controversy.

The most basic definition of the West is of a place. Western civilization is now typically thought to comprise the regions of Europe, the Americas, Australia, and New Zealand. However, this is a contemporary definition of the West. The inclusion of these places in the West is the result of a long history of European expansion through colonization. In addition to being a place, Western civilization also encompasses a cultural history—a tradition stretching back thousands of years to the ancient world. Over this long period the civilization we now identify as Western gradually took shape. The

"What Is the West?"

The West: Encounters & Transformations begins with an essay to engage students in the task of defining the West and to introduce them to the notion of cultural encounters. "What Is the West?" guides students through the text by providing a framework for understanding how the West was shaped. Structured around the six questions of What? When? Where? Who? How? and Why?, this framework encourages students to think about their understanding of Western civilization. The essay serves as a blueprint for using this textbook.

NEW! "Encounters & Transformations"

These features, which appear in about half the chapters, illustrate the main theme of the book by identifying specific encounters and showing how they led to significant transformations in the culture of the West. These features show, for example, how encounters among nomadic tribes of Arabia led to the rapid spread of Islam; how the Mayas' interpretation of Christian symbols transformed European Christianity into a hybrid religion; how the importation of chocolate from the New World to Europe changed Western consumption patterns and the rhythms of the Atlantic economy; and how Picasso's encounter with African art led to the transformation of modernism. Each of these essays concludes with a question for discussion.

Encounters & Transformations

Ships of the Desert: Camels from Morocco to Central Asia

A remarkable thing happened when the Arab followers of the dynamic new religion of Islam encountered the humble beast of burden the camel. The camel helped make Arab armies lethal in battle, which meant that the message of Islam spread rapidly through conquest. In addition the caravan trade that transported goods on the backs of camels brought the Arabs into contact with a vast stretch of the world from Spain to China. In the exchanges that took place along the caravan routes, Islamic religious ideas were widely disseminated, and Arab merchants gained access to a lucrative trade that enriched Muslim cities. The success of the caravan trade changed the very appearance of large parts of the West by making obsolete the old Roman roads and the shipping lanes that had unified the Mediterranean, Europe, and North Africa in the ancient world. Narrow camel tracks replaced roads; oases and cities along the caravan routes supplanted ports in economic significance.

Before Muhammad began to recite, the camel had already transformed the life of Arabia. Camels were highly efficient beasts of burden, especially in arid regions, because of their bodies' capacity to conserve water. Able to drink as much as twenty-eight gallons at a time, camels can last four to nine days without water and travel great distances in this period. The fat in their humps allows camels to survive for even longer without food. As pack animals, camels are more efficient than carts pulled by animals because they can traverse roadless rough terrain and cross rivers without bridges. They require fewer people to manage them on a journey than do wheeled vehicles.

Arab fighters were especially menacing because they developed the "North Arabian saddle" that let them ride the one-humped Arabian camel with comfort in battle. The new saddle required only one rider who could grasp the camel's reins with one hand while slashing downward at enemy troops with a sword in his other hand. Warriors on camels could attack infantry with speed and crushing force. By 300 C.E., camel-breeding Arab tribesmen, empowered by their new military technology, inaugurated the "Caravan Age." The Arabs seized control of the lucrative spice trade routes and became an economic, military, and political force by exploiting and guarding the wealth of the caravans.

After Muhammad established his community in Mecca, Islam literally "took off" on camelback. Tribesmen on camels proved an unstoppable force as they spread Islam first throughout Arabia and the Middle East, and then with lightning speed across North Africa into Spain and Central Asia. Camels played a significant role in the expanding Islamic economy because they made long-distance trade extremely profitable. The transformations the camel brought were most evident in the former

Roman provinces wh[...] mous Roman roads h[...] primary conduit of la[...] Thousands of miles c[...] nected the provinces[...] Empire and let troop[...] from one front to and[...] ever, camels changed[...] Because these "ships[...] do not need paved r[...] routes did not have t[...] Roman road systems,[...] chants bypassed then[...] New trade routes acr[...] and other harsh terra[...] to camels quickly de[...] Morocco to Central A[...] astonishing conseque[...] 700 paved roads start[...] pear. Because camels[...] walk on narrow path[...] streets and wide mar[...] carts and wagons tha[...] Greek and Roman cit[...] use. Bazaars with nar[...] lanes appropriate to [...] sprung up to replace [...] and wheeled vehicle[...] peared in these lands[...] just roads and the sh[...] that changed. There [...] consequences as wel[...] caravan traffic reache[...] China, bringing Chin[...] Chinese ideas to the [...]

Question for D[...]
How might the history [...] have differed had not [...] replaced the system of [...]

The Camel Caravan
This modern photograph shows a string of camels cross-

Focus Questions

The introduction to each chapter includes a statement of the main question that the entire chapter addresses. It also includes a set of questions that the individual sections of the chapter seek to answer. Each of these questions is then repeated at the beginning of the relevant section of the chapter. The reason for this strategy is to remind the student that the purpose of studying history is not only to learn what happened in the past but also to explain and interpret the course of events. This pedagogical strategy reinforces the approach that the essay, "What is the West?," introduces at the beginning of the book.

"Justice in History"

Found in every chapter, this feature presents a historically significant trial or episode in which different notions of justice (or injustice) were debated and resolved. The "Justice in History" features illustrate cultural encounters within communities as they try to determine the fate of individuals from all walks of life. Many famous trials dealt with conflicts over basic religious, philosophical, or political values, such as those of Socrates, Jesus, Joan of Arc, Charles I, Galileo, and Adolf Eichmann. Other "Justice in History" features show how judicial institutions, such as the ordeal, the Inquisition, and revolutionary tribunals, handled adversarial situations in different societies. These essays, therefore, illustrate the way in which the basic values of the West have evolved through attempts to resolve disputes, contention, and conflict.

Each "Justice in History" feature includes two pedagogical aids. "Questions of Justice" helps students explore the historical significance of the episode just examined. These questions can also be used in classroom discussion or as student essay topics. "Taking It Further" provides the student with a few references that can be consulted in connection with a research project.

"The Human Body in History"

Found in about half of the chapters, these features show that the human body, which many people tend to understand solely as a product of biology, also has a history. These essays reveal that the ways in which various religious and political groups have represented the body in art and literature, clothed it, treated it medically, and abused it tell a great deal about the history of Western culture. These features include essays on the classical nude male body, the signs of disease during the Black Death, bathing the body in the East and the West, and the contraceptive pill. Concluding each essay is a single question for discussion that directs students back to the broader issues with which the chapter deals.

Primary Source Documents

In each chapter we have presented a number of excerpts from primary source documents—from "Tales of the Flood" to "Darwin's 'Descent of Man'"—in order to reinforce or expand upon the points made in the text and to introduce students to the basic materials of historical research.

Maps and Illustrations

Artwork is a key component of our book. We recognize that many students often lack a strong familiarity with geography, and so we have taken great care to develop maps that help sharpen their geographic skills. Complementing the book's standard map program,

Justice in History

The Trial of Joan of Arc

After only fifteen months as the inspiration of the French army, Joan of Arc fell into the hands of the English, who brought her to trial for witchcraft. The English needed to stage a kind of show trial to demonstrate to their own demoralized forces that Joan's remarkable victories were the result not of military superiority but rather of witchcraft. In the English trial, conducted at Rouen in 1431, Joan testified that her mission to save France was in response to voices she heard that commanded her to wear men's clothing. On the basis of this evidence of a confused or double gender identity, the ecclesiastical tribunal declared her a witch and a relapsed heretic. The court sentenced her to be burned at the stake.

Political motivations governed the 1431 English trial for witchcraft, but Joan's...

distinctions that were alien to her. When they wanted to know if the voices were those of angels or saints, Joan seemed perplexed and responded, "This voice comes from God . . . I am more afraid of failing the voices by saying what is displeasing to them than answering you."[7] The judges kept pushing, asking if the saints or angels had heads, eyes, and hair. Exasperated, Joan simply replied, "I have told you often enough, believe me if you will."

The judges reformulated Joan's words to reflect their own rigid scholastic categories and concluded that her "veneration of the saints seems to partake of idolatry and to proceed from a pact made with devils. These are less divine revelations than lies invented by Joan, suggested or shown to her by the demon in illusive appari-

to prove bad behavior...

The Human Body in History

The Ecstasy of Teresa of Avila: The Body and the Soul

Teresa of Avila (1515–1582, canonized St. Teresa in 1622) eloquently expressed the intimate connection between physical and spiritual experiences that was a common feature of Catholic mysticism. She was a Spanish Carmelite nun whose accounts of her own mystical experiences made her a model for other nuns throughout the world. Filled with religious ardor, she devoted herself to an ascetic regime of self-deprivations so intense that she fell ill and suffered paralysis.

Often afflicted by an intense pain in her side, Teresa reported that an angel had stuck a lance tipped with fire into her heart. This "seraphic vision," which became the subject of Gianlorenzo Bernini's famous sculpture in Santa Maria della Vittoria in Rome (1645–1652), epitomized the Catholic Reformation sensibility of understanding spiritual states through physical feelings. In Teresa's case, her extreme bodily deprivations, paralysis, and intense pain conditioned how she experienced the spiritual side of her nature. Many have seen an erotic character to the vision, which may be true, but the vision best demonstrates a profound psychological awareness that bodily and spiritual sensations cannot be precisely distinguished. As Teresa put it, "it is not bodily pain, but spiritual, though the body has a share in it—indeed, a great share." She described the paralysis of her soul and her body as interconnected: "The soul is unable to do either this or anything else. The entire body contracts and neither arm nor foot can be moved." She then described, in remarkably graphic terms, her repeated vision:

It pleased the Lord that I should

sion. I would see beside me, on my left hand, an angel in bodily form—a type of vision which I am not in the habit of seeing, except very rarely . . . I pleased the Lord that I should see this angel in the following way. He was not tall, but short, and very beautiful, his face so aflame that he appeared to be one of the highest types of angel who seem to be all afire. . . . In his hands I saw a long golden spear and at the end of the iron tip I seemed to see a point of fire. With this he seemed to pierce my heart several times so that it penetrated to my entrails. When he drew it out, I thought he was drawing them out with it and he left me completely afire with a great love for God. The pain was so sharp that it made me utter several moans; and so excessive was the sweetness caused me by this intense pain that one can never wish to lose it, nor will one's soul be content with anything less than God. . . . So sweet are the colloquies of love which pass between the soul and God that if anyone thinks I am lying I be-

seech God, in His give him the same

Visions such as th... difficult to interpret... was going on in tho... quies between Teres... visions with intense... receive divine illumi... tion between her sou... Her sensibility about... relationship between... and spiritual experie... especially pronounc... sixteenth-century Ca... and suffering were u... a form of penance, a... body could play a po... redemptive role in e... tuality. The best way... this world was in bo... because through pai... escaped the temptati... flesh and renounced... tions of the world.

For Discussion

How was pain underst... religious value? What v... around Teresa that mig... preoccupation with pai...

An angel is about to pierce her side with an arrow.

St. Teresa lies su... ness in the air in a swo... a vision.

At that point Oliver Cromwell (1599–1658), the commander in chief of the army and the most prominent member of the Council of State after 1649, had himself proclaimed Protector of England, Scotland, and Ireland. Cromwell had been a leader of the revolution, a zealous Puritan who had provided crucial support for the execution of the king and the establishment of the republic. At the same time, however, Cromwell feared that the Levellers and now the radical Puritans of the Barebones Parliament would destroy the social order. The establishment of the Protectorate, in which Cromwell shared legislative

Allegorical View of Cromwell as Savior of England

litical achievement of their cousin, Louis XIV of... the same time, however, they realized that they c... return to the policies of their father, much less a... of Louis. Neither of them attempted to rule i... without Parliament, as Charles I had. Their mai... was to destroy the independence of Parliament... it with their own supporters and use the pre... weaken the force of the parliamentary statute... they objected.

The main political crisis of Charles II's reig... attempt by a group of members of Parliament,... the Earl of Shaftesbury (1621–1683) and know...

DOCUMENT

John Locke Justifies the Glorious Revolution

John Locke wrote Two Treatises of Government between 1679 and 1682, during the reign of Charles II. The main purpose of the book was to justify armed resistance against Charles, who was pursuing absolutist policies, including attacks on the freedom of the English Parliament. Locke did not publish the Two Treatises, however, until after the Glorious Revolution of 1688. In order to justify that revolution, Locke wrote two new paragraphs, claiming that when a king abandons his responsibility to enforce the law, as James II had when he fled to France in December 1688, the government was dissolved and the people had the right to form a new one, as they had when they offered the crown to William and Mary in February 1689.

There is one more way whereby such a government may be dissolved, and that is when he who has the supreme executive power neglects and abandons that charge, so that the laws already made can no longer be put in execution. This is demonstrably to reduce all to anarchy, and so effectually to dissolve the government. For laws not being made for themselves, but to be by their execution the

bonds of the society, to keep every part of the body in its due place and function, when that totally ceases, government visibly ceases, and the people become a confused multitude, without order or connection. Wh... is no longer the administration of justice, for the s... of men's rights, nor any remaining power within th... munity to direct the force, or provide for the neces... the public, there is certainly no government left. W... laws cannot be executed, it is all one as if there wer... and a government without laws is, I suppose, a my... politics, unconceivable to human capacity, and inc... with human society.

In these and in the like cases, when the governm... dissolved, the people are at liberty to provide for th... selves, by erecting a new legislative, differing from... by the change of persons or form, or both, as they... it most for their safety and good. For the society ca... by the fault of another, lose the native and original... has to preserve itself, which can only be done by a... legislative and a fair and impartial execution of the... made by it.

Source: From Two Treatises of Government by John Lock...

we include maps focusing on areas outside the borders of Western civilization. These maps include a small thumbnail globe that highlights the geographic area under discussion in the context of the larger world. Fine art and photos also tell the story of Western civilization, and we have included more than 350 images to help students visualize the past: the way people lived, the events that shaped their lives, and how they viewed the world around them.

Chronologies and Suggested Readings

Each chapter includes chronological charts and suggested readings. Chronologies outline significant events, such as "The End of World War II," and serve as convenient references for students. Each chapter concludes with an annotated list of suggested readings. These are not scholarly bibliographies aimed at the professor, but suggestions for students who wish to explore a topic in greater depth or to write a research paper. A comprehensive list of suggested readings is available on our book-specific website, www.ablongman.com/levack2e.

Glossary

We have sought to create a work that is accessible to students with little prior knowledge of the basic facts of Western history or geography. Throughout the book we have explained difficult concepts at length. For example, we present in-depth explanations of the concepts of Zoroastrianism, Neoplatonism, Renaissance humanism, the various Protestant denominations of the sixteenth century, capitalism, seventeenth-century absolutism, nineteenth-century liberalism and nationalism, fascism, and modernism. Key concepts such as these are identified in the chapters with a degree symbol (°) and defined as well in the end-of-text Glossary.

MyHistoryLab Icons

Throughout the text, you will see icons that will lead students to additional resources found on MyHistoryLab.com. These resources fall into four categories:

The **document** icon directs students to primary source documents that support the material they are reading in the textbook. In addition, most documents offer headnotes and analysis questions that focus students' reading.

The **image** icon leads students to photos, cartoons, and artwork that relate to the topic they are reading. Most images include a descriptive, contextualized headnote and analysis questions.

The **map** icon refers to maps, many of which are interactive and contain headnotes and questions designed to help students visualize the material they are learning. Printable map activities from Longman's outstanding geography workbooks allow students to interact with maps.

The **video** icon leads students to video clips that focus on the regions, people, or events discussed in the text.

A Note About Dates and Transliterations

In keeping with current academic practice, *The West: Encounters & Transformations* uses B.C.E. (before the common era) and C.E. (common era) to designate dates. We also follow the most current and widely accepted English transliterations of Arabic. *Qur'an*, for example, is used for *Koran; Muslim* is used for *Moslem*. Chinese words appearing in the text for the first time are written in pinyin, followed by the older Wade-Giles system in parentheses.

Supplements

For Qualified College Instructors

Instructor's Resource Manual

0-321-42735-1

In this manual written by Sharon Arnoult, Midwestern State University, each chapter contains a chapter outline, significant themes, learning objectives, lesson enrichment ideas, discussion suggestions, and questions for discussing the primary source documents in the text.

Test Bank

0-321-42731-9

Written by Susan Carrafiello, Wright State University, this supplement contains more than 1,200 multiple-choice and essay questions. All questions are referenced by topic and text page number.

TestGen-EQ Computerized Testing System

0-321-42573-1

This flexible, easy-to-master computerized test bank on a dual-platform CD includes all of the items in the printed test bank and allows instructors to select specific questions, edit existing questions, and add their own items to create exams. Tests can be printed in several different fonts and formats and can include figures, such as graphs and tables.

Companion Website (www.ablongman.com/levack2e)

Instructors can take advantage of the Companion Website that supports this text. The instructor section includes teaching links, downloadable maps, tables, and graphs from the text for use in PowerPoint, PowerPoint lecture outlines, and a link to the Instructor Resource Center.

Instructor Resource Center (IRC) (www.ablongman.com/irc)

Through the Instructor Resource Center, instructors can log into premium online products, browse and download book-specific instructor resources, and receive immediate access and instructions to installing course management content. Instructors who already have access to CourseCompass or Supplements Central can log in to the IRC immediately using their existing login and password. First-time users can register at the Instructor Resource Center welcome page at www.ablongman.com/irc.

MyHistoryLab (www.myhistorylab.com)

MyHistoryLab provides students with an online package complete with the entire electronic textbook and numerous study aids. With several hundred primary sources, many of which are assignable and link to a gradebook, pre- and post-tests that link to a gradebook and result in individualized study plans, videos and images, as well as map workbook activities with gradable quizzes, the site offers students a unique, interactive experience that brings history to life. The comprehensive site also includes a History Bookshelf with fifty of the most commonly assigned books in history classes and a History Toolkit with tutorials and helpful links. Other features include gradable assignments and chapter review materials; a Test Bank; and Research Navigator.

Delivered in CourseCompass, Blackboard, or WebCT, as well as in a non-course-management version, MyHistoryLab is easy to use and flexible. MyHistoryLab is organized according to the table of contents of this textbook. With the course management version, instructors can create a further customized product by adding their own syllabus, content, and assignments, or they can use the materials as presented.

PowerPoint Presentations

These presentations contain PowerPoint slides for each chapter and may include key points and terms for a lecture on the chapter, as well as full-color images of important maps, graphs, and charts. The presentations are available for download from www.ablongman.com/levack2e and www.ablongman.com/irc.

Text-Specific Transparency Set

0-321-42732-7

Instructors can download files with which to make full-color transparency map acetates taken from the text at www.ablongman.com/irc.

History Video Program

Longman offers more than one hundred videos from which qualified adopters can choose. Restrictions apply.

History Digital Media Archive CD-ROM

0-321-14976-9

This CD-ROM contains electronic images, interactive and static maps, and media elements such as video. It is fully customizable and ready for classroom presentation. All images and maps are available in PowerPoint as well.

Discovering Western Civilization Through Maps and Views

0-673-53596-7

Created by Gerald Danzer, University of Illinois at Chicago, and David Buissert, this unique set of 140 full-color acetates contains an introduction to teaching history through maps and a detailed commentary on each transparency. The collection includes cartographic and pictorial maps, views and photos, urban plans, building diagrams, and works of art. Available to qualified college adopters on Longman's Instructor Resource Center (IRC) at www.ablongman.com/irc.

For Students

Study Guide

Volume I: 0-321-42733-5
Volume II: 0-321-42734-3

Containing activities and study aids for every chapter in the text, each chapter of the *Study Guide* written by Carron Fillingim, Louisiana State University, includes a thorough chapter outline; timeline; map exercises; identification, multiple-choice and thought questions; and critical-thinking questions based on primary source documents from the text.

Companion Website (www.ablongman.com/levack2e)

Providing a wealth of resources for students using *The West: Encounters & Transformations,* Second Edition, this Companion Website contains chapter summaries, interactive practice test questions, and Web links for every chapter in the text.

Research Navigator and Research Navigator Guide

0-205-40838-9

Research Navigator is a comprehensive Website comprising four exclusive databases of credible and reliable source material for research and for student assignments: EBSCO's ContentSelect Academic Journal & Abstract Database, the *New York Times* Search-by-Subject Archive, *Financial Times* Article Archive and Company Financials, and "Best of the Web" Link Library. The site also includes an extensive help section. The Research Navigator Guide provides your students with access to the Research Navigator website and includes reference material and hints about conducting online research. Available to qualified college adopters when packaged with the text.

Mapping Western Civilization: Student Activities

0-673-53774-9

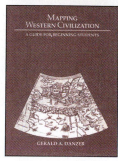

Created by Gerald Danzer, University of Illinois at Chicago, this FREE map workbook for students is designed as an accompaniment to *Discovering Western Civilization Through Maps and Views.* It features exercises designed to teach students to interpret and analyze cartographic materials such as historical documents. Available to qualified college adopters when packaged with the text.

Western Civilization Map Workbook

Volume I: 0-321-01878-8

Volume II: 0-321-01877-X

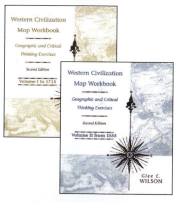

The map exercises in these volumes, created by Glee Wilson at Kent State University, test and reinforce basic geography literacy while building critical-thinking skills. Available to qualified college adopters when packaged with the text.

Study Card for Western Civilization

0-321-29233-2

Colorful, affordable, and packed with useful information, Longman's Study Cards make studying easier, more efficient, and more enjoyable. Course information is distilled down to the basics, helping students quickly master the fundamentals, review a subject for understanding, or prepare for an exam. Because they're laminated for durability, they can be kept for years to come and used whenever necessary for a quick review. Available to qualified college adopters when packaged with the text.

MyHistoryLab (www.myhistorylab.com)

MyHistoryLab provides students with an online package complete with the entire electronic textbook, numerous study aids, primary sources, and chapter exams. With several hundred primary sources and images, as well as map workbook activities with gradable quizzes, the site offers students a unique, interactive experience that brings history to life. The comprehensive site also includes a History Bookshelf with fifty of the most commonly assigned books in history classes and a History Toolkit with tutorials and helpful links.

Longman Atlas of Western Civilization

0-321-21626-1

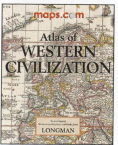

This fifty-two-page atlas features carefully selected historical maps that provide comprehensive coverage for the major historical periods. Each map has been designed to be colorful, easy to read, and informative, without sacrificing detailed accuracy. This atlas makes history—and geography—more comprehensible.

A Short Guide to Writing About History, Fifth Edition

0-321-22716-6

Written by Richard A. Marius, late of Harvard University, and Melvin E. Page, Eastern Tennessee State University, this engaging and practical text helps students get beyond merely compiling dates and facts; it teaches them how to incorporate their own ideas into their papers and to tell a story about history that interests them and their peers. Covering both brief essays and the documented resource paper, the text explores the writing and researching processes; identifies different modes of historical writing, including argument; and concludes with guidelines for improving style.

Penguin-Longman Partnership

The partnership between Penguin Books and Longman Publishers offers a discount on the following titles when bundled with any Longman history survey textbook. Visit www.ablongman.com/penguin for more information.

Available Titles

Peter Abelard, *The Letters of Abelard and Heloise*

Dante Alighieri, *Divine Comedy: Inferno*

Dante Alighieri, *The Portable Dante*

Anonymous, *Early Irish Myths & Sagas*

Anonymous, *The Epic of Gilgamesh*

Anonymous, *The Song of Roland*

Anonymous, *Vinland Sagas*

Hannah Arendt, *On Revolution*

Aristophanes, *The Birds and Other Plays*

Aristotle, *The Politics*

Louis Auchincloss, *Woodrow Wilson* (Penguin Lives Series)

St. Augustine, *The Confessions of St. Augustine*

Jane Austen, *Emma*

Jane Austen, *Persuasion*

Jane Austen, *Pride and Prejudice*

Jane Austen, *Sense and Sensibility*

Edward Bellamy, *Looking Backward*

Richard Bowring, *Diary of Lady Murasaki*

Charlotte Brontë, *Jane Eyre*

Charlotte Brontë, *Villette*

Emily Brontë, *Wuthering Heights*

Edmund Burke, *Reflection on the Revolution in France and on the Proceedings in Certain Societies in London Relative to that Event*

Benvenuto Cellini, *The Autobiography of Benvenuto Cellini*

Geoffrey Chaucer, *The Canterbury Tales*

Marcus Tullius Cicero, *Cicero: Selected Political Speeches*

Miguel de Cervantes, *The Adventures of Don Quixote*

Bartolome de las Casas, *A Short Account of the Destruction of the West Indies*

René Descartes, *Discourse on Method and Related Writings*

Charles Dickens, *Great Expectations*

Charles Dickens, *Hard Times*

John Dos Passos, *Three Soldiers*

Einhard, *Two Lives of Charlemagne*

Olaudah Equiano, *The Interesting Narrative and Other Writings*

M. Finley (ed.), *The Portable Greek Historians*

Benjamin Franklin, *The Autobiography and Other Writings*

Jeffrey Gantz (tr.), *Early Irish Myths and Sagas*

Peter Gay, *Mozart* (Penguin Lives Series)

William Golding, *Lord of the Flies*

Grimm & Grimm, *Grimms' Fairy Tales*

Thomas Hardy, *Jude the Obscure*

Herodotus, *The Histories*

Thomas Hobbes, *Leviathan*

Homer, *The Iliad*

Homer, *The Iliad* (Deluxe)

Homer, *Odyssey Deluxe*

Homer, *Odyssey: Revised Prose Translation*

The Koran

Deborah Lipstadt, *Denying the Holocaust*
Machiavelli, *The Prince*
Bill Manley, *The Penguin Historical Atlas of Ancient Egypt*
Karl Marx, *The Communist Manifesto*
Colin McEvedy, *The New Penguin Atlas of Ancient History*
Colin McEvedy, *The New Penguin Atlas of Medieval History*
John Stuart Mill, *On Liberty*
Jean-Baptiste Molière, *Tartuffe and Other Plays*
Sir Thomas More, *Utopia and Other Essential Writings*
Robert Morkot, *The Penguin Historical Atlas of Ancient Greece*
Sherwin Nuland, *Leonardo Da Vinci*
George Orwell, *1984*
George Orwell, *Animal Farm*
Plato, *Great Dialogues of Plato*
Plato, *The Last Days of Socrates*
Plato, *The Republic*
Plutarch, *Fall of the Roman Republic*
Marco Polo, *The Travels*
Procopius, *The Secret History*
Jean-Jacques Rousseau, *The Social Contract*
Sallust, *The Jugurthine Wars, The Conspiracy of Cataline*
Chris Scarre, *The Penguin Historical Atlas of Ancient Rome*
Desmond Seward, *The Hundred Years' War*
William Shakespeare, *Four Great Comedies: The Taming of the Shrew, A Midsummer's Night Dream, Twelfth Night, The Tempest*

William Shakespeare, *Four Great Tragedies: Hamlet, Macbeth, King Lear, Othello*
William Shakespeare, *Four Histories: Richard II, Henry IV: Part I, Henry IV: Part II, Henry V*
William Shakespeare, *Hamlet*
William Shakespeare, *King Lear*
William Shakespeare, *Macbeth*
William Shakespeare, *The Merchant of Venice*
William Shakespeare, *Othello*
William Shakespeare, *The Taming of the Shrew*
William Shakespeare, *The Tempest*
William Shakespeare, *Twelfth Night*
Mary Shelley, *Frankenstein*
Aleksandr Solzhenitsyn, *One Day in the Life of Ivan Denisovich*
Sophocles, *The Three Theban Plays*
Robert Louis Stevenson, *The Strange Case of Dr. Jekyll and Mr. Hyde*
Suetonius, *The Twelve Caesars*
Jonathan Swift, *Gulliver's Travels*
Tacitus, *The Histories*
Various, *The Penguin Book of Historical Speeches*
Voltaire, *Candide, Zadig and Selected Stories*
Carl von Clausewitz, *On War*
von Goethe, *Faust, Part 1*
von Goethe, *Faust, Part 2*
Edith Wharton, *Ethan Frome*
Willet, *The Signet World Atlas*
Gary Wills, *Saint Augustine* (Penguin Lives Series)
Virginia Woolf, *Jacob's Room*

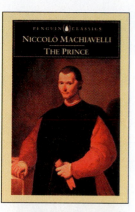

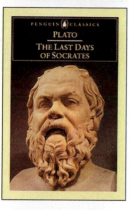

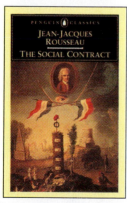

Longman Library of World Biography Series

Each interpretive biography in the new Library of World Biography series focuses on a figure whose actions and ideas significantly influenced the course of world history. Pocket-sized and brief, each book relates the life of its subject to the broader themes and developments of the time. Longman Publishers offers your students a discount on the titles below when instructors request that they be bundled with any Longman history survey textbook. Series titles include:

Ahmad al-Mansur: Islamic Visionary by Richard Smith (Ferrum College)
Alexander the Great: Legacy of a Conqueror by Winthrop Lindsay Adams (University of Utah)
Benito Mussolini: The First Fascist by Anthony L. Cardoza (Loyola University)
Fukuzawa Yûkichi: From Samurai to Capitalist by Helen M. Hopper (University of Pittsburgh)
Ignatius of Loyola: Founder of the Jesuits by John Patrick Donnelly (Marquette University)

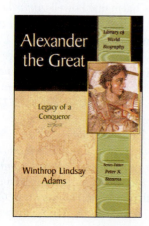

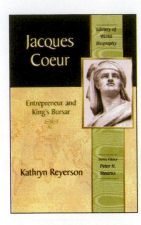

Jacques Coeur: Entrepreneur and King's Bursar by Kathryn L. Reyerson
    (University of Minnesota)
Katô Shidzue: A Japanese Feminist by Helen M. Hopper (University of Pittsburgh)
Simón Bolívar: Liberation and Disappointment by David Bushnell (University of Florida)
Vasco da Gama: Renaissance Crusader by Glenn J. Ames (University of Toledo)
Zheng He: China and the Oceans in the Early Ming, 1405–1433 by Edward Dreyer
    (University of Miami)

Acknowledgments

In writing this book we have benefited from the guidance of many members of the superb editorial staff at Longman. We would like to thank our acquisitions editor Janet Lanphier for helping us refine and develop this second edition. David Kear, our development editor, gave us valuable criticisms and helped us keep our audience in mind. Heather Johnson superintended the copyediting and proofreading with skill and efficiency, while Christine Buese helped us locate the most appropriate illustrations. Sue Westmoreland, the executive marketing manager for history, offered many creative ideas for promoting the book.

The authors wish to thank the following friends and colleagues for their assistance: Kenneth Alder, Joseph Alehermes, Karl Appuhn, Sharon Arnoult, Nicholas Baker, Paula Baskovits, Paul-Alain Beaulieu, Kamilia Bergen, Timothy Breen, Peter Brown, Peter Carroll, Shawn Clybor, Jauabeth Condie-Pugh, Patricia Crone, Tracey Cullen, Arthur Eckstein, Susanna Elm, Benjamin Frommer, Cynthia Gladstone, Dena Goodman, Stefka Hadjiandonova, Matthias Henze, Stanley Hilton, Kenneth Holum, Mark Jurdjevic, Werner Kelber, Cathleen Keller, Anne Kilmer, Jacob Lassner, Robert Lerner, Nancy Levack, Richard Lim, David Lindenfeld, Brian Maxson, Sarah Maza, Peter Mazur, Laura McGough, Roderick McIntosh, Susan K. McIntosh, Glenn Markoe, William Monter, Randy Nichols, Scott Noegel, Monique O'Connell, Carl Petry, Michael Rogers, Karl Roider, Sarah Ross, Michele Salzman, Paula Sanders, Regina Schwartz, Ethan Shagan, Julia M. H. Smith, James Sidbury, and Rachel Wahlig.

We would also like to thank the many historians who gave generously of their time to review during the various stages of development of our second edition. Their comments and suggestions helped to improve the book. Thank you:

Melanie A. Bailey, *South Dakota State University*
Brett Berliner, *Morgan State University*
Alfred S. Bradford, *University of Oklahoma*
Linda Charmaine Powell, *Amarillo College*
Daniel Christensen, *California State University, Fullerton*
William L. Cumiford, *Chapman University*
Rebecca Durrer, *Columbia College*
Steven Fanning, *University of Illinois at Chicago*
Sean Farrell, *Northern Illinois University*
Judy E. Gaughan, *Colorado State University*
Jennifer Hedda, *Simpson College*
David Hudson, *California State University, Fresno*
Rebecca Huston, *Hinds Community College*
Barbara A. Klemm, *Broward Community College*
Molly McClain, *University of San Diego*
Randall McGowen, *University of Oregon*

John A. Nichols, *Slippery Rock University*
James T. Owens, *Oakton Community College*
Elizabeth Propes, *Mesa State College*
Miriam Raub Vivian, *California State University, Bakersfield*
Anne Rodrick, *Wofford College*
Jarbel Rodriguez, *San Francisco State University*
Jacquelyn A. Royal, *Lee University*
Jutta Scott, *South Carolina University*
Susan O. Shapiro, *Utah State University*
Steven E. Sidebotham, *University of Delaware*
David Stone, *Kansas State University*
Charles R. Sullivan, *University of Dallas*
Mary C. Swilling, *University of Mississippi*
Larissa Juliet Taylor, *Colby College*
Jonathan Ziskind, *University of Louisville*

We would also like to thank the historians whose careful reviews and comments on the first edition helped us revise the book for its second edition. Our thanks for your contributions:

Henry Abramson, *Florida Atlantic University*
Patricia Ali, *Morris College*
Joseph Appiah, *J. Sergeant Reynolds Community College*
Sharon L. Arnoult, *Midwestern State University*
Arthur H. Auten, *University of Hartford*
Clifford Backman, *Boston University*
Suzanne Balch-Lindsay, *Eastern New Mexico University*
Wayne C. Bartee, *Southwest Miami State University*
Brandon Beck, *Shenandoah University*
James R. Belpedio, *Becker College*
Richard Berthold, *University of New Mexico*
Cynthia S. Bisson, *Belmont University*
Richard Bodek, *College of Charleston*
Melissa Bokovoy, *University of New Mexico*
William H. Brennan, *University of the Pacific*
Morgan R. Broadhead, *Jefferson Community College*
Theodore Bromund, *Yale University*
April A. Brooks, *South Dakota State University*
Nathan M. Brooks, *New Mexico State University*
Michael Burger, *Mississippi University for Women*
Susan Carrafiello, *Wright State University*
Kathleen S. Carter, *High Point University*
William L. Combs, *Western Illinois University*
Joseph Coohill, *Pennsylvania State University–New Kensington*
Richard A. Cosgrove, *University of Arizona*
Leonard Curtis, *Mississippi College*
Miriam Davis, *Delta State University*
Alexander DeGrand, *North Carolina State University*
Marion Deshmukh, *George Mason University*
Janusz Duzinkiewicz, *Purdue University, North Central*
Mary Beth Emmerichs, *University of Wisconsin, Sheboygan*
Steven Fanning, *University of Illinois at Chicago*
Bryan Ganaway, *University of Illinois at Urbana–Champaign*
Frank Garosi, *California State University–Sacramento*
Christina Gold, *Loyola Marymount University*
Ignacio Götz, *Hofstra University*
Louis Haas, *Duquesne University*
Linda Jones Hall, *Saint Mary's College of Maryland*
Paul Halsall, *University of North Florida*
Donald J. Harreld, *Brigham Young University*
Carmen V. Harris, *University of South Carolina at Spartanburg*
James C. Harrison, *Siena College*
Mark C. Herman, *Edison Community College*
Curry A. Herring, *University of Southern Alabama*
Patrick Holt, *Fordham University*
W. Robert Houston, *University of South Alabama*
Lester Hutton, *Westfield State College*

Jeffrey Hyson, *Saint Joseph's University*
Paul Jankowski, *Brandeis University*
Padraic Kennedy, *McNeese State University*
Joanne Klein, *Boise State University*
Theodore Kluz, *Troy State University*
Skip Knox, *Boise State University*
Cynthia Kosso, *Northern Arizona University*
Ann Kuzdale, *Chicago State University*
Lawrence Langer, *University of Connecticut*
Oscar E. Lansen, *University of North Carolina at Charlotte*
Michael V. Leggiere, *Louisiana State University at Shreveport*
Rhett Leverett, *Marymount University*
Alison Williams Lewin, *Saint Joseph's University*
Wendy Liu, *Miami University, Middletown*
Elizabeth Makowski, *Southwest Texas State University*
Daniel Meissner, *Marquette University*
Isabel Moreira, *University of Utah*
Kenneth Moure, *University of California–Santa Barbara*
Melva E. Newsom, *Clark State Community College*
John A. Nichols, *Slippery Rock University*
Susannah R. Ottaway, *Carleton College*
James H. Overfield, *University of Vermont*
Brian L. Peterson, *Florida International University*
Hugh Phillips, *Western Kentucky University*
Jeff Plaks, *University of Central Oklahoma*
Thomas L. Powers, *University of South Carolina, Sumter*
Carole Putko, *San Diego State University*
Barbara Ranieri, *University of Alabama at Birmingham*
Elsa M. E. Rapp, *Montgomery County Community College*
Marlette Rebhorn, *Austin Community College*
Roger Reese, *Texas A&M University*
Travis Ricketts, *Bryan College*
Thomas Robisheaux, *Duke University*
Bill Robison, *Southeastern Louisiana University*
Mark Ruff, *Concordia University*
Frank Russell, *Transylvania University*
Marylou Ruud, *The University of West Florida*
Michael Saler, *University of California–Davis*
Timothy D. Saxon, *Charleston Southern University*
Daniel A. Scalberg, *Multnomah Bible College*
Ronald Schechter, *College of William and Mary*
Philip Skaggs, *Grand Valley State University*
Helmut Walser Smith, *Vanderbilt University*
Eileen Solwedel, *Edmonds Community College*
Sister Maria Consuelo Sparks, *Immaculata University*
Ilicia J. Sprey, *Saint Joseph's College*
Charles R. Sullivan, *University of Dallas*
Frederick Suppe, *Ball State University*

Frank W. Thackery, *Indiana University Southeast*
Frances B. Titchener, *Utah State University*
Katherine Tosa, *Muskegon Community College*
Lawrence A. Tritle, *Loyola Marymount University*

Clifford F. Wargelin, *Georgetown College*
Theodore R. Weeks, *Southern Illinois University*
Elizabeth A. Williams, *Oklahoma State University*
Mary E. Zamon, *Marymount University*

BRIAN LEVACK
EDWARD MUIR
MEREDITH VELDMAN
MICHAEL MAAS

Meet the Authors

Brian Levack grew up in a family of teachers in the New York metropolitan area. From his father, a professor of French history, he acquired a love for studying the past, and he knew from an early age that he too would become a historian. He received his B.A. from Fordham University in 1965 and his Ph.D. from Yale in 1970. In graduate school he became fascinated by the history of the law and the interaction between law and politics, interests that he has maintained throughout his career. In 1969 he joined the history department of the University of Texas at Austin, where he is now the John Green Regents Professor in History. The winner of several teaching awards, Levack teaches a wide variety of courses on British and European history, legal history, and the history of witchcraft. For eight years he served as the chair of his department, a rewarding but challenging assignment that made it difficult for him to devote as much time as he wished to his teaching and scholarship. His books include *The Civil Lawyers in England, 1603–1641: A Political Study* (1973), *The Formation of the British State: England, Scotland and the Union, 1603–1707* (1987), and *The Witch-Hunt in Early Modern Europe* (1987 and 1995), which has been translated into eight languages.

His study of the development of beliefs about witchcraft in Europe over the course of many centuries gave him the idea of writing a textbook on Western civilization that would illustrate a broader set of encounters between different cultures, societies, and ideologies. While writing the book, Levack and his two sons built a house on property that he and his wife, Nancy, own in the Texas hill country. He found that the two projects presented similar challenges: It was easy to draw up the design, but far more difficult to execute it. When not teaching, writing, or doing carpentry work, Levack runs along the jogging trails of Austin, and he has recently discovered the pleasures of scuba diving.

Edward Muir grew up in the foothills of the Wasatch Mountains in Utah, close to the Emigration Trail along which wagon trains of Mormon pioneers and California-bound settlers made their way westward. As a child he loved to explore the broken-down wagons and abandoned household goods left at the side of the trail and from that acquired a fascination with the past. Besides the material remains of the past, he grew up with stories of his Mormon pioneer ancestors and an appreciation for how the past continued to influence the present. During the turbulent 1960s, he became interested in Renaissance Italy as a period and a place that had been formative for Western civilization. His biggest challenge is finding the time to explore yet another new corner of Italy and its restaurants.

Muir received his Ph.D. from Rutgers University, where he specialized in the Italian Renaissance and did archival research in Venice and Florence, Italy. He is now the Clarence L. Ver Steeg Professor in the Arts and Sciences at Northwestern University and former chair of the history department. At Northwestern he has won several teaching awards. His books include *Civic Ritual in Renaissance Venice* (1981), *Mad Blood Stirring: Vendetta in Renaissance Italy* (1993 and 1998), and *Ritual in Early Modern Europe* (1997 and 2005).

Some years ago Muir began to experiment with the use of historical trials in teaching and discovered that students loved them. From that experience he decided to write this textbook, which employs trials as a central feature. He lives beside Lake Michigan in Evanston, Illinois. His twin passions are skiing in the Rocky Mountains and rooting for the Chicago Cubs, who manage every summer to demonstrate that winning isn't everything.

Meredith Veldman grew up in the western suburbs of Chicago in a close-knit, closed-in Dutch Calvinist community. In this immigrant society, history mattered: the "Reformed tradition" structured not only religious beliefs but also social identity and political practice. This influence certainly played some role in shaping Veldman's early fascination with history. But probably just as important were the countless World War II reenactment games she played with her five older brothers. Whatever the cause, Veldman majored in history at Calvin College in Grand Rapids, Michigan, and then earned a Ph.D. in modern European history, with a concentration in nineteenth- and twentieth-century Britain, from Northwestern University in 1988.

As associate professor of history at Louisiana State University, Veldman teaches courses in nineteenth- and twentieth-century British history and twentieth-century Europe, as well as the second half of "Western Civ." In her many semesters in the Western Civ. classroom, Veldman tried a number of different textbooks but found herself increasingly dissatisfied. She wanted a text that would convey to beginning students at least some of the complexities and ambiguities of historical interpretation, introduce them to the exciting work being done now in cultural history, and, most important, tell a good story. The search for this textbook led her to accept the offer made by Levack, Maas, and Muir to join them in writing *The West: Encounters & Transformations*.

The author of *Fantasy, the Bomb, and the Greening of Britain: Romantic Protest, 1945–1980* (1994), Veldman is also the wife of a Methodist minister and the mother of two young sons. They reside in Baton Rouge, Louisiana, where Veldman finds coping with the steamy climate a constant challenge. She and her family recently returned from Manchester, England, where they lived for three years and astonished the natives by their enthusiastic appreciation of English weather.

Michael Maas was born in the Ohio River Valley, in a community that had been a frontier outpost during the late eighteenth century. He grew up reading the stories of the early settlers and their struggles with the native peoples, and seeing in the urban fabric how the city had subsequently developed into a prosperous coal and steel town with immigrants from all over the world. As a boy he developed a lifetime interest in the archaeology and history of the ancient Mediterranean world and began to study Latin. At Cornell University he combined his interests in cultural history and the classical world by majoring in classics and anthropology. A semester in Rome clinched his commitment to these fields—and to Italian cooking. Maas went on to get his Ph.D. in the graduate program in ancient history and Mediterranean archaeology at the University of California at Berkeley.

He has traveled widely in the Mediterranean and the Middle East and participated in several archaeological excavations, including an underwater dig in Greece. Since 1985 he has taught ancient history at Rice University in Houston, Texas, where he founded and directs the interdisciplinary B.A. program in ancient Mediterranean civilizations. He has won several teaching awards.

Maas's special area of research is late antiquity, the period of transition from the classical to the medieval worlds, which saw the collapse of the Roman Empire in western Europe and the development of the Byzantine state in the East. During his last sabbatical, he was a member of the Institute for Advanced Study in Princeton, New Jersey, where he worked on his current book, *The Conqueror's Gift: Ethnography, Identity, and Imperial Power at the End of Antiquity* (forthcoming). His other books include *John Lydus and the Roman Past: Antiquarianism and Politics in the Age of Justinian* (1992), *Readings in Late Antiquity: A Sourcebook* (2000), and *Exegesis and Empire in the Early Byzantine Mediterranean* (2003).

Maas has always been interested in interdisciplinary teaching and the encounters among different cultures. He sees *The West: Encounters & Transformations* as an opportunity to explain how the modern civilization that we call "the West" had its origins in the diverse interactions among many peoples of antiquity.

THE WEST

What Is the West?

MANY OF THE PEOPLE WHO INFLUENCE PUBLIC OPINION—POLITI-cians, teachers, clergy, journalists, and television commenta-tors—refer to "Western values," "the West," and "Western civilization." They often use these terms as if they do not re-quire explanation. But what *do* these terms mean? The West has always been an arena within which different cultures, religions, values, and philosophies have interacted, and any definition of the West will inevitably arouse controversy.

The most basic definition of the West is of a place. Western civilization is now typically thought to comprise the regions of Europe, the Americas, Australia, and New Zealand. However, this is a contemporary definition of the West. The inclusion of these places in the West is the result of a long history of European expansion through colonization. In addition to being a place, Western civilization also encompasses a cultural history—a tradition stretching back thousands of years to the ancient world. Over this long period the civilization we now identify as Western gradually took shape. The many characteristics that identify any civilization emerged over this time: forms of government, economic systems, and methods of scientific inquiry, as well as religions, languages, literature, and art.

Throughout the development of Western civilization, the ways in which people identified themselves changed as well. People in the ancient world had no such idea of the common identity of the West, only of being mem-bers of a tribe, citizens of a town, or subjects of an empire. But with the spread of Christianity and Islam between the first and seventh centuries, the notion of a distinct civilization in these "Western" lands subtly changed. People came to identify themselves less as subjects of a particular empire and more as members of a community of faith—whether that community com-prised followers of Christianity, Judaism, or Islam. These communities of faith drew lines of inclusion and exclusion that still exist today. Starting

The Temple of Hera at Paestum, Italy Greek colonists in Italy built this temple in the sixth century B.C.E. Greek ideas and artistic styles spread throughout the ancient world both from Greek colonists, such as those at Paestum, and from other peoples who imi-tated the Greeks.

about 1,600 years ago, Christian monarchs and clergy began to obliterate polytheism (the worship of many gods) and marginalize Jews. From a thousand to 500 years ago, Christian authorities strove to expel Muslims from Europe. Europeans developed definitions of the West that did not include Islamic communities, even though Muslims continued to live in Europe and Europeans traded and interacted with the Muslim world. The Islamic countries themselves erected their own barriers, seeing themselves in opposition to the Christian West, even as they continued to look back to the common cultural origins in the ancient world that they shared with Jews and Christians. During the Renaissance in the fifteenth century, these ancient cultural origins became an alternative to religious affiliation for thinking about the identity of the West. From this Renaissance historical perspective Jews, Christians, and Muslims descended from the cultures of the ancient Hebrews, Greeks, and Romans. Despite all their differences, the followers of these religions shared a history. In fact, in the late Renaissance a number of thinkers imagined the possibility of rediscovering the single universal religion that they thought must have once been practiced in the ancient world. If they could just recapture that religion they could restore the unity they imagined had once prevailed in the West.

A Satellite View of Europe
What is the West? Western civilization has undergone numerous transformations throughout history, but it has always included Europe.

The definition of the West has also changed as a result of European colonialism, which began about 500 years ago. When European powers assembled large overseas empires, they introduced Western languages, religions, technology, and culture to many distant places in the world, making Western identity a transportable concept. In some of these colonized areas—such as North America, Argentina, Australia, and New Zealand—the European newcomers so outnumbered the indigenous people that these regions became as much a part of the West as Britain, France, and Spain. In other European colonies, especially in European trading outposts on the Asian continent, Western culture failed to exercise similar levels of influence.

As a result of colonialism Western culture sometimes merged with other cultures, and in the process both were changed. Brazil, a South American country inhabited by large numbers of indigenous peoples, the descendants of African slaves, and European settlers, epitomizes the complexity of what defines the West. In Brazil, almost everyone speaks a Western language (Portuguese), practices a Western religion (Christianity), and participates in Western political and economic institutions (democracy and capitalism). Yet in Brazil all of these features of Western civilization have become part of a distinctive culture, in which in-

digenous, African, and European elements have been blended. During Carnival, for example, Brazilians dressed in indigenous costumes dance in African rhythms to the accompaniment of music played on European instruments.

For many people today, the most important definition of the West involves adherence to a certain set of values, the "Western" values. The values typically identified as Western today include universal human rights, toleration of religious diversity, equality before the law, democracy, and freedom of inquiry and expression. However, these values have not always been part of Western civilization. They came to be fully appreciated only very recently as the consequence of a long and bloody history. In fact, there is nothing inevitable about these values, and Western history at various stages exhibited quite different ones. For example, the rulers of ancient Rome did not extend the privileges of citizenship to all the inhabitants of the empire until a century after it had reached its greatest size. The extent to which women could participate in public life was limited by law. Rich and powerful people enjoyed more protection under the law than did slaves or humble people. Most medieval Christians were completely convinced that their greatest contribution to society would be to make war against Muslims and heretics and to curtail as much as possible the actions of Jews. Western societies seldom valued equality until quite recently. Before the end of the eighteenth century, few Westerners questioned the practice of slavery; a social hierarchy of birth remained powerful in the West through the entire nineteenth century; most Western women were excluded from equal economic and educational opportunities until well into the twentieth century. Swiss women did not get the vote until 1971 (and in one canton not until 1990). Also in the twentieth century, Nazi Germany and the Soviet Union demonstrated that history could have turned out very differently in the West. These totalitarian regimes in Europe rejected most of the Western values so prized today and terrorized their own populations and millions of others beyond their borders through massive abuses of human rights. The history of the West is riddled with examples of leaders who stifled free inquiry and who censored authors and journalists. These examples testify to the fact that the values of Western societies have always been contended, disputed, and fought over. In other words, they have a history. This text highlights and examines that history, demonstrating how hard values were to formulate in the first place and how difficult they have been to preserve.

The Shifting Borders of the West

The geographical setting of the West also has a history. This textbook begins about 10,000 years ago in what is now Iraq and it ends in Iraq, but in the meantime the Mesopotamian region is only occasionally a concern for Western history. The West begins with the domestication of animals, the cultivation of the first crops, and the establishment of long-distance trading networks in the Tigris, Euphrates, and Nile River valleys. Cities, kingdoms, and empires in those valleys gave birth to the first civilizations. By about 500 B.C.E., the civilizations that are the cultural ancestors of the modern West had spread from southwestern Asia and North Africa to include the entire Mediterranean basin—areas influenced by Egyptian, Hebrew, Greek, and Roman thought, art, law, and religion. By the first century C.E. the Roman Empire drew the map of what historians consider the heartland of the West: most of western and southern Europe, the coastlands of the Mediterranean Sea, and the Middle East.

The West is now usually thought to include Europe and the Americas. However, the borders of the West have in recent decades come to be less about geography than culture, identity, and technology. When Japan, an Asian country, accepted human rights, democracy, and industrial capitalism after World War II, did it become part of the West? Most Japanese might not think they have adopted "Western" values, but the industrial power and stable democracy of a traditional Asian country that had never been colonized by a European power complicates the idea of what is the West. Or consider the Republic of South Africa, which until 1994 was ruled by the white minority, people descended from European immigrants. The oppressive regime violated human rights, rejected full legal equality for all citizens, and jailed or murdered those who questioned the government. Only when that government was replaced through democratic elections and a black man became president did South Africa fully embrace what the rest of the West would consider Western values. To what degree was South Africa part of the West before and after these developments?

Russia long saw itself as a Christian country with a tradition of cultural, economic, and political ties with the rest of Europe. The Russians have intermittently identified with their Western neighbors, but their neighbors were not always sure about the Russians. After the Mongol invasions of the thirteenth and fourteenth centuries much of Russia was isolated from the rest of the West; during the Cold War from 1949 to 1989, Russian communism and the Western democracies were polarized. When was Russia "Western" and when not?

Thus, when we talk about where the West is, we are almost always talking about the Mediterranean basin and much of Europe (and later, the Americas). But we will also show that countries that border "the West," and even countries far from it, might be considered Western in many aspects as well.

The Astrolabe

The mariner's astrolabe was a navigational device intended for use primarily at sea. The astrolabe originated in the Islamic world and was adopted by Europeans in the twelfth century—a cultural encounter that enabled Europeans to embark on long ocean voyages around the world.

Asking the Right Questions

So how can we make sense of the West as a place and an identity, the shifting borders of the West, and Western civilization in general? In short, what has Western civilization been over the course of its long history—and what is it today?

Answering these questions is the challenge this book poses. There are no simple answers to any of these questions, but there is a method for finding answers. The method is straightforward. Always ask the *what, when, where, who, how,* and *why* questions of the text.

The *What* Question

What is Western civilization? The answer to this question will vary according to time and place. In fact, for much of the early history covered in this book, Western civilization as we know it today did not exist as a single cultural entity. Rather, a number of distinctive civilizations were taking shape in the Middle East, northern Africa, and Europe, each of which contributed to what later became Western civilization. But throughout time the idea of Western civilization slowly began to form. Thus the understanding of Western civilization will change from chapter to chapter. The most extensive change in the place of the West was through the colonial expansion of the European nations between the fifteenth and twentieth centuries. Perhaps the most significant cultural change in the West came with acceptance of the values of scientific inquiry for solving human and philosophical problems, an approach that did not exist before the seventeenth century but became one of the distinguishing characteristics of Western civilization. During the late eighteenth and nineteenth centuries, industrialization became the engine that drove economic development in the West, and during the twentieth century industrialization in both its capitalist and communist forms dramatically gave the West a level of economic prosperity unmatched in the non-industrialized parts of the world.

The *When* Question

When did the defining characteristics of Western civilization first emerge, and for how long did they prevail? Dates frame and organize each chapter, and there are numerous short chronologies offered. These resources make it possible to keep track of what happened when. Dates have no meaning by themselves, but the connections *between* them can be very revealing. For example, dates show that the agricultural revolution that permitted the birth of the first civiliza-

tions unfolded over a span of about 10,000 years—which is more time than was taken by all the other events and developments covered in this textbook. Wars of religion plagued Europe for nearly 200 years before Enlightenment thinkers articulated the ideals of religious toleration. The American Civil War—the war to preserve the union, as President Abraham Lincoln termed it—took place at exactly the same time as other wars were being fought to achieve national unity in Germany and Italy. In other words, by paying attention to other contemporaneous wars for national unity the American experience seems less peculiarly an American event.

By learning when things happened, one can identify the major causes and consequences of events and thus see the transformations of Western civilization. For instance, the ability to produce a surplus of food through agriculture and the domestication of animals was a prerequisite for the emergence of civilizations. The violent collapse of religious unity after the Protestant Reformation in the sixteenth century led some Europeans to propose the separation of church and state two centuries later. And during the nineteenth century many Western states—in response to the enormous diversity among their own peoples—became preoccupied with maintaining or establishing national unity.

The *Where* Question

Where has Western civilization been located? Geography, of course, does not change very rapidly, but the idea of where the West is does. The location of the West is not so much a matter of changing borders but of how people identify themselves. The key to understanding the shifting borders of the West is to study how the peoples within the West thought of themselves. These groups include Muslims and the peoples of eastern Europe (such as the Soviet Union during the Cold War), which some people have wanted to exclude from the West. In addition, the chapters trace the relationships between the West (as it was constituted in different periods) and other, more distant civilizations with which it interacted. Those civilizations include not only those of East Asia and South Asia but also the indigenous peoples of sub-Saharan Africa, the Americas, and the Pacific islands.

The *Who* Question

Who were the people responsible for making Western civilization? Sometimes they were anonymous, such as the unknown geniuses who invented the mathematical systems of ancient Mesopotamia. At other times the makers of the

West were famous—saints such as Joan of Arc, creative thinkers such as Galileo Galilei, or generals such as Napoleon. But history is not made only by great and famous people. Humble people, such as the many millions who migrated from Europe to North America or the unfortunate millions who suffered and died in the trenches of World War I, can also influence the course of events.

Perhaps most often this book encounters people who were less the shapers of their own destinies than the subjects of forces that conditioned the kinds of choices they could make, often with unanticipated results. When during the eleventh century farmers throughout Europe began to employ a new kind of plow to till their fields, they were merely trying to do their work more efficiently. They certainly did not recognize that the increase in food they produced would stimulate the enormous population growth that made possible the medieval civilization of thriving cities and magnificent cathedrals. Answering the who question requires an evaluation of how much individuals and groups of people were in control of events and how much events controlled them.

The *How* Question

How did Western civilization develop? This is a question about processes—about how things change or stay the same over time. This book identifies these processes in several ways. First, the theme of encounters and transformations has been woven throughout the story. What is meant by encounters? When the Spanish *conquistadores* arrived in the Americas some 500 years ago, they came into contact with the cultures of the Caribs, the Aztecs, the Incas, and other peoples who had lived in the Americas for thousands of years. As the Spanish fought, traded with, and intermarried with the natives, each culture changed. The Spanish, for their part, borrowed from the Americas new plants for cultivation and responded to what they considered serious threats to their worldview. Many native Americans, in turn, adopted European religious practices and learned to speak European languages. At the same time, they were decimated by European diseases to which they had never before been exposed. They also witnessed the destruction of their own civilizations and governments at the hands of the colonial

Map 1   Core Lands of the West

The geographical borders of the West have changed substantially throughout history.

Cortés Meets Montezuma

As the Spanish fought, traded, and intermarried with the native peoples of the Americas during the fifteenth and sixteenth centuries, each culture changed.

powers. Through centuries of interaction and mutual influence, both sides became something other than what they had been.

The European encounter with the Americas is an obvious example of what was, in fact, a continuous process of encounters with other cultures. These encounters often occurred between peoples from different civilizations, such as the struggles between Greeks and Persians in the ancient world or between Europeans and Chinese in the nineteenth century. Other encounters took place among people living in the same civilization. These include interactions between lords and peasants, men and women, Christians and Jews, Catholics and Protestants, factory owners and workers, and capitalists and communists. Western civilization developed and changed through a series of external and internal encounters.

Second, features in the chapters formulate answers to the question of how Western civilization developed. For example, each chapter contains an essay titled "Justice in History." These essays discuss a trial or some other episode involving questions of justice. Some "Justice in History" essays illustrate how Western civilization was forged in struggles over conflicting values, such as the discussion of the trial of Galileo, which examines the conflict between religious and scientific concepts of truth. Others show how efforts to resolve internal cultural, political, and religious tensions helped shape Western ideas about justice, such as the

essay on the *auto-da-fé*, which illustrates how authorities attempted to enforce religious conformity. At the end of each "Justice in History" feature are several questions tying that essay to the theme of the chapter.

Some chapters include two other features as well. Essays titled "The Human Body in History" demonstrate that even the body, which is typically understood as a product of genetics and biology, has a history. These essays show that the ways in which Western people understand their bodies, how they cure them, how they cover and uncover them, and how they adorn them tell us a great deal about the history of Western culture. For example, the book explores how the bodies of World War I soldiers afflicted with shell shock were treated differently from women experiencing similar symptoms of hysteria. Shell-shocked soldiers gave people a sense of the horrors of war and stimulated powerful movements in Europe to outlaw war as an instrument of government policy.

The "Encounters and Transformations" features show how encounters between different groups of people, technologies, and ideas were not abstract historical processes but events that brought people together in a way that transformed history. For example, when the Arabs encountered the camel as an instrument of war, they adopted it for their own purposes and were able to conquer their neighbors very quickly and spread Islam far beyond its original home in Arabia.

The *Why* Question

Why did things happen in the way they did in history? This is the hardest question of all, one that engenders the most debate among historians. To take one persistent example, why did Hitler initiate a plan to exterminate the Jews of Europe? Can it be explained by something that happened to him in his childhood? Was he full of self-loathing that he projected onto the Jews? Was it a way of creating an enemy so that he could better unify Germany? Did he really believe that the Jews were the cause of all of Germany's problems? Did he merely act on the deeply seated anti-Semitic tendencies of the German people? Historians still debate the answers to these questions. These questions raise issues about human motivation and the role of human agency in historical events. Can historians ever really know what motivated a particular individual in the past, especially when it is so notoriously difficult to understand what motivates other people in the present? Can any individual determine the course of history? The *what, when, where, who,* and *how* questions are much easier to answer, but the *why* question, of course, is the most interesting one, the one that cries out for an answer.

This book does not always offer definitive answers to the *why* question, but it attempts to lay out the most likely possibilities. For example, historians do not really know what disease caused the Black Death in the fourteenth century, which killed about one-third of the population in a matter of months. But they can answer many questions about the consequences of that great catastrophe. Why were there so many new universities in the fourteenth and fifteenth centuries? It was because so many priests had died in the Black Death, creating a huge demand for replacements. The answers to the *why* questions are not always obvious, but they are always intriguing, and finding them is the joy of studying history.

The Beginnings of Civilization, 10,000–2000 B.C.E.

I N 1991 HIKERS TOILING ACROSS A GLACIER IN THE ALPS BETWEEN AUSTRIA AND Italy made a startling discovery: a man's body stuck in the ice. They alerted the police, who soon turned the corpse over to archaeologists. The scientists determined that the middle-aged man had frozen to death about 5,300 years ago. Ötzi the Ice Man (his name comes from the Ötztal Valley where he perished) quickly became an international celebrity as the world's oldest freeze-dried human. The scientists who examined Ötzi believe that he was a shepherd herding flocks of sheep and goats to mountain pastures when he died. A few grains of wheat on his clothing suggested that he lived in a farming community. Copper dust in his hair hinted that Ötzi may also have been a metalworker, perhaps looking for ores during his journey. An arrowhead lodged in his back indicated a violent cause of death, but the exact circumstances remain mysterious.

Ötzi's gear was state-of-the-art for his time. His possessions showed deep knowledge of the natural world. He wore leather boots insulated with dense grasses chosen for protection against the cold. The pouch around his waist contained stone tools and fire-lighting equipment. The wood selected for his bow offered special strength and flexibility. In his light wooden backpack Ötzi carried containers to hold burning embers, as well as dried meat and nutritious seeds to eat on the trail. The arrows in his quiver featured a natural adhesive that tightly bound bone and wooden points to the shafts. The most noteworthy find among Ötzi's possessions was his axe. Its handle was made of wood but its head was copper—a remarkable innovation at a time when most tools were made of stone. Ötzi was ready for almost anything—except the person who shot him in the back.

Ötzi lived at a transitional moment, at the very end of what archaeologists call the Neolithic Age, or "New Stone Age," when people made refinements in tool-making techniques over those of previous ages. For example, Neolithic artisans carved remarkably delicate arrowheads and blades that

CHAPTER OUTLINE

- Culture, Agriculture, and Civilization

- The Birth of Civilization in Southwest Asia

- The Emergence of Egyptian Civilization

- The Transformation of Europe

Papyrus Harvest This painted wall sculpture from the Tomb of Nefer and Kahay in Saqqara Egypt dates to the fifth dynasty, 2494–2345 B.C.E. It shows farmers harvesting papyrus, the plant that grows along the banks of the Nile. Records were kept on papyrus, making it an essential element of Egyptian society and government.

Ötzi the Ice Man
This artist's recreation shows Ötzi in his waterproof poncho carrying his state-of-the-art tools.

could be used for a variety of tasks, from hunting to sewing. The Neolithic Age was a long period of revolutionary change lasting from about 10,000 to about 3000 B.C.E. that altered human existence on Earth forever. Even the most advanced technological developments of the twentieth century did not reshape human life as profoundly as did those of the Neolithic era.

This chapter traces humanity's first steps toward the civilizations that developed in Southwest Asia, Egypt, and Europe—regions that made crucial contributions to the development of Western civilization. First we will consider the most fundamental encounter of all—the relationship between humans and the natural world. Many thousands of years of human interaction with nature led to food production through agriculture and the domestication of animals. This revolutionary achievement let humans develop new, settled forms of communities: first villages, then cities, and eventually kingdoms and empires. Civilizations grew from the foundations of agriculture and the domestication of an-

imals. The growth of civilization also depended on constant interaction among communities that lived far apart. Once people were settled in a region, they began trading for commodities that were not available in their homelands. As trade routes extended over long distances and interactions among diverse peoples proliferated, ideas and technology spread.

How did the encounters between these early human societies create the world's first civilizations? To answer this question, this chapter asks the following questions:

- What is the link between the food-producing revolution of the Neolithic era and the emergence of civilizations?
- What transformed the earliest settled communities in Southwest Asia into the first cities, kingdoms, and empires in history?
- How did civilization take shape along the Nile River in Egypt?
- How and why did food production and the use of metals transform the lives of the men and women who populated Europe in the Neolithic Age?

Culture, Agriculture, and Civilization

- What is the link between the food-producing revolution of the Neolithic era and the emergence of civilizations?

Anthropologists use the term culture° to describe all the different ways that humans collectively adjust to their environment, and organize and transmit their experiences and knowledge to future generations. We can understand a people's culture as a web of interconnected meanings that enable them to understand themselves and their place in the world. Each culture is distinctive; thus we use labels—"Greek culture" or "American culture." Yet all cultures constantly borrow from their neighbors and change over time.

We often use *culture* and *civilization* interchangeably, yet in the history of human development, civilization has a specific definition. Archaeologists define civilization° as a society differentiated by levels of wealth and occupation in which people lived in cities. With cities, human populations achieved the critical mass necessary to develop specialized occupations, as well as a level of economic production high enough to sustain complex religious and cultural practices. As villages evolved into cities, their social organization grew more complicated. The labor of most people supported a small group of political and religious leaders. A city's leaders controlled the mechanisms of not only government and warfare but also the distribution of food and wealth. They augmented their authority by building temples to the gods and participating in religious rituals that linked divinity with kingship. Thus, in early civilizations three kinds of power—economic, political, and religious—converged.

The Food-Producing Revolution

Food production made civilization possible. For the first thousands of millennia of their existence, modern humans, known as *Homo sapiens sapiens*° ("most intelligent people"), did not produce food. Between 200,000 and 100,000 years ago, *Homo sapiens sapiens* first appeared in Africa and began to spread to other continents. Scientists refer to this stage of human history as the Paleolithic Age, or Old Stone Age, because people made tools by cracking rocks and using their sharp edges to cut and chop. *Homo sapiens sapiens'* use of tools demonstrated adaptation to new environments and practical needs. They scavenged for wild food and became shrewd observers of the natural environment. They followed migrating herds of animals, hunting with increasing efficiency as their weapons improved. They also created beautiful works of art by carving bone and painting on cave walls. By

DOCUMENT

Cave Drawings

45,000 years ago, these humans had reached most of Earth's habitable regions, except for Australia, the islands of the South Pacific, and North and South America.

The end of the last Ice Age about 15,000 years ago ushered in an era of momentous change: the food-producing revolution. As the Earth's climate became warmer, causing changes in vegetation, humans began to interact with the natural environment in new ways. The warmer climate allowed cereal grasses to spread quickly over large areas; hunter-gatherers learned to collect these wild grains and grind them up for food. Some groups of hunter-gatherers settled in semipermanent camps near rivers and wetlands, where wild grains grew. When people learned that the seeds of wild grasses could be transplanted and grown in new areas, the domestication of plants was under way (see Map 1.1).

At the same time that people discovered the benefits of planting seeds, they also began domesticating pigs, sheep, goats, and cattle, which eventually replaced wild game as the main source of meat. Domestication° occurs when humans manipulate the breeding of animals in order to serve their own purposes—for example, making wool (lacking on wild sheep), laying extra eggs (not done by undomesticated chickens), and producing extra milk

Map 1.1 The Beginnings of Food Production

This map shows early farming sites discovered by archaeologists where the first known production of food occurred in ancient Southwest Asia.

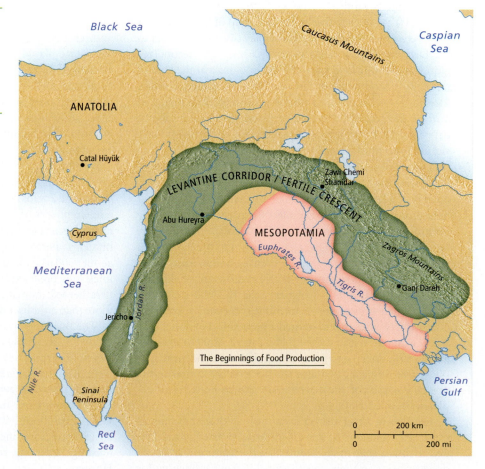

Black Sea

Caucasus Mountains

Caspian Sea

ANATOLIA

Catal Hüyük

Zawi Chemi
Shanidar

LEVANTINE CORRIDOR / FERTILE CRESCENT

Abu Hureyra

Cyprus

MESOPOTAMIA

Euphrates R.

Zagros Mountains

Mediterranean Sea

Tigris R.

Ganj Dareh

Jordan R.

Jericho

The Beginnings of Food Production

Nile R.

Persian Gulf

Sinai Peninsula

Red Sea

0   200 km
0   200 mi

(wild cows produce only enough milk for their offspring). The first signs of goat domestication occurred about 8900 B.C.E. in the Zagros Mountains in Southwest Asia. Pigs, which adapt very well to human settlements because they eat garbage, were first domesticated around 7000 B.C.E. By around 6500 B.C.E. domesticated cattle, goats, and sheep had become widespread.

Farming and herding required hard work, but the payoff was enormous. Even simple agricultural methods could produce about fifty times more food than hunting and gathering. Thanks to the increased food supply, more newborns survived past infancy. Populations expanded, and so did human settlements. With the mastery of food production, human societies developed the mechanisms not only to feed themselves, but also to produce a surplus, which could then be traded for other resources. Such economic activity allowed for economic specialization and fostered the growth of social, political, and religious hierarchies.

The First Food-Producing Communities

In Southwest Asia, where sufficient annual rainfall enabled crops to grow without irrigation, people began cultivating food in three separate areas. Archaeologists have named the first area the Levantine Corridor° (also known as the Fertile Crescent°)—a twenty-five-mile-wide strip of land that runs from Jericho in the Jordan River valley of modern Israel to the Euphrates River valley in today's Iraq. The second region was the hilly land north of Mesopotamia at the base of the Zagros Mountains in the western part of modern Iran. The third was Anatolia, or what is now the central region of Turkey. In each of these three regions, archaeological evidence reveals how human societies made the revolutionary shift to food production.

The small settlement of Abu Hureyra near the center of the Levantine Corridor illustrates how agriculture developed over a long period at a single site. Humans first settled here around 9500 B.C.E. They fed themselves primarily by hunting gazelles and gathering wild cereals. But sometime between 8000 and 7700 B.C.E., they began to plant and harvest a small number of grains. Eventually they discovered that crop rotation—planting different crops in a field each year—resulted in a much higher yield. By 7000 B.C.E. Abu Hureyra had grown into a farming community, covering nearly thirty acres that sustained a population of about 400. A few generations later, the inhabitants of Abu Hureyra began herding sheep and goats to supplement their meat supply. These domesticated animals became the community's primary source of meat when the gazelle herds were depleted about 6500 B.C.E.

Families in Abu Hureyra lived in small dwellings built of mud brick containing several rooms. Archaeological evidence shows that many women in the community developed arthritis in their knees, probably from crouching for

hours on end as they ground grains. Thus we assume that while men hunted and harvested, women performed the labor of grinding grains and preparing food. The division of labor along gender lines indicates a growing complexity of social relations within communities.

To the south of Abu Hureyra, at the southwestern end of the Levantine Corridor, the farming village of Jericho offers a second example of the way the food-producing revolution led to greater social complexity. Jericho began to develop rapidly after 8500 B.C.E. Located at an old hunting-gathering site along a stream in the Jordan River valley near modern Jerusalem, Jericho expanded to encompass nearly ten acres after its inhabitants started cultivating crops, including wheat, barley, lentils, and peas. They soon learned that if they let a field lie fallow for a season, the soil would be richer and more productive the following year. Archaeological evidence shows how Jericho's growing wealth enabled the community to evolve. The inhabitants developed more elaborate political, religious, and economic structures. Fairly sophisticated engineering projects, such as the digging of a nine-foot-deep ditch around the village as a flood control device and the erection of a massive stone wall to protect against attackers, indicate the emergence of some form of political organization. Other findings hint at religious beliefs. Jericho's people buried their dead within the settlement, sometimes under the floors of their houses. They placed plastered skulls of their deceased on the walls, a practice that may suggest worship of the family's ancestors.

Archaeological evidence also reveals that long-distance commerce played a part in the lives of these villagers. They exchanged agricultural goods for turquoise from the Sinai Peninsula, shells from the Mediterranean and Red Seas, and most important of all, obsidian from Anatolia. This volcanic stone was the most important commodity in the Neolithic Age because it could be used for making sharp-edged tools such as arrowheads, spear points, and sickles for harvesting crops.

The second region of village settlement, the lands at the foot of the Zagros Mountains north of Mesopotamia, reveals a different sort of development pattern from that exhibited in the Levantine Corridor. Archaeologists have unearthed a hunter-gatherer camp at Sawi Chemi Shanidar, dating to about 9000 B.C.E. In this settlement, the domestication of animals long predated the development of agriculture. The settlers herded animals, but they did not cultivate crops for more than a thousand years.

The third region of early settled communities, Anatolia, followed patterns more like those of the Levantine Corridor. Around 8500 B.C.E. a few simple settlements appeared. The villagers raised pigs and traded obsidian for materials from far away, such as the highly prized blue lapis lazuli stones from northeastern Afghanistan. A thousand years later, about 7400 B.C.E., Anatolians began cultivating a variety of crops, including wheat and lentils. They started herding sheep at roughly the same time as the Abu Hureyra villagers, and domesticated dogs for hunting, herding, and protection. Many new villages sprang up in this region during the next millennium. The farmers lived in rectangular houses. More than mere huts, these houses featured plastered walls, hearths, courtyards, and ovens for baking breads.

Sometime after 6000 B.C.E. Anatolian communities grew more complex, with the emergence of religious beliefs and social hierarchies. For example, the Anatolian town of Çatal Hüyük consisted of thirty-two acres of tightly packed houses that the townspeople rebuilt more than a dozen times as their population expanded. Çatal Hüyük controlled the obsidian trade from Anatolia to the Levantine Corridor. The wealth from this trade fostered the emergence of social differences. The townspeople buried some of their dead with jewelry and other riches, a practice that indicates distinctions between wealthy and poor members of the society.

The long-distance obsidian trade sped up the development of communities in the Levantine Corridor, the Zagros Mountains, and Anatolia. These trade networks of the Neolithic Age laid the foundation for commercial and cultural encounters that would shape the development of civilizations for the next 5,000 years.

The Birth of Civilization in Southwest Asia

■ What transformed the earliest settled communities in Southwest Asia into the first cities, kingdoms, and empires in history?

By 6000 B.C.E., settled communities that depended on farming and herding had become the norm throughout Southwest Asia. With better and more plentiful food, such communities expanded steadily. Prosperity further stimulated commerce, and merchants from different regions began traveling regularly to one another's villages to trade. Mesopotamia, the dry floodplain bounded by the Tigris and Euphrates Rivers, became the meeting place of peoples and ideas from across an enormous geographical area. Over time, these Mesopotamian village communities began to resemble one another and a more uniform culture developed. The development of this more uniform culture set the stage for the emergence of civilization in Southwest Asia.

Sumer: A Constellation of Cities in Southern Mesopotamia

About 5300 B.C.E. the villages in Sumer, an ancient name for southern Mesopotamia, began a dynamic civilization that would flourish for 3,000 years. At the height of this civiliza-tion, Sumerians (who called themselves "the black-headed people" because of their characteristic dark hair) lived in thriving cities governed by leaders who controlled agricultural production, regulated long-distance trade, and presided over the worship of the gods.

Sumerian civilization was linked to water. Over centuries, the Sumerians learned to control the unpredictable waters of the Tigris and Euphrates Rivers. Sumerians first dug their own small channels to divert floodwaters from the two great rivers to irrigate their dry lands. Then they discovered that by combining the labor force of several villages, they could build and maintain irrigation channels on a large scale. The lands irrigated by river water provided rich yields of crops that fed Sumer's growing population. Villages blossomed into cities that became the foundation of Sumerian civilization.

By 2500 B.C.E., about twelve major cities in Sumer had emerged that controlled the Mesopotamian floodplain in an organized fashion. Some cities achieved impressive dimensions. Uruk, for example, covered about two square miles by 2500 B.C.E. and had a population estimated at between 10,000 and 50,000 people, including the peasants living in the countryside, many of whom labored to provide food for the urban populations as well as for themselves.

These cities served as the economic centers of southern Mesopotamia. Craft specialists such as potters, toolmakers, and weavers gathered in these urban settings to purchase food, swap information, and sell their goods. By providing markets for outlying towns, the cities spun a web of economic interdependence. Long-distance trade, made easier by the introduction of wheeled carts drawn by oxen, enabled merchants to bring timber, ores, building stone, and luxury items unavailable in Mesopotamia from Anatolia, the Levantine Corridor, Afghanistan, and Iran. With the introduction of the potter's wheel, Sumerian artisans could mass-produce containers for trade and storage of grain and other commodities.

Within the cities, an elite, headed by a king, controlled all economic resources. Centralized authorities directed the necessary labor for irrigation and water control, maintained warehouses for storing surplus grains, and distributed food to workers who labored on building projects for the king. Archaeological excavations reveal that the elite— priests, aristocrats, important civil administrators, and wealthy merchants—lived in luxurious houses near the temples, while everyone else crowded into small mud-brick houses with few comforts. Control over the economic resources of their cities enabled kings to supply armies and lead them into battle. Sumerian kings frequently waged war against one another in an effort to increase their territory and power. This rivalry prevented Sumerian cities from uniting politically, but the kings maintained diplomatic relations with one another as well as with rulers throughout Southwest Asia and Egypt, primarily to protect their trading networks. Safe trade links helped tie the Sumerian cities together and fostered a common Sumerian culture.

Through trade and warfare and from the many diplomats, soldiers, travelers, and slaves who passed through Mesopotamia's cities, the Sumerians knew much about the natural resources, economic organization, and customs that characterized the foreign peoples around them. The world known to them extended from India to the east to the Caucasus Mountains to the north; to Egypt and Ethiopia to the south; and to the Mediterranean Sea to the west. Sumerians strongly believed that the gods favored them over all other peoples, and they developed intense prejudices against their neighbors, accusing them of cowardice, stupidity, and treachery.

Religion—powerfully influenced by Mesopotamia's volatile climate—played a central role in daily life. Sumerians knew firsthand the famine and destruction that could result from sudden floods, storms, and winds. They envisioned each of these natural forces as a god who, like a human king or queen, had to be pleased and appeased. The all-powerful king Anu, the father of the gods, ruled the sky. Enlil was master of the wind and guided humans in the proper use of force. Enki ruled the Earth and rivers and guided human creativity and inventions. Inanna was the goddess of love, sex, fertility, and warfare. Sumerians believed that in order to survive they must continually demonstrate their subservience to the gods, and their practice of constantly feeding these deities with sacrifices was one way of doing so.

The Sumerian worldview revolved around religious belief. Each Sumerian city was protected by one god or goddess. The deity's temples served as the center of the city and the focus of religious life. In Uruk, for example, two enormous temples dominated the community: the Ziggurat of Anu (the supreme sky god) and the Temple of Heaven Precinct. This latter complex of buildings contained a colonnaded courtyard and a large limestone temple dedicated to Inanna (also known as Ishtar), the goddess of love and war and the city's special guardian. All Sumerian cities had similar temples that towered over the city, reminding all the inhabitants of the omnipresent gods who controlled their destiny.

Sumerians told exciting stories about their gods and heroes. One of the most popular figures in Sumerian ballads was the legendary king Gilgamesh of Uruk. Part god and part man, Gilgamesh—accompanied by his stalwart companion, Enkidu—embarked on many adventures that delighted Mesopotamian audiences for thousands of years.

DOCUMENT

The Clash Between Civilization and Nature: The Taming of Enkidu

The Sumerians saw their civilization as tightly linked to nature, as this passage from the tale of Gilgamesh suggests. This excerpt tells how Enkidu, Gilgamesh's companion, first became civilized. Originally living like a wild animal, Enkidu prevents hunters from trapping game. But city officials send him a prostitute who tames him by having sex with him for a week, and introducing him to cooked food, beer, and clothing. As a result of this epic sexual encounter, Enkidu loses his ability to talk to the animals. The episode teaches that civilization imposes control on natural forces, transforming them in the process. In the figure of the prostitute we see nature controlled and regulated by the city—a metaphor for the Sumerians' civilization.

In the wilderness the goddess Aruru created valiant
    Enkidu . . .
He knew neither people nor settled living . . .
He ate grasses like gazelles,
And jostled at the watering hole with the animals . . .
Then Shamhat [the prostitute] saw him—a primitive,
A savage fellow from the depths of the wilderness! . . .
Shamhat unclutched her bosom, exposed her sex,
And Enkidu took in her voluptuousness.
She was not restrained, but took his energy . . .

For six days and seven nights Enkidu stayed aroused,
And had intercourse with the prostitute,
Until he was sated with her charms.
But when he turned his attention to the animals,
The gazelles saw Enkidu and darted off,
The wild animals distanced themselves from his body . . .
Enkidu knew nothing about eating bread for food,
[nor] of drinking beer he had not been taught to.
The prostitute spoke to Enkidu, saying:
"Eat the food, Enkidu, it is the way one lives.
Drink the beer, as it is the custom of our land."
Enkidu ate the food until he was sated,
He drank the beer—seven jugs!—and became expansive
    and sang with joy!
He was elated and his face glowed.
He splashed his shaggy body with water,
And rubbed himself with oil and turned into a human.
He put on some clothing and became like a warrior.
He took up weapons and chased lions so shepherds could
    rest at night.
With Enkidu as their guard, the herders could lie down.

Source: Excerpts from Kovacs, Maureen Gallery, translator, *The Epic of Gilgamesh,* with an Introduction and Notes. Copyright © 1985, 1989 by the Board of Trustees of the Leland Stanford Junior University. With the permission of Stanford University Press, www.sup.org.

The tale describes how the gods created Enkidu to be Gilgamesh's companion and balance the king's rash disposition. Together the two men battled monsters and set out on long journeys in search of adventure. As a result of his travels, Gilgamesh became a wiser king and his subjects benefited from his new wisdom.

Sumerian culture exerted an enormous impact on the peoples of ancient Southwest Asia. Sumerians devised the potter's wheel, and also the wagon and the chariot, which proved essential for daily transportation and warfare. The Sumerians were skilled architects, as their ziggurats and city walls reveal. Their irrigation systems show their mastery of hydraulic engineering. They also developed detailed knowledge about the movement of the stars, planets, and the moon—especially as these movements pertained to agricultural cycles.

The Sumerians also made impressive innovations in mathematics. The first numerals (symbols for numbers) emerged around the same time as writing. Archaeologists have found many Sumerian tablets that show multiplication tables, square and cube roots, and exponents, as well as other practical information such as how to calculate compound interest on loans. Sumerian numeracy has left a lasting imprint on Western culture. The Sumerians divided the circle into 360 degrees, and developed a counting system based on sixty in multiples of ten—a system still in use in the way we tell time.

Perhaps the Sumerians' most important cultural innovation was their development of writing. The Sumerians devised a unique script used to record their language. Historians call the symbols that were pressed onto clay tablets with sharp objects cuneiform°, or wedge-shaped, writing. The earliest known documents written in this language come from Uruk about 3200 B.C.E. Researchers believe, however, that the roots of cuneiform writing date back 10,000 years, when people began to cultivate crops and domesticate animals in Southwest Asia. To keep track of quantities of produce and numbers of livestock, villagers began using small clay tokens of different shapes to represent and record these quantities. The tokens took the uncertainty out of transactions, reducing conflict because parties to a transaction no longer had to rely simply on memory or spoken agreements. After several centuries, people stopped using tokens and simply impressed the shapes directly on a flat piece of clay or tablet with a pointed stick.

As commodities and trading became more complex, the number of symbols multiplied. By 3000 B.C.E. the number of symbols had been streamlined from about a thousand to approximately 500, but learning even 500 signs re-

Cuneiform Texts
This clay tablet, written on in cuneiform, or "wedge-shaped" letters, is early in the development of the script. Dating from about 3000 B.C.E., it lists what are probably temple offerings under the categories day one, day two, and day three.

quired intensive study. The scribes, the people who mastered these signs, became valued members of the community. Sumerian cuneiform writing spread, and other peoples of Mesopotamia and Southwest Asia began adapting it to record information in their own languages.

From Akkad to the Amorite Invasions

The political independence of Sumer's cities ended around 2340 B.C.E. Conquered by a warrior who took the name Sargon ("true king"), Sumer's cities found themselves swallowed up by Mesopotamia's first great empire. Sargon came from Akkad, a region in Mesopotamia north of Sumer. Sargon's people, the Akkadians, had lived in Mesopotamia for more than a thousand years. The Akkadians began to migrate into Mesopotamia from their original homes somewhere in the Levantine Corridor during the late fourth millennium B.C.E. Their settlements grew in size, and although they intermingled with the native Sumerian population they preserved their own language and customs.

By bringing cities with very different languages, culture, and traditions under his rule, Sargon (r. ca. 2340–ca. 2305 B.C.E.) created a dynamic empire that endured for more than a century. The term empire° identifies a kingdom or any other type of state that controls foreign territories, either on the same continent or overseas. The realm that Sargon had established reached its greatest extent about 2220 B.C.E. Controlling a large empire posed new challenges for Akkadian rulers. To surmount them, Sargon and his successors imitated and expanded on the governing methods they observed in individual Sumerian cities. For example, to secure the loyalty of their many subjects, Akkadian kings presented themselves as symbols of unity in the form of semidivine figures. After a king's death, his subjects worshiped him as a god. Some monarchs claimed to be gods while they were alive.

Raising the revenues to meet the costs of running their enormous empire presented another problem for Akkadian kings. The king paid for all the public buildings, irrigation projects, and temples throughout his realm, as well as for the immense army required to defend, control, and expand it. Monarchs generated revenues in several ways. One key source of revenue was the leasing out of the vast farmlands that belonged to the king. Kings also required conquered peoples to pay regular tribute in the form of trade goods, produce, and gold and silver. In addition, Akkadian kings depended on the revenue generated by commerce. They placed heavy taxes on raw materials imported from foreign lands.

In fact, most Akkadian kings made long-distance trade the central objective of their foreign policy. They signed treaties with foreign kings and sent military expeditions as far as Anatolia and Iran to obtain timber, metals, luxury goods, and construction materials. Akkadian troops protected these international trade routes and managed the maritime trade in the Persian Gulf, where merchants brought goods by ship from India and southern Arabia.

The cities of Mesopotamia prospered under Akkadian rule. Even so, Akkadian rulers could not hold their empire together for reasons that historians do not completely understand. One cause was marauding tribes from the Zagros Mountains, who repeatedly infiltrated the kingdom and caused tremendous damage. Akkadian kings lost control of their lands and a period of anarchy began about 2103 B.C.E. "Who was king? Who was not king?" lamented a writer during this time of troubles. The kingdom finally collapsed about 2100 B.C.E.

With the fall of Akkad, the cities of Sumer regained their independence, but they were quickly reunited under Ur-Nammu (r. ca. 2112–ca. 2095 B.C.E.), king of the Sumerian city of Ur. Ur-Nammu established a powerful dynasty that lasted for more than a century. The kings of Ur strengthened the central government by turning formerly independent cities and their territories into provinces and appointing administrators to govern them.

Ur's kings also centralized economic production in their empire. The royal administration controlled most long-distance trade and developed a vigorous industry in woolen garments and leather goods. Ur's rulers supported thousands of artisans and laborers who were paid in beer and various agricultural products. The materials the artisans produced were traded throughout Southwest Asia. Wealth also flowed to the kings of Ur from farming and herding. The kings owned huge herds of livestock that grazed on royal estates, but ordinary people were not permitted to possess agricultural lands. Most of Ur's citizens worked either as tenant farmers on estates owned by the king and the political leaders, or as slaves. Each year government officials collected tens of thousands of cattle and hundreds of

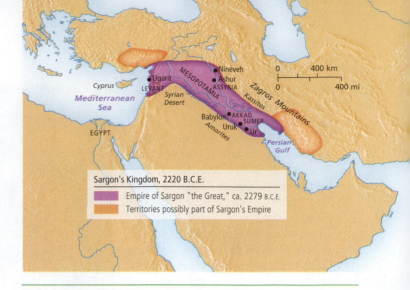

Map 1.2 Sargon's Empire, 2220 B.C.E.
Sargon of Akkad created an empire that included many distinct ethnic groups. For the first time in history, rulers had to struggle with the resistance of diverse subject peoples.

DOCUMENT

The Legend of King Sargon

The Akkadian king Sargon inspired many legends. The following story tells how his mother, a priestess, bore him in secret and put him in a basket in the river, from which a water bearer rescued him. The document explains how Sargon eventually became king of the Mesopotamians through the favor of the goddess Ishtar. The tale of a baby found in the bulrushes who achieves greatness was a Sumerian story already old in Sargon's day. A similar tale about the prophet Moses would be recorded in the Hebrew Bible more than a thousand years later. The recurrence of such literary motifs over a period of more than 3,000 years indicates the pervasive influence of Sumerian culture on subsequent civilizations of Southwest Asia.

Sargon, the mighty king, king of Agade, am I.
My mother was a high priestess, my father I knew not . . .
My mother, the high priestess, conceived me, in secret she
   bore me.
She set me in a basket of rushes, with bitumen she sealed
   my lid.
She cast me into the river which rose not over me.
The river bore me up and carried me to Akki, the drawer of
   water. . . .
Akki, the drawer of water, took me as his son and reared me.
Akki, the drawer of water, appointed me as his gardener.
While I was a gardener, Ishtar granted me her love.
And for four and [. . .] years I exercised kingship.
The black-headed people I ruled, I governed. . . .

Source: From *Chronicles Concerning Early Babylonian Kings*, by L. W. King. London: British Museum, 1907.

thousands of sheep and redistributed them to temples throughout the kingdom for use in sacrifices.

The most important innovation in Ur occurred in the realm of the law. Ur-Nammu compiled the first known collection of laws in ancient Mesopotamia. His laws reveal his determination to provide social justice for his subjects. The custom of writing down laws so that citizens and later generations could refer to them became a strong tradition in Western civilization.

The kings of Ur used political innovations, economic centralization, and legal codification to strengthen their hold over Sumer's cities; they did not, however, challenge or change the key facets of Sumerian culture. Ur's monarchs continued the long Mesopotamian tradition of building elaborate temple complexes featuring ziggurats, palaces, and tombs to demonstrate their piety. Like earlier Mesopotamian rulers, Ur's kings considered themselves gods. They placed their tombs in the temple complex of the moon god Nanna, Ur's special protector.

Despite their sophisticated government, the kings of Ur could not stave off political fragmentation. About 2000 B.C.E., seminomadic peoples known as Amorites began invading Mesopotamia from the steppes to the west and north. They seized fortified towns, taking food and supplies and causing widespread destruction. Their invasions destabilized the economy of Mesopotamia as well as of other regions of Southwest Asia. Peasants fled from the fields, and with no food or revenues, inflation and famine overcame the empire. Ur collapsed, and Mesopotamia shattered once again into a scattering of squabbling cities. Taking advantage of the political turmoil and attracted by the abundant food supplies, tribes of Amorites settled in Mesopotamian lands.

Ziggurat of Ur
Built of mud-brick, the Ziggurat of Ur was the focal point of religious life. This vast temple was built by King Ur-Nammu of the Third Dynasty (2112–2095 B.C.E.) and restored by the British archaeologist Sir Leonard Woolley in the 1930s.

New Mesopotamian Kingdoms: Assyria and Babylonia

Within a few generations, the Amorites absorbed the culture of the Mesopotamian urban communities they had conquered. Two new kingdoms, Babylonia and Assyria, emerged in the lands once controlled by Sumer and Akkad and coexisted for more than two centuries. The phenomenon of invaders absorbing the culture of sophisticated communities they conquered and then creating something new would often be repeated as Western civilization evolved.

Ashur, the major city in Assyria, began as a trading hub on the upper Tigris River some time before 2000 B.C.E. The discovery of bronze making may be one reason that Assyria's power began to expand. Bronze, an easily worked but very hard metal, became highly valued for both military and ornamental uses. By 1900 B.C.E. the Assyrians had established an extensive trading network in metals as well as agricultural products such as barley and wool that reached as far as Anatolia and Syria. They also controlled and operated about a dozen trading colonies throughout these regions.

By 1762 B.C.E., however, Assyria and all of Mesopotamia fell under the rule of King Hammurabi of Babylon, one of humanity's first great empire builders. The kingdom of Babylonia, a mixture of Sumerian and Amorite cultures, emerged about 1800 B.C.E. as the dominant power in southern Mesopotamia. To secure their rule and enrich their coffers, Babylonian kings embarked on the conquest of neighboring lands. Their capital city, Babylon, grew wealthy. Under the leadership of Hammurabi (r. 1792–1750 B.C.E.), Babylonia gained control of all of Mesopotamia, including the Assyrian realm. Impressed by his own victories, Hammurabi called himself "King of the Four Quarters of the World."

Hammurabi also called himself the "King of Justice," a well-deserved title because his historical legacy is a rigorous system of justice codified in law. The 282 civil, commercial, and criminal laws contained in the Law Code of Hammurabi unveil the social values and everyday concerns of Babylonia's rulers. For example, the irrigation system on which Babylonian agriculture depended is a frequent focus of the code. Many laws related specifically to damages and personal responsibility with regard to irrigation. Similarly, the code buttressed Babylon's social hierarchy by drawing legal distinctions between classes of people. The crimes of aristocrats were treated more leniently than were the offenses

DOCUMENT
Hammurabi's Law Code

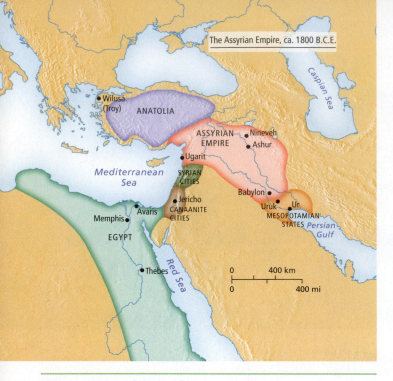

Map 1.3 Assyrian Empire, ca. 1800 B.C.E.
The Assyrians combined warfare and commerce to create their empire in Mesopotamia.

of common people, while slaves were given no rights at all. At the same time, however, Hammurabi's Code introduced one of the fundamentals of Western jurisprudence: the idea that the punishment must suit the crime. One law reads: "If a man has opened his channel for irrigation and has been negligent and allowed the water to wash away a neighbor's field, he shall pay grain equivalent to the crops of his neighbors."[1] Through its introduction of such abstract principles as "an eye for an eye," Hammurabi's Code helped shape legal thought in Southwest Asia for a millennium. It is possible that it later influenced the laws of the Hebrews, and thus through the Hebrew Bible continues to mold ideas about justice to this day.

Babylonian society contained a private sector of merchants, craftspeople, farmers, and sailors. With no ties to the temples or the king, these free people grew prosperous. Merchants traveling by land and sea brought textiles and metals as well as luxury items such as gold and silver jewelry and gems from Anatolia, Egypt, Iran, Afghanistan, and lands along the Persian Gulf and Red Sea. This private sector enjoyed a degree of personal freedom unique in ancient Mesopotamia.

Nevertheless, Hammurabi and his successors imposed increasingly heavy taxes on their subjects. These financial demands provoked great resentment, and when Hammurabi died, many Babylonian provinces successfully revolted. The loss of revenue weakened the Babylonian imperial government. Successive kings tried to maintain their control by increasing the number of bureaucrats to enforce laws and to collect taxes, but such measures only made the government top-heavy. By 1500 B.C.E. it collapsed.

The Emergence of Egyptian Civilization

■ How did civilization take shape along the Nile River in Egypt?

As the civilizations of Mesopotamia rose and fell, another emerged far to the south: Egypt. A long and narrow strip of land in the northeast corner of the African continent, Egypt depended for its survival on the Nile, the world's longest river, which flows north into the Mediterranean Sea from one of its points of origin in eastern Africa 4,000 miles away. The northernmost part of Egypt, where the Nile enters the Mediterranean, is a broad and fertile delta. In ancient times, Egypt controlled an 850-mile strip of land along the Nile. The river flooded annually from mid-July to mid-October, leaving behind rich deposits of silt ideal for planting crops. In its ancient days, the Nile abounded with fish, water birds, and game on the shore. The rich banks of the Nile provided an ideal setting for agriculture and settled communities.

Historians organize the long span of ancient Egyptian history into four main periods: Predynastic (10,000–3000 B.C.E.), the Old Kingdom (3000–2200 B.C.E.), the Middle Kingdom (2040–1785 B.C.E.), and the New Kingdom (1600–1100 B.C.E., discussed in Chapter 2). Times of political disruption between the kingdoms are called intermediate periods. Despite these periods of disruption, the Egyptians maintained a remarkably stable civilization for several millennia.

The Old Kingdom, ca. 3500–2200 B.C.E.

Like the peoples of Mesopotamia, the Egyptians were originally hunter-gatherers who slowly turned to growing crops and domesticating animals. Small villages, in which people could coordinate their labor most easily, appeared along the banks of the Nile between 5000 and 4000 B.C.E. By 3500 B.C.E., Egyptians could survive comfortably through agriculture and herding. With the transition to settled life complete, Egyptian society began to develop in many new ways. Small towns grew quickly in number along the Nile, and market centers connected by roads emerged as hubs where artisans and merchants exchanged their wares.

Towards the end of the Predynastic period, between 3500 and 3000 B.C.E., energetic trade along the Nile River resulted in a shared culture and unified way of life. Towns along the Nile grew into small kingdoms, whose rulers constantly warred with one another, attempting to grab more land and extend their power. The big consumed the small, and by 3000 B.C.E., the towns had been absorbed into just two kingdoms: Upper Egypt in the south and

Lower Egypt in the north. These two then united, forming what historians term the Old Kingdom.

With the unification of Egypt under one king, a new era dawned for this civilization. In the newly built capital city of Memphis, the Egyptian kings established themselves as the focal points of religious, social, and political life. Under the kings' careful supervision, the Old Kingdom stabilized and took on many of the characteristics of early civilizations we have seen in Mesopotamia, such as semi-divine kingship, literate bureaucracies, a centralized economy, and strong support of long-distance trade.

Egyptian monarchs considered themselves gods as well as kings and believed that

DOCUMENT

Elders' Advice to Their Successors

Ra, the sun god and creator of the universe, had chosen them to rule as his representatives on Earth. In their role as religious leaders, kings claimed to control even the Nile and its life-giving floods. To the Egyptians, the presence of the kings meant that cosmic order reigned, and that the kingdom was protected against forces of disorder and destruction. The rulers steadily amassed more power, and by 2600 B.C.E. they owned the largest and richest agricultural lands.

The power of the kings was highly centralized. Authority began with the king and passed to his court officials and then to provincial governors who delegated power to the mayors of cities and villages. Administrators collected Egypt's surplus produce—coinage would not be used in Egypt for another 2,000 years—and then the kings' officials redistributed it throughout the kingdom. Surplus crops fed the armies that protected Egyptian territories and long-distance trade as well as the peasants who labored on public works such as temples, roads, and irrigation projects.

The job of keeping records of the kings' possessions and supervising food production fell to the scribes, who were trained in hieroglyph writing. This form of writing involved a set of several thousand signs called *hieroglyphs,* literally "sacred carvings." Hieroglyphs represent both sounds (as in our alphabet) and objects (as in a pictorial system). The hieroglyph system was very complex, all the more so because it diverged from the spoken Egyptian language. Consequently, learning hieroglyphs for literary or administrative purposes meant acquiring a second language and took years of schooling to master. It was worth the effort, however, for knowledge of hieroglyphs gave scribes great power. For 3,000 years, these royal bureaucrats kept the machinery of Egyptian government running despite the rise and fall of dynasties.

Narmer the Unifier of Egypt
Carved pieces of stone called *palettes* were originally crafted in the Predynastic period as holders for cosmetics, but they evolved into objects with important religious and symbolic functions. This sample shows King Narmer of Hierakonpolis, who lived about 3100 B.C.E. With his right hand he holds a mace and is about to smash the skull of an enemy. He stands on two dead enemies, as a servant behind him carries his sandals. A falcon god, Horus (*Hierakonpolis* means "City of the Falcon"), sits in a papyrus plant holding an enemy's severed head. Narmer wears the White Crown of Upper Egypt and a bull's tail, symbolizing his virility. On the other side, he wears the Red Crown of Lower Egypt, which he has conquered.

Like bureaucrats, priests in the king's service grew powerful. Priests came from elite families, often the king's, and their positions passed from father to son. They owned vast estates, including the temples to the god they served, and they became enormously wealthy. In addition, they often played a major role in political life. Kings sought their advice to ensure that in their leadership they were implementing the will of the gods.

Religious Beliefs in the Old Kingdom

Egypt's religion was polytheistic°. Egyptians believed that many gods controlled their destinies. Ra, the sun god, was one of the most important Egyptian deities. Embodying the power of Heaven over Earth, Ra had created the universe and everything in it. He journeyed across the sky every day in a boat, rested at night, and returned in the morning to resume his eternal journey. By endlessly repeating the cycle of rising and setting, the sun symbolized the harmonious order of the universe that Ra established. The sun's reappearance at dawn every day gave Egyptians the hope of life after death.

Evil, however, constantly threatened the order of the universe in the form of Apopis, a serpent god whose coils could trap Ra's boat like a reef in the Nile. Ra's cosmic journey could continue only if proper worship and justice existed among humans. To make this possible, Ra created Egypt's kings, who shared in his divine nature and who ruled as his representatives on Earth.

Gods and Kings in Mesopotamian Justice

Mesopotamian kings placed a high priority on ruling their subjects justly. Shamash, the sun god and protector of justice, named two of his children Truth and Fairness. In the preface to his law code, Hammurabi explained the relationship between his rule and divine justice:

At that time, Anu and Enlil [two of the greatest gods], for the well-being of the people, called me by name, Hammurabi, the pious, god-fearing prince, and appointed me to make justice appear in the land [and] to destroy the evil and wicked, so that the strong might not oppress the weak, [and] to rise like Shamash over the black-headed people [the people of Mesopotamia].[2]

Courts in Mesopotamian cities handled cases involving property, inheritance, boundaries, sale, and theft. A special panel of royal judges and officials handled cases involving the death penalty, such as treason, murder, sorcery, theft of temple goods, or adultery. Mesopotamians kept records of trials and legal decisions on clay tablets so that others might learn from them and avoid additional lawsuits.

A lawsuit began when an individual brought a dispute before a court for trial and judgment. The court consisted of three to six judges chosen from among the town's leading men, who typically included merchants, scribes, and officials in the town assembly. The judges could speak with authority about the community's principles of justice.

Individuals involved in the dispute spoke on their own behalf and presented testimony through witnesses, written documents, or statements made by leading officials. Witnesses took strict oaths to tell the truth in a temple before the statue of a god. Once the parties presented all the evidence, the judges made their decision and pronounced the verdict and punishment.

Sometimes the judges asked the defendants to clear themselves by letting the god in whose name the oath was taken make the judgment. The accused person would then undergo an ordeal or test in which he or she had to jump into a river and swim a certain distance underwater. Individuals who survived were considered innocent. Drowning constituted proof of guilt and a just punishment rendered by the gods.

The following account of one such ordeal comes from the city of Mari, about 1770 B.C.E. In this case a queen was accused of casting spells on her husband. The maid whom she forced to undergo the ordeal on her behalf drowned, and we do not know whether the queen received further punishment:

Concerning Amat-Sakkanim . . . whom the river god overwhelmed . . . : "We made her undertake her plunge, saying to her, 'Swear that your mistress did not perform any act of sorcery against Yarkab-Addad her lord; that she did not reveal any palace secret nor did another person open the missive of her mistress; that your mistress did not commit a transgression against her lord.' In connection with these oaths they had her take her plunge; the river god overwhelmed her, and she did not come up alive."[3]

This account illustrates the Mesopotamian belief that sometimes only the gods could make decisions about right and wrong. Kings willingly allowed the gods to administer justice in their kingdoms. In this way, divine justice and royal justice became part of the same system.

By contrast, the following trial excerpts come from a homicide case in which humans, not gods, made the final judgment. About 1850 B.C.E., three men murdered a temple official named Lu-Inanna. For unknown reasons they told the victim's wife, Nin-dada, what they had done. King Ur-Ninurta of the city of Isin sent the case to be tried in the city of Nippur, the site of an important court. When the case came to trial, nine accusers asked that the three murderers be executed. They also requested that Nin-dada should be put to death because she had not reported the murder to the authorities. The accusers said:

They who have killed a man are not worthy of life. Those three males and that woman should be killed in front of the chair of Lu-Inanna, the son of Lugal-apindu, the religious official.

In her defense, two of Nin-dada's supporters pointed out that she had not been involved in the murder and therefore should be released:

Granted that the husband of Nin-dada, the daughter of Lu-Ninurta, has been killed, but what had the woman done that she should be killed?

The court agreed with this latter argument on the grounds that Nin-dada was justified in keeping silent because her husband had not provided for her properly. Then the members of the Assembly of Nippur faced the three murderers and said:

A woman whose husband did not support her . . . why should she not remain silent about him? Is it she who killed her husband? The punishment of those who actually killed him should suffice.

In accordance with the decision of the court, the defendants were executed.

This approach to justice—using witnesses, evaluating evidence, and rendering a verdict in a court protected by the king—demonstrates the Mesopotamians' desire for fairness. This court decision became an important precedent that later judges frequently cited.

Questions of Justice

1. How would a city benefit by letting a panel of royal officials make judgments about life-and-death issues? How would the king benefit?
2. These trials demonstrate that the enforcement of justice in Mesopotamia depended on the interaction of religious, social, and political beliefs. How does this interaction help us understand Mesopotamian civilization?

Taking It Further

Greengus, Samuel. "Legal and Social Institutions of Ancient Near Mesopotamia," in *Civilizations of the Ancient Middle East*, ed. Jack M. Sasson, vol. 1, pp. 469–484. 1995. Describes basic principles of law and administration of justice, with a bibliography of ancient legal texts.

Kuhrt, Amélie. *The Ancient Middle East: ca. 3000–330 B.C.*, vol. 1. 1995. An authoritative survey combining archaeological and textual evidence.

Hammurabi stands because his status is lower than Shamash's. He raises his hand in a gesture of respect and speaks directly to the god.

The god, seated on a throne, wears a crown of horns, a scepter, and a ring. Flames rise from his shoulders.

Hammurabi's code was written in Babylonian cuneiform script. This stone copy stands taller than seven feet.

The Law Code of Hammurabi
This copy of Hammurabi's Code shows Hammurabi receiving the law directly from the sun god, Shamash.

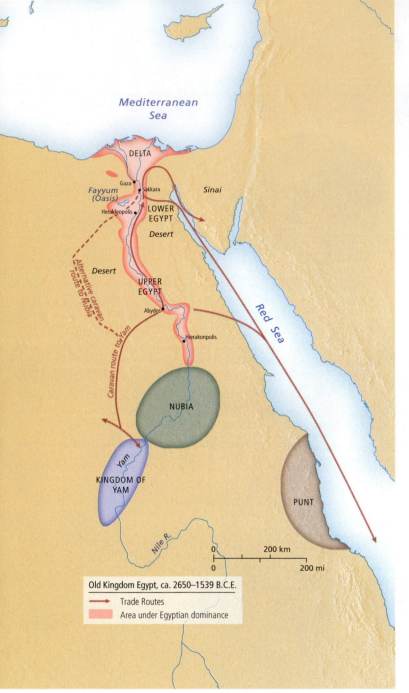

Mediterranean Sea

DELTA

Gaza

Sakkara

Sinai

Fayyum (Oasis)

Herakleopolis

LOWER EGYPT

Desert

Desert

Alternative caravan route to Nubia

UPPER EGYPT

Abydos

Hierakonpolis

Red Sea

Caravan route to Yam

NUBIA

Yam

KINGDOM OF YAM

PUNT

Nile R.

0   200 km

0   200 mi

Old Kingdom Egypt, ca. 2650–1539 B.C.E.

→ Trade Routes

Area under Egyptian dominance

Map 1.4   Old Kingdom Egypt, ca. 3000–2200 B.C.E.
During the Old Kingdom, Egyptians traded with the kingdom of Yam, Nubia, and the land of Punt (modern Somalia). Egyptian rulers built pyramids in Lower (northern) Egypt.

The Pyramids

With their emphasis on the afterlife, Egyptians took great pains to provide proper housing for the dead. Many tombs were built as monuments to the dead person's wealth and social status. These structures provided not only a resting place for the corpse but a symbolic entryway to the next life. Members of the elite were buried in expensive tombs filled with ivory furniture and other luxurious goods, but kings had the grandest tombs of all.

Burial customs in the Old Kingdom grew ever more elaborate. For the first several centuries of the Old Kingdom, kings built their tombs in the city of Abydos, the homeland of the first kings. The tombs consisted of an underground room with a special compartment for the royal corpse. The king's treasures filled nearby underground rooms. Above the ground sat a small palace featuring courtyards and halls suitable for a royal afterlife. The earliest of these tombs, dating to about 2800 B.C.E., contains the bones of animals and people sacrificed to accompany the ruler into the next world.

About 2680 B.C.E., architects began building a new kind of royal tomb. The defining feature was a great four-sided monument of stone in the shape of a pyramid. Elaborate temples in which priests worshiped statues of the king surrounded the monument. The structure also included compartments where the king could dwell in the afterlife in the same luxury he enjoyed during his life on Earth. King Djoser, the founder of the Old Kingdom, built the first pyramid complex at Saqqara near Memphis. Known today as the Step Pyramid, this structure rests above Djoser's burial place and rises high into the air in six steps, which represent a ladder to Heaven.

For the next 2,000 years, kings continued building pyramids for themselves and smaller ones for their queens, with each tomb becoming more architecturally sophisticated. The walls grew taller and steeper and contained hidden burial chambers and treasure rooms. The Great Pyramid at Giza, built around 2600 B.C.E. by King Khufu (or Cheops), stood as the largest human-made structure in the ancient world. It consists of more than two million stones that weigh an average of two and a half tons each. Covering thirteen acres, it reaches over 480 feet into the sky.

Building the pyramid complexes was a long and enormously costly task. In addition to the architects, painters,

IMAGE

The Pyramids at Giza

Egyptians also worshiped Osiris, the son of the sky and the Earth, as god of the dead. According to Egyptian belief, Osiris was murdered by his brother Seth, god of chaos, after Osiris married their sister Isis, goddess of fertility. Seth cut Osiris into pieces and scattered them over the Earth, but Isis gathered the pieces and restored Osiris to life. The death and resurrection of Osiris symbolized the natural cycles of regeneration and rebirth that the Egyptians witnessed each spring as their fields bore new crops. After his regeneration, Osiris became king of the underworld, where he judged the dead. Egyptians associated this powerful deity with mummification, by which they tried to preserve bodies after death. Representations of Osiris appeared in pyramids, where the mummies of kings rested for eternity.

sculptors, carpenters, and other specialists employed on the site throughout the year, stone masons supervised the quarrying and transportation of the colossal building blocks. Peasants, who were organized into work gangs and paid and fed by the king, provided the heavy labor when the Nile flooded their fields every year. As many as 70,000 workers out of a total population estimated at 1.5 million sweated on the pyramids every day. Entire cities sprang up around pyramid building sites to house the workmen, artisans, and farmers. The construction of enormous pyramids stopped after 2400 B.C.E., probably because of the expense, but smaller burial structures continued to be built for many centuries.

The Middle Kingdom, ca. 2040–1785 B.C.E.

Around 2200 B.C.E. the Old Kingdom collapsed, due to economic decline, the deterioration of royal authority, and a cycle of terrible droughts that triggered a breakdown of law and order. For 200 years, anarchy and civil war raged in Egypt during what historians call the First Intermediate Period. Finally, the governors of Thebes, a city in Upper Egypt, set out to reunify the kingdom. In 2040 B.C.E., Mentuhotep II consolidated his rule and established a vigorous new monarchy, initiating the Middle Kingdom (see Map 1.5).

Rulers in the Middle Kingdom defined a new role for themselves. They still viewed themselves as gods, but their rule became less despotic. Although they continued building large temple complexes to house themselves in the afterlife, these structures were not as grandiose as the Old Kingdom pyramids. The highly centralized bureaucracy opened to men of any social standing, as long as they could read and write hieroglyphs. Wealth spread more widely. The kings launched many public-works projects for the benefit of their subjects. Amenemhet I (r. 1991–1962 B.C.E.) and his successors transformed the marshy Fayyum Oasis, fifty miles southwest of Memphis, into a well-irrigated agricultural community that yielded abundant crops even in dry years.

Greater concern for the lives and needs of ordinary people also characterized the religious life of the Middle Kingdom. Because it stressed moral conduct more than the performance of rituals open only to the wealthy, the religion of the Middle Kingdom comforted more people with the hope of a satisfying afterlife.

DOCUMENT

Hymns of Praise to a Victorious King

These passages come from a collection of hymns of praise to King Sesostris III of the Middle Kingdom. Written on a papyrus scroll, the hymns were probably read aloud in an elaborate ritual when Sesostris, who lived in the northern city of Memphis, visited a town in southern (Upper) Egypt. References to "Two Lands" and his "double crown" refer to the symbolic unity of all of Egypt that this king represents. The Bowmen are raiders from Nubia, evidently a considerable problem during Sesostris's reign. The praise includes more general allusions to other enemies as well. Needless to say, the king triumphs over all of them and wins the universal devotion of his subjects.

I.

Hail to you, Son of Re [the sun god], our Horus,
   Divine of Form!
Land's protector who widens its borders,
Who smites foreign countries with his crown;
Who holds the Two Lands in his arms' embrace;
Who subdues foreign lands by a motion of his hands;
Who slays Bowmen without a blow of the club;

Who shoots the arrow without drawing the string;
Whose terror strikes the Bowmen in their land,
Fear of whom smites the Nine Bows.
Whose slaughter brought death to thousands of Bowmen,
Who had come to invade his borders. . . .
His majesty's tongue restrains Nubia.
His utterances make Asiatics flee. . . .

II.

How the gods rejoice:
You have strengthened their offerings!
How the people rejoice:
You have made safe their frontiers!
How your forbears rejoice:
You have enriched their portions!
How Egypt rejoices in your strength:
You have protected its customs!
How the people rejoice in your guidance:
Your might has won increase for them! . . .

Source: From Miriam Lichtheim, *Ancient Egyptian Literature: The Old and Middle Kingdoms,* Volume 1. Copyright © 1973 by The Regents of the University of California. Reprinted by permission.

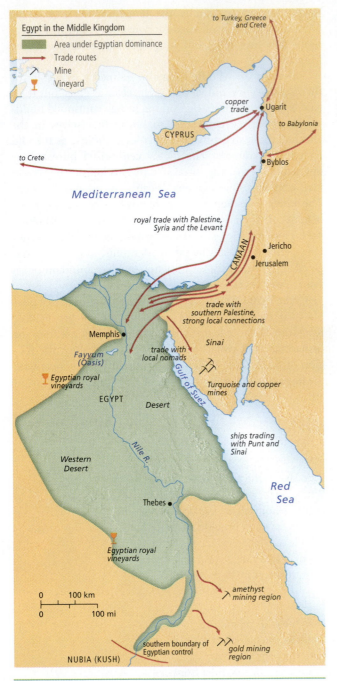

Map 1.5   Egypt in the Middle Kingdom
During the Middle Kingdom, Egyptian merchants traded extensively with Southwest Asia and the cities of the eastern Mediterranean. Turquoise and copper mines in the Sinai were heavily exploited.

Egyptian Encounters with Other Civilizations

During both the Old and Middle Kingdoms, Egypt's kings sought to protect the trade routes along which raw materi-

als and luxury goods were imported. Rulers did not hesitate to use force when necessary to protect their commercial interests. Some of them sent their armies to make punitive attacks in the western desert and in Sinai to stop raiders from robbing trade caravans. Other kings tried to maintain good relations with the chief trading cities of Syria and Palestine in order to stimulate trade.

From the earliest years of the Old Kingdom, Egypt cultivated friendly ties with the Mediterranean port city of Byblos, north of Beirut in modern Lebanon. Exchanges between Byblos and Egypt benefited both sides. Egyptians imported timber from Byblos for the construction of tombs and learned many shipbuilding techniques. The people of Byblos gained technical skills, especially in masonry and engineering, from the Egyptians, and also adopted some of the Egyptian gods. Thoth, the god of writing, became Taut in Byblos.

During the Old and Middle Kingdoms, Egyptian interactions with Nubia, the territory to the south, proved economically important. Egyptian merchants systematically exploited its natural resources of gold, timber, and animal skins. They enslaved many Nubians and transported them for labor in Egypt. Agents of Egyptian rulers, called Keepers of the Gateway of the South, tried to protect the merchants by keeping the peace with the warlike Nubian tribes. Slowly, Egyptian monarchs made their presence more permanent. About 1900 B.C.E., king Amenemhet built ten forts at strategic locations where trade routes from the interior of Africa reached the Nile River. Egyptian merchants placed the gold, ivory, and other natural resources that reached these forts into boats, which they sailed northward along the Nile to Egypt. Egyptians came to depend on these vast resources of Nubia.

Commercial connections between Egypt and other African lands were less important. Egyptian merchants traded with the land of Punt (modern Somalia) for spices and rare woods, and they opened turquoise mines in the Sinai. During the Old Kingdom, some merchants traded for skins, ivory, incense, and slaves among the peoples living in the Kingdom of Yam, located at the tributaries of the Nile River in the interior of eastern Africa, but the Egyptians abandoned trade with Africa south of Nubia during the Middle Kingdom.

With the desert on both sides of the Nile Valley protecting Egypt from invasion by foreign enemies, the Egyptians developed a distinctive culture characterized not only by economic prosperity but also by a powerful sense of self-confidence and optimism. Attracted by Egypt's stability and prosperity, peoples from different lands sought to settle in the Nile Valley. They took Egyptian names and assimilated into Egyptian culture. The government settled these immigrants, as well as war captives, throughout the kingdom where they could mix quickly with the local inhabitants. This willingness to accept newcomers into their kingdom lent Egyptian civilization even more vibrancy. During the last years of the Middle Kingdom, many merchants and large numbers of settlers moved into Egypt from Syria and Palestine. Around 1750 B.C.E., one such group from Syria, called the Hyksos, took control of Egypt and changed the direction of Egyptian history. As we shall see in Chapter 2, the Second Intermediate Period was marked by both foreign invasion and internal division.

The Transformation of Europe

■ How and why did food production and the use of metals transform the lives of the men and women who populated Europe in the Neolithic Age?

The elements that produced civilization in Mesopotamia and Egypt began to appear about 10,000 years ago. Western history claims the cultures that developed in these regions as remote ancestors. But in Europe, the core territory of Western civilization today, civilization developed later than in the floodplains of Mesopotamia and the Levantine Corridor. Because the climate was colder and forests had to be cleared, food production was more difficult in Europe. Consequently Europeans made the transition from hunting and gathering to food production much more slowly. The food-producing revolution that had begun in Southwest Asia around 8000 B.C.E. spread to Europe a thousand years later when farmers, probably from Anatolia, ventured to northern Greece and the Balkans. It took another 4,000 years for the inhabitants of Europe to clear forests and to establish farms and grazing lands. By 2500 B.C.E., most of Europe's hunting and gathering cultures had given way to farming societies. New patterns of wealth, prestige, and inheritance had begun reshaping some communities but Europeans did not yet live in cities. Without the critical mass of people and possessions that accompanied city life, Europeans could not yet develop the specialized religious, economic, and political classes that characterize a "civilization." The transition to food production, however, laid the economic foundations of subsequent European cultures (see Map 1.6).

As farmers and herders spread across Europe, people adapted to different climates and terrain. A variety of cultures evolved from these differences. Archaeologists have named the different cultures of Neolithic Europe after some distinguishing feature of their pottery, tools, methods of constructing houses, or burial customs.

The Linear Pottery Culture

By 5000 B.C.E. one of the most important of these cultures, the Linear Pottery culture, had spread across Europe from

CHRONOLOGY	
The Beginnings of Civilization	
150,000 years ago	Modern humans first appear in Africa
45,000 years ago	Modern humans spread through Africa, Asia, and Europe
15,000 years ago	Ice Age ends
10,000 years ago	Food production begins
9,500–3,000 years ago	Settled villages, domesticated plants and animals, and long-distance trade appear in Mesopotamia, Anatolia, and Egypt
7000–2500 B.C.E.	Agriculture spreads through Europe
3000 B.C.E.	Sumerian civilization develops in Mesopotamia
3000–2200 B.C.E.	Old Kingdom in Egypt
3200 B.C.E.	First known written documents in cuneiform appear
2040–1785 B.C.E.	Middle Kingdom in Egypt
1900 B.C.E.	Assyria grows powerful through trade and conquest
1800 B.C.E.	Babylonian civilization emerges; Hammurabi's law code prepared
1750–1560 B.C.E.	Hyksos rule in Egypt

modern-day Netherlands to Russia. Archaeologists call it the Linear Pottery culture because its people decorated their pottery with parallel lines. Their customs varied slightly in different regions, but they shared many similarities as well. For example, the Linear Pottery farmers lived in small villages of about sixty people. They built clusters of permanent family farmsteads made of timber and thatch, and rebuilt them over many generations. These farm families cultivated barley and other grains and kept sheep, goats, dogs, and, most important, cattle, which provided wealth and prestige. From gifts of jewelry and other luxury goods left in graves, archaeologists theorize that women were held in high esteem, perhaps because the people in these communities traced ancestry through them.

After about 4500 B.C.E., villages consisting of several hundred people began to appear in northern Europe, and the trend toward cultural diversity accelerated. In different regions, people used different kinds of pottery and probably spoke distinct languages.

As Linear Pottery settlements slowly spread, competition for farmlands and grazing lands stiffened. Archaeologists believe that men who controlled the livestock—the source of wealth and prestige—developed political authority. These early European elites tried to increase their influence by seizing the lands and herds of others. Conflicts broke out among groups, and people fortified their villages with defensive works. These struggles marked the beginnings of warfare in Europe.

During this era, the peoples of the Linear Pottery communities began building communal tombs with huge stones called *megaliths*. Megaliths survive in regions from Scandinavia to Spain and on islands in the western Mediterranean. The best-known example of a megalithic structure is Stonehenge, a monument in England. People began to build Stonehenge about 3000 B.C.E. as a ring of pits. Later generations reconstructed it several times, adding large stones. Stonehenge took its final form about 1600 B.C.E., when builders positioned immense stones, each weighing several tons, in standing positions. Stonehenge possibly measured the movement of stars, the sun, and the planets, and perhaps served as a place for religious ceremonies.

Around the same time early Europeans began experimenting with metallurgy, the art of using fire to shape metals such as copper into items such as tools or jewelry. Knowledge of metallurgy spread slowly across Europe from the Balkans, where people started to mine copper about 4500 B.C.E. Metallurgy would eventually prove as revolutionary as food production, but its beginnings were very modest. At first, people worked with copper only part of the year. Ötzi the Ice Man, for example, may have been both a shepherd and a coppersmith. Gradually, as copper tools and ornaments became more widely used, metalworkers became specialists. As villages became larger, wealthier inhabitants demonstrated their social status by wearing precious copper jewelry. Trade in metals flourished, changing Europe's economy by creating long-distance trading networks. In turn, these networks provided the basis for the meeting and blending of different cultural assumptions and ideas.

The Battle Axe Cultures

Between 3500 B.C.E. and 2000 B.C.E. the Battle Axe cultures gradually replaced the Linear Pottery cultures across Europe. Named for the stone and copper battle axes used in warfare, Battle Axe peoples cultivated many different types of crops and lived in rectangular single-family thatched dwellings. They may also have been the first peoples to domesticate the horse.

One of the better understood Battle Axe cultures is that of the Kurgan peoples, who made their homes on the edges of the Russian steppes beginning about 3000 B.C.E. A warrior culture, the Kurgan people had to cross long distances to trade for the copper they needed for their weapons. They began to migrate from southern Russia about 3500 B.C.E. As they traveled, their culture spread far to the west and south.

Scholars theorize that the Kurgan peoples brought with them a language that became the ancestor of the tongues spoken by half the world's population today. The majority of the languages spoken in Europe, the Americas, and other lands colonized by Europeans, as well as Persian and Armenian spoken in Southwest Asia, share similarities in vocabulary and grammar inherited from an Indo-European parent language. Most historians argue that the Kurgan peoples spoke this parent language, which then spread throughout Europe in the course of their migrations. The development of the Indo-European languages represents a foundation of Western civilization: the languages we speak.

Technology and Social Change

As the peoples of Europe developed their diverse cultures, their societies became socially stratified. One important tool that helped alter human relationships in early Europe was the plow, which became widely used around 2600 B.C.E. Once plow technology took hold, agricultural life in Europe underwent substantial changes over the course of a mere 200 years. The use of plows meant that fewer people were needed to cultivate Europe's heavy soils. With more people available to clear forest lands, new settlements sprang up and farming communities spread. The expansion of land

---

Map 1.6   Neolithic Cultures in Europe
During the Neolithic period, most of the peoples of Europe changed their way of life from hunting and gathering to food production. In the process, many new cultures developed.

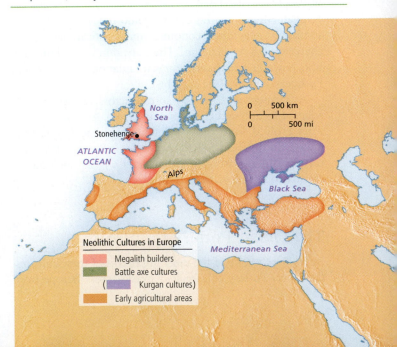

Stonehenge
This megalithic monument consists of two circles of standing stones with large blocks capping the circles. It was built without the aid of wheeled vehicles or metal tools, and the stones were dragged from many miles away.

under cultivation enabled farmers to move out from old family-controlled lands and start new homes. As a result, opportunities for individual initiative and the accumulation of wealth increased. Some farmers could afford trade goods of high prestige, and they passed their lands and possessions to their descendants, who used their inherited resources to acquire even more wealth. By exchanging these expensive and prestigious objects, men cultivated friendships and loyalty, established political and military ties, and formalized mutual obligations. Growing divisions resulted between rich and poor, the powerful and the weak.

Such changes were evident in western Europe between about 2600 and 2400 B.C.E. For the first time, individual graves played a prominent role in burial customs, which may indicate the emergence of new forms of authority based on the preeminence of individual men in the community, particularly those who controlled land and inheritances. The tombs contain weapons and luxury goods, suggesting not only that these individuals were wealthy and powerful men who could afford expensive symbols of their prestige and power, but also that they were warriors as well as or instead of farmers.

As warriors gained power, wealth, and influence in their communities, they emerged as political leaders, and they passed their wealth, political power, and social status down to their sons. These families came to dominate their societies. Historians call these elite groups nobles or aristocrats. The presence of male-dominated groups, designated by birth, that controlled the greatest wealth and enjoyed the greatest privileges in society remained unchallenged in Europe and a defining characteristic of Western civilization until the eighteenth century.

Conclusion

Civilization and the West

This chapter has described the change in human patterns of life from nomadic hunting and gathering to living in settled communities in which food was produced through agriculture and domestication of animals. This transformation took more than 8,000 years. The changes in food production led to the development of village settlements. Powerful elites emerged, and an individual's social status and gender defined what kind of work he or she performed. Soon human communities took on new characteristics. In Southwest Asia and Egypt, civilizations arose by about 3000 B.C.E. that were based on cities and devoted their resources to irrigation, warfare, and worship. The invention of writing enabled communities to record their laws and traditions. It also reinforced the long-distance trade that linked communities throughout Southwest Asia and beyond. Trade among these cities led to the encounters of different peoples. They exchanged new food production technologies, advances in crafts, new approaches to government and administration, and stories and religious ideas.

These changes unfolded over many centuries and did not happen everywhere at the same time. Europe lagged behind Southwest Asia and Egypt in the development of cities and the emergence of civilization. By the end of the Neolithic Age, "the West" did not yet exist, but from the civilizations of Egypt and Southwest Asia, Western civilization would inherit such crucial components as systems of writing and numeracy, the idea of a law code based on abstract principles, and gender-based divisions of labor and power.

By 3000 B.C.E., the rulers of Egypt and Mesopotamia had spun a web of interrelated economies and shared political interests. Over the next millennium, cities such as Ur and Ashur grew powerful under the watchful eyes of ambitious kings who constantly fought with one another. But these kings did not yet possess the skills needed to rule vast empires for an extended period of time. As we will see in the next chapter, they would soon learn.

Suggestions for Further Reading

For a comprehensive list of suggested readings, please go to www.ablongman.com/levack2e/chapter1

Andrews, Anthony P. *First Cities.* 1995. An excellent introduction to the development of urbanism in Southwest Asia, Egypt, India, China, and the Americas.

Bogucki, Peter. *Forest Farmers and Stockherders: Early Agriculture and Its Consequences.* 1988. A clear synthesis of archaeological evidence from northern Europe.

Cunliffe, Barry, ed. *The Oxford Illustrated Prehistory of Europe.* 1994. An important synthesis of recent research by leading archaeologists.

Fagan, Brian. *People of the Earth: An Introduction to World Prehistory.* 1998. A comprehensive textbook that introduces basic issues with a wealth of illustrations and explanatory materials.

Harris, David R., ed. *The Origins and Spread of Agriculture and Pastoralism in Eurasia.* 1996. A collection of detailed essays by noted experts that draw on the latest research.

Kemp, Barry J. "Unification and Urbanization of Ancient Egypt," in *Civilizations of the Ancient Middle East,* ed. Jack M. Sasson, vol. 2, pp. 679–690. 1995. Describes the emergence of towns and political unification of the early phases of Egyptian history.

Kuhrt, Amélie. *The Ancient Middle East: ca. 3000–330 B.C.,* vol. 1. 1995. An authoritative and up-to-date survey that combines archaeological and textual evidence in a lucid narrative with rich documentation.

Murnane, William J. "The History of Ancient Egypt: An Overview," in *Civilizations of the Ancient Middle East,* ed. Jack M. Sasson, vol. 2, pp. 691–718. 1995. A good place to start for a "big picture" of ancient Egyptian history.

Quirke, Stephen. *Ancient Egyptian Religion.* 1992. A brilliant synthesis and explanation of basic Egyptian beliefs and practices.

Redford, Donald B. *Egypt, Canaan, and Israel in Ancient Times.* 1993. A distinguished Egyptologist discusses 3,000 years of uninterrupted contact between Egypt and southwestern Asia.

Schmandt-Besserat, Denise. *How Writing Came About.* 1996. A highly readable and groundbreaking argument that cuneiform writing developed from a method of counting with tokens.

Shaw, I., ed. *The Oxford History of Ancient Egypt.* 2001. Provides excellent discussions of all aspects of Egyptian life.

Spindler, Konrad. *The Man in the Ice: The Discovery of a 5,000-Year-Old Body Reveals the Secrets of the Stone Age.* 1994. A leader of the international team of experts interprets the corpse of a Neolithic hunter found in the Austrian Alps.

Trigger, Bruce G. *Early Civilizations: Ancient Egypt in Context.* 1995. A leading cultural anthropologist examines Old and Middle Kingdom Egypt through comparison with the early civilizations of China, Peru, Mexico, Mesopotamia, and Africa.

Notes

1. *Code of Hammurabi,* trans. J. N. Postgate, 55–56. Cited in Postgate, *Early Mesopotamia: Society and Economy at the Dawn of History* (1992), 160.

2. Samuel Greengus, "Legal and Social Institutions of Ancient Near Mesopotamia," in *Civilizations of the Ancient Middle East,* ed. Jack M. Sasson, vol. 1 (1995), 471.

3. Ibid., 474.

The International Bronze Age and Its Aftermath: Trade, Empire, and Diplomacy, 1600–550 B.C.E.

2

I N 1984, SCUBA-DIVING ARCHAEOLOGISTS BEGAN TO EXCAVATE THE WRECK OF A rich merchant ship that sank about 1300 B.C.E. at Uluburun, off the southern coast of Turkey. Its cargo of raw materials and exotic luxury objects revealed a prosperous world of international trade and cultural exchange. A partial inventory includes ebony logs, ostrich eggshells, elephant tusks, and a trumpet carved from a hippopotamus tooth from Egypt. From Southwest Asia came exquisitely worked gold jewelry as well as nearly a ton of scented resin, perhaps intended for use as incense in religious worship. Finely painted storage jars from the island of Cyprus held pomegranates and probably olive oil. The archaeologists also recovered swords, daggers, and arrowheads, as well as hinged wooden writing boards with a thick wax surface on which business accounts could be recorded.

The most valuable portion of the cargo that the divers lifted from the ocean floor, however, consisted of 354 flat copper bars, each weighing about fifty pounds, and several bars of tin. When melted and mixed together, these metals produce bronze°. This alloy, which is much tougher than copper or tin by themselves, lends itself to the making of dishes, jewelry, tools, and especially weapons. The use of bronze ushered in a new era in the ancient world.

About 3200 B.C.E. people living in northern Syria and Iraq began making bronze. The technology spread slowly throughout Southwest Asia and into Egypt and Europe. Because deposits of tin and copper are not always present in the same areas, merchants traded over long distances to obtain the ores

House of the Admiral This lively wall painting, which may depict a religious celebration, comes from the so-called House of the Admiral on the island of Thera, midway between Crete and Greece. The painting is about twenty-two feet long and a foot and a half high. Created about 1500 B.C.E., before a volcanic explosion destroyed the settlement on Thera, this painting shows scenes of busy maritime activity outside a harbor town.

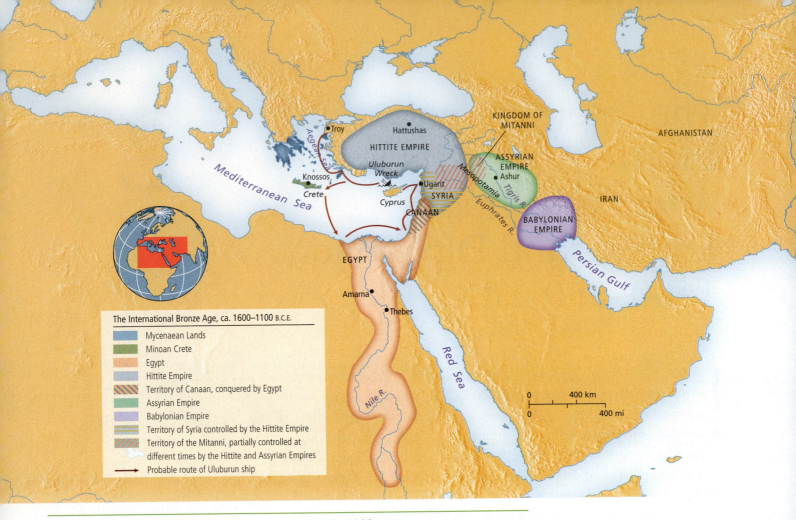

Map 2.1 The International Bronze Age, ca. 1600–1100 B.C.E.

For 500 years, networks of commerce and diplomacy tied together the distinct cultures of Egypt, Greece, Anatolia, and Southwest Asia.

with which to forge the prized alloy. As they traded, they spread knowledge about bronze technology among diverse peoples. By 1600 B.C.E., when peoples throughout Southwest Asia, Egypt, and Europe had mastered bronze making, the International Bronze Age began (see Map 2.1).

The new international trade in bronze provides the key to understanding how four separate regions became linked in a large area of political and cultural influence and thus began to lay the foundations of Western civilization. Egyptians controlled the first region, which consisted of their territories along the Nile in northeastern Africa and lands under their control in Southwest Asia. To the north, the Hittites dominated a second region in Anatolia (modern Turkey). To the east, Mesopotamia, the third region, contained the kingdoms of the Assyrians and the Babylonians. In the west, the fourth major region lay in the eastern Mediterranean where the Minoans on Crete and the Myceneans on mainland Greece developed maritime kingdoms. Several small mercantile kingdoms developed on the eastern edge of the Mediterranean region, serving as buffers between the great powers. These different cultures depended on an international trade network

to obtain the metals and other goods they needed for everyday life.

The continued quest for new sources of wealth spurred rulers in Egypt, the Hittite kingdom, Assyria, and Babylonia to conquer large realms and construct enormous, multiethnic empires. Yet these same rulers recognized that constant warfare interrupted trade and interfered with the successful management of territories. Discovering the advantages of international cooperation for the first time, rulers during this period developed a system of diplomacy that produced long periods of peace—an unprecedented achievement. That the Uluburun cargo ship could stop at so many ports and take on board merchandise from so many different kingdoms illustrates the benefit of these peaceful times.

This chapter examines how the peoples of the International Bronze Age and its aftermath engaged in a series of commercial, technological, and cultural exchanges. How, in other words, did the varied encounters between Bronze Age societies transform both international relations and these societies themselves? To understand these transformations, we shall consider the following questions:

- How did Egypt during the New Kingdom use warfare and diplomacy to develop an empire that reached from Nubia to Mesopotamia?
- What were the political, religious, and cultural traditions of the Hittite Empire in Anatolia and the Assyrian and Babylonian Empires in Mesopotamia?
- What were the characteristics of the Mediterranean civilizations of Minoan Crete, Mycenaean Greece, Ugarit, and Troy, and what roles did they play in international trade and politics?
- What forces brought the International Bronze Age to a close and how did the Phoenicians, Assyrians, and Babylonians build new kingdoms and empires in its wake?

Civilization of the Nile: The Egyptian Empire

- How did Egypt during the New Kingdom use warfare and diplomacy to develop an empire that reached from Nubia to Mesopotamia?

Egypt played a central role in the economic, diplomatic, and cultural networks that shaped the International Bronze Age. A prosperous new phase of Egyptian history began when the Middle Kingdom ended about 1650 B.C.E. During the next 500-year period, Egyptians created a vast multiethnic empire stretching from Africa to Southwest Asia. Under the direction of talented and aggressive rulers, Egyptian imperial civilization reached its greatest height.

From the Hyksos Era to the New Kingdom

Egyptian history changed course abruptly at the end of the Middle Kingdom when the Hyksos, a people from northern Palestine whose name meant "peoples of foreign lands" in Egyptian, invaded Egypt and established a new regime in the northern delta region. The Hyksos introduced to Egypt an advanced military technology that was revolutionizing warfare throughout Southwest Asia, Anatolia, and Greece. This technological innovation consisted of a chariot with wheels of bronze spokes. Two young men wearing bronze chain-mail armor rode into battle on each chariot, one driving the horses, the other shooting bronze-tipped arrows at the enemy. Troops of trained charioteers and bowmen easily outmaneuvered the traditional massed infantry forces and inflicted terrible ca-

sualties from a distance. Chariot warfare reshaped the economic policies and foreign relations of Egypt and all the other kingdoms and empires of the International Bronze Age. To meet the enormous expenses of training and supplying armies of charioteers, rulers carefully organized domestic resources and tried to acquire more wealth through trade and conquest.

About 1550 B.C.E. King Ahmose I (r. ca. 1569–ca. 1545 B.C.E.) mastered the new military tactics and technology and expelled the Hyksos from Egypt. Historians call the period of renewed Egyptian self-rule that began with Ahmose the New Kingdom (ca. 1550–1150 B.C.E.). Ahmose's new dynasty continued the highly centralized system of government that had been developed in the Middle Kingdom, but also added a powerful new force: a permanent, or standing, army. For the first time in Egyptian history, a ruler could count on the readiness of highly trained regiments of charioteers and infantrymen to go to war whenever he wished. Troops would also remain as garrisons in conquered lands. The standing army thus extended the ruler's reach and influence abroad. In this era, Egypt pushed its territorial boundaries into Asia, reaching as far as the Euphrates River (see Map 2.2).

During the New Kingdom, Egypt's kings first took the title *pharaoh*, which means "great house"—or master of all Egyptians. Pharaohs exercised wide-ranging and unrivaled political power. Egyptians believed that the gods entrusted their safekeeping to the pharaoh's care and that he had the final authority in matters of government, law, religion, and warfare. In return for the authority granted him by the gods, the pharaoh had the duty of maintaining peace and order in Egypt and bringing this order to the entire world. He did this by caring for the temples and cults of the gods, conquering Egypt's enemies, and ruling wisely.

Egypt during the New Kingdom developed a highly organized bureaucracy that helped the pharaoh maintain order. Egypt was divided into two major administrative regions: Upper Egypt in the south, governed from the city of Thebes, and Lower Egypt in the north, ruled from the city of Memphis. Regional administrators raised taxes and drafted men to work on the pharaoh's building projects. The chief minister of state, the vizier, superintended the administration of the entire kingdom. Every year the vizier decided when to open the canal locks on the Nile so that farmers' fields could be irrigated. He supervised the Egyptian treasury and the warehouses into which produce was paid as taxes.

Temples also played an essential part in the government of Egypt. Priests collected taxes, organized building projects, and administered justice among the thousands of peasants who labored in the vast estates attached to the temples. The temple of Amun at Karnak, for example, controlled a workforce of nearly 100,000 people.

VIDEO

The Temple of Karnak

The Mummy

The burial practices of the ancient Egyptians provide a window into their society. They reveal Egyptian attitudes about life, death, and the afterlife. Egyptians believed that a person could have an afterlife only if the person's body remained in recognizable form after death.

The Egyptians also thought that every human possessed three spirits active after death: the Ka, Ba, and Akh. The Ka was a person's life force, created at birth but set free at death to live in his or her tomb, where the spirit inhabited the deceased's statue and cared for the body. The Ba could take many shapes and travel outside the tomb, and it accompanied the corpse to final judgment. The Ba comprised all the qualities that made a person unique; without a body to return to, the Ba and the deceased's personality would vanish forever. The Akh represented a person's immortality and lived among the stars. These three spirits could survive only if the body did not decay, and so preserving the corpse became a central issue in burial practice.

Egyptians began experimenting with embalming or mummification between 3000 and 2600 B.C.E. and continued to develop the art for the next 3,000 years. The rise of Christianity in Egypt in the second and third centuries C.E. ended the practice of preserving corpses. Ancient records and modern scientific investigation have uncovered the secrets of mummification. Embalming took place within seventy days after death. By means of a metal hook, highly trained experts extracted the brains through the nostrils and discarded them. Sometimes they filled the skull with linen cloth and resin. Through an incision below the ribs the embalmers removed all the organs except for the heart. (That organ represented a person's life and would be examined by the gods on Judgment Day.) The embalmers wrapped the liver, lungs, stomach, and intestines individually and placed them in separate containers within a chest carved from alabaster. Next the embalmers thoroughly dried the corpse by packing it with natrun, a natural compound of sodium carbonate and bicarbonate. After drying for forty days, the skin shriveled and the embalmers padded the body with aromatic packing materials to re-create as lifelike an appearance as possible. The priests then added hairpieces and artificial eyes. They applied a layer of resin over the face and body followed by a coat of paint—red for men and yellow for women.

Customarily, embalmers placed magical amulets on the corpse to protect the deceased in the next world. They also decorated the body with expensive jewelry and insignia of rank. Then they tightly wrapped the corpse in long strips of linen. Before placing the corpse in a shroud, they fitted the face with a painted linen mask. The masks of royalty were made of gold.

Finally the corpse was placed in its coffin, which was painted with a stylized portrait of the deceased. The dead person's family and friends carried the coffin to the tomb. After the proper prayers, the priest conducting the burial ceremony touched the eyes, ears, nose, and mouth painted on the coffin to enable the dead person to see, hear, smell, and breathe for eternity. Then the priest and family sealed the tomb. When prepared in such a fashion, a body could last forever.

For Discussion

What does the practice of mummification reveal about Egyptian attitudes toward death and the boundaries between life and death?

Mummy of Ramesses II
Both a science and an art, mummification preserved the body of King Ramesses II (r. 1279–1213 B.C.E.) for more than 3,000 years. This near-perfect example of a mummy is the product of an Egyptian tradition of preserving the body after death that began at the beginning of Egyptian history.

In the New Kingdom, women played an important role. Under Egyptian law, women and men had complete equality in matters of property, business, and inheritance. In addition to preparing foods, weaving cloth, and caring for livestock and children, women arranged burials and worshiped at tombs to ensure an afterlife for departed family members. Some women held priesthoods. The most powerful, the "God's Wife of Amun," was often a member of the royal family. This priestess had administrative responsibilities as well as the obligation to perform religious rituals. The wives of priests and officials formed musical groups called "Singers of Amun" that sang, clapped, and danced to the accompaniment of stringed instruments during religious rituals.

Military Expansion and Diplomatic Networks: Building an Empire in Canaan and Nubia

During the New Kingdom, pharaohs conquered territories far beyond the borders of Egypt. The military power that came from chariot warfare technology, and the ability of the pharaoh to use the great wealth of the country to support a large army, made these conquests possible. A well-developed logistical system also contributed to Egypt's military strength. With food and supplies carefully prepared in advance by government administrators, the Egyptian army regularly waged war far from home.

Egyptian attitudes toward non-Egyptians also encouraged the imperial expansion of the New Kingdom. Egyptians divided the world into two groups: themselves (whom they referred to as "The People") and everyone else. Egyptians were people who lived in the Nile Valley and spoke Egyptian. The other peoples known to the Egyptians were the Nubians, Libyans, and the inhabitants of Southwest Asia. Egyptians believed that forces of chaos resided in foreign lands where the pharaoh had not yet imposed his will. Thus it was the pharaoh's responsibility to crush all foreign peoples and bring order to the world.

In their drive to establish order in the world, Egyptian rulers in the New Kingdom clashed with kingdoms in

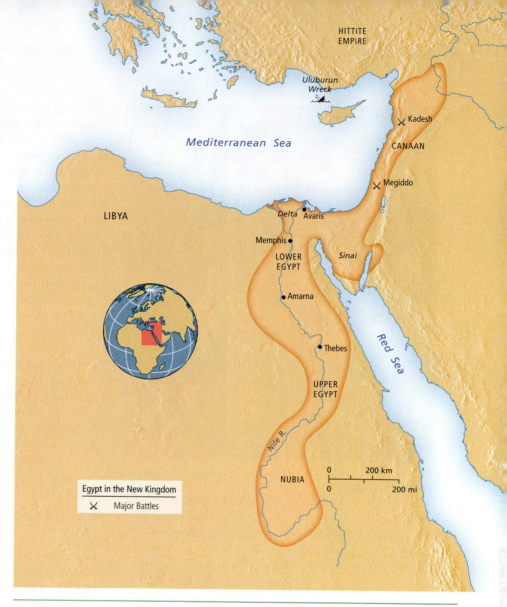

Map 2.2   Egypt in the New Kingdom

During the New Kingdom, Egyptians conquered Nubia, Canaan, and parts of Southwest Asia as far as the Euphrates River. They created a prosperous, multiethnic empire.

Anatolia, Syria, and Mesopotamia. Under the dynamic leadership of Thutmose I (r. 1504–1492 B.C.E.), the armies of Egypt conquered southern Palestine. A coalition of Syrian cities slowed further advance, but by the end of the reign of the great conqueror Thutmose III (r. 1458–1425 B.C.E.), Egypt had extended its control over all the lands between the Orontes River in Syria and the Euphrates in Mesopotamia. The western portion of this region, called Canaan (modern-day Lebanon, Israel, and parts of Jordan and Syria), provided the Egyptians with additional wealth, both because of Canaan's own natural resources and because Canaan was a vital trading center with ties to Mesopotamia and beyond.

The New Kingdom also expanded its territorial grip southward, seizing the populous and prosperous African land known in antiquity as Nubia or Kush (modern

Enemies of Egypt

These tiles found at the mortuary temple of Pharaoh Ramesses III were made around 1170 B.C.E. They depict Egypt's enemies with such great attention to details of clothing, hairstyle, and stereotyped physical features that we can know the ethnicity of the men. From left to right: a Libyan with tattooed arms, a Nubian with black skin, and a bearded Syrian. All wear handcuffs, a sign of their defeat and Egypt's triumph.

Akkadian, the Mesopotamian language used for international communication, these letters show that Egyptian pharaohs were in regular contact with the rulers of neighboring peoples, as well as with their own officials in Canaan and Syria. In their correspondence, the monarchs referred to themselves as "Great Kings" and addressed one another as "brother," despite their constant rivalry. By using these titles, the rulers recognized each other's authority and created a sense of international community. They cemented their ties by arranging marriages among the royal families and exchanging lavish gifts. By these means they could guard their frontiers and protect the merchants who crisscrossed their territories.

Egypt gained more than enormous wealth from its empire. The cultural encounter between Egyptians and the people they conquered resulted in an exchange of ideas and traditions. Egyptian speech adopted hundreds of Canaanite words. Many fairy tales about exotic lands modeled on Southwest Asia made their way into Egyptian literature. Numerous gods of conquered peoples entered Egyptian life as well. For example, Baal and Astarte, who were worshiped widely in Southwest Asia, became popular Egyptian divinities.

Pharaohs: Egypt's Dynamic Leaders

Egypt's success during the New Kingdom hinged in large part on the talents of its pharaohs. These rulers defined all aspects of Egyptian life, from empire building and trade to agriculture and worship.

Hatshepsut the Female Pharaoh and Thutmose III the Conqueror

One of the most remarkable rulers of the New Kingdom was Hatshepsut (1479–1458 B.C.E.), the first female pharaoh. With the aid of trusted advisers, Hatshepsut pursued policies of peace, though her armies waged war when necessary to secure Egypt's possessions in Southwest Asia.

Because pharaohs had always been men, all of the images of kingly power were male and the elaborate rituals of ruling presumed a male ruler. Hatshepsut carefully adapted her image to these expectations. For example, in the inscriptions and paintings of the great funerary temple that she built near Thebes, Hatshepsut is represented as a man, the son of the god Amun-Re. In more private contexts, she referred to herself as a woman. Several decades after Hatshepsut's death, her name was systematically removed from monuments throughout Egypt, probably to inform the gods that Egypt had returned to "proper" male kingship.

Thutmose III (r. 1458–1425 B.C.E.) succeeded his mother Hatshepsut and began a reign marked by military glory. He led his armies into Canaan seventeen times during his reign. In one of his greatest victories at Megiddo (in mod-

Sudan). Nubia was extremely rich in gold and other natural resources, while trade routes from central and eastern Africa that converged in Nubia further augmented its wealth. In order to gain control of these riches, Egyptian forces conquered Nubia about 1500 B.C.E. An Egyptian governor, called the King's Son of Kush, ruled the vast region in the pharaoh's name, but Egyptian control depended on the cooperation of Nubian princes who organized local labor and guaranteed the regular delivery of tribute. In return for this collaboration, the princes were permitted to govern their communities. To strengthen further their grip on Nubia, pharaohs encouraged Egyptians to migrate to Nubia and establish communities along the Nile River. These Egyptian colonies increased the population of Nubia and exploited the fertile river lands for the benefit of the pharaoh.

Although willing to use war to further their imperial interests, the pharaohs grew to prefer diplomatic means. Evidence of their diplomacy comes from an archive of documents discovered at Tell el-Amarna in 1887 C.E. Written in

Hatshepsut as a Bearded Pharaoh

Although she was a woman, tradition required that Hatshepsut be depicted as a man.

ern Israel) Thutmose captured more than 900 war chariots from his enemies. To maintain Egyptian authority throughout his empire, Thutmose established permanent garrisons in conquered territories, just as Ahmose had done when the territory had first been conquered. Thutmose cultivated a triumphant military atmosphere at court that was quite different from that of Hatshepsut, yet he also wrote literary works and pursued an interest in science. From Syria he brought back samples of the region's flowers and plants and had them painted on temple walls. Under his influence, Egyptian artists perfected their ability to capture detail, movement, and emotion in painting and sculpture.

The Amarna Period: The Beginnings of Diplomacy

Four decades after Thutmose III's reign, Egypt experienced a religious revolution, begun when Pharaoh Amenhotep III (r. 1388–1351 B.C.E.) turned away from traditional beliefs and practices. Amenhotep called the sun Aten and worshipped his physical form, the sun seen in the sky. The pharaoh's son, Amenhotep IV (r. 1351–1334 B.C.E.), changed his own name to Akhenaten ("one useful to Aten") and with his religious advisers took the revolutionary step of declaring that Aten was the only god. Thus the Egyptians in the Amarna Period first developed monotheism°, the idea of a single, all-powerful god.

Full of religious enthusiasm, Akhenaten and his queen, Nefertiti, abandoned the capital of Thebes and built a new city where no temple had ever stood. Left open to the sun, the city received the first rays of light as each day dawned. Because the modern name for this site is Tell el-Amarna, historians refer to this period of religious ferment as the Amarna Period. Akhenaten attacked the worship of other gods, closed down many temples, and appropriated their wealth and lands for himself. Paintings and sculptures no longer depicted Aten in the traditional way, as a falcon-headed god, but instead represented the deity as a simple disc with radiating beams of light. Akhenaten forbade the celebration of ancient public festivals to the other gods and even the mention of their names. His agents chiseled their names from monuments and buildings across the land.

Akhenaten gradually lost the support of the general population as well as that of the priests who administered the temples of other gods. The people of Egypt were unwilling to abandon the many traditional gods who played such an important role in their daily lives. After Akhenaten's death, the royal court returned to Memphis and then to Thebes. Akhenaten's monotheistic religion thus did not survive him.

The Battle of Kadesh and the Age of Ramesses

After Akhenaten's death, rule of Egypt passed through the hands of several men before Ramesses I took the throne in 1292 B.C.E. and established a new dynasty, the nineteenth in Egyptian history. The greatest king of the nineteenth dynasty was Ramesses II (r. 1279–1213 B.C.E.), who ruled

---

DOCUMENT

A Hymn to Aten Sung by the Pharaoh

The following Egyptian hymn was sung to Aten, the sun god, by the pharaoh. It describes a single god who created the universe:

Splendid you rise, O living Aten, eternal lord!
You are radiant, beauteous, mighty,
Your love is great, immense.
Your rays light up all faces,
Your bright hue gives life to hearts,
When you fill the Two Lands with your love.
August God who fashioned himself,
Who made every land, created what is in it,
All peoples, herds, and flocks,
All trees that grow from soil; they live when you dawn
   for them,
You are mother and father of all that you made.
I am your son who serves you, who exalts your name,
Your power, your strength, are firm in my heart;
You are the living Aten whose image endures,
You have made the far sky to shine in it,
To observe all that you made . . .

Source: From Miriam Lichtheim, *Ancient Egyptian Literature: The Old and Middle Kingdoms, Volume II.* Copyright © 1976 by the Regents of the University of California. Reprinted by permission.

Egyptian Tomb Robbers on Trial

In New Kingdom Egypt a council called a *kenbet,* composed of the local governor and temple priests, combined the functions of prosecutor, judge, and jury. There was no counsel for the defendants. At the village level people might bring lawsuits against one another at the *kenbet,* and women and men alike represented themselves at trial. Another court, the Great Kenbet, handled all cases of property and taxation affecting state revenues as well as all offenses against the pharaoh and the government. This court consisted of high officials of the government and was headed by the pharaoh's chief administrator, the vizier.

One of the most serious crimes in Egypt was robbing tombs. People accused of this crime were interrogated by the authorities, who routinely used beatings and torture to extract confessions. The Great Kenbet then delivered a verdict. Conviction of tomb robbing carried the death penalty. Lesser crimes not related to tomb robbing could result in confiscation of property, beatings, forced labor, and body mutilation.

The following document comes from the trial record of tomb robbers in the Great Tombs of the pharaohs in the Valley of the Kings.[1] These tombs were situated a few miles from the Nile River at Thebes, where most of the New Kingdom pharaohs and their families were buried. The trials were conducted over a period of several summer days during the reign of Ramesses IX (r. 1125–1107 B.C.E.). The vizier, assisted by the overseer of the granary and treasury and two royal stewards, conducted the proceedings, which were written on a papyrus scroll unearthed in 1872 C.E. The account shows how justice was carried out in the New Kingdom.

Examination. The herdsman Bukhaaf of the temple of Amun was brought. The Vizier said to him, "When you were about that business in which you engaged and the god caught you and brought and placed you in the hand of pharaoh, tell me all the men who were with you in the Great Tombs." Bukhaaf replied, "As for me, I am a field worker of the temple of Amun. The woman came to the place where I was and she said to me, 'some men have found something that can be sold for bread; let's go so you may eat it with them.'" [Bukhaaf gives some misleading testimony that does not deceive the Kenbet.] *Bukhaaf was examined with the stick [i.e., beaten]. "Stop, I will tell," he said. The Vizier said to him, "Tell the story of your going to attack the Great and Noble Tombs." Bukhaaf said, "It was Pewer, a workman of the City of the Dead [the Tombs] who showed us the tomb of Queen Hebrezet." The Vizier and the others said to him, "In what condition was the tomb that you went to?" Bukhaaf said, "I found it already open." He was examined with the stick again. "Stop," he said, "I will tell." The Vizier said to him, "Tell what you did." He said, "I brought away the inner coffin of silver and a shroud of gold and silver together with the men who were with me. And we broke them up and divided them among ourselves."*

[Bukhaaf's punishment is not recorded, but it was in all likelihood death.]

On the third day of the trial of thieves, a carpenter Thewenani was examined for a different robbery. He proclaimed his innocence and swore a great oath, "If I speak untruth may I be mutilated and sent to Ethiopia."

Despite several beatings and torture, Thewenani would not confess, and the vizier let him off with the warning that if he was accused again, he would be sentenced to death. Later that day, Ese, the wife of the gardener Ker who had been implicated in stealing silver from the Great Tombs in still another case, was brought before the Kenbet. She swore an oath to be truthful or be mutilated and placed on a stake. She denied any connection with the robbery, but one of the officials at the trial asked her how she had suddenly gotten rich enough to buy several slaves. Her answer that she had saved the money from selling the produce of her garden did not convince the Kenbet, which brought in her slave to give testimony against her. Her fate is not recorded.

Why did Egyptian officials prosecute tomb robbers with such energy? They considered tomb robbing a serious crime for both religious and economic reasons. Egyptians were deeply concerned about the afterlife and stressed the proper treatment of the dead. They believed that when people died they were judged by the god Osiris. If they had lived good lives, their bodies would live again. The families of the deceased had the obligation to provide food and water at the graveside for the dead to eat. They also were required to remember the name of the dead. "Provide water for your father and mother who rest in the desert valley. . . . Let the people know that you are doing it and then your son will do the same for you," advised one religious text.[2] In Egyptian

The jackal-headed god Anubis leads Hunefer into the courtroom, where his heart is weighed against a feather on giant scales.

Because the feather and the heart weigh the same, it means that the court decides that Hunefer has led a just life.

The god of wisdom, Thoth, stands by the scale, and records the result of weighing.

Horus leads Hunefer to the great god Osiris who judges and rules the dead. Hunefer can look forward to a peaceful eternity.

Osiris

Judgment Day
Painted about 1285 B.C.E., this papyrus scroll shows the trial of a man called Hunefer on the day of judgment.

eyes, robbing a tomb violated basic principles of religious behavior. It was a monstrous sacrilege.

The many gifts placed in a grave with the dead person were intended to make the deceased person's afterlife as comfortable as possible. Pharaohs and the wealthy elite of Egypt filled their tombs with luxury items of incalculable value—an irresistible lure for thieves. In addition to their profound desire to prevent sacrilege, Egyptian officials worried that plundering this treasure and putting it back into circulation would cause prices to fall and thereby derail the economy. From the point of view of Egyptian officials, tomb robbers deserved nothing less than death. Only this way would justice be served.

Questions of Justice

1. To what extent do both the living and the dead play a part in this trial?
2. The "International Bronze Age" witnessed the rise of strong, highly centralized states. What do these tomb raiders' trials reveal about the links between law, religion, and central state power?

Taking It Further

Goelet, Ogden. "Tomb Robbery Papyri," in *The Oxford Encyclopedia of Ancient Egypt*, ed. Donald B. Redford, vol. 3, pp. 417–418. 2001. Provides the latest analysis of the documents relating to the trials of tomb robbers as well as further bibliography.

Kruchten, Jean-Marie. "Law," in *The Oxford Encyclopedia of Ancient Egypt*, ed. Donald B. Redford, vol. 2, pp. 277–282. 2001. An excellent overview of Egyptian law with helpful suggestions for further reading.

for sixty-six years. Ramesses's efforts to restore Egyptian authority in Syria brought him into conflict with the king of the Hittites, Muwatallis, who wanted to conquer some of Egypt's possessions for himself. In 1274 B.C.E. the armies of Ramesses and Muwatallis clashed in a battle at the city of Kadesh in northern Syria. Muwatallis's huge Hittite army, with about 3,500 chariots and 37,000 infantry, caught the Egyptians by surprise, but in a last-minute counterattack led by the pharaoh himself, Egyptian troops rallied and pushed their enemy back. The battle ended in a stalemate, with heavy losses on both sides.

The Battle of Kadesh°, perhaps because of its indecisive outcome, resulted in a treaty between the two kings. Writing in Akkadian, the Egyptian and Hittite monarchs signed a treaty of friendship and cooperation in 1269 B.C.E. Ramesses formally abandoned Egyptian claims to the city of Kadesh and northern Syria. In return, the Hittite monarch acknowledged Egypt's right to control Canaan, establishing a boundary between the two states. The two powers also agreed to give one another aid and military assistance in case of invasion by a third party or in the event of internal rebellions. The Battle of Kadesh thus yielded nearly a century of peace between the Hittites and the Egyptians. During this period commerce flourished, benefiting both realms. With peace established with the Hittites, Egypt enjoyed many decades of prosperity under Ramesses II's rule.

VIDEO

Abu Simbel

Civilizations of Anatolia and Mesopotamia: The Hittite, Assyrian, and Babylonian Empires

■ What were the political, religious, and cultural traditions of the Hittite Empire in Anatolia and the Assyrian and Babylonian Empires in Mesopotamia?

Egypt was only one of several large, highly centralized empires that developed during the International Bronze Age. As we can see on Map 2.1, Egypt's main rivals were the Hittite Empire in Anatolia and the Assyrian and Babylonian Empires in Mesopotamia.

The Growth of Hittite Power: Conquest and Diversity

By about 1650 B.C.E., the Hittites had established control over the rich plateau of Anatolia (modern Turkey). Like the Egyptians, the warlike Hittites were among the first people to use the new chariot warfare technology. For two cen-

turies Hittite power gradually expanded across Anatolia and into western Mesopotamia, as well as southward into Syria where the Hittites stood face to face with the Egyptian Empire. Within a century Hittite conflict with Egypt led to the Battle of Kadesh, as we saw earlier. The expanding Hittite Empire played a prominent role in the network of trade and communication of the International Bronze Age. From the carefully kept inventory tablets that have survived, historians know that the Hittites made great profits by trading textiles, grains, and metals to markets as far away as Cyprus and the Aegean, Syria, and Mesopotamia in return for metals and luxury goods.

At the top of the Hittite Empire was the Great King, who ruled in the name of the supreme God of Storms. Like Egyptian rulers, the Great King owned the land of all his subjects, and he gave agricultural estates to the noblemen who served as his officials. In return they supplied the soldiers and charioteers he demanded for the army. The Great King also strengthened ties of allegiance throughout his empire by requiring his officials and subordinate monarchs to swear oaths of loyalty to the main Hittite gods. The Great King gave further unity to the empire by playing the role of chief priest of all the gods who were worshiped by the many different communities under his control.

Hittite kings worked hard to provide uniform justice throughout their realm for rich and poor, male and female alike. This proved a complex undertaking because as the Hittite Empire expanded, it grew increasingly multiethnic, absorbing many smaller kingdoms with their own languages and cultural traditions. The many different peoples who made up the Hittite Empire were permitted to follow their own customs and laws. Administering justice thus required close cooperation between subject peoples' local authorities and the Great King's legal officials. The Hittite tongue served as the official language of law and government, but the empire's cultural diversity and ties abroad forced the Hittites to keep records in other languages as well. The Hittites' use of cuneiform script, borrowed from nearby Mesopotamia, provides evidence of extensive cultural interaction with that region.

The Hittites spoke of their "thousand gods" because their religion drew from the empire's many subjects as well as from neighboring regions. The imperial government deliberately brought the statues of the gods of its subjects to its capital city of Hattushas and built many temples for them in an effort to promote the unity of all the people under the Great King's rule. Hittites believed that their gods were present in the form of their statues and that the gods wished to communicate with their human worshipers. Priests appointed by the Great King managed this "conversation" by making appropriate offerings to the deities at fixed intervals in an elaborate calendar of festivals and holy days. According to Hittite belief, properly worshiped gods would protect the empire as well as any individuals who might pray to them privately. In the Hittite afterlife, the souls of the deceased lived in a huge palace ruled by the Goddess of Death in the Underworld, located far below the Earth's surface.

The Mesopotamian Empires

The kingdoms of Mesopotamia, which rivaled the Hittite Empire in wealth and power, had an equally vital place in the political, commercial, and cultural networks of the International Bronze Age. During this period, two powerful empires emerged in Mesopotamia: Babylonia in the south and Assyria in the north.

The Kingdom of Babylonia

By about 1600 B.C.E. people known as Kassites infiltrated Mesopotamia as raiders, soldiers, and laborers. Their language and precise place of origin are unknown, but by 1400 B.C.E. they had gradually gained control of most of southern Mesopotamia. For the next 250 years, until about 1150 B.C.E., Kassite monarchs maintained order and prosperity in Babylonia, establishing the longest-ruling dynasty in ancient Southwest Asian history.

During these centuries, Babylonia enjoyed a golden age. Kassite kings politically unified Babylonia's many cities through a highly centralized administration that closely controlled both urban centers and countryside. These skilled monarchs won the loyalty of individuals of all ranks and temple priesthoods by giving them tracts of land. The Kassite kings gained a reputation for fair rule and for that reason were popular with their subjects. The government spent lavishly on temples, public buildings, and projects such as canals throughout the kingdom.

Under Kassite rule, Babylonia became renowned as a center of trade, culture, and learning. Science, medicine, and literature flourished during this period. With encouragement from the Kassite kings, who wished to demonstrate their full integration into Babylonian society, scribes systematically copied the works of earlier Mesopotamian cultures to preserve their intellectual legacy. Treatises on omens, astrology, and medicine gathered an enormous body of knowledge. Babylonian doctors earned fame throughout Southwest Asia. Gula, the goddess of healing known as the Great Physician, was the divine patron of a religious center where doctors received their training.

In literature, the Babylonian creation epic *Enuma Elish* tells the story of the origin of the world by Marduk, the god of Babylon and sole lord of the universe. The order that Marduk creates reflects the organized rule that the Kassite kings provided for Babylonia. Babylonian authors also wrote versions of the *Epic of Gilgamesh,* the Sumerian story about the establishment of civilization that we discussed in Chapter 1. These two great works were translated into many languages and entertained people throughout Southwest Asia for more than a thousand years.

DOCUMENT

Hittite Military Rituals

Religious rituals and magic played an important role in every aspect of Hittite life, including warfare. Hittite warriors believed that the gods were usually on their side in battle. They thought that if the gods saw them as impure, they would suffer defeat in combat. After a purification ritual, defeated Hittite soldiers could return to soldiering with renewed morale and vigor. The following document explains the ritual of purification that soldiers performed after a military defeat:

If our troops are defeated by the enemy, they perform the Far-Side-Of-The-River-Ritual. On the far side of the river, they cut in half a person, a billy goat, a puppy, and a piglet. Half of each they place on this side and half on that side (of the river). In front they build a gate of hawthorn. . . . Over the top they draw a rope. In front, on either side, they light a fire. The troops go through the middle. When they reach the river, they sprinkle them with water. Afterward they perform the Ritual-Of-The-Battlefield for them in the usual way [and can return to battle].

Source: From Richard H. Beal, "Hittite Military Organization" in *Civilizations of the Ancient Near East 4V*, edited by Jack Sasson, Charles Scribner's Sons, © 1995 by Charles Scribner's Sons. Reprinted by permission of The Gale Group.

The Kingdom of Assyria

Babylonia's chief rival for dominance in the Mesopotamian region during the International Bronze Age lay to the north: Assyria. Around 1350 B.C.E. Assyria recovered from more than a century of submission to the neighboring kingdom of Mittani in Syria. Under the skillful rule of Ashur-Uballit (ca. 1365–1330 B.C.E.) the Assyrian kingdom began a new phase of expansion. Like the rulers of the Egyptians and the Hittites, Ashur-Uballit and his successors understood the value of close diplomatic ties with other great powers. As a letter found in Egypt reveals, he tried to win the favor of the pharaoh:

> Thus speaks Ashur-Uballit, king of Assyria. May everything be well with you, your house, your land, your chariots and your troops. . . . I am sending you a beautiful chariot, two horses, and a bead of authentic lapis-lazuli [a valuable gemstone] as your greeting gift . . . My messenger will see how you are and how your country is, and then may he come back to me.[3]

Like their rivals, however, Ashur-Uballit and other Assyrian kings were also quite willing to go to war to safeguard their economic interests. To that end, Assyrian kings pushed westward, clashing with the Hittites over trade, metal ores, and timber. The Assyrians built a string of garrisons on their border with the Hittite kingdom and seized territories in northern Syria that had come under Hittite control. Assyrian kings also competed with Babylonia for control of copper, tin, horses, and other prized natural resources in the hilly lands to Mesopotamia's north and east. The mighty ruler Tukulti-Ninurta I (r. 1244–1208 B.C.E.) led his armies to victory over Babylonia and by the time of his death Assyria controlled all the lands extending from northern Syria to southern Iraq—the greatest reach Assyria would ever attain. Even though Babylonia would reassert its independence within the next twenty years, Assyria dominated Mesopotamian affairs for the next two centuries.

Civilizations of the Mediterranean: The Minoans and Mycenaeans

■ What were the characteristics of the Mediterranean civilizations of Minoan Crete, Mycenaean Greece, Ugarit, and Troy, and what roles did they play in international trade and politics?

The Egyptian, Babylonian, and Assyrian Empires of the International Bronze Age were each rooted in civilizations that had emerged thousands of years before. In Europe, however, the cold climate and extensive forests slowed the development of city life and therefore of civilization. It was not until the International Bronze Age that two vigorous and distinctive civilizations developed in the eastern Mediterranean: the Minoan civilization of Crete and the Mycenaean civilization on mainland Greece.

Several smaller coastal cities and kingdoms situated on the eastern Mediterranean participated in the brisk trade that so characterized the International Bronze Age. These coastal kingdoms served as buffer states between Egypt, Mycenaean Greece, and the Hittite Empire. The two most prosperous, the mercantile kingdoms of Ugarit and Troy, played a "middleman" role in the trading and diplomatic networks that developed during these centuries.

Minoan Crete

About 2000 B.C.E. small urban communities on the island of Crete began to import copper and tin from the eastern Mediterranean. Sir Arthur Evans, the late-nineteenth-century British archaeologist who first discovered the remains of these communities, named them "Minoan," after the Cretan king Minos in Greek mythology. In the course of the second millennium B.C.E., the Minoans developed a busy merchant navy that traded with Greece, Egypt, and the coastal communities of the eastern Mediterranean. Crete became a thriving center of long-distance trade. Minoan

Snake Goddess

One of the most important divinities of Minoan civilization was the Snake Goddess. Here she (or her priestess) is captured in typical pose and dress: She grasps a snake in each outstretched hand and wears a tight-fitting, layered dress that exposes her breasts. A sacred cat perches on her head.

civilization was the most brilliant in the Mediterranean until the sixteenth century B.C.E., when it was surpassed by that of the Mycenaeans.

Despite the rich array of artifacts and sites unearthed by archaeologists, the basic beliefs of Minoan religion remain a mystery. Historians do know that Minoans worshiped the powerful Mistress of Animals at some mountaintop shrines, and that in their homes they prayed to a goddess whom they always depicted as holding a snake. Statues show this Snake Goddess (or her priestess) wearing a many-tiered skirt, with breasts exposed and snakes coiled around her outstretched arms.

The Minoan economy revolved around four major urban administrative centers, called palaces, at Knossos,

Phaistos, Mallia, and Zakros. The Knossos palace alone occupied three acres. At its center stood a courtyard surrounded by hundreds of rooms intended as living quarters for the governing and religious elite, administrative headquarters, shrines for religious worship, and warehouses for storing crops and wine. These warehouses, which could hold more than a quarter of a million gallons of wine or olive oil, show the Minoan rulers' tight control over the production of wealth on Crete. Palace administrators told farmers how much to grow and collected the produce from them, then gave back sufficient food for their subsistence. Palace officials also controlled the specialized artists who produced the crafts that were traded abroad.

IMAGE

The Toreador Fresco

The Minoan elites lived in great luxury in palaces connected to warehouses. Vivid frescoes (plaster painted while it is still wet) of sea creatures, flowers, court officials and acrobats in bright garments, and scenes of daily life adorned their walls. The residents enjoyed indoor plumbing and running water, comforts that most people in the West would not enjoy until the nineteenth century C.E. The palaces had no fortifications, suggesting that the Minoans felt quite safe on their island.

Like other monarchs, Minoan rulers carefully kept precise records of their wealth and possessions on clay tablets. Accountants recorded long lists of the livestock, produce, raw materials, and merchandise brought to the palace warehouses, as well as land holdings, debts, and payments made to the palace. These administrators used a form of writing known as Linear A, a simplified hieroglyphic script that developed on Crete around 1700 B.C.E., probably influenced by Egyptian writing. Linguists have not entirely deciphered the script.

Minoan mercantile documents found in ports along the eastern coast of the Mediterranean as well as the excavation of Minoan trading posts on the islands of the central Aegean Sea, on the island of Rhodes, and in other locations along the eastern Mediterranean coast reveal the international reach of Minoan travel and commerce. Minoan merchants sold their wares on the Greek mainland, and Minoan delegations brought rich gifts to the courts of Egyptian pharaohs. Exporting luxury goods—jewelry of precious metals and stones, painted vases, and delicate figures carved in the deep blue gemstone called lapis lazuli°—to eager foreign buyers made the Minoans wealthy.

Minoan prosperity and power came to a sudden and unexplained end around 1450 B.C.E. At that time all of the Cretan towns and palaces were destroyed except for Knossos, which fell about seventy-five years later. Excavations reveal that immediately after the destruction of the Minoan palaces, artifacts from mainland Greece appeared on Crete and throughout the Aegean. Graves on Crete began to contain Greek-style weapons and armor. Archaeologists do not know whether Mycenaean Greeks from the mainland caused the collapse of Minoan power or

merely took advantage of it, but it is certain that invaders from Greece took control of Crete and its trade networks around this time. The international economy and the balance of maritime power in the eastern Mediterranean shifted from the island of Minoan Crete to the mainland of Mycenaean Greece.

Mycenaean Greece

A German archaeologist, Heinrich Schliemann, first brought the Bronze Age civilization of mainland Greece to light in 1876 C.E. Determined to prove that the epic poems of the Greek poet Homer about the Trojan War were based in fact, Schliemann first dug at Troy (see next section) and then at the fortress of Mycenae, the home of the Greek king Agamemnon in Homer's *Iliad*. He made spectacular finds of golden treasures and sophisticated architecture at Mycenae, which archaeologists today believe was only one of perhaps six kingdoms on the Greek mainland. The name *Mycenaean* refers both to the kingdom of Mycenae and, more generally, to the culture of Greece during the International Bronze Age. Mycenaean civilization lasted from around 1600 to 1100 B.C.E.

By 1400 B.C.E. a uniform Mycenaean civilization had reached its apex throughout southern Greece and in Mycenaean settlements abroad. The larger Mycenaean communities consisted of heavily fortified palaces with outlying agricultural lands. As on Crete, the Mycenaean palaces functioned as administrative centers of food collection and distribution. They also served as manufacturing centers that produced pottery, jewelry, tapestries, and other trade goods. Literate bureaucrats living in the palaces were essential in governing the Mycenaean kingdoms. Like their counterparts in Crete and Southwest Asia, they recorded long lists of livestock, slaves, farm produce, land holdings, taxes, and tribute taken from peasants and slaves. They also kept detailed records of imported and exported luxury goods and raw materials. These administrative records were written on clay tablets in a script known as Linear B, an early form of the Greek language spoken today.

The most influential kingdom in southern Greece during this period was located at Mycenae, where kings governed from a citadel looking down on a broad agricultural plain. This center of power reveals much about life in Bronze Age Greece. Thirty royal burials consisting of deep shafts arranged in two circles on the citadel and dating from 1600 to 1450 B.C.E. suggest a highly warlike people. The graves contain bronze swords, daggers, spearheads, and stone arrowheads and blades. The skeletons of the rulers buried in these graves stood nearly six feet tall, which made them tower over the general population. Apparently they enjoyed better nutrition than their subjects, whose graves reveal more diminutive skeletons. The many gold and silver drinking vessels and pieces of jewelry found in the graves further demonstrate that the Mycenaean leaders enjoyed tremendous luxury.

The Mycenaean kings also relied on aristocratic warriors, who enforced the monarchs' decisions and served as military officers during wartime. As in Egypt, Anatolia, and Southwest Asia, elite warriors used light, fast-moving chariots pulled by horses. They also took their favorite weapons of war with them to the grave, suggesting that they valued military prowess very highly.

The Mycenaeans took advantage of the peaceful conditions in the eastern Mediterranean that diplomatic ties between Egypt and the Hittite Empire had helped create. With the collapse of Minoan Crete, they assumed control of commerce across the Aegean Sea and the eastern Mediterranean. During the fourteenth and thirteenth centuries B.C.E., Mycenaean merchants extended Minoan commercial routes, establishing strong links with Egyptians and the inhabitants of Ugarit and other coastal towns. Ships carried Mycenaean commodities in large clay vessels painted with distinctive designs as far west as Spain and northern Italy.

Mycenaean rulers also forged diplomatic ties with Egyptian monarchs. Ambassadors of Pharaoh Amenhotep III visited Crete and the Greek mainland, including Mycenae, where they presented ceremonial plaques bearing the pharaoh's name. In the interest of maintaining good relations and brisk commerce, Egyptian and Mycenaean rulers avoided war with each other during this period, but Mycenaean relations with the Hittites were not quite so cordial. To extend and protect their trade routes, some

Mycenaean Greeks settled on the coast of Asia Minor, a sphere of Hittite influence. There they engaged in trade, piracy, and warfare with surrounding communities. Hittite documents dating to the fourteenth century B.C.E. tell of meddling Mycenaean kings who slipped away to sea in their ships, out of the reach of landbound Hittite forces.

Two Coastal Kingdoms: Ugarit and Troy

Many independent cities existed along the border regions between Egypt, Mycenaean Greece, and the Hittite Empire. A string of these small communities stretched along the seacoast from the Aegean Sea to the Gaza Strip and served as a buffer between the three major powers. The two most notable of these cities were Ugarit and Troy.

Ugarit: A Mercantile Kingdom

Directly east of Cyprus on the Syrian coast lay the port city of Ugarit, which controlled a small but influential kingdom of about 2,000 square miles. Ugarit became a highly cultured city with international connections because of its rich natural resources. The fertile plain offered arable land for grape vines, olive trees, and grains, while the heavily forested surrounding hills provided timber for shipbuilding and construction. Perhaps Ugarit's greatest asset was a fine natural harbor that made the city a hub of international trade. Merchant ships like the one that sank at Uluburun sailed to Ugarit from Cyprus and the Aegean, the coast of

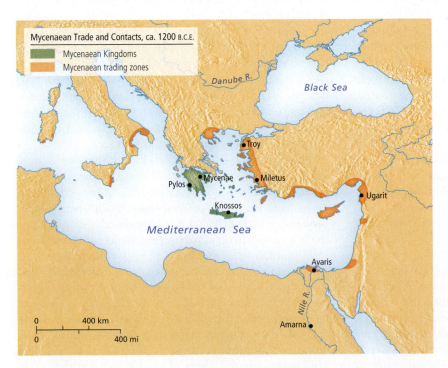

Map 2.3 Mycenaean Trade and Contacts, ca. 1200 B.C.E.
The Mycenaean Greeks traded extensively with communities throughout the eastern Mediterranean world, including Egypt, the coastal towns of Asia Minor, and Canaan. Sometimes their commerce was little more than raiding and piracy.

Mycenaean Trade and Contacts, ca. 1200 B.C.E.
- Mycenaean Kingdoms
- Mycenaean trading zones

The Millawanda Letter

About 1300 B.C.E., a Hittite king wrote the following letter to an unknown Mycenaean king, complaining of the behavior of a lesser ruler on the Aegean coast of Asia Minor who had defied the Hittite king's commands. Millawanda was the Hittite name for the coastal town in Asia Minor where the Mycenaeans had established a stronghold.

The author's insistence on the formalities of diplomatic communication is striking. The letter indicates the significant role of international diplomatic relations among the great powers, but it leaves some questions unanswered: Was the Mycenaean kingdom of Ahhijawa on Rhodes, on Cyprus, or in Greece? What was the previous trouble over the city of Wilusa (another name for Troy)? And what was the fate of the messengers?

I have to complain of the insolent and treacherous conduct of . . . Tawagalawas. We came into contact in the land of Luqqa [in southwest Asia Minor]; and he offered to become a vassal of the Hittite Emperor. . . . I order him, if he desires to become a vassal of mine, to make sure that no troops of his are to be found in Ijalanda [an unknown location] when I arrive there. And what do I find when I arrive at Ijalanda? The troops of Tawagalawas fighting on the side of my enemies. I defeat them, take many prisoners, devastate the district, scrupulously keeping the fortress of Atrija intact out of respect for my treaty with you. Now comes a Hittite subject, Pijamaradus, . . . who steals my 7000 prisoners, and makes off to your city Millawanda (Miletus). I command him to return to me: he disobeys. I write to you:

you send a surly message, unaccompanied by gift or greeting. . . . So I go to fetch him. I enter your city Millawanda, for I have something to say to Pijamaradus, and it would be well that your subjects there should hear me say it. But my visit is not a success. I ask for Tawagalawas: he is not at home. I should like to see Pijamaradus: he has gone to sea. . . . Are you aware, and is it with your blessing, that Pijamaradus is going around saying that he intends to leave his wife and family, and incidentally my 7000 prisoners, under your protection, while he makes continual inroads into my territory? Kindly tell him either to settle down peacefully in your country, or to return to my country. Do not let him use Ahhijawa as a base for operations against me. You and I are friends. There has been no quarrel between us since we came to terms in the matter of Wilusa [Troy]: the trouble there was all my fault, and I promise you that it shall not happen again. As for my military occupation of your city Millawanda, please consider it a friendly visit. I am sorry that in the past you have had occasion to accuse me of being aggressive and of sending impolite messages: I was young then and carried away in the heat of action. I may add that I also have had harsh words from you, and I suggest that the fault may not lie with ourselves but with our messengers. Let us bring them to trial, cut off their heads, mutilate their bodies, and live henceforward in perfect friendship.

Source: From Denys L. Page, *History and the Homeric Iliad,* Copyright © 1959 by The Regents of the University of California. Reprinted by permission.

---

western Anatolia, and Egypt. Caravans laden with goods arrived from Mesopotamia, the Hittite lands, and Canaan. People from all these places settled in Ugarit, whose population is estimated at 10,000 inhabitants. Another 25,000 people lived as farmers in the Ugarit countryside.

In Ugarit's spacious houses archaeologists have excavated numerous baked clay tablets containing legal, financial, literary, diplomatic, and religious texts written in Ugaritic, the local Semitic language. The tablets demonstrate the literacy of the Ugaritic elite. Young people studied their own language in school while also mastering foreign languages useful in trade and diplomacy. The tablets show an innovative alphabet. In it, each spoken sound was represented by just one letter or sign. This Ugaritic alphabet was the ancestor of all modern alphabets that follow the same principle of one sign per spoken sound.

Ugarit was always overshadowed by mighty Egypt to the south and the combative Hittite Empire to the north. To

maintain Ugarit's independence, the port city's rulers had to be clever diplomats. Archaeologists have unearthed records of treaties made between the kings of Ugarit and Hittite, Assyrian, and other rulers in Southwest Asia. These treaties show that Ugarit played an influential role in international diplomacy.

Troy: A City of Legend

Troy, the best known and yet most mysterious of all Bronze Age cities, has captured the popular imagination for 3,000 years, but archaeology cannot explain the origins of the people who lived there, or even their language. Historians do know that like Ugarit, Troy was a city embedded in the intricate web of trade, diplomacy, and warfare that linked the societies of the International Bronze Age.

Situated in northwest Asia Minor on a promontory overlooking a bay about six miles from the Aegean Sea, this city has become immortal as the site of the Trojan War in

Homer's epic poems the *Iliad* and the *Odyssey*. Composed about 750 B.C.E., these stories were legends, not history. Still, they formed part of an enduring oral tradition that began in the International Bronze Age and reflect social conditions and perhaps even events that actually occurred.

Archaeologists have unearthed numerous distinct layers of occupation and construction in Troy, as generations of inhabitants rebuilt their city from about 3000 to 1200 B.C.E. Around 1700 B.C.E. the inhabitants of Troy VI (meaning the sixth major layer of occupation) constructed huge gateways and a royal palace consisting of many spacious mansions. A fortified citadel, Troy VI was built with monumental blocks of masonry similar to that used by the Hittites and the Mycenaeans, suggesting that techniques of military engineering had spread among these kingdoms. The Trojans prospered in the fifteenth and fourteenth centuries B.C.E. by trading with Mycenaean Greeks, Hittites, Cypriots, and merchants from Ugarit. But around 1270 B.C.E., an earthquake tumbled the mighty walls of Troy VI and the city went up in flames. The Trojans' prosperity and influence ended.

Heinrich Schliemann, the first archaeologist to excavate Troy, erroneously concluded that Troy VI was the city destroyed by Mycenaean Greeks in Homer's *Iliad*. Later archaeologists proved that Greeks had nothing to do with the city's collapse. Most archaeologists believe that if there is even a kernel of truth in Homer's stories about the Greek destruction of Troy, it must lie in the violent end of Troy VIIa, the modest city built within the rubble of Troy VI's fortress walls by the survivors of the earthquake. This new version of the city also fell to ruin about 1190 B.C.E., probably as the result of warfare. Hittite royal documents indicate that at this time Mycenaeans were raiding the coastlands of Asia Minor in search of slaves and booty, and Linear B tablets from the Greek mainland list slaves captured on the Asia Minor coast. These records suggest that Troy VIIa may well have fallen prey to a Mycenaean attack. Some historians believe that in the centuries following Troy VIIa's destruction, the story of a Mycenaean raid slowly took on epic proportions as generations of Greek bards told and retold it. Older tales recounting the glory of Troy VI may have augmented the legend of the Trojan War.

The "Death Mask of Agamemnon"

This thin gold mask, about eleven inches long, was found at the citadel of Mycenae in the tomb of a ruler who died about 1550 B.C.E. Heinrich Schliemann, who excavated the tomb, mistakenly jumped to the conclusion that it was the death mask of King Agamemnon, who led the Greek forces during the Trojan War, as told in Homer's *Iliad*. Later archaeologists have discovered that this king died several centuries before the period that Homer described.

The End of the International Bronze Age and Its Aftermath

■ What forces brought the International Bronze Age to a close, and how did the Phoenicians, Assyrians, and Babylonians build new kingdoms and empires in its wake?

The intricate diplomatic, cultural, and economic interconnections between Egypt, Southwest Asia, Anatolia, and Greece broke between 1200 and 1100 B.C.E. These formerly vibrant civilizations plummeted into a dark age marked by invasions, migrations, and the collapse of stable governments. The era of prosperity and international cooperation ended abruptly. In the aftermath of these turbulent events, however, the people of Southwest Asia from the Mediterranean coast to Mesopotamia gradually developed new and powerful kingdoms with distinctive cultures.

The Raiders of the Land and Sea

Developments in Mycenaean Greece and the Hittite Empire were pivotal in bringing the International Bronze Age to an end. The collapse of Hittite and Mycenaean power contributed to migrations throughout the eastern Mediterranean. People fled their homes in search of new lands to settle. Overcoming all resistance, these displaced groups plundered cities and brought destruction to the entire eastern Mediterranean as they moved southward.

Warfare among the many competitive kingdoms of Mycenaean Greece probably began this chain of disasters. These conflicts resulted in the breakdown of the palace-centered economic system about 1150 B.C.E. When the Mycenaean kingdoms collapsed, the economy disintegrated as well. Literacy disappeared because without palace inventories to record, there was no need for scribes to learn Linear B. Trade and population declined rapidly, and many Greeks migrated to the coast of Asia Minor. The Greek language and some religious beliefs survived, but the crafts, artistic styles, and architectural traditions of Mycenaean life were forgotten. In contrast to the brilliance of Mycenaean civilization, the poverty and hardship of the era that followed merit the name "dark age."

For the Hittite Empire, a deadly combination of economic decline and invasions early in the twelfth century B.C.E. triggered the government's collapse. The subject kingdoms in the western regions of the Hittite Empire began to rebel, and peasants fled their lands. The Hittites became ever more dependent on foreign sources of grain, forcing their rulers to import larger supplies from Egypt and Syria. Rebellions occasionally blocked these shipments, worsening the Hittites' plight. By the first decade of the twelfth century B.C.E. an enemy force of uncertain origin stormed through the Hittite Empire and burned the capital city of Hattushas. With no effective leadership, Hittite power soon crumbled.

As Hittite and Mycenaean power collapsed, migrating peoples surged across the eastern Mediterranean. In Egyptian documents these people are referred to as Raiders of the Land and Sea°. They came from many places, impelled not only by political instability and economic decline, but also by earthquakes, plague, and climate change. The raiders included pirates and mercenaries, as well as migrating groups that traveled with their families and livestock in search of new lands. The raiders' movements destabilized all the regions linked together by the trading and diplomatic networks of the International Bronze Age. Moving south through Syria and Palestine, the raiders destroyed Ugarit and other coastal cities. Bound together in a loose confederation, the raiders moved further south toward Egypt in search of land and food. By 1170 B.C.E., the Egyptian Empire had lost control of Syria and Canaan. Ugarit fell at the same time. Groups of raiders settled on the Mediterranean coast and extended their power inland. Organized political life in Canaan disintegrated and the last of the Bronze Age cities collapsed by about 1100 B.C.E. One group of raiders, the Peleset People, who settled on the coast of Canaan, are known to us as the Philistines, a name that survives in the modern word *Palestine*.

Egypt was able to marshal its military might and avoid total destruction at the hands of the Raiders of the Land and Sea, but it slipped into a long economic and military decline. Drought, poor harvests, and inflation ruined the Egyptian economy, while weak rulers struggled unsuccessfully to hold Egypt together. The bonds between Upper and Lower Egypt were severed, and the land of Egypt split once again into separate kingdoms.

In Mesopotamia, the kingdoms of Babylonia and Assyria also experienced an economic and political breakdown. Historians attribute this decline primarily to invasions by seminomadic peoples originating in Syria and the Iranian Plateau. Their monarchs lost power and political influence, but the Assyrians and Babylonians nevertheless maintained their identity as distinct peoples throughout these troubled centuries.

After the International Bronze Age ended about 1100 B.C.E., two regions acquired special importance: the eastern coast of the Mediterranean, where the Phoenicians established a maritime culture, and Mesopotamia, where the kingdoms of Assyria and Babylonia revived. (We will examine the civilization of the Hebrews, which also emerged in the aftermath of the International Bronze Age, in Chapter 3.)

The Phoenicians: Merchants of the Mediterranean

Two hundred years after the International Bronze Age drew to a close, a dynamic maritime civilization took shape in the independent port cities that stretched along the eastern Mediterranean seaboard. Byblos, Tyre, and Sidon were the most powerful of these cities. These seafaring people, whom historians call Phoenicians, continued the commercial traditions of Ugarit and other small Bronze Age kingdoms. By following old Minoan and Mycenaean trade routes of the International Bronze Age, they created a large commercial sphere of influence. Hundreds of their ships crisscrossed the Mediterranean and ventured into the Atlantic Ocean in search of trade. By 950 B.C.E. they had established extensive trade and political connections with peoples of the Levant and spread their civilization into the

Mediterranean world as far as North Africa, Italy, and Spain.

The search for metal ores motivated much of Phoenician commerce. Phoenician metal prospectors located deposits of precious ores in North Africa, Spain, Italy, Britain, and France. They traded with the local inhabitants in these regions who had been working the mines for centuries. In this way Phoenician traders established economic connections with lands that would later become the center of Western civilization (see Map 2.4). The enterprising Phoenicians also learned techniques of smelting metals for weapons, tools, and jewelry that had been developing in European lands since the International Bronze Age, and they transmitted this knowledge to Southwest Asian peoples. In return, they brought back Asian and Egyptian artistic styles to western Mediterranean lands.

By 800 B.C.E., Carthage ("New City"), a colony located on the northern coast of modern Tunisia, had become the chief Phoenician city in the west. For this reason, Phoenician culture in the western Mediterranean is called Carthaginian. With its magnificent harbor and strategic location midway between the Levant and the straits of Gibraltar, Carthage controlled trade between the eastern and western Mediterranean. Its inhabitants developed a land-based empire on the North African coast and in Spain. Phoenicians were more interested in trading than settling, however. Their approach to trade facilitated good relations with the southern Mediterranean's native inhabitants, especially in Sicily and Italy.

Phoenician religion showed remarkable continuity through time and across the Mediterranean. Many of their gods and goddesses had also been worshiped by Southwest Asian peoples during the International Bronze Age. Even though the deities' names differed among many Phoenician cities, their roles as protectors and warriors remained the same. The chief gods were Baalat ("Lady of the Heavens") and her husband Baal ("Lord of the Heavens"), who represented the order of the natural world and protected the Phoenicians from danger. Many parents killed their firstborn son as an offering to the Lord and Lady of the Heavens at moments of crisis or as an offering for the fulfillment of a personal vow. Child sacrifice continued at Carthaginian settlements, often secretly, as late as 200 C.E. In the western Mediterranean, the Lady of the Heavens became associated

Map 2.4   Phoenician Expansion, ca. 600 B.C.E.

Several centuries after the collapse of the International Bronze Age, adventurous merchants from the eastern Mediterranean coast developed a commercial empire across the Mediterranean Sea. By 600 B.C.E. Carthage had become the chief Phoenician city in the western Mediterranean. It controlled the resources of North Africa and parts of Spain.

with the practice of sacred prostitution, in which every sexual union between a priestess and a male believer symbolized the fertility and regenerative power of the Lady of the Heavens.

The Phoenicians' most lasting cultural contribution to the peoples of the Mediterranean world was the alphabet. The Phoenicians developed a system of writing based on that of Ugarit in which each letter represented a single sound. Thus the alphabet could be used to record the sounds of any language. The Phoenician alphabet spread throughout the Mediterranean world, where the Greeks and then the Romans adopted it. In this way it became the source of all alphabets and writing in the West.

Known mainly as accomplished sailors and merchants, the Phoenicians did not develop a large, centralized state. Their cities, therefore, became vulnerable to attack by larger empires and lost their independence in the fifth century B.C.E. Their strong mercantile and seafaring culture, however, lasted into Roman times. As we will see in Chapter 4, Carthage grew into a vast Mediterranean empire and became Rome's greatest enemy.

Mesopotamian Kingdoms: Assyria and Babylon, 1050–550 B.C.E.

The decline of both Assyria and Babylonia at the end of the International Bronze Age did not result in their outright disappearance as kingdoms. Torn apart by invasions, they nevertheless managed to survive. Beginning in about 1050 B.C.E., the Assyrian and then the Babylonian imperial regimes began to regain effective control over their territories, reestablish their commercial power, and reconquer neighboring lands.

Neo-Assyrian Imperialism

After 1000 B.C.E., the Assyrian kings slowly reasserted their dominance in northern Mesopotamia. In 745 B.C.E., Tiglath-Pileser III (r. 745–727 B.C.E.) ascended the Assyrian throne and ushered in a century of rapid expansion. This Neo-Assyrian Empire was the first in history to control the Tigris, Euphrates, and Nile River valleys, where civilization had first emerged two millennia before (see Map 2.5). By 500 B.C.E., Nineveh, the Neo-Assyrian capital city, boasted at least 500,000 inhabitants.

Neo-Assyrian rulers, who called themselves "Kings of the Universe," developed a highly militarized empire. To terrify their victims and aid their conquests, they cultivated a reputation for extreme cruelty. Assyrian armies tortured, butchered, and enslaved the inhabitants of defeated cities. Then, after carting off everything of value, they burned the cities to the ground. News of their atrocities spread to neighboring areas, which quickly and understandably surrendered.

CHRONOLOGY	
ca. 3200 B.C.E.	Bronze making begins in Northern Syria and Iraq
ca. 2000 B.C.E.	Minoans build first palaces built on Crete
ca. 1650–1600 B.C.E.	International Bronze Age begins; Hittite Kingdom emerges
ca. 1550 B.C.E.	New Kingdom begins in Egypt
ca. 1450 B.C.E.	First palaces built at Mycenae in Greece; Linear B script develops
ca. 1400 B.C.E.	Kassites gain control of Babylonia
ca. 1351–1334 B.C.E.	Amenhotep IV (Akhenaten) rules in Egypt; Amarna Period
ca. 1190 B.C.E.	Troy VIIa falls
ca. 1244–1208 B.C.E.	Tukulti-Ninurta I conquers Babylonia
ca. 1200–1150 B.C.E.	International Bronze Age ends
ca. 1000 B.C.E.	Aramaeans invade Assyria
ca. 900 B.C.E.	Phoenician civilization develops
ca. 750 B.C.E.	Phoenician alphabet reaches Greece
721 B.C.E.	Assyria conquers Northern Kingdom of Israel
603 B.C.E.	Neo-Assyrian Empire falls
612–539 B.C.E.	Neo-Babylonian Empire emerges; astronomy flourishes

Like their predecessors during the International Bronze Age, the Neo-Assyrian rulers grew wealthy from agriculture and trade. They also exploited their subjects more harshly than previously. Provincial administrators imposed crippling taxes and systematically drained away their subjects' resources. With these revenues, the kings could maintain armies of more than 100,000 men. At the same time, the government strengthened the economy by rebuilding cities, increasing the amount of land under cultivation, and building roads to improve trade and communications throughout the empire.

As the Assyrians conquered more and more peoples, they faced problems that have troubled empires ever since: How can subject peoples be controlled and what degree of cultural independence should they be permitted to retain? Assyrian solutions were thoughtful yet violent. Assyrian rulers permitted their subjects to continue their traditions and religious practices without interference. If they rebelled

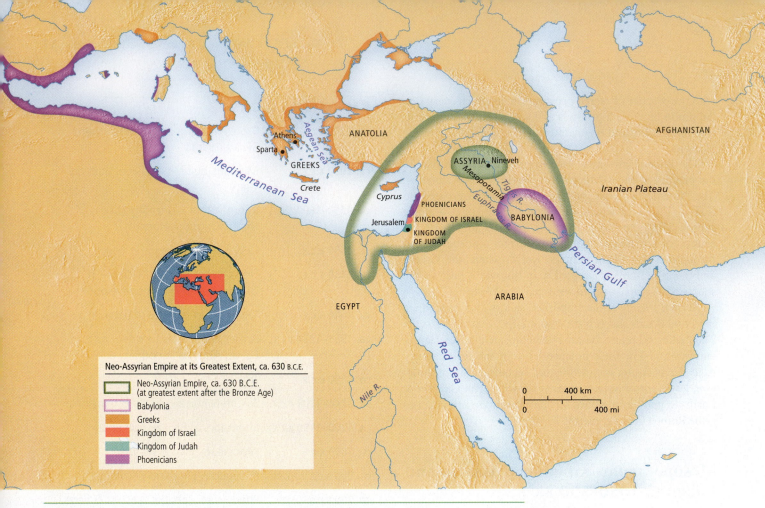

Map 2.5   The Neo-Assyrian Empire at Its Greatest Extent, ca. 630 B.C.E.
By 630 B.C.E., the Assyrians had recovered their strength and established the Neo-Assyrian Empire. This huge realm included Mesopotamia, the Israelite kingdoms, Phoenicia, and parts of Egypt.

against Assyrian authority, however, the army would crush them and deport entire populations to distant corners of the empire. Some Assyrian rulers depopulated entire regions. Perhaps as many as a million and a half people were forced from their homes by Assyrian deportation policies.

Ashurbanipal (r. 669–626 B.C.E.), the last strong ruler of the Neo-Assyrian Empire, attempted to create a uniform culture throughout his vast realm. At his command, scholars collected subject peoples' written knowledge, translated it into Akkadian, and distributed copies on clay tablets throughout Assyrian lands. Ashurbanipal did not succeed in imposing a standardized culture on the empire, but he was the first monarch to try to organize the diverse cultural inheritances of his many subject peoples.

Despite its prosperity and efficient administration, the Neo-Assyrian model of imperial rule failed to bring lasting unity to its peoples. Subject peoples who had endured brutal treatment at the hands of Assyrian administrators nursed a bitter resentment and revolted as soon as possible. The most significant of these rebels was the Babylonian king Nabopolassar in southern Mesopotamia (r. 625–605 B.C.E.). He allied himself with Persian kings and began a successful revolt against Assyrian rule. By 603 B.C.E., the Assyrian Empire collapsed again, this time for good.

The Neo-Babylonian Empire

After Nabopolassar acquired Assyrian territory, he built the Neo-Babylonian (or Chaldean) Empire into the most powerful in Southwest Asia, which lasted until 539 B.C.E. His son, the brilliant general Nebuchadnezzar II (r. 604–562 B.C.E.), conquered lands that had broken free when Assyrian rule collapsed (see Map 2.6). Babylonian armies seized Egypt, Syria, Phoenicia, and the kingdom of Judah, where they destroyed the city of Jerusalem and exiled many Jews to Babylon. (We will learn more about this exile in Chapter 3.)

With the wealth acquired from these conquests, Nebuchadnezzar made his capital city, Babylon, one of the most luxurious in the ancient world. A moat flooded with waters from the Euphrates River surrounded Babylon's eight miles of walls. The Ishtar Gate, which opened onto a grand avenue leading to the temple of Marduk, Babylon's greatest god, was decorated with glazed, brightly colored tiles. According to tradition, Nebuchadnezzar built the "Hanging Gardens of Babylon" for a favorite wife who

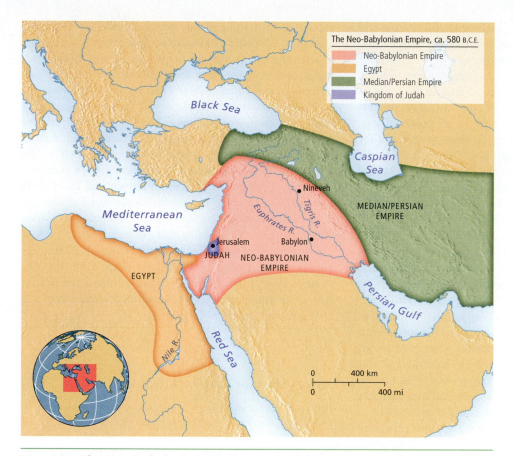

Map 2.6   The Neo-Babylonian Empire, ca. 580 B.C.E.
By ca. 580 B.C.E., the Neo-Babylonian Empire had replaced the Neo-Assyrian Empire as the dominant power in the Middle East.

Ishtar Gate

The magnificently tiled Ishtar Gate, right, provided a dramatic entrance to Babylon, the capital city of the Neo-Babylonian Empire. Babylonian artists used brightly colored tiles to create complicated three-dimensional depictions of animals, including lions, which represented royal power. The gate now rests in a museum in Berlin.

missed her mountainous homeland. Splendid flowers and plants cascaded down the slopes of a terraced hillside that from a distance seemed to float in the air.

The Neo-Babylonian Empire comprised a constellation of wealthy cities in which life revolved around the uninterrupted worship of Marduk. At the center of each community stood a magnificent temple to the all-powerful god. The Babylonians considered proper worship essential for the prosperity of their communities. They looked to the king to provide the peaceful conditions in which they could worship their gods without interruption. The king, for his part, expected his subjects to obey his commands, and he counted on the priests to bolster his authority.

Religion not only gave the Babylonians a profound sense of spiritual security, it also expanded their scientific knowledge. The Babylonians believed that proper interpretation of the celestial bodies through astronomy could help them understand the will of the gods. Building on the Sumerians' mathematical and astronomical legacy, Babylonian astronomers patiently observed and recorded the movements of the stars, the planets, and the moon. They kept a continuous log of observations between 747 B.C.E. and 61 C.E., an astonishing achievement. Starting around 500 B.C.E., they had accumulated so much astronomical data that they could perform complicated mathematical computations to predict eclipses of the moon and sun. They also calculated the first appearance of the new moon every month, which enabled them to devise a calendar. These brilliant astronomers' calculations, which Persians and Greeks would later adopt, helped lay the foundation of Western science. From these able scientists, the West inherited the names of many constellations, the zodiac, and many complex mathematical models of astronomical phenomena.

Conclusion

The International Bronze Age and the Emergence of the West

The International Bronze Age and its aftermath marked two early but crucial phases in the formation of Western civilization. Within a large geographical area centered on the eastern Mediterranean but stretching far beyond its shores, an intricate network of political, commercial, and cultural ties was established among cities and kingdoms that had previously lived in relative isolation from each other. The forces that exposed the cultures of these areas to each other were the expansion of international trade; the development of a new military technology; the growth of large, multiethnic empires; and the establishment of diplomatic relations among rulers. Long before it was possible to identify what we now call the West, the exchange of commodities, the spread of religious ideas, the growth of common political traditions, the dissemination of scientific and technological techniques, and the borrowing of one language from another created a complex pattern of cultural diffusion over a vast geographical area.

During subsequent centuries the content of such cultural interaction would change, and the geographical area within which these exchanges took place would shift as well, first to the lands controlled by Persia, then to the Hellenistic world conquered by Alexander the Great, and later still to the sprawling Roman Empire. All these shifts took place as the result of imperial expansion and consolidation, a process that began with the formation of multiethnic empires discussed in this chapter. Each period of expansion, moreover, involved new cultural encounters among different peoples. In the next chapter we will continue to look at the aftermath of the International Bronze Age, as we explore a series of encounters between Persians, Hebrews, and Greeks.

Suggestions for Further Reading

For a comprehensive list of suggested readings, please go to
www.ablongman.com/levack2e/chapter2

Bryce, Trevor. *The Kingdom of the Hittites.* 1998. The latest synthesis of Hittite history and culture.

Cline, Eric H., and Diane Harris-Cline, eds. *The Aegean and the Orient in the Second Millennium: Proceedings of the 50th Anniversary Symposium, Cincinnati, 18–20 April 1997, Aegaeum 18.* 1998. A collection of papers by experts providing state-of-the-art discussions of all aspects of the connections among Bronze Age civilizations of the eastern Mediterranean and Middle East.

Dickinson, Oliver. *The Aegean Bronze Age.* 1994. Now the standard treatment of the complex archaeological data.

Dothan, Trude, and Moshe Dothan. *People of the Sea: The Search for the Philistines.* 1992. A recent, highly popularized survey of the archaeological material.

Drews, Robert. *The End of the Bronze Age: Changes in Warfare and the Catastrophe ca. 1200 B.C.* 1993. A controversial but well-argued analysis that offers new solutions to the question of why the Bronze Age ended.

Fitton, J. Lesley. *The Discovery of the Greek Bronze Age.* 1996. A lucid and well-illustrated study of the archaeologists who brought the Greek Bronze Age to light in the nineteenth and early twentieth centuries.

Harding, A. F. *The Mycenaeans in Europe.* 1984. Exploration of the trade and cultural connections between Mycenaeans and the rest of Europe.

Hornung, Erik. *History of Ancient Egypt: An Introduction,* trans. David Lorton. 1999. A concise and lucid overview of Egyptian history and life.

Knapp, A. Bernard. *The History and Culture of Ancient Western Asia and Egypt.* 1988. A reliable archaeological and historical overview without excessive detail.

Kuhrt, Amélie. *The Ancient Middle East, ca. 3000–330 B.C.,* 2 vols. 1995. A magisterial, up-to-date overview, with an excellent bibliography. The place to start for a continuous historical narrative of the region.

Macqueen, James G. *The Hittites and Their Contemporaries in Asia Minor.* 1986. This account stresses the interconnections of Hittites and other peoples.

Markoe, Glenn. *Phoenicians.* 2000. The best and most up-to-date treatment of Phoenician society by a noted expert.

Page, Denys. *History and the Homeric Iliad.* 1959. An entertaining and provocative examination of the historical context of the events described in Homer's *Iliad.*

Redford, Donald B. *Egypt, Canaan and Israel in Ancient Times.* 1992. An excellent, detailed synthesis of textual and archaeological evidence that emphasizes interconnections among cultures.

Schulz, Regine, and Matthias Seidel, eds. *Egypt: The World of the Pharaohs.* 1999. A sumptuously illustrated collection of essays on all aspects of Egyptian society and life by leading experts.

Traill, David. *Schliemann of Troy: Treasure and Deceit.* 1995. A fascinating discussion of the motivations and methods of the archaeologist who discovered the Bronze Age.

Walker, Christopher, ed. *Astronomy Before the Telescope.* 1996. A fascinating collection of essays about astronomy in the premodern period, which makes clear Western civilization's enormous debt to the Babylonians.

Wood, Michael. *In Search of the Trojan War.* 1985. A valuable introductory discussion of the archaeological and historical problems of placing Homer's Trojan War in its Bronze Age context.

Notes

1. T. Eric Peet, *The Great Tomb Robberies of the Twentieth Egyptian Dynasty,* 2 vols. (1930; reprinted in one volume, 1977). Contains texts and translations of this and other trials.

2. Regina Schulz and Matthias Seidel, eds., *Egypt: The World of the Pharaohs* (1998), 485.

3. Translated in Amélie Kuhrt, *The Ancient Middle East,* vol. 1 (1995), 350–351.

Persians, Hebrews, and Greeks: The Foundations of Western Culture, 1100–336 B.C.E.

3

I N THE SECOND HALF OF THE SIXTH CENTURY B.C.E., CYRUS THE GREAT, A Persian king from southern Iran, created the largest empire the world had ever seen, with territories in Asia, the Middle East, Africa, and Europe. According to one of the many legends surrounding this celebrated ruler, Cyrus grew restless as a young man under the rule of another king. He summoned the Persian tribal leaders who owed him allegiance and instructed them to spend a day clearing land with sickles. When they finally stopped their backbreaking labor, he invited them to a magnificent banquet. After the men had devoured the last delicacy, Cyrus asked them which they enjoyed more, tasting the wonderful food or sweating in the fields. The chieftains shouted in unison that they preferred the wine and fine foods. Cyrus then proclaimed:

> *Men of Persia, follow me and I promise that you will enjoy this sort of luxury for the rest of your lives, but if you do not, your lives will be full of painful toil with no such rewards from your present masters.*[1]

Without hesitation the men joined Cyrus in his successful revolt. Under his able leadership the Persians conquered more than twenty-three different peoples in territories ranging from the eastern Mediterranean coast to central Asia. Cyrus's successors added Egypt and parts of Greece and India to the Persian Empire. With its huge expanse and the stable government it provided to an enormous mix of cultures, the Persian Empire marked a turning point in the history of the ancient world.

This chapter examines the civilizations that developed during the six centuries following the collapse of the International Bronze Age around

Persian Art Persian artists drew freely from the artistic traditions of their subject peoples. This illustration shows how they put their own stamp on the Babylonian art of ceramic tile. The tiles show two members of the elite imperial guard, known as the Immortals. The details of their uniforms appear in vivid color. Soldiers like these in Xerxes' army attacked the Greeks in the fifth century B.C.E.

1100 B.C.E. When long-distance trade in copper and tin broke down, iron became the preferred metal for making tools and weapons throughout the ancient world. As a result of the widespread use of iron, archaeologists refer to the new period as the Iron Age. Its most significant features, however, were not its metal products but its distinctive religious, political, and cultural innovations. These innovations, which became fundamental to Western civilization, originated in a series of encounters between Persians and other peoples, particularly the Hebrews and Greeks.

For two centuries after Cyrus's death in 530 B.C.E., the Persian Empire prospered as its leaders methodically expanded their territory abroad and shrewdly managed their many subject peoples. The interaction of local cultures with that of Persia made an indelible impression on the history of the West. From their Assyrian and Babylonian subjects, the Persians inherited—and improved on—a political legacy of ruling a multiethnic empire. They also benefited from a scientific tradition that stretched back to the Sumerians. The Persians' capacity to borrow and adapt the most useful features of other cultures strengthened their own highly organized and justly administered empire.

Two peoples who established their own political identities during this era of Persian imperial dominance made even more important contributions to Western culture. From the Hebrews, who benefited from Persian rule and eventually were granted a measure of religious autonomy within the empire, came a tradition of monotheism, the worship of only one god. Monotheism became the main characteristic of the Hebrews' religion, Judaism, and it later became central to Christianity and Islam as well. Thus the three great religions of the West, which traced their origins back to the same roots, all professed a belief in only one god.

The other people who developed their cultural traditions in a world dominated by Persia were the Greeks. The most distinctive contribution of the Greeks to the West was the political tradition of democracy°, the conviction that people should share equally in the government of their communities, devise their own political institutions, and select their own leaders. Democratic institutions originated in the Greek city-state of Athens, which never succumbed to Persian military power, in the sixth century B.C.E. Following their victories over the Persians in the following century, Athenians were free to develop their democratic institutions in an atmosphere of great economic stability and security.

Victories over the Persians also made it possible for Athenian artists and thinkers to flourish. During what is known as the Classical Age of Greece, Athenians established philosophical schools that laid the foundations of Western philosophy, wrote dramas that grappled with fundamental moral questions, and created a distinctive Greek classical style in sculpture and architecture that has continued to be a source of inspiration in the West up to the present day.

This chapter addresses the major question of how the cultural traditions of the peoples of the Persian Empire, the Hebrews, and the Greeks laid the foundations of Western culture. More specifically, the major sections of this chapter will ask the following questions:

- How did the Persian Empire bring the peoples of the Middle East together in a stable realm, and what elements of Persian religion and government have influenced Western thought?
- What political and religious beliefs and institutions gave Hebrew civilization its unique character, and what consequences came of its interactions with the Assyrians, Babylonians, and Persians?
- How did Greek city-states develop in the framework of a larger world dominated by Persia?
- What were the intellectual, social, and political innovations of Greece in the Classical Age?

Persia: An Empire on Three Continents

- How did the Persian Empire bring the peoples of the Middle East together in a stable realm, and what elements of Persian religion and government have influenced Western thought?

Persian history began about 1400 B.C.E., when small groups of people started migrating with their herds and flocks into western Iran from areas north of the Caspian Sea. Over five centuries these settlers slowly coalesced into two closely related groups, the Medes and the Persians.

The Medes organized a loose confederation of tribes in western Iran and began to expand their territory. By about 900 B.C.E., they established mastery over all the peoples of the Iranian Plateau, including the Persians. In 612 B.C.E., with the assistance of the Babylonians, the Medes conquered the Assyrians. Then they pushed into central Asia Minor (modern Turkey), Afghanistan, and possibly farther into central Asia. In the sixth century, under the leadership of Cyrus the Great (r. 550–530 B.C.E.), Persia broke away from Medean rule and soon conquered the kingdom of the Medes. Under the guidance of this brilliant monarch and his successors, the Persians acquired a vast empire. They followed a monotheistic religion, Zoroastrianism, and governed their subjects with a combination of tolerance and firmness.

Cyrus the Great and Persian Expansion

After ascending the Persian throne about 550 B.C.E., Cyrus embarked on a dazzling twenty-year career of conquering neighboring peoples. His military genius and organizational skills transformed the small kingdom near the Persian Gulf into a giant multiethnic empire that stretched from India to the Mediterranean Sea. Cyrus's swift victory over the Medes put Persia at the center of the Middle East and thrust it into face-to-face encounters with a diverse array of peoples.

Cyrus expanded his empire beyond Persia in several stages. In 546 B.C.E. he conquered Asia Minor, where he first came into contact with Greeks living on the westernmost coast and islands, a region called Ionia. Cyrus conquered these Ionian Greek cities and installed loyal Greek administrators. Next he defeated the kingdom of Babylonia in 539 B.C.E., thus gaining control of the entire Mesopotamian region. After that he brought Afghanistan under his control and fortified it against the raids of the Scythian nomads who lived on the steppe lands to the north of his realm. These fierce warriors posed a perpetual threat to the settled territories of Persia.

With his borders expanded and secured, Cyrus turned his attention to the welfare of his Persian homeland. Dissatisfied with his capital city of Susa, he founded a spacious new capital city called Pasargadae. Builders, craftsmen, artists, and merchants flocked to it from Asia Minor, Egypt, Mesopotamia, and Greece. Inspired by Cyrus's leadership, these artisans turned the new capital into a cosmopolitan city of great ethnic diversity.

After Cyrus died in 530 B.C.E. while fighting against steppe nomads north of Persia, his son Cambyses II (r. 529–522 B.C.E.) continued his father's policy of expansion by subduing Egypt and the wealthy Phoenician port cities. The capture of Phoenicia gave the Persians a new strategic advantage. With control of Phoenician naval resources, the Persian Empire could reach overseas in a way that the landlocked Hittites could not during the International Bronze Age. Phoenician fleets became an integral part in Persia's invasion of Greece, as we will see later in this chapter. By the time of Cambyses's death in 522 B.C.E., Persia had become the mightiest empire in the world, with territorial possessions spanning Europe, Asia, the Middle East, and Africa (see Map 3.1).

To ensure that they could easily communicate with their subjects, the Great Kings of Persia established an elaborate system of roads to link their provinces. Special officials maintained supply stations at regular intervals along these roads. The chief branch of this system, called the Royal Road, stretched between Asia Minor and the Persian homeland. Persian road building was an indication of the sophistication of the Great Kings in managing an empire. These roads not only facilitated the transportation of soldiers and commercial goods from one part of the empire to another, but they also made possible the flow of ideas and the transmission of cultural traditions.

A Government of Tolerance

The key to maintaining power in such a diverse empire lay in the Persian government's treatment of its many ethnic groups. The highly centralized Persian government wielded absolute power, but it rejected the brutal model of the Assyrian and Babylonian imperial system in favor of a more tolerant approach.

After conquering Babylonia Cyrus began a popular policy of allowing peoples exiled by the Babylonians to return to their homelands. Though Cyrus was Zoroastrian, he made a proclamation to the Babylonians presenting himself as an agent of their chief god, Marduk:

> I am Cyrus, the king of the world. Marduk, the great god, rejoices at my pious acts . . . I gathered all their peoples and led them back to their abodes . . . and at the order of Marduk . . . I had all the gods [of exiled peoples] installed in their sanctuaries . . . May all the gods whom I have led back to their cities pray daily for the length of my days.[2]

Subject peoples were permitted to worship freely if they acknowledged the political supremacy of the Great King. In this way the Persians won the loyalty and gratitude of their ethnically diverse subjects throughout the empire.

The firm but tolerant methods of governing developed by the Persian government provided a legacy for Western civilization. As we will see in Chapter 4, Macedonian rulers continued to permit subjects to worship as they wished in the Hellenistic period following Alexander the Great's conquest of Persia.

Zoroastrianism: An Imperial Religion

The Great Kings of Persia and the Persian people followed Zoroastrianism°, a monotheistic religion that still exists today. Its founder, the prophet Zarathustra, known more commonly by his Greek name Zoroaster, lived and preached sometime between 1500 and 1200 B.C.E. His message spread widely throughout Iran for a thousand years before it became Persia's chief faith.

Persians transmitted Zoroaster's teachings, known collectively as the *Avesta*, through oral tradition until scribes recorded them in the sixth century C.E. According to Zoroaster, Ahura Mazda (Lord Wisdom), the one and only god of all Creation, is the cause of all good things in the universe. He represents wisdom, justice, and proper order among all created things. Another eternal being, Angra Mainyu (or Ahriman), opposes him. This spirit of destruction and disorder threatens Ahura Mazda's benevolent arrangement of creation.

CHRONOLOGY

Persia

550 B.C.E.	Cyrus starts the Persian Empire; Zoroastrianism becomes the empire's religion
546 B.C.E.	The Persians conquer Asia Minor
539 B.C.E.	The Persians capture Babylon
530 B.C.E.	Cyrus dies fighting Scythian steppe nomads
525 B.C.E.	Persian troops conquer Egypt
522 B.C.E.	Darius becomes king; the Achaemenid dynasty begins
490 B.C.E.	Greeks stop Persian invasion of Greece at Marathon
480–479 B.C.E.	Xerxes' invasion of Greece fails

In Zoroastrian belief, Ahura Mazda will eventually triumph in this struggle with the forces of evil, leaving all creation to enjoy a blissful eternity. Until then, the cosmic fight between Ahura Mazda's forces of light and Angra Mainyu's forces of darkness gives meaning to human existence and lays the foundation for a profoundly ethical way of life. Ahura Mazda requires humans to contribute to the well-being of the world. Everyone has the responsibility of choosing between right and wrong actions.

At the last Day of Judgment, sinners who have not listened to Ahura Mazda's instructions, such as those succumbing to the "filth of intoxication," will suffer eternal torment in a deep pit of terrible darkness. Those who have lived ethical lives will live eternally in a world purged of evil. In a period of transformation called "the Making Wonderful," the dead will be resurrected, and all will live together in the worship of Ahura Mazda.

The Great Kings of Persia believed themselves to be Ahura Mazda's earthly representatives. They committed their energies to fighting the forces of disorder active in their world. In this way, Zoroastrianism provided an ideological support for the Persian Empire's wars of conquest and consolidation at home. The Great Kings lavishly supported the Zoroastrian church, and its priests, called magi, established the faith as the empire's official religion. They built grand temples with sacred fires throughout Persian lands. Because Zoroastrian worship at fire altars occurred wherever Persian power expressed itself, the religion became a reminder to subject peoples of an enduring imperial presence around them. Although the Persian Empire tolerated other religions, Zoroastrianism became the official religion that supported the emperor.

Zoroastrian beliefs have played an important role in shaping the three great Western religions: Judaism, Christianity, and Islam. The Zoroastrian belief that God was opposed by an powerful spirit of evil contributed to the gradual development of the Jewish belief in Satan, who appears in the later books of the Hebrew Bible, into a demon with a distinct personality. Early Christians developed the concept of Satan, later known as the Devil, more clearly during the first century C.E., when they transformed him into a cosmic force of evil against whom Christians must engage in combat. The prophecy of a final struggle against the Devil, followed by the establishment of the kingdom of God on Earth, was incorporated into Revelation, the last book of the New Testament. The Zoroastrian idea of a final

Darius the Great Giving an Audience
In this carved panel from the Treasury of the Palace at Persepolis, the Great King Darius (r. 522–486 B.C.E.) is shown receiving a dignitary who has come to speak with him. Darius is seated on his throne and holds a staff of office. Subject kings from all over the Persian Empire also came to court to pay their respects and bring tribute.

judgment, followed by an afterlife in Heaven or Hell, became a central concept in Christianity and Islam.

The Achaemenid Dynasty

DOCUMENT

Persian Royal Inscription

In 522 B.C.E., a Persian nobleman, Darius, seized the imperial throne by murdering one of the sons of Cyrus the Great and initiated the Achaemenid dynasty. Named for a legendary ancestor, Achaemenes, the new dynasty inaugurated an epoch of territorial expansion and cultural activity that lasted until the Macedonian conqueror Alexander the Great overwhelmed Persia in 330 B.C.E. Darius built a new capital city at Persepolis. Like Cyrus before him, Darius drew workmen, artists, and material resources from among the many peoples of his vast empire. Greeks, Egyptians, Babylonians, and Scythians, among others, made the imperial capital a glittering city crowded with luxurious palaces where people of many cultures came together in the service of the Great King.

From this power center, Darius controlled an efficient administration. He expanded and improved Persia's roads, set up a postal system, and standardized measures and coinage. He also reorganized Cyrus's system of provincial government, dividing the empire into twenty provinces called *satrapies*. Each province paid an annual sum to the central government based on its productivity. The provincial governors, Persian noblemen called *satraps*, collected these taxes and gathered military recruits. In addition, the provincial capitals imitated Persepolis, maintaining administrative archives and serving as local centers of tax collection and bureaucracy. As we will see in the next chapter, this system of administration served as a model for later empires, particularly that of Alexander the Great.

By 513 B.C.E. Darius had greatly expanded his empire. On his northeastern frontier he annexed portions of India as far as the Indus River. He built a canal in Egypt that linked the Mediterranean and Red Seas. But his conquests on the northwestern frontier of the Persian Empire had the greatest impact on Western civilization because they brought Persia into direct contact with the Greeks. Eager to

Map 3.1 The Persian Empire at Its Greatest Extent

The Persian Empire begun by Cyrus about 550 B.C.E. grew to include all of the Middle East as far as India, Egypt, and northern Greece. This multiethnic, multireligious empire governed its many peoples firmly but tolerantly.

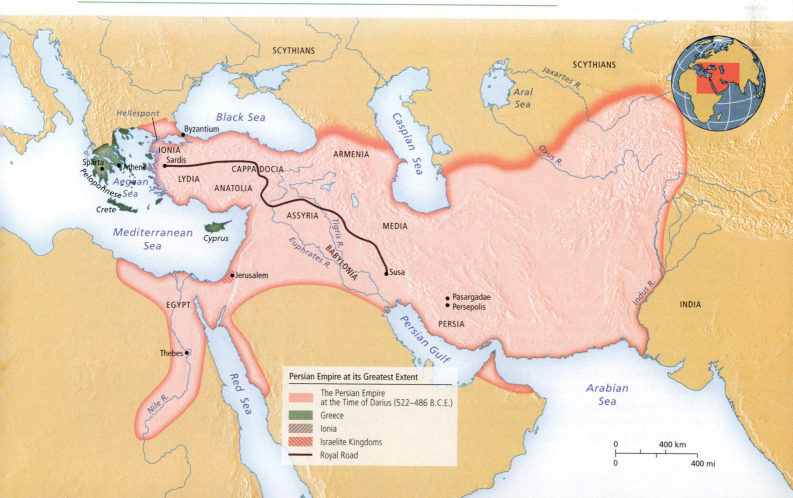

conquer Greece, Darius sent troops across the Hellespont, the channel of water that separates Europe from Asia, in order to establish military bases in the north of Greece. Such incursions along the Greek frontier were only a small part of Darius's grand imperial strategy, but to the Greeks the growing Persian presence caused profound anxiety. The stage was now set for the confrontation between the Persians and the Greeks, a confrontation that demonstrated the limits of Persian imperialism.

Hebrew Civilization and Religion

■ What political and religious beliefs and institutions gave Hebrew civilization its unique character, and what consequences came of its interactions with the Assyrians, Babylonians, and Persians?

One of the most influential civilizations in the West has been that of the Jews, a people who originated in the Middle East during the International Bronze Age. As we saw in Chapter 2, the Raiders of the Land and Sea destroyed many Canaanite cities around 1100 B.C.E. and caused great upheaval among the local populations. At about the same time, different groups of seminomadic pastoralists, called *Hapiru* ("landless people"), began to migrate into the hill country of Canaan, where they settled, herded their flocks, and began farming. Some historians think that this settlement was the origin of the biblical Hebrews, who gradually cohered into tribes and then kingdoms.

The Settlement in Canaan

If these historians are correct, sometime around 1100 B.C.E. one small group of wandering Hapiru arrived in Canaan, bringing with them the seeds of a powerful new religious belief. They gave allegiance to only one god. Belief in this deity gave them a strong sense of identity and distinguished them from the Canaanite peoples, who worshiped many gods. These followers of one god became known as Hebrews, then Israelites, and later Jews. Many centuries later, their traditions explained that a leader called Moses had led them from slavery in Egypt to freedom in Canaan, and that he had communicated God's law to them. Known today as the Ten Commandments, these laws forbid such acts as murder, theft, lying, and worshiping other gods. Later biblical laws were built on these principles.

By absorbing new members and conquering other groups, a loose confederation of tribes gained control of most of Canaan during the eleventh century B.C.E. Impressed by the Hebrew victories, many Canaanites began to worship the Hebrew God and joined the Hebrew tribes. Gradually these various tribes came to believe that they all shared a common history and a common ancestor, Abraham, who had traveled to Canaan from his home in Mesopotamia long before Moses. According to biblical tradition, Abraham was the first person to worship only one god. For this reason, he is considered the first Hebrew monotheist and the ancestor of the Jews.

The Hebrew tribes built shrines to their God throughout Canaan. The most important religious site was the shrine in the town of Shiloh, where they celebrated their allegiance to their God and settled disputes about property, inheritance, and crime. They kept their most sacred object, the Ark of the Covenant, in this shrine. The Ark of the Covenant was a gold-covered box that reputedly contained a divine and mysterious power. Concealed from the sight of everyone but the priests who organized God's worship, the Ark symbolized the connection between God and his followers as well as the unity of all the Hebrew tribes.

The confederation of Hebrew tribes faced many enemies in Canaan. The most serious threat came from the Philistines, who were descendants of a group of Raiders of the Land and Sea called the Peleset. They controlled the Mediterranean coastal plain in Canaan and pushed relentlessly at the Hebrews living in the inland hills. Around 1050 B.C.E., a Philistine army defeated the Hebrew tribes in battle, captured the Ark of the Covenant, and destroyed Shiloh. According to traditions recorded in the Bible, the desperate Hebrews chose a king to give them stronger leadership, even though tribal tradition was hostile to the notion of kings. The tribes chose Saul to be the first king about 1020 B.C.E., and he retrieved the Ark from the Philistines. Some twenty years later, a popular warrior in Saul's court named David succeeded Saul as king and reigned from approximately 1000 to 962 B.C.E.

The Israelite Kingdoms

David was a talented monarch. By establishing a strong alliance among the Hebrew tribes of northern and southern Canaan, he defeated the Philistines permanently and built a prosperous kingdom. Called the Israelite monarchy by historians, this kingdom lay sandwiched between the empires in Egypt and Mesopotamia (see Map 3.2). By imitating the government institutions of these neighboring states, David transformed the nature of Israelite society. He set up a centralized bureaucracy run by professional soldiers, administrators, and scribes. David established a census as the basis for tax collection and military conscription, and he created a royal court complete with a harem. Jerusalem, an old Canaanite city, served as the capital of his new kingdom. He moved the Ark of the Covenant from Shiloh to Jerusalem, bringing the worship of the Hebrew God under the control of the monarchy.

During the reign of David's son Solomon (ca. 962–922 B.C.E.), the kingdom of Israel enjoyed peace and prosperity.

VIDEO
The Old City of Jerusalem

One of Solomon's greatest achievements was the construction of a grand temple in Jerusalem to serve as the house of God and a resting place for the Ark of the Covenant. Constructed with the technical assistance of architects and artisans from the neighboring Phoenician kingdom of Tyre and the forced labor of Solomon's subjects, the Jerusalem temple became the focal point of religious worship in his kingdom.

Solomon pursued an ambitious foreign policy devoted to developing long-distance commerce. He controlled the major trade routes running from Egypt and Arabia to Syria,

Map 3.2 The Israelite Monarchy
The kingdom established by David (ca. 1000–962 B.C.E.) and expanded by his son Solomon (ca. 962–922 B.C.E.) unified the Hebrew tribes of Canaan. At Solomon's death, the realm split into two smaller kingdoms. Assyrian armies destroyed the northern kingdom of Israel in 722 B.C.E., and Babylonian forces destroyed the southern kingdom of Judah in 586 B.C.E.

and under his supervision Israelite merchants prospered as middlemen in an expanding system of international commerce. Under his leadership, the kingdom enjoyed substantial control over the trade of horses sent south from Asia Minor and chariots sent north from Egypt. Solomon developed his own corps of charioteers to protect these trade routes from bandits.

With the assistance of Phoenician shipbuilders, Solomon constructed a merchant fleet for trade in the Red Sea. His merchants sailed as far south as Somalia, the portion of the African coast that touches the Arabian Sea, from where they brought jewels, gold, ivory, and other items of luxury. In addition, Solomon also developed overland trade with Arabia and established economic ties with the kingdom of Sabaea (Sheba) in Yemen. According to tradition, the Queen of Sheba visited Solomon, bringing delightful gifts, including spices from East Asia. What Solomon's merchants traded in return is uncertain. Solomon developed diplomatic relations with Egypt, as well as the seafaring Phoenicians, and other kingdoms in Africa and Middle East. He married foreign princesses in order to cement diplomatic ties, and he permitted his wives to build shrines in Jerusalem to gods of their homelands.

When Solomon died in 922 B.C.E., his heirs' inability to placate the northern Israelite tribes, who felt that Solomon had favored his own tribe of Judah at their expense, caused the Israelite kingdom to break into two parts. The kingdom of Israel, in the northern region of the former kingdom, established its capital at Shechem and remained reasonably stable in comparison to its southern rival. In the southern kingdom of Judah, Solomon's successors retained Jerusalem as its capital, but political stability remained elusive for them due to dynastic instability and quarrels among the leaders. Only for two brief periods did the kingdom of Judah enjoy stable government. During the two centuries after 922 B.C.E., however, both of the two successor kingdoms struggled to survive under the shadow of the far more powerful neighboring empires of Assyria and Babylonia. The gap between the rich and the poor in both kingdoms widened in the course of these tumultuous centuries. The upper classes grew extremely wealthy from trade and the accumulation of land, which they acquired from the indebted poor. In their anguish the poor called out for social justice, a cry heard by the prophets.

The Hebrew Prophets

As kings and aristocrats became more rapacious, and as taxes increased, more and more debt-ridden peasants lost their farms to rich landholders. The poor found champions in the Hebrew prophets. These men spoke out on behalf of the downtrodden with words they believed to be inspired by God. These social critics strongly censured what they saw as religious and moral decay among the landowners and kings, such as the worship of Canaanite gods, a practice that remained widespread. They urged the entire population toward moral reform and spiritual consciousness. The prophet Elijah, who lived in the ninth century B.C.E., proclaimed that kings should not break the laws with impunity but should conform to the same laws as everyone else. The principle that kings and rulers are not above the law remained as a basic political idea in what eventually became the West. In the next century, another champion of social justice named Amos mocked the irony and hypocrisy of the royal court's celebrating lavish religious ceremonies in God's name while the poor starved. Isaiah, a prophet who lived in Jerusalem, demanded that people attempt to establish a just society in order to avert divine punishment. He had no patience for religious observance empty of personal commitment. According to Isaiah, God said:

> *What need have I of all your sacrifices? . . . I am sated with burnt offerings of sacrificial rams . . . Incense is offensive to me. . . . Though you pray at length, I will not listen. Your hands are stained with crime. Wash yourselves clean; Put your evil doings away from my sight. Cease to do evil; learn to do good; devote yourself to justice; aid the wronged. Uphold the rights of the orphan. Defend the cause of the widow. (Isaiah 1:11–17)*

Preoccupied with internal problems, the Israelites failed to note the growing power of the neighboring Assyrian Empire. As we saw in Chapter 2, Assyrian armies under the command of King Tiglath-Pileser conquered the Israelite kingdom in 733 B.C.E. Eleven years later, when the Israelite ruler refused to pay tribute, the Assyrians destroyed the kingdom and deported nearly 30,000 Israelites to Mesopotamia, a standard Assyrian practice with defeated enemies. The deported Israelites, who became known as the Lost Ten Tribes, eventually forgot their cultural identity in their new homes and disappeared from the historical record. The kingdom of Israel had come to an undignified end.

The kingdom of Judah, however, survived. By accepting the overlordship of the Assyrians and later the Babylonians, who had replaced the Assyrians as the dominant power in the Middle East by the late seventh century B.C.E., Judah escaped Israel's fate. After the destruction of the northern kingdom, a mood of religious reform spread throughout Judah. People began to believe that God had destroyed the kingdom of Israel in anger, though they disagreed about the causes of his rage and how to appease him.

To regain God's favor, some of Judah's leaders insisted on the absolute primacy of the temple in Jerusalem as the place for religious worship on the assumption that God disapproved of his followers' worshiping him at many shrines instead of only one. By insisting on Jerusalem as the sole place of worship, the priests of Jerusalem increased their power. With the help of the king's soldiers, the temple priests in Jerusalem violently suppressed all other shrines to God scattered across the land. The consequences were greater uniformity of worship among the Hebrews and a centralized religious authority. These developments enhanced a sense of Hebrew identity.

Some Hebrew prophets, however, sought to appease God by countering this trend. They challenged the supremacy of the Jerusalem priests and emphasized the need for personal reform and the creation of a just society. One of these prophets was Jeremiah, who began preaching in 627 B.C.E. In the tradition of Isaiah, he placed little value on the strength of the temple priesthood's prayers on Judah's behalf. He predicted that God would cause the Babylonians to destroy Judah because its people were corrupt. Jeremiah's predictions proved correct. When Judah revolted against the Babylonians in 598 B.C.E., the Babylonian king Nebuchadnezzar sent a large army to crush the rebellion. The next year he captured Jerusalem and deported Judah's king and high priests to Babylonia. Ten years later, when another revolt broke out, Babylonian forces burned Jerusalem to the ground and demolished Solomon's temple, the spiritual and political center of the kingdom of Judah. Perhaps as many as 20,000 people were deported to Babylonia, an event historians call the Babylonian Exile°.

IMAGE

The Wailing Wall

The Babylonian Exile

After the destruction of the Jerusalem temple in 587 B.C.E., the Hebrew exiles living in Babylonia struggled to maintain their cultural and religious identity. But Babylonian culture influenced their religious practice. Babylonian astronomy contributed to the institution of a seven-day week (and perhaps sabbath worship on the seventh day). The Hebrews developed a calendar that adopted Babylonian names of months. For example, the Babylonian month Nissanu is the same as the Hebrew month Nisan. Like the Babylonians, the Hebrew exiles structured their calendar around seasonal festivals. The exiles added their own new religious celebrations to the structure provided by the Babylonian calendar. The Hebrews observed a New Year's Day and a Day of Atonement in the autumn. In the spring they celebrated Passover, the commemoration of the departure of the Hebrews from Egypt under the leadership of Moses.

Sometime after the year 538 B.C.E., an anonymous author, known to biblical scholars as Second Isaiah (because he wrote some of the chapters of the Book of Isaiah), comforted the dispirited Hebrews in Babylonia. Trying to find meaning in the destruction of the kingdoms of Israel and Judah, he explained that God's primary interest lay in the human spirit, not in earthly kingdoms. The god described by Second Isaiah was a truly universal god who alone governs all creation and shapes the lives of all the peoples of the world. This vision of a single, universal deity not bound by time or place was perhaps the greatest legacy of Hebrew civilization to the West.

Second Isaiah promised that God would return his people to Jerusalem and that Cyrus the Great King of Persia would serve as God's agent in this task. The reference to the

Persian king suggests that Second Isaiah wrote sometime around 538 B.C.E., when Cyrus instituted his policy permitting all peoples exiled by the Babylonians to return to their homelands. Many of the Hebrew exiles in Babylonia returned to their old homes, now governed by Persia, and attempted to revive traditional religious life in Jerusalem.

The Second Temple and Jewish Religious Practice

Nearly two generations passed before the Hebrews, with Persian assistance, finished building a new temple in Jerusalem, called the Second Temple. In 458 B.C.E., with the authority of the Persian king, a leader called Ezra the Scribe began to organize and regulate religious practices. He instituted regular sabbath worship and began a program of teaching religious law to the population. For the next 500 years this restored temple worship was the center of religious life. Historians call the Hebrews who lived after the completion of the Second Temple Jews. Henceforth, the people are known as Jews and their religion is called Judaism.

Ezra and other religious thinkers believed that God had destroyed the kingdoms of Israel and Judah before the Babylonian Exile because the people had failed to observe religious law properly. For this reason, knowledge of the law (or Torah) through study and observance now became all-important for the preservation of the Jewish community and Jewish identity. In particular, the priesthood in Jerusalem, which controlled secular and religious affairs, insisted on very strict observance of laws concerning temple sacrifice and ritual. The priests also made a decision that determined the status of women in Jewish society. By deciding that descent through the mother determined Jewish identity, they assigned women a crucial role in determining membership in the Jewish community. In this one respect the priests enhanced the status of Jewish wives.

Despite these reforms, the public role of women in organized worship grew quite restricted. Prior to the Babylonian Exile, women participated in worship as priestesses, singers, and dancers. Canaanite religion gave a high status to female goddesses of fertility, and Israelite women sometimes participated in their cults. In the Second Temple period, however, the Jews worshiped only one male god and denied all other deities. Women could not enter the most sacred portions of the temple where the main sacrifices were performed because according to religious law the blood of menstruation and childbirth made them ritually unclean. Many of these ancient attitudes regarding the place of women in religious and family life have survived to the present day, especially in the exclusion of women from the most sacred rituals and responsibilities in some forms of Judaism and Christianity.

The Hebrew Bible

After the Second Temple was built in 515 B.C.E., the Hebrew Bible (called the Old Testament by Christians)

CHRONOLOGY

The Israelite Kingdom

ca. 1100 B.C.E.	The International Bronze Age ends; Hapiru arrive in Canaan
ca. 1000–922 B.C.E.	David and Solomon rule the Israelite kingdom
922 B.C.E.	The Israelite kingdom splits into Judah (southern kingdom) and Israel (northern kingdom)
ca. 800 B.C.E.	Prophets begin to preach moral reform
721 B.C.E.	Assyrians destroy northern kingdom (Israel)
587 B.C.E.	Babylonians defeat southern kingdom (Judah) and destroy Jerusalem and Solomon's temple
538 B.C.E.	Cyrus of Persia permits Israelites to return to Palestine and rebuild the temple

slowly took the shape it has today. Like many other peoples in the ancient Middle East, the Jews believed that their God had chosen them to serve him. They believed that historical events described in the Bible illustrate and interpret that relationship. As a historical document, the Bible provides a chronology of the world from the moment of its creation and gives an account of the early development of the Hebrew people. Drawn from a variety of oral and written sources, and composed many centuries after the events they describe, the biblical accounts condense and simplify a very complex process of migration, settlement, and religious development.

Many details in the Bible have been confirmed by non-Hebrew sources, but the Bible must be understood primarily as an expression of religious meaning through historical traditions of different sorts. It combines highly detailed narratives with folklore, prophecies, parables, stories, and poems. The Bible provides far more than the narration of events. It explains God's presence in human lives and establishes a moral vision of human existence. As a result no book has had more influence on the religious thought of the West.

For many people, the significance of the Hebrew Bible lies in the religious principles that its stories illustrate. The book describes a single God who protects the Earth and his chosen people, the Hebrews. Historical events demonstrate his concern for them, for he punishes and rewards his people in accordance with their actions. In the Hebrew Bible, events such as the restoration of the temple in Jerusalem by

Isaiah Scroll

Discovered in a cave near the Dead Sea in 1947 and now housed in the Shrine of the Book in Jerusalem, this text of the biblical book of Isaiah was written between about 300 and 100 B.C.E., making it nearly a thousand years older than the next surviving manuscript of Isaiah. The two copies of the book of Isaiah differ in only a few minor details, demonstrating the care with which biblical texts were copied and passed on by generations of scribes.

Cyrus have significance in terms of a divine plan and the fulfillment of prophecy. As part of this divine plan, God expects his followers to follow a strict code of compassionate, ethical behavior toward their fellow human beings. As a religious work the Hebrew Bible provides the basis of Judaism. In conjunction with the New Testament, written in the first century C.E., it is the core text of Christianity. Muslims also recognize both the Hebrew and Christian texts as holy writings, superseded only by the Qur'an.

Greece Rebuilds, 1100–479 B.C.E.

■ How did Greek city-states develop in the framework of a larger world dominated by Persia?

As we saw in Chapter 2, at the end of the International Bronze Age Greek civilization entered a period of bitter poverty and political instability. This period, known as the Dark Age, lasted until about 750 B.C.E., when a period designated by historians as the Archaic Age began. The Archaic Age was marked by economic growth at home and many Greek encounters with Phoenicians and Persians abroad (see Map 3.3). This period of revival set the stage for Greece's Classical Age, a time of great cultural achievement.

The Dark Age, ca. 1100–750 B.C.E.

Compared with the wealth and splendor of Mycenaean communities in the Bronze Age, Greek life in the Dark Age was quite gloomy. Few new settlements were established on the mainland, and urban life disappeared. Maritime trade declined precipitously and the economies controlled by the

Map 3.3 Greece in the Archaic and Classical Ages

During the Archaic and Classical Ages, Greek cities spread from Greece to the shores of the Black Sea and as far west as Italy and southern France. This map shows the Greek heartland: the mainland, the islands of the Aegean Sea, and Ionia. Although never unified politically in the Archaic and Classical Ages, the people in these cities spoke Greek, worshiped the same gods, and shared a similar culture.

palaces broke down. Because there was no longer a need for scribes to record inventories, Linear B writing dropped out of use entirely. A serious decline in agriculture led to a steep decrease in food production and population.

A slow economic recovery began in the Greek world about 850 B.C.E., when the population began to grow again and when trade became brisker. Because of the harsh living conditions on the mainland during the Dark Age, many Greeks had abandoned their homes and moved to a region called Ionia that encompassed the coasts and islands of western Asia Minor. Relatively isolated from other Greek communities, these pioneers developed their own distinctive Ionian variation of the Greek language. By 800 B.C.E. the Ionian Greeks were regularly interacting with the Phoenicians in the eastern Mediterranean. These seafarers forged a connection between Greeks and the cultures of the Middle East that exerted a lasting impact on Greek society because it marked the end of Greek isolation (see Map 2.5).

The Archaic Age, ca. 750–479 B.C.E.

Between about 750 and 650 B.C.E., many fresh ideas poured into Greece from the Middle East through contact with the Phoenicians and other peoples. Historians call this exciting period the Archaic Age. Encounters with Middle Eastern poets, merchants, artisans, refugees, doctors, slaves, and spouses brought innovations to Greece: new words such as *tyrant* and *gold*; new economic practices such as the use of coinage and charging interest on loans; new myths and literary themes (such as the story of the Great Flood; see document on page 69); new ritual procedures for sacrificing

The Alphabet and Writing in Greece

Sometime around the middle of the eighth century B.C.E., Greek merchants brought the alphabet to Greece. They adopted this system of letters from seafaring Phoenicians whom they encountered while trading in the eastern Mediterranean. To write down their business transactions, Phoenicians used an alphabet of twenty-two letters derived from the one invented in the Bronze Age at Ugarit. Recognizing the potential of writing, the Greeks quickly adapted the Phoenician script to the Greek language and began to read and write. By 650 B.C.E. the Greek alphabet and the literacy that went with it spread widely, following trade routes throughout the Mediterranean world. The Greek alphabet reached Italy and eventually the Romans, whose adaptation of the alphabet is the one we use today.

The adoption of the alphabet deeply affected Greek society because it let information of all sorts be preserved in written form—and widely shared. The alphabet is easy to learn because each letter represents one sound, and therefore many people in the Greek world began to exploit the potential of reading and writing.

Unlike the cultures of Mesopotamia and Egypt, in which writing was the specialized expertise of an elite scribal class, the more open Greek culture never limited writing to a particular group. People of all sorts employed it. For example, government officials began to write down laws, which for the first time became available for all members of the community to see. Having written laws posted in public helped to undercut the ancient privileges of the aristocracy to interpret the oral law, something they often did arbitrarily and unjustly. Thus written laws

contributed to the development of fairer political institutions in the Greek poleis. Merchants kept track of shipments, payments, loans, and debts, thereby helping the economies of Greek communities to thrive and become more complex.

Perhaps the most significant development of all, however, was the beginning of written literature. The first works of literature to be rendered in writing were the *Iliad* and the *Odyssey* of Homer, the product of a long tradition of oral transmission combined with the particular genius of Homer, who gave them their final written form. These tales became central to Greek culture.

But soon writers were not just recording oral poetry, they were composing original poetry to be read and recited. Tragedians composed the intense dramas that explored fundamental questions of human psychology. Mythological tales were set down and considered critically, leading eventually to the development of scientific thought (see text on Ionian philosophers). As soon as historians could read the accounts of

earlier historians, they began to criticize them in different ways, and the Western tradition of critical history took root.

Thus the adoption of the alphabet transformed Greek society. Reading and writing—which depend on the alphabet—helped shape the Greek intellectual legacy that we value so highly today. But the importance of the alphabet and of reading and writing in the West is still far more profound: Western civilization is based on the writing and interpretation of texts. Sacred books, legal codes, scientific inquiries, and the rich and varied traditions of literature are fundamental to who we are and how we experience the world. And they were made possible by the alphabet and the advent of reading and writing.

Question for Discussion

Why was the alphabet essential to the development of Greek literature?

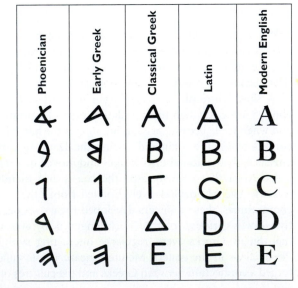

Chart of the Development of the Alphabet
This chart shows how the first five letters of the Phoenician alphabet developed into the first five letters of the English alphabet.

Tales of the Flood

In one of the most popular tales of the Classical Age, a god destroys the Earth in a great flood but permits some humans to survive on a boat and repopulate the Earth once the waters subside. Here we see excerpts from three versions of the flood story composed by Babylonians, Hebrews, and Greeks. The similarities among the texts suggest that the story may have originated in an earlier Mesopotamian culture and then spread to these three cultural traditions.

The Epic of Gilgamesh: How the Gods Spared Uta-napishti

[Everything I owned] I loaded aboard:
all the silver I owned I loaded aboard,
all the gold I owned I loaded aboard,
all the living creatures I had I loaded aboard.
I sent on board all my kith and kin,
the beasts of the field, the creatures of the wild, and
   members of every skill and craft . . .
. . . For six days and [seven] nights,
there blew the wind, the downpour,
the gale, the Deluge, it flattened land.
But the seventh day when it came,
the gale relented, the Deluge ended.
The ocean grew calm, that had thrashed like a woman in
   labour,
the tempest grew still, the Deluge ended . . .
Enlil [a powerful god] came up inside the boat,
[and blessed Uta-napishti and his wife, saying:]
In the past Uta-napishti was a mortal man,
but now he and his wife shall become like us gods!

The Hebrew Bible: The Story of Noah and the Ark

Then the Lord said to Noah, "Go into the ark with all your household, for you alone have I found righteous before Me in this generation. Of every clean animal you shall take seven pairs, males and their mates, and of every animal that is not clean, two, a male and its mate. Of the birds of the sky, also. . . . For in seven days I will make it rain upon the earth, forty days and forty nights, and I will blot out from the earth all existence that I created. And Noah did just as the Lord commanded him. . . . And on the seventh day the waters of the Flood came upon the earth. . . . [When the Flood had ended] God spoke to Noah, saying, come out of the ark, together with your wife, your sons, and your sons' wives. Bring out with you every living thing of all flesh that is there with you: birds, animals, and everything that creeps on earth; and let them swarm on the earth and be fertile and increase on earth.

Greek Mythology: Deucalion's Story

In this Greek tale, King Deucalion survives because his father, the god Prometheus, warns him.

When Zeus, the king of the gods, decided to destroy humankind . . . Deucalion by the advice of Prometheus constructed a chest, and having stored it with provisions he embarked in it with Pyrrha, his wife. But Zeus, by pouring heavy rain from Heaven flooded the greater part of Greece, so that all men were destroyed, except for a few who fled to high mountains in the neighborhood. . . . But Deucalion, floating in the chest over the sea for nine days and as many nights, drifted to Mount Parnassus, and there, when the rain ceased, he landed and sacrificed to Zeus . . . And Zeus . . . allowed Deucalion to choose whatever he wished, and he chose to create men. At the bidding of Zeus, he picked up stones and threw them over his head, and the stones became men, and the stones that Pyrrha threw became women. . . .

Sources: From *The Epic of Gilgamesh: The Babylonian Epic Poem and Other Texts in Akkadian and Sumerian,* translated by Andrew George (Allen Lane The Penguin Press, 1999). Translation copyright © 1999 by Andrew George. Reproduced by permission of Penguin Books Ltd.; from *Tanakh, A New Translation of The Holy Scriptures According to the Traditional Hebrew Text,* 1985, Exodus 7–8. Published by the Jewish Publication Society; and reprinted by permission of the publishers and the Trustees of the Loeb Classical Library from *Apollodorus: Volume I,* Loeb Classical Library Volume L 121, translated by J. G. Frazer, Cambridge, Mass.: Harvard University Press, 1921. The Loeb Classical Library® is a registered trademark of the President and Fellows of Harvard College.

animals; new gods and goddesses (such as Dionysus, the god of wine); and new inventions of convenience (such as parasols to provide shade).

By far the most valuable import from the Phoenicians was the alphabet. As we saw in Chapter 2, the Phoenicians, who had been using an alphabet of twenty-two letters for at least three centuries, introduced the system to Greece sometime just before 750 B.C.E. The adoption of the alphabet, to which the Greeks added vowels, was one of the developments that marked the beginning of the Archaic Age. Because an alphabet records sounds, not words, it can be adjusted easily for any language. Greeks quickly recognized the potential of the new system, and quickly adopted it throughout their communities. Greeks learned to write and read, first for business purposes and then for pleasure. They began to record their oral traditions, legends, and songs. At the same time, they began to compose an entirely new literature and write down their laws.

Homer's Epic Poems

Two of the greatest works of literature ever composed, the *Iliad* and the *Odyssey*, were soon written down in the new alphabet. A Greek poet named Homer, who probably lived around 750 B.C.E., is credited with composing these poems, but they were certainly not entirely his personal invention. The stories of the *Iliad* and the *Odyssey* drew from a large and widely recited cycle of tales about the legendary Trojan War that wandering poets had recited for centuries. The poets had elaborated on the stories so much over time that all historical accuracy was lost. Nevertheless, many details in the poems, especially about weapons and armor no longer used in Homer's day, suggest that the earliest versions of the poems were first recited in the International Bronze Age and may be very loosely based on events of that time.

The body of poems of which the *Iliad* and the *Odyssey* were a part tells how an army of Greek warriors sailed to Troy, a wealthy city on the northwest coast of Asia Minor, to recover a beautiful Greek princess, Helen, who had been stolen by a Trojan prince. After ten years of savage fighting, the Greeks finally stormed Troy and won the war, though their greatest fighters had died in battle. When the surviving heroes returned to Greece, they were met with treachery and bloodshed.

The genius of Homer lay in his retelling of these old stories. He did not relate the entire saga of the Trojan War because he knew that his audiences were familiar with it. Instead, he selected certain episodes in which he emphasized aspects of human character and emotion in the midst of violent conflict in fresh ways. In the *Iliad*, for example, he describes how the hero Achilles, the mightiest of all the Greeks fighting at Troy, grows angry when his commander-in-chief Agamemnon steals his favorite concubine. In a rage, Achilles withdraws from the battle and returns to fight only to avenge his best friend who had been killed by Hector, the mainstay of the Trojan defense. Achilles eventually slays Hector, but does not relinquish his fury until Hector's father, Priam, the king of Troy, begs him to return his son's corpse for proper burial. "Honor the Gods, Achilles, and take pity upon me, remembering your own father," implores King Priam. "Yet I am still more pitiful than he. I have endured more than any other mortal: I kiss the hand of the man who has killed my sons." Achilles relents and weeps, his humanity finally restored after so much killing. In Homer's hands, the story of Achilles' anger becomes a profound investigation into human alienation and redemption.

The *Odyssey* tells a different kind of story. The hero of this poem, the Greek king Odysseus, wants nothing more than to return to his wife after the fall of Troy. His trek takes ten years, full of suspenseful adventures as he sails about in the Mediterranean Sea. Odysseus's endless patience, relentless cunning, intellectual curiosity, and deep love for his family finally brings him home. Due to their very human strengths and weaknesses, Achilles and Odysseus are two of the most finely drawn characters in Western literature.

The Polis

In addition to telling epic tales that glorified heroes of the past, Greeks in the Archaic Age experimented with new forms of social and political life. They developed a new style of community called the polis° (plural *poleis*), or city-state. A polis was a self-governing community consisting of an urban center with a defensible hilltop called an acropolis° and all the surrounding land farmed by citizens of the polis. Greek cities varied in size from a few square miles to several hundred. All contained similar institutions: an assembly in which the men of the community gathered to discuss and make decisions about public business; a council of male elders who offered advice on public matters; temples to gods who protected the polis and whose goodwill was necessary for the community's prosperity; and an open area in the center of town called an *agora*, which served as a market and a place for informal discussions.

Living in a polis provided an extremely strong sense of community. A person could be a citizen of only one polis, and every citizen was expected to place the community's interests above all other concerns. Even the women, who were citizens but not permitted to play a role in public life, felt powerful ties to their polis. While only citizens had full membership in a polis, enjoying the greatest rights and bearing the greatest responsibilities, every city had noncitizens from other communities. Some of these noncitizens had limited rights and obligations, whereas slaves had no rights at all.

Colonization and the Settlement of New Lands

A population boom during the Archaic Age forced Greeks to emigrate because the rocky soil of the mainland could not provide enough food. From about 750 to 550 B.C.E., cities such as Corinth and Megara on the mainland and Miletos in Ionia established more than 200 colonies overseas.

Greek emigrants traveled by boat to foreign shores. Many colonists settled on the Aegean coast north into the Black Sea region, which offered plentiful farmlands. The important settlement at Byzantium controlled access to the agricultural wealth of these Black Sea colonies. Greeks established many new cities in Sicily and southern Italy, as well as on the southern coast of France and the eastern coast of Spain. By 600 B.C.E. Greeks had founded colonies in North Africa in the region of modern Libya and on the islands of Cyprus and Crete. Greek merchants also set up a trading community on the Syrian coast and another in the Egyptian delta, with the pharaoh's permission.

New Greek cities such as Syracuse and Tarentum in Italy, Massilia (Marseilles) in France, and Neapolis (Naples) in Italy gave land-hungry settlers the opportunity to prosper

Athenian

(front)

(back)

Jewish Second Temple Period

(front)

(back)

Athenian Coinage

The coins made in Athens displayed the head of Athena on one side, and her sacred bird, the owl, on the other side. The coin shown at the top dates to the height of the Athenian Empire, about 450 B.C.E. On the bottom, another coin of similar weight and appearance is called a Jehud (from the Persian name of the province of Judah). Minted near Jerusalem, its front shows a face based on Athena. Its back shows an owl and Hebrew writing. The similarities of these coins reveal the international influence of Athenian coinage and the importance of standard weights in long-distance trade.

through farming, manufacturing, and trade. The colonists obtained metal ores, timber, and slaves from the regions they settled and began growing wheat, olives, and wine for export. Merchants carried the goods to markets all over the Mediterranean. The overseas world of the Greeks prospered, and a vibrant Greek culture with common language, gods, and social institutions spread throughout the Mediterranean and into the Black Sea.

Although all of the Greek colonies maintained some formal religious ties with their mother city-states, or *metropoleis,* they were self-governing and independent. Some colonies failed, but others grew rich and populous enough to send out their own colonies. Because the Greek colonists seized territory by force and sometimes slaughtered the local inhabitants, relations with the people already living in these lands were often quite tense.

The Greek adoption of coinage spurred commercial activity among many Greek communities. Coinage first replaced barter as a medium of exchange in western Asia Minor about 630 B.C.E. as a form of portable wealth that could be used to buy goods and services. Minted from pre-

cious metals and uniform in weight, coins helped people standardize the value of goods, a development that revolutionized commerce. By 600 B.C.E. Greeks living in Ionia and on the Greek mainland began to mint their own coins. Each city-state used a distinctive emblem to mark its currency. When Athens became the dominant economic power in the Aegean during the second half of the fifth century B.C.E., Athenian coinage became the standard throughout the Greek world and far beyond.

Greek colonization played a critical role in shaping Western civilization by creating wealthy centers of Greek culture in Italy and the western Mediterranean. Sometimes overshadowed in the historical record by city-states of the Greek mainland, such as Athens, Sparta, and Corinth, the impressive new poleis spread Greek civilization, language, literature, religion, and art far beyond Greece itself. The colony of Syracuse in Sicily, for example, grew to be larger than any city in Greece. Greek communities deeply influenced local cultures and would make a tremendous impact on Etruscan and Roman civilization in Italy, as we will see in Chapter 4. Overseas colonies also prepared the way for the rapid explosion of Greek culture that followed the conquests of Alexander the Great.

Elite Athletic Competition in Greek Poleis

Athletic contests called panhellenic° games, because they drew participants from the entire Greek world, were a mainstay of aristocratic Greek culture in the Archaic Age. As many as 150 cities regularly offered aristocratic men the chance to win glory through competition in chariot racing, discus throwing, wrestling, foot racing, and other field events. Through sports the Greeks found a common culture that allowed them to express their Greek identity and honor the gods at the same time.

The Olympic Games, which originated in 776 B.C.E., carried the most prestige. Every four years Greek athletes from southern Italy to the Black Sea gathered in the sacred grove of Olympia in central Greece to take part in games dedicated to Zeus, the chief Greek god. The rules required the poleis to call truces to any wars, even if they were in the middle of battle, and allow safe passage to all athletes traveling to Olympia. Records show the naming of champions at Olympia from 776 B.C.E to 217 C.E. The Roman emperor Theodosius I, who was a Christian, abolished the games in 393 C.E. because they involved the worship of Greek gods.

The Hoplite Revolution

The new wealth flowing through the Greek world transformed everyday life. For the first time, men who were not aristocrats could afford to purchase weapons of war. Called hoplites°, these heavily armed infantry used their own funds to purchase helmets, shields, swords, shin guards, and thrusting spears. Hoplites entered the battlefield in massed ranks, four to eight deep, a formation called a phalanx°. Each man relied for protection on the man to his right, whose shield protected his own sword arm. Cooperation was all-important, for if the line broke, the individual soldier became more vulnerable. Fighting in massed units like this replaced the combat between individual aristocrats and their retinues that had characterized Greek warfare in earlier periods.

Greeks glorified battling in this close-knit manner. Hoplite fighting generated a sense of pride and common purpose that had political consequences, as hoplites demanded a political voice in the communities for which they fought. Their growing confidence directly challenged aristocratic families who traditionally held tight control over community decision making.

In many poleis, new political leaders arose to champion the cause of the hoplite citizenry. These political leaders were known as tyrants°, a word borrowed from the Middle East that originally did not have the negative connotation it carries today. Tyrants typically came from the ruling classes, but they found their political support among the hoplites and the poor who felt otherwise left out of the political life

of the community. When tyrants seized power in a polis, they served the interests of the community as a whole, not just the aristocrats. They promoted overseas trade, built harbors, protected farmers, and began public-works projects to employ citizen workers and to beautify their cities. They also cultivated alliances with other tyrants in other poleis to establish peace and prosperity. Most important, the tyrants' authority enabled a broad range of Greek citizens to participate in government for the first time.

But tyrannies contained a fatal flaw. The power of the tyrant was handed down from father to son, and the successors rarely inherited their fathers' qualities of leadership. As a result, the tyrannies often became oppressive and unpopular, especially among the hoplites and poor who had sup-

---

DOCUMENT

Tyrtaeus: The Glory of Hoplite Warfare

During the mid-seventh century B.C.E., *the Spartan poet Tyrtaeus wrote many poems glorifying warfare on behalf of the polis. Spartan troops sang his poems as they marched into combat. This poem explains why young men should seek glory and avoid shame by fighting in the front ranks.*

It is a noble thing for a good man to die fighting in the front
    lines for his country;
but to abandon his city and fertile fields, to be reduced to
    poverty,
this is most grievous of all things, for then a man wanders
    from place to place
with his beloved mother and elderly father, his small
    children and lawful wife. . . .
And so, since a wanderer receives no recognition, neither
    honor nor respect nor mercy,
let us fight with all our might for this land, and die for our
    children,
never caring to spare our lives.
Stand together and fight, then, O young men; take no step
    in shameful flight.
Be not overcome by fear, but let the heart be great and
    strong in your breast,
never flinching when you face the enemy. . . .
So let every man bite his lip, and, with both feet firmly on
    the ground,
take his place for battle.

ported the tyrants in the first place. Few of them lasted more than two generations.

Two of the most important poleis on the Greek mainland, Sparta and Athens, both experienced hoplite revolutions, but the two poleis developed very different political and social systems. In Sparta, the hoplite class formed an egalitarian elite that had consistently opposed the rule of tyrants but ruled the rest of the population in an authoritarian manner. Athenians, on the other hand, developed into a democracy, including the entire population in the political process.

Sparta: A Militarized Society

Cut off from the rest of Greece by high mountain ranges to the west and north, Sparta dominated the Peloponnese, the southernmost part of Greece. Until about 700 B.C.E. Spartans lived very much like other Greeks except that their hoplite forces achieved political power without the aid of tyrants, whom they despised. Rapid expansion in the Peloponnese prompted Spartans to develop a highly militarized way of life among the Greeks. All political power rested with a corps of warrior hoplites that comprised the entire population of male citizens. The Spartan hoplites, who called themselves "the Equals," controlled all the polis's land and spent their time in military training.

The Spartan military system grew more elaborate after 700 B.C.E. when the Spartans conquered Messenia, a fertile region in the western Peloponnese. To maintain control over the Messenians, who vastly outnumbered them, the Spartans brutally reduced the Messenians to the status of helots°, a level barely higher than beasts of burden. Technically free, helots were nevertheless bound to the land and forced to farm. If a Spartan master sold the land to another Spartan, the helots stayed with the land. Helots paid half of their produce to their Spartan masters and could be murdered with impunity. Controlling the helots through terror became the Spartans' preoccupation.

In Sparta's social hierarchy free subjects stood one level above the helots. These individuals included merchants, manufacturers, and other businessmen who lived in communities throughout Spartan territories. Free subjects paid taxes and served in the army when necessary, but they were not Spartan citizens.

The male and female citizens of Sparta stood at the top of the social pyramid. They devoted themselves completely to a military way of life. The greatest responsibility of all Spartan citizens was to fulfill the needs of the polis. From early childhood, boys trained to become soldiers and girls trained to become the mothers of soldiers. Boys left home at age 7 to live in barracks, where they mastered the skills of battle. They learned that their comrades-in-arms played a more important role in their lives than their own families. Young married Spartan men were not permitted to live with their wives, but had to sneak away from their barracks at night to visit them.

DOCUMENT

Greek Versus Barbarian

In the following excerpt Hippocrates of Kos (d. ca. 400 B.C.E.), known as the Father of Medicine, explains the forms of government of the Near East and the character of the people, whom he calls Asiatics. Like other Greeks of his time, Hippocrates believed in the superiority of Greek civilization. In this passage, he explains that the climatic zones in which people live determine the characteristics of their culture.

The small variations of climate to which the Asiatics are subject, extremes of both heat and of cold being avoided, account for their mental flabbiness and cowardice . . . They are less warlike than Europeans and tamer of spirit, for they are not subject to those physical changes and the mental stimulation that sharpen tempers and induce recklessness and hot-headedness . . . Such things appear to me to be the cause of the feebleness of the Asiatic race, but a contributory cause also lies in their customs; for the greater part is under monarchical rule . . . Even if a man be born brave and of stout heart, his character is ruined by this form of government.

Source: From Paul Cartledge, *The Greeks: A Portrait of Self and Others,* 1993. Reprinted by permission of Oxford University Press.

Contempt for pain and hardship, blind obedience to orders, simplicity in word and deed, and unabashed courage were the chief Spartan virtues. Cowardice had no place in this society. Before sending their men to war, wives and mothers warned, "Come home with your shield—or on it!" Sparta's splendidly trained armies won a reputation as the most ferocious force in all of Greece.

After its conquest of Messenia, Sparta strengthened its presence further by organizing the Peloponnesian League, an informal alliance of most of the poleis in the Peloponnese. Spartans avoided wars far from home, but they and their allies joined with the Athenians and other Greeks in resisting Persia's aggression against Greece, as we will see shortly.

Athens: Toward Democracy

Athens, the best known polis of ancient Greece, made an incalculably rich contribution to the political, philosophical, artistic, and literary traditions of Western civilization. The first democracy in the ancient world, Athens developed principles of government that remain alive today. Athens's innovative form of government and the flowering of its intellectual life stemmed directly from its response to tyranny and Persian aggression.

In the eighth and seventh centuries B.C.E., the Athenians settled Attica, the territory surrounding their city, rather

CHRONOLOGY

Greece Rebuilds

ca. 1100 B.C.E.	Mycenaean palaces collapse; the Dark Age begins
850 B.C.E.	Greek population begins to grow; trade and settlements increase
776 B.C.E.	Traditional date of first Olympic Games
750–720 B.C.E.	Homer composes the *Iliad* and the *Odyssey*
750 B.C.E.	City-states emerge, overseas colonization begins; Greeks adopt the alphabet from the Phoenicians
700–650 B.C.E.	Hoplite armor and tactics develop; Spartans conquer Messenia
670–500 B.C.E.	Tyrants rule many city-states
600 B.C.E.	Coins are first minted in Lydia in Asia Minor; science and philosophy start in Ionia
594 B.C.E.	Solon reforms Athenian Constitution
ca. 560–510 B.C.E.	Peisistratus and sons rule as tyrants in Athens; Sparta is dominant in Peloponnese
508 B.C.E.	Cleisthenes' democratic reforms unify Attica

than sending colonists abroad. In this way, Athens gained more land and a larger population than any other polis on the Greek mainland. By the beginning of the sixth century, aristocrats controlled most of the wealth of Attica, and many of the Athenian peasants became heavily indebted to them, pledging their bodies as collateral on loans. They risked being sold into slavery abroad if they could not repay the debt.

With civil war between the debt-ridden peasantry and the aristocracy on the horizon, both segments of the population of Attica agreed to let Solon, an Athenian statesman known for his practical wisdom, reform the political system. In 594 B.C.E. Solon (ca. 650–570 B.C.E.) enacted several reforms that limited the authority of the aristocracy and enabled all male citizens to participate more fully in Athenian public life. These reforms created the institutions of public political life from which democracy eventually developed. Solon cancelled debts, eliminated debt-slavery, and raised enough funds to buy back enslaved Athenians. Then he took additional steps to give all Athenian men a greater voice in governing their city. Taking advantage of a rise in literacy, Solon directed scribes to record his new laws on wooden panels for the whole community to see. This diminished aristocratic control of the interpretation of Athenian law and ensured that the laws would be enforced fairly for all Athenian citizens, regardless of their status.

Solon next organized the population into four classes based on wealth. Only men in the two richest classes could hold the highest administrative office of *archon* and be elected to the highest court, traditionally a base of aristocratic authority. From the third class, Solon created the *boule,* a council of 400 men who prepared the agenda for the general citizen assembly. Men from the fourth and poorest class, who could not afford hoplite weapons, could vote in the citizen assembly, though they could not be elected to any office. Finally, men of any class could serve on a new court that Solon established. Women and slaves had no voice in government at all. These changes provided a temporary solution to Athens's problems.

After a generation of internal peace, Athenian aristocrats began to chafe at their loss of power and rebelled against Solon's system. In ca. 560 B.C.E. a nobleman named Peisistratus (ca. 590–528 B.C.E.) seized power and ruled Athens as a tyrant. Like other tyrannies in Greece, Peisistratus's regime initially enjoyed widespread support. He sponsored building projects, supported religious festivals, encouraged trade and economic development, and supported the arts. He initiated a vigorous tradition of Athenian intellectual life by inviting artists and poets to come to Athens from all over Greece. His sons, however, abused their power, and jealous aristocrats assisted by Sparta toppled the family's rule in 510. Peisistratus's surviving son fled to Persia.

Two years later, the assembly selected a nobleman named Cleisthenes to reorganize Athens. By cleverly rearranging the basic political units of Attica, Cleisthenes unified Attica and made Athens the center of all important political activity. Building upon Solon's reforms, he set the basic institutions of democracy in place with a new council of 500 male citizens drawn from throughout Attica, which made decisions for the community. He ensured that every male citizen had a permanent voice in government, broke the power of aristocratic families, and set up the lasting, fundamental structures of Athenian democracy. The strength of Cleisthenes' new system would be tested in the face of invasions by Persia in the fifth century B.C.E.

The Persian Wars, 490–479 B.C.E.

Around 510 B.C.E. the Persian king Darius conquered the Ionian Greek poleis. The Persians ruled their new subjects fairly, but the Ionian Greeks nevertheless revolted in 499 B.C.E. Ionian Greek rebels traveled to Sparta and Athens to ask for assistance against the Persians. The Spartans refused to send any troops when they learned how far away Ionia was. The Athenians, however, sent an expeditionary force that helped the rebels burn Sardis, a Persian provincial capital. The Persians crushed the rebellion in 494 B.C.E., but they did not forget the role of Athens in it.

The Marathon Campaign

In 490 B.C.E., after four years of meticulous planning, a Persian army crossed the Aegean Sea in the ships of their Phoenician subjects. They landed at the beach of Marathon, some twenty-six miles from Athens. The vicinity around Marathon was the traditional stronghold of Peisistratus, the former Athenian tyrant. The Persians brought Peisistratus's son Hippias with them, planning to install him as the new tyrant of Athens.

To save their city, the Athenians marched to Marathon, and with the aid of troops from a neighboring polis (Spartan reinforcements arrived too late), the outnumbered Greek army overcame the Persian forces. Their surprising victory at Marathon demonstrated that a well-trained hoplite force could defeat a far more numerous foe. It also showed that Cleisthenes' democratic reforms had unified Attica so firmly that its citizens had no interest in helping the Persians restore tyranny. Democracy worked.

Athenian Naval Power and the Salamis Campaign

After Marathon, Athens embraced even more dramatic reforms. A new political leader named Themistocles persuaded his fellow citizens to spend the proceeds from a rich silver mine in Attica on a new navy and port. By 480 B.C.E. Athens possessed nearly 200 battleships, called triremes°. With three banks of oars manned by the poorest citizens of the polis, the triremes transformed Athens into a naval powerhouse. The entire male citizen body of Athens, not just the aristocrats and hoplites, could now be called to arms. The Athenian navy embodied Athenian democracy in action in which every male citizen had an obligation to defend his homeland.

The battle of Marathon dealt a shameful blow to the Persians' pride that they resolved to avenge, but a major revolt in Egypt and Darius's death in 486 B.C.E. prevented them from invading Greece again for nearly a decade. In 480 B.C.E., Xerxes I, the new Persian Great King, launched a massive invasion of Greece. He brought an overwhelming force of some 150,000 soldiers, a navy of nearly 700 mostly Phoenician vessels, and ample supplies. His troops crossed from Asia into Europe by means of a bridge of boats over the Hellespont, while the navy followed a parallel path by sea in order to supply the troops. They intended to smash Athens.

Terrified by the magnitude of the Persian army, fewer than 40 of the more than 700 Greek poleis joined the defensive coalition that had formed in anticipation of the invasion. Under the leadership of Sparta, the Greek allies planned to hold back the Persian land force in the north, while the Athenian navy sailed north to attack the invaders at sea. The Spartan king Leonidas led the coalition. Under his command, a Greek force stopped the Persians at the pass of Thermopylae until a traitor revealed an alternate path through the mountains. On the last day of the battle, Leonidas, his entire force of 300 valiant Spartans, and several thousand allies died fighting.

Their sacrifice was not in vain. The disaster at Thermopylae gave the Athenians precious time to evacuate their city and to station their highly maneuverable fleet in the narrow straits of Salamis, just off the Athenian coast. In a stunning display of naval skill, the Athenian triremes defeated the Persian navy in a single day of heavy fighting. Xerxes returned to Persia and withdrew most of his forces to Asia Minor, but he left a large army in northern Greece.

Early in 479 B.C.E., a combined Greek army once again stopped the Persians at the battle of Plataea, north of Attica.

Warfare at Sea

In the classical world navies relied on long rowed vessels with bronze battering rams. This painting of a war galley was made about 550 B.C.E. and shows soldiers, oarsmen, and a man at the helm. Athenians perfected the war galley. Their ships could reach a speed of more than nine nautical miles per hour for short distances.

In this battle a large contingent of Spartans led a decisive final charge. That same year, the combined naval forces of Greece defeated the Persian navy off the Ionian coast. Without a single substantial military success, Xerxes gave up the attempt to conquer Greece.

The Classical Age of Greece, 479–336 B.C.E.

■ What were the intellectual, social, and political innovations of Greece in the Classical Age?

The defeat of mighty Persia by a handful of Greek cities shocked the Mediterranean world. Xerxes' failure did not seriously weaken Persian society, but it greatly strengthened the Greeks, not only by boosting their economy and by enhancing their own position in the Mediterranean but also for what we would now call their self-image. After the defeat of the Persians, the Greeks exhibited immense confidence in their ability to shape their political institutions and to describe and analyze their society and the world around them. In the political realm, the emboldened Athenians created a powerful empire that made them the dominant power in the Greek world. During this time democratic institutions flourished in Athens. Yet the very success of Athens sowed the seeds of its demise. After alienating many of the other Greek poleis, Athens lost the long and bitter Peloponnesian War with Sparta.

The distinguishing feature of the Classical Age was its remarkable level of creativity, especially in drama, science, history writing, philosophy, and the visual arts. Despite the turmoil of the Persian and Peloponnesian Wars, Greek society remained rigidly hierarchic with strictly defined gender roles and a large class of slaves who performed much of the heavy labor. The structures of Greek society provided many male citizens with the leisure time for debating public affairs in a democratic fashion, for attending plays, and for speculating about philosophical issues. The many deities of the Greek pantheon were the subject of much Greek art. Greeks worshiped these gods in temples that established the Classical style, which was imitated by Romans and other peoples throughout subsequent centuries. None of the Greek cities produced as many creative men as Athens, which makes its experience as an empire and a democracy particularly revealing.

The Rise and Fall of the Athenian Empire

With the Persian threat to Greece nearly eliminated, Athens began a period of rapid imperial expansion. This aggressive foreign policy backfired. It set off waves of discord among the other Greek city-states that led to war and the eventual collapse of the Athenian Empire.

From Defensive Alliance to Athenian Empire

After the battle of Plataea, the Greek defensive alliance set out to clear the Persians once and for all from the Ionian coast. The Spartans soon grew disillusioned with the effort and withdrew their troops, leaving Athenians in charge. In the winter of 478 B.C.E., Athens reorganized the alliance, creating the Delian League°, named for the small island of Delos where the members met. Athens contributed approximately 200 warships to continue attacks against the Persians, while the other members supplied ships or funds to pay for them. The league ultimately gathered a naval force of 300 ships. By 469 B.C.E. it drove the last Persians from the Aegean.

With the Persians ousted, several poleis tried to leave the league, but the Athenians forced them to remain. The Athenians were rapidly turning the Delian League into an Athenian Empire organized for their own benefit. In subsequent decades the Athenians established military garrisons and intervened in the political life of many cities of the league by imposing heavy taxes and establishing many rules and financial regulations. Several open revolts broke out, but no polis in the empire could overcome Athens's might. In 460 B.C.E. Athens sent approximately 4,000 men and 200 warships to assist in an Egyptian revolt against Persia, but Persian troops destroyed the entire expeditionary force. Sobered by this fiasco, the Athenians moved the treasury of the Delian League from Delos to Athens, claiming that they were protecting it from Persian retaliation. In fact, the Athenians spent the league treasury on public buildings in Athens, including the Parthenon. Athenian policy had become indifferent to the original purpose of the league, but the revenues generated by the league's exploitation simultaneously enabled democracy to flourish at home.

Democracy in the Age of Pericles

The chief designer of the Athenian Empire was Pericles, an aristocrat who dominated Athenian politics from 461 B.C.E. until his death in 429 B.C.E. During the so-called "Age of Pericles," Athenian democracy at home and empire abroad reached their peak.

During the Age of Pericles, about 40,000 citizen men lived in Athens. Only men over age 18 could participate in the city's political life. Women, foreigners, slaves, and other imperial subjects had no voice in public life.

The representative council of 500 men established by Cleisthenes continued to administer public business. The citizen assembly met every ten days and probably never had more than 5,000 citizens in attendance, except for the most important occasions. The assembly made final decisions on issues of war, peace, and public policy by majority vote. Because men gained political power through debate in the assembly, a politician's rhetorical skills played an all-important role in convincing voters.

Ten officials called *generals* were elected every year by popular vote to handle high affairs of state and to direct Athens's military forces. Generals typically were aristocrats who had proven their expertise. Pericles, for example, was reelected almost continually for more than twenty years.

The vast increase in public business multiplied the number of public administrators running the empire. By the middle of the fifth century, Athens had about 1,500 officials in its bureaucracy. Now responsible for administrating the Delian League, boards of assessors determined the amount of money its members would pay. Many legal disputes arose among cities in the league, forcing Athens to increase the number of its courts. Because of the constant need for jurors and other office holders, Pericles began paying wages for public service, the first such policy in history. Jurors were chosen by lot, and trials lasted no more than a day to expedite cases, save money, and prevent jury tampering.

Athenians took steps to ensure honesty in public affairs. Every official who spent public revenues had his account books examined at the beginning and at the end of his term in office. Citizens meeting in the assembly had regular opportunities to write down the name of any other citizen they disliked or distrusted on a broken piece of pottery called an *ostrakon*. If a sufficient number of citizens singled out the same person, he would be expelled from Athenian lands for ten years, though his property would remain intact for his return. This procedure, called ostracism°, provided a way to get rid of corrupt or overly ambitious politicians. A strong sense of shared identity and common purpose resulted from these democratic institutions and attracted men of all social classes to public service.

Additional reforms by Pericles gave women a more important role in Athenian society. Before 451 B.C.E., children born to Athenian men and their foreign wives attained full citizenship. Pericles' new law allowed citizenship only if both parents were Athenian citizens. As a result, Athenian citizen women took pride in giving birth to the polis's only legitimate citizens. Nevertheless, citizen women continued to be denied full freedom of action in public life.

Conflict with Sparta: The Peloponnesian War

Sparta and its allies felt threatened by growing Athenian power. Between 460 and 431 B.C.E., Athens and a few allies fought intermittently with Sparta and the Peloponnesian League. War broke out between the two sides in 431 B.C.E., dragging on until 404 B.C.E. (see Map 3.4). In the beginning of the conflict, called the Peloponnesian War, the Spartans repeatedly raided Attica in the hope of defeating Athenian forces in open battle.

Thanks to Athens's fortifications and the two parallel five-mile-long walls connecting the city to its main port of Piraeus, the Athenians endured the devastating Spartan in-

CHRONOLOGY

Classical Greece

490 B.C.E.	Battle of Marathon; first Persian invasion stopped
480–479 B.C.E.	Xerxes invades Greece and is defeated
478 B.C.E.	Delian League formed; expansion of Athenian democracy and imperialism
450s B.C.E.	Pericles ascendant in Athens; Herodotus writes his *Investigations* (*Histories*)
477–432 B.C.E.	Parthenon built in Athens; sophists active
431–404 B.C.E.	Peloponnesian War; Thucydides writes his *History*
429 B.C.E.	Death of Pericles; Euripides and Sophocles active
415–413 B.C.E.	Athens's campaign in Sicily fails
405 B.C.E.	Sparta defeats Athens at Aegospotami
399 B.C.E.	Trial and death of Socrates
399–347 B.C.E.	Plato writes *Dialogues* and founds Academy

vasions. Safe behind their fortifications, they relied on their navy to deliver food and supplies from cities of the Athenian Empire that Spartan armies could not reach. The Athenians also launched attacks from the sea against Spartan territory almost at will. With the hope that their greater resources would sustain them until victory, the Athenians fought on. Although plague struck the overcrowded city in 430 B.C.E., killing almost one-third of the population including Pericles, Athens and Sparta continued to fight.

In 421 B.C.E., Spartan and Athenian generals agreed to a fifty-year truce, but a mere six years later war broke out again. The reckless policies of Alcibiades, an Athenian general, started a new round of warfare. A nephew of Pericles, Alcibiades lacked his uncle's wisdom. In 415 B.C.E. he persuaded the Athenians to send an expeditionary force of 5,000 hoplites to invade Sicily and take its resources for the war effort. Just as the fleet was about to sail, Alcibiades' enemies accused him of profaning a religious festival, and he fled to Sparta. After two years of heavy fighting, the Athenian expedition ended in utter disaster. Syracusan soldiers captured every Athenian ship and either slaughtered the Athenian soldiers or sold them into slavery.

The Collapse of Athenian Power

The Peloponnesian War dragged on for another ten years, but Athens never fully recovered from the catastrophic loss of men and ships in Sicily. At the suggestion of Alcibiades,

Map 3.4   The Peloponnesian War

During this long conflict that lasted from 431 to 404 B.C.E., the forces of Athens and its allies struggled with Sparta and its allies for control of mainland Greece. Though Sparta defeated the Athenian Empire, Athens survived as an influential force in Greek social, political, and economic life.

the Spartans established a permanent military base within sight of Athens, which enabled them to control Attica. When 20,000 slaves in the Athenian silver mines escaped to freedom under the Spartans, Athens lost its main source of revenue. The final blow came when Lysander, the Spartan commander in chief, obtained money from Persia, which continued to maintain an active interest in Greek affairs and built a navy strong enough to challenge Athenian sea power. At the battle of Aegospotami on the Hellespont, Lysander's navy sank every Athenian ship. Athens surrendered in 404 B.C.E.

The victorious Spartan forces pulled down Athens's long walls stretching to Piraeus, but they refused to burn the city to the ground as some enemies of Athens demanded, because Athens had been Sparta's valiant ally in the Persian Wars. Instead, the Spartans set up an oligarchy°, or government by a few. Led by the "Thirty Tyrants," a violent and conservative political faction, the oligarchy soon earned the hatred of Athenian citizens. Within a year they overthrew the tyrants and restored democracy.

Sparta's victory did not bring peace to the Greek world. Following the defeat of the Athenian Empire, the Spartans began a shortsighted attack on Persian provinces in Asia Minor. Angered by Sparta's aggression, the Persians retaliated by financing Athens and other poleis to fight Sparta. Bitter war raged among the Greek poleis, but finally agents of the Persian Great King negotiated the King's Peace in 386 B.C.E. With this treaty the Persians promised not to intervene again in Greek affairs. In return the Greek cities of Asia Minor would remain under Persian control. The war-weary Greek states eagerly agreed. For the next two decades, the Greek city of Thebes dominated Greek affairs after defeating Sparta in 371 B.C.E., but wars among different poleis continued on a small scale. When not fighting other Greeks, many Greek hoplites fought as mercenaries for Persian kings in the period after the Peloponnesian War. These Greek soldiers learned that well-trained, highly disciplined hoplite troops were more than a match for the Persian army. In the next chapter we will see how the kingdom of Macedonia to the north of Greece benefited from this important lesson.

The Social and Religious Foundations of Classical Greece

Amid the violence of the Classical Age, the Greek poleis developed a vibrant way of life in which men and women had distinct roles to play, one that freed men for involvement in public affairs. Greek men and women lived very different lives, guided by strict rules of behavior. A hierarchy of gender roles determined individuals' access to public space, legal rights, and opportunities to work. In this emphatically patriarchal society, only men held positions of public authority, controlled wealth and inheritance, and enjoyed the right to participate in political life. Women were expected to engage in domestic activities, out of sight of non-family members. At the bottom of society slaves of both genders were completely subject to their masters.

Gender Roles

Greek women were expected to marry early in puberty, typically to men at least ten years older. Through marriage legal control of women passed from father to husband. In the case of divorce, which only men could instigate, the husband had to return his wife's dowry to her father. Greek houses were small and usually divided into two parts. In the brighter front rooms husbands entertained their male friends at dinner and enjoyed active conversation and social interaction with other males. Wives spent the majority of their time in the more secluded portions of the home, supervising the household slaves, raising children, dealing with their mothers-in-law, and weaving cloth.

Greek men feared that their wives would commit adultery, which carried the risk of illegitimate offspring and implied that husbands could not control their possessions or access to their homes. Consequently, Greek men strictly monitored and closely controlled women's sexual activity. Because men considered females powerless to resist seduction, respectable women rarely ventured out in public without a chaperone. Slaves went to market and ran errands. To the typical Greek husband, the ideal wife

(a)

(b)

(c)

Male Views of Women: Subservient or Out of Control?

In male-dominated Greek communities, men idealized passive women and had great anxiety about losing control over them. (a) This Athenian vase of the fifth century B.C.E. reflects Greek men's view of a properly subordinate woman. In the image, the wife bids goodbye to her young husband, who is going off to war. Her place is at home, tending to chores until his return. (b) This vase depicts male fears about females freed from social constraints. It depicts women as wild, drunken, and potentially murderous followers of Dionysus, god of wine. (c) Greek men's worst nightmare was women fighting back. This vase portrays an Amazon, a mythological female warrior, fighting on horseback. According to myth, Amazons fought in battle like men and ruled themselves.

stayed out of public sight, dutifully obeyed him, and was satisfied by sexual relations with him three times a month. She was not supposed to mind if he had relations with prostitutes or adolescent boys. Above all, she was expected to produce legitimate children, preferably sons, who would continue the family line and honorably serve the polis.

Women who worked outside the home did so primarily in three capacities: as vendors of farm produce or cloth in the marketplace, as priestesses, and as prostitutes. Female vendors in the marketplace came from the lower classes. Their skills in weaving cloth and making garments, as well as in growing vegetables in their gardens, gave them the opportunity to supplement the family income.

Priestesses served the temples of goddesses such as Hera in Argos and Athena in Athens. In classical Athens, more than forty publicly sponsored religious cults had female priests. These women gained high prestige in their communities. Greeks believed that some women possessed a special spirituality that made them excellent mediums through whom divinities often spoke. Such women served as oracles, as in the temple of Apollo at Delphi. They attracted visitors from all over the Mediterranean world who wanted to discern the gods' wishes or learn what the future might bring.

Prostitutes lived in all Greek cities, but unlike priestesses, their profession was considered shameful. In Athens, most prostitutes were slaves from abroad. Some women worked as elite courtesans called *hetairai*°. Because Greek men did not think it possible to have intellectual exchanges with their spouses, they hired hetairai to accompany them to social gatherings and to participate in stimulating conversations about politics, philosophy, and the arts. Like ordinary prostitutes, hetairai also were expected to be sexually available for pay.

The most famous of all hetairai was Aspasia, who came to Athens from the Ionian city of Miletus. She became Pericles' companion, and their son gained Athenian citizenship by special vote of the assembly. Aspasia participated fully in the circle of scientists, artists, and intellectuals who surrounded Pericles and made Athens "the school of Greece." According to legend, she taught rhetoric and regularly conversed with the philosopher Socrates.

The Athenian orator Demosthenes famously summed up Greek attitudes toward women with these words: "We have hetairai for the sake of pleasure, regular prostitutes to

Male Homosexuality
This painted vase displays a common homo-erotic scene, the courting of an un-bearded youth by an older man. The youth holds a garland that suggests athletic victory.

care for our physical needs, and wives to bear legitimate children and be loyal custodians of our households."[3]

In classical Greece, where men considered women intellectually and emotionally inferior, some men believed that the best sort of friendship was found in male relationships. It was not uncommon for Greek men, especially prominent members of society, to have adolescent boys as lovers. In these relationships the older man often assumed the role of mentor to his younger companion. Some poleis institutionalized such relationships. In the city of Thebes, for example, the elite "Sacred Band" of 150 male couples led the city's hoplites into battle during the fourth century B.C.E. These men were considered the best warriors because they would not endure the shame of showing cowardice to their lovers. The Sacred Band could defeat even Spartan warriors.

Slavery: The Source of Greek Prosperity

Unlike free citizens of a polis, slaves were totally under the control of other people and had no political or legal rights. Masters could kill them without serious penalty and could demand sexual favors at any time. Slavery existed in every polis at every social level. The slave population expanded in the period after 600 B.C.E. as poleis prospered and demands for labor increased.

Most information about Greek slavery comes from Athens, which was the first major slave society that is well documented. Between about 450 and 320 B.C.E., the thriving polis had a total population of perhaps a quarter of a million people, one-third of whom were enslaved. The proportion of slaves to free people was similar in other poleis. In the Archaic Age the Athenian aristocracy began to rely on slave labor to work their large landed estates. Most of these slaves had fallen into bondage for debt, but after Solon made the enslavement of Athenian citizens illegal in 594 B.C.E., the wealthy turned to sources outside Attica. Many slaves were captured during the Persian Wars, but most

DOCUMENT

Aristotle on Slavery

slaves were either the children of slaves or purchased from the thriving slave trade in non-Greek peoples from around the Aegean.

Athenians and other Greeks relied on slaves to perform an enormous variety of tasks. The city of Athens owned slaves who served as a police force, as public executioners, as clerks in court, and in other public capacities. Most slaves, however, were privately owned. Some labored as highly skilled artisans and businessmen who lived apart from their owners but were required to pay them a high percentage of their profits. Every Greek household had male and female slaves who performed menial tasks. Some rich landowners owned gangs of slaves who worked in the fields. Others rented slaves to the polis to labor in the silver mines, where they were worked to death under hideous conditions.

Slavery did not necessarily last until a person's death. A few slaves won their freedom through the generosity of their owners. Others saved enough money from their trades to buy their freedom. Freed slaves could not become citizens. Instead, they lived as resident foreigners in the polis of their former masters and often maintained close ties of loyalty and obligation to them.

Slavery was so widespread in Athens because it was extremely profitable. The Athenian political system evolved to permit and support the exploitation of noncitizen slaves to benefit the citizen class. The slaves were primarily responsible for the prosperity of Athens and gave the aristocrats the leisure to engage in intellectual pursuits and to create the rich culture that became part of the core of Western civilization.

Religion and the Gods

Religion permeated Greek life. It provided a structured way for Greeks to interact with the deities who exercised considerable influence over their lives. Greeks worshiped many gods, whom they asked for favors and advice. Every city kept a calendar of religious observances established for certain days. Festivals marked phases in the agricultural year, such as the harvest or sowing seasons, and initiation ceremonies marked an individual's transition from childhood to adulthood.

Above all, Greeks gave their devotion to the gods who protected the city. For instance, during the annual Panathenaea festival in Athens, the entire population, citizens and noncitizens alike, honored the city's patron goddess Athena with a grand procession and numerous sacrifices. Every fourth year, the celebration was expanded to include major athletic and musical competitions. In a joyous parade, the citizens would convey a robe embroidered with mythological scenes to the statue of Athena in her temple, called the Parthenon, or House of the Virgin Goddess, that stood on the Acropolis hill in the center of the city.

The Acropolis and the Parthenon
The Acropolis of Athens, crowned by the Parthenon, stood as a symbol of Athenian imperial culture.

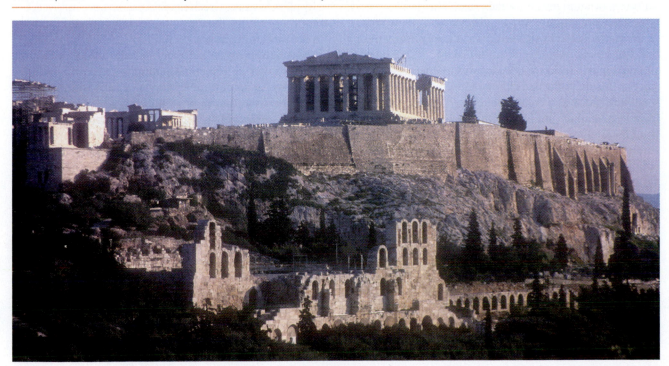

Although every polis had its own set of religious practices, people throughout the Greek world shared many ideas about the gods. Like the Greek language, these shared religious beliefs gave a common identity to Greeks. They also distinguished them from so-called barbarians who worshiped strange gods in ways the Greeks considered uncivilized.

Most Greeks believed that immortal and enormously powerful gods and goddesses were all around them. These deities often embodied natural phenomena such as the sun and moon, but Greeks attributed very human personalities and desires to them. Because these divine forces touched every aspect of daily life, human interactions with them were unavoidable and risky, for the gods could be as harmful as they were helpful to humans.

The Greeks believed that the twelve greatest gods lived on Mount Olympus in northern Greece as a large and quite dysfunctional family. Zeus was the father and king; Hera was his sister and wife; and Aphrodite was the goddess of sex and love. The jealous clan also included Apollo, god of the sun, prophecy, and medicine; Ares, the god of war; and Athena, the goddess of wisdom. Greek mythology developed a set of stories about the Olympian gods that have passed into Western literature and art.

In addition to their home on Mount Olympus, the gods also maintained residences in cities. Temples served as the gods' living quarters. They displayed the wealth and piety of every polis, for Greek cities spared no expense to employ the finest architects and best materials. Rows of carved marble columns surrounded the central room and supported the temple's roof. Sculptural decorations on the temple walls that told stories about the gods were painted with bright colors, but today they have been bleached white by centuries of sunlight and weathering. The god's likeness, typically a large statue, stood at the center of these rectangular marble structures, facing an altar in front of the building.

Worship at Greek temples consisted of offerings and sacrifices. Outside in the open air, worshipers offered the gods small gifts, such as a small bouquet of flowers, a pinch of incense, or a small grain cake. On especially important festivals the Greeks sacrificed live animals to their gods. Priests and priestesses supervised these rituals. The god inside the temple watched the priests prepare the sacrifice, heard the sacrificial animals bleat as their throats were slit, and listened to women howl as blood poured from the beasts. Finally, the god smelled the aroma of burning meat as the victim was cooked over the flames. Satisfied, the god awaited the next sacrifice.

In addition, Greeks took pains to discern the future. They hired religious experts to analyze their dreams and to predict the future based on the examination of the internal organs of specially sacrificed birds. Greeks and non-Greeks alike traveled to consult the priestess of Apollo, the so-called Oracle of Delphi, at a shrine in central Greece. If the god chose to reply to a particular query, he spoke through the mouth of his oracle, a priestess who would lapse into a trance. Priests stood nearby to record and explain the oracle's utterances, which often could have more than one interpretation. When King Croesus of Lydia asked the oracle what would happen if he went to war with the Persians, Apollo told him that "a great kingdom will fall." Croesus never dreamed it would be his own.

Intellectual Life

In the Classical Age, Greeks investigated the natural world and explored the human condition with astonishing freshness and vigor. Their legacy in drama, science, philosophy, and the arts continued to inspire people in many subsequent periods of history. The term *Renaissance*, which is applied to several cultural movements in later periods, refers to attempts to recapture the intellectual vitality of the Greek Classical Age as well as that of the Romans, which drew heavily from it.

Greek Drama

Greek men examined their society's values through public dramatic performances. Peisistratus, the tyrant of Athens, introduced plays around 550 B.C.E. Initially, plays were performed in annual festivals dedicated to Dionysus, the god of wine, and authors entered their plays in competition. Dramatic productions soon became a mainstay of Greek life. In their plays set in the mythical past, the playwrights explored issues relevant to contemporary society. Above all, Greeks who attended the plays (only men were allowed) could expect to be educated and entertained. Fewer than fifty plays from the Greek classical period have survived, but they count among the most powerful examples of literature in the Western tradition.

In tragedies Athenian men watched stories about the terrible suffering underlying human society. In many of these plays an important aristocrat or ruler is destroyed by a fatal personal flaw beyond his or her ability to control. With an unflinching gaze, playwrights examined conflicts between violent passion and reason and between the laws of the gods and those of human communities. Their dramas depicted the terrible consequences of vengeance, the brutality of war, and the relationship of the individual to the polis. In the plays of the three great Athenian tragedians—Aeschylus, Sophocles, and Euripides—characters learn vital lessons through their suffering, and the audience learns them, too.

Aeschylus (525–456 B.C.E.) believed that the gods were just and that human suffering stemmed directly from human error. His most powerful works include a trilogy called the *Oresteia*. This collection of three plays expresses the notion that a polis can survive only when courts made up of citizens settle matters of murder, rather than leaving justice to family vendettas. The cycle of retaliation that tormented the family of King Agamemnon of Mycenae for generations finally ends when Athena and her citizens provide the hideous deities of violent revenge an honorable resting place in Athens.

Another of Aeschylus's plays, *The Persians,* reflected the triumphal mood of Athenians after the defeat of the Persians at Salamis and the Persian withdrawal from Greece. This play shows the tragic consequences of Xerxes' limitless arrogance and ambition. Aeschylus also makes a sharp distinction, for the first time in Greek literature, between Greek civilization and foreign barbarism. This distinction developed into a major theme in Greek thought, and it still is used to categorize cultures today.

In the plays of Sophocles (ca. 496–406 B.C.E.), humans are free to act, but they are trapped by their own weaknesses, their history, and the will of the gods. In *Antigone,* a young woman buries her outlaw brother in accordance with divine principles but in defiance of her city's laws, knowing that she will be executed for her brave act. The misguided king who wrote the law and ordered her death realizes too late that a polis will prosper only if human and divine laws come into proper balance. In *Oedipus the King,* Oedipus unknowingly kills his father and marries his mother. When he learns what he has done, Oedipus blinds himself. Although he knows that fate caused his tragedy, he understands that he was the one who committed the immoral acts.

Like Sophocles' works, the plays of Euripides (ca. 484–406 B.C.E.) portray humans struggling against their fates. In these works, the gods have no human feeling and are capable of bestial action against humans. Unlike other writers of his day, Euripides showed remarkable sympathy for women, who often fall victim to war and male deceit in his plays. At the end of *The Trojan Women,* the despairing Trojan queen Hecuba stands amid the smoldering ruins of her vanquished city, lamenting the cruel life as a slave that awaits her: "Lead me, who walked soft-footed once in Troy, lead me a slave where earth falls sheer away by rocky edges, let me drop and die withered away with tears."[4]

In addition to the tragedies, Greeks delighted in irreverent comedies. Performances of comedy probably began in the seventh century B.C.E. as lewd sketches associated with Dionysus, the god of wine and fertility. The playwright Aristophanes of Athens (ca. 450–388 B.C.E.) proved a master at presenting comedy as social commentary. No person, god, or institution escaped his mockery. Although fully committed to Athenian democracy, Aristophanes had no patience for hypocritical politicians or self-important intellectuals. His comic plays are full of raunchy sex and allusions to the day's issues, containing withering sarcasm, silly puns, and outrageous insults. Audiences howled at the fun, but these plays always carried a thought-provoking message as well. *The Birds* is an apt example. In this satire, Aristophanes tells the story of two down-on-their-luck Athenians who flee the city looking for peace and quiet. On their trek they have to deal with an endless stream of Athenian bureaucrats and frauds, whom Aristophanes mercilessly skewers. Finally the travelers seize power over the Kingdom of the Birds—and then transform it into a replica of Athens. This satire of Athenian imperialism shows Athenians helpless to avoid their own worst instincts.

Scientific Thought in Ionia

Greek science began about 600 B.C.E. in the cities of Ionia, when a handful of men began to ask new questions about the natural world. Living on the border between Greek and Persian civilizations, these Greek thinkers encountered the vigorous Babylonian scientific and mathematical traditions that still flourished in the Persian Empire. Following the method of carefully observing the natural world and systematically recording data, these men began to reconsider traditional Greek explanations for natural phenomena. They rejected notions of gods who arbitrarily inflicted floods, earthquakes, and other disasters on humanity. Instead, they looked for general principles that could explain each natural phenomenon. To these investigators, the natural world was orderly, knowable by means of careful inquiry, and therefore ultimately predictable. These scientists inquired about the physical composition of the natural world, tried to formulate the principles of why change occurs, and began to think about proving their theories logically.

Thales of Miletus (ca. 625–547 B.C.E.), the first of these investigators, theorized that the Earth was a disk floating on water. When the Earth rocked in the water, he proposed, the motion caused earthquakes. Thales traveled to Egypt to study geometry and established the pyramids' height by calculating the length of their shadows. Perhaps influenced by Egyptian and Babylonian teachings, he believed that water gave rise to everything else. His greatest success as an astronomer came when he predicted a solar eclipse in 585 B.C.E.

One of Thales' students, Anaximander (ca. 610–547 B.C.E.), wrote a pioneering essay about natural science called *On the Nature of Things.* Anaximander became the first Greek to create a map of the inhabited world. He also argued that the universe was rational and symmetrical. In his view, it consisted of Earth as a flat disk at its center, held in place by the perfect balance of the limitless space around it. Anaximander also believed that change occurred on Earth through the tension between opposites, such as hot versus cold and dry versus wet.

A third great thinker from Miletus, Anaximenes (ca. 545–525 B.C.E.), suggested that air is the fundamental substance of the universe. Through different processes, air could become fire, wind, water, earth, or even stone. His conclusions, along with those of Thales and Anaximander, may seem odd and unsatisfactory today, but these men were pioneers in the scientific exploration of the natural world.

Dragons and Serpents

Current archaeological research suggests that the dragons and serpents appearing in Greek mythology represent ancient attempts to explain dinosaur fossils. Greek vase painters illustrated these stories with such accuracy that paleontologists today can identify the dinosaur. This vase, painted about 550 B.C.E., shows the hero Hercules and the princess Hesione fighting the sea monster that had been holding her captive. Scientists believe that the monster's head might have been modeled on the skull of *Samotherium,* a giant giraffe that lived about eight million years ago. Many fossils of this creature have been found in Greece and Turkey.

Their brave willingness to remove the gods from explanations of natural phenomena, and their effort to provide arguments in defense of their theories, established the foundations of modern scientific inquiry and observation.

These Milesian thinkers sparked inquiry in other parts of the classical Greek world as well. Soon other investigators developed their own theories. Heraclitus of Ephesus (ca. 500 B.C.E.) argued that fire, not gods, provided the true origin of the world. Leucippus of Miletus (fifth century B.C.E.) and Democritus of Abdera (ca. 460–370 B.C.E.) proposed that the universe consisted entirely of an endless number of material atoms. Too small to be seen, these particles floated everywhere. When the atoms collided or stuck together, they produced the elements of the world we live in, including life itself. These atomists had no need for gods in their explanations of the natural world.

The Origins of Writing History

The Western tradition of writing history has its roots in the work of Herodotus (ca. 484–420 B.C.E.), who grew to adulthood in the Ionian city of Halicarnassus. This Greek author concerned himself with finding the general causes of human events, not natural phenomena. He called his work *Investigations* (the original Greek meaning of the word *history*), and he attempted to explain the Persian Wars. He believed this conflict deserved to be analyzed and remembered because it had been the greatest war ever fought. For Herodotus, "the war between the Greeks and the non-Greeks" was just one episode in an unending cycle of violence between barbarian and civilized, between oppressed and free.

Gods appear in Herodotus's narrative but do not play a causal role in events. Instead, Herodotus attempted to show that humans always act in accordance with the general principle of reciprocity; that is, people predictably respond in equal measure to what befalls them. He described reciprocal violence in legends, such as that of the Trojan War, and recounted the conquest of Lydia by Cyrus the Great in the sixth century. He tells how the Greeks became involved in Persian affairs and finally triumphed over Persian aggression.

Herodotus, Histories

Herodotus traveled widely. He frequently visited Athens, where he read portions of his analysis of the Persian War to appreciative audiences. He also made voyages to Egypt, Babylonia, and other foreign lands, gathering information about local religions and customs. Herodotus relished the differences among cultures, and his narrative brims with vivid descriptions of exotic habits in far-off lands.

Although he considered Greeks superior to other peoples, Herodotus raised basic questions about cultural encounters that still engage us today. How can we judge whether one culture's customs are better than another's? Is it possible to evaluate a foreign culture on its own terms or are we doomed to view things through our own eyes and experiences only? Herodotus made description and analysis of foreign cultures an integral part of his "investigations." Today historians justly refer to him as the "Father of History."

Western civilization also owes an incalculable debt to Thucydides of Athens (d. ca. 400 B.C.E.), who further advanced the science of writing history. His brilliant *History of the Peloponnesian War* stands as perhaps the single most influential work of history in the Western tradition because it provides a model for analyzing the causes of human events and the outcomes of individual decisions. In it he combines meticulous attention to accuracy and detail with a broad moral vision. To Thucydides, the Peloponnesian War represented a profound tragedy. At one time under the wise leadership of Pericles, Athens epitomized all that was good about a human community. In this "school of Greece," culture flourished and creativity and political accomplishment had no limits. Unfortunately, Athenians, like all humans, possessed a fatal flaw, the unrelenting desire to possess more. Never satisfied, they followed unprincipled leaders after Pericles' death, embarking on foolhardy adventures that eventually destroyed them.

In Thucydides' analysis, humans, not the gods, are entirely responsible for their own triumphs and defeats. As an analyst of the destructive impact of uncontrolled power on a society, Thucydides has no match. Even more than Herodotus, he set the standard for historical analysis in the West.

Nature Versus Custom and the Origins of Philosophical Thought

The Greeks believed that their communities could prosper only when governed by just political institutions and fair laws. They questioned whether the political and moral standards of the day were rooted in nature or whether humans had invented them and preserved them as customs. They wondered whether absolute standards should guide polis life or whether humans are the measure of all things. No one has answered these questions satisfactorily to this day, but one of the legacies of classical Greece is that they were asked at all.

During the fifth century B.C.E., a group of teachers known as sophists°, or wise men, traveled throughout the Greek-speaking world. They shared no common doctrines, and they taught everything from mathematics to political theory with the hope of instructing individuals in the best ways to lead better lives. The best-known among them was Protagoras (ca. 485–440 B.C.E.), who questioned the existence of gods and absolute standards of truth. All human institutions, Protagoras argued, were created through human custom or law and not through nature. Thus, because truth is relative, an individual should be able to defend either side of an argument persuasively.

Socrates (469–399 B.C.E.), an Athenian citizen, challenged the sophists' notion that there were no absolutes to guide human life. He spent his days trying to help his fellow Athenians understand the basic moral concepts that governed their lives by relentlessly asking them questions. Because Socrates wrote nothing himself, we know of his ideas chiefly through the accounts of his student Plato of Athens (ca. 428–347 B.C.E.), who made his teacher the central figure in his own philosophical essays.

Plato established a center called the Academy in Athens for the purpose of teaching and discussion, and earned a towering reputation among Greek philosophers. Like Socrates, he rejected the notion that truth and morality are relative concepts. Plato taught that absolute virtues such as goodness, justice, and beauty do exist, but on a higher level of reality than human existence. He called these eternal, unchanging absolutes Forms°. In fact, in Platonic thought, the Forms represent true reality. Like shadows that provide only an outline of an object, what we experience in daily life is merely an approximation of this true reality. Plato's theories about the existence of absolute truths and how humans can discover them continue to shape Western thought. In particular, Platonic theory emphasizes how the senses deceive us and how the truth is often hidden. Truth

Symposium

At drinking parties called *symposia,* men would gather to enjoy an evening meal, complete with dancing girls, musicians, and wine. After dinner they often discussed serious issues, including matters of philosophy and ethics. This cup was painted in Athens about 480 B.C.E. It shows a young man reclining on a couch while a young woman dances for his pleasure.

The Trial and Execution of Socrates the Questioner

In 399 B.C.E. the people of Athens tried and executed Socrates, their fellow citizen, for three crimes: for not believing in Athenian gods, for introducing new gods, and for corrupting the city's young men. The charges were paradoxical, for Socrates had devoted his life to investigating how to live ethically and morally. Although Socrates could have escaped, he chose to die rather than betray his most fundamental beliefs. Socrates wrote nothing down, yet his ideas and the example that he set by his life and death make him one of the most influential figures in the history of Western thought.

Born in Athens in 469 B.C.E., Socrates fought bravely during the Peloponnesian War. Afterward he openly defied the antidemocratic Thirty Tyrants whom the Spartans had installed in Athens. Socrates did not seek a career in politics or business. Instead he spent his time thinking and talking, which earned him a reputation as an eccentric. His friends, however, loved and deeply respected him.

Socrates did not give lectures. Instead, he questioned people who believed they knew the truth. By asking them such questions as "What is justice? Beauty? Courage?" and "What is the best way to lead a good life?" Socrates revealed that they—and most people—do not truly understand their most basic assumptions. Socrates did not claim to know the answers, but he did believe in the relentless application of rational argument in the pursuit of answers. This style of questioning, known as the Socratic method, infuriated complacent men because it made them seem foolish. But Socrates' method delighted people interested in taking a hard look at their most cherished beliefs.

Socrates attracted many followers. His brightest student was the philosopher Plato, to whom Socrates was not only a mentor, but a hero. Plato wrote a number of dialogues, or dramatized conversations, in which Socrates appears as a questioner, pursuing the truth about an important topic. Four of his dialogues—*Euthyphro, Apology, Crito,* and *Phaedo*—involve Socrates' trial and death.

The trial began when three citizens named Lycon, Meletus, and Anytus accused Socrates before a jury of 501 men. After hearing the charges, Socrates spoke in his own defense, but instead of showing any remorse, he boldly defended his method of questioning. Annoyed by Socrates' stubbornness, the jury convicted him.

Athenian law permitted accusers as well as defendants to suggest alternative penalties. When the accusers asked for death, Socrates responded with astonishing arrogance. He suggested instead that Athens pay him upkeep for making the city a better place. Outraged by this response from Socrates, the jury chose death by an even wider margin. Socrates accepted their verdict calmly.

While Socrates sat in prison waiting for his execution, a friend named Crito offered to help him escape. Socrates refused to flee. He told Crito that only a man who did not respect the law would break it, and that such a man would indeed be a corrupting influence on the young. Socrates pointed out that he had lived his life as an obedient Athenian citizen and would certainly not break the law now. Human laws may be imperfect, he admitted, but they permit a society to function. Private individuals should never disregard them. To the end he remained a loyal citizen.

On his final day, with his closest friends around him, Socrates drank a cup of poison and died bravely. Plato wrote, "This is the way our dear friend perished. It is fair to say that he was the bravest, the wisest, and the most honorable man of all those we have ever known."[5]

Historians and philosophers have discussed Socrates' case since Plato's time. Were the accusations fair? What precisely was his crime? In the matter of corrupting Athens's youth, there is no doubt that at least two of his most fervent young followers, Alcibiades and Critias, had earned terrible reputations. Alcibiades had betrayed his city in the Peloponnesian War. Critias was one of the most violent of the Thirty Tyrants. Many Athenians suspected Socrates of influencing them, even though these men represented everything he opposed.

Charges of impiety were harder to substantiate, but Athenians took them seriously. His fellow citizens knew that Socrates always participated in Athenian religious life. But during his defense Socrates admitted that his views were not exactly the same as those of his prosecutors. His claim to have a divine *daimon* or "sign" who sat on his shoulder and gave him advice was eccentric though not actually sacrilegious. Many Athenians thought this daimon was a foreign god rather than Socrates' metaphor for his own mental processes.

The reasons for Socrates' prosecution lie much deeper than the official charges. His trial and execution emerged from an anti-intellectual backlash bred in the frustrations of Athens's defeat in

Socrates on Trial

Many sculptors made portraits of Socrates in the centuries after his death. Though Socrates was viewed as a hero who died for his beliefs, this sculptor did nothing to glamorize him in this portrait. Socrates was famous for the beauty of his thoughts—and the ugliness of his face.

the Peloponnesian War and in the Thirty Tyrants' rule. Even though Athenians had restored democracy, deep-seated resentments sealed Socrates' fate. In many societies throughout history, especially democratic ones like that of Athens that grant freedom to explore new ideas, people who fear change and creativity often strike out at artists, intellectuals, and innovators in times of stress. Athenians resented Socrates because he challenged them to think. He wanted them to live better lives, and they killed him.

Questions of Justice

1. What does this trial reveal about the nature of Athenian justice?
2. What does this trial tell us about the attitude of Athenians toward philosophy?

Taking It Further

Brickhouse, Thomas C., and Nicholas D. Smith. *Socrates on Trial.* 1989. A thorough analysis of Socrates' trial.

Stokes, Michael. *Plato: Apology, with Introduction, Translation, and Commentary.* 1997. The best translation, with important commentary.

can be discovered only through careful, critical questioning rather than through observation of the physical world. As a result, Platonic thought emphasizes the superiority of theory over scientific investigation.

According to Plato, humans can gain knowledge of the Forms. This is possible because we have souls that are small bits of a larger eternal Soul that enters our bodies at birth, bringing knowledge of the Forms with it. Our individual bits of Soul always seek to return to their source, but they must fight the constraints of the body and physical existence that stand in the way of their return. Mortals can aid the Soul in its struggle to overcome the material world by using reason to seek knowledge of the Forms. This rational quest for absolutes, Plato argued, is the particular responsibility of the philosophers, but all of us should do our best to embark on this search.

In his great political work, *The Republic,* Plato described how people might construct an ideal community based on the principles he had established. In this ideal state, educated men and women called the Guardians would lead the polis because they were capable of comprehending the Forms. They would supervise the brave Auxiliaries who defended the city. At the bottom of society were the Workers who produced the basic requirements of life. Workers were the least capable of abstract thought.

Plato and his student Aristotle (384–322 B.C.E.) stand as the two greatest thinkers of classical Greece. Aristotle founded his own school in Athens, called the Lyceum. Unlike his teacher, Aristotle did not envision the Forms as separate from matter. In his view, form and matter are completely bound together. For this reason, we can acquire knowledge of the Forms by carefully observing the world around us and classifying what we find. Following this theory, Aristotle rigorously investigated a large range of subjects, including animal and plant biology, aesthetics, psychology, and physics. His theories regarding mechanics (the study of motion) and his argument that the sun and planets revolve around the Earth acquired great authority among medieval thinkers and were not effectively challenged until the Scientific Revolution of the late sixteenth and seventeenth centuries.

Aristotle's idea regarding politics had an equally important impact on Western thought. In contrast to Plato, who described an ideal state, Aristotle analyzed the political communities that actually existed in his day, the Greek poleis. This empirical approach to politics, which paralleled his approach to studying the natural world, led him to conclude that human beings were by nature "political animals" who had a natural tendency to form political communities. By living in such societies they learned about jus-

tice, which was essential to the state and which was its guiding principle. Aristotle's view that the people themselves, not the gods, formed the state proved immensely important in the history of Western thought. It has survived in modern democracies, especially in the United States, where the Constitution proclaims that the people themselves established the government and determined how it should be structured.

The Arts: Sculpture, Painting, and Architecture

Like philosophers and dramatists during the Classical Age, Greek sculptors, painters, and architects pursued ideal beauty and truth. Classical artists believed the human body was beautiful and an appropriate subject of their attention. They also valued the human capacity to represent in art the ideals of beauty, harmony, and proportion found in nature.

Classical Greek men celebrated their ability to make rational judgments about what was beautiful and pleasing to the eye—and to create art that embodied those judgments. To create a statue that was an image of physical perfection, sculptors copied the best features of several human models while ignoring their flaws. They strove to depict the muscles, movement, and balance of the human figure in a way that was both lifelike in its imitation of nature and yet idealized in the harmony and symmetry of the torso and limbs. This balance between realism and idealism, as well as the belief that the human male body came closest to perfection and that men embodied the most admirable virtues, ex-

IMAGE

Myron, The Discus Thrower

The Male Nude in Greek Sculpture: Polyclitus's Spear-Carrier

This Roman replica of a bronze statue of a warrior, probably Achilles, by the Greek sculptor Polyclitus of Argos, reflects the desire of Greek artists to depict the ideal man. The spear-carrier's anatomy is perfectly proportioned, and his muscles indicate the discipline and preparation for battle. He is the perfect male citizen, balanced and controlled yet poised to fight. The original statue has not survived.

plains the proliferation of male statues—many of them nude—throughout the Greek world.

Greek painters explored movement of the human body as well as colors and the optical illusion of depth. The figures that they depicted on vases and on walls became increasingly lively and realistic as the Classical Age unfolded. Artists portrayed every sort of activity from religious worship to erotic fun, but regardless of the subject, they shared a similar goal: to create a lifelike depiction of the human figure.

In a similar effort to capture ideals of perfection, Greek architects designed their buildings, especially temples, to be symmetrical and proportional. They used mathematical ratios that they observed in nature to shape their designs. The buildings they created show a grace, balance, and harmony that have inspired architects for more than two millennia.

The temple of Athena in Athens, called the Parthenon or "House of the Virgin Goddess," stood as the greatest triumph of classical Greek architecture (see illustration on page 81). Built on the Acropolis of Athens, the temple symbolized Athens's imperial glory. Using funds appropriated from the Delian League, Athenians built the huge temple between 447 and 432 B.C.E. and dedicated it to their divine protector. The architects Ictinus and Callicrates achieved a superb example of structural harmony, perfectly balancing all the building's elements according to mathematical proportions copied from nature. For the Parthenon's sacred inner room, Phidias, a friend of Pericles, sculpted a statue of Athena made of gold and ivory over a wooden core and decorated it with gems and other precious metals. The temple also displayed an elaborate series of carved and brightly painted marble panels depicting the mythology of Athena. The Parthenon remained nearly intact until 1687 C.E., when powder kegs stored inside exploded, causing irreparable damage.

Conclusion

The Cultural Foundations of the West

During the period from 1100 to 336 B.C.E., several of the elements of what would later be considered Western culture came into being. The peoples responsible for this legacy—Persians, Hebrews, and Greeks—did not have a conception of "the West" as a distinct cultural realm, but their religious, philosophical, and political traditions later became essential components of the Western cultural tradition. These traditions arose in a world dominated by Persia. Some of them came directly from Persia itself. Persians preserved and transmitted older Middle Eastern traditions of science, mathematics, astronomy, and navigation, which they bequeathed to the Greeks

and then to the people of the western Mediterranean, North Africa, and eventually Europe. At the same time the official religion of Persia, Zoroastrianism, had a demonstrable impact on Judaism and subsequently on two other great monotheistic religions of the West—Christianity and Islam.

Other Western cultural traditions developed among the people who either were permitted a degree of religious autonomy within the Persian Empire or who successfully resisted conquest by Persian armies. The Persian policy of tolerating other religions allowed the Hebrews to develop their distinctive version of monotheism and the ethical teachings encapsulated in the Bible. These beliefs entered into the mainstream of Western religious culture. In Greece, where Persian expansion met its limits, the democratic institutions of the Athenian polis became well established. Under the political and cultural leadership of Athens, Greek civilization thrived, producing the most enduring artistic and philosophical contributions of the ancient world to Western culture. Many of these traditions were transmitted to a broader geographical area by the Macedonian king, Alexander the Great, who conquered the Greeks and destroyed the Persian Empire. To these military achievements, and the cultural effects of his victories, we now turn.

Suggestions for Further Reading

For a comprehensive list of suggested readings, please go to www.ablongman.com/levack2e/chapter3

Boardman, John. *Persia and the West: An Archaeological Investigation of the Genesis of Achaemenid Art.* 2000. A brilliantly illustrated study that stresses intercultural influences in every aspect of Persian art.

Boyce, Mary. *A History of Zoroastrianism.* Vol. 2. 1975. This authoritative examination provides a masterful overview of the religion of the Persian Empire.

Burkert, Walter. *The Orientalizing Revolution: Near Eastern Influence on Greek Culture in the Early Archaic Age,* trans. Margaret Pinder and Walter Burkert. 1993. Explains how the Semitic East influenced the development of Greek society in the Archaic Age.

Cohn, Norman. *Cosmos, Chaos, and the World to Come: The Ancient Roots of Apocalyptic Faith.* 1993. Expert critical analysis of apocalyptic religions in the West, including Zoroastrianism, ancient Judaism, Christianity, and other faiths.

Finkelstein, Israel, and Neil Asher Silberman. *The Bible Unearthed: Archaeology's New Vision of Ancient Israel and the Origin of the Sacred Texts.* 2001. An important archaeological interpretation that challenges the narrative of the Hebrew Bible and offers a reconsideration of biblical history.

Gottwald, Norman K. *The Hebrew Bible: A Socio-Literary Introduction.* 1985. Combines a close reading of the Hebrew Bible with the latest archaeological and historical evidence.

Just, Roger. *Women in Athenian Law and Life.* 1989. Provides an overview of the social context of women in Athens.

Kuhrt, Amélie. *The Ancient Near East, ca. 3000–330 B.C.* Vol. 2. 1995. This rich and comprehensive bibliography is a remarkably concise and readable account of Persian history with excellent discussion of ancient textual evidence. Many important passages appear in fluent translation.

Lindberg, David C. *The Beginnings of Western Science: The European Scientific Tradition in Philosophical, Religious, and Institutional Context, 600 B.C. to A.D. 1450.* 1992. This highly readable study provides an exciting survey of the main developments in Western science.

Markoe, Glenn. *Phoenicians.* 2000. The best and most up-to-date treatment of Phoenician society by a noted expert.

Murray, Oswyn. *Early Greece.* 1983. A brilliant study of all aspects of the emergence of Greek society between the Dark Age and the end of the Persian Wars.

Osborne, Robin. *Greece in the Making, 1200–479 B.C.* 1996. An excellent narrative of the development of Greek society with special regard to the archaeological evidence.

Stewart, Andrew. *Art, Desire, and the Body in Ancient Greece.* 1997. A provocative study that examines Greek attitudes toward sexuality and art.

Walker, Christopher, ed. *Astronomy Before the Telescope.* 1996. A fascinating collection of essays about astronomy in the pre-modern period, which makes clear our enormous debt to the Babylonians.

Wieshöfer, Josef. *Ancient Persia from 550 B.C. to A.D. 650,* trans. Azizeh Azodi. 1996. A fresh and comprehensive overview of Persian cultural, social, and political history that relies on Persian evidence more heavily than on biased Greek and Roman sources.

Notes

1. Based on Herodotus, *History,* vol. 1, trans. Rex Warner (2000), 125–126.

2. James B. Pritchard, *Ancient Near Eastern Texts Relating to the Old Testament.* 3rd ed. with supplement (1969), 315–316.

3. Demosthenes, *Orations,* 59.122.

4. From Euripides, *The Trojan Women,* trans. Peter Levi, in John Boardman, Jasper Griffith, and Oswyn Murray, eds., *The Oxford History of the Classical World* (1986), 169.

5. Plato, *Phaedo,* 1.118.

The Hellenistic World and the Roman Republic, 336–31 B.C.E.

4

ONE EVENING AFTER DINNER IN 193 B.C.E., AT THE PALACE OF A GREEK king in Asia Minor, two battle-hardened generals from different lands debated the identity of the greatest military commander of all time. Both generals came from aristocratic backgrounds. One had grown up in Rome, the other in Carthage, an imperial city on the coast of North Africa. They conversed in Greek, the language of diplomacy and culture that was used throughout the Mediterranean and the Middle East. The Carthaginian was Hannibal, a military genius who had led the armies of Carthage in a savage war against Rome between 218 and 201 B.C.E. and who now lived in exile. The Roman, who was visiting Asia Minor as part of a diplomatic mission, was Publius Cornelius Scipio Africanus. This equally brilliant general had defeated Hannibal and ended the bloodiest war in Rome's history. When Scipio asked Hannibal who he thought was the world's greatest general, Hannibal named the legendary Macedonian conqueror Alexander the Great. With a smile Scipio then asked his former foe, "What if *you* had defeated *me*?" "In that case," replied the Carthaginian in a flattering tone, "I would be the greatest general of them all."

This anecdote illuminates some fundamental elements of a period that historians call the Hellenistic Age. First, it reveals a cosmopolitan, Greek-based culture in which a Carthaginian general, whose native tongue was a Semitic language, and a Latin-speaking Roman aristocrat could easily communicate. Second, these two warriors shared knowledge of the history of Mediterranean lands, politics, and diplomatic etiquette. Most of all, both admired Alexander the Great, who had made their cosmopolitan world possible. Scipio, Hannibal, and doubtless their host sought to imitate the Macedonian king. Alexander and the civilization he had inaugurated had set the standard for success in the minds of men from very different cultural backgrounds.

Celt and Wife This dramatic statue epitomizes the mixing of cultures in the Hellenistic Age. The statue is a Roman copy in marble of a bronze original made at Pergamum in Asia Minor by a Greek sculptor. The artist tells the tragic story of a defeated Celt. Rather than be captured alive, he has just killed his wife and is at the precise moment of taking his own life. In typically Hellenistic style, the artist combines anatomical accuracy with psychological agony.

The Hellenistic period began when Alexander (r. 336–323 B.C.E.) conquered the Persian Empire, extending Greek culture as far east as Afghanistan and India. Greeks called themselves *Hellenes,* and thus historians use the terms *Hellenism* and *Hellenistic* to describe the complex cosmopolitan civilization that developed in the wake of Alexander's conquests. This civilization offered a rich variety of goods, technologies, and ideas to anyone who knew or was willing to learn Greek. Just as people throughout the world today study English because it is the primary language used in science and technology, global business, and international politics, Greek became the common tongue used in trade, politics, and intellectual life.

Political borders did not limit Hellenistic civilization. After Alexander died, the empire he had built fragmented into smaller kingdoms that often fought one another. Despite the instability and warfare, however, Hellenistic culture thrived within Alexander's successor kingdoms. It also spread far beyond the lands conquered by Alexander, mainly in the western Mediterranean, where it had a profound effect on the civilizations of North Africa, Europe, and especially Rome. Romans, Jews, Persians, Celts, Carthaginians, and other peoples all absorbed elements of Greek culture—its philosophy, religion, literature, and art. Hellenism gave a common language of science and learning to diverse peoples speaking different languages and worshiping different gods. Hellenism thus gave a cultural unity to a vast area stretching from Europe in the west to Afghanistan in the east. Large portions of this cultural realm ultimately became what historians call the West.

The spread of Hellenistic culture over this vast area involved a series of cultural exchanges. Greek culture offered great prestige and possessed a powerful intellectual appeal to non-Greek peoples, but it also posed a threat to their local, traditional identities. Instead of simply accepting Greek culture, these non-Greek peoples engaged in a process of cultural adaptation and synthesis. In this way Hellenism, which throughout this period remained open to outside influences, absorbed foreign scientific knowledge, religious ideas, and many other elements of culture. These elements then entered the mainstream of Hellenistic culture and were transmitted to the greater Hellenistic world. Some of the basic components of Western civilization originated in these cultural encounters between Greek and non-Greek peoples. These include the seven-day week, beliefs in Hell and Judgment Day, the study of astrology and astronomy, and technologies of metallurgy, agriculture, and navigation.

The Hellenistic era and the age of independent Hellenistic kingdoms came to a close in 31 B.C.E., when the Roman politician and military commander Octavian (later known as Augustus) won control of the Mediterranean world, the Middle East, Egypt, and parts of Europe. This political development did not, however, put an end to the influence of Hellenistic culture. By forging a new, more resilient civilization in which Greeks, Romans, and many other peoples intermingled in peace, the Romans created their own version of Hellenism and introduced it to western Europe.

The main question this chapter seeks to answer is how the encounter between Greeks and the many peoples of the Middle East and Europe, especially the Romans, laid the foundation of Western civilization. In order to answer this main question, the individual sections of the chapter ask the following more specific questions:

- How did Alexander the Great create an empire in which Greek civilization flourished in the midst of many diverse cultures?
- What were the distinguishing features of Hellenistic society and culture, and what was the result of encounters between Greeks and non-Greeks?
- How did the Roman Republic come to dominate the Mediterranean world during the Hellenistic Age, and how did Roman rule over the Hellenistic East affect Rome's development?
- What political and social changes brought the Roman Republic to an end?

The Warlike Kingdom of Macedon

- How did Alexander the Great create an empire in which Greek civilization flourished in the midst of many diverse cultures?

The Hellenistic Age had its roots in Macedon, a kingdom to the north of Greece that was rich in timber, grain, horses, and fighting men. Most Macedonians lived in scattered villages and made a living by engaging in small-scale farming, raiding their neighbors, and trading over short distances. Relentless warfare against wild Thracian and Illyrian tribes to the north and west kept Macedonians constantly ready for battle.

Macedonians spoke a dialect of Greek, but their customs and political organization differed from those of the urbanized Greek communities that lay to their south. Unlike democratic Athens, Macedon had a hereditary monarchy. Cutthroat struggles for ascendancy in the royal family trained Macedonian kings to select the best moment to deliver a lethal blow to any enemy. Maintaining centralized political control over their territory proved a constant problem for Macedon's kings because independent-minded nobles resented their rule. Only the army of free citizens could

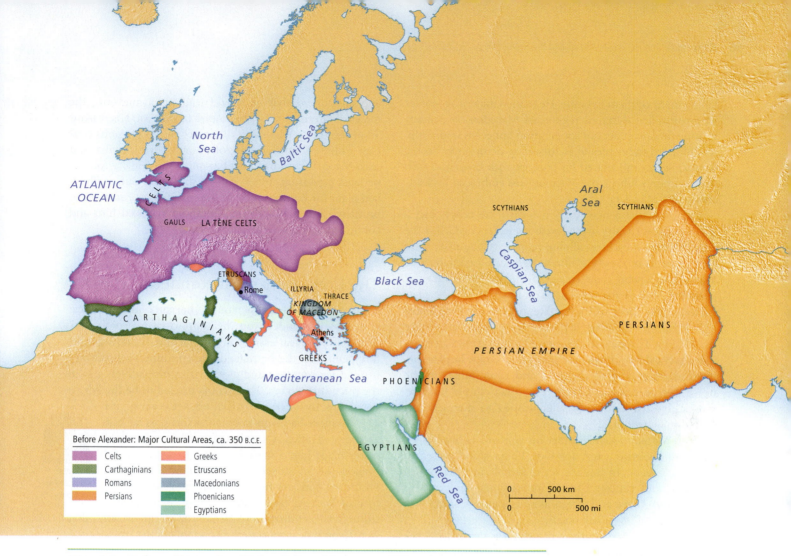

Map 4.1 Before Alexander: Major Cultural Areas, ca. 350 B.C.E.
During the Hellenistic Age, Greek culture influenced many cultures. This map shows the realms of
the Persians, Celts, Romans, Carthaginians, and Phoenicians, whose societies would participate in
the Hellenistic Age.

legitimize a king's reign. In return for their support, the soldiers demanded the spoils of war. As a result, Macedonian
kings had to wage war continually to obtain that wealth and
keep their precarious position on the throne.

Unity and Expansion Under King Philip

Throughout most of the Classical Age of Greece these fierce
Macedonian highlanders knew little of city life and seemed
like savages to sophisticated Greeks. When cities started to
appear in Macedon in the fifth century B.C.E., Macedonian
aristocrats began to emulate the culture of classical Greece.
The members of the royal family, for example, claimed the
Greek hero Hercules as their ancestor. This move won them
the right to compete in the Olympic Games, which were
open only to Greeks. Macedonian aristocrats also offered

rich stipends to Greek playwrights and scholars to lure
them to their capital city of Pella.

In the political realm, however, Macedon shrewdly
avoided Greek affairs. During the Persian Wars (490 B.C.E.
and 480–479 B.C.E.), Macedonian kings pursued a cautious
and profitable policy of friendship with the Persian invaders. During the convulsions of the Peloponnesian War
(431–404 B.C.E.) and its turbulent aftermath, Macedon
refrained from exploiting Athens, Sparta, and the other
Greek cities as they bled to exhaustion. The lack of Greek
entanglements, however, could not ease the tensions between kings and nobles. In 399 B.C.E., Macedon slipped
into a forty-year period of anarchy. Just as Macedon was
on the verge of disintegration, King Philip II (382–336
B.C.E.) stepped forward and transformed the Macedonian
kingdom.

A ruthless opportunist with a gift for military organization, Philip consolidated his power by eliminating his rivals,

killing many of them in battle. He unified the unruly nobles who controlled different regions of Macedon by demonstrating the advantages of cooperation under his leadership. As Philip led the nobles to victory after victory over hostile frontier tribes and shared his plunder with them and with the common soldiers, the Macedonians embraced his leadership (see Map 4.1).

Philip created a new army in which the nobles had a special role as cavalry armed with heavy lances. Called the Companions, they formed elite regiments bound to their king by oaths of loyalty. Philip reorganized the infantry, or foot soldiers, who were recruited mainly from the rural peasantry, into phalanxes. The main function of these phalanxes, unlike those of the hoplites, was to use long lances to hold off the enemy while the cavalry galloped in to strike a fatal blow. This new strategy gave Philip's armies an enormous tactical advantage over traditional Greek hoplite formations. After seizing the gold and silver mines of the north Aegean coast of Greece, Philip had ample funds to hire additional armies of mercenaries to augment his Macedonian troops.

With Macedon firmly under his control, its borders secure and his army eager for loot, Philip stood poised to strike at Greece. In 349 B.C.E. he seized several cities in northern and central Greece, inaugurating a decade of diplomacy, bribery, and threats as he maneuvered for power over the rest of the Greek poleis.

Recognizing that Philip represented a threat to Greek liberty, the brilliant Athenian orator Demosthenes organized resistance among the city-states. In 340 B.C.E., when Philip attempted to seize the Bosporus, the link to Athens's vital Black Sea trade routes, the poleis took action. Demosthenes delivered a series of blistering speeches against Philip known as "the Philippics" and assembled an alliance of cities. In 338 B.C.E., however, Philip crushed the allied armies at the battle of Chaeronea in central Greece. In this confrontation Philip's 18-year-old son Alexander led the Companions in a charge that won the day for the Macedonians.

Philip imposed Macedonian rule over Greece by establishing a coalition of Greek cities called the League of Corinth, of which he was the leader. He also established Macedonian garrisons at strategic sites and forbade Greek cities to change their form of government without his approval. For the Greek poleis, the age of autonomy had passed forever.

Philip next cast his eyes on the Persian Empire. In 337 B.C.E. he cloaked himself in the mantle of Greek culture and announced that he would lead his armies and the forces of Greece against the empire to the east. His reason? To avenge Persia's invasion of Greece in the previous century. Philip's shrewd linking of classical Greek civilization with Macedonian force now became a rallying cry for imperialist expansion under Philip's direction. But as Philip laid plans for his assault on Persia in 336 B.C.E., an assassin murdered him. Philip's son Alexander replaced him and continued his plans to invade the East.

The Conquests of Alexander

A man of immense personal charisma and political craftiness, Alexander won the support of his soldiers by demonstrating fearlessness in combat and displaying military genius on the battlefield. He combined a predatory instinct for conquest and glory with utter ruthlessness in the pursuit of power. These traits proved to be the key to his success. By the time of his death, at the age of just 33, Alexander had won military victories as far east as India, creating a vast empire. Alexander's successes made him a legend during his lifetime, and millions of his subjects worshiped him as a god. Historians consider him a pivotal figure in the history of Western civilization because his conquests led to the dissemination of Hellenistic culture in lands that were to become important components of the West.

VIDEO

Greek Heritage in Turkey

Alexander the Great
This silver coin minted about 315 B.C.E. shows Alexander wearing an elephant scalp, which refers to his battles in India; a diadem, which was a symbol of kingship; and ram's horns, which alludes to a connection with Zeus, king of the gods.

After brutally consolidating power in Macedonia and Greece following his father's death, Alexander launched an invasion of Persia. With no more than 40,000 infantry and 5,000 cavalry, Alexander crossed the Hellespont—the narrow strait dividing Europe from Asia where the Black Sea meets the Aegean Sea—and marched into Persian territory in 334 B.C.E. Darius III, the Great King of Persia who had ascended the throne two years earlier, proved no match for Alexander's tactical brilliance. The young Macedonian king won his first great victory in battle over Persian forces at the Granicus River, giving him control over Asia Minor with its rich Greek coastal cities and fleets. He then marched into Syria, where he broke the main Persian army near the town of Issus in 333 B.C.E. Just as he had done at the battle of the Granicus River, Alexander led the Macedonian cavalry's victorious charge into the teeth of the enemy. From this victory Alexander gained control of the entire eastern coast of the Mediterranean Sea and the Persian naval bases located there.

When the maritime city of Tyre succumbed to Alexander's siege in 332 B.C.E., Darius panicked and offered the young Macedonian his daughter and all of his empire west of the Euphrates River in return for peace. Alexander rejected the offer and marched into Egypt, where the inhabitants welcomed him as a liberator from their Persian masters. From Egypt he advanced into Mesopotamia, where he crushed Darius once again on the battlefield at Gaugamela near the Tigris River.

When Alexander entered Babylon in triumph he once again received an enthusiastic welcome as a liberator. From Babylon his forces ventured southeast to Persepolis, the Persian capital, which Alexander captured in January 330 B.C.E. He plundered the city and burned it to the ground. The enormous wealth he acquired from Persepolis paid for all of his military activities for the next dozen years and invigorated the entire Macedonian economy. Darius escaped the destruction of his capital but was soon murdered by his own nobles. The once-powerful Persian Empire lay in ruins.

Alexander had fulfilled his father's pledge to gain vengeance against Persia, but he had no intention of slowing down his march of conquest (see Map 4.2). He pushed past the tribesmen of the harsh Afghan mountain ranges to penetrate Central Asia. Then in 327 B.C.E. he entered the

Map 4.2 Macedon and the Conquests of Alexander the Great

Alexander led troops from his Macedonian homeland as far east as the Indus Valley. He defeated the Persian Empire and incorporated it into his kingdom. This map shows the route of Alexander's march of conquest and the sites of his most important victories.

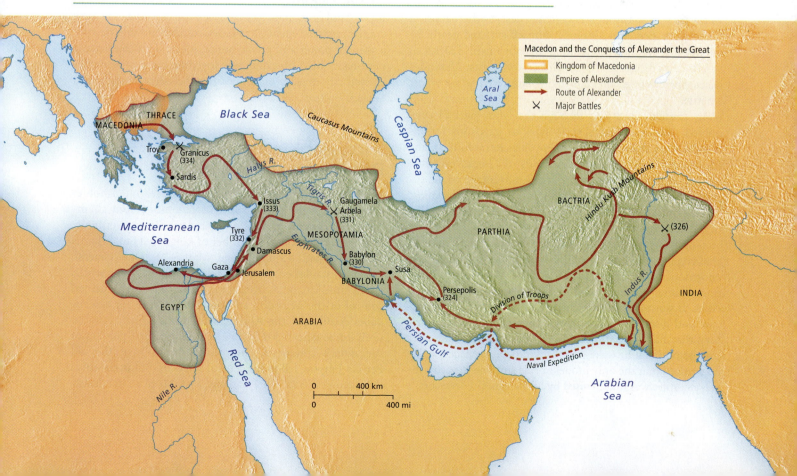

territory that is modern Pakistan through the Khyber Pass. There he defeated Poros, an Indian king, but then the tide of fortune slowly turned against him. After crossing the Indus River and advancing into India, his exhausted armies refused to go any farther. The route he chose for his return westward passed through a scorching desert, where most of his soldiers died, and Alexander himself suffered nearly fatal wounds. While recuperating at Babylon in 323 B.C.E., where he had begun to plan further conquests, Alexander succumbed to fever after a drinking bout. He had never lost a battle.

In strategic locations through the lands he had conquered, Alexander established cities as garrisons for his troops. More than a dozen of these cities received the name Alexandria in his honor. Thousands of Greeks migrated east to settle in the new cities to take advantage of the expanded economic opportunities for trade and farming. These Greek settlers became the cultural and political elite of the new cities.

Governing an empire of this size proved to be a difficult challenge. It was much easier for Alexander to conquer an enormous empire than to rule it. The Macedonian kingdom that he led was geared to seizing land and plundering cities. It was another task entirely to create the infrastructure and discipline necessary for ruling an immense territory that had little linguistic or cultural unity. Alexander understood that he was no longer king of just Macedon. He recognized that the only model of rule suitable to such a diverse empire was that devised by his Persian predecessors: a Great King presiding over a hierarchy of nobles who governed Persian territory, and subject kings who ruled non-Persian regions.

Necessity thus forced Alexander to bring his Macedonian troops and his new Persian subjects together in an uneasy balance. To that end, Alexander persuaded his army to proclaim him "King of Asia"—that is, the new Great King. With his Companions he simply took over the government of the former Persian Empire from the top. He included a handful of loyal Persians in his administration by making them regional governors or satraps, while offering other Persians minor roles in his regime.

These practical steps promised to bring order to the empire. By adopting the elaborate Persian role of the Great King, Alexander demonstrated to his foreign subjects that his regime stood for security and continuity of orderly rule. His proud Macedonian soldiers, however, ultimately stymied his efforts. They refused to grovel before him as Persian royal ceremony dictated. And though Alexander may well have thought of himself as a god, they refused to worship him while he lived. Instead, they saw Alexander's recruitment of 30,000 Persian troops into their army as a threat to the traditional relationship between Macedonian soldiers and their king. They also resented the marriages with the daughters of Persian noblemen that Alexander forced on them in order to unite Macedonians and Persians—although no Persian nobles received Greek wives. The Macedonian troops expected to keep all the spoils of victory for themselves. They wanted to be conquerors, not partners in a new government. They failed to understand that men of other cultures within the new empire might be equally loyal to Alexander and thus deserve a share of power and public honor. Alexander's charismatic personality held his conquests together, but his death destroyed any dreams of cooperation between Persians and Greeks.

Successor Kingdoms: Distributing the Spoils

Alexander left no adult heir, and the Macedonian nobles who served as his generals fought viciously among themselves for control of his conquered territory. Eventually these generals created a number of kingdoms out of lands Alexander had acquired (see Map 4.3). One general, Ptolemy, established the Ptolemaic dynasty in Egypt, which lasted until 30 B.C.E. Antigonus "the One-Eyed" gained control of the Macedonian homeland, where his descendants established the Antigonid dynasty, which survived until Rome defeated it in 167 B.C.E. The largest portion of Alexander's conquests, comprising the bulk of the old Persian Empire, fell to his general Seleucus. But in the mid-third century B.C.E., the Parthians, a people from northeast-

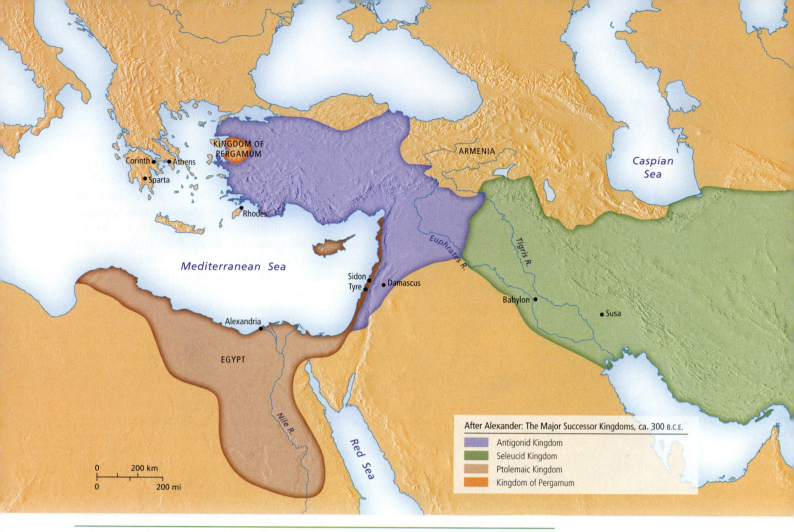

Map 4.3 After Alexander: Major Successor Kingdoms, ca. 300 B.C.E.

After Alexander's death, his generals quarreled and broke the empire into several smaller kingdoms.

ern Persia, shook off Seleucid rule and created a vigorous state. By 150 B.C.E. the Seleucids ruled only Syria.

Smaller kingdoms were also carved out of the areas Alexander had conquered. Bactria (in northern Afghanistan) came under the rule of a Greek-speaking government that would control it well into the second century B.C.E. In 303 B.C.E. the Indian king Chandragupta Maurya conquered the easternmost Indian territories and incorporated them into his own non-Greek kingdom in India. Another lesser successor kingdom emerged in Asia Minor. Centered on the city of Pergamum, a buffer between the Seleucid and Antigonid kingdoms, it was ruled by the Attalid dynasty.

Following the example of Macedon itself, the Hellenistic successor states all maintained a monarchical form of government, in which a king ruled the people with the support of the army and highly regimented bureaucracies. The members of the administrative hierarchy were all Greeks and Macedonians; indigenous people were not recruited into the ruling elite. Greek was the language of rule in the successor kingdoms. The talented queen Cleopatra (69–30 B.C.E.), who was the last descendant of Ptolemy to rule in Egypt, was the first of her line ever to speak Egyptian. Greek-speaking monarchs were nonetheless aware that they needed to cultivate the goodwill of their non-Greek-speaking subjects. As one monarch asked in a Hellenistic political dialogue, "How can I accommodate myself to all the different races in my kingdom?" A subject answered: "By adopting the appropriate attitude to each, making justice one's guide."

The king towered over Hellenistic society, holding authority over all his subjects and bearing ultimate responsibility for their welfare. Following the example of Alexander, Hellenistic monarchs earned legitimacy by leading their troops into wars of conquest. A king embodied the entire community that he ruled. He was at once the ruler, father, protector, savior, source of law, and god of all his subjects. His garb reinforced his elevated position—kings arrayed themselves in battle gear with a helmet or Macedonian sombrero, crowns, purple robes, scepters, and special seal rings. Monarchs earned the loyalty of their subjects and glorified their own rule by establishing cities, constructing public buildings, and rewarding their inner circle.

Ptolemaic King of Egypt

This golden ring depicts Ptolemy VI, who ruled Egypt from 176 to 145 B.C.E. Although he and his court spoke only Greek, he is depicted as a pharaoh wearing a double crown, the age-old symbol of Egyptian monarchy. The image on the ring demonstrated the integration of old and new political symbols in Egypt during the Hellenistic Age.

DOCUMENT

Descriptions of Alexandria

Ptolemy II, who ruled in Egypt from 283 to 246 B.C.E., exemplifies these notions of Hellenistic kingship. Ptolemy expanded his dominions by conquering parts of Asia Minor and Syria from rival monarchs. He also expanded the bureaucracy, refined the taxation system, and funded many new military settlements. With his support, merchants established new trading posts on the Red Sea, where they engaged in commerce with merchants from India and other eastern lands. Ptolemy patronized the arts and sciences by building impressive research institutes and libraries. He transformed Egypt's capital city of Alexandria, founded by Alexander in Egypt in 331 B.C.E., into the leading center of Greek culture and learning in the Hellenistic world. To reinforce his authority and majesty, he encouraged his subjects to worship him as a god.

This worship of Hellenistic monarchs drew from indigenous traditions throughout the Middle East, but in its Hellenistic form it had a political rather than a spiritual significance. People worshiped their kings as a spontaneous expression of gratitude for the protection and the peace that good government made possible. For example, when the Antigonid king Demetrius "the Besieger" captured Athens in 308 B.C.E., the pragmatic Athenians sang a song in honor of their new master: "The other gods either do not exist or are far off, either they do not hear, or they do not care; but you are here and we can see you, not in wood and stone but in living truth."[1] Deification legitimized a king's right to rule. In turn the ruler cult, in which monarchs were worshiped as gods, channeled all-important loyalty directly to the king.

In addition to the loyalty of their subjects, Hellenistic kings also depended on permanent professional armies to wage the military campaigns so essential to maintaining their authority and to defending their territories. Hellenistic kings fought wars over much larger territories than those that had led to squabbles among Greek city-states in previous centuries. The conquest of such territories required an increase in the size of field armies. The Athenian hoplites had numbered about 10,000 in the fifth century B.C.E., but in the Hellenistic Age kings routinely mustered armies of between 60,000 and 80,000 men. Many soldiers came from military colonies established by the kings. In return for land, the men of these Greek-speaking colonies were obliged to serve generation after generation in the king's army and to police the native, non-Greek populations.

Hellenistic Society and Culture

- **What were the distinguishing features of Hellenistic society and culture, and what was the result of encounters between Greeks and non-Greeks?**

Chronic warfare among Hellenistic monarchs made political unity among the Hellenistic kingdoms impossible. Nevertheless, the social institutions and cultural orientation of Greek-speaking people in all these kingdoms gave them a unity that their monarchs could not achieve.

Cities: The Heart of Hellenistic Life

Alexander and his successors seized dozens of Greek city-states scattered across the eastern Mediterranean and founded dozens of new glittering urban communities in all the territories they conquered. Hellenistic cities were much more than garrisons put in place to enforce the conquerors' power. They continued traditions of learning, art, and architecture, as well as traditions of citizen participation in public life that had flourished in the classical poleis. Most important, people in cities throughout the Hellenistic world spoke a standard version of Greek called Koine° that gave them a sense of common identity. Greek city life defined Hellenistic civilization.

On the surface, many of the institutions of the classical poleis remained the same: magistrates, councils, and popular assemblies ran the cities' affairs, and some form of democracy remained the ideal in local government. Yet beneath the surface, the poleis had undergone radical changes. Because kings wielded absolute power, once-independent cities such as Athens and Corinth lost their freedom to make peace or wage war. They now served as the bureaucratic centers that administered their rulers' huge kingdoms.

Hellenistic kings preferred to maintain the illusion of the cities' independence and rarely intervened in urban affairs, permitting considerable freedom in local government. Nonetheless, Hellenistic methods and those of classical Greece differed in one important way. Democracies had developed in Greece during the Archaic and Classical Ages to protect the interests of the poor as well as the rich. Now, in the Hellenistic Age, the wealthy dominated society and government while the condition of the poor deteriorated. Rich men appointed by the king controlled all the courts, held all the magistracies, and represented all the cities at the court of the kings, who in return showered these civic leaders with honors. Through land grants, tax immunities, and other favors, the monarchs developed networks of personal ties that bound civic leaders to them. In return, these urban elites did more than serve their king. They spent their vast fortunes on behalf of their cities, building magnificent temples, gymnasiums, and other structures for their fellow citizens.

Hellenistic kings and aristocrats spent fortunes turning their cities into showcases of art and design. Distinctive styles of building and ornamentation quickly spread from the east to Carthage, Rome, and other communities in the western Mediterranean. Laying out streets on a grid plan became standard in the Mediterranean world, lending a sense of order to urban space. Stone theaters for plays and spectacles, council halls, and roofed colonnades called *stoas* sprang up everywhere, as did baths with heated pools and gymnasium complexes with sports facilities and classrooms.

In all the major Greek cities of the Hellenistic world, architects built on a monumental scale, integrating sculpture with surrounding buildings and the natural landscape. Temple precincts reveal designers' delight in sweeping vistas across carefully planned terraces and grand stairways. Redefined by these features, the natural setting served as a backdrop for the temple and its processions and rituals.

The freestanding sculpture that decorated public spaces in Hellenistic cities took classical Greek forms in new directions. Turning away from representations of ideal perfection, Hellenistic artists delighted in exploring the movement of the human body and varieties of facial expression. Their subjects ranged from alluring love goddesses to drunks and haggard old boxers. Artists enjoyed portraying the play of fabrics across the human body to accentuate the contours of male and female flesh. Sometimes painted in

Greek Athletics and Culture

This model of the Greek city of Priene in modern Turkey depicts it as it looked in the fourth century B.C.E. The gymnasium complex, with its exercise fields and long colonnade, can be seen at the bottom of the picture. Athletic competition was a significant part of Greek culture. Every self-respecting Greek city had at least one gymnasium. More than just sports centers, gymnasiums served as centers of education and social life for Greek-speaking communities. In these clusters of colonnaded porticoes, wealthy young men of the city learned the basics of Greek literature, rhetoric, science, and music from teachers paid with public funds. For centuries gymnasiums produced leaders and carriers of Hellenistic culture. Here lies the paradox of Hellenism: At the same time that gymnasiums created a shared culture and sense of unity over an enormous geographical extent, they also established a sense of exclusivity and distance from people who did not speak Greek.

Aphrodite of Melos: The Hellenistic Portrayal of the Perfect Female

Perhaps the best-known female statue surviving from antiquity is that of Aphrodite of Melos, popularly known as the Venus di Milo (her Italian name). Sculpted from marble in the second century B.C.E., the goddess is half-nude. She rests on her right foot and seems to step forward toward the viewer. Though her arms are missing today, originally one arm was probably raised to cover her breasts in a gesture of modesty. Her facial expression is serene. The garment draped loosely around her hips gave an artist the opportunity to explore the play of thin cloth over her thighs, expressing his delight in movement and physicality. Somewhat more sedate than other voluptuous representations of Aphrodite, the goddess of love, this statue portrays a male vision of a perfect woman, highly sexual but also charmingly modest.

Nude statues of Aphrodite meant to be erotic and provoke sexual feelings in men became popular in the Hellenistic Age as the result of changing male attitudes about women. Greek women in the Classical Age led secluded lives at home, with no role to play in warfare, politics, debate, or intellectual pursuits. Men appreciated women primarily as mothers and maintainers of the household, not as objects of sexual desire. Statues of women in the Classical Age generally presented them as heavily draped to protect their bodies from the stares of men. In this misogynistic environment, homoeroticism flourished, and men idealized young men as suitable objects of their love and sexual desire.

In the Hellenistic Age, Greek women achieved more social freedom. Although still excluded from politics, women won greater legal rights and participated more fully in activities outside the home. One consequence of women's changed status in the polis was that men began to appreciate them more fully as objects of sexual desire. Male intellectuals debated whether sex with young men or with young women was better for men, and male artists began portraying women as an erotic ideal. Men created nudes like Aphrodite of Melos for other men to enjoy. It is not known what Hellenistic women thought of these statues.

For Discussion

What does this work of art tell us about attitudes toward sexuality and the status of women in the Hellenistic Age?

In order to appreciate the beauty of a work of art, is it necessary to understand the values of the society in which it was made? Is it possible for a work of art to be meaningful or beautiful at another time or place but not today?

Aphrodite of Melos
Aphrodite, the goddess of sexual love, displayed the perfection of the female form. This marble statue found on the Greek island of Melos was carved in the second century B.C.E.

bright colors, these statues explored human frailty and homeliness as often as they celebrated beauty and lofty emotions.

As we saw in Chapter 3, citizenship in the city-states of classical Greece was a carefully limited commodity that gave people a sense of identity, guaranteed desirable rights and privileges, and demanded certain responsibilities. The territories controlled by any city-state were relatively small, yet even Athens at the height of its empire never considered giving Athenian citizenship to all of the people it ruled outside Attica. In contrast, during the Hellenistic Age, large kingdoms containing many cities were the basic political units. People were subjects of a king and citizens of their particular cities. To be sure, some philosophers played with the idea of a universal citizenship of all humankind, but there was no notion of a citizenship shared by all the people in one kingdom. Citizenship lost its political force because individual cities had lost their political autonomy. In a sharp break with earlier practice, important individuals sometimes gained the honor of citizenship in more than one city, something that Greeks in the Classical Age would have found inconceivable.

Hellenistic cities contained more diverse populations than had classical poleis. Alexandria, in Egypt, the largest and most cosmopolitan of Greek cities, boasted large communities of Macedonians, Greeks, Jews, Syrians, and Egyptians. Although these groups lived in different areas of the city and often fought violently with one another, they all participated to varying degrees in the Hellenistic culture of the city. For example, Alexandrian Jews who spoke Greek translated the Hebrew Bible into Greek, a version called the Septuagint°, so that they could more easily read and understand it.

In some older cities such as Babylon and Jerusalem, deep-seated cultural and religious traditions prevented the complete penetration of Greek civilization. Many traditional customs and forms of religious worship, such as the Babylonian worship of the great god Marduk, continued untouched by the Greek way of life. Even the Greek language found limited use in local government. In Mesopotamian cities, for example, local administrators continued to use Aramaic, the local language. The leading families of these cities learned Greek, however, so they could communicate with the members of the king's government and gain political influence.

New Opportunities for Women

One measure of the status of women in a society is the level of female infanticide. Greek parents in the Classical Age routinely abandoned unwanted female babies, leaving them to die. In Hellenistic families, however, particularly those of the Ptolemaic nobility, baby girls were raised in greater numbers than before. Greek women in Egypt, as well as

many other Hellenized lands, enjoyed full citizenship and held religious offices. Many owned land and property, paying taxes as men did, but they could enter into business contracts only of minimal value.

Women in the upper levels of Hellenistic society had the opportunity to wield considerably more power than was conceivable for aristocratic women in the classical Greek period. The wives of Hellenistic kings emerged as models of the new, more powerful Hellenistic woman. Inscriptions engraved in stone praise Hellenistic queens for demonstrating such traditional female virtues as piety and for producing sons. As public benefactors, these women built sanctuaries and public works, sponsored charioteers at the Olympic Games, and provided dowries for poor brides. Queens sometimes exerted real authority, supporting and commanding armies. For example, in Egypt the Ptolemaic queen Arsinoë II (r. 276–270 B.C.E.), sister and wife of Ptolemy II of Egypt, directed the armies and navies of the Ptolemaic kingdom in their conquest of Phoenicia and much of the coast of Asia Minor. Egyptian sources refer to her as Pharaoh, a royal title usually reserved for men. The reverence paid to her was also related to the worship of the goddess Isis, with whom she was often identified.

To a lesser extent, opportunities for nonaristocratic Greek women also increased during the Hellenistic Age. In Alexandria young women received education in dancing, music, rudimentary reading and writing, and scholarship and philosophy. Often the daughters of scholars became scholars in their own right. Although their work is lost, we know that women wrote about astronomy, musical theory, and literature, and many female poets competed for honors. A few Hellenistic women distinguished themselves as portrait painters, architects, and harpists. Despite these accomplishments, women still had fewer rights and opportunities than men, and they remained under the supervision of their male relatives. In Egypt, a woman still could not travel overnight without her husband's permission.

Hellenistic Literature, Philosophy, and Science

The Hellenistic Age witnessed the continuation of some trends in classical Greek scholarship while promoting some striking innovations in literature, philosophy, and science.

Literature: Poetry and History Writing

Much Hellenistic literature has vanished, but some surviving works give a glimpse of creativity and originality, which often combined urbanity and thoughtful scholarship. Hellenistic poets turned to frivolous themes because the repressive political climate discouraged questioning of authority. Light comedy became immensely popular, especially in the hands of the playwright Menander of Athens (ca. 300 B.C.E.). This clever author delighted audiences with escapist, frothy tales of temporarily frustrated love and happy endings. These plays, known now as New Comedy, developed from the risqué satires of classical Athens. They featured vivid street language and a cast of stock characters: crotchety parents, naive young men and silly young women, tricky slaves, and wicked pimps.

Theocritus (ca. 300–ca. 260 B.C.E.), who came from Syracuse but wrote in Alexandria in the 270s B.C.E., invented a new genre called pastoral poetry. His verses described idyllic life in the countryside, but his coarse herdsmen reflect the sadness and tensions of city life. Of all the Hellenistic poets, Theocritus has had the most wide-ranging and enduring influence, providing a model for pastoral verse in Rome, Shakespeare's England, and even nineteenth-century Russia. The other great poet from Alexandria, Callimachus (ca. 305–240 B.C.E.), combined playfulness with extraordinary learning in works ranging from *Collections of Wonders of the World* to his moving love poems, the *Elegies*. His poetry provides the best example of the erudite style known as Alexandrianism, which demonstrated a command of meter and language and appealed more to the intellect than to the emotions.

Powerful Hellenistic monarchs influenced the writing of history. Kings wanted flattering accounts of their deeds, not the probing, critical independence of mind that Thucydides had offered in the classical period. Some writers resisted these pressures, however. Hieronymous of Cardia, a professional administrator who lived to age 104, described nearly three generations of political intrigue that followed Alexander's death. His conclusion? Fortune, not the efforts of mighty kings, determines the affairs of men.

Philosophy: The Quest for Peace of Mind

The study of philosophy continued to flourish in the Hellenistic world. Plato's Academy and Aristotle's Lyceum remained in operation in Athens, drawing intellectually curious men from around the Mediterranean. In this environment several new schools of philosophy arose. Three of them in particular—the Epicureans, the Stoics, and the Cynics—shared the common goal of overcoming what they called disturbance, thereby acquiring an inner tranquility or peace of mind. According to Xenocrates (d. 314 B.C.E.), the head of the Platonic Academy, the purpose of studying philosophy "is to allay what causes disturbance in life."

The first of these philosophical schools, the Epicureans°, was founded by Epicurus of Samos (341–271 B.C.E.). Known by its meeting place, the Garden, this school was open to women and slaves as well as free men. Because Epicurus believed that "the entire world lives in pain," he urged people to gain tranquility in their troubled souls through the rational choice of pleasure. The word *epicurean* today denotes a person of discriminating taste who takes pleasure in eating and drinking, but the pleasure Epicurus sought was intellectual, a perfect harmony of body and mind. To achieve this harmony Epicurus recommended a

virtuous and simple life, characterized by plain living and withdrawal from the stressful world of politics and social competition. Epicurus also reassured his students that they should fear neither death nor the gods. There was no reason to fear death because the soul was material; hence there was no afterlife. Nor was there any reason to fear the gods, who lived in a happy condition far from Earth, unconcerned with human activity. With these fears assuaged, humans could find inner peace.

The main rival to Epicureanism was Stoicism°, the school established by Zeno of Cition (ca. 335–ca. 263 B.C.E.) at Athens in 300 B.C.E. Taking its name from the Stoa Poikile (the Painted Portico) where Zeno and his successors taught, Stoicism remained influential well into the time of the Roman Empire. Stoics believed that all human beings have an element of divinity in them and therefore participate in one single indissoluble cosmic process. They could find peace of mind by submitting to that cosmic order, which Stoics identified with nature or fate. Thus the word *stoic* today carries the meaning of a person who responds to pain or misfortune without showing passion or feeling. Stoics believed that wise men did not allow the vicissitudes of life to distract them. Rather than calling for withdrawal from the world, like the Epicureans, Stoicism encouraged people to participate actively in public life. Because Stoicism accepted the status quo, many kings and aristocrats embraced it. They wanted to believe that their success formed part of a cosmic, divine plan.

Cynics° took a different approach to gaining peace of mind. Inspired by Antisthenes (ca. 445–360 B.C.E.), a devoted follower of Socrates, the Cynics taught that the key to happiness was the rejection of all needs and desires. To achieve this goal, Cynics rejected all pleasures and possessions, leading a life of asceticism. Diogenes (ca. 412–324 B.C.E.), the chief representative of this philosophy, made his home in an empty barrel. Cynics manifested contempt for the customs and conventions of society, including wealth, social position, and prevailing standards of morality. One prominent Cynic, Crates of Thebes (ca. 328 B.C.E.), caused a public scandal when he did the unthinkable: He took his wife, the philosopher Hipparchia, out for a meal in public instead of leaving her at home where respectable women belonged. The word *cynic* today usually refers to a person who sneeringly denies the sincerity of human motives and actions. Some Cynics took the doctrine of Diogenes to extremes by satisfying, rather than denying, their simplest natural needs. Their behavior, which included public masturbation and defecation, repelled so many people that their philosophy failed to have a lasting impact.

Explaining the Natural World: Scientific Investigation

While Athens remained the hub of philosophy in the Hellenistic Age, the Ptolemaic kings made Alexandria the preeminent center of scientific learning. These monarchs sponsored scientific research and lectures on the natural world by professional scholars at an institution called the Museum. Nearby, the Library housed hundreds of thousands of texts that attempted to organize the knowledge of the world. In addition to summarizing the work of previous scholars, Hellenistic scientists sought to depict the world as

Comedy Mosaic from Pompeii
Brilliant decorative mosaics have survived in great numbers from the Hellenistic world. Often derived from Greek paintings, which have entirely disappeared, these scenes give a vivid glimpse into everyday life. This mosaic is based on a scene from a comedy performed in a theater. We can almost hear the music as street entertainers play and dance in front of a rich man's house.

it actually was. This emphasis on realism involved the rejection of some of the more speculative notions that had characterized classical Greek science.

In mathematics, Euclid (ca. 300 B.C.E.) produced a masterful synthesis of the knowledge of geometry in his great work, the *Elements*, which remained the standard geometry textbook until the twentieth century. Euclid demonstrated how one could attain knowledge by rational methods alone—by mathematical reasoning through the use of deductive proofs and theorems. Equally famous as a theorist and engineer was Archimedes of Syracuse (ca. 287–212 B.C.E.), who calculated the value of pi (the ratio of a circle's circumference to its diameter) and measured the diameter of the sun. A sophisticated mechanical engineer, Archimedes reputedly said: "Give me a fulcrum and I will move the world." Archimedes put his scientific knowledge to work in wartime. During the Roman siege of Syracuse in 212 B.C.E., he built a huge reflecting mirror that focused the

CHRONOLOGY

Hellenistic Literature, Science, and Philosophy

ca. 445–360 B.C.E.	Antisthenes founds the Cynic School at Athens
390–320 B.C.E.	Heraclides of Pontus notes that some planets orbit the sun
ca. 350 B.C.E.	First books on human anatomy are written
310–230 B.C.E.	Aristarchus of Samos establishes heliocentric theory
ca. 310–230 B.C.E.	Pytheas of Marseilles explores coasts of the North Sea
ca. 295 B.C.E.	Ptolemy I founds Museum and Library in Alexandria in Egypt; Menander of Athens writes New Comedy; Zeno of Cition teaches Stoicism at Athens; Euclid writes *Elements of Geometry*
287–212 B.C.E.	Archimedes of Syracuse calculates the value of pi
276–194 B.C.E.	Eratosthenes of Cyrene calculates the Earth's circumference
ca. 190–127 B.C.E.	Hipparchus of Nicaea argues that the Earth is the center of the universe
140s B.C.E.	Polybius writes history of Rome's rise to world power
60s–40s B.C.E.	Cicero writes on rhetoric and philosophy at Rome
129–199 C.E.	Galen codifies Hellenistic medical knowledge

bright Sicilian sun on Roman warships, burning holes in their decks.

Astronomy advanced as well during the Hellenistic Age. In their research, Hellenistic investigators borrowed from the long tradition of precisely recorded observation of the heavens that Babylonian and Egyptian scholars had established. This intersection of Middle Eastern and Greek astronomical work produced one of the richest new areas of knowledge in the Hellenistic world. For example, Heraclides of Pontus (ca. 388–312 B.C.E.) anticipated a heliocentric (sun-centered) theory of the universe when he observed that Venus and Mercury orbit the sun, not Earth. Aristarchus of Samos (ca. 310–230 B.C.E.) established the idea that the planets revolve around the sun while spinning on their own axes. Eratosthenes of Cyrene (ca. 276–194 B.C.E.) made a calculation of the Earth's circumference that came within 200 miles of the actual figure.

The sun-centered view never caught on because of fierce opposition from the followers of Aristotle, whose geocentric (Earth-centered) theories had become canonical. Instead, Hipparchus of Nicaea (ca. 190–127 B.C.E.), who produced the first catalog of stars, insisted that the Earth was the center of the universe. The geocentric view of the universe prevailed until the sixteenth century C.E., when the Polish astronomer Nicholas Copernicus, who had read the work of Heraclides and Aristarchus, provided mathematical data to support the heliocentric theory (see Chapter 16).

Medical theory and research also flourished in the great Hellenistic cities. Diocles, a Greek doctor of the fourth century B.C.E. who combined theory and practice, wrote the first handbook on human anatomy and invented a spoonlike tool for removing arrowheads from the human body that physicians used on King Philip of Macedon. Doctors during this period believed that human behavior as well as disease were products of the interactions of fluids in the body, called humors. They argued about whether to categorize the humors as hot, cold, wet, and dry; as earth, water, fire, and air; or as blood, phlegm, yellow bile, and black bile. Praxagoras of Cos (late fourth century B.C.E.) argued that the body contained more than a dozen kinds of humors. He also studied the relation of the brain to the spinal cord. Other doctors, such as Herophilus and Erasistratus, who lived in Alexandria in the fourth century B.C.E., systematically dissected human cadavers. They also may have practiced vivisection, operating on living subjects to study their organs. There is some evidence that with the king's permission they conducted experiments on condemned criminals who had not yet been executed, a practice that is outlawed today. Through dissection these physicians learned a great deal about the human nervous system, the structure of the eye, and reproductive physiology.

The Hellenistic medical tradition continued long after the Hellenistic age came to an end. Galen (129–199 C.E.), the greatest doctor of antiquity, organized Hellenistic medical knowledge, producing accurate, realistic descriptions of human anatomy, and formulated a theory regarding the motion of the blood from the liver to the veins that was not replaced until William Harvey discovered the circulation of the blood in the seventeenth century (see Chapter 16). Galen's theories, like many other aspects of Hellenistic culture, had a profound impact on Western scholarship during the Middle Ages.

Encounters with Foreign Peoples

During the Hellenistic Age, Greeks encountered large numbers of foreign peoples, and the effects of these interactions laid some of the foundations of the West. The encounters took place when Greeks explored the unknown regions in Africa and Europe; when Hellenistic culture met with resistance from Babylonians, Egyptians, and Hebrews; and when Celtic peoples migrated to the boundaries of the Hellenistic world.

Exploring the Hellenistic World

A spirit of inquiry—combined with hunger for trade and profit—drove men to explore and map the unknown world during the Hellenistic Age (see Map 4.4). Explorers supported by monarchs ventured into the Caspian, Aral, and Red Seas. By the second century B.C.E., Greeks had established trading posts along the coasts of modern Eritrea and Somalia, where merchants bought goods, particularly ivory, transported from the interior of Africa. Hellenistic people also craved pepper, cinnamon, and other spices and luxury goods from India, but Arab middlemen made direct trade nearly impossible. One intrepid navigator named Eudoxus made an unsuccessful attempt to find a sea route to India by sailing down both the east and west coasts of Africa, but he never got farther than Morocco.

The most ambitious and successful of all Hellenistic explorers was Pytheas of Marseilles (ca. 380–306 B.C.E.). Setting out from the Greek city of Gades (the modern Spanish port of Cadiz) in about 310 B.C.E., he sailed around Britain and reported the existence of either Iceland or Norway. He may even have reached the Vistula River in Poland. Throughout his journeys Pytheas contributed much to navigational knowledge by recording astronomical bearings and natural wonders such as the northern lights.

As these explorers expanded geographical horizons, Greeks developed a lively though condescending interest in the different peoples of the world. Greeks considered themselves culturally superior to non-Greek-speaking peoples,

Map 4.4 Hellenistic Trade and Exploration
During the Hellenistic Age, merchants traveled widely across the breadth of the Mediterranean and throughout the Near East. They sailed into the Persian Gulf and Indian Ocean on commercial ventures. Some explorers sailed along the east and west coasts of Africa as well as Europe's Atlantic coast, reaching Britain and the North Sea.

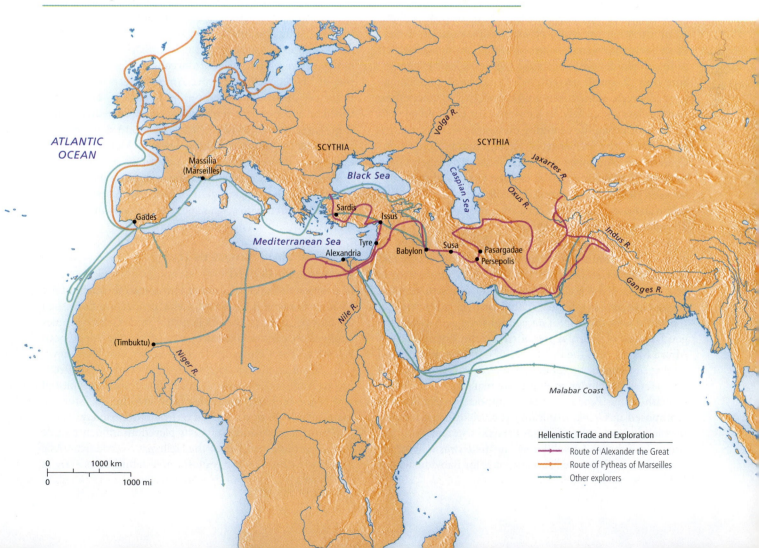

including Jews, Babylonians, Celts, steppe nomads, and sub-Saharan Africans who lived beyond the borders of Hellenistic kingdoms. Greeks considered all of these peoples barbarians. Despite this prejudice, educated men and women throughout the Hellenistic world enjoyed reading accounts in Greek of foreign peoples' customs, myths, natural history, and forms of government.

Knowledge about different peoples often came from non-Greek intellectuals who translated their accounts into Greek. For example, Berosus, a Babylonian priest, wrote a history of his people that provided Greek readers with extensive astronomical knowledge as well. Manetho, an Egyptian priest, composed a history of his land. Hecataeus of Abdera, a Greek, wrote a popular history arguing that Egypt was the site of the origin of civilization. Most of what was known in the West about India until the Middle Ages derived from the reports of Megasthenes, a Seleucid diplomat. Information about the histories and belief systems of their neighbors entertained intellectuals and helped Hellenistic rulers govern their conquered peoples.

Resistance to Hellenistic Culture

Despite this curiosity among educated Greeks about foreign customs, a great barrier of mutual incomprehension and suspicious resentment separated Greeks and their subjects. Language was one such barrier. In most kingdoms, administrators conducted official business only in Greek. Few Greek settlers in the cities or even in far-flung, isolated military colonies ever bothered to learn the local languages, and only a small percentage of the local populations learned Greek. Many communities preferred to ignore their Greek rulers completely. In Babylonia, for example, age-old patterns of urban life centering on temple worship continued outside the influence of Greek culture. Some non-Greeks, however, hoped to rise in the service of their Greek masters. They made an effort to learn Greek and to assimilate into Hellenistic culture. Their collaboration with Greek rulers alienated them from their own people and provoked divisions within native societies.

Many people conquered by the Greeks continued to practice their traditional religions. Still stunned by the loss of their empire, some aristocratic Persians found solace in practicing Zoroastrianism, the traditional Persian religion. As we have seen in Chapter 3, Zoroastrianism teaches that the world is in the grip of an eternal struggle between the good forces of light, represented by the divine creator, Ahura Mazda, and the evil forces of darkness, represented by Angra Mainyu, the demonic destroyer. These Persians interpreted Alexander as Angra Mainyu's agent. In the aftermath of the Persian defeat an important religious text (composed in Greek, ironically) predicted that a military messiah would soon restore Persia's true religion and rulers. In Babylon a book known as the *Dynastic Prophecy* (ca. 300 B.C.E.) expressed similar hopes for Babylonians.

Resentful voices also rang out in Egypt. The *Demotic Chronicle* (ca. 250 B.C.E.) and *The Oracle of the Potter* (ca. 250 B.C.E.) maintained that the Ptolemies had brought the punishment of the gods to Egypt by displacing the pharaohs and interfering with religious customs. One day, the book assured readers, a mighty king would expel the conquerors. Not coincidentally, a series of open rebellions erupted in Egypt about the same time that these works gained popularity.

The Jewish response to Hellenism produced the best-known account of resistance, preserved in the Hebrew Bible as the First and Second Book of Maccabees. After Alexander's death in 323 B.C.E., Jerusalem and Jewish Palestine passed to the control of the Ptolemies and then the Seleucids. The Ptolemaic monarchs at first tolerated Jewish religion and welcomed the rapid assimilation of Jerusalem's priestly aristocracy into Greek culture. Under the rule of these Hellenized priests, a gymnasium and other elements of Greek culture first appeared in Jerusalem. At the same time, however, traditional Jewish worship at the temple in Jerusalem continued.

The situation changed in 167 B.C.E., when the Seleucid king Antiochus IV Epiphanes tried to demonstrate his authority by further Hellenizing the city; when the Jews resisted, his soldiers desecrated the temple by introducing foreign worship there, an abomination in Jewish eyes. Initially, Antiochus intended to advertise his own strength, not to suppress Jewish practice, but his plan backfired. A family of Jewish priests, the Maccabees, began a religious war of liberation. They drove Antiochus's armies out of Palestine, purified the Temple in Jerusalem, and established an independent Jewish kingdom under their rulership. Later, when Jewish writers sought to explain their actions to the Greek-speaking Jews of Alexandria, they described their struggle in terms of resistance to Hellenism. However, the Maccabean dynasty that had led the victorious struggle against Hellenism soon adopted many Greek customs, causing deep rifts within Jewish society.

Celts on the Fringes of the Hellenistic World

In addition to the Greek culture that spread throughout the Mediterranean and Near East, Celtic civilization flourished in Europe during the Hellenistic Age. Celtic peoples emerged in continental Europe north of the Alps about 750 B.C.E. The Celts, who lived in tribes that were never politically unified on a large scale, shared common dialects, metal- and pottery-making techniques, and agricultural and home-building methods. They are the ancestors of many peoples of northern and central Europe today.

Through trade and war, Celts played an influential role on the northern margins of the Hellenistic world from Asia Minor to Spain. Trading routes were established as early as the eighth century B.C.E., but commerce was often interrupted by war. The military activities of Celtic tribes restricted the expansion of Hellenistic kingdoms, thereby pressuring them to strengthen their military capacities.

Archaeologists call the first Celtic civilization in central Europe Hallstatt° culture, because of excavations in Hallstatt, Austria. Around 750 B.C.E., Hallstatt Celts started to spread from their homeland into Italy, the Balkans, Ireland, Spain, and Asia Minor, conquering local peoples on the way. These people left no written records, so we know little of their political practices. The luxury goods and weapons left in their graves, however, indicate a stratified society led by a warrior elite. Hallstatt sites were heavily fortified, suggesting frequent warfare among communities. Men gained status through competitive exchange of gifts, raiding, and valor in battle. In southern France, Celts encountered Hellenistic civilization at the Greek city of Massilia (modern Marseilles). There they participated in lively trade along the Rhône River for Greek luxury goods, including wine and drinking goblets.

In the middle of the fifth century B.C.E. a new phase in Celtic civilization began, called La Tène° culture, which takes its name from a site in modern Switzerland. More weapons appeared in tombs than in the Hallstatt period, indicating intensified warfare. La Tène Celts developed new

centers of wealth and power, especially in the valleys of the Rhine and Danube Rivers. They also founded large, fortified settlements in these regions as well as in present-day France and England.

La Tène craftsmen benefited from new trade routes across the Alps to northern Italy, the home of Etruscan merchants and artisans. Etruscans traded bronze statuettes to the Celtic north, and they may have also introduced the two-wheeled fighting chariots found in aristocratic Celtic tombs. Greek styles in art reached the Celts through these Etruscan intermediaries, but Celtic artists developed their own distinctive style of metalwork and sculpture. Many Celtic communities began to use coinage, which they adopted from the Greeks.

For about a century relations between the Celtic and Mediterranean peoples centered on trade, but around 400 B.C.E. overpopulation in central Europe instigated massive migrations of Celtic tribes. In 387 B.C.E. one migrating group of Celts sacked the city of Rome. Their invasion had an unexpected effect on Roman military technology: The Romans began to use the highly effective Celtic short sword, which became the standard weapon of the Roman legions.

This period of hostile migrations lasted until 200 B.C.E. Some Celts traveled to lands that are Slavic today (Slovakia

---

DOCUMENT

A Jewish Martyr for a Hellenistic Audience

This excerpt from the narrative of II Maccabees in the Greek version of the Hebrew Bible tells the tragic tale of an old Jew who endured martyrdom for his refusal to compromise with Hellenistic life. Written for a Greek-speaking Jewish audience in Alexandria, the story is told with many allusions to Plato's account of the death of Socrates, demonstrating how Greek ideas had influenced even the enemies of Hellenism.

Eleazar, one of the foremost teachers of the Law, a man already advanced in years and of most noble appearance, had his mouth forced open, to make him eat a piece of pork. But he, resolving to die with honour rather than to live disgraced, walked of his own accord to the torture of the wheel. . . . The people supervising the ritual meal, forbidden by the law, because of the time for which they had known him, took him aside and privately urged him to have meat brought of a kind he could properly use, prepared by himself, and only pretend to eat the portions of sacrificial meat as prescribed by the king; this action would enable him to escape death, by availing himself of an act of kindness prompted by their long friendship. But having taken a noble decision worthy of his years and the dignity of his great age and the well-earned distinction of his grey hairs, worthy too of his impeccable conduct from boyhood and about all of the holy legislation established by God himself, he answered accordingly, telling them to send him at once to Hades. "Pretence, he said, does not befit our time of life. Many young people would suppose that Eleazar at the age of ninety had conformed to the foreigners' way of life and because I had played this part for the sake of a paltry brief spell of my life, might themselves be led astray on my account; I should only bring defilement and disgrace on my old age. Even though for the moment I avoid execution by man, I can never elude the grasp of the Almighty. Therefore if I am man enough to quit this life here and now, I shall have left the young a noble example of how to make a good death, eagerly and generously, for the venerable and holy laws." So saying he walked straight to the wheel . . .

Source: Excerpt from *The New Jerusalem Bible,* copyright © 1985 by Darton, Longman & Todd, Ltd. and Doubleday, a division of Random House, Inc. Reprinted by permission.

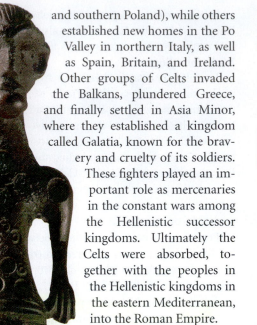

and southern Poland), while others established new homes in the Po Valley in northern Italy, as well as Spain, Britain, and Ireland. Other groups of Celts invaded the Balkans, plundered Greece, and finally settled in Asia Minor, where they established a kingdom called Galatia, known for the bravery and cruelty of its soldiers. These fighters played an important role as mercenaries in the constant wars among the Hellenistic successor kingdoms. Ultimately the Celts were absorbed, together with the peoples in the Hellenistic kingdoms in the eastern Mediterranean, into the Roman Empire.

Rome's Rise to Power

■ **How did the Roman Republic come to dominate the Mediterranean world during the Hellenistic Age, and how did Roman rule over the Hellenistic East affect Rome's development?**

From Rome's Capitoline Hill a tourist today can look down on the Roman Forum and see a large field of broken buildings and monuments. These remains lie at the heart of what was once an enormous empire extending from northern England to Iraq and from Morocco to the Black Sea. On the western slope of the neighboring Palatine Hill, archaeologists have uncovered hut foundations from the city's earliest occupants in the tenth century B.C.E. How the Roman Empire emerged from this crude village above a swamp remains one of the most remarkable stories in the history of the West.

During the Hellenistic Age, Rome expanded from being a relatively small city-state with a republican form of government into a vast and powerful empire. As it conquered the peoples who ringed the Mediterranean—the Carthaginians, the Celts, and the Hellenistic kingdoms of Alexander's successors—Rome incorporated these newcomers into the political structure of the republic. Trying to govern these sprawling territories with institutions and social traditions suited for a city-state overwhelmed the Roman Republic° and led to the establishment of a new form of government, the Roman Empire, by the end of the first century B.C.E.

Roman Origins and Etruscan Influences

Interaction with outsiders shaped the story of Rome from its very beginning. Resting on low but easily defensible hills covering a few hundred acres above the Tiber River, Rome lies at the intersection of north-south and east-west trade routes that

Celtic Warriors
These two Celtic statuettes of fighting men reveal the impact of Hellenistic art on native traditions. The first warrior, who stands stiffly and without a well-articulated anatomy, is the product of Celtic artistic traditions untouched by Greek art. The second figure shows the influence of Greek styles. He is well-balanced to throw a spear. His muscles are clearly understood and he turns convincingly in space.

had been used in Italy since the Neolithic Age. Romans used these same routes to develop a thriving commerce with other peoples, many of whom they eventually conquered and absorbed into their Roman polity.

Settlements began in Rome about 1000 B.C.E., but we know little about the lives of these first inhabitants. So small was the scale of village life that clusters of huts on the different hills may have constituted entirely different communities. What would one day be the Forum°—the place of assembly for judicial and other public business—was an undrained marsh, which villagers used as protection and burial grounds.

Control of the Tiber River crossing and trade allowed Rome to grow quickly. Excavated graves from the eighth century B.C.E. reveal that a wealthy elite or aristocracy had already emerged. Women evidently shared the benefits of increased prosperity. One grave contained a woman buried with her chariot, a symbol of authority and status. In the course of the seventh century the Roman population increased rapidly. Extended families or clans emerged as a force in Roman life. Throughout this early period of Roman history, according to Roman legend, kings exercised political authority.

Historians think that Latin, the Roman language, was only one of at least 140 distinct languages and dialects spoken by Italy's frequently warring communities during the first four centuries of Rome's existence. During this period, Romans developed their military skills in order to defend themselves against their neighbors. Nevertheless, the Romans had amicable relations with some neighbors—particularly the Etruscans, who lived northwest of Rome.

In the sixth and seventh centuries B.C.E., Etruscan culture strongly influenced that of Rome. Like the Romans, the Etruscans° descended from indigenous prehistoric Italian peoples. By 800 B.C.E., they were firmly established in Etruria (modern Tuscany), a region in central Italy between the Arno and Tiber rivers. By the sixth century B.C.E. they controlled territory as far south as the Bay of Naples and

Map 4.5 Celtic Expansion, Fifth to Third Century B.C.E.

During the Hellenistic Age, Celtic peoples migrated into many parts of Europe and Asia Minor. This map shows their routes.

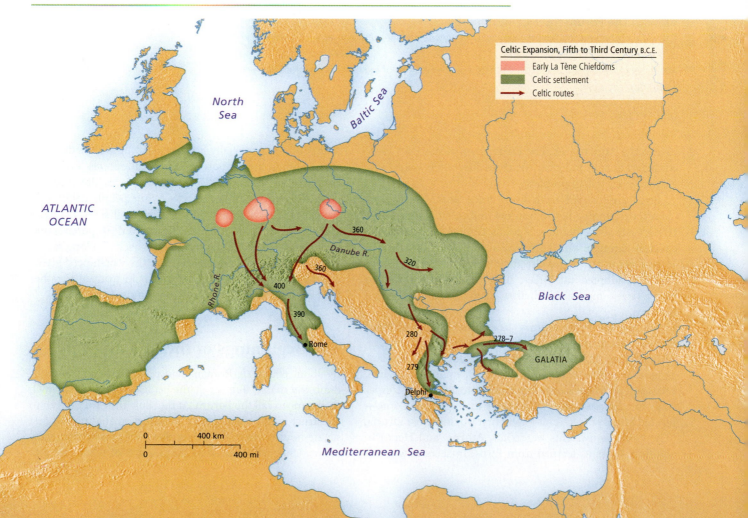

View of the Forum from Capitoline Hill
This view down into the Forum valley was taken from the site of the temple of Jupiter, Rome's mightiest god. All victory processions after a successful war would have ended at this temple, where sacrifices were made. Now tourists visit the remains of buildings from which Rome ruled an international empire.

east to the Adriatic Sea. The Etruscans maintained a loose confederation of independent cities that often waged war against other Italian peoples.

Etruscans carried on a lively trade with Greek merchants, exchanging native iron ore and other resources for Greek vases and other luxury goods. Commerce became the conduit through which Etruscans and later Romans absorbed many aspects of Greek culture. The Etruscans, for example, adopted the Greek alphabet and subscribed to many Greek myths, which they later transmitted to the Romans.

During the sixth century B.C.E., the Etruscans ruled Rome, influencing its religion and temple architecture. Although the Etruscans and Romans spoke different languages, a common culture deriving from native Italian, Etruscan, and Greek communities gradually evolved, especially in religious practice. The three main gods of Rome—Jupiter, Minerva, and Juno—were first worshiped in Etruria. (The Greek equivalents were Zeus, Athena, and Hera.) In addition, Romans learned from Etruscan seers how to in-

terpret omens, especially how to learn the will of the gods by examining the entrails of sacrificed animals. Etruscans also gave the Romans a distinctive temple architecture that differed from that of the Greeks. While people could walk around a Greek temple and see it from all sides, Etruscan and eventually Roman temples featured deep porches and were placed on a high platform at the back of a long sacred enclosure. This positioning directed the worshipers' attention to the god's temple and the altar in front of it rather than the building's placement in the landscape.

The Beginnings of the Roman State

By about 600 B.C.E. Romans had prospered sufficiently to drain the marsh that lay at the center of their city, which they came to call the Forum. At the same time they began to construct temples and public buildings, including the first senate house, where the elders met to discuss community affairs. Under the rule of its kings, some of whom were of

Etruscan origin, Rome became an important military power in Italy. Only free male inhabitants of the city who could afford their own weapons voted in the citizen assembly, which made public decisions with the advice of the senate. Poor men could fight but not vote. Thus began the struggle between rich and poor that would plague Roman life for centuries.

About 500 B.C.E., when Rome had become a powerful city with perhaps as many as 35,000 inhabitants, the Romans put an end to kingship and began a new system of government that historians call the Roman Republic. According to legend, in 509 B.C.E. a courageous aristocrat named Brutus overthrew the tyrannical Etruscan king, Tarquin the Arrogant. After the coup, Roman aristocrats established several new institutions in place of the kingship that structured political life for 500 years. An assembly comprising Rome's male citizens, called the Centuriate Assembly because of the units of 100 into which the population was divided, managed the city's legislative, judicial, and administrative affairs. As in the Greek poleis, only men participated in battle and public life. Each year, the assembly elected two chief executives called consuls, who could apply the law but whose decisions could be appealed. As time went on, the assembly also selected additional officers to deal with legal and financial responsibilities. A body of elders, called the Senate, comprising about 300 Romans who had held administrative offices, advised the consuls, though they had no formal authority. Priests performed religious ceremonies on behalf of the city.

Hatred of kings, which became a staple of Roman political thought, prevented any one man from becoming too prominent. A relatively small group of influential families held real power within the political community, by both holding offices and working behind the scenes. This kind of government is known as an oligarchy, or "the rule of the few."

To celebrate the end of the monarchy, the people of Rome built a grand new temple to Jupiter on the Capitoline Hill, looking down on the Forum. Probably at the same time the Romans also established the community of Vestal Virgins as caretakers of the sacred fire and hearth in the Temple of Vesta, one of Rome's most ancient religious sites. In such ways the welfare of Rome became a shared public concern.

Tensions between the rich and the poor shaped political and social life at Rome during the Republic. At the top of the social hierarchy stood the patricians°, aristocratic clans whose high status extended to the days of the kings. These men, including the legendary Brutus, had been responsible for toppling the monarchy. Because they monopolized the magistracies and the priesthoods, they occupied most of the seats in the Senate. Other rich landowners and senators with lesser pedigrees, as well as the prosperous farmers who made up the army's phalanxes, joined the patricians in resisting the plebeians°, the poorest segments of society. The

plebeians demanded more political rights, such as a fair share of distributed public land and freedom from debt bondage. These efforts of poor Romans to acquire a political voice, called the Struggle of the Orders°, accelerated during the fifth century B.C.E., when Rome experienced a severe economic recession.

A victory in the plebeians' struggle came in 494 B.C.E., when they won the right to elect two tribunes each year as their spokesmen. Tribunes could veto magistrates' decisions and so block arbitrary judicial actions by the patricians. Then, in 471 B.C.E., a new Plebeian Assembly gave plebeians the opportunity to express their political views in a formal setting, although without the formal authority to enact actual legislation. About 450 B.C.E., the plebeians took another major step forward with the publication of the Law of the Twelve Tables. Until that time, Romans did not write down their laws, and aristocrats often arbitrarily interpreted and applied laws to the disadvantage of the poor. The plebeians pressed for codification and public display of the law to ensure that the rights of all free Romans would be recognized and respected. The Twelve Tables covered all aspects of life from the proper protection of women ("Women shall remain under the guardianship [of a man] even when they have reached legal adulthood") and debt bondage ("Unless he pays his debt or someone stands surety for him in court, bind him in a harness, or in chains . . . ") to religious matters. Even when cruel, the law could now be applied uniformly.

The plebeians continued to make their presence felt in Roman life. In 445 B.C.E., a new law permitted marriage between plebeians and patricians. This enabled wealthy plebeians to marry into aristocratic families. A high point came in 367 B.C.E., when politicians agreed that one of each year's two consuls should come from the plebeian class. The plebeians now were fully integrated within the Roman government. Moreover, around the same time Romans limited the amount of public land that could be distributed to any citizen. The new arrangement prevented aristocrats from seizing the lion's share of conquered territories and permitted poor citizen soldiers to receive a share of captured land. The last concession to the plebeians came in 287 B.C.E., when the decisions of the Plebeian Assembly became binding on the whole state. The plebeians acquired their political strength and full acceptance in the political arena by simple extortion: They threatened to leave the army if the aristocratic elite failed to meet their demands. Without the plebeians, who constituted the bulk of the Roman army, the Republic could not protect itself from invaders or conquer new lands.

The political success of the plebeians resulted in the formation of a new upper class in Rome, consisting of wealthy patrician and plebeian families. At the same time a new underclass of slaves emerged as the result of military expansion in Italy. Poor Roman farmers eagerly settled in newly conquered territories. These farmers in turn served as soldiers in further wars of expansion in which Romans enslaved other conquered peoples. Thus a self-perpetuating cycle of conquest, settlement, and enslavement began to take shape, reaching full development after 200 B.C.E.

Roman Territorial Expansion

During the period of the Republic, Rome conquered and incorporated all of Italy, the vast Carthaginian Empire in northern Africa, and Spain, and many of the lands inhabited by Celtic people to the north and west of Italy (see Map 4.6). As a result of these conquests, the Roman state found it necessary to change the methods of government established in the fifth century B.C.E.

Winning Control of Italy

The new political and military institutions that developed in Rome enabled the Romans to conquer the entire Italian peninsula by 263 B.C.E. In the process the Romans learned the fundamental lessons necessary for ruling much larger territories abroad. Romans began to expand their realm by allying with neighboring cities in Italy. For centuries, Rome and the other Latin-speaking peoples of Latium (the region of central Italy where Rome was situated) had belonged to a

loose coalition of cities called the Latin League. Citizens of these cities shared close commercial and legal ties and could intermarry without losing citizenship rights in their native cities. More important, they forged close military alliances with one another.

In 493 B.C.E. Rome successfully led the Latin cities in battle against fierce hill tribes who coveted Latium's rich farmlands. From the success of this venture, Rome learned the value of political alliances with neighbors. Rome and its allies next confronted the Etruscans. In 396 B.C.E. they overcame the Etruscan city of Veii through a combination of military might and shrewd political maneuvering. From this experience, the Romans discovered the uses of careful diplomacy.

A temporary setback to Rome's expansion occurred in 387 B.C.E., when a raiding band of Celts from the Po Valley in the north of Italy defeated a Roman army and plundered the city of Rome before returning home. Only after a generation did Romans recover from this disaster and reassert their preeminence among their allies. Still, they had learned that tenacity and discipline enabled them to endure even a serious military reversal.

The next major step in Rome's expansion came in 338 B.C.E., when Roman troops smashed a three-year revolt of its Latin allies, who had come to resent Rome's overlordship. The peace settlement set the precedent for Rome's future expansion: Rome permitted defeated peoples to become citizens, giving them either partial or full citizenship depending on the treaty it struck with each community. The conquered allies were permitted to continue their own customs, and were not forced to pay tribute. Rome asked for only two things in return: loyalty and troops. All allied communities had to contribute soldiers to the Roman army in wartime. With the huge new pool of troops, Rome became the strongest power in Italy.

In return for their military service and support of Rome, the newly incorporated citizens, especially aristocrats from the allied communities, received a share of the profits of war. They also received the guarantee of Roman protection from internal dissension or outside threats. Those communities not granted full Roman citizenship rights could hope to earn it if they served Roman interests faithfully. Some communities joined the Roman state willingly. Others, particularly the Samnites of south central Italy, resisted bitterly, but to no avail.

Romans continued their march through Italy, becoming embroiled in the affairs of Greek cities of the "toe" and "heel" of the boot-shaped Italian peninsula. Some of these Greek cities invited King Pyrrhus of Epirus, a Hellenistic adventurer, to wage war against Rome on their behalf. Pyrrhus invaded southern Italy with 25,000 men and twenty elephants. Though he defeated Roman armies in two great battles in 280 B.C.E., he lost nearly two-thirds of his own troops and withdrew from Italy. "Another victory like this and I'm finished for good!" he said to a comrade,

CHRONOLOGY

Rome's Rise to Power

ca. 509 B.C.E.	Roman Republic is created
508 B.C.E.	Romans sign treaty with Carthage
494 B.C.E.	Tribunes of the Plebeians created
474 B.C.E.	Plebeian Assembly is created
ca. 450 B.C.E.	Twelve Tables of Law is published
387 B.C.E.	Celts sack Rome
287 B.C.E.	Laws of Plebeian Assembly become binding on all Romans
280 B.C.E.	Pyrrhus of Epirus is defeated
264–241 B.C.E.	First Punic War
218–201 B.C.E.	Second Punic War
215–168 B.C.E.	Wars with Macedon
149–146 B.C.E.	Third Punic War
148–146 B.C.E.	Macedon and Greece become a Roman province
67–62 B.C.E.	Pompey establishes Roman control over Asia Minor, Syria, and Palestine

giving rise to the expression "a Pyrrhic victory," which is a win so costly that it is ruinous. Without Pyrrhus's protection, the Greeks in southern Italy could not withstand Rome's legions, and by 263 B.C.E. Rome ruled all of Italy.

The Struggle with Carthage

By the third century B.C.E., imperial Carthage dominated the western Mediterranean region. From the capital city of Carthage located on the north African coast near modern Tunis, Carthaginians held rich lands along the African coast from modern Algeria to Morocco, controlled the natural resources of southern Spain, and dominated the sea lanes of the entire region. Phoenician traders had founded Carthage in the eighth century B.C.E., and the city's energetic merchants carried on business with Greeks, Etruscans, Celts, and eventually Romans.

Hellenistic culture deeply affected Carthage as it did other Mediterranean and Middle Eastern cities. During the Classical Age, Carthaginian trade with the Greek cities in Sicily, and likely with Greek artisans in north Africa, introduced many elements of Greek culture to Carthage. For example, Carthaginians worshiped the Greek goddess of agriculture, Demeter, and her daughter, Kore (also called Persephone), in an elegant temple served by Carthaginian priests and priestesses. By the fourth century B.C.E. the Carthaginian Empire was playing an integral role in the economy of the Hellenistic world by exporting agricultural products, raw materials, metal goods, and pottery.

Rome and Carthage were old acquaintances. Eager for widespread recognition at the beginning of the Republic, Roman leaders signed a commercial treaty with Carthage. Several centuries of wary respect and increasing trade followed. In 264 B.C.E., just as Rome established power throughout the Italian peninsula, a complicated war between Greek cities in Sicily drew Rome and Carthage into conflict. When a Carthaginian fleet went to help a Greek city in Sicily, another city asked Rome for assistance in dislodging them. The aristocratic Senate refused, but the Plebeian Assembly, eager for the spoils of war, voted to intercede. Rome invaded Sicily, setting off the First Punic War, so called because the word *Punic* comes from the Latin word for *Phoenician*.

The First Punic War between Rome and Carthage for control of Sicily lasted from 264 to 241 B.C.E. During this time the Romans learned how to fight at sea, cutting off the Carthaginian supply lines to Sicily. In 241 B.C.E. Carthage signed a treaty in which it agreed to surrender Sicily and the surrounding islands and to pay a war indemnity over the course of a decade. Roman treachery, however, wrecked the agreement. While the Carthaginians struggled to suppress a revolt of mercenary soldiers, Rome seized Corsica and Sardinia, over which Carthage had lost effective control,

CHRONOLOGY

Imperial Carthage

ca. 850 B.C.E.	Phoenicians found Carthage
600s B.C.E.	Carthage expands in North Africa, Sardinia, southern Spain, and Sicily
508 B.C.E.	Carthage makes treaty with Rome
500–200 B.C.E.	Conflicts with Greeks in Sicily
264–241 B.C.E.	Carthage fights First Punic War against Rome
218–203 B.C.E.	Hannibal fights in Italy
218–201 B.C.E.	Carthage fights Second Punic War against Rome
202 B.C.E.	Battle of Zama; Hannibal is defeated near Carthage
149–146 B.C.E.	Carthage fights Third Punic War against Rome; end of Carthaginian Empire
146 B.C.E.	Destruction of the city of Carthage

and demanded larger reparations. Roman bad faith stoked Carthaginian hatred and desire for revenge.

War did not resume for another two decades. Under the able leadership of Hamilcar Barca (r. 238–229 B.C.E.), Carthage put its energy into developing resources in Spain, while Rome campaigned against Celts living in the Po Valley and fierce tribes on the Adriatic coast. During these years trade between Rome and Carthage continued, reaching new heights. Soon, however, the rapid growth of Carthaginian power in Spain led to renewed conflict with Rome. The Second Punic War (218–201 B.C.E.) erupted when Hamilcar's son, Hannibal, 25 years old and eager for vengeance, ignored a Roman warning and captured Saguntum, a Spanish town with which Rome had formal ties of friendship. In an imaginative and daring move, Hannibal then launched a surprise attack on Italy by crossing the Alps and invading from the north. With an army of nearly 25,000 men and eighteen elephants, he crushed the Roman armies sent against him. In the first major battle, at the Trebia River in the Po Valley, 20,000 Romans died. At Lake Trasimene in Etruria in 216 B.C.E., another 25,000 Romans fell. In the same year at Cannae, 50,000 men perished in Rome's worst defeat ever.

Despite these staggering losses, the Romans persevered and eventually defeated the Carthaginian general. They succeeded, first of all, because Hannibal lacked sufficient logistical support from Carthage to capitalize on his early victories and take the city of Rome. Second, most of Rome's allies in Italy proved loyal. They had often seen Romans prevail in the past and knew that the Romans took fierce revenge on disloyal friends. Thus the Roman policy of including and

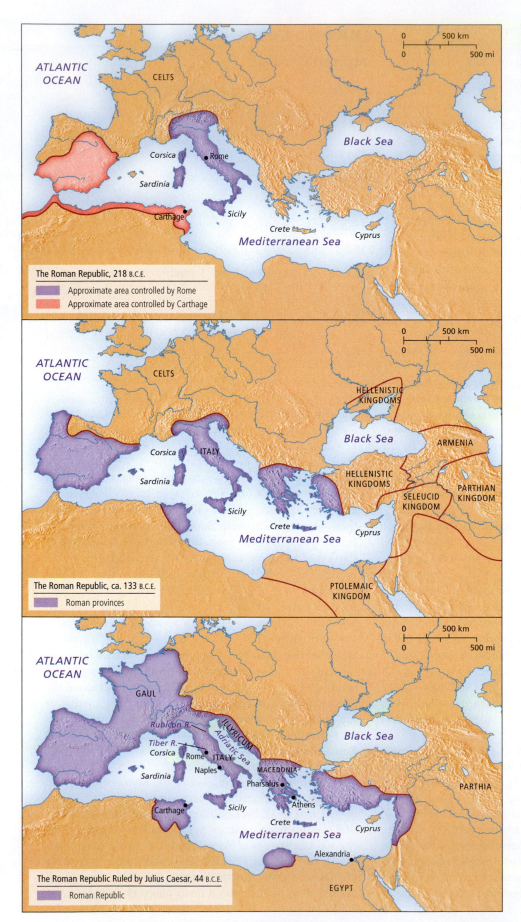

The Roman Republic, 218 B.C.E.

- Approximate area controlled by Rome
- Approximate area controlled by Carthage

The Roman Republic, ca. 133 B.C.E.

- Roman provinces

The Roman Republic Ruled by Julius Caesar, 44 B.C.E.

- Roman Republic

Map 4.6   The Roman Conquest of the Mediterranean During the Republic

Armies of the Roman Republic conquered the Mediterranean world during the Hellenistic Age, overcoming the Carthaginian Empire, the Hellenistic successor kingdoms, and many Celtic peoples in Spain and Gaul.

protecting allies paid off. A third reason for Hannibal's defeat was the indomitable Roman spirit. The Romans simply refused to stop fighting, even after suffering devastating casualties.

The turning point in the war came when Roman commanders adopted a new strategy. After incurring so many defeats, the army dared not face Hannibal in open battle. Instead, Fabius, the Roman commander in Italy, avoided open battle and used guerilla tactics to pin down Hannibal in Italy, thus earning the nickname "the Delayer," while Publius Cornelius Scipio Africanus, the Roman general introduced at the beginning of this chapter, took command of Roman forces in Spain. Within a few years he defeated Carthaginian forces there, cutting completely the thin lines of logistical support to Hannibal. In 204 B.C.E., Scipio led Roman legions into Africa, forcing Carthage to recall Hannibal from Italy in order to protect the city.

In one last effort Hannibal confronted Scipio on Carthaginian soil. At the battle of Zama near Carthage in 202 B.C.E., fortune finally deserted Hannibal. Scipio put an end to his string of victories, forcing him into exile. Hannibal had won every battle but his last. Though Scipio spared Hannibal's life and did not destroy Carthage, the peace treaty transferred all of Carthage's overseas territories to Roman control.

Because the war against Hannibal had claimed so many Roman lives, many vengeful Romans agitated for the total destruction of Carthage. In particular, the statesman Marcus Porcius Cato (234–149 B.C.E.), who ended every public utterance with the demand "Carthage must be destroyed!" goaded Romans to violate the peace treaty and resume war with its old adversary. The Third Punic War (149–146 B.C.E.) resulted in the destruction of Carthage. Survivors were enslaved, and the city was burned to the ground and plowed under with salt. Its territories were reorganized as the Roman provinces of Africa.

DOCUMENT

Plutarch, *The Life of Cato the Elder*

Conflict with the Celts

Celtic peoples in western Europe fiercely resisted Roman military expansion. After Carthaginian power ended in the Iberian peninsula (modern Spain and Portugal) following the Punic Wars, Romans struggled for more than a century to establish their control over the region's natural resources, particularly its metals and rich farmlands. Not until the reign of Augustus (31 B.C.E.–14 C.E.) did the Romans bring the Iberian peninsula under complete control. The constant fighting drained Rome's manpower and contributed to severe economic and political turmoil in the Republic during the second century B.C.E.

Relations with the Celts had not always been acrimonious. The Roman colonies along the Mediterranean coast that formed an administrative unit called "the Province" (modern Provence) traded peacefully and actively with their Gallic Celtic neighbors. By the late second century B.C.E., Rome made military alliances with the Aedui, a Celtic

CHRONOLOGY

The World of the Celts

ca. 400 B.C.E.	Celts expand from central Europe
ca. 390–386 B.C.E.	Celts invade Italy and plunder Rome
281 B.C.E.	Celts kill Macedonian king in battle
279 B.C.E.	Celts invade Greece
270s B.C.E.	Celts establish kingdom in Asia Minor
100s B.C.E.	Romans campaign against Celts in Spain
58–50 B.C.E.	Julius Caesar fights Celts in Gaul

tribe that lived further inland. Peace with the Celts, however, ended in 58 B.C.E., when the Roman general Julius Caesar invaded the part of Gaul that lies across the Alps. There he found numerous Celtic tribes with sophisticated political systems dominated by warrior aristocrats. After eight years of bloody conquest and massacre, Caesar conquered Gaul, turning the region into several Roman provinces that within a century became an integral part of the Roman Empire.

From the sack of Rome by Celts in the fourth century B.C.E. to the incorporation of some Celtic lands into the Roman state at the end of the Republic, the Celts were a significant factor in Roman life. In his *History*, Polybius suggested that the constant threat of Celtic invasion contributed to the growth of Roman military force. The Roman Republic was geared for constant warfare, and the Celts frequently were the enemy. Thus the Celts shaped Roman foreign policy as well as the Roman allocation of military resources.

Rome and the Hellenistic World

By the end of the Punic Wars, Rome had become involved in the affairs of the vigorous Hellenistic kingdoms of the East. Initially reluctant to take direct control of these regions, Roman leaders gradually changed their policies. They assumed responsibility for maintaining order and gradually established absolute control over the entire eastern Mediterranean region.

The Macedonian Wars

Rome waged three wars against Macedon between 215 and 168 B.C.E. that resulted in mastery of Macedon and Greece. The First Macedonian War (215–205 B.C.E.) began when the Macedonian king, Philip V (221–179 B.C.E.), had made an alliance with Hannibal after the Roman defeat at the battle of Cannae. The results of the conflict were inconclusive.

Rome entered a second war with Macedon (205–197 B.C.E.) because Philip and the Seleucid king Antiochus III of

Syria had agreed to split the eastern Mediterranean between them. The poleis of Greece begged Rome for help, and Rome responded by ordering Philip to cease meddling in Greek affairs. Philip refused, and Roman forces easily defeated him with the support of Greek cities. In 196 B.C.E. the Roman general Titus Quinctius Flamininus declared the cities of Greece free and withdrew his forces.

These cities were not truly free, however. Rome installed oligarchic governments on whose support the Romans could rely. These unpopular regimes perpetuated the class distinctions of Rome. When Antiochus III sent an army to Greece to free it of Roman control, Rome struck back again, defeating him in 189 B.C.E. Rome imposed heavy reparations but claimed no territory, preferring to protect the newly freed Greek cities of Asia Minor and Greece from a distance.

Rome's policy of control from a distance changed after a third war with Macedon (172–168 B.C.E.). A harsher attitude took hold in Rome when a new Macedonian king tried to supplant Rome as protector of Greece. After a smashing victory, Rome imposed crippling terms of surrender on Macedon. Rome chopped Macedon into four separate republics and strictly forbade marriage and trade across the new borders. Roman troops ruthlessly stamped out all opposition, destroying seventy cities that objected to Rome's presence and selling 150,000 people into slavery.

When some Greek cities tried to pull away from Roman control and assert their independence, the heel of Rome came down hard. To set an example of the danger of resistance, the Roman commander Mummius burned the opulent city of Corinth to the ground and enslaved its inhabitants. For weeks afterward, ships carrying plunder and slaves from the fallen city docked in Italy.

The Encounter Between Greek and Roman Culture

Romans had interacted with Greek culture to some degree for centuries, first indirectly through Etruscan intermediaries, and then through direct contact with Greek communities in southern Italy and Sicily. During the second century B.C.E., when Rome acquired the eastern Mediterranean through its wars with Macedon, the pace of Hellenism's intellectual influence on Rome accelerated. In addition to fine statues and paintings, Greek ideas about literature, art, philosophy, rhetoric, and education poured into Rome after the Macedonian wars.

This Hellenistic legacy challenged many Roman assumptions about the world. But there was a paradox in the reaction of Roman aristocrats to Hellenism. Many noblemen in Rome felt threatened by the novelty of Hellenistic ideas. They preferred to maintain their conservative traditions of public life and thought. They also wanted to present to the world the image of a strong and independent Roman culture, untainted by traditions from other cultures. Thus during the second century B.C.E., Romans occasionally tried to expel Greek philosophers from their city

because they worried that Greek culture might corrupt traditional Roman values. At the same time, many Romans truly admired the sophistication of Greek political thought, art, and literature, and they wished to participate in the Hellenistic community.

Consequently many aristocrats learned Greek but refused to speak it while on official business in the East. While Latin remained the language spoken in the Senate house, senators hired Greek tutors to instruct their sons at home in philosophy, literature, science and the arts, and Greek intellectuals found a warm welcome from Rome's upper class. Cato the Censor, the senator who had insisted that Rome destroy Carthage, embodied the paradox of maintaining public distance from Greek culture while privately cherishing it. He cultivated an appearance of forthrightness and honesty, traditional Roman values that he claimed were threatened by Greek culture. He publicly denounced Greek oratory as unmanly, while drawing upon his deep knowledge of Greek rhetoric and literature to write his speeches praising Roman culture.

Before their exposure to the Hellenistic world in the second century B.C.E., Romans had little interest in literature. Their written efforts consisted mainly of inscriptions of laws and treaties on bronze plaques hung from the outer walls of public buildings. Families kept records of the funeral eulogies of their ancestors, while priests maintained simple lists of events and religious festivals. By ca. 240 B.C.E., Livius Andronicus, a former Greek slave, began to translate Greek dramas into Latin. In 220 B.C.E., a Roman senator, Quintus Fabius Pictor, wrote a history of Rome in the Greek language—the first major Roman prose work. In the next century, Polybius, a Greek historian who stood watching with Scipio Aemilianus while Carthage burned, made a major contribution to the writing of Roman history. Taken to Rome from Greece as a hostage in the 160s B.C.E., Polybius came to realize the futility of opposing Roman force. His *History,* written in the analytical tradition of the Greek historian Thucydides, traces Rome's astounding rise to world dominance in a mere fifty-three years and includes moralizing attacks on the abuse of power.

Hellenistic culture also had a major impact on Roman drama. Two Roman playwrights, Plautus (ca. 250–184 B.C.E.) and Terence (ca. 190–159 B.C.E.), took their inspiration from Hellenistic New Comedy and injected some fun into Roman literature. Their surviving works offer entertaining glimpses into the pitfalls of everyday life while also reinforcing the aristocratic values of the rulers of Rome's vast new domains.

Many educated Romans found Greek philosophy extremely attractive. The theory of matter advanced by the Hellenistic philosopher Epicurus, whose ethical philosophy we have already discussed, gained wide acceptance among Romans. Epicurus believed that everything has a natural cause: that "nothing comes from nothing." Romans learned about Epicurus's theories of matter and the infinity of the universe from the poem *On the Nature of the Universe* by the Roman poet Lucretius (d. ca. 51 B.C.E.), who wrote in Latin. The Hellenistic ethical philosophy that held the greatest appeal to Romans was Stoicism, because it encouraged an active public life. Stoic emphasis on the mastery of human difficulties appealed to aristocratic Romans' sense of duty and dignity. The great Roman orator and politician Marcus Tullius Cicero (106–43 B.C.E.), in particular, combined Stoic ideas in a highly personal yet fully Roman way. Cicero stressed moral behavior in political life while urging the attainment of a broad education. Cicero's high-minded devotion to the Republic won him the enmity of unscrupulous politicians. He was murdered in 43 B.C.E. because he made a series of public speeches accusing Antony of being a threat to Republican freedom.

Despite their openness to Greek philosophy, many members of the Roman ruling elite objected to foreign religious practices. In 186 B.C.E., for example, the Senate suppressed the popular orgiastic cult of the wine god Bacchus, not simply to protect public morals, as they claimed, but to demonstrate and extend their authority over religious worship. Nevertheless, at crucial moments Rome welcomed foreign gods. In 204 B.C.E., two years before the end of the war with Hannibal, the Senate imported the image of the nature goddess Cybele, called the Great Mother, to Rome in order to inspire and unify the city. The cult of Cybele flourished in the Hellenistic kingdom of Pergamum, where devotees worshiped her in the form of an ancient and holy rock. A committee of leading citizens brought this sacred boulder to a new temple on the Palatine Hill amid wild rejoicing. When the ship carrying the rock got stuck in the Tiber River, legend has it that a noble lady, Claudia Quinta, towed the ship with her sash. Not only did Rome defeat Hannibal soon after the arrival of Cybele's sacred stone, but the move cemented Roman relations with Pergamum.

The massive infusion of Hellenistic art following the Macedonian wars inevitably affected public taste. The most prestigious works of art decorated public shrines and spaces throughout the city. Many treasures went to private collectors. Greek artists soon moved to Rome to enjoy the patronage of wealthy Romans. Although copyists made replicas of Greek masterpieces, distinctively Roman artistic styles also emerged, just as they did in rhetoric, literature, philosophy, and history writing. In portrait sculpture, especially, a style developed that unflinchingly depicted all the wrinkles of experience on a person's face. In this way the venerable Roman tradition of carving ancestral busts merged with Greek art.

Circular Temple

This circular temple from the city of Rome near the Tiber River dates to the late second century B.C.E. It is the earliest surviving marble temple in Rome. The plan of the temple as well as the original marble of the columns and much of the rest of the building came from Greece.

In architecture, the magnificent temple of Fortune at Praeneste (first century B.C.E.), a town near Rome, combined Italian and Hellenistic concepts to produce the first great monument demonstrating a genuinely Greco-Roman style. By the end of the Republic, Romans had gained enough confidence to adopt the intellectual heritage of Greece and put it to their own ends without fear of seeming "too Greek."

Life in the Roman Republic

During the Hellenistic Age, Rome prospered from the acquisition of new territories. A small number of influential families dominated political life, sometimes making decisions about war from which they could win wealth and prestige. The Roman Republic remained strong because these ruling families took pains to limit the amount of power any one man or extended political family might attain.

Patrons and Clients

The ruling families of Rome established political networks that extended their influence through all levels of Roman society. These relationships depended on the traditional Roman institution of patrons and clients°. By exercising

A Corrupt Roman Governor Is Convicted of Extortion

Governors sent by the Roman Senate to rule the provinces wielded absolute power, which often corrupted them. One such man was Gaius Verres, who was convicted in 70 B.C.E. in a court in Rome for his flagrant abuse of power while governor of Sicily. The courtroom drama in which Verres was found guilty reveals one of the deepest flaws of the Roman Republic: the unprincipled exploitation of lands under Roman control. It also reveals one of Rome's greatest strengths: the presence of men of high ethical standards who believed in honest government and fair treatment of Roman subjects. The trial and its result reveals Republican Rome at its best and worst.

While governor from 73 to 71 B.C.E., Verres had looted Sicily with shocking thoroughness. In his pursuit of gold and Greek art, Verres tortured and sometimes killed Roman citizens. His outraged victims employed the young and ambitious lawyer Marcus Tullius Cicero (106–43 B.C.E.) to prosecute Verres. They could not have chosen a better advocate.

The prosecution of Verres marks the beginning of Cicero's illustrious career as one of the most active politicians and certainly the greatest orator of the Republic. Cicero also stands as one of the most influential political philosophers of Western civilization, one who hated the corruption of political life and opposed tyranny in any form. His many works have influenced political thinkers from antiquity to the present.

In the Roman Republic, only senators and equestrians between ages 30 and 60 could serve on juries for civil crimes such as those committed by Verres. All adult male citizens had the right to bring a case to court, but women had less freedom to do so. After swearing oaths of good faith, accusers read the charges in the presence of the accused, who in turn agreed to accept the decision of the court.

When trials began, the prosecutor was expected to be present, but the accused could decline to attend. The prosecution and the defense both produced evidence, then cross-examined witnesses. Since a Roman lawyer could discuss any aspect of the defendant's personal or public life, character assassination became an important—and amusing—rhetorical tool.

After deliberating, the jury delivered its verdict and the judge gave the penalty required by law, generally fines or periods of exile. No provisions for appeal existed, but pardon could be obtained by a legislative act.

Cicero worked this system to his advantage in his prosecution of Verres. He nimbly quashed an attempt to delay the trial until 69 B.C.E., when the president of the court would be a crony of Verres. Then, with a combination of ringing oratory and irrefutable evidence of Verres's crimes, Cicero made his case. The following excerpt from his speech shows Cicero's mastery of persuasive rhetoric:

Judges: at this grave crisis in the history of our country, you have been offered a peculiarly desirable gift . . . For you have been given a unique chance to make your Senatorial Order less unpopular, and to set right the damaged reputation of these courts. A belief has taken root which is having a fatal effect on our nation—and which to us who are senators, in particular, threatens grave peril. This belief is on everyone's tongue, at Rome and even in foreign countries. It is this: that in these courts, with their present membership, even the worst criminal will never be convicted provided that he has money. . . . And at this very juncture Gaius Verres has been brought to trial. Here is a man whose life and actions the world has already condemned—yet whose enormous fortune, according to his own loudly expressed hopes, has already brought him acquittal! Pronounce a just and scrupulous verdict against Verres and you will keep the good name which ought always to be yours. . . . I spent fifty days on a careful investigation of the entire island of Sicily; I got to know every document, every wrong suffered either by a community or an individual. . . .

For three long years he so thoroughly despoiled and pillaged the province that its restoration to its previous state is out of the question. . . . All the property that anyone in Sicily still has for his own today is merely what happened to escape the attention of this avaricious lecher, or survived his glutted appetites. . . . It was an appalling disgrace for our country.

. . . In the first stage of the trial, then, my charge is this. I accuse Gaius Verres of committing acts of lechery and brutality against the citizens and allies of Rome, and many crimes against God and man. I claim that he has illegally taken from Sicily sums amounting to forty million sesterces. By the witnesses and documents, public and private, which I am going to cite, I shall convince you that these charges are true.[2]

Republican Portrait of Cicero
This portrait of Cicero captures his uncompromising personality. The style of depicting every wrinkle conforms both to Hellenistic interest in psychological portraiture and traditional Roman directness. In the Republican period this type of portraiture was enormously popular.

Cicero's speech was persuasive, and the jury found Verres guilty. Verres went into exile in Marseilles to avoid his sentence, but he did not avoid punishment altogether. Justice—relentless and ironic—caught up with him some years later during the civil wars that followed Julius Caesar's death. Mark Antony, who was also a connoisseur of other people's wealth, wanted Verres's art collection for himself and so put Verres's name on a death list to obtain it. The former governor of Sicily was murdered in 43 B.C.E.

In his prosecution of Verres, Cicero delivered more than an indictment of one corrupt man; for a brief moment he revealed some of the deepest, fatal flaws of the Roman Republic. The trial inspired some short-term reforms, but not until the reforms of the emperor Augustus did the relationship between Roman administrators and provincial populations become more fair.

Questions of Justice

1. What does Verres's trial reveal about weaknesses in the Roman Republic?
2. Cicero's speech illustrates his disdain for corruption and tyranny. What are the tensions between personal morality and the requirements of governing a large empire?

Taking It Further

Gruen, Erich S. *The Last Generation of the Roman Republic.* 1974. A magisterial analysis of the Republic's decline, with emphasis on legal affairs.

Rawson, Elizabeth. *Cicero, A Portrait.* 1975. This book gives a balanced account of Cicero's life.

influence on behalf of a social subordinate, a powerful man (the patron) would bind that man (the client) to him in anticipation of future support. In this way complex webs of personal interdependency influenced the entire Roman social system. The patron-client system operated at every level of society, and it was customary for a man of influence to receive his clients on matters of business at his home the first thing in the morning. In a modest household the discussion might involve everyday business such as shipping fish, arranging a marriage, or making a loan. But in the mansion of a Roman aristocrat a patron might be more interested in forging a political alliance. When several patron-client groups joined forces, they became significant political factions under the leadership of one patron.

Pyramids of Wealth and Power

Like its political organization, Rome's social organization demonstrated a well-defined hierarchy. By the first century B.C.E., a new, elite class of political leaders had emerged in Rome, composed of both the original patrician families and wealthy plebeians who had been able to attain membership in the Senate through their service in the various public offices. The men of this leadership class dominated the Senate and formed the inner circle of government. From their ranks came most of the consuls. They set foreign and domestic policy, led armies to war, held the main magistracies, and siphoned off the lion's share of the Republic's resources.

Beneath this elite group came the equestrian class. Equestrians normally abstained from public office, but were often tied to political leaders by personal obligation. They were primarily businessmen who prospered from the financial opportunities that Rome's expansion provided. For example, during the Republic, equestrian businessmen could bid on contracts to collect taxes in different areas. The man awarded the contract was permitted to collect taxes—with few restraints on his methods. After paying the Senate the amount agreed upon in the contract, he could keep any other tax funds that he had gathered. Many equestrians accumulated fortunes in this way.

Next in rank came the mass of citizens who were known as plebeians. As we have seen, this group had acquired political representation and influence, but the Plebeian Assembly had gradually come under the control of politicians who were the clients of aristocratic patrons. These wealthy plebeian politicians, who had become members of a new ruling class, had little interest in the condition of the large body of poor plebeians, which now had no direct means to express its political will. The demands of army service kept many plebeians who had small farms away from their land for long periods of time. Rich investors seized this opportunity to create huge estates by grabbing the bankrupt farms and replacing the free farmers with slaves captured in war. Sometimes impoverished plebeians became dependent tenant farmers on land they had once

owned themselves. As a result, these plebeians turned more and more to leaders who would protect them and give them land.

Rome's Italian allies had even fewer rights than the plebeians, despite their service in the Roman armies. Although millions of allies inhabited lands controlled by Rome, only a privileged few of the local elites received Roman citizenship. The rest could only hope for the goodwill of Roman officials.

At the bottom of the Roman hierarchy were slaves. By the first century B.C.E., about two million slaves captured in war or born in captivity lived in Italy and Sicily, amounting to about one-third of the population. Romans considered the slaves to be pieces of property, "talking tools," whom their owners could exploit at will. Freed slaves owed legal obligations to their former masters and were their clients. The brutal inequities of this system led to violence. The slave gangs who farmed vast estates in Sicily revolted first. In 135 B.C.E. they began an ill-fated struggle for freedom that lasted three years and involved more than 200,000 slaves.

Thirty years later another unsuccessful outburst began in southern Italy and Sicily because slave owners refused to comply with a senatorial decree to release any slaves who once had been free allies of Rome. 30,000 slaves took up arms between 104 and 101 B.C.E. The most destructive revolt occurred in Italy during the years from 73 to 71 B.C.E. An army of more than 100,000 slaves led by the Thracian gladiator Spartacus (gladiators were slaves who fought for public entertainment) battled eight Roman legions totaling about 50,000 men before being crushed by the superior Roman military organization.

The Roman Family

A Roman *familia* typically included not just the husband, wife, and unmarried children, but also their slaves and often freedmen and others who were dependent on the household. Legitimate marriages required the agreement of both husband and wife. Women usually married at puberty, and men did so in their twenties. In most families only two or three children survived infancy. Although Roman men could have only one wife at a time, men frequently cohabited with women to whom they were not married (concubines). Having a concubine was perfectly acceptable, but doing so was legal only if both parties involved had no living spouse.

The Roman family mirrored the patterns of authority and dependency found in the political arena. Just as a patron commanded the support of his clients regardless of their status in public life, so the male head of the household directed the destiny of all his subordinates within the *familia*. A man ruled his *familia* with full authority over the purse strings and all of his descendants until he died. The head of the family, or *paterfamilias*, held power of life and death over his wife, children, and slaves, though few men exercised this power. In practice, women and grown children often had a great deal of independence, and aristocratic women often exerted a strong influence in political life, though always from behind the scenes.

Upper-class Romans placed great value on the continuity of the family name, family traditions, and control of family property through the generations. For these reasons they often adopted males, even of adult age, to be heirs, especially if they had no legitimate sons of their own. Legitimate offspring always took the name of their father, and in case of divorce, which could be easily obtained, continued to live with him. Illegitimate offspring stayed with the mother.

With very few exceptions Roman women remained legally dependent on a male relative. In the most common form of marriage, a wife remained under the formal control of the *paterfamilias* to whom she belonged before her marriage—in most cases, her father. In practice this meant that the wife retained control of her own property and the inheritance she had received from her father. A husband in this sort of marriage would have to be careful to avoid the anger of his wife's father or brothers, and so he might be inclined to treat his wife more justly. Another form of marriage brought the wife under the full control of her husband after the wedding. She had to worship the family gods of her husband's household and accept his ancestors as her own. If her husband died, one of his male relatives became the woman's legal protector.

The stability of family life through the generations desired by free Romans was impossible for slaves to attain. Former female slaves (freedwomen) remained tied to their former masters with bonds of dependency and obligation. Roman law did not recognize marriage between slaves. Some Roman handbooks explaining how to use slaves to maximum advantage advocated letting slaves establish conjugal arrangements. Owners could, however, shatter such alliances by selling the enslaved partners or their offspring.

Beginnings of the Roman Revolution

- **What political and social changes brought the Roman Republic to an end?**

The inequalities of wealth and power in Roman society led to the disintegration of the Republic. The rapid acquisition of territories and enormous wealth overseas heightened those differences. Roman reformers' attempts to face the new economic realities met with fierce resistance from those who profited the most from imperial rule: politicians, governors, high military personnel, and businessmen. These men sought personal glory and political advantage even if it came at the Republic's expense. Their quest for political prominence through military adventure, coupled with deep-seated flaws of political institutions, eventually overwhelmed the Republic's political structure and brought about a revolution—a decisive, fundamental change in the political system.

The Gracchi

During the second century B.C.E., more and more citizen farmers in Italy lost their fields to powerful landholders, who replaced them with slaves on their estates. As a result, the slave population of Italy increased dramatically. Some members of the political elite feared the danger inherent in these developments. If citizen farmers failed to meet the property requirements for military service and pay for their own weapons, as they traditionally had done, Rome would lose its supply of recruits for its legions.

Two young brothers, Tiberius and Gaius Gracchus, attempted some reforms. Although their mother was an aristocrat (the daughter of Scipio Africanus), she had married a wealthy plebeian. Thus, the brothers were legally plebeian, and they sought influence through the tribunate, an office limited to plebeians. As a tribune, Tiberius Gracchus (162–133 B.C.E.) convinced the Plebeian Assembly to pass a bill limiting the amount of public land that one man could possess. The new law required that the excess land from wealthy landholders be redistributed in small lots to poor citizens. While the land redistribution was in progress, conservative senators ignited a firestorm of opposition to Tiberius Gracchus. He responded by running for a second term as tribune, which was a break with precedent. Fearing revolution, a clique of senators in 133 B.C.E. arranged for assassins to club Tiberius to death. Land redistribution did not cease, but a terrible precedent of public violence had been set.

A decade later, when Tiberius's brother Gaius Gracchus became tribune in 123 B.C.E., he turned his attention to the problem of extortion in the provinces. With no checks on their authority, many corrupt governors forced provincials to give them money, valuable goods, and crops. Gaius Gracchus attempted to stop these abuses. In an attempt to dilute the power of corrupt provincial administrators chosen from the Senate and to win the political support of equestrians in Rome, he permitted equestrian tax collectors to operate in the provinces and to serve on juries that tried extortion cases. Gaius also tried to speed up land redistribution. But when he attempted to give citizenship to Rome's Italian allies in order to protect them from having their land confiscated by Romans, he lost the support of the Roman people, who did not wish to share the benefits of citizenship with non-Romans. In 121 B.C.E. Gaius committed suicide rather than allow himself to be murdered by a mob sent by his senatorial foes.

The ruthless suppression of the Gracchi (the Latin plural form of *Gracchus*) and their supporters lit the fuse of political and social revolution at Rome. By attempting to effect change through the Plebeian Assembly, the Gracchi unwittingly paved the way for less scrupulous aristocrats to seek power by falsely claiming to represent the interests of the poor. The introduction of assassinations into the public debate signaled the end of political consensus among the oligarchy. Rivalry among the elite combined with the desperation of the poor in an explosive blend, with the army as the wild card. If an unscrupulous politician were to join forces with poverty-stricken soldiers, the Republic would be in peril.

Gaius Marius (157–86 B.C.E.) became the first Roman general to play this wild card. He rose to power when the angry Roman poor made him their champion. Despite his equestrian origins, this experienced general won the consulship in 107 B.C.E. A special law of the Plebeian Assembly put him in command of the legions fighting King Jugurtha in Numidia in North Africa, and he brought the war to a quick and successful conclusion. Then in response to a new threat from Germanic tribes seeking to invade Italy, Marius trained a new army and trounced the invaders.

In organizing his army Marius made some radical changes. He eliminated the property requirement for enlistment, thereby opening the ranks to the very poorest citizens in the countryside and in Rome. These soldiers swore an oath of loyalty to their commander in chief, who in return promised them farms after a victorious campaign. Marius's reforms put generals in the crossfire of the long-running political struggle between the Senate and the Plebeian Assembly, the two institutions authorized to allocate lands won in war.

Marius achieved great personal power, but he did not use it against the institutions of the Republic. When he left public life in old age, the Roman Republic lurched ahead to its next major crisis: a revolt of the Italian allies.

War in Italy and Abroad

In 90 B.C.E. Rome's loyal allies in Italy could no longer endure being treated as inferiors when it came to distribution of land and booty. They launched a revolt against Rome known as the Social War (from the Latin word *socii*, which means "allies"). The confederation of allies demanded not independence but participation in the Roman Republic. They wanted full citizenship rights because they had been partners in all of Rome's wars and thus felt entitled to share in the fruits of victory. The allies lost the war, but soon afterward Rome granted citizenship to all Italians. Rome's new citizens quickly became a potent force in Roman political life. Their presence in the political arena tilted the political scales away from the wealthy in Rome toward the population of Italy in general.

DOCUMENT

The Ruinous Effects of Conquest

Roman conquests in Italy damaged the economy of newly captured rural areas. The following excerpt from the work of the Roman historian Appian, written in the second century C.E., describes the process of Roman settlement in newly taken territories in Italy, and the consequences of that settlement. The reforms of the Gracchi were intended to correct some of these problems.

The Romans, as they subdued the Italian peoples successively in war, seized a part of their lands and built towns there, or established their own colonies in already existing towns, using them as garrisons. Of the land thus acquired by war they assigned the cultivated part forthwith to settlers, or leased or sold it. Since they had no leisure as yet to allot the part which then lay desolated by war (this was generally the greater part), they proclaimed that in the meantime those who were willing to work it might do so for a share of the yearly crops—a tenth of the grain and a fifth of the fruit. From those who kept flocks, a tax was fixed for the animals, both oxen and small cattle. This they did in order to multiply the Italian race, which they considered to be the most laborious of peoples, so that that they might have plenty of allies at home. But the very opposite happened; for the rich, getting possession of the greater part of the undistributed lands, and being emboldened by the lapse of time to believe that they would never be dispossessed, and adding to their holding the small farms of their poor neighbors, partly by purchase and partly by force, came to cultivate vast tracts instead of single estates, using for this purpose slaves as laborers and herdsmen, lest free laborers be drawn from agriculture into the army. . . . Thus the governing class became enormously rich and the number of slaves multiplied throughout the country, while the Italian peoples dwindled in numbers and strength . . .

Source: From *A History of Rome through the Fifth Century, Volume 1, The Republic,* edited by A. H. M. Jones (New York: Walker and Company, 1968), p. 104.

The Social War in Italy was followed by wars abroad. The aristocrat Lucius Cornelius Sulla (138–78 B.C.E.), consul in 88 B.C.E., was setting out with an army to put down a serious provincial revolt in Asia Minor when the Plebeian Assembly turned command of his troops over to Marius, whose military reforms had aided the poor. In response, Sulla marched from southern Italy to Rome and reestablished his control by placing his own supporters into positions of authority in the Senate, the Plebeian Assembly, and various administrative offices.

However, only a year later, when Sulla returned to Asia Minor to resume command of the war against King Mithradates of Pontus, Marius and the other consul, Cinna, won back political control of Rome. They declared Sulla an outlaw and slaughtered his supporters. When Sulla returned to Italy in 82 B.C.E., at the head of a triumphant and loyal army, he seized Rome after a battle in which about 60,000 Roman soldiers died, and then murdered 3,000 of his political opponents. The Senate named him dictator, which gave him complete power. With the support of the aristocratic Senate, whose power he hoped to restore, Sulla crippled the political power of the plebeians. In particular, he restricted the powers of tribunes to propose legislation because they had stirred up so much political instability for fifty years. After restoring the peace and the institutions of the state, Sulla surprised many people by resigning as dictator in 80 B.C.E. Like Marius, Sulla was unwilling to destroy the Republic's institutions for the sake of his own ambition. It was enough for him to have restored peace and the preeminence of the Senate. Nevertheless, he had set a precedent for using armies in political rivalries. In the next fifty years the Senate conspicuously failed to restrain generals backed by public armies, thereby contributing to the collapse of the Republic.

The First Triumvirate

The Roman Republic's final downward spiral of social turmoil was provoked by three men: Pompey (Gnaeus Pompeius, 106–48 B.C.E.), Marcus Licinius Crassus (ca. 115–53 B.C.E.), and Gaius Julius Caesar (100–44 B.C.E.). Pompey, the general who suppressed a revolt in Spain, and Crassus, the wealthiest man in Rome who had been one of Sulla's lieutenants, joined forces to crush the slave revolt of Spartacus in 71 B.C.E. Backed by their armies, they then coerced the Centuriate Assembly into naming them consuls for 70 B.C.E., even though Pompey was legally too young and had not yet held the prerequisite junior offices.

During their consulship, Pompey and Crassus made modest changes to Sulla's reforms. They permitted the tribunes to propose laws again and let equestrians serve on juries. After their year in office they retired without making further demands. Pompey continued his military career. He received a special command in 67 B.C.E. to clear pirates from the Mediterranean in order to protect Roman trade. The following year Pompey crushed another rebellion in Asia Minor. He reorganized Asia Minor and territories in the Middle East, creating new provinces and more client kingdoms subservient to Rome.

When Pompey returned to Rome he asked the Senate to grant land to his victorious troops. The Senate, jealous of his success and afraid of the power he would gain as the patron of so many troops, would not comply. To gain land for his soldiers and have his political arrangements in Asia

CHRONOLOGY

Social Conflict in Rome and Italy

133 B.C.E.	Tiberius Gracchus initiates reforms
123–122 B.C.E.	Gaius Gracchus initiates reforms
107 B.C.E.	Marius serves his first consulship
104–100 B.C.E.	Marius holds consecutive consulships
90–88 B.C.E.	Rome fights "Social War" with Italian allies
88 B.C.E.	Sulla takes Rome
82–80 B.C.E.	Sulla serves as dictator
77–71 B.C.E.	Pompey fights Celts in Spain
73–71 B.C.E.	Spartacus's slave revolt
70 B.C.E.	Cicero prosecutes Verres in court

Minor and the Middle East ratified, Pompey made an alliance with two men even more ambitious and less scrupulous than he: his old ally Crassus and Gaius Julius Caesar, the ambitious descendant of an ancient patrician family. The three formed an informal alliance historians call the First Triumvirate°. With their influence now combined, no man or institution could oppose them. Caesar obtained the consulship in 59 B.C.E., despite the objections of many senators. By using illegal means that would return to haunt him, he directed the Senate to ratify Pompey's arrangements in the Middle East and Asia Minor and to grant land to his troops. He arranged for Crassus's clients, the equestrian tax collectors, to have their financial problems resolved at public expense.

As a reward for his efforts on behalf of the triumvirate, the perpetually debt-ridden Caesar arranged to receive the governorship of the Po Valley and the Illyrian coast for five years after his consulship ended. Later he extended that term for ten years. During this time, he planned to enrich himself at the expense of the provincials. As he set out for his governorship, he assumed command of Transalpine Gaul (northwest of the Alps) when its governor died. This put Caesar in a position to operate militarily in all of Gaul—and ultimately to conquer it.

Julius Caesar and the End of the Republic

Caesar's determination to conquer Gaul lay in pursuing personal advantage. He knew that he would win glory, wealth, and prestige in Rome by conquering new lands, and so he promptly began a war (58–50 B.C.E.) against the

Celtic tribes of Transalpine Gaul. A military genius, Caesar chronicled his ruthless tactics and military successes in his *Commentaries on the Gallic War,* as famous today for its elegant Latin as for its unflinching glimpse of Roman methods and justifications of conquest. In eight years Caesar conquered the area of modern France and Belgium, turning these territories into Roman provinces. He even briefly invaded Britain. His intrusion into Celtic lands led to their eventual Romanization. The French language developed from the Latin spoken by Roman soldiers. Similarly Spanish, Italian, Portuguese, and Romanian also derived from the tongue of Roman conquerors and are called "Romance" languages.

The Career of Julius Caesar

Meanwhile, the other members of the triumvirate, Crassus and Pompey, also sought military glory. The wealthy Crassus raised an army out of his own pocket, reputedly asserting, "If you can't afford to pay for an army, you shouldn't command it!" His attempt to conquer the Parthians, the successors to the Persian Empire, ended in disaster in 53 B.C.E. in Syria. The Parthians killed Crassus, destroyed his army, and captured the military insignia (metal eagles on staffs, called standards) that each legion proudly carried into battle. Pompey again assumed the governorship of Spain, but stayed in Rome while subordinates waged war there against Spain's Celtic inhabitants.

In Rome, a group of senators grew fearful of Caesar's power, ambitions, and arrogance. They appealed to Pompey for assistance, and he brought the armies loyal to him to the aid of the Senate against Caesar. The Senate then asked Caesar to lay down his command in Gaul and return to Rome. Caesar knew that if he complied with this request he would be indicted on charges of improper conduct or corruption as soon as he returned to Rome. Facing certain conviction, Caesar refused to return for a trial. In 49 B.C.E. he left Gaul and marched south with his loyal troops against the forces of the Senate in Rome. Recognizing the enormity of his gamble ("I've thrown the dice!" he said when he crossed the Rubicon River, the boundary of land under direct control of the Senate), he deliberately plunged Rome into civil war. Because of his victories in Gaul and his generosity to the people of Rome, Caesar could pose as the people's champion while seeking absolute power for himself. Intimidated by Caesar's forces and public support, Pompey hastily withdrew to Greece, but Caesar overtook and defeated him at Pharsalus, a town in Thessaly, in 48 B.C.E. When Pompey fled to Egypt high officials of the Ptolemaic pharaoh's court immediately murdered him to win Caesar's favor.

It took Caesar more than two years to complete his victory over the Senate and return to Italy in 45 B.C.E. Back in Rome, he had himself proclaimed dictator for life and assumed complete control over all aspects of government, flagrantly disregarding the traditions of the Republic. Because he did not live to fully implement his plan, his long-term goals for the Roman state remain unclear, but he probably intended to establish some version of Hellenistic monarchy.

Once in power, Caesar permanently ended the autonomy of the Senate. He enlarged the Senate from 600 (its size at the time of Sulla) to 900 men, and then filled it with his supporters. He also established military colonies in Spain, North Africa, and Gaul to provide land for his veterans and to secure those territories. He adjusted the chaotic Republican calendar by adding one day every fourth year, creating a year of 365.25 days. The resulting "Julian" calendar lasted until the sixteenth century C.E. He regularized gold coinage and urban administration and planned a vast public library. At his death, plans for a major campaign against Parthia were underway, suggesting that conquest would have remained a basic feature of his rule.

Caesar seriously miscalculated by assuming he could win the support of his enemies by showing clemency to them and by making administrative changes that disregarded Republican precedent. These changes earned Caesar the resentment of traditionalist senators who failed to recognize that the Republic could never be restored. On March 15, 44 B.C.E., a group of idealistic senators, led by Cassius and Brutus, stabbed Caesar to death at a Senate meeting. The assassins claimed that they wanted to restore the Republic, but in reality they had only unleashed another brutal civil war.

Marcus Antonius (Mark Antony), who had been Caesar's right-hand man, stepped forward to oppose the conspirators. He was soon joined by Octavian, Caesar's grandnephew and legal heir. Though Octavian was only 19, he gained control of some of Caesar's legions and compelled the Senate to name him consul. Marcus Lepidus, commander of Caesar's cavalry, joined Mark Antony and Octavian to form the Second Triumvirate°. The new trio coerced the Senate into granting them power to rule Rome legally.

At the battle of Philippi, a town in Macedonia, in 42 B.C.E., forces of the Second Triumvirate crushed the army of the senators who had assassinated Caesar. But soon Antony, Octavian, and Lepidus began to struggle among themselves for absolute authority. Lepidus soon dropped out of the contest, while Antony and Octavian maneuvered for control of Rome. Reluctant to begin open warfare, they agreed to separate spheres of influence. Octavian took Italy and Rome's western provinces, while Antony took the eastern provinces.

In Egypt, Antony joined forces with Cleopatra VII, the last descendant of the Hellenistic monarch Ptolemy. Both stood to gain from this alliance: Antony would gain the resources of Egypt in his quest to gain complete power over the eastern provinces, while Cleopatra would strengthen her rule in Egypt. In response to this alliance, Octavian launched a vicious propaganda campaign. Posing as the conservative protector of Roman tradition, he accused

Antony of surrendering Roman values and territory to an evil foreign seductress. The inevitable war broke out in 31 B.C.E. At the battle of Actium, in Greece, Octavian's troops defeated Antony and Cleopatra's land and naval forces. The couple fled to Alexandria, in Egypt, where they committed suicide a year later.

The 31-year-old Octavian now stood as absolute master of the Roman world. He had a clear vision of the problems that had destroyed the Republic, and from its ashes he planned to rebuild the Roman state. Under the leadership of Octavian, who came to be known as the emperor Augustus, Rome created a new political system, the Roman Empire, in which Octavian had unprecedented power over a vast geographical area.

The new world order that Octavian created brought an end to the Hellenistic Age. Rome now ruled all the lands that Alexander the Great had conquered, except for Persia and the territories farther to the east, and Hellenistic culture would now have to accommodate the realities of Roman rule. As we will see in the next chapter, Octavian succeeded where Alexander had failed: He created a world empire that had the infrastructure it needed to endure, and the peaceful conditions that enabled its culture to flourish and spread.

CHRONOLOGY

The Collapse of the Ro...

60 B.C.E.	The First Triumvir...
58–50 B.C.E.	Julius Caesar con... Gaul
53 B.C.E.	Crassus is killed in the Parthian War
49 B.C.E.	Caesar crosses Rubicon River and begins civil war
48 B.C.E.	Battle of Pharsalus; Pompey is killed in Egypt
45 B.C.E.	Caesar wins civil war
47–44 B.C.E.	Caesar serves as dictator
44 B.C.E.	Caesar is murdered; civil war breaks out
43 B.C.E.	The Second Triumvirate is formed; Cicero is murdered
42 B.C.E.	Battle of Philippi; Caesar's assassins are defeated
31 B.C.E.	Octavian defeats Antony and Cleopatra and gains absolute power

Conclusion

Defining the West in the Hellenistic Age

During the Hellenistic Age the cultural and geographical boundaries of what would later be called the West began to take shape. These boundaries encompassed the regions where Hellenistic culture penetrated and had a lasting influence. The lands within the empire of Alexander the Great, all of which lay to the east of Greece and Egypt, formed the core of this cultural realm, but the Hellenistic world also extended westward across the Mediterranean, embracing the lands ruled by Carthage from North Africa to Spain. Hellenism also reached the edges of the lands inhabited by Celtic peoples. Most of all, Hellenistic culture left a distinctive mark on Roman civilization in Italy. In all these locations Greek culture interacted with those of the areas it penetrated, and the synthesis that resulted became one of the main foundations of Western civilization.

During the period of the Roman Empire, which will be the subject of the next chapter, a new blend of Hellenistic and Latin cultures, in which Hellenism was an important but not the dominant component, took shape. The geographical arena within which this culture flourished was that of the vast Roman Empire, covering a large part of Europe, North Africa, and the Middle East. The culture that characterized this empire gave a new definition to what we now call the West.

Suggestions for Further Reading

For a comprehensive list of suggested readings, please go to www.ablongman.com/levack2e/chapter4

Boardman, John, Jasper Griffin, and Oswyn Murray, eds. *Greece and the Hellenistic World.* [*The Oxford History of the Classical World.*] 1988. A synthesis of all aspects of Hellenistic life, with excellent illustrations and bibliography.

Cohn, Norman. *Cosmos, Chaos, and the World to Come: The Ancient Roots of Apocalyptic Faith.* 1993. This brilliant study explains the development of ideas about the end of the world in the cultures of the ancient world.

Cornell, T. J. *The Beginnings of Rome: Italy and Rome from the Bronze Age to the Punic Wars (ca. 1000–264 B.C.).* 1996. A synthesis of the latest evidence with many important new interpretations.

Crawford, Michael. *The Roman Republic,* 2nd ed. 1992. This overview by a leading scholar lays a strong foundation for further study.

Cunliffe, Barry. *The Ancient Celts.* 1997. This source analyzes the archaeological evidence for the Celtic Iron Age, with many illustrations and maps.

Barry, ed. *The Oxford Illustrated Prehistory of Europe.* ..6. A collection of well-illustrated essays on the development of European cultures from the end of the Ice Age to the Classical period.

Gardner, Jane F. *Women in Roman Law and Society.* 1986. Explains the legal position of women in the Roman world.

Green, Peter. *Alexander to Actium: The Historical Evolution of the Hellenistic Age.* 1990. A vivid interpretation of the world created by Alexander until the victory of Augustus.

Gruen, Erich S. *The Hellenistic World and the Coming of Rome.* 1984. An extremely important study of how Rome entered the eastern Mediterranean world.

Kuhrt, Amélie, and Susan Sherwin-White, eds. *Hellenism in the East: The Interaction of Greek and Non-Greek Civilizations from Syria to Central Asia After Alexander.* 1987. These studies help us understand the complexities of the interaction of Greeks and non-Greeks in the Hellenistic world.

Pollitt, J. J. *Art in the Hellenistic Age.* 1986. A brilliant interpretation of the development of Hellenistic art.

Notes

1. Athenaios, 253 D; cited and translated in J. J. Pollitt, *Art in the Hellenistic Age* (1986), 271.

2. From *Selected Works* by Cicero, translated by Michael Grant (Penguin Classics 1960, second revised edition 1971). Copyright © Michael Grant 1960, 1965, 1971. Reproduced by permission of Penguin Books Ltd.

Enclosing the West: The Early Roman Empire and Its Neighbors, 31 B.C.E.–235 C.E.

5

N THE MIDDLE OF THE SECOND CENTURY C.E., AELIUS ARISTIDES, AN ARISTO-cratic Greek writer who held Roman citizenship, visited Rome, where he gave a long public oration in honor of the imperial capital. His words reveal what the Roman Empire meant to a wealthy, highly educated man from Rome's eastern provinces: "Rome is to the whole world what an ordinary city is to its suburbs and surrounding countryside . . . you have given up the division of nation from nation . . . you have separated the human race into Roman and non-Romans."

Aristides' description of the empire as one grand city with a unified culture set off from the "barbarian" peoples in the world is an exaggeration. Nevertheless it points to the key element of the Romans' success—a willingness to share their culture with their subjects and to assimilate them into the political and social life of the empire. Aristides understood that Roman culture flourished primarily in cities, and he believed that Roman urban life was the mark of civilization. He dismissed with a contemptuous sniff those not fortunate enough to live as Romans. In Aristides' opinion, Rome's destiny was to bring civilization to the rest of the world. His satisfied view of the Roman Empire demonstrates how successfully Rome had created a sense of common purpose among its elite citizens.

During its first two and a half centuries of existence, the Roman Empire brought cultural unity and political stability to an astonishingly diverse area stretching from the Atlantic Ocean to the Persian Gulf. Imperial rule disseminated Roman culture throughout not only the Mediterranean region and the Middle East, but also much of northwestern Europe. Within imperial Rome's parameters—intellectual, religious, political, and geographic—the basic outlines of what we call the West today were drawn.

Marcus Aurelius This magnificent bronze statue shows the emperor Marcus Aurelius (r. 161–180 C.E.) raising his right hand in a gesture of command, compelling the viewer to obey. A triumph of the art of bronze casting, this statue conveys the majesty of the Roman Empire.

This chapter examines the Roman Empire at the height of its power (ca. 31 B.C.E.–235 C.E.). We will see how its encounters with far-flung subject populations helped shape its development. Autocratic and exploitative, the Roman imperial system nonetheless provided the climate for rich developments in social, religious, and political life. Military force maintained the imperial system, but the peace and prosperity that accompanied Roman rule persuaded many subject peoples of its benefits. The new regime established a stable governing system that brought a nearly unbroken peace to the Mediterranean world for more than two centuries. Historians call this era the *Pax Romana*°, the Roman Peace. In these centuries Roman culture slowly took root across western Europe, North Africa, and the Middle East, transforming the lives of local populations. In the eyes of millions of people during these years, Rome ceased to be an unfamiliar and predatory occupying power. They came to regard Rome as a civilizing agent that provided unity and common culture. But others, particularly the slaves whose labor fueled the Roman economy and the small farmers whose taxes supported the Roman state, experienced Rome as an oppressive ruler.

This chapter analyzes imperial Rome's constantly evolving political and cultural community as three concentric circles of power—the imperial center, the provinces, and the frontiers and beyond. In the imperial center stood not only the emperor but also the Roman senate, the chief legal and administrative institutions, and the city of Rome itself, an important model of the Roman way of life. In the second circle, provincial populations struggled with the challenges raised by the imposition of Roman culture and politics and in the process contributed to the construction of a new imperial culture. The outermost circle of the empire, its frontier zones and the lands beyond, included Romans living within the empire's borders as well as the peoples who lived on the other side, but who nonetheless interacted with Rome through trading and warfare. Throughout the chapter we will explore what it meant to be a Roman in each of these concentric circles.

How did the encounters between the Romans and the peoples they conquered transform the Mediterranean world and create a Roman imperial culture? Four questions guide this exploration:

- How did the Roman imperial system develop and what roles did the emperor, senate, army, and Rome itself play in this process?
- How did provincial peoples assimilate to or resist Roman rule?
- How did Romans interact with peoples living beyond the imperial borders?
- What was the social and cultural response to the emergence and consolidation of empire?

The Imperial Center

- How did the Roman imperial system develop and what roles did the emperor, senate, army, and Rome itself play in this process?

After civil wars left the Roman Republic in ruins, a new political system emerged from its ashes. Rome continued to acquire and rule huge territories far from Italy. Its form of government, however, changed from a republic, in which members of an oligarchy competed for power that they shared by serving in elected offices, to an empire, in which one man, the emperor, held absolute power for life. Roman culture, with its strict social divisions and political structures, its distinctive forms of architecture and art, its shared intellectual and religious life, and its legal system defining the rights of citizens and subjects, was now securely anchored by an imperial system based on force (see Map 5.1).

Imperial Authority: Augustus and After

As we saw in Chapter 4, Julius Caesar's heir, Octavian, destroyed the Republic while pretending to preserve it. Octavian wrenched the state from the spiral of civil war and claimed that he had restored normal life to the Republic. In his own eyes, as well as those of a people weary of bitter civil war, Octavian was the savior of Republican Rome. In public affairs, however, nothing could have been further from the truth. Behind a carefully crafted façade of restored Republican tradition, Octavian created a Roman version of a Hellenistic monarchy, like those of Alexander the Great's successors in the eastern Mediterranean. By neutralizing all of his political enemies in the Roman Senate; vanquishing his military rivals, such as Antony and Cleopatra; and establishing an iron grip on every visible mechanism of power, Octavian succeeded where Julius Caesar and other less able Republican politicians had failed: He achieved total mastery of the political arena at Rome. No one successfully challenged his authority.

To mask his tyranny, Octavian never wore a crown and modestly referred to himself as *Princeps,* or First Citizen. He took several steps to create a political position in Rome that was all-powerful and at the same time unobtrusive. In 27 B.C.E., as he boasted in the official account of his reign, Octavian "transferred the Republic from his power into that of the Senate and the Roman people." This abdication was a carefully organized sham. In reality, he maintained absolute political control over Rome. Following his instructions, the powerless Senate showered honors on him, including the title "Augustus" (which is how we will refer to him throughout the rest of this chapter). This invented title illustrates well the political cleverness of Rome's absolute master. "Augustus" implied a uniquely exalted, god-like authority in the community, but the word had no previous associations with kingship. Augustus "accepted" the Senate's plea to remain consul and agreed to exercise control over the frontier provinces where the most troops were stationed, including Spain, Gaul, and Syria. The senators rejoiced, calling Augustus "sole savior of the entire empire."

In 23 B.C.E. Augustus took further steps to establish his paramount position. He had held the consulship every year since the end of the civil war in 31 B.C.E., but he recognized that holding the power of a consul year after year was inconsistent with his claim to have restored the Republic. So in 23 B.C.E. he renounced the consulship and shrewdly arranged for the Senate to grant him unprecedented power, but disguised by Republican trappings. He assumed the powers of a tribune, which included the right to conduct business in the Senate, the right to veto, and immunity from arrest and punishment. He could now legally intercede in all government activities and military affairs by virtue of "greater authority" granted to him by the Senate. Other generals continued to lead the legions into battle, but always in his name. Other magistrates continued to administer the state in accordance with the traditional responsibilities of their office, but no one was chosen without his approval.

Augustus selected or approved all his provincial governors. He assumed direct control over particularly rich provinces, such as Egypt, and those, such as Germany, that required a strong military presence to ward off invaders and control the recently conquered population. The Roman Senate maintained authority over peaceful provinces such as Greece and Sicily. Yet even in these provinces, Augustus intervened whenever he wished.

Map 5.1   The Roman Empire at Its Greatest Extent

The Roman Empire reached its greatest extent during the reign of Trajan (r. 98–117 C.E.). Stretching from the north of Britain to the Euphrates River, the empire brought together hundreds of distinct ethnic groups.

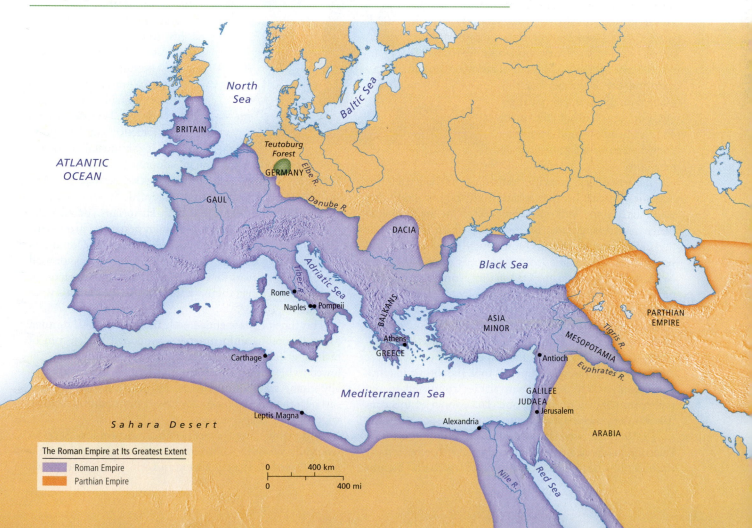

The Roman Empire at Its Greatest Extent
- Roman Empire
- Parthian Empire

0   400 km
0   400 mi

Augustus: A Commanding Presence
This imposing statue of Augustus dating to 19 B.C.E. depicts him as a warrior making a gesture of command. His face is ageless, the carving on his armor celebrates peace and prosperity, and his posture is balanced and forceful.

Later rulers, accepting the trappings of monarchy more openly than Augustus, used the title *imperator,* or emperor. Despite this change, the imperial system established by Augustus long survived his death, even when the throne was occupied by men such as Caligula (r. 37–41 C.E.), who tried to have his favorite horse elected to the Senate, or Nero (r. 54–68 C.E.), who murdered both his wife and his mother.

The Problem of Succession

Augustus, following the example of the Hellenistic world, hoped to establish a hereditary monarchy, in which power passed down through his family. When he died in 14 C.E., his stepson Tiberius (r. 14–37 C.E.) took control of the empire without opposition. A hereditary monarchy was now in place. Some senators muttered occasionally about restoring the Republic, but this remained an idle—and very dangerous—dream. Neither the army nor the people would have supported a Senate-led anti-imperial rebellion.

The hereditary principle remained unchallenged for centuries, in part because it staved off the instability that would have come with open competition for the throne. In the dynasty inaugurated by Augustus, which is known as the Julio-Claudian dynasty and which lasted almost 100 years, every ruler came from Augustus's extended family. Nero, the last of Augustus's family line, committed suicide in 68 C.E. He left no heirs and so no obvious successors to the throne. Four men contended for the throne.

During this "Year of the Four Emperors," Rome learned what the historian Tacitus later called the "secret of empire"—that troops far from the imperial city could choose emperors. Four different emperors took the throne in quick succession, as different Roman armies competed to put their commanders on the throne. The winner of this contest was the general Titus Flavius Vespasianus, or Vespasian (r. 69–79 C.E.), who learned of Nero's death while in Palestine breaking the back of a great Jewish rebellion. By the end of 69 C.E. Vespasian defeated his rivals and became

the first emperor who did not come from the Roman nobility. Born into the equestrian class, he built his reputation on his military prowess.

The Flavian dynasty that Vespasian established lasted twenty-five years until the death of his last son, Domitian (r. 81–96 C.E.). A conscientious and able monarch, Domitian nevertheless ruled with an openly autocratic style. He executed many aristocratic senators, creating a reign of terror among Rome's elite. Fittingly, a group of senators murdered him.

To avoid the chaos of another succession crisis, the Senate cooperated with the army in choosing a new emperor, the elderly Nerva (r. 96–98 C.E.). They hoped that this highly respected man who had no sons would ensure a smooth transition to the next regime, and so he did. Under pressure from the restless military establishment, Nerva adopted the vigorous and experienced general Trajan (r. 98–117 C.E.) as his son and heir. He thus inaugurated the era historians call the Antonine Age. For almost a century, Rome enjoyed competent rule, to a large degree because Nerva's practice of adopting highly qualified successors continued. After Trajan adopted Hadrian (r. 117–138 C.E.), Hadrian in turn adopted Antoninus Pius (r. 138–161 C.E.). Antoninus adopted Marcus Aurelius (r. 161–180 C.E.) to succeed him. Historians consider the Antonine age a high point of Roman peace and prosperity. The Roman historian Tacitus, who survived Domitian's tyranny to live during Nerva's and Trajan's reigns, praised these latter emperors for establishing "the rare happiness of times, when we may think what we please, and express what we think."

This time of peace ended with another imperial murder. Marcus Aurelius unfortunately abandoned the custom of picking a highly qualified successor, and instead was followed to the throne by his incompetent, cruel, and eventually insane son Commodus (r. 180–192 C.E.). In 192 C.E., several senators arranged to have Commodus strangled, triggering another civil war.

A senator from North Africa, Septimius Severus, emerged victorious from this conflict and assumed the imperial throne in 193 C.E. Fluent in Latin, Greek, and Punic,

The Accomplishments of Augustus

In 14 C.E., the 76-year-old Augustus composed a text detailing his achievements. He ordered that the text be engraved on bronze tablets and erected outside his mausoleum after his death. As the following excerpts show, Augustus presented himself as the savior rather than the destroyer of Republican traditions.

At the age of nineteen, on my own initiative and at my own expense, I raised an army by means of which I liberated the Republic, which was oppressed by the tyranny of a faction [Antony and his supporters] . . . Those who assassinated my father* I drove into exile, avenging their crime by due process of law; and afterwards when they waged war against the state, I conquered them twice on the battlefield [at Philippi in 42 B.C.E.].

I waged many wars throughout the whole world by land and by sea, both civil and foreign, and when victorious I spared all citizens who sought pardon. Foreign peoples who could safely be pardoned I preferred to spare rather than to extirpate. About 500,000 Roman citizens were under military oath to me. Of these, when their terms of service were ended, I settled in colonies or sent back to their own municipalities a little more than 300,000, and to all of these I allotted lands or granted money as rewards for military service. . . .

The dictatorship offered to me [in 22 B.C.E.] by the people and by the senate, both in my absence and in my presence, I refused to accept. . . . The consulship, too, which was offered to me at that time as an annual office for life, I refused to accept. In [19, 18, and 11 B.C.E.], though the Roman senate and people unitedly agreed that I should be elected sole guardian of the laws and morals with supreme authority, I refused to accept any office offered me which was contrary to the traditions of our ancestors. . . .

I repaired the Capitol and the theater of Pompey with enormous expenditures on both works, without having my name inscribed on them. I repaired the conduits of the aqueducts which were falling into ruin in many places because of age . . . I completed the Julian Forum and the basilica which was between the temple of Castor and the temple of Saturn, . . . and when the same basilica was destroyed by fire, I enlarged its site and began rebuilding the structure, which is to be inscribed with the names of my sons. . . .

I gave a gladiatorial show three times in my own name, and five times in the names of my sons or grandsons; at these shows about 10,000 fought. Twice I presented to the people in my own name an exhibition of athletes invited from all parts of the world, and a third time in the name of my grandson. I presented games in my own name four times, and in addition twenty-three times in the place of other magistrates. . . . Twenty-six times I provided for the people in my own name or in the names of my sons or grandsons, hunting spectacles of African wild beasts in the circus or in the Forum or in the amphitheaters; in these exhibitions about 3,500 animals were killed. . . .

I brought peace to the sea by suppressing the pirates. In that war I turned over to their masters for punishment nearly 30,000 slaves who had run away from their owners and taken up arms against the state. The whole of Italy voluntarily took an oath of allegiance to me and demanded me as its leader in the war in which I was victorious at Actium [in 31 B.C.E.]. . . . I extended the frontiers of all the provinces of the Roman people . . . I restored peace. . . .

Augustus refers here to his adoptive father, Julius Caesar.

Source: Augustus, *The Accomplishments of Augustus* (14 C.E.). From Naphtali Lewis and Meyer Reinhold (eds.), Roman *Civilization: Selected Readings*, 3rd ed., Vol. 1 (New York: Columbia University Press, 1990), pp. 561–572.

---

the Phoenician language still widely spoken in North Africa, Septimius Severus exemplified the ascent of provincial aristocrats to the highest levels of the empire. The Severan dynasty he established lasted until 235 C.E. Septimius Severus could afford to ignore the Senate because he was popular with the army—he raised its pay for the first time in more than 100 years. But when the last emperor of his dynasty, Severus Alexander (r. 222–235 C.E.), attempted to negotiate with the German tribes by offering them bribes, his own troops killed him because they wanted the cash for themselves. Once again, the murder of an emperor provoked civil war. Fifty years of political and economic crises followed the end of the Severan dynasty. As we

will see in the next chapter, the imperial structure that emerged after this time of crisis differed significantly from the Augustan model.

The Emperor's Role: The Nature of Imperial Power

Under the Augustan imperial system, four main responsibilities defined the emperor's role. First, the emperor both protected and expanded imperial territory. Only the emperor determined foreign policy and made treaties with other nations. Only the emperor waged war—both defensive wars to protect the empire from its enemies and aggressive campaigns of conquest. Generals fighting under

CHRONOLOGY

Emperors of Rome

	27 B.C.E.–14 C.E.	Augustus
JULIO-CLAUDIAN DYNASTY	14–37 C.E.	Tiberius
	37–41 C.E.	Caligula
	41–54 C.E.	Claudius
	54–68 C.E.	Nero
	68–69 C.E.	Galba
	69 C.E.	Otho
	69 C.E.	Vitellius
FLAVIAN DYNASTY	69–79 C.E.	Vespasian
	79–81 C.E.	Titus
	81–96 C.E.	Domitian
	96–98 C.E.	Nerva
	98–117 C.E.	Trajan
	117–138 C.E.	Hadrian
	138–161 C.E.	Antoninus Pius
ANTONINE DYNASTY	161–180 C.E.	Marcus Aurelius
	161–169 C.E.	Lucius Verus
	180–192 C.E.	Commodus
	193 C.E.	Pertinax
	193 C.E.	Didius Julianus
	193–211 C.E.	Septimius Severus
	211–217 C.E.	Caracalla
SEVERAN DYNASTY	211–212 C.E.	Geta
	217–218 C.E.	Macrinus
	218–222 C.E.	Elagabalus
	222–235 C.E.	Severus Alexander

Augustus's orders conquered huge tracts of Spain, Germany, and the Balkans. The emperor Trajan won great glory by conquering the rich Dacian kingdom north of the Danube River between 101 and 106 C.E. Other emperors smashed internal revolts or fought long border wars. From Augustus's reign onward, the northern frontier along the Rhine and Danube Rivers saw occasional, bitter warfare with various Germanic peoples. Marcus Aurelius had to pawn palace treasures to finance campaigns against confederations of Germanic tribes along the Danube frontier.

The emperor's second responsibility was to administer justice and to provide good government throughout his dominions. In theory all citizens could appeal to the emperor directly for justice. In addition, the emperor and his staff responded to questions on points of law and administration from provincial governors and other officials who ruled in the emperor's name. Emperors provided emergency relief after natural disasters, looked after the roads and infrastructure of the empire, and financed some public buildings in many provincial cities.

The emperor's third responsibility stemmed from his religious role. As *Pontifex Maximus,* or High Priest, the emperor supervised the public worship of the great gods of Rome, particularly Jupiter, as well as the goddess Roma. Emperors and subjects alike believed that in order to fulfill Rome's destiny to rule the world, they must make regular sacrifices to the gods.

Finally, the emperor gradually became a symbol of unity for all the peoples of the empire. He embodied the empire and served as the focal point around which all life in the empire revolved. Inevitably, the emperor seemed more than human, even worthy of worship, for he was the guarantor of peace, prosperity, and victory for Rome, and he had infinitely more power than anyone else alive.

Worship of the emperor began with Augustus. He was reluctant to call himself a god because Roman tradition opposed such an idea, but he permitted his spirit to be worshiped in a paternal way, as a sort of *paterfamilias* or head of a universal family of peoples of the empire. He also referred to himself as the "son of a god"—in this case Julius Caesar, whom the Senate had declared divine. After Augustus, imperial worship became more pronounced, although only a few emperors, such as Domitian, emphasized their divinity during their lifetimes. Most were content to be worshiped after death, assuming that the Senate would declare them gods after their funerals. On his deathbed, Vespasian managed to joke, "I guess I'm becoming a god now."

In Rome's eastern provinces such as Egypt and Syria, where people for thousands of years had considered their kings divine, the worship of the emperor spread quickly. Each city's official calendar marked the emperor's day of accession to the throne. Soon, cities across the empire worshiped the emperor on special occasions through games, speeches, sacrifices, and free public feasts in which people ate the flesh of the animals sacrificed in the emperor's honor. At magnificent temples, priests conducted elaborate public rituals to venerate the emperor.

This cult of the emperor provided a focus of allegiance for the diverse peoples of the empire and so served as a unifying force. Although most people would never see their ruler, he was in their prayers and their public spaces every day. In addition to encouraging worship or veneration in public ceremonies throughout the empire, emperors made their presence felt by building and restoring roads, temples, harbors, aqueducts, and fortifications. These public works demonstrated the emperor's unparalleled patronage and concern for the public welfare. In turn, local leaders emulated his generosity in their own cities.

Other elements of material culture also made the imperial presence real for the emperor's subjects. Coins, for example, provided a glimpse of the emperor's face and a phrase that characterized some aspect of his reign. Slogans such as "Restorer of the World," "Concord with the Gods," and "The Best Ruler—Sustenance for Italy" brought the ruler's message into every person's pocket. Statues of the emperor served a similar purpose. (One statue of an emperor found in Carthage had a removable head, so that when a new ruler ascended the throne, the town leaders could save money by replacing only the head.) In his own portraits, Augustus tended toward the conventions of classical Greek portraiture that presented him as remote and ageless. In contrast, his successors placed portraits of their faces on their coins and statues, making them easily identifiable in surviving sculpture.

Emperors also used military and sporting victories to make their presence felt throughout the empire. In the Republic, conquest had brought wealth and glory to its many generals. In contrast, in the new imperial system, only the emperor could take credit for victory in war. Imperial propaganda described the emperor as eternally triumphant. Sporting events, too, glorified the emperor. At the Circus Maximus in Rome, a chariot racetrack where a quarter of a million people could gather to cheer their favorite charioteer, as well as in racetracks throughout the empire, enthusiastic crowds shared the pleasure of the competition with the emperor or his representatives.

Aqueducts: The Pont du Gard
This graceful aqueduct, now known as the Pont du Gard, was built about 14 C.E. to carry water to the city of Nîmes, in the south of France, from its surrounding hills. Romans were highly sophisticated hydraulic engineers, and waterworks like this aqueduct were a common feature of all the large cities of the empire.

The City of Rome

The city of Rome stood as a monument to the paramount authority of the emperor. Augustus boasted that he had found Rome built of brick and left it built of marble. Though an exaggeration, this claim nevertheless reveals the effect of monarchy on Rome's urban fabric. Every emperor wanted to leave his mark on the city of Rome as a testimony to his generosity and power. As Rome grew, it became the model for cities throughout the empire. Its public spaces and buildings provided a stage for the acting out of basic activities of imperial rule (see Map 5.2).

The center of political and public life in the city of Rome was the Forum, an area filled with many imposing buildings—administrative headquarters such as the treasury and records office, law courts, and the Senate House. Roman laws were inscribed on gleaming bronze tablets and placed on the outer walls of these buildings, testimony to the principles of justice and order that formed the framework of the Roman state. Basilicas, colossal colonnaded halls in which Romans conducted public business ranging from finance to legal trials, crowded against the sides of the Forum.

Because public and religious life were intertwined, the Forum also contained many grand temples of the gods who controlled Rome's destiny. For example, the goddess Concordia, who represented political agreement among Romans, had a gleaming shrine. Jupiter, Rome's chief god, had a huge marble temple on the Capitoline Hill looking down on the Forum. An altar to the goddess Victory stood in the Senate, where generals took oaths of allegiance to the emperor before marching to war.

The Forum particularly highlighted the emperor's power within the imperial system. Emperors built huge arches in the Roman Forum to celebrate their triumphs. After a victorious military campaign, emperors paraded through the Forum on the Sacred Way, passed under the arches, and finished at the temple of Jupiter. Delighted crowds watched defeated kings pass by in chains and marveled at huge floats piled high with loot. In the victory

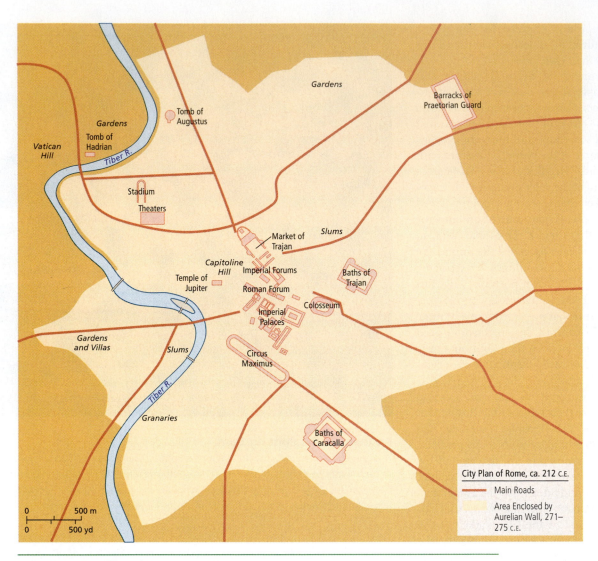

Map 5.2   The City of Rome, ca. 212 C.E.
This diagram shows the main public buildings of the imperial capital. Most cities elsewhere in the empire imitated this urban plan.

parade, slaves carried grandiose paintings that depicted important battles and other scenes of the war.

The might of the emperor was on display not only in the Forum but throughout the city of Rome. Emperors spent gigantic sums on baths, stadiums, and additional forums. Trajan's Forum, by far the biggest, included libraries of Greek and Latin texts, an enormous basilica for public business, a multistoried marketplace not unlike a modern mall, shops, and a marble column thirty-eight meters high on which was carved the story of Trajan's victorious Dacian Wars. The emperor Caracalla was renowned for constructing the biggest and most expensive bathing complex. The Colosseum, built by Vespasian and Titus, replaced Nero's private pleasure pond and provided a spot in the very heart of the city where as

The Colosseum

many as 50,000 happy spectators could watch the slaughter of men and animals at the emperor's expense. Romans could also go to the Circus Maximus to see horse-drawn chariots compete for victory under the emperor's auspices. Emperors also built and maintained theaters, libraries, parks, and markets for the public's enjoyment.

Other impressive monuments dotted the city's landscape. The tombs of Augustus and his family stood in the Field of Mars, a region of the city full of public buildings. Hadrian's mausoleum was just across the Tiber River. A great map of the empire built by Augustus delighted viewers while at the same time asserting imperial claims to control of the world. Emperors built their palaces on the Palatine Hill, which looked down on the Forum from the east, and great men's mansions covered nearby hills.

To erect these monumental buildings, the Romans pioneered certain architectural techniques and styles. They were the first to build extensively in concrete, which allowed them to develop new methods of construction. The concrete vault, for example, made possible the enormous baths and public buildings that graced the streets of Rome. The Pantheon, built by Hadrian, is the largest ancient roofed building still standing today. With a diameter of 142 feet, its dome has no interior supports.

IMAGE

Dome of the Pantheon

The wealthy of Rome lived in luxury that would not be equaled in the West for centuries. By the time of Trajan's reign, eleven aqueducts provided Rome with 300 million gallons of water every day. Prosperous Romans could have fresh water for drinking and bathing pumped directly into their homes. The aqueducts also supplied the enormous demands of the imperial bath complexes built for the entire population.

In stark contrast to the gleaming homes and public buildings were the filthy slums of the poor. Unlike wealthy Romans, the impoverished majority of Rome's inhabitants lived in the valleys between Rome's seven hills or by the Tiber River, where they crowded into apartment buildings up to six stories high. Each building contained several apartments, consisting of small rooms without plumbing, fireplaces, or proper ventilation. Lacking proper foundations, apartment buildings often collapsed and could easily become firetraps. (Perhaps it is not a surprise, then, that Augustus established the first professional fire department in Western history.)

The Agents of Control

The emperor stood at the heart of the imperial system devised by Augustus. But the imperial center also included other agents of control. The Roman Senate continued to play a significant administrative role in the new system. As it grew to represent not just the aristocracy of the city of Rome, but a new ruling elite drawn from the provinces, the Senate solidified networks of power and communications that tied the imperial center to its outlying regions. The army, too, constituted an important element of the imperial center. It not only conquered new territories and ensured the emperor's rule throughout the empire, it also served as a force of Romanization°, bringing Roman cultural and political practices to distant regions.

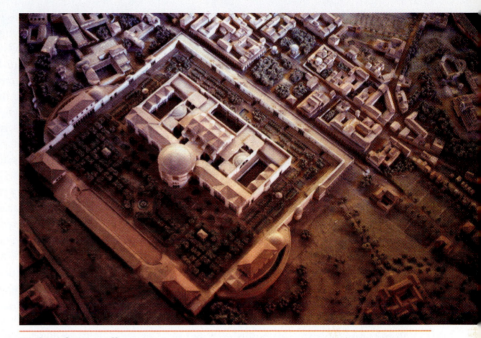

Baths of Caracalla

The gigantic bath complex built by Caracalla in 212–216 C.E. (seen here in an architect's reconstruction) covers more than fifty acres in central Rome. It contained numerous pools heated to different temperatures, exercise grounds, and rooms for reading and relaxation. With walls covered in colored marble, statues, and works of art prominently displayed, the baths were a visual treat for the public. The building's structure demonstrates Roman architectural planning and hydraulic engineering at their finest. One of the bathing pools has been converted to a stage where today theater productions are performed.

The Roman Senate: From Autonomy to Administration

In the imperial system fashioned by Augustus, the Senate continued to function, but with a more restricted role. To maintain the illusion that he had saved rather than destroyed the Republic, Augustus took pains to show respect for the Senate. He allowed its members to compete among themselves for promotion and honor in his service. He permitted the old Republican offices such as tribune and consul to remain in place, and encouraged ambitious men in Rome to compete for them. Augustus also emphasized integrity in the service of the state and sent able senators to govern provinces, thereby reducing corruption.

In these ways the basic machinery of government inherited from the Republic continued to operate—but in conformity with the emperor's wishes. In the new imperial system, the emperor, not the Senate, controlled military, financial, and diplomatic policy. Free political debate was silenced. Because he wanted to avoid the ruthless competition for power that had destroyed the Republic, Augustus eliminated his opponents and filled the Senate with loyal supporters.

Deprived of its autonomy, the Senate became an administrative arm of imperial rule. Senators served as provincial governors, army commanders, judges, and financial officers. They managed the water and grain supplies of the city of Rome, and some of them served on the emperor's advisory council. Aristocratic senators learned to serve the empire faithfully even if they disliked the emperor.

Emperors often brought new men into the Senate from the provinces as a reward for their support, with the belief that Rome grew strong through admitting the best of its provincials to the highest levels of government. Broadening Senate membership in this way enabled more and more of the Romanized elites of the empire to feel they had a stake in the imperial enterprise. Some Roman-born senators, however, balked at such inclusiveness. The emperor Claudius (r. 41–54 C.E.) caused considerable dismay among the snobbish Roman senators when he admitted a few new members from Gaul. Nevertheless, the numbers of provincials in the Roman Senate increased in the first two centuries. By the end of the third century C.E. more than half of Rome's senators came from outside Italy.

While the emperor's relationship with the Senate was of primary importance, other social ranks also played crucial roles in imperial administration. Many members of the equestrian class served in government positions. In addition, many emperors employed freedmen (former slaves) on their administrative staffs and benefited from their loyalty and competence. During Claudius's reign, some senators complained that the freedmen in his administration possessed more influence and easier access to the emperor than did the senators themselves.

The Roman Army and the Power of the Emperor

Like the Senate and administration, the Roman army was a crucial component of imperial rule. The army could make or break an emperor—something that every ruler understood. Without the army's support, Augustus would never have succeeded in transforming the Republic into his imperial system. In 41 C.E., after the death of Caligula, soldiers of the palace guard dragged the lame, stammering Claudius from behind a curtain and forced him to take the throne, as a means of ensuring imperial continuity—and their own livelihoods. When Vespasian took the throne in 69 C.E. with the support of his troops, no one in Rome, least of all the emperors, could doubt the power of the army to influence political affairs. After 235 C.E., many emperors, including Aurelian (r. 270–275 C.E.) and Diocletian (r. 284–305 C.E.), rose through the ranks and became emperor due to the support of their fellow soldiers.

Augustus created a highly efficient professional army that would be the bulwark of the empire for nearly two and a half centuries. His first step was to reduce the army from 60 to 28 legions, so that the troops now totaled 150,000 citizens. (Trajan later added two more legions.) To solidify the loyalty of these legions, Augustus established regular terms of service as well as an ample retirement benefit. He also violated Roman tradition with the creation of the elite Praetorian Guard, which consisted of one and a half legions stationed in Rome to serve as a ceremonial escort for the emperor, maintain order in the city, and enforce the emperor's will throughout Italy.

The strength of the army was augmented by subject peoples who were not citizens. These subjects served as auxiliary troops. After completing their years of service, auxiliaries received Roman citizenship—an important incentive for recruitment. The combined legions and auxiliaries brought the military strength of the Roman army to 300,000 men.

Legionaries enlisted for twenty-five years but only about half survived this term of service. Short life expectancy rather than death in battle kept the figure low, although regular rations and medical care may have helped soldiers live longer than civilians. A soldier with special skills, such as literacy, could rise through the ranks to have significant responsibilities and perhaps become an officer. For those who survived their period of enlistment, Augustus established military colonies in Italy and the provinces of Africa, Spain, and Asia. He rewarded more than 100,000 veterans with grants of land in return for their military service. Later emperors continued the same practice.

The imperial army epitomized many of the values central to Roman imperial culture. It maintained a very high degree of organization, discipline, and training—characteristics on which Romans prided themselves. To the Romans, strict military discipline distinguished their soldiery from disorganized barbarians. Military punishments were notoriously ferocious. For example, if a soldier fell asleep during sentry duty, his barrackmates were required to beat him to death. But tight discipline and vigorous training did produce highly professional fighters. To keep in fighting trim, troops constantly drilled in weaponry, camp building, and battle formations. A Roman soldier was expected to march twenty miles in four hours—while carrying his forty-pound pack and swimming across any rivers encountered along the way.

Life in the Roman Provinces: Assimilation, Resistance, and Romanization

■ How did provincial peoples assimilate to or resist Roman rule?

Beyond the city of Rome and the imperial center lay the second concentric circle of power, the Roman Empire's provinces. In these diverse regions some people assimilated readily to Roman ways, while others fiercely resisted. Unlike the Greeks of the Classical Age,

Romans in the imperial era were willing to include their subjects in the political and cultural life of the empire. Anyone could adopt the practices of Roman daily life, while formal grants of Roman citizenship gave many people the legal rights and privileges that Roman citizens enjoyed.

The Roman way of life manifested itself most noticeably in cities. Modeling themselves on an idealized version of the imperial capital, provincial cities became "little Romes." They served the empire's purposes by funneling wealth from its massive hinterland into imperial coffers. As Roman culture came to predominate in urban centers, however, the division between city and countryside widened. Provincial urban elites benefited from government that was more efficient and orderly than it had been during the Republic. In contrast, rural inhabitants, who formed the majority of the empire's population, faced economic exploitation and threats to their traditional ways of life. Social unrest always boiled beneath the surface of the Roman peace. Yet of the many revolts against Roman authority, only one ever succeeded. Roman military brutality kept most subject peoples in check, but so, too, did the more positive aspects of imperial rule. Many provincial people came to think of themselves as beneficiaries rather than as victims of the Roman Empire.

The Army: A Romanizing Force

More than any other institution, the army mirrored the growth of the Roman Empire from a diverse collection of conquered territories to a well-organized state with a common culture. During the Republic, soldiers tended to be drawn from the city of Rome and surrounding regions—a natural consequence of the fact that Roman soldiers were required to be Roman citizens. In the course of the first two and a half centuries of imperial rule, however, the number of troops from Italy steadily diminished as territories under Roman rule increased.

The army was a significant Romanizing force throughout the imperial era. Army bases in far-flung regions provided the first taste of Roman culture and language to provincial peoples. The army introduced provincial recruits to the Latin language, Roman religion, social organization, and values. Oaths of loyalty bound soldiers to the emperor and Rome, neither of which most legionaries would ever see. Latin, the language of command and army administration, provided another common bond to men whose mother tongues reflected the empire's ethnic diversity. Many inscriptions on soldiers' tombstones reveal that a simplified version of Latin developed in the army. (This language became the ancestor of French, Spanish, and other Romance languages.)

Roman soldiers who settled in the provinces also served as a Romanizing force. Soldiers could not legally marry during their military service but many men reared families anyway with local women. Septimius Severus pragmatically abandoned the restriction against marriage in the army at the end of the second century C.E. At retirement, most soldiers stayed near the bases in which they had been stationed. Many towns arose full of former military personnel and their friends, families, and small businesses. These towns helped transmit Roman culture and values to provincial peoples.

Sports Riot!

In 59 C.E. a riot broke at the amphitheater of Pompeii between the Pompeians and spectators from the neighboring town of Nuceria who had come to see the gladiatorial games. Badly outnumbered, many Nucerians were killed and many others badly wounded. As punishment, the amphitheater was closed for ten years.

Each of the legions with a contingent of auxiliary troops was stationed as a permanent garrison in a province with an elaborate logistical infrastructure to provide weapons, food, and housing. Legions had a standard chain of command to organize officers and men. The architecture of camps and fortification, as well as weapons, armor, and tactics, followed the same conventions across the empire, thus reinforcing the army's role as a Romanizing force. Generals and staff officers often had postings in different provinces during their careers, so there developed a strong sense of shared enterprise.

After conquering new territories and peoples, Roman armies remained in place as occupying forces. Initial relations tended to be hostile. The Romans spoke a different language from that of their subjects, worshiped different gods, and enforced strange and unwelcome rules. The tension between Roman armies and provincial populations never entirely went away, but gradually the conquered peoples became Romanized. As the occupying Roman forces settled in and raised families with local women, defeated peoples started to assimilate into Roman culture. They adopted Roman customs and language, and provincial elites began to enter Roman politics. Romanization transformed the provinces from occupied zones where shattered communities obeyed foreign masters to well-integrated territories in which Roman culture flourished.

Administration and Commerce

Conquered lands were quickly organized into provinces. One of the chief accomplishments of the Augustan state was establishing a well-managed and prosperous provincial system that lasted until the late third century C.E. A governor ruled over each province: He administered justice, supervised tax collection, and orchestrated the flow of slaves, timber, metals, horses, spices, and other treasures back to Rome. Although the Roman Empire at its height had about 50 million inhabitants, only a few thousand men participated directly in imperial administration in the provinces. Most administrative work was performed at the local level by city councilors, who in turn were loosely supervised by imperial governors and their staffs. The governors' responsibilities included protecting the frontiers, collecting taxes, administering justice, and suppressing rebellions.

This structure of government gave rise to an administrative-military class that drew its members from both the senatorial and the equestrian orders. In the service of the emperor, these men enjoyed splendid careers, climbing the ladder of success through appointments in different provinces. As a group, they provided a cadre of officials with empire-wide experience. Gnaeus Julius Agricola is an apt example. The father-in-law of the historian Tacitus, Agricola had a brilliant military career under the Flavian emperors. During his five years as governor of Britain, he

DOCUMENT

Agricola the General

The historian Tacitus wrote a biography of his father-in-law, the general and administrator Gnaeus Julius Agricola (49–93 C.E.). Agricola had a glittering military career under the Flavian emperors. As commander in chief of Roman forces in Britain from 78 to 83 C.E., he subdued most of the island and advanced deep into Scotland. Agricola encouraged urbanization and Mediterranean customs such as public bathing and chariot racing. In the following selection, Tacitus considers the implications of deliberate Romanization.

The following winter passed without disturbance, and was employed in salutary measures. For, to accustom to rest and repose through the charms of luxury a population scattered and barbarous and therefore inclined to war, Agricola gave private encouragement and public aid to the building of temples, courts of justice and dwelling houses, praising the energetic and reproving the indolent. Thus an honourable rivalry took the place of compulsion. He likewise provided a liberal education for the sons of the chiefs, and showed such a preference for the natural powers of the Britons over the industry of the Gauls that they who lately disdained the tongue of Rome now coveted its eloquence. Hence, too, a liking sprang up for our style of dress and the toga became fashionable. Step by step they were led to things which dispose to vice, the lounge, the bath, the elegant banquet. All this in their ignorance they called civilization, when it was but a part of their servitude.

Source: From Tacitus, "Agricola 21" in *Complete Works of Tacitus,* edited by Moses Hadas, translated by Alfred John Church and William Jackson Brodribb (New York: The Modern Library, 1942).

brought that distant province firmly under Roman control. Agricola epitomized loyalty to the state, experience in military affairs, and a thoughtful approach to drawing the elites of defeated enemies into the imperial way of life.

Extensive transport and commercial networks also helped both to connect the many provinces of the vast Roman Empire and to spread the Roman way of life. More than 40,000 miles of roads crisscrossed the empire. These roads, however, were built to move troops, not goods; throughout the Roman era transporting goods by land remained far more expensive than moving them by water. Rivers and the Mediterranean Sea were the primary conduits of trade. With pirates quelled by the Roman navy, shipping flourished. Improvements in harbors, ports, and linking canal systems further encouraged the growth of long-distance trade around the Mediterranean.

The Cities

The empire's territory consisted of a honeycomb of cities. Each "cell" in the structure constituted one administrative unit comprising the main urban center as well as the surrounding lands and villages. The Romans called each of these cells a *civitas*°, or city. Without the cities, Rome could not have held together the huge territories conquered by its armies. As centers for tax collection and law courts, cities were the locations where the imperial administrators interacted with provincial aristocrats, who had influence over the local population. Through cities, the empire's vast territories were linked to the imperial center.

More than a thousand cities dotted the imperial map (see Map 5.3). In regions where Roman urban traditions were little-known, the Romans created new urban centers. Cities such as Lugdunum (Lyons) in France or Eburacum (York) in Britain were created in the first years of conquest as centers of Roman culture and authority. In contrast, in regions throughout the Mediterranean where urban culture had deep roots, provincial cities such as Athens or Jerusalem had long been centers of learning or religion.

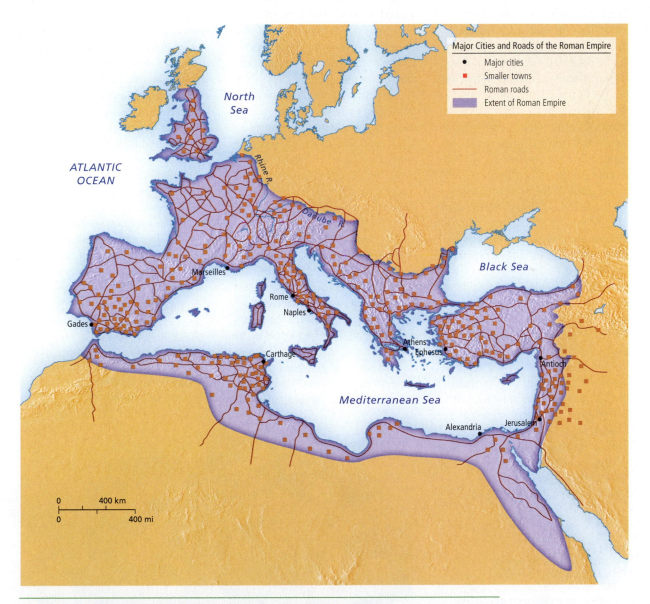

Map 5.3   Major Cities and Roads of the Roman Empire
Thousands of miles of roads linked the cities of the Roman Empire. Used primarily as military highways, the roads also helped merchants travel with their wares. When they crossed imperial frontiers, merchants traded with many peoples eager for Roman goods, especially wine and luxury objects.

The Roman City: Agent of Cultural Transformation

Between the second century B.C.E. and the first century C.E., Roman armies conquered much of western Europe. The Celtic peoples who inhabited these regions did not dwell in cities like those in Italy and the Mediterranean world. They lived in small villages scattered over the landscape. But as soon as the bloodshed of conquest was over, the Roman conquerors began to establish cities. These new urban foundations imitated Mediterranean cities, and especially an idealized notion of the city of Rome, in their physical and architectural layout. All of them had a forum in the center of town, flanked by a council house (modeled on the Roman Senate), basilicas, and temples—temples to the community's gods as well as the chief gods of the Roman Empire, to the emperor, and to Rome itself. In addition, the cities provided all the amenities and requirements of Mediterranean urban life, such as bathhouses, brothels, arenas for gladiatorial combat and wild beast hunts, and slave markets. Two main streets intersected in the heart of the town, connecting the city to the larger Roman road system that linked the provinces together and that let local farmers bring their produce into market.

The emergence of these cities meant more than political or economic development. Through their architecture and layout, as well as the lifestyle they promoted, provincial cities became agencies of cultural change, the stages on which the Roman way of life was acted out. In these cities, provincial peoples encountered Rome not just as a military conqueror but also as a cultural force. Thus the cities played an essential role in the process known as Romanization, in which local populations slowly acquired the characteristics of Roman life: They started to speak Latin, worship Roman gods, employ Roman architecture and styles of art, and habituate themselves to the Roman way of life.

This cultural transformation was particularly marked in the ranks of the local aristocratic elites. Often the leaders of the conquered communities who were willing to go along with the Romans were rewarded with Roman citizenship. They took a leading role in their city's senate, administering the city and its agricultural lands and collecting taxes. They paid for public buildings out of their own pockets to demonstrate their civic-minded generosity, just as Roman aristocrats did throughout the empire and especially in the city of Rome itself. In return for their cooperation, these local grandees could expect rewards from Rome. Some even entered the Roman Senate.

For Romans, the cities symbolized a transformation from the old way of life of conquered peoples to the Roman style of living, a transformation from barbarism to civilization. Romanization was a two-way street, however. Just as much as the local populations assimilated the notion of Roman cultural superiority, adopting aspects of Roman life and benefiting materially from their encounter with Roman culture, Rome took something in return. By drawing these provincial peoples into the imperial matrix, Rome grew more cosmopolitan. Roman art and literature reflected images and themes drawn from provincial cultures. Roman life differed subtly from one province to another as local cultures made their presence felt on the dominant Roman forms. These differences ranged from provincial accents in spoken Latin to specialized cuisines and agricultural techniques. Yet all the provinces—and the cities in them—were Roman.

Question for Discussion

For Romans, the cities symbolized a transformation from barbarism to civilization. What characteristics, then, defined "civilization" to the Romans? What alternative definitions of "civilization" were available?

Little Romes

The amphitheater at the Tunisian town of El-Djem (the ancient city of Thysdrus) was built in the early third century C.E. and was one of the largest in the empire. Like the Colosseum in Rome, which it imitated, this arena could seat more than 20,000 spectators at gladiatorial fights and other entertainments. These public activities were popular throughout the empire.

Some urban hubs, such as Carthage and Alexandria, teemed with several hundred thousand people.

Certain common patterns characterized urban life throughout the empire. All cities governed themselves. A city council modeled on the Roman Senate presided over each city's affairs. Only a handful of the community's wealthiest men served in the city council and held the various magistracies and priesthoods. Council membership passed from father to son. Wealthy women held no administrative office and had no role in public decision making, though they sometimes presided as priestesses in civic religious observances. The male citizens of each city voted on local issues and elected town officials. City councils managed the grain supply, arranged for army recruitment, supervised the marketplaces, administered justice in local law courts, and most important of all, collected taxes for the central government. Councilors paid out of their own pockets for the upkeep of public works, aqueducts, and baths, and funded religious festivals and public amusements. As provincial officials performed their public responsibilities on behalf of their hometowns, they imitated the efforts of that greatest patron of all, the emperor himself. The city councilors were the "mouthpiece of Rome."

The Countryside

Control of the countryside was the key to the prosperity of the imperial system. The wealthiest men owned the most land. Landholdings, however, varied greatly in size and distribution. The emperor was the greatest property owner, controlling millions of acres of land throughout the empire. Augustus, for example, personally owned the entire province of Egypt. Like Augustus, wealthy Roman investors owned properties in many different regions of the empire. Some of these landed magnates chose to enter a life of public service either in Rome or in their home cities. Others preferred to enjoy the benefits of their enormous wealth away from the risks of political life.

At the bottom of the pyramid toiled the peasants, who lived in the countryside and performed the agricultural labor that made local landowners rich. The circumstances of peasant life varied greatly throughout the empire. Some peasants owned small farms sufficient to maintain their families, perhaps with the assistance of seasonal wage laborers or a few slaves. Others rented their lands from landlords to whom they owed payment in the form of produce, money, or labor. Degrees of dependency on landlords varied as well. Extremely fierce penalties for inability to pay rents ranged from enslavement to other forms of bondage.

All landowning peasants faced one constant threat—the possibility that a more powerful landowner might seize their fields by force. When this happened, peasants had little hope of getting their land back. The imperial system favored the property rights of the wealthy and worked to the disadvantage of the rural poor. Cities gobbled up the peasants' crops; government officials extorted taxes from them; and landlords and soldiers bullied them. Rabbi Hanina ben Hama, who lived in Palestine about 240 C.E., stated bluntly that the empire established cities "in order to impose upon the people forced labor, extortion and oppression." In addition to this relentless exploitation, famine, natural disasters, and debt constantly threatened the peasants' very survival.

Despite these hardships, the peasantry during the empire's first three centuries managed to produce enough surplus crops to maintain the imperial system, especially the army with its ravenous demands for supplies and foods. Indeed, agricultural productivity during this era was remarkable, considering the low yields of farms, the difficulty and expense of transportation, and the rudimentary farming technology of the time. Some historians estimate that Europe did not see a comparable level of agricultural productivity again until the seventeenth century.

Food staples in the Mediterranean region included olives, grains, and wines. Dates were a coveted sweet, because the Romans did not have sugar. In more northern regions butter replaced oil and beer substituted for wine. Large flocks of sheep and herds of cattle provided necessary wool and leather.

Terrain and climate as much as investment and local farming custom determined the methods of agricultural exploitation. In Sicily and parts of southern Italy, chain gangs of slaves predominated, working on vast estates. Migrant workers labored in the olive groves of North Africa, while seasonal movement of grazing animals predominated in hilly regions of Italy and the Balkans. In Egypt, the annual flooding of the Nile determined the rhythms of agricultural life and made the Nile Valley one of the empire's chief producers of grain.

Revolts Against Rome

Conquest by Roman armies could be a long and brutal ordeal. After the shock of military defeat and surrender to Roman generals came the imposition of the administrative structures of Roman rule and the mechanisms of economic exploitation. Not surprisingly, resentment simmered among conquered peoples. Revolts against Roman authority often followed soon after a subject people's initial defeat, while freedom was still a living memory. The stories of several revolts illustrate that subject peoples rarely adjusted smoothly to Roman rule and that Roman force usually—but not always—proved overwhelming.

Arminius and the Revolt in Germany

In 9 C.E. Arminius, chieftain of a Germanic tribe called the Cherusci, led the only successful military revolt against Roman rule. As a young man serving in an auxiliary

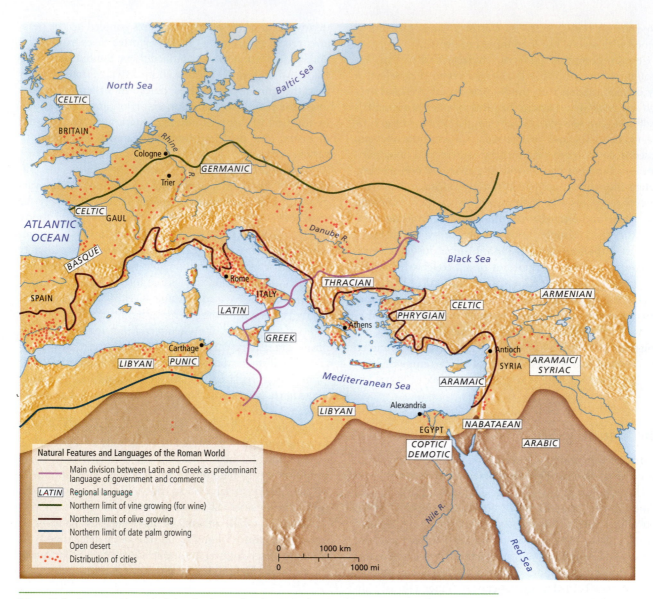

Map 5.4   Languages and Agriculture in the Roman Empire

The 50 million inhabitants of the Roman Empire spoke many different languages, but the two most dominant were Greek in the eastern regions and Latin in the west. Another important division was that between the wine-drinking regions in the south and the beer-drinking territories in the north.

regiment in the Roman army, Arminius earned Roman citizenship, learned to speak Latin, and gained the rank of equestrian. Arminius seemed to be a real friend of Rome, but the Cherusci had a history of belligerence and resistance. Arminius's tribal ties proved stronger than his loyalty to the empire. The Romans underestimated the pugnacity of their new Germanic subjects and sent the wrong man, Lucius Varus, to be their governor. Varus was a peacetime administrator, not a general. His previous experience in Syria and North Africa had not prepared him for the challenges he encountered east of the Rhine River. He imposed economic exploitation and taxation—the hallmarks of the

Roman peace—on the Cherusci too quickly. Not used to a monetary economy, debt, and foreign control, the tribe and its allies rose in revolt, led by Arminius.

Arminius lured the unsuspecting Varus into a trap in the Teutoburg Forest, slaughtering Varus and three entire Roman legions. A relief army under the command of the future emperor Tiberius contained the disaster, but nevertheless, when Augustus died in 14 C.E., all of Rome's legions were on the west side of the Rhine. No emperor ever again attempted to conquer Germany. One lasting result of Arminius's successful revolt is the linguistic distinction that still cuts across Europe. Whereas French and Italian derive from Latin, German does not because the tribes living between the Rhine and Elbe Rivers managed to throw off the Roman yoke in 9 C.E.

Boudica's Revolt in Britain

Fifty years after Arminius's victory, another major uprising broke out in Britain, led by Boudica, the queen of the people known as the Iceni. The revolt had a long, complex history. In the decades following the initial conquest of the island by the emperor Claudius in 43 C.E., the Romans consolidated their power by playing favorites among the local tribes. They encouraged tribes not under Roman control to ally themselves with Rome as client states. Under King Prasutagus, the Iceni were one of these client states that supplied troops to the Roman army in return for Roman protection. Before King Prasutagus died in 60 C.E., he named the Roman emperor his co-heir with his wife, Boudica, and his daughters. Within a few years the emperor Nero pushed Boudica aside and incorporated the kingdom of the Iceni directly into the Roman state. Emboldened by their new dominance over the Iceni, the agents of the tyrannical Roman governor abused Boudica and raped her daughters.

The queen then led her forces into open rebellion. With the aid of several neighboring tribes who also resented the Roman presence in Britain, Boudica destroyed a legion and leveled several cities, including Camulodunum, a major imperial cult center with a temple dedicated to Rome and the emperor. Resistance ended quickly after Roman forces routed Boudica's troops and the queen took her own life.

The Britons learned that resistance to Rome was futile. The Romans learned a lesson as well: Subject peoples should be treated more justly. The next Roman governor of Britain adopted more lenient administrative policies.

The Revolt of Julius Civilis in Gaul

Like Arminius, Julius Civilis was a Germanic tribal leader who had served in the Roman army. Julius Civilis was both a Roman citizen and a prince of his tribe, the Batavi. Like the Iceni in Britain, the Batavi had supplied troops but not tribute to Rome for several decades. Civilis was serving as a commander of Roman auxiliary troops in Gaul when civil war broke out in Rome in 69 C.E. following Nero's death. Quick to seize an opportunity, Julius Civilis led an army—consisting not only of Batavians but also men from several unconquered German tribes and some restless Gallic tribes—against Roman legionary bases depleted by the civil war.

Despite his career in Roman military service and his involvement in provincial politics, Civilis presented himself to his Batavian followers in religious terms, with native-style oaths of allegiance sworn in a sacred grove. He also maintained close ties with a Batavian prophet, who may

CHRONOLOGY

Political and Military Events

31 B.C.E.	Octavian defeats Mark Antony and controls Mediterranean world
27 B.C.E.	Octavian adopts the name Augustus
9 C.E.	Varus and three legions are defeated; Romans abandon Germany
30 C.E.	Jesus executed in Palestine
63 C.E.	Revolt of Boudica crushed in Britain
66–70 C.E.	Jewish Revolt; Temple and Jerusalem destroyed
69 C.E.	"Year of the Four Emperors"
101–106 C.E.	Trajan conquers Dacia
115–116 C.E.	Trajan conquers Mesopotamia; Rome reaches greatest extent
122–128 C.E.	Hadrian's Wall built in Britain
132–135 C.E.	Hadrian crushes Jewish revolt in Judaea
168 C.E.	Marcus Aurelius defeats the Marcomanni
212 C.E.	Antonine Decree grants Roman citizenship to all free inhabitants of the empire
235 C.E.	Fifty years of political turmoil begin

have predicted that Civilis would lead his people to freedom. But unlike the revolt of Arminius, the revolt of Civilis failed. The new emperor Vespasian brought stability back to the frontier through a combination of diplomacy and swift military action.

Jewish Revolts

Augustus had created the province of Judaea and annexed it to the Empire in 6 C.E. A series of mediocre governors and heavy taxation caused Judaea's economy to decline. Famines and banditry became common, and political discontent mounted among the Jews. Open rebellion almost broke out when the emperor Caligula (r. 37–41 C.E.) ordered that his statue be placed in the Temple in Jerusalem, an unthinkable sacrilege for the Jews. Only Caligula's death in 41 C.E. prevented the beginning of war between Rome and the Jews of Judaea.

Under Roman rule, a significant divide opened up within the Jewish community. Some members of the Jewish priestly caste became devoted to Greek and Roman culture, and the landed elite benefited directly from Roman rule. Ordinary Jews, however, suffered from high taxation and viewed their leaders as collaborators with an occupying and godless power. These Jews gave their loyalty and respect to the

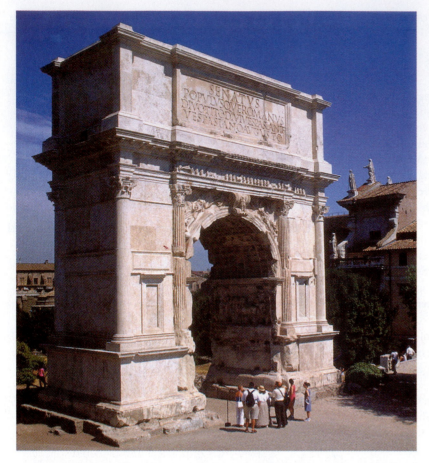

Arch of Titus
This triumphal arch built at the end of the first century C.E. honors the recently deceased Titus for crushing the Jewish revolt of 66–70 C.E. Marble reliefs inside the arch represent the loot from the Temple of Jerusalem carried in the triumphal parade.

scribes, men of learning who devoted their lives to copying religious texts and interpreting the Bible. These learned and religious men had little stake in preserving Roman rule.

Sixty years of Roman mismanagement combined with a desire for independence sparked a massive revolt in Judaea in 66 C.E. Jews stopped offering sacrifices for the emperor's health and formed their own government. They appointed regional military commanders, chose a leader by lot, abolished debt, and issued their own coinage imprinted with messages of freedom. Internal political conflicts within the Jewish community, however, weakened the rebellion and proved as fatal to their cause as the might of Roman legions. In 70 C.E. imperial forces captured Jerusalem, destroyed the Temple, and enslaved an estimated two million people. The victorious generals were Vespasian and his son Titus, both of whom later became emperors.

Despite their overwhelming defeat in 70 C.E., Jewish communities continued to resist Rome. During Trajan's reign, minor revolts broke out in the eastern Mediterranean (115–118 C.E.). Revolts erupted again in 132–135 C.E., prompted by Hadrian's attempt to forbid the Jewish ritual circumcision of male infants. This latter revolt was led by Simon Bar Kochba, or "Son of the Star," who may have claimed to be a messiah, a leader who would end foreign oppression and inaugurate a new era for the Jewish nation.

Other rebellions occurred under the emperors Antoninus Pius (r. 138–161 C.E.) and Septimius Severus (r. 193–211 C.E.). The last major Jewish uprising occurred in Palestine in the fourth century C.E. All of these revolts failed.

Several conclusions may be drawn from these instances of resistance. In each of the western revolts, the Romans overestimated their ability to pacify subject peoples soon after conquering them. Even a tribal leader's service in the Roman auxiliary forces did not blunt tribal identity and allegiance. The rebel leaders appealed to their fellow tribespeople in traditional rather than in Roman terms. It required more than one generation after conquest for tribal elites to embrace the imperial system.

In the case of the Jewish revolt of 66–70 C.E., the Romans misunderstood the nature of leadership and loyalty in Judaea's Jewish society. The Romans allied themselves with members of the Jewish elite whom the majority of Jews distrusted and refused to follow. The continuation of Jewish opposition to Roman rule demonstrates that a population with a strong sense of religious identity rooted in a set of sacred texts could resist—and survive—the overwhelming power of Rome. Most rebels lacked this focus. Within a few generations they assimilated fully into Roman society. The Jews never did so.

Law, Citizenship, and Romanization

In the early days of the empire, Roman law set Romans apart from the bulk of the empire's peoples, who followed their own laws. For example, Jews could live according to Jewish law or Athenians by Athenian law, as long as they paid their taxes to the emperor and did not cause trouble. If a Jew or an Athenian held Roman citizenship, however, he or she could also enjoy the rights and benefits of Roman law. A Roman citizen possessed crucial legally defined rights, including the guarantee of freedom from enslavement. Male citizens had the right to compete for public magistracies, vote in public assemblies, serve in the legions, and make an appeal in a criminal trial.

As the Roman Empire expanded during the first and second centuries C.E., conditions of peace and prosperity encouraged the spread of both Roman-style cities and Roman citizenship, and thus the dominance of Roman law. In this way, Roman law tied the vast empire together. No matter where they lived in the empire, Roman citizens took pride in their centuries-old legal tradition, and in their rights of citizenship. Roman law thus helped erode the local loyalties and traditions of the diverse provincial peoples and so furthered the process of Romanization, of creating a Roman imperial culture.

Then, in 212 C.E., Emperor Aurelius Antoninus (r. 211–217 C.E.), nicknamed Caracalla, issued what became known as the Antonine Decree°. This ruling was a milestone because it granted citizenship to all free men and women within the empire, presumably to increase the tax base. By formally eliminating the distinction between Roman conquerors and subject peoples, the Antonine Decree enabled Roman law to embrace the entire population. This legal uniformity further strengthened provincial loyalty to Rome. Provincial allegiances to their own traditions and laws that had coexisted with Roman imperial law for centuries began to diminish.

Roman law not only served as an important element in Romanization, it also had a significant role in shaping the culture of the West in three specific ways. First, Roman law distinguished between civil law and criminal law. Civil law dealt with all aspects of family life, property and inheritance, slavery, and citizenship. It also dealt with legal procedure and the settling of disputes. Civil law, therefore, defined relations among different classes of Roman society and enabled courts to judge disputes among citizens. Criminal law addressed theft, homicide, sexual crimes, treason, and offenses against the government. These distinctions between civil and criminal law created by the Romans have become standard in the legal systems of nations that are part of Western civilization.

Roman law had a second significant impact on the West in its tradition of codification and interpretation. By the time of Hadrian, a board of professional jurists—directly supervised by the emperor—directed imperial legal affairs. Combining legal scholarship, teaching, and administrative careers, these legal experts collected and analyzed earlier laws and the opinions of their predecessors. Papinian, Paul, and Ulpian, who lived in the early third century C.E., were the greatest of these specialists. They wrote hundreds of books of commentary that shaped the interpretation of Roman law for centuries, were passed on to the lawyers of medieval Europe, and continue to influence Italian, French, and Spanish legal traditions today, as well as the legal system of the state of Louisiana.

One crucial such interpretative tradition is that under the principle of what the Romans called "equity," or fairness, jurists should consider the spirit or intent rather than simply the letter of the law. On the basis of equity, Roman jurists argued that an accuser bears the burden of proof: A defendant does not have to prove he or she is innocent; rather, he or she must be proven guilty.

Finally, and perhaps most important, the Roman concept of "the law of nature" shaped Western ideas of justice. This concept stemmed from Stoicism, with its ideal of an underlying rational order to all things. From the Stoic assumption of rational order the idea developed that certain principles of justice are part of nature itself. Ideally, at least, laws of human societies should conform to the law of nature. Hence the Romans developed the idea that codes of law, although the product of particular societies and circumstances, are based on universally applicable principles. This idea would become a foundation of Western civilization. Building on this Roman idea, later thinkers would insist that all human beings had inalienable rights and that all individuals should be treated as equals under the law.

Equality under the law did not, however, exist in the Roman imperial age. Roman citizens had more rights than noncitizens, and not all Roman citizens had the same rights. In the first century C.E. the vast differences in wealth that divided citizens began to take on legal significance. By the third century C.E., the wealthy upper class, generally called *honestiores* or "better people," and the poor, called *humiliores* or "humbler people," acquired different legal rights, especially in criminal law. For example, *honestiores* convicted of crimes could not be tortured and if they were convicted of a capital crime, they received a quick death by sword. The "humbler people" received the most gruesome punishments, such as being crucified or thrown to wild animals in the arena.

The stronger legal distinction between better and humbler peoples was only one aspect of the law that shifted to reflect the new hierarchies of imperial Rome. During the Republic the Senate gave advice on legal matters to magistrates or citizen assemblies that had official authority to issue laws. During the empire control of law shifted into the emperor's hands. Whether the emperor was issuing a decree on his own initiative, making a general policy in response to an inquiry from a provincial administrator, or making a technical ruling on a point of law in consultation with legal experts on his staff, his decisions had the same status as any law issued by a citizen assembly during the Republic. The idea that the emperor was above the law and that his wishes had the force of law was widely accepted by the early third century C.E.

The Frontier and Beyond

■ How did Romans interact with peoples living beyond the imperial borders?

In Virgil's *Aeneid,* the great god Jupiter promises Rome "imperial rule without limit." But by the time of Hadrian's reign, the limits of the empire were clear. The third concentric circle of the Roman world consisted of the frontier—the outermost regions of the empire and beyond.

Like the generals of the Republic and the Hellenistic kings, Augustus set out to conquer as much land as possible in order to win glory and demonstrate his power. During his reign large portions of Germany and the Danube River basin came under Roman rule. His successors continued to add new lands to the empire. Claudius brought Britain into the Roman fold in 43 C.E., and by 117 C.E. Trajan had conquered Dacia (modern Romania), Mesopotamia, and parts of Arabia bordering the Red Sea. At this point the empire reached its greatest territorial extent.

But after Trajan, emperors turned their attention from conquest to consolidation. Trajan's successor, Hadrian, abandoned Mesopotamia because it was too expensive to control. He organized Rome's frontier with a series of carefully planned fortifications, including the renowned wall that still crosses the north of Britain and bears his name. His successors continued to fortify both the natural and manmade borders of the empire.

By the early second century C.E., regularly spaced military bases and fortresses dotted the empire's northern border while armed naval forces patrolled the Rhine and Danube, and Hadrian's wall stretched across Britain. In the East, another line of military defenses extended from the Black Sea to the Nile. In North Africa as well, a perimeter of fortifications indicated the limits of cultivable land along the empire's southernmost edge.

These were lines of not only political but also cultural demarcation. For the Romans, the boundaries between the empire and its unconquered neighbors symbolized a cultural division between civilization and barbarism. Romans used this distinction to help define their place in the world and to justify their conquest and absorption of other peoples.

Emperors systematically and heavily fortified these lines of political and cultural demarcation. Despite the resources spent on maintaining these borders, however, they remained highly permeable. These borders represented the limits of Roman authority, but they could not prevent non-Romans from entering the empire altogether.

Hadrian's Wall
This massive fortification epitomizes the second-century-C.E. military concept of the fortified frontier; stretched across northern Britain, it separated the Roman provinces to its south from the "barbarians" to the north.

Rome and the Parthian Empire

Although the Roman Empire dominated a huge expanse of territory, it did have one formidable rival: the Parthian Empire (Parthia) to the east. This realm stretched from the Euphrates River to the Indus River (covering modern Iran and Pakistan). Unlike the poorly organized and politically unstable Celtic and Germanic tribes the Romans confronted in western Europe, the Parthian Empire was highly structured and enormously powerful. It replaced the successor states of Alexander the Great in Iran in the mid-third century B.C.E. The Parthian Empire ended in 224 C.E., when another Iranian dynasty, the Sasanian, rose to power.

The structure of the highly stratified Parthian society included a king and warrior aristocracy; a middle range of doctors, artisans, and traders; and a large class of peasants. In addition Parthia contained many subject peoples with their own cultures, such as Babylonians, Jews, and Armenians. Unlike Rome, Parthia did not permit subject peoples and internal minorities to enter the ruling elite. The Parthian Empire did tolerate practice of various religions, although Zoroastrianism was the main religion of the Parthian state.

The Romans knew the Parthians as fierce warriors. Parthia's specially bred battle horses, which were famous as far away as China, made heavily armed Parthian cavalrymen and their archers worthy opponents of Rome's legions. Glory-seeking Roman generals of the late Republic found Parthia an attractive but dangerous target. Augustus, however, inaugurated a new Roman policy toward Parthia, just as he initiated changes in so many other aspects of Roman rule. Augustus—and most of the Roman emperors after him—preferred diplomacy to open conflict with Parthia because they knew they could not conquer and assimilate such a vast territory. Trajan's ambitious conquest of the Parthian provinces of Armenia and Mesopotamia in 115–116 C.E. broke with this consensus on the advantages of diplomacy, but only briefly. Trajan's successor, Hadrian, abandoned these territories because he knew that they overextended Rome's resources.

The most important result of the rivalry between Parthia and Rome was the exchange of products, technology, and ideas between their peoples. Romans highly prized Parthian steel and leather, as well as the exotic spices traded through Parthia from even farther east. The Romans also adopted some military technology and tactics from Parthia, particularly the use of heavily armed cavalry. By the fourth century C.E. these units constituted the core of Roman military might.

There was also an erratic exchange of nonmilitary technological expertise between the two empires. From the Parthians, the Romans learned new techniques of irrigating fields. In turn, Roman hydraulic engineers and masons went to Persia to help construct a great dam for the Parthian king. *Via,* the Latin word for "paved road," entered the Persian language, an indication that other Roman specialists worked in Parthia as well.

Religious ideas also flowed in both directions. Many people in the Roman Empire studied Parthian astrology and magic, while Jewish scholars in the Roman Empire maintained close ties with the Jewish academies in the Parthian province of Babylonia. It was Christianity, however, that was the most directly influenced by this religious interchange between the Parthians and the Romans. The Persian Mani (216–276 C.E.), founder of a religion called Manichaeism, preached that an eternal conflict between forces of light and darkness caused good and evil to intermingle. God's soul had become trapped in matter, and Jesus, the son of God, had come to Earth to retrieve God's soul. Mani taught that all those who followed him and turned their back on earthly possessions would be redeemed. Mani's contempt for the material world colored much of early Christian belief.

Roman Encounters with Germanic Peoples

The peoples living north of the Rhine and Danube Rivers, not the Parthians, posed the greatest threat to Rome during the first two and a half centuries C.E. Called "Germans" by the Romans, these peoples never used that term among themselves or thought of themselves as one group. Numbering in the tens of millions, most of them spoke their own dialects and did not understand the language of other tribes. Lacking political unity, different Germanic peoples constantly grouped and regrouped, taking new names and following new leaders. Led by aristocratic warriors, they often fought bitterly among themselves.

In the early years of Augustus's reign, Roman legions conquered large portions of what is now called Germany between the Rhine and the Elbe Rivers. Arminius's successful revolt in 9 C.E. drove out the Romans, however, and Roman civilization never took root in northern Europe. The Rhine and Danube Rivers became the symbolic boundary between Romans and their northern enemies. Most of Rome's legions were stationed along this boundary to defend against attacks from their northern neighbors.

Tribes along the northern border sometimes fragmented into pro- and anti-Roman factions. Romans supported kings who would favor their cause by fighting Rome's enemies beyond the borders and supplying troops to the auxiliary regiments of the Roman army. Occasionally for short periods of time, Germanic tribes formed loose confederations under the leadership of charismatic warlords in order to invade the empire themselves. For example, the Marcomanni, meaning "men of the borderlands," constituted one of these hostile confederations during the reign of Marcus Aurelius. Seeking land and booty, this confederation of many armed groups attacked the Roman

Empire with more than a hundred thousand men. Only after fourteen years of brutal war did Marcus Aurelius crush this force.

Tacitus,
Germania

During long periods of peace, the people on either side of the border had the opportunity to interact with one another through military service and trade. Through extensive trade with Roman merchants, mostly Italians and Syrians, many Germanic aristocrats developed a taste for Mediterranean luxuries, including wine and jewelry. By the second century C.E. some chose to live in Roman-style villas in imitation of Roman aristocrats. Many Germanic men gained exposure to Roman civilization when they served in the Roman army as auxiliary troops. Discharged after the standard twenty-five years of service, many of these men returned to their homes with Roman money in their purses, a smattering of Latin, and knowledge of the riches and power of the Roman Empire.

By the end of the second century C.E. the weight of different peoples pressing on Rome's northern borders began to crack the imperial defenses. With the end of the Severan dynasty in 235 C.E., the empire entered a period of unrelieved disasters that lasted nearly fifty years. Invading groups from north of the Rhine and Danube Rivers pushed into the empire as far south as central Italy in search of plunder and land on which to settle. The Romans ultimately marshaled the military resources to repel the invaders and restore the empire's security late in the third century C.E. As we will see in the next chapter, however, the restored Roman Empire differed radically from the system Augustus inaugurated.

Economic Encounters Across Continents

The Roman empire stood on the edge of an almost global economic web. Trade routes linked the Mediterranean basin, the East African coast, the Persian Gulf, and the Red Sea with India's western Malabar coast, as well as with lands across the Bay of Bengal in Southeast Asia and China. One Roman account from the first century C.E., *Voyage Around the Red Sea*, written by an unknown author, describes a vast international commercial network.

Encounters with China

More than 3,000 forbidding miles separated the empires of Rome and China. Chinese documents from the first century C.E. mention ambassadors sent to Rome who reached as far as the Persian Gulf, and in 166 C.E. emperor Marcus Aurelius sent ambassadors to China, but the two empires never established formal ties.

Silk, not diplomatic links, bound Rome and China together. From the second millennium B.C.E. until the sixth century C.E., when Western entrepreneurs finally succeeded in smuggling the eggs of silkworms and the seeds of mulberry trees out of China, the Chinese possessed a monopoly on silk production. Far superior to wool and linen both in texture and in its ability to retain brightly colored dyes, silk was one of the most desired commodities in Roman society. In the Republican era, silk was so rare that even the wealthiest Romans could afford only small pieces, which they tended to wear as brooches.

Then, during the age of Augustus, Romans learned to use the monsoon winds to travel from southeastern Egypt across the Indian Ocean to the western coast of India, a journey that took about 40 days. Every year approximately 120 ships made this journey, lured by the promise of vast profits from the silk trade. In India, they would exchange glass, gold, wine, copper, and other items for silk. By the time this trade occurred, the price of the silk would have multiplied several times, as payments were made to each middleman along the 8,000-kilometer "Silk Road" that ran from northern China across the sweltering deserts, towering mountains, and treacherous salt flats of southern Asia and down through modern Afghanistan to the Indian coast. Yet silk was so precious that a successful journey would guarantee a Roman merchant a profit a hundred times larger than his original investment.

Roman demand for silk, spices (especially pepper), and other luxury items from the

Wineship
Found in Germany, this energetic but unsophisticated sculpture of the second century C.E. depicts wine merchants hurrying their cargo to thirsty customers somewhere on the Rhine River. Because grapes could not be cultivated in this northern region, wine was a luxury there. Common people drank beer.

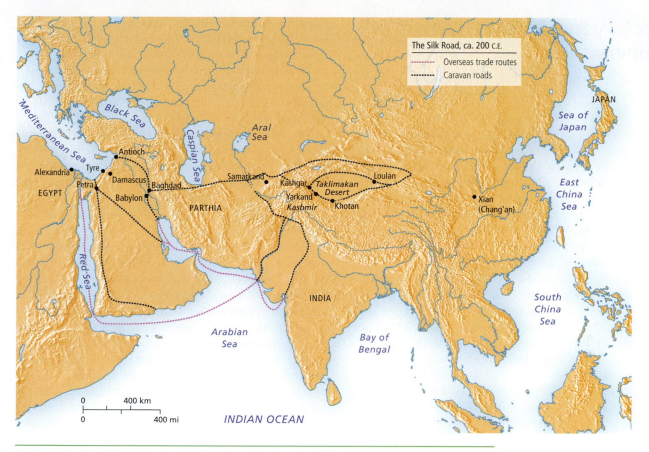

Map 5.5   The Silk Road
The first-century C.E. development of sea routes to supplement the overland parts of the journey greatly strengthened this cross-continental trading network.

Far East eventually produced a trade imbalance. As early as the first century C.E., Pliny the Elder griped, "And by the lowest reckoning India, China, and the Arabian Peninsula take from our Empire many thousands of pounds of gold every year—that is the sum which our luxuries and our women cost us." Pliny's concern was not unfounded: Many historians view the drain of hard currency to the East to pay for luxury goods as a key economic weakness of the Roman Empire, particularly from the third century onward.

Encounters with Africa

In addition to traveling to India and trading with China, Romans did some exploring in sub-Saharan Africa. Roman coins found deep in the interior of Africa suggest that they may have had commercial dealings with peoples there as well. To the Romans, however, "Africa" was one of their provinces bordering the Mediterranean Sea—the region we know as North Africa today—not the vast continent that lay to the south, beyond the Sahara Desert. Only in the European Middle Ages would the name *Africa* come to stand for the entire land mass of the continent.

The Romans knew little about sub-Saharan Africa. In 146 B.C.E., the Roman general Scipio sent the historian Polybius on an expedition down the west coast of Africa. Polybius's expedition got as far as Senegal and a place Scipio called Crocodile River. In the first century C.E., a Roman military expedition that marched south from a base in North Africa in pursuit of some raiders may have reached Chad. One hundred years later, an intrepid Roman officer named Julius Maternus traveled south for four months, reaching a place "where the rhinoceroses gather." He emerged in the Sudan, where he found the Nile and returned home.

The Romans used the word *Aethiopians* ("the People with Burned Faces") to refer to the peoples who lived south of the Sahara desert. Most of their knowledge of these peoples came from the Egyptians, who regularly traded with peoples living in the extreme south of the Nile River valley. From the Egyptians they learned of a place of fabulous wealth and exotic creatures. It would take many centuries, however, before European peoples viewed Africa as anything other than a fantasyland.

Society and Culture in the Imperial Age

■ What was the social and cultural response to the emergence and consolidation of empire?

The same central theme that characterized Roman politics after Augustus also characterized Roman society in the imperial age—the illusion of continuity with the Republic, masking fundamental change. The social pyramid described in Chapter 4 remained intact—senators at the top, followed by equestrians, plebeians and peasants, freedmen, and slaves. Important changes, however, occurred within the pyramid, as imperial rule altered social and economic relationships.

The shift from republic to empire also had a profound influence on Roman culture and religious belief. In their works, writers, poets, and historians explored the ambivalence of life under stable but autocratic rule. At the same time, the spread of religious cults promising salvation hinted that many people under Roman rule found life less than stable, and looked outside the political sphere for safety. Christianity, which emerged during the Augustan era, possessed a special appeal to the classes of society that benefited the least from imperial governance.

The Upper and Lower Classes

In the Roman Empire, aristocrats continued to stand at the top of the social pyramid, enjoying the greatest wealth, power, and prestige. Roman emperors recognized three social groups, or orders, as having aristocratic status. The first order, the senators of Rome, occupied a place of honor at the very top of the social pyramid. The Roman Senate was not a hereditary aristocracy, but Augustus encouraged the sons of senators to follow in their fathers' footsteps, and he offered financial incentives to senators to have children and perpetuate their family line. Despite these efforts, most of the oldest Roman senatorial families died out by the end of the first century C.E., due to death in war, failure to produce heirs, and falling victim to political intrigues. With the approval of the emperor, new aristocratic families emerged to take their place and serve in the Senate. These senators came from Roman families that had grown in wealth and prestige through service to the emperor. Many new senators also stemmed from the provinces and came to Rome to be in the Senate and serve as imperial officials. All senators, and their descendants for three generations, had the right to wear a broad purple stripe on their togas (formal clothing) as a badge of honor.

Below the senators stood the equestrian order, which was much larger than the senatorial order. Like senators, equestrians had to possess high birth and wealth—but to a lesser degree. The equestrian order flourished in the imperial age. Many equestrians continued to follow business careers as they had during the Republic, but the expansion of the empire provided them with new opportunities for public service. Equestrians staffed the diplomatic, fiscal, and military services, and a few were admitted to the Senate by the emperor.

The third aristocratic order consisted of the city councilors who served in the councils of every Roman city throughout the provinces. Like senators and equestrians of the city of Rome, they were expected to be wealthy, of respectable birth, and of good moral character. In many cities, the sons of freedmen (men who had once been slaves) were permitted to be city councilors.

These three aristocratic orders represented only a tiny fraction of the empire's population. Below them came the plebeians—Rome's poor but free underclass of citizens. Though not included in political life, plebeians living throughout the empire benefited in some ways from imperial rule. In the city of Rome, for example, they received a daily allotment of free grain. (Approximately half of Rome's population of one million depended on the daily gifts of grain.) With little incentive to work and deprived of the responsibilities of political participation, the plebeians enjoyed much free time. By the first century C.E., Romans had approximately 100 days designated as holidays. The plebeians demanded a steady diet of entertainment, such as the bloody gladiatorial combats in the Colosseum and the exciting chariot races in the Circus Maximus. Thus plebeian life in the city of Rome became dependent on "bread and circuses": free grain and free entertainment.

Plebeians needed bread and circuses to compensate not only for their loss of political power but also for their poor living conditions. Crowded into vile tenement slums with little light and no plumbing, the poor lived in misery. Disease kept the birth rate and life expectancy very low. Probably more than a quarter of all infants died within their first five years, and a third of those who survived were dead by age 10. The average Roman man died at age 45, and the average woman at age 34.

Poor people lived in similarly wretched conditions in every Roman city, but without the free distributions of grain. They relied on local aristocrats to provide food in times of emergency and to provide public entertainments. Plebeians in the countryside made their living primarily by farming, and they provided the bulk of troops in the Roman army.

Slaves and Freedmen

Slavery was one of the harshest facts of life in the Roman Empire. Slaves made up a huge percentage of Roman society, at the very bottom of the social order. Of the city of Rome's approximately one million inhabitants, an estimated 400,000 were slaves during the early empire. When Augustus took control of Rome, slaves constituted 35 to 40 percent of the total population of Italy.

Everyone accepted that humans could be reduced to property. Millions of slaves inhabited the empire, holding the lowest possible status in a society in which social and legal status meant everything. No Roman citizen ever objected to slavery as an institution. Some high-minded Stoic philosophers, who noted the common humanity of slaves and owners, did criticize slavery, but only because they feared its corrupting effect on the masters. They had no concern for the condition of the slaves themselves. Later Christian writers living within the empire stressed that slaves should obey their masters "with fear and trembling."

The victims of a brisk international trade in humans, most slaves entered the empire through conquest. Others were enslaved from birth, having been born of a slave mother. There was never a shortage of slaves, and sometimes after a successful military campaign, such as Trajan's defeat of the Dacians in 106 C.E., the market was glutted.

Ownership of slaves reflected a person's status. The emperor himself owned tens of thousands of slaves who labored on his estates throughout the empire. Rich men, too, possessed them in huge numbers. Even poor artisans and teachers might hold one or two. Former slaves who had gained their freedom (freedmen) also owned slaves. Slaves were permitted to earn money, with the result that even some slaves owned slaves.

Slaves used for domestic service or in commerce and crafts were the lucky ones. Many slaves worked on the great plantations, or latifundia°, as part of large slave gangs. The absentee owners cared little for the welfare of these slaves. Latifundia slaves often labored in chains and slept in underground prisons. The slaves sent to work in the mines experienced even worse conditions. For them, only a wretched death lay ahead. Female slaves were spared the horrors of working in the fields and mines, but they were valued far less than were male slaves.

Dehumanized by their enslavement and stripped of their identity when taken from family and home, slaves lived in fear of their masters, who could abuse them physically or sexually with impunity. Violence lay at the heart of this institution, for ultimate control of slaves rested on force. In 61 C.E. when Pedanius Secundus, the chief administrator of the city of Rome, was killed by one of his slaves, all the other 400 slaves in his household were executed in accordance with Roman custom, on the assumption that some of them surely must have known the killer's intention. Romans, in common with the Greeks and other ancient peoples, believed that the only way to compel a slave to tell the truth was through torture. Thus, any testimony provided by a slave in court was valid only if it was extracted by torture. In the face of such brutality, slaves had few options. Slaves could try to escape, but if caught were branded on the forehead. Slave revolts never succeeded.

Despite their utter lack of freedom, many slaves formed emotional and sexual relationships with one another. Epitaphs on graves demonstrate that they used conventional terms of affection and marriage bonds such as husband and wife, although Roman law did not recognize these informal slave marriages. Some slave owners permitted slave marriages because they understood that slaves with families would be less likely to rebel. Complete submissiveness and the goodwill of their masters were necessary to hold a slave family together.

Slavery was not, however, necessarily a permanent condition. Slaves might obtain their freedom through manumission. Through this carefully regulated legal procedure, a master granted freedom to a slave as a reward for faithful service or docile behavior, or even out of genuine affection. Of course manumission worked to the best interests of the owner: The merest hope of manumission kept most slaves docile. Moreover, Roman law established limits to manumission. No more than 100 slaves could be freed at the death of an owner, and the slave had to be at least 30 years old and the owner at least 25.

Despite these restrictions, the freedmen constituted an important class in Roman society. Freedmen made up only about 5 percent of Rome's population, but their enterprise and ambition marked them as some of the more successful members of Roman society. Many former slaves worked in business or as skilled laborers, teachers, and doctors. Unlike in other ancient societies, freedmen rid themselves of the taint of slavery in only one generation. A freed slave had only partial citizen rights, but his or her children became full Roman citizens, who could freely marry other citizens. The historian Tacitus records a remark made in a senatorial debate about this phenomenon: "Not without good reason had our ancestors, in distinguishing the position of the different orders, thrown freedom open to all." Tacitus noted that some senators and many equestrians could point to exslaves among their ancestors.

Slavery remained a part of Mediterranean economic and social life until the early Middle Ages, but in the second century C.E. the role of slaves in the economy began to diminish. As Roman emperors concentrated on consolidating rather than expanding the borders of the empire, the supply of slaves dwindled, and the cost of slaves rose. Thus, slave owning may have become less economically viable.

Women in the Roman Empire

Women in the senatorial and equestrian ranks possessed far more freedom than was usual in the ancient world. By 250 C.E., the form of marriage by which a woman passed from the control of her father to that of her husband had almost entirely died out. Women remained, at least theoretically, under the control of their father or legal guardian. In practice, this form of marriage gave a woman more freedom, in large part because her husband no longer controlled her dowry. Some women used this freedom to move more into the public view, taking part in banquets, attending the gladiatorial battles at the Colosseum and the races at the Circus Maximus, and presiding over literary salons. Wealthy women owned property, made investments, and became public benefactors. Many high-ranking women were educated in the liberal arts and lived a cultivated lifestyle. Their surviving portraits (carved in stone) reveal a restrained physical elegance. The portraits of several wives and daughters of emperors even appeared on coins.

As these coins suggest, at the highest level of society some women possessed real political power, though expressed behind the scenes. Livia, married to Augustus for fifty-two years, possessed a great deal of influence during his reign and worked actively to ensure the succession of her son Tiberius. The emperor Hadrian may have received his throne in part because of the influence of his cousin Trajan's wife, Plotina. At Plotina's funeral, Hadrian admitted, "She often made requests of me, and I never once refused her." The empress Julia Domna survived her husband Septimius Severus to become an important political power during the reign of her son Caracalla.

Lives of Luxury

A woman pours perfume in this wall painting from around 20 B.C.E. Only the wealthy could afford perfume and paintings.

The vast majority of women, of course, were not immortalized in stone or coin. We have scanty evidence about the lives of non-aristocratic women in the Roman Empire. Women do, however, appear in some records as moneylenders, shopkeepers, and investors, and there is evidence that some women became doctors while others prospered as artists. Most women probably married and gave birth to three or four children. If they survived childbirth, which many of them did not, then they would very likely see at least one or two of their children die before reaching adulthood.

Although literary evidence demonstrates that many aristocratic Roman men cherished their daughters, the practice of female infanticide remained common throughout Roman society. The expected ratio of female to male births is 105 to 100. In second-century Rome, however, the rate was 100 to 131. Unwanted babies—not only girls but also the sick and malformed, as well as some born outside marriage—were killed through exposure: The baby was left on a pile of garbage or by the roadside. Not all died; often, the babies were picked up and raised as slaves.

Literature and Empire

Writers during the reign of Augustus embodied the tensions and uncertainties of living in a society that had exchanged freedom for stability. The presence of imperial autocracy, as well as Rome's expanding might, affected literary production in different ways.

The work of the historian Livy (59 B.C.E.–12 C.E.) illustrates the fine line walked by writers in an age of autocracy. Livy wrote a massive history of Rome, called *From the Foundation of the City,* that traced Rome from its origins until his own time. Though less than a fifth of this work survives, we see that Livy presented Rome's rise to world mastery as a series of instructive moral and patriotic lessons. He showed how Rome grew to world power because of both its military and its moral strength. Although proud of Rome's greatness, Livy also believed that with power came decadence. He did not gloss over the ruthlessness with which Augustus waged the civil war that destroyed the Republic, nor did he veil his criticism of what he perceived as Rome's moral and political decline. Augustus made his displeasure with Livy's open criticism known, yet he did not punish the historian, perhaps because Livy also expressed the hope that Augustus would restore Rome's glory.

Ovid (43 B.C.E.–17 C.E.) was not so fortunate. His tragic career demonstrated the risks of offending an emperor. Ovid's brilliant love elegies had made him the darling of Rome. His lighthearted descriptions of Roman sexual life were contrary to the ideals of Augustus's legislation on marriage, while his book *Metamorphoses* developed themes of change and impermanence that indirectly challenged the idea of a stable state under Augustus's leadership. In 8 C.E., Ovid's erotic poem "The Art of Love," along with an obscure scandal involving Augustus's daughter, earned him the hostility of the emperor. Augustus exiled Ovid to a squalid village on the Black Sea, where he died in sorrow.

The poet Horace (65–8 B.C.E.), son of a wealthy freedman, walked a more careful path. He avoided political entanglements and maintained close ties to Augustus. His poetry on public themes praised Augustus for bringing peace and the hope of a moral life to the world. Throughout his work, Horace urged serene appreciation of life's transient joys. In his most famous verse (*Odes* I.11.6ff) he sings, "Be wise, taste the wine, and since our time is brief, be moderate in your aspirations. Even as we speak, greedy life slips away from us. Grasp each day (*carpe diem*) and do not pin your hopes on tomorrow."

Virgil stands as the greatest of the Roman poets. Drawing on Hellenistic poetic forms, Virgil wrote of the wisdom, safety, and serenity found in an idealized country life—with the terrible uncertainties of civil war providing a silent backdrop. At Augustus's request Virgil composed the *Aeneid*°, an epic poem that legitimized and celebrated the emperor's reign. Ostensibly the poem was about the mythic foundation of the Roman state by the hero Aeneas, a Trojan prince fleeing the destruction of his native city by the Greeks. But through a series of cinematic "flash-forwards," Virgil presented the entire history of the Roman people as culminating in the reign of Augustus. In the *Aeneid,* the emperor brings to completion the nearly unendurable efforts of his Trojan ancestor.

Although the *Aeneid* praises Augustus, Virgil was not just a propagandist for the imperial regime. Virgil praised those aspects of peace and fulfillment of duty that he genuinely valued, but he questioned the costs of warfare and empire on human beings by subtly investigating the toll imposed by the demands of public duty on individual character. In the *Aeneid* Virgil's hero Aeneas is deeply tempted by his love for the Carthaginian queen Dido to abandon his mission of founding Rome. But Aeneas overcomes his private desire in favor of the destiny of Rome: He abandons Dido to continue his divinely inspired mission. At the end of the poem, Aeneas stands victorious— but a psychological ruin. He has given everything to his duty. Virgil makes his readers wonder about the costs of such utter public service.

Seneca (ca. 4 B.C.E.–41 C.E.), who combined philosophical interests with literary skill, accepted the imperial system. He intended his writings to give sound advice to rulers. Deeply influenced by Stoicism, Seneca courageously acknowledged how hard it was to control one's human weaknesses and live a truly moral life. His integrity and rhetorical brilliance earned him the unenviable task of being Nero's tutor when the emperor was still an impressionable 12-year-old boy. For eight years Seneca guided Nero, and the empire enjoyed good government. As Nero matured, however, he found other, less decent advisers. Appalled by his student's descent into corruption, Seneca plotted to kill Nero. When he was caught, he killed himself.

Practitioners of the art of public speaking (rhetoric) had to grapple most directly with the new realities of the imperial age. Autocratic government made free political debate impossible. Nevertheless, opportunities for public speech still abounded: Law cases still had to be tried in court, and emperors had to be bathed in praise at regular intervals. Thus, rhetoric blossomed in the new imperial world. Quintilian (ca. 35–ca. 90 C.E.) exemplifies the new kind of imperial rhetorician. He rose to prominence in Rome as a teacher and speaker, becoming the tutor in the royal household of the emperor Domitian. His masterpiece, *Training in Oratory,* calls for clarity and balance in speaking. It also rather wistfully suggests that an orator might guide the Senate and the state, as Quintilian's model Cicero had done during the days of the Republic.

The historian and rhetorician Tacitus (ca. 56–ca. 118 C.E.) took a more realistic approach than Quintilian. In his *Dialogue on Orators* he argued—correctly—that political autocracy had killed true oratory, reducing it to mere public entertainment and ceremonial flourishes. Sardonic and terse, Tacitus's historical accounts covering the first century of the Augustan age displayed a deep understanding of human psychological reaction to the harsh political realities of early imperial tyranny. Although Tacitus's career flourished under the tyrannical Domitian, he hated political oppression and he never abandoned his love for the best of Roman ideals. In the *Agricola*, his biography of his father-in-law, Tacitus affirmed that good men could serve their country honorably, even under bad rulers. The *Agricola* thus inadvertently revealed an important accomplishment of Augustus's imperial system: It had tamed the competitive energies of Rome's aristocrats, transforming them into an efficient governing class.

Eager to contemplate the cultural superiority of the Roman Empire over other peoples, Rome's ruling elite took a strong interest in the habits of non-Romans. In his *Geography,* Strabo (64 B.C.E.–ca. 25 C.E.), a native Greek and a Roman citizen, wrote a detailed account of the many peoples ruled by Rome, stressing how Roman civilization could change foreign cultures for the better. He suggested that Rome's rulers and administrators should "bring together cities and peoples into a single Empire and political management." Drawing on Hellenistic and Greek traditions of writing about foreign cultures, Strabo placed the Roman Empire at the center of the inhabited world.

In addition to geography, other forms of scientific writing made great strides in the early centuries of the Roman Empire. Claudius Ptolemy of Alexandria maintained the high standards of the Hellenistic science tradition that continued to flourish under Roman rule. Writing in the second half of the second century C.E. (we do not know the dates of his birth or death), Ptolemy composed definitive works in many fields. Using the division of spheres into units of 60 first developed by the Sumerians and perfected by the Babylonians, Ptolemy's *Almagest* proved the theories and tables necessary to compute the positions of the sun, the moon, and five known planets. He accepted the Greek theory that the sun revolves around the Earth. Western astronomers used his maps of the heavens for nearly 1,500 years. His *Geography* gave readings in longitude and latitude and provided information for drawing a world map, which remained the basis of cartography until the sixteenth century. Translated from Greek into Arabic, Ptolemy's books became standard in the medieval Islamic world. Eventually they were translated into Latin and so passed back into use in western Europe during the Middle Ages.

Roman medicine also helped shape Western practices for hundreds of years. The physician Galen (131–201 C.E.) was one of the most prolific writers in the imperial period: A fire in 191 C.E. destroyed many of his manuscripts, yet enough of his work survives today to fill twenty volumes in Greek. His writings ranged from philosophy to philology, but his medical theory and practice proved the most influential. Galen sought to make medicine a science. He insisted on the importance of dissection in understanding the physical body, and stressed the need for experimentation. For most of his career Galen worked in Rome, but he served for four years as physician to the gladiators in his hometown of Pergamum, where he was able to study firsthand the impact of trauma on the human body.

Galen's influence on Western medicine was not wholly positive. He viewed disease as the result of an imbalance in the body's four "humors," or basic bodily fluids (blood, bile, urine, phlegm). Too much blood, for example, meant fever. To restore the balance, Galen taught, the physician should apply leeches or cut open a vein, and thereby drain the patient of "excess" blood. The practice of bloodletting, and the humoral theory on which it was based, remained central in Western medical practice into the early decades of the nineteenth century.

Religious Life

Religious expression in the Roman Empire took many forms. The imperial government made no effort to impose uniform belief, so subject peoples freely worshiped many gods and maintained their traditional religious rituals. Within many religious cultures, trends that first appeared in the Hellenistic Age continued, but important new changes emerged during the imperial era. Judaism was transformed during this period. At the same time, an entirely new religion, Christianity, emerged from Jewish roots. This new faith grew to become the dominant religion in the empire by 400 C.E. and eventually suppressed polytheistic religions.

DOCUMENT

Galen the Physician

Galen, the greatest physician of the imperial age, described in vivid terms how peasants in the countryside often were very close to starvation.

As soon as summer was over, those who live in the cities, in accordance with their universal practice of collecting a sufficient supply of grain to last a whole year, took from the fields all the wheat, with the barley, beans and lentils, and left to the rustics only those annual products which are called pulses and leguminous fruits; they even took away a good part of these to the city. So the people in the countryside, after consuming during the winter what had been left, were compelled to use unhealthy forms of nourishment. Through the spring they ate twigs and shoots of trees, bulbs and roots of unwholesome plants, and they made unsparing use of what are called wild vegetables, whatever they could get hold of, until they were surfeited; they ate them after boiling them whole like green grasses, of which they had not tasted before even as an experiment. I myself in person saw some of them at the end of spring and almost all at the beginning of summer afflicted with numerous ulcers covering their skin and inflamed tumours, others from spreading boils, others had an eruption resembling . . . leprosy.

Source: From Galen, translated by G. E. M. de Ste. Croix in *The Class Struggle in the Ancient Greek World.* Copyright © 1981 by G. E. M. de Ste. Croix. Reprinted by permission of Gerald Duckworth & Co. Ltd.

Polytheism in the Empire

Syncretism°, the practice of equating two gods and fusing their cults, was a common feature of imperial religious life. Like many other Mediterranean peoples, the Romans often identified a foreign god with their own deities. For example, Julius Caesar described the Gallic god of commerce as Mercury, because Mercury served the same function in Roman religion. Romans did not care that other people throughout the empire might worship Jupiter or Juno or any other Roman god in different ways, or might give the gods different attributes. Syncretism, then, helped unify the diverse peoples and regions under Roman rule. Through syncretism, shared religious experiences spread across the empire.

Imperial subjects worshiped the emperor and Rome, the protectors of the entire empire. In addition, each city in the empire had its own gods, whom people imagined as dwelling within the temples dedicated to them. Worshipers gathered in front of the temples to offer sacrifices at altars located in front of the shrines. On religious holidays, thousands of city dwellers participated in parades and feasted at the great banquets that followed the sacrifice of many specially selected animals at temple altars. Particularly elaborate celebrations attracted pilgrims and visitors from afar.

The gods worshiped in specific cities and at specific holy sites generally were of great antiquity. Gods such as Athena in Athens or Jupiter in Rome were as old as the town itself. People believed that these gods would protect and benefit their communities if the residents made the proper sacrifices. Although a deity might be associated with a similar

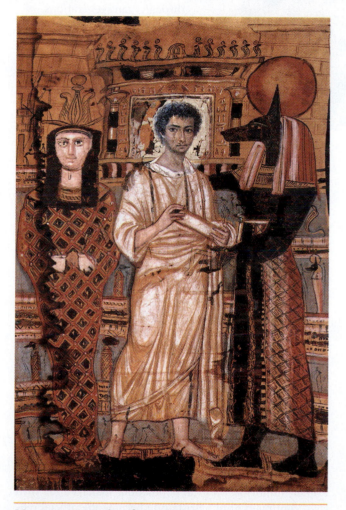

Mummy Wrapping from Egypt

This painted linen cloth was wrapped around a mummy in an Egyptian burial during the second century C.E. It shows the Egyptian god Osiris (on the left) and the jackal-headed god Anubis (on the right). Between them is the deceased man, dressed in Roman clothing. His portrait has been carefully painted and added separately. This wrapping and portrait show the continuity of ancient Egyptian religion during Roman imperial rule.

god in another town, its worship in each city had a unique quality, deeply intertwined with the history and architecture of the town itself. For example, Hercules protected many places, but his temple in each town was connected to a different local myth about him.

Some religious cults transcended their places of origin and spread widely, particularly among slaves, freedmen, and the urban poor who felt lost in the sprawl of the empire's big cities. The anonymity of life in big cities for the poor contributed to the spread of religions that offered a measure of identity and community and a kind of salvation as well. Religions that promised victory over death or liberation from the abuses and pain of daily existence possessed a wide appeal and spread quickly across the empire.

The goddess Isis, for example, who originated in Egypt, offered freedom from the arbitrary abuses of fate to her many followers throughout the empire. The story of Isis revolved around the death and resurrection of her husband Osiris (also called Serapis); her initiates believed that they, too, would experience life after death. Moreover, Isis—often depicted holding her baby son Horus—represented the universal mother and so attracted believers with her promise of compassionate nurture.

In his work *The Golden Ass,* the Roman writer Apuleius (ca. 125–ca. 170 C.E.) describes the goddess's protective power. Full of eroticism and magic, the story tells of Lucius, a carefree young Romeo, who is turned into a miserable donkey when caught spying on a gorgeous witch. After many comic misadventures in which Lucius learns how uncertain fate can be, Isis restores him to human form. In gratitude, Lucius thanks Isis for caring "for the troubles of miserable humans with a sweet mother's love." He joins her religion and becomes her priest.

Another popular religion that promised salvation to its initiates was that of Mithras, a sun god. Artists depicted Mithras slaying a bull, an archetypal sacrifice that his followers reenacted in secret ceremonies. Limited to men, worship of Mithras took place in underground chambers in which small groups held banquets, recited sacred lessons about the celestial journey of the soul after death, and made sacrifices to the god in imitation of his killing of the bull. Because this religion stressed both physical courage and performance of duty, it particularly attracted soldiers and administrators.

The most important religion of an eastern god whose worship spread throughout the Roman Empire was that of the Unconquered Sun. Originating in Syria, this deity came to be associated with Apollo and Helios, two Greco-Roman sun gods. When Elagabalus, the high priest of the Syrian sun god (El-Gabal), became Roman emperor (r. 218–222 C.E.), he built a huge temple dedicated to his god in Rome, and designated December 25 as a special day of worship to the deity. Within fifty years, the Unconquered Sun became the chief god of imperial and official worship.

Mithras Slays the Bull
Made around 100 C.E., this sculpture shows Mithras, a god of the sun, in the sacred act of sacrificing a bull. Mithras was a savior god whose followers received salvation. Limited to men only who were organized in strict hierarchies, the worship of Mithras occurred throughout the empire. Worshipers met for fellowship, a communal meal, and worship in small, private chambers.

The greatest product of the rabbinic tradition of this era was the Mishnah, a collection of opinions, decisions, and homilies to explain the law to unlearned people. Jewish teachers had begun accumulating this material in Hellenistic times, but it was completed around the year 220 C.E. In their desire to prepare a manageable body of material for reference and teaching, rabbis undertook a task not unlike that of the Roman jurists. But unlike Roman compilations, which drew from written texts, the Mishnah drew largely from oral law that had been memorized and transmitted through many generations.

Compiled by Rabbi Judah the Prince and his school, the Mishnah consists of sixty-three books, each dealing with a particular aspect of law, ranging from matters of ritual purity to calendrical issues to civil and criminal law. Among the many moral principles stressed by the Mishnah, saving life was paramount. According to the Mishnah, no person could save his or her own life by causing another's death, and no person could be sacrificed for the welfare of the community. Moreover, to save a life, any person could break any Jewish religious law, except those forbidding idolatry, adultery, incest, or murder. In Jewish thought, saving one life symbolized saving humanity. A radical idea slowly emerged from this principle: Since all humans are made in God's image, they should all have equal rights. This idea contributed to the gradual decline of slave holding among Jews.

Only the rise of Christianity would displace the worship of the Unconquered Sun.

Gnosticism, which originated in the Hellenistic Age, continued its influence in the Roman Empire, affecting Judaism, Christianity, and many polytheistic religions. Gnostics believed that the material world of daily life is incompatible with the supreme god. They thought that sparks of divinity (sometimes considered the human soul) are imprisoned within the body. Only a redeemer sent from the supreme god could release these divine sparks.

The Origins of Rabbinic Judaism

Following the Roman devastation of Judaea and the destruction of the Temple in Jerusalem in 70 C.E., a new kind of community-based religious life began to develop among Jews in Judaea and other lands. Since the sixth century B.C.E., communities of Jews had lived outside Palestine, but after the Romans ransacked Judaea, the Diaspora° ("dispersion of population") came to characterize Jewish life. Jerusalem ceased to serve as the focus of Judaism's religious ceremony, although not of Jewish religious thought and aspiration. More concretely, the entire religious practice of ritual animal sacrifice centered on the Temple disappeared. So, too, did the priesthood. The rabbi ("my master" in Hebrew) gradually replaced the priest in the role of religious instructor and community guide. Scholars trained in the Jewish law, rabbis interpreted and taught the Torah, the first five books of the Hebrew Bible. By 200 C.E., synagogues emerged as communal centers in which rabbis studied Jewish law and passed judgment on disputes. Gradually synagogues developed into centers where the Jewish community would celebrate the Sabbath and pray together.

In addition to the rabbis who led individual Jewish communities, an official called the Patriarch represented the Jews as a whole to the emperor. The Romans appointed the Patriarch and gave him the highest political authority in Jewish affairs in the empire. The Patriarch's responsibilities included collecting taxes for Rome and choosing judges for Jewish courts. The Romans gave the Patriarch the rank of senator, as the representative of all the Jews in the empire. This arrangement, a clear example of how Roman authorities let local populations manage their own laws, continued until Christianity became the official religion of the empire in the fifth century C.E. Christian emperors then began persecuting Jews and limiting their participation in public life.

The Emergence of Christianity

The emergence of Christianity forced the Romans to deal with an entirely new community within the empire. Christianity was more than a new set of religious beliefs; Christians had a new sense of shared identity, a new sense of history, and a new perception of the Roman system. The

A Jewish Offering

According to the Greek inscription, Jacob, a local leader, left this gold medallion to the synagogue in fulfillment of a vow. Jacob made his offering somewhere in the eastern Mediterranean region some time after the third century C.E. The medallion shows a menorah, the seven-branched lampstand, and other objects of Jewish ritual.

number of Christians gradually grew until they came to dominate the religious life of the empire. Within 400 years of the death of its founder, Christianity became the official imperial religion.

The founder of Christianity was a Jew named Yeshua ben Yosef, known today as Jesus of Nazareth (ca. 4 B.C.E.– ca. 30 C.E.). Born during the reign of Augustus, Jesus grew to manhood in the Jewish community of Galilee, in northern Palestine. Around age 30 he began to travel through Palestine with a band of followers, urging men and women to repent their sins because God would soon come to rule the Kingdom of Heaven on Earth. Jesus' followers believed him to be the messiah, an important figure in Jewish prophetic writings whose coming would inaugurate a new age of freedom for God's people. Like many other contemporary Jewish teachers, Jesus insisted that having the right intent in carrying out God's law mattered more than conforming to the outward performance of the law. When asked to identify the greatest commandment, Jesus replied, "You must love the Lord your God with all your heart, with all your soul, and with all your mind. This is the greatest and the first commandment. The second resembles it: You must love your neighbor as yourself. On these two commandments hang the whole Law." Jesus urged his listeners and followers to regard themselves and others as God's children, and taught them to recognize God as their loving Father.

In 30 C.E. Jesus entered Jerusalem to preach his message. He dared to challenge some of the Jewish elites who controlled the Jewish Temple under Roman supervision, and caused a near-riot. This dangerous act led the Roman authorities to arrest, try, and convict him as a revolutionary. Sentenced to death, Jesus died by crucifixion, the usual form of capital punishment in the Roman Empire for noncitizens.

Jesus' followers, however, insisted that he still lived, that he rose from the dead three days after being executed, and that he appeared to them a number of times in the forty days between his resurrection from the dead and his ascent into Heaven. They proclaimed him as not only the Jewish messiah, but as the Son of God who died on the cross as part of the divine plan. In Christian theology, Jesus' brutal death at the hands of the Romans became a loving sacrifice: The sinless Son of God endured the punishment that sinful men and women deserved. Christians, then, regarded Jesus as their savior, as the God whose intervention in human history rescued them from their sins and whose spirit continued to guide them in their earthly lives.

Jesus recorded none of his ideas in writing, but his followers transmitted his teachings orally for several decades after his death and then in the 50s and 60s C.E. began to write them down. By about 120 C.E. they had compiled an authoritative body of texts that recorded Jesus' life and words, which Christians

DOCUMENT

The Gospel According to Luke

The Trial of Jesus in Historical Perspective

In 30 C.E. Roman authorities in the city of Jerusalem in the Roman province of Judaea tried and executed a Jewish teacher known as Jesus of Nazareth, whose teachings lie at the foundation of Christianity, the faith of hundreds of millions of people in the world today. Although an insignificant event at the time, the trial of Jesus and its interpretation made and continues to make a profound impact on Western civilization.

Information about Jesus' trial comes from the New Testament books of Matthew, Mark, Luke, and John. These narratives, called the Gospels, were written thirty to sixty years after Jesus' death. They relate that during three years of teaching and miraculous healing in the Roman provinces of Galilee and Judaea, Jesus earned the resentment of certain segments of the Jewish religious leadership by disregarding aspects of Jewish religious law. According to the Gospels, when Jesus entered the Temple precinct in Jerusalem, he angered the temple elites by denouncing their hypocrisy and by overturning the tables of money changers. The priests then conspired to kill him. They paid one of Jesus' followers to reveal his whereabouts, arrested him on either the night before or the night of the Passover feast, and tried him immediately before the Sanhedrin, the highest Jewish court, which met that same night in the house of the Jewish high priest. The Sanhedrin found Jesus guilty of the crime of blas-

phemy for claiming to be the messiah, the Son of God.

Lacking the authority to put Jesus to death, the Jewish leaders brought Jesus before Pontius Pilate, the Roman governor, and demanded that he execute Jesus. Pilate hesitated, but the priests persuaded him by insisting that Jesus threatened the emperor's authority with his claim to be king of the Jews. Pilate's soldiers crucified Jesus, but according to the Gospel accounts, the real blame for Jesus' death lay with the Jews, who had demanded his execution. In all four Gospels, Jewish crowds in Jerusalem reject Jesus and cry out, "Crucify him!" to a reluctant Pontius Pilate.

The Gospel accounts of Jesus' arrest, trial, and crucifixion offer some difficulties for historians: Portions of these narratives conflict with what scholars understand about the conduct of trials by Jewish authorities or Roman administrators. For example, the evidence that we have indicates that the Sanhedrin did not hold trials at night; it did not meet in the house of the high priest; and it did not convene on a Jewish feast day or the night before a feast.

Far more important than these issues, however, is the question of the crime of blasphemy. According to Jewish law Jesus would not have blasphemed by claiming to be the messiah. Originating in ceremonies of anointing kings, the word *messiah* had many interpretations in Judaism as a kingly figure of power—but not as a divine being. Some scholars, though, argue that the Jewish leaders could have construed as blasphemy both Jesus' criticisms of Temple Judaism and his inferred claim to sit in God's presence (and thus to share in God's rule).

The issue of Jesus' blasphemy remains unclear but there is little debate about the importance of Jesus' confrontation with the Jewish elites in the Temple. Jesus had committed a very dangerous act by denouncing the priests in Jerusalem. These men, especially the high priest himself, owed their positions of power to the Roman overlords and were responsible for maintaining order. Many Jews in the temple elite saw Jesus as an agitator who posed a threat to their authority. Jesus was first brought before the Sanhedrin, the Jewish court permitted by the Romans to deal with affairs within the Jewish community. The Romans had appointed all seventy-one members of the court, including Caiaphas, the high priest who led it. These court members knew that if they could not control Jesus, the Romans would certainly replace them. The Sanhedrin could not punish Jesus under Jewish law, but it could send him before Roman magistrates on a

The Scales of Justice
This coin shows the goddess Aequitas, who represents the idea of fairness in Roman justice.

Early Christian Symbols
Some of the earliest Christian symbols decorate this Roman tombstone.

The anchor represents hope.

The fish stands for Jesus. The Greek word for fish, icthus, is an anagram of the Greek words for "Jesus Christ Son of God and Savior."

charge that the Romans would not hesitate to prosecute—stirring up rebellion.

Jesus' popularity with the common people and the disturbance in the Temple precinct would have been enough to arouse Roman suspicion. Roman officials usually responded to real or imagined threats to the political order by crucifixion. In the eyes of Pontius Pilate, a cautious magistrate, Jesus constituted a threat to public order, and so deserved execution. He would not have been reluctant to kill him.

Why, then, do the Gospels tend to shift the blame for Jesus' death from Pontius Pilate, who most certainly ordered Jesus' execution, and place it on the Jewish community? We know that the Gospel narratives began to be written down in an atmosphere of growing hostility and suspicion between Jews and Christians. Moreover, after Roman armies destroyed the Jerusalem Temple in the Jewish rebellion of 66–70 C.E.,

Christians wanted to disassociate themselves from Jews in Roman eyes, hoping to persuade Roman authorities to think of them not as rebels but rather as followers of a lawful religion. Such concerns may have shaped the Gospel writers' tendencies to emphasize the role of Jewish leaders in Jesus' death and to deemphasize Pilate's responsibility.

The Gospels also relate that before he died Jesus predicted the destruction of the Jewish Temple in Jerusalem. Many early Christians came to believe that the fall of the Temple and the savage repression of the Jewish rebellion served as divine punishment for the Jews who had caused Jesus' death. These interpretations of Jesus' trial and execution, and of the destruction of the Jewish community in Palestine, helped poison Christian-Jewish relations for two millennia. From the first century C.E. through the twentieth, important segments of the Christian community blamed "the Jews" for Jesus' crucifixion.

Questions of Justice

1. What does the trial of Jesus show about Roman methods of provincial administration—and about the limitations of these methods? Who had power in Judaea?
2. In Christian theology, Jesus died for the sins of the world. In theological terms, then, all sinners—all human beings—bear responsibility for Jesus' death. Why, then, does it matter if the Gospels place the blame for Jesus' crucifixion on Jews instead of Romans?

Taking It Further

Crossan, John Dominic. *Who Killed Jesus: Exposing the Roots of Anti-Semitism in the Gospel Story of the Death of Jesus.* 1997. A highly engaging investigation.

Johnson, Luke Timothy, John Dominic Crossan, and Werner H. Kelber. *The Jesus Controversy.* 1999. Three experts discuss the problems of finding who Jesus "really was."

Sherwin-White, A. N. *Roman Society and Roman Law in the New Testament.* 1963. A leading Roman historian puts the New Testament in its Roman context.

call the New Testament. Christians held that Jesus' teachings contained in the New Testament built on the teachings of the Hebrew Bible—the "Old" Testament. Consequently, they tended to interpret the Hebrew Bible in light of Christianity. For example, Christians read the prophetic writings of the Hebrew Bible as predictions of Jesus' birth, death, and resurrection.

For many decades after Jesus' death, his followers still thought of themselves as Jews. The word *Christian* (which comes from the Greek word *Christos,* meaning "the anointed one" or "messiah") was first used in the Syrian city of Antioch in the second half of the first century C.E. Christianity, however, eventually diverged from Judaism. Most scholars agree that the work and teaching of Paul of Tarsus (d. ca. 65 C.E.) played a crucial role in this development. An educated Jew, Paul fiercely opposed the new Christian teachings until he had a vision of Jesus calling him to Christian service. Paul became as ardent in his advocacy of Christianity as he had been in his opposition. The most effective early Christian missionary, he traveled throughout Asia Minor, inaugurating and developing Christian communities. Even more important, Paul wrote letters that circulated among these communities. These letters, written in the 50s C.E., constitute our earliest written Christian documents and articulate key doctrines of the Christian faith—doctrines that helped divide Christianity from Judaism.

In Paul's writings, the Christian view of Jesus' crucifixion as a divine sacrifice to atone for human sin was first fully developed. Paul taught that the only way a man or a woman could join God after death for an eternity of peace and happiness was by belief in Jesus as the Son of God and as the savior of humanity. Through participating in the ritual of the Eucharist (also called Holy Communion or the Lord's Supper), Christians recalled Jesus' sacrifice of himself on the cross. Paul preached this message of sacrifice and salvation to the Jews of the Diaspora and, significantly, to non-Jews. Paul encouraged Christian converts from outside Judaism to abide by certain Jewish laws, but he did not require that they be circumcised, a key Jewish initiation rite, or that they follow Jewish dietary restrictions.

Paul was executed as a troublemaker by the Romans in 65 C.E.; five years later the Roman army destroyed the Jewish Temple and devastated Judaea. After the fall of the Temple, Judaism and Christianity took their own distinctive paths. Yet, for all their fundamental differences of belief, Christianity and Judaism shared characteristics that distinguished them from other religions of antiquity. Both Christianity and Judaism combined a statement of belief with a social ethic. Their ethical systems embodied values that strengthened the religious community. Both, for example, protected the underprivileged—widows, orphans, and the poor—in their communities. Both religious communities also had an internal organization that did not depend on Rome. Their leaders (bishops for Christians and rabbis for Jews) gave judgments based on law that was separate from the Roman justice system. Finally, both Judaism and Christianity were monotheistic. Jews and Christians believed that that there is only one God, with whom contact is direct and immediate. To the Romans, who believed in many gods, this monotheism was the strangest aspect of the two faiths. Worshiping only one god made no sense to Romans, with their tradition of making sacrifices to many gods.

The Spread of Christianity

Christianity drew many of its first converts from socially marginalized groups, such as women, noncitizens, and slaves. Indeed, Jesus' message was revolutionary in the way it overturned conventional boundaries of class, gender, and ethnicity. Paul's writings in the New Testament illustrate this perspective. Paul encouraged a communal life in which all followers of Jesus were equal in the eyes of God. As he wrote to a small Christian community in Galatia in Asia Minor, "For in Christ Jesus . . . there is no longer Jew or Greek, there is no longer slave or free, there is no longer male or female; for all of you are one in Christ Jesus." Paul therefore urged the entry of gentiles (non-Jews) into the Christian community, believing that Jesus' teachings would one day unify the entire human race.

Christianity continued to attract the poor and outcast, but by the middle of the second century C.E., an important change occurred within the ranks of Christian adherents. Many new converts to the faith were men and women who had already been educated in Greek philosophy. They began to analyze and understand Christianity in the terms with which they were familiar: the abstract ideas of the Hellenistic philosophical tradition. Rather than dismiss the philosopher Plato, for example, they argued that his ideas about the supremacy of the soul and what it meant to lead a good life anticipated the teachings of Jesus.

Because it eventually led to Christianity's assimilation of much of classical culture, this encounter between Christians and the intelligentsia of the Mediterranean world transformed the Christian faith. As Christians explained their faith to educated gentiles in the language of traditional philosophical education, they won even more converts. They developed methods of analyzing biblical texts drawn from philosophy and rhetoric. The language of Christianity and Greek and Latin intellectual life fused.

Much of this development centered on the works of a group of Christian writers, whom historians call Apologists°. The Apologists publicly defended their faith to learned non-Christian audiences (just as Socrates had defended his beliefs in Plato's *Apology*—hence the name *Apologists*). In the process, they helped shape the Christian response to the challenges of Hellenist philosophy and cosmology. One of the most important of the Apologists, Justin Martyr (ca. 100–165 C.E.), sought to make Christianity comprehensible to other intellectuals like himself who had not grown up as Christians. Justin insisted that Christian beliefs accorded with rational thought and that Christianity was the culmination of intellectual developments that had begun in the classical past.

Justin Martyr's embrace of Greek philosophy was typical of Apologist thought. Another Apologist, Clement of Alexandria (ca. 150–216 C.E.), wrote that the study of Greek philosophy could prepare a Christian to understand Jesus' teachings. Origen (ca. 184–255 C.E.), the most profound thinker among the Apologists, was as much a classical scholar as a churchman. A talented editor and commentator on biblical texts, he also made significant contributions to Christian theology. He and Clement laid the groundwork for the integration of classical Greek philosophy and culture with Christianity. This complex step was of great importance in the development of Western civilization because it not only enhanced the appeal of Christianity among educated believers but also ensured the transmission of many Greek philosophical ideas to what would become Western culture.

The Apologists faced stiff opposition from within the Christian community because many churchmen viewed classical learning with deep suspicion. Tertullian (ca. 160–240 C.E.), Origen's influential contemporary, argued forcefully for the separation of Christianity from the learning and culture of the non-Christian world. He worried that the mingling of religious cults so common in his day might corrupt Christianity. Tertullian summed up his opposition to classical culture: "What has Athens to do with Jerusalem? What is there in common between the philosopher and the Christian? . . . After the Gospel we have no need for further research." Christians like Tertullian mistrusted the power of the human intellect and stressed the need to remain focused on the divine revelation of the Christian Scriptures. Yet Tertullian could not stop the integration of Christianity with classical learning. By the third century C.E. Christians could no longer ignore the Mediterranean world in which they lived.

And that world could no longer ignore them. Many of Christianity's core concepts, such as its ideas about personal salvation, the equality of individual men and women before God, and the redemption of humanity from sin, distinguished it from the empire's polytheistic faiths. Most strikingly, Christianity firmly rejected the existence of multiple gods and sought to convince followers of other religions that they stood in error. This conversionist impulse (called *proselytizing*), in addition to Christians' close community life and failure to engage in the public life of Roman culture, won them suspicion and persecution. Claudius expelled Christians from Rome, and in 64 C.E., Nero blamed Christians for a destructive fire that consumed central Rome. (Popular legend blamed him, equally wrongly.) Hundreds of Christians died in the arena before cheering crowds.

By the second half of the first century C.E., many Roman officials perceived Christians as potential enemies of the state because they refused to join in the worship of the emperor. Christians called the men and women who died rather than renounce their beliefs *martyrs,* or witnesses for their faith. Tertullian chided his Roman persecutors, "We multiply whenever we are mown down by you; the blood of Christians is [like] seed."

In their vision of all humanity united under a single God and their desire to replace other forms of religious expression with the worship of this one God, Christians were truly revolutionary. Christians eventually succeeded in displacing all polytheist religions within the Roman Empire. Although polytheism still exists in many parts of the world today, it is nearly absent from the West. A fundamental part of how many peoples understood the world changed radically as a result of the Christian revolution.

Conclusion

Rome Shapes the West

The map of the Roman Empire outlined the heart of the regions included in the West today. Rome was the means by which cultural and political ideas developed in Mediterranean societies and spread into Europe. This quilt of lands and peoples was acquired mostly by conquest. An autocratic government held the pieces together. Although Roman authorities permitted no dissent in the provinces, they allowed provincial peoples to become Roman. Being Roman meant that one had specific legal rights of citizenship, not that one belonged to a particular race or ethnic group. Thus, in addition to expanding the boundaries of the empire and patrolling its borders, the Roman army brought a version of Roman society to subject peoples. By imitating Roman styles of architecture and urban life, the cities, too, helped spread Roman civilization. Moreover, the elites of these cities helped funnel the resources of the countryside into the emperor's coffers, and so sustain the imperial system.

For two and a half centuries the *Pax Romana* inaugurated by Augustus fostered a remarkable degree of cultural uniformity within the empire's boundaries. Rome's civilization, including its legal system, its development of cities, and its literary and artistic legacy, made it the foundation of Western civilization as we know it today. The legal precedents established by Roman jurists remain valid in much of Europe. Latin and Greek literature of the early Roman Empire has entertained, instructed, and inspired readers in the West for nearly 2,000 years. Until very recently all educated people in the West could read Latin and many could read Greek, and looked to the works of the Romans for their model in prose style. Many of our public buildings and memorial sculptures continue to adhere to the artistic and architectural models first outlined in Rome. The Roman Empire was the most important and influential model of an imperial system for Europeans until modern times. Of equal importance, the monotheism and ethical teachings of Judaism and Christianity have been prominent forces in shaping Western ideals and attitudes.

A debilitating combination of economic weakness, civil war, and invasions by northern peoples would almost destroy the Roman Empire in the third century C.E. How the Roman Empire recovered and was transformed in the process is the story of the next chapter.

Suggestions for Further Reading

For a comprehensive list of suggested readings, please go to www.ablongman.com/levack2e/chapter5

Beard, Mary, John North, and Simon Price. *Religions of Rome.* 1995. The first volume contains essays on polytheist religions, and the second contains translated ancient sources.

Gardner, Jane F. *Women in Roman Law and Society.* 1987. Discusses issues pertaining to women in Rome.

Garnsey, Peter, and Richard Saller. *The Roman Empire: Economy, Society, and Culture.* 1987. Stresses the economic and social foundations of the Roman Empire.

Hornblower, Simon, and Antony Spawforth, eds. *The Oxford Classical Dictionary,* 3rd ed. 1996. This encyclopedia treats all aspects of Roman culture and history.

Isaac, Benjamin. *The Creation of Racism in Classical Antiquity.* 2004. A highly readable discussion of ancient social prejudices and discriminatory stereotypes that influenced the development of modern racism.

Markus, Robert. *Christianity in the Roman World.* 1974. An excellent study of the growth of Christianity.

Ramage, Nancy H., and Andrew Ramage. *Roman Art,* 4th ed. 2005. An excellent, beautifully illustrated introduction to Roman art and architecture.

Romm, James. *The Edges of the Earth in Ancient Thought: Geography, Exploration, and Fiction.* 1992. An exciting introduction to the Roman understanding of real and imaginary peoples.

Scott, Sarah, and Jane Webster, eds. *Roman Imperialism and Provincial Art.* 2003. A collection of essays that explores new approaches to the cultural interconnections between the Romans and the peoples they ruled.

Talbert, Richard, ed. *The Barrington Atlas of the Classical World.* 2000. This atlas contains the best maps available.

Webster, Graham. *The Roman Imperial Army,* 3rd ed. 1985. Discusses military organization and life in the empire.

Wiedemann, Thomas. *Emperors and Gladiators.* 1992. An important study of the ideology and practice of gladiatorial combat.

Wolfram, Herwig. *The Roman Empire and Its Germanic Peoples.* 1997. Examines the interrelation of Romans and Germans over several centuries.

Woolf, Greg. *Becoming Roman: The Origins of Provincial Civilization in Gaul.* 1998. The best recent study of Romanization.

Late Antiquity: The Age of New Boundaries, 250–600

6

URING THE LAST WEEK OF AUGUST IN 410, AN EVENT OCCURRED THAT stunned the Roman world. A small army of landless warriors—no more than a few thousand men—led by their king Alaric, forced their way into the city of Rome and plundered it for three days. For more than a year Alaric had been threatening the city in an attempt to extort gold and land for his people. When his attempts at extortion failed, he resorted to attacking the city directly. Because Alaric's followers, the Visigoths, were Christian, they spared Rome's churches and took care not to violate nuns. But that left plenty of loot—gold, silver, and silks—for them to cart away.

For these warriors and their families, who had first invaded the Roman Empire from their homelands in southern Russia thirty years earlier, pillaging the most opulent city in the Mediterranean world was a pleasant interlude in a long struggle to secure a permanent home. For the Romans, however, the looting of Rome was an unfathomable disaster. They could scarcely believe that their capital city, the gleaming symbol of world rule, had fallen to an army of people they considered barbarian thugs, one of several Germanic tribes that invaded the Roman Empire. "If Rome is sacked, what can be safe?" lamented the Christian theologian Jerome when he heard the news in far-off Jerusalem. His remark captures the outrage and astonishment felt by Roman citizens everywhere, Christian and non-Christian alike, who believed that their empire was divinely protected and would last forever.

To understand how the Visigoths managed to sack Rome, we must examine late antiquity, the period between about 250 and 600, which bridged the classical world and the Middle Ages. During this critical era in the

The Vienna Genesis Written in silver ink on purple-dyed parchment, this sumptuous manuscript of the first book of the Bible, now in a museum in Vienna, Austria, was created in the sixth century, probably for a member of the imperial court in Constantinople. The Greek text at the top portion of the page tells the story of Susanna at the Well, which is illustrated at the bottom of the page. Though the illustration tells a biblical story, certain details reflect conditions in late antiquity, such as fortified cities and the growing importance of camels in travel and commerce. The seated, semi-nude female in the lower left is derived from polytheist religion. She personifies the stream from which the more modestly dressed Susanna gathers water.

development of Western civilization, the Roman Empire underwent radical transformation. After its recovery from a half century of near-fatal civil war, foreign invasion, and economic crisis, Rome experienced a hundred years of political reform and economic revival. Yet by the middle of the fifth century, the political unity of the Mediterranean world had come to an end. The Roman Empire collapsed in western Europe. In its place, new Germanic kingdoms developed in Italy, Gaul, Britain, Spain, and North Africa. These kingdoms would serve as the foundation of western medieval Europe.

In contrast, the Roman Empire in the East managed to hold together and prosper. The empire's eastern provinces were held together by the new capital, the city of Constantinople (modern Istanbul in Turkey). Until their empire fell to the Turks in 1453, the inhabitants of this eastern realm considered themselves Romans. In both Constantinople (where Roman political administration was maintained) and the new kingdoms of the West (where it was not) Rome's cultural legacy continued.

Late antiquity witnessed not only the collapse of the Roman Empire in the western provinces but also the emergence of Christianity as the dominant religion throughout the imperial realm. From there it spread beyond the imperial borders, bringing new notions of civilization to the people of Europe, North Africa, and the Middle East. In this era one did not have to be Roman to be Christian, but it was necessary to be Christian to be civilized. Once Christianity became dominant the cultural boundaries between Christians, Jews, and polytheists hardened. Henceforth, Western civilization was for most people a Christian civilization, and the borders that separated peoples were not just political ones, as in the ancient world, but religious ones. The encounter between the Roman Empire and Christianity raised the question, how were both the culture of the empire and the practice of Christianity transformed?

- How did the Roman Empire successfully reorganize following the instability of the third century?
- How did Christianity become the dominant religion in the Roman Empire, and what impact did it exert on Roman society?
- How did Christianity enable the transformation of communities, religious experience, and intellectual traditions inside and outside the empire?
- How and why did the Roman Empire in the West disintegrate?

Crisis and Recovery in the Third Century

- How did the Roman Empire successfully reorganize following the instability of the third century?

In the years between 235 and 284, the Roman Empire staggered under waves of political and economic turmoil. The very institutions of the army and the office of the emperor, which had made the Roman Empire the dominant power in the Mediterranean, seemed incapable of standing up to new threats. Rival generals competed for the throne, chronic civil war shook the empire's very foundation, and invaders hungry for land and plunder broke through the weakened imperial borders. As a consequence the economy collapsed and the imperial administration broke down. However, by the end of the third century, the emperor Diocletian managed to arrest the process of disintegration by shoring up the empire with drastic administrative and social reforms.

The Breakdown of the Imperial Government

In 235, the assassination of Emperor Severus Alexander, the last member of the Severan dynasty, precipitated a crisis in the imperial administration. Military coup followed military coup as ruthless generals with nicknames like "Sword-

The Walls of Rome

The emperor Aurelian built a twelve-mile circuit of walls around Rome in the 270s to protect the city from Germanic invaders. Twenty feet high and twelve feet thick, the walls had eighteen major gates. The Gate of Saint Sebastian, seen here, had additional towers added in later years. That Rome should need protective walls would have been unthinkable during the early empire.

Subjugation of Valerian

Persian kings built their tombs in a cliff six miles north of Persepolis, the old Persian capital. Here at Naqsh-i Rustam, a carving depicts the Great King Shapur I (239–272) on horseback holding the arm of his prisoner, the Roman emperor Valerian. The previous Roman emperor, Philip (known as "the Arab"), kneels in supplication. Shapur bragged about his accomplishments: "When I first came to rule, the Roman emperor Gordian gathered an army from the whole empire of the Romans, Goths, and Germans and came to Mesopotamia against my empire. . . . and we annihilated the Roman army. Then the Romans proclaimed Philip the new emperor . . . and he came to plead with me, and he paid 500,000 gold pieces as ransom and became our tributary. . . . And when I marched against Carrhae and Edessa [Roman cities in Syria], the Emperor Valerian advanced against us. . . . We fought a great battle . . . and I captured the Emperor Valerian myself with my own hands."

in-Hand" competed for the throne. In the latter half of the third century, not one of more than four dozen emperors and would-be emperors died a natural death. Gallienus clung to the throne longest: his reign lasted fifteen years (253–268). Most emperors held power for only a few months. Preoccupied with merely staying on the throne, they neglected the empire's borders, leaving them vulnerable to attack.

This situation had dire consequences for the empire. Foreign invaders attacked both eastern and western provinces throughout late antiquity. To the Romans' deep shame, Emperor Valerian was captured in battle by the Great King of Persia in 260. Warbands from across the Rhine River reached as far south as Italy, forcing the em-

peror Aurelian to build a great wall around the city of Rome in 270. Many other cities across the empire constructed similar defenses. The Roman military system and the Roman economy buckled under the pressure of invasions and civil war. Inflation spun out of control and coins lost their value. With the decline of the value of money the government was forced to pay soldiers in produce and supplies rather than cash. Not surprisingly, resentment boiled among the troops.

As a consequence of the political turmoil in the empire, the seat of power shifted from Rome to provincial cities. Unlike their predecessors, the soldier-emperors of this era, who came mostly from frontier provinces, had little time to cultivate the support of the Roman Senate. Instead, they held court in cities close to the embattled frontiers. Towns far from Rome, such as York in Britain or Trier in Gaul, had long functioned as military bases and supply distribution centers. Now they served as imperial capitals whenever the emperor resided there.

With the emperor on the move and with armies slipping from imperial control, political power fragmented. Political decentralization injured the empire further. Some cities and provinces took advantage of the weakened government to try to break away from Roman control. In the early 260s and 270s a large portion of Gaul known as the Gallic Empire briefly established independence. A few years later, Zenobia, the queen of Palmyra (r. 267–272), a city in Syria that had grown wealthy from the caravan trade, rebelled against Rome, and a bitter war ensued. The emperor Aurelian's troops finally crushed Palmyra in 272 and led Zenobia in chains through the streets of Rome in a triumphal procession. Such triumphs, however, were few and far between in these years.

The Restoration of Imperial Government

Diocletian (r. 284–305) stepped in to rescue the empire from its chaotic condition near the end of the third century. Drawing partly on innovations of his immediate predecessors and partly on his brilliant organizational talents, he launched a succession of military, administrative, and economic reforms that had far-reaching consequences. Not since the reign of Augustus had the Roman Empire been so fundamentally transformed.

Diocletian's Reforms

After ruling alone for two years, Diocletian recognized that the enormous responsibilities of imperial rule overburdened a single ruler, and so he took the dramatic step of dividing the administration of the empire into two parts. In 286 he chose a co-ruler, Maximian, to govern the western half of the empire, while he continued to rule in the east, residing for much his early rule in the city of Nicomedia (in modern Turkey), strategically located at the point where Asia meets Europe. Based in Rome, Maximian maintained a separate administrative system and his own army. Then, in 293, Diocletian and Maximian subdivided their territories by appointing two junior-level emperors. These junior rulers administered their territories in the eastern and western parts of the empire with their own bureaucracies and armies.

Through this system of shared government called the tetrarchy° or rule of four, Diocletian hoped not only to make the imperial government more efficient, but also to put an end to the bloody cycle of imperial assassinations. Although he had gained the throne by murdering his predecessor, he knew that the empire's survival depended on a

The Tetrarchs
Stolen by crusaders during the Middle Ages from its original site near Constantinople, this statue of the tetrarchs now is built into a wall of the cathedral of San Marco in Venice. To depict their solidarity and readiness for war, the tetrarchs are presented as fierce soldiers in military uniform, holding their swords with one hand and clasping their colleague's shoulder with the other. Each pair of figures shows one junior emperor and one senior emperor, who has more worry lines in his forehead as a sign of his greater responsibilities.

reliable succession strategy. To that end, Diocletian dictated that the junior emperors were to step into the senior emperors' place when they retired. Then they themselves were to select two new talented and reliable men to be junior emperors and their eventual replacements. Thus supreme power was to be handed down from capable ruler to capable ruler, and the constant cycle of assassinations and civil wars was to be broken.

Diocletian sought to enhance imperial authority by heightening the grandeur of the emperor's office. He used the title *dominus*, or lord, more freely than any emperor before him. Everything that had to do with the emperor was referred to as sacred or divine, suggesting his closeness to the gods. During public ceremonies he arrayed himself in gorgeous robes of purple silk. He required his officials to prostrate themselves before him and kiss the hem of his gown before they spoke to him. Diocletian as well as his fellow tetrarchs claimed that specific gods had singled them out for glory and victory. Jupiter was Diocletian's special protector, while Mars (the god of war) and Hercules guarded other tetrarchs. By emphasizing his special ties to the mightiest god of Rome, Diocletian set himself apart from the rest of the imperial court, thereby heightening his authority and prestige.

To restore Roman military power that had been weakened during the crises of earlier decades, Diocletian reorganized the Roman army, raising its size to about 400,000 men, an increase of 50,000 soldiers. In order to protect the empire from invaders, he stationed most of these troops along the borders of the empire and built several new mili-

tary roads in the western and eastern parts of the empire. He also supported forces of heavily armed cavalry that could race to trouble spots whenever necessary. At the same time, Diocletian sought to reduce the army's involvement in political affairs. Although he was a soldier himself, he recognized that the army had played a disruptive role in earlier decades by constantly engaging in civil wars. He created many new legions but reduced the size of each in order to limit its commander's power as well as to increase its maneuverability. He placed the legions under new, loyal commanders. With these military reforms in place, Diocletian was able to secure the empire's borders once again and suppress internal revolts (see Map 6.1).

Reorganizing the army was only one part of Diocletian's vision of reform. To restore efficient government, he also embarked on a thorough reorganization of the empire's administrative system. He redrew the map of the realm, drastically reducing the size of provinces. He set up a civil governor and a military commander within each province and

Map 6.1   The Roman Empire in Late Antiquity
Following the reforms of Diocletian, the Roman Empire enjoyed a century of stable government, with the same borders as in earlier centuries.

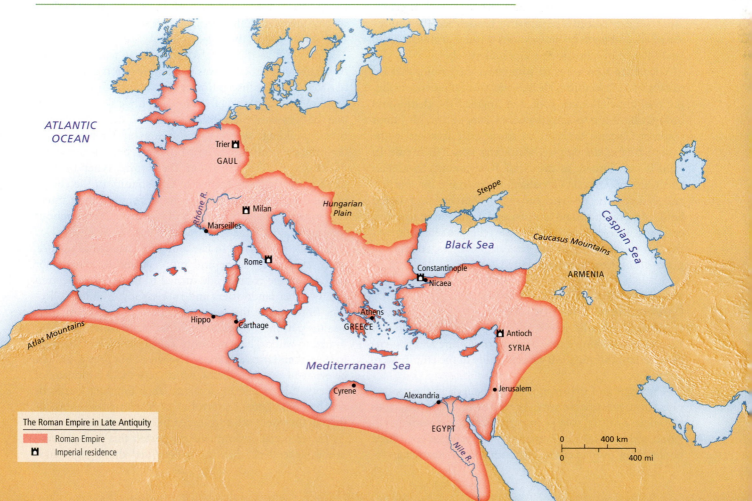

gave them separate civilian and military bureaucracies. These changes further reduced the risk of rebellion by limiting the power of any single civilian official. This administrative overhaul resulted in a significant expansion of the numbers of bureaucrats and military commanders.

Maintaining the expanded civilian and military apparatus created by the tetrarchy, especially in an era of rampant inflation, demanded full use of the empire's financial resources as well as far-reaching economic reforms. To halt the declining value of money, Diocletian attempted to freeze wages and prices by imperial decree. He also increased taxes and endeavored to make tax collection more effective through the establishment of a regular—and deeply resented—census to register all taxpayers. Despite the fact that senators, army officers and other influential citizens were undertaxed or not taxed at all, the new tax system generated enough revenues to fund the now enormous machinery of government.

The greatest tax burden fell on those least able to pay it: the peasants. These agricultural workers were required by law to remain in the places in which they were registered by the census. Sons were supposed to follow in their fathers' professions. This attempt to maintain the agricultural tax base was successful, but it lessened social mobility, and the gap between rich and poor continued to grow, a feature characteristic of late antique society. Fewer rich men controlled more of the empire's land and the wealth it generated than ever before. The emperor himself was the wealthiest of all, adding to his possessions through confiscation of lands owned by cities and private individuals.

Diocletian took steps to strengthen the empire that led to religious persecution. He believed that failure to worship the traditional Roman gods had angered the deities and brought hardship to the empire. In 303, he and his junior emperor Galerius initiated an attack on Christians in the eastern part of the empire, which was under their rule. In what is now known as the Great Persecution°, Diocletian and Galerius forbade Christians to assemble for worship and ordered the destruction of all churches and sacred books. Several thousand women and men refused to cooperate and were executed. Due to the religious sensibilities of the two co-emperors in the western provinces, attempts at persecution there were halfhearted.

Foundations of Late Antique Government and Society

Diocletian's reforms stabilized and preserved the Roman Empire, establishing a new foundation for life and government in late antiquity. All aspects of life in the empire were affected.

The quality of urban life slowly changed in the reorganized imperial government. As we saw in Chapter 5, cities played an essential role in imperial Rome's economic, religious, and cultural life: Romans saw themselves as civilized because they lived in cities. The number of Roman cities remained largely unchanged in late antiquity, but the weight of the new tax system and the costly bureaucracy of the increasingly centralized imperial government transformed many traditions of urban daily life. To finance imperial projects, emperors confiscated most city-owned lands and revenues, resulting in a reduction of funds to spend on civic life: games, chariot races, public buildings, and maintenance of urban infrastructure, such as roads and aqueducts.

Furthermore, the city councilors, who had the responsibility of raising the tax revenues required by the central government, grew increasingly frustrated. If they could not gather the amount of tax revenues that the government demanded every year, they would have to pay the difference from their own pockets. Failure to do so could lead to public flogging with lead-tipped whips—a punishment as humiliating as it was painful. Once considered a great honor, being a city councilor began to lose its appeal. Because a position in the imperial bureaucracy granted immunity from service in city government, with its crushing fiscal obligations, many ambitious men turned to the imperial bureaucracy to win the honors, status, and power that used to come with positions in the city government. Some cities benefited from the newly expanded imperial superstructure, especially administrative centers and the capitals of the many new provinces. Most cities, however, lost a great deal of their autonomy because of the growth of the imperial bureaucracy. Meanwhile, both the wealth and numbers of city aristocrats, the traditional leaders and patrons of their communities, dwindled.

One result of this shift in power away from the traditional urban aristocracy was the deterioration of the fabric of urban life. The inscriptions in marble attached to public buildings reveal a gradual decline in public spending by all but the very wealthiest citizens. As civic monuments and public buildings decayed, restoration and repair rather than the construction of new buildings became the order of the day in cities throughout the empire. When the empire's governing elite turned to Christianity in the course of the fourth century, private donors shifted their interests and built many churches and monasteries throughout the empire.

The life of peasants in late antiquity changed as well. As some men grew richer and more powerful, many poor peasants in the countryside turned to them for protection against other landowners and ruthless imperial tax collectors. In return for this protection, these peasants gave their wealthy patrons ownership of the farms on which they continued to work. These peasants, called *coloni*, lost the right to leave their farms and move elsewhere, but they could not be evicted from their farms, which gave them a measure of security. Coloni had to perform labor for their landlords and had only limited control of their own possessions, although they were still considered free Roman citizens.

The imperial government supported this form of economic dependency because it benefited the biggest landholders—including the emperor—who needed a stable workforce tied to the land to make agriculture profitable and to supply recruits for the army. The coloni system (called the colonate) also promised the emperor a reliable source of tax revenues. Over time, landowners particularly in the western provinces began to develop private armies to protect their vast country estates and the peasants who labored on them. This usurpation of the role of the central government weakened the authority of the emperor and his administration in the western provinces. In contrast, the eastern provinces of the empire remained prosperous into the sixth century. Private estates grew in size, but the imperial administrators maintained tight control of the economy.

The economic strength of the eastern provinces was matched by the development of political strength in that part of the empire. In late antiquity, the center of power within the empire shifted decisively to the east, where wealth and political might were increasingly concentrated. Cities such as Antioch in Syria and eventually the new capital of Constantinople became the wealthiest and most powerful urban centers in the empire.

Christianizing the Empire

■ How did Christianity become the dominant religion in the Roman Empire, and what impact did it exert on Roman society?

When Diocletian died, he left the eastern provinces of the empire, at least, stronger militarily, administratively, and economically than they had been for nearly a century. The steps he had taken to eradicate Christianity, however, turned out to be a failure. The new faith gathered momentum despite the hostility of Diocletian and other polytheist emperors. Within a year of Diocletian's resignation as emperor, an ambitious young man began his quest to become the sole emperor of Rome, and his subsequent conversion transformed the Christians from a persecuted minority to the dominant force in the empire.

Constantine: The First Christian Emperor

In 305, Diocletian stepped down from the imperial throne and insisted that his co-emperor in the west, Maximian, retire as well. Diocletian expected a peaceful succession to occur. It did, but just barely. As planned the two junior emperors, Galerius and Constantius, took Diocletian's and Maximian's places. But just one year later, Constantius died in Britain. Abandoning the principles of the tetrarchy, the

troops stationed in Britain in 306 proclaimed Constantius's son, Constantine (ca. 280–337), to be his replacement. The ambitious young general set out to assert sole rule over the Roman Empire. In 312 he smashed the army of Maxentius, his last rival in the west, at the battle of the Milvian Bridge over the Tiber River at Rome. Twelve years later he defeated Licinius, the tetrarch ruling in the east. Constantine then rejoined the western and eastern halves of the empire together with himself as absolute ruler. Thus both the divided rule of the empire and the system of succession through co-emperors that Diocletian implemented came to an end.

In other ways, however, Constantine continued along Diocletian's reformist path. Under Constantine the empire's eastern and western sectors retained separate administrations. To improve the administrative chain of command, Constantine installed new officials called praetorian prefects in each sector. These rulers were directly accountable to the emperor. He also retained Diocletian's emphasis on a large field army, but ensured that heavily armored cavalry troops were trained for rapid deployment to trouble spots.

The imperial bureaucracy and army remained immense, and so taxes remained high. Under Diocletian coins had been losing their value, which contributed to the rampant inflation of prices and made the burden of taxes on the poor ever harder to sustain. To remedy the situation, Constantine reformed the coinage system. He recognized that the existing coins had become so debased they were effectively worthless, so he created a new gold coin—the *solidus*, which had a fixed weight of gold content. The creation of the solidus stabilized the economy by restoring the value of currency. The new coin ended the inflationary spiral that had contributed so much to the political and social turmoil of the third century and remained the standard coin in the Mediterranean world for 800 years.

Unlike Diocletian, Constantine embraced the new religion of Christianity. Most emperors had associated themselves with a divine protector. Constantine chose the sun god Apollo as his first divine companion. But the night before the pivotal battle at the Milvian Bridge in 312, Constantine experienced a revelation, which he interpreted as a sign from the Christian God. After triumphing in battle, Constantine attributed his success to Christ's favor. Later in his reign, writers described Constantine's victory as a miracle. Though it was not unusual for an emperor to embrace a new god, Constantine's particular choice made a difference. Because monotheistic Christianity repudiated rival gods and alternative forms of worship, Constantine's conversion led to the eventual Christianization of the entire empire. Constantine did not order his subjects to accept Christianity or forbid polytheist worship. He did, however, encourage widespread and public practice of his new faith. Before Constantine Christian worship had been conducted in the privacy of homes, but he lavished funds on church buildings. He obtained the gold for his new solidus coinage

DOCUMENT

Eusebius on the Vision and Victory of Constantine

by looting the treasures that had been stored for centuries in polytheist temples. Now yoked to the imperial office, Christianity quickly gained strength across the empire and became a potent challenge to traditional modes of religious expression.

To glorify his name, Constantine founded a new capital city, Constantinople, the "City of Constantine," on the site of the Greek city Byzantium in 324. Constantine's choice of location reveals a shrewd eye for strategy. The city lay at the juncture of two military roads that linked Europe and Asia and controlled access to the Black Sea. From this convenient spot the emperor could monitor the vast resources of the empire's eastern provinces. Like Diocletian, Constantine recognized that the wealth and power of the empire lay in the East.

The growth of Constantine's new city of Constantinople paralleled the growth of Christianity. Constantine did not intend to establish an exclusively Christian city as an alternative to Rome. He built no more than three churches and left the city's many temples to older gods intact. Within a generation, however, Constantinople became a Christian center, and the traces of polytheism in the city disappeared. Constantinople continued to grow in size and splendor, as palaces, monuments, churches, bathhouses, public buildings, and colonnaded streets appeared on a scale befitting the New Rome, as Constantinople came to be known. In addition to serving as an administrative center and an imperial capital, Constantinople came to symbolize the kingdom of Heaven in the minds of Christians. As God ruled from his throne in the court of Heaven, so the emperor ruled in Constantinople. The emperor, whom God had chosen to rule, thus provided the essential link between the celestial and earthly kingdoms. Christian monotheism created a new conception of the Roman Empire. One Roman law was wedded to one faith shared by all its subjects and led by one emperor who was God's representative on Earth.

Constantine's capital also became a strongly fortified city. In response to the threat of attack by Vandal pirates, the emperor Theodosius II erected massive defensive walls around the city in 413. In future centuries these fortifications would protect the city—and indeed, the empire—from ruin on several occasions. With a new Senate formed on the model of the Senate of the city of Rome, a steady supply of grain from Egypt to feed the capital's inhabitants, and plenty of opportunities for trade, Constantinople attracted people from all over the empire. The city rapidly grew in size, reaching perhaps several hundred thousand inhabitants by the early sixth century.

The Spread of Christianity

Before the fourth century Christianity had grown through traveling missionaries who established congregations in most cities of the empire. After Constantine successive em-

perors promoted Christianity, which mushroomed rapidly throughout the empire during the fourth century. With imperial support, church leaders transformed the face of cities by building churches and leading attacks on the institutions and temples of polytheist worship.

MAP

Spread of Latin Christianity in Western Europe

The Rise of the Bishops

As Christianity spread, it grew more complex in its internal organization. Shortly after Paul of Tarsus (ca. 5–67) had established the theological grounding of the new religion, a distinction developed between the laity—the ordinary worshipers—and the priests, who led the worship, administered the sacraments, and acted as pastors for the laity. This distinction between the laity and the priesthood remained a central feature of the administration of Christianity. Much of the early growth of Christianity occurred in cities. In imitation of the hierarchic Roman urban administration, Christian priests developed their own structures to exercise authority over the laity. Just as an imperial official directed each city's political affairs with a staff of assistants, so each city's Christian community came to be led by a chief pastor, called a bishop, who in turn had a staff of subordinate priests and deacons. Just as a provincial governor controlled the political affairs of all of the cities and rural regions in his province, so the bishop of the main city of a province held authority over the other bishops and priests in the province. This main or head bishop came to be called a *metropolitan* (because he resided in the chief city, the metropolis, of the province) in the east, an *archbishop* in the west. Through this hierarchy of metropolitans, archbishops/bishops, priests, and deacons, the scattered communities of believers were linked together into what emerged as the Christian Church.

With its sophisticated administrative structure, the Church grew quickly, and bishops became important authorities in their cities. A bishop's main task was to supervise the religious life of his *see* or diocese, which comprised not only the city itself but also its surrounding villages and agricultural regions. Such supervision involved explaining Christian principles and teaching the Bible to these communities. Bishops soon became far more than religious teachers. As the Church grew wealthy from the massive donations of emperors such as Constantine and the humbler offerings of pious women and men throughout the empire, bishops used these resources to help the poor. They cared for the general welfare of orphans, widows, sick people, prisoners, and travelers. When famine struck southern Gaul in the fifth century, for example, the bishop of Lyons sent so much food from his church estates that the Rhône and Saône Rivers as well as all the roads to the south were jammed with grain transports.

Constantine incorporated the Church's bishops into the imperial government by permitting them to act as judges in civil actions. This policy soon entangled them in secular politics. Litigants could choose to be tried before a bishop rather than a civil judge. The decisions of a bishop had the same legal authority as those made by civil judges and could not be appealed. Using the rhetorical skills they had learned in Roman schools, bishops were also the advocates of their cities before provincial governors or the imperial court. In many ways they usurped the role of the traditional urban aristocracy. For example, when the people of Antioch in Syria rioted and smashed a statue of the emperor, it was the local bishop, not a local aristocrat, who intervened with the emperor to prevent imperial troops from massacring the city's people.

Bishops also administered the financial affairs of their communities. Sometimes bishops used this money for political purposes. In an attempt to win influence and political support, Cyril, bishop of Alexandria from 412 to 444, spent 2,500 pounds of gold on general expenses and bribes to court officials and other clergymen during just one visit to Constantinople. In contrast, in regions without wealthy cities, the bishops were often hard pressed to find enough money to function effectively. British bishops going to a Church conference in 359 could do so only with financial assistance from the government.

By 400 Rome had become the most important see in western Europe. The bishop of Rome came to be called the "pope"—the papa or father of the other western bishops. By the middle of the fifth century the emperor formally recognized the pope's claim to have preeminence over other bishops. A number of factors explain why the office of the bishop of Rome evolved into the papacy°. Together with Jerusalem, Rome was a site of powerful symbolic importance to Christians. Both the Apostle Peter, the first among Jesus' disciples, and Paul of Tarsus, the traveling teacher who took a leading role in spreading Christianity beyond its Jewish origins, died as martyrs in Rome. Early Christians considered Peter to have been the first bishop of Rome who passed on his authority to all subsequent popes.

The tradition that Peter was the first among the disciples received support from a conversation between Jesus and Peter recorded in the Gospel of Matthew. Punning on Peter's name, Jesus told him, "You are Peter [*petrus*] and upon this rock [*petram*] I will build my church, and the gates of Hell shall not avail against it. And I will give to you the keys of the kingdom of heaven." Early Christians interpreted these words to mean that Jesus had given Peter special authority, including the power to absolve a sinner's guilt, and that the Church was to be led by those who inherited Peter's position. What came to be called the doctrine of the Petrine Succession declared that just as Peter was specially anointed by Jesus, so subsequent bishops in Rome (the popes) were anointed with special, God-given powers.

In this way popes claimed to be the chief bishops of the Christian world. They insisted that their spiritual authority took precedence over that of rival bishops in four other imperial cities: Constantinople, Jerusalem, Alexandria in Egypt, and Antioch in Syria. The bishops of these leading religious centers, however, also claimed spiritual descent from Jesus' apostles. They did not accept papal authority and often quarreled bitterly with the pope over matters of faith and politics. The tensions among these bishops of the empire's most important Christian communities led to divisions between the eastern and western parts of the empire that have lasted until the present day.

Through the authority of the bishops, the Church began functioning almost as an administrative arm of the government, although it still had its own internal organization. Indeed, when Roman rule collapsed in western Europe in the fifth century, the Church survived the crisis and stepped in to fill the vacuum of public leadership.

Christianity and the City of Rome

Christianity transformed the appearance of Roman cities. Constantine set an example of public and private spending on churches, hospitals, and monastic communities that conformed to Christian values. The first churches in Rome were built to honor Christian martyrs of earlier centuries, including the great basilicas built over the presumed burial sites of Sts. Paul and Peter. One of the great churches that

---

Central Nave of Santa Maria Maggiore

The church of Santa Maria Maggiore, dedicated to Mary, the mother of Jesus, was built in Rome in the 430s. Like other churches of the late antique period, Santa Maria Maggiore followed the plan of a Roman public building, a basilica, but added an altar in the semicircular apse at one end. Stories from the Bible were presented in mosaics on the walls above the columns. They decorated the church and provided lessons for illiterate worshipers.

Constantine built in Rome was called "Saint Paul Outside the Walls." This imposing structure marked the burial spot of Paul of Tarsus. Constantine also financed the construction of another grand church on the presumed site of Peter's martyrdom and burial, in an obscure cemetery on what was called the Vatican hill, just outside Rome's wall and across the Tiber River. St. Peter's Basilica was an imposing structure, with five aisles punctuated with marble columns. Its altar rested over Peter's grave. (Today the papal cathedral of St. Peter stands on that same spot, in the heart of the Vatican, the city of the pope.) The construction of these churches signaled that Jesus' disciples Peter and Paul had replaced Rome's mythical founders Romulus and Remus as the city's sacred patrons. In other places, too, Christian saints took the place of traditional gods and heroes as protectors of city life. With the construction of Christian churches, spending and construction on traditional buildings such as temples, bathhouses, and public entertainment facilities such as the circuses gradually declined.

Although Rome became a vital center of Christianity, the city's inhabitants did not adopt the Christian faith overnight. Throughout the fourth century, the huge temples and shrines of the old gods clustered in Rome's center continued to attract many worshipers, including influential senators. Church authorities hesitated to close these time-honored places of worship because they did not have legal authority to do so. Even after imperial laws in 391 and 392 forbade polytheist worship, sacrifices, and other religious rites, the ancient temples stood empty for a long time, because Christians believed that demons inhabited them. At the prompting of Rome's bishops, other public buildings, such as the large basilicas that had been used to conduct public business of many sorts, including legal trials, were turned into churches.

With the proliferation of new Christian houses of worship in Rome and other cities came new religious festivals and rituals, which gradually replaced traditional celebrations. Christians marked the anniversaries of the martyrdom of saints on the calendar. Sometimes a Christian holiday (a holy day) competed with a non-Christian holiday. For example, Rome's churchmen designated December 25 as the birthday of Christ to challenge the popular festival of the Unconquered Sun, which fell on the same day. Other Christian holidays also aimed to draw worshipers away from the rites of older gods. By the early sixth century the Church had filled the calendar with many days devoted to Christian ceremonies. Christmas and Easter (which commemorates Jesus' death and resurrection) as well as days for worshiping specific martyrs supplanted traditional Roman holidays. These festivals thus changed the patterns of urban community life throughout the empire. Not all of the traditional Roman holidays disappeared, however. Those that Christians considered harmless continued to be observed as civic holidays. These included New Year's Day, the accession days of the emperors, and the days that celebrated the founding of Rome and Constantinople.

One additional development in the Christian shaping of time was the use of the letters A.D. as a dating convention. A.D. stands for *anno domini*, or "in the year of our Lord," referring to the year of Jesus' birth. The convention began in 531, when Dionysius Exiguus, a monk in Rome, established a simple system for determining the date of Easter every year. He began his calendar with the birth of Jesus in the year 1 (zero was unknown in Europe at this time) and started counting from there. Although he was probably a few years off in his determination of the year of Jesus' birth, his system slowly came into general use by the tenth century. In modern secular societies where Christianity is not the universal belief, the abbreviation A.D. has been replaced by C.E.—meaning "in the Common Era"—to designate years (as is done in this textbook). In both systems, however, the year 1 still refers to Jesus' birth. Regardless of what designation is used—A.D. or C.E.—the Christian system has become the standard dating convention around the world.

Old Gods Under Attack

Many people today identify themselves as members of a religious community—as Christians, Buddhists, Hindus, Jews, or Muslims. For the most part these faiths are mutually exclusive—there are no Muslim Christians, for example. In late antiquity, however, before Christianity became the dominant religion in the Roman Empire, people prayed to gods of all sorts. Different deities met different needs, and the worship of one did not preclude worship of another. Some divinities—such as Isis, who promised life after death—had elaborate cults throughout the empire. The empire's great gods—Jupiter, Juno, and Minerva—had temples in cities everywhere and were formally worshiped on state occasions. In the countryside as well a variety of deities protected laborers and ensured fertility of plants, animals, and the farmers themselves.

To Christians, this diverse range of religious expression was intolerable. They labeled all polytheistic worship with the derogatory term paganism° and made a determined effort to eradicate it.

After converting to Christianity in 312, Constantine ordered the end of the persecution of Christians. Although Christianity did not become the "official" religion of the empire for nearly a century, tolerance for non-Christian beliefs and practices began to fade. In the fourth century, imperial laws forbade sacrificing animals on the altars outside the old gods' temples. Constantine's son, Constantius II (r. 337–361), ordered the Altar of Victory removed from the Senate House in Rome. Since Augustus's reign, generals had sworn oaths of allegiance to the emperor at this altar before marching to battle. State funding for polytheistic worship gradually stopped. Instead of temples, emperors built churches with money collected from the taxpayers.

During the fourth century bishops and monks, often in collusion with local administrators, led attacks on polytheist shrines and holy places. For example, in 392 the bishop and parishioners of Alexandria destroyed the city's Temple of Serapis, known for its huge size, its magnificent architecture, and the devotion of the local community to it. Similar clashes erupted in many cities across the empire. Libanius, an aristocrat from Antioch, complained to Emperor Theodosius in 390 about the destruction caused by gangs of zealous monks: "This black-robed tribe . . . hasten to attack the temples with sticks and stones and bars of iron, and in some cases, disdaining these, with hands and feet. Then utter desolation follows, with the stripping of roofs, demolition of walls, the tearing down of statues and the overthrow of altars, and the [polytheist] priests must either keep quiet or die."[1]

One emperor tried to restore traditional religion. Julian the Apostate (r. 360–363), who had been raised as a Christian in Constantine's court, rejected Christianity and tried to reinstate the old religions when he came to the throne. But his death during a campaign against Persia eliminated any hope for a restoration of pre-Christian ways. Emboldened by this turn of events, an increasingly zealous Church establishment attacked polytheism with renewed vigor. Emperor Theodosius I (r. 379–395) and his grandson Theodosius II (r. 402–450) forbade all forms of polytheistic worship, and non-Christian practice lost the protection of the law.

Because polytheism was not a single, organized religion, it offered no systematic opposition to government-supported attacks, but there were influential opponents to the Christianization of the empire. In sharp contrast to the pious Christian court at Constantinople, the conservative aristocracy of the city of Rome clung hard to the old gods. In 384, their spokesman unsuccessfully begged the emperor for tolerance. Quintus Aurelius Symmachus, a highly respected nobleman who had pleaded unsuccessfully for the return of the Altar of Victory, argued that Rome's greatness had resulted from the observance of ancient rites. His pleas fell on deaf ears. By the middle of the fifth century the aristocracy of the city of Rome had accepted Christianity.

A Female Priest
This foot-high ivory panel shows a female priest making a sacrifice at an altar to an unnamed god or goddess. *Symmachorum* means "of the family of the Symmachi," an aristocratic Roman clan in which some members defended the old gods in the face of Christianity. This elegant plaque commemorates some now-forgotten event in the family's life.

Many less influential people also struggled to maintain ancient forms of worship. Sometimes they fought with monks to preserve the shrines of the gods their families had worshiped for generations. But with the empire's resources pitted against them, they could not resist for long. People increasingly began to join Christian communities, though often without fully understanding what the religion required of them. Surviving records of sermons reveal that church leaders preached for centuries afterward against the surprising persistence of "pagan" habits among their congregants. Priests repeatedly explained the risks to salvation that lurked in age-old festivals, bawdy public entertainments, and even regular bathing, which was considered a sinful pleasure.

Eventually, this priestly diligence paid off. The pace of conversion accelerated in the fifth and sixth centuries. Emperor Justinian (r. 527–565) sponsored programs of forced conversion in the countryside of Asia Minor, where tens of thousands of his subjects still followed ancient ways. Eradicating polytheism in the Roman Empire meant far more than the substitution of one religion for another. Polytheism lay at the heart of every community, influencing every activity, every habit of social life, in the pre-Christian world. To replace the worship of the old gods required a true revolution in social and intellectual life. Completing that revolution became the challenge of the new Christian communities.

New Christian Communities and Identities

■ How did Christianity enable the transformation of communities, religious experience, and intellectual traditions inside and outside the empire?

The spread of Christianity produced new kinds of identities based on faith and language. Christianity solidified community loyalties and allegiances by providing a shared belief system and new opportunities for participation in religious culture. Yet at the same time, Christianity opened up new divisions and gave rise to new hostilities. Certain new groups were respected and revered; others found themselves marginalized or persecuted. As Christians debated how to interpret the doctrines of their faith, sharp divisions emerged among them. Because Christians spoke Greek, Latin, Coptic, Syriac, Armenian, and other languages, different religious interpretations and rituals sometimes took hold, creating distinct communities. As a result, new religious zones identified with different spoken languages and different interpretations of Christian texts appeared within the empire.

The Creation of New Communities

Christianity fostered the growth of large-scale communities of faith by providing a well-defined set of beliefs and values. These basic beliefs and values had to be integrated with daily life and older ways of thinking. Thus Christianity required followers to study and interpret the Bible, the religion's sacred text. The religion also demanded allegiance to one God and a complex set of doctrines. Weaving these elements into daily life resulted in a strong sense of Christian identity and common purpose. This new Christian identity competed with and at times replaced older identities linked to Roman citizenship or shaped by regional or urban loyalties.

Christian Doctrine and Heresy

The foundations of Christian doctrine were in two texts, the Hebrew Bible, which Christians called the Old Testament, and Jesus' teachings, contained in the New Testament. The Old and New Testaments gave a focal point to Christian worship, and their interpretation shaped Christian communities. Both testaments contained powerfully evocative narratives, moral teachings, poems, and parables, the precise meanings of which were not always self-evident. Every week the priest read to parishioners from these sacred texts. As Christian communities developed, interpretation of that faith by its followers became all-important. The Church decided what interpretations of the Bible were correct and expected all members of the community to accept these doctrines. In this way, Christian teaching contrasted sharply with secular (nonreligious) education in the Roman Empire, which was intended only for the urban elite. Christian teaching was meant for all. It required all people to live according to a shared interpretation of the Bible and the meaning of Jesus' life, death, and resurrection.

The Church soon ran into difficulties over interpretation of the texts, as Church leaders disagreed about the meanings of many biblical passages. Councils of bishops met frequently to try to resolve doctrinal differences and produce statements of the faith that all parties could accept. Two theological questions generated the most disagreement—the nature of the Trinity and the nature of Jesus Christ.

Christians believe that one God created and governs Heaven and Earth. This monotheistic foundation, however, undergirded a complex theological system in which the one God was understood to exist in three distinct "persons," each fully and absolutely God—God the Father, God the Son, and God the Holy Spirit—or the Holy Trinity. Church leaders argued about the precise relation of the three persons to one another and within the Trinity. Were the Son and the Holy Spirit of the same essence as the Father? Were they equally divine? Did the Father exist before the Son?

These debates over the Trinity were intimately connected to the second issue of contention with the early Church—the question of the nature of Jesus. At one extreme, some Christian scholars believed that Jesus was entirely divine and had no human nature. This emphasis on Jesus' divinity made his death on the cross and his resurrection irrelevant, for God could not suffer and die. It also severed the links between Jesus and his human followers by emphasizing that Jesus was entirely "transcendent" or "other," entirely beyond human comprehension or human limitations. At the other extreme, some Christians taught that Jesus was entirely human and not at all divine, thus challenging both the belief in the Trinity and what most other Christians understood as Jesus' mission on Earth.

The questions of the nature of the Trinity and the nature of Jesus erupted in the first great Christian controversy of late antiquity: the dispute between the Arians and the Athanasians. The Arians followed Arius of Alexandria (ca. 250–336), a priest steeped in Greek philosophy. Arians asserted that God the Father created Jesus and so Jesus could not be equal to or of the same essence as God the Father. Arians argued that the Trinitarian idea that Jesus as God the Son was both fully divine and fully human was illogical. The Athanasians, followers of the Bishop Athanasius of Alexandria (293–373), were horrified by what they saw as the Arians' attempt to degrade Jesus' divinity. They argued that Christian truths were beyond human logic and that Jesus was fully God, equal to and of the same substance as God the Father, yet also fully human.

The Arian-Athanasian dispute resulted in perhaps the most influential of the many church meetings held in late antiquity: the Council of Nicaea. In 325, Emperor Constantine summoned the bishops to Nicaea, a town near Constantinople, to reach a decision about the relationship among the divine members of the Holy Trinity. The bishops produced the Nicene Creed, which is still recited in Christian worship today. The creed states that God the Son (Jesus Christ) is identical in nature and essence to God the Father, Athanasian belief. More than a century later, the Council of Chalcedon of 451 reinforced the Nicene Creed. The assembled bishops agreed that Jesus was both fully human and fully divine, and that these two natures were entirely distinct though united.

The Nicene Creed and the decisions of the Council of Chalcedon became the correct, or orthodox°, interpretation of Christian teaching because they had the support of most bishops and the imperial court. Still, some bishops and other religious leaders continued to debate conflicting interpretations of the Bible, and many ordinary Christians continued to hold beliefs that clashed with those defined as orthodox. People who held the orthodox point of view considered such alternative doctrines to be false beliefs, or heresies°, and they labeled the supporters of such alternative beliefs *heretics*.

Communities of Faith and Language

The doctrinal differences between orthodox and unorthodox or heretical Christian groups helped cement different communal and even ethnic identities in late antiquity. Several geographic zones of Christians emerged that held different interpretations of Christian doctrine. They produced Bibles, sermons, and religious ceremonies in their native languages. A central zone based in Constantinople and including North Africa, Gaul, Italy, the Balkans, and much of western Europe contained Christians called Chalcedonians°, or orthodox. (In the Latin-speaking western provinces they were also called Catholics.) These believers followed the decision of the Council of Chalcedon in 451 that defined Christ's divine and human natures as equal but entirely distinct. In late antiquity, the emperors in Constantinople and the popes in Rome—as well as the most of the population of the Roman Empire—were Chalcedonian Christians.

Although the Christians in this zone agreed on fundamental matters of doctrine, they differed culturally by producing Bibles, delivering sermons, and conducting religious ceremonies in their native languages—Latin in the western part of the central zone, mostly Greek (but also Syriac, Armenian, and Coptic) in the eastern. In western Europe, Latin was the language of Christian literature and church ritual. About 410, the monk Jerome finished a new Latin translation of the Bible, which replaced earlier Latin versions. This translation, called the Vulgate Bible, became the standard Bible in European churches for many centuries.

The western Church's use of Latin kept the door open for the transmission of all Latin texts into a world defined by Christianity. This ensured the survival of Roman legal, scientific, and literary traditions, even after Roman rule had evaporated in western Europe. Latin also forged a common bond among different political communities of the empire's western sector. Latin served as an international language among the ruling elites in western Europe, even though they spoke different languages in their daily lives. Thus, church-based Latin served as a powerful unifying and stabilizing influence. The Latin language combined with Christianity to spur the development of Latin Christendom°—the many peoples and kingdoms in western Europe united by their common religion and shared language of worship and intellectual life.

In the eastern provinces of the Roman Empire, Christianity had a different voice. There a Greek-based Church developed. Greek was the language of imperial rule and common culture in that region, and Greek became the language of the eastern Christian Church. In addition to the New Testament, which had been originally written in Greek, eastern Christians used a Greek version of the Hebrew Bible (the Old Testament) called the Septuagint, which Greek-speaking Jews had prepared in Alexandria in the second century B.C.E. for their own community. The Septuagint combined with the Greek New Testament to become the authoritative Christian Bible throughout most of Rome's eastern provinces.

In a second zone in the eastern Mediterranean and beyond were Anti-Chalcedonians, usually known by the derogatory term of Monophysites° (literally "one nature"). They did not accept the teaching of the Council of Chalcedon about the combination of the divine and the human in Christ as being "in two natures." Instead, they believed that Christ had one nature in which the divine and human coexist, though neither mixed nor divided. As a leading Anti-Chalcedonian bishop in Alexandria explained, "if there are two natures, there are necessarily two persons, but if there are two persons, there are also two Christs." Three Anti-Chalcedonian communities had developed by the end of late antiquity. The kingdom of Armenia in the Caucasus mountain region of eastern Asia Minor, which had become in about 300 the first kingdom in the world to accept Christianity, which was a dozen years before Constantine's conversion, eventually accepted the doctrines of Anti-Chalcedonian Christianity in the late fourth century. When the Bible was translated into Armenian about 400, a rich Christian literature developed among the peoples of Armenia. Christianity in its Anti-Chalcedonian form helped foster a strong sense of ethnic identity among the Armenians.

An Anti-Chalcedonian community also appeared in Egypt, among the native Egyptian speakers, called Copts. Like the Armenians, the Copts developed a vibrant Christian culture expressed in the Egyptian language. Christianity took root in Egypt during the first century, and a Coptic Bible, completed in late antiquity, solidified a Coptic community that has survived to the present day.

In the Middle East, another distinctively Anti-Chalcedonian community was forged among the inhabitants of Syria. These Christians spoke Syriac, a Semitic language spoken by many people within the region. The Syriac Bible probably appeared in the second century. As was the case with Armenian and Coptic peoples, a vast literature of biblical interpretation, sermons, commentaries, and church documents was gradually created, forming the basis of Syriac-speaking Christian culture. In the sixth century the Syriac church developed its own hierarchy of priests and bishops independent of the Chalcedonian church in Constantinople.

The Ascetic Alternative

The idea that the human body, with all its physical needs, stands in the way of spiritual progress had long existed in the ancient Mediterranean world. Over the centuries, it has become deeply rooted in Western culture. As we saw in Chapter 3, in the fifth century B.C.E. Plato had argued that human souls are only bits of the great Soul that dwells in an unchanging celestial realm far above our earthly world. These bits of soul reside only temporarily in the human body during a person's life. By pursuing the philosophical life people might overcome the constraints of the human body and the material world and free these bits of soul to return to their source. Living a philosophical life meant combining a rigorous intellectual pursuit of knowledge with a disregard for physical needs. Greek and Roman philosophers following Plato dreamed of freeing their souls to ascend to a higher realm.

Christian ascetics took a different direction. They sought to suppress their physical needs to the extent that God might enter their bodies and work through them. Making contact with God required constant preparation, as one might prepare for an athletic competition. For this reason Christian ascetics struggled to deny the physical self in all its manifestations. Many relied on deprivation, going without food and sleep. They would also punish their bodies through self-flagellation. Still others rejected human contact, living in uncomfortable places such as atop a pillar or at the bottom of a dry well. All ascetics struggled to abstain from sex and to reject social standards of cleanliness, which they viewed as mere vanity.

Christian ascetic practice could also take subtler forms than physical abuse. Some followers rejected their families and communities, spurned all knowledge except for the content of the Bible, and even denied the significance of the passage of time by insisting that each day was a new beginning. In all of these ways ascetics freed themselves from the practices that ordered and gave meaning to everyday life. In monasteries and nunneries men and women submitted to the absolute rule of abbots and abbesses in their quest to suppress individual aspirations.

Winning the endless battles against the desires of the self and the lures of the Devil made ascetics holy in the eyes of their fellow Christians. Once an ascetic achieved communion with God, that divine presence within the ascetic radiated a curative power. Uniquely situated on the border between the divine and the human, holy ascetics sometimes channeled their power to the benefit of the human community by performing healing miracles and mediating disputes.

The ascetic movement revealed a profound shift in ideas about the body, the accessibility of divinity, and the nature of sexuality. From the ascetic perspective, the human body ceased to be a beautiful gift to be glorified in statuary and song. Instead it became an obstacle to spiritual communion with God. An ascetic life was not just a suppression of sexual desires but a victory over them. For Christians, following an ascetic life was not a cowardly flight from the problems of the world. Rather, it represented a courageous encounter with personal demons and the evils of society. Through ascetic discipline, men and women challenged their own physical existence as well as the basic values of the everyday Mediterranean world.

For Discussion

How did religious beliefs affect the ways that Christians understood their bodies in late antiquity? What do these beliefs about the human body and sexuality tell us about late antique society?

The shell above Symeon's head symbolizes his sainthood.

Symeon, who wears the robes of a monk, resists the devil with the help of a holy text that he holds on his lap.

In this silver plaque Symeon threatened by the devil, w taken the form of a serper

Symeon the Pillar Saint
The fifth-century ascetic saint Symeon lived atop a pillar in Syria. Crowds gathered to watch him perform holy acts of bodily mortification and to ask his advice and blessing.

In addition to the Chalcedonian and Anti-Chalcedonian regions in late antiquity, a third zone of Christians consisted of the Arians. As described earlier, Arians° believed that Jesus was not equal to or of the same essence as God the Father. Most of the people who followed Arian Christianity were the Goths and other Germanic settlers who converted to Christianity in the fourth century, when they still lived north of the Danube River and in southern Russia. When they invaded the Roman Empire in the fifth century, they seized political control of Rome's western provinces. Because of religious differences with the Roman Christians who followed Chalcedonian Christianity, the two groups did not intermarry, and the Arians were able to maintain their ethnic identity in the face of the much larger Roman population whom they ruled. While the Goths were still north of the Danube, a Gothic priest named Ulfila devised a Gothic alphabet and used it to translate the Bible. A Christian Gothic culture thrived in the western zone despite its minority status.

In all of these three zones, variations of the Christian faith expressed in different languages formed the seedbed of ethnic communities, some of which survive to the present day, such as the Armenians, Copts, and Greek-speaking Orthodox Christians. Yet at the same time, the spread of Christianity weakened other local groupings. As language-based Christian communities spread inside and outside the empire, many local dialects and languages disappeared. Throughout most of western Europe the Celtic languages began to fade away during late antiquity. In the east the old languages of Asia Minor were gone by the end of the sixth century. Only the languages in which Christianity found textual expression survived.

The Monastic Movement

Near the end of the third century, a new Christian spiritual movement took root in the Roman Empire. Known today as asceticism°, this movement called for Christians to subordinate their physical needs and desires to a quest for spiritual union with God. Asceticism both challenged the emerging connection between the political and religious authorities and rejected the growing wealth of the Church.

The life of an Egyptian Christian, Antony, provided a model for future ascetics. Around 280 Antony sold all his property and walked away from his crowded village near the Nile into the desert in search of a higher spirituality. A few decades later, Athanasius, the Bishop of Alexandria who had argued against the Arians, composed a biography, the *Life of Antony,* telling how Antony overcame all the temptations the Devil could conjure up, from voluptuous naked women to opportunities for power and fame. Vividly describing the struggle between asceticism ("the discipline") and the lures of everyday life ("the household"), Athanasius's work became one of the most influential books in Western literature. It captured the spiritual yearnings of thousands of men and women, inspiring them to imitate Antony by following "the discipline" to seek God through a rejection of the ties of the household and material world. Asceticism appealed to those who desired an alternative to everyday political and social life, especially family life with its coercive parental authority, marriage, sexuality, and children that distracted from the contemplation of God.

Ascetic discipline required harsh and often violent treatment of the body. The first ascetics, called anchorites or hermits, lived alone in the most inaccessible and uncomfortable places they could find, such as a cave in a cliffside, a hole in the ground, or on top of a pillar. In addition to praying constantly in their struggle to overcome the Devil and to empty themselves of human desires so that God could enter and work through them, these men and women starved and whipped themselves, rejecting every comfort, including human companionship.

Over time, however, many Egyptian ascetics began to construct communities for themselves. The result was the monastic movement°. Because these communities, called monasteries, often grew to hold a thousand or more members, they required organization and guidance. Leaders like the Egyptian Pachomius (ca. 292–346), known as the "Searcher of Hearts," emerged to provide clear instructions for regulating monastic life and to offer spiritual guidance to the members of the monasteries. (The male inhabitants of monasteries are called monks, or solitary men; women are called nuns.)

Monastic communities soon multiplied in the eastern provinces of the Roman Empire, especially near Jerusalem in Palestine, where Jesus had lived centuries earlier. Basil of Caesarea (ca. 330–379) wrote a set of guidelines that was widely followed in eastern lands. Highly educated in Greek and Roman literature and philosophy as well as Christian theology, Basil repudiated extreme ascetic practices. He viewed the monastery as a community of individuals living and working together while pursuing their individual spiritual growth. Through his writings, Basil encouraged monks to discipline their souls through productive labor and voluntary poverty rather than through long bouts of self-inflicted physical tortures. He also insisted that monks should devote the greater part of their day to religious contemplation and prayer. In the monasteries, the monks typically shared meals and worship but engaged in ascetic discipline and prayer alone.

After spreading throughout the eastern provinces, monasticism made its way into western Europe. The desert, so accessible to monks in Egypt, became a metaphor for any desolate place where a person could live as an ascetic in the quest for God. John Cassian (ca. 365–ca. 433), for example, carried monastic ideas from Egypt to Gaul, where he found his "desert" in the rugged islands of the coast near modern Marseilles. He established two monasteries there. Cassian and other monks wrote rule books explaining how to organize and govern monastic life for the many communities that sprang up in Italy and Gaul.

Rule of St. Benedict

Drawing from the ideas of these earlier monastic rules written in Greek, Benedict of Nursia (ca. 480–547) wrote a Latin *Rule* that became the foundation of monasticism in western Europe. Benedict built a monastery on Monte Cassino near Naples in 529. Like Basil of Caesarea, Benedict emphasized voluntary poverty and a life devoted to prayer. Benedict, however, placed a greater stress on labor. Fearing that the Devil could easily tempt an idle monk, Benedict wanted his monks to keep busy. He therefore ordered that all monks perform physical labor for parts of every day when they were not sleeping or praying.

In the western Roman Empire monasticism played a central role in preserving classical learning and thus allowing its integration into Christian culture in later centuries. Much of the responsibility for the preservation of the classical intellectual tradition lay with the monasteries founded by Benedict. This group of monks, called the Benedictine order, established many monasteries throughout western Europe, modeled on Benedict's original monastery of Monte Cassino. Benedict himself was wary of classical teaching, but he wanted the monks and nuns under his supervision to be able to read religious books. At least basic education had to become part of monastic life. Benedictine monasteries provided an education not only to their inhabitants but also to any eager scholar from the surrounding communities. The Benedictine definition of "manual labor" expanded to include the copying of ancient manuscripts and Benedictine monasteries developed significant libraries. As monasteries that followed Benedict's *Rule* spread throughout Europe, they served as centers of education and also succeeded in preserving much Latin literature.

Monasticism, Women, and Sexuality

The monastic movement opened new avenues for female spirituality and offered an alternative to marriage and childbearing. In the first monastic communities, men and women lived separately to reduce sexual temptation, but within the confines of these communities, gender was irrelevant. It was just one more difficult physical boundary to cross over on the path to finding God. By joining monastic communities and leaving the routines of daily life behind, women could gain independence from the obligations of male-dominated society. As Christian monasticism spread, ascetic women began to create communities of their own. They lived as celibate sisterhoods of nuns, dedicated to spiritual quest and service to God.

The wives or daughters of wealthy and powerful families were typically the founders of female monastic communities. Such women wielded an authority and influence that would not have been available to them otherwise. For example, Melania the Younger (383–439), the daughter of a wealthy Roman senatorial family, decided to sell her vast estates and spend the proceeds in religious pursuits. When the Roman Senate objected to the breaking up of Melania's family estates, Melania successfully appealed to the empress, who interceded with the legal authorities to enable her to dispose of her property. (Melania's slaves also objected because they did not want to be sold separately to raise cash for her religious projects, but Melania ignored them.) Melania spent her fortune on building monasteries in the Holy Land of Palestine. Most women lacked the financial resources to make such dramatic gestures, but they could imitate Melania's accomplishment on a modest scale.

Monasticism also reinforced negative ideas about women and sexuality in the Church. During the late antique era an increasingly negative view of women emerged in the writings of churchmen. Christian writers branded women as disobedient, sexually promiscuous, innately sinful, and naturally inferior to men. They interpreted Genesis, the first book of the Bible, to mean that women bore a special curse. In their reading of the Genesis account, Eve, the first woman, seduced Adam, the first man. For this reason late

DOCUMENT

An Aristocratic Woman Chooses Poverty and a Religious Life

Melania the Younger (383–439) became a saint because of her generosity and piety. The daughter of an enormously wealthy senatorial family in Rome, she married at an early age but remained loyal to ascetic principles of poverty and virginity. In their early twenties, she and her husband, who was equally rich, sold their estates and gave their money to charity. This description comes from a biography of Melania written by one of the nuns in a monastery founded by Melania in Jerusalem:

It was as if she hoped that by the virtuous practice of almsgiving alone she might obtain mercy; as the Lord said, "blessed are the merciful, for they shall obtain mercy." Her love for poverty exceeded everyone else's. As she testified to us shortly before her departure of the Lord, she owned nothing at all except for about fifty coins of gold for the offering and even this she sent to a very holy bishop, saying "I do not wish to possess even this from our patrimony." Nor only did she offer to God that which was her own, she also helped others to do the same. Thus many of those who loved Christ furnished her with their money, since she was a faithful and wise steward. She commanded these monies to be distributed honestly and judiciously according to the request of the donor.

Source: *Life of Melania the Younger*, 30.35, trans. Elizabeth A. Clark (NY/Toronto: Mellon Press, 1984), 48, 51.

antique Christians blamed Eve—and women collectively—for humanity's expulsion from the Garden of Eden and for all the woes human beings had suffered ever since. Yet at the same time Christians also believed that God would save the souls of women as well as men, and they honored Mary for her role in bringing Jesus, and therefore salvation, into the world. In many ways women occupied a position in the Christian religious imagination comparable to that held by Jews: They were considered guilty as a group of a terrible deed, yet they were accepted as a necessary part of God's plan for humanity.

Male ascetics preached and practiced sexual abstinence as an important self-denying discipline. In ascetic thought, women were linked to the corrupt world of the flesh against which the Christian must exercise unceasing vigilance. The ascetic retreat into the desert or monastery was a flight from temptation, and that meant a flight from women. As ascetic ideas gained in prominence, celibacy became a Christian ideal, with sexual relations within the confines of marriage viewed as distinctly second-best.

Jews in a Christian World

Until Christianity became the official religion of the Roman Empire, Jews had been simply one among hundreds of religious and ethnic groups who lived under Roman rule. Although polytheist Romans considered Jews eccentric because they worshiped only one god and refused to make statues of him, they still respected the Jewish people's faith. Prior to the fourth century, Jews had enjoyed full citizenship rights and appeared in all professions and at all levels of society.

Christianity slowly erased all this. According to Christian belief, Jews had been the chosen people of God until the appearance of Jesus, who displaced them from their place in God's plan. Christians criticized Jews for failing to accept that Jesus' teachings had supplanted those of the Hebrew Bible, and blamed them collectively for Jesus' crucifixion. Christians viewed the Diaspora (the dispersion of Jews around the world after the destruction of Jerusalem by the Roman army in 70) as God's way of punishing the Jews.

With the advance of Christianity within the empire, conditions for Jews declined. Beginning in the fourth century, Roman laws began to discriminate against Jews, forbidding them to marry Christians, own Christian slaves, or accept converts into their faith. With the support of Christian imperial officials, Church leaders sometimes forced entire communities of Jews to convert to Christianity on pain of death. A notable exception to this downward spiral was that Jews still retained the right to remain members of city councils. Although organized resistance among scattered Jewish communities was impossible, many Jews refused to accept the deepening oppression. Their resistance ranged from acts of violence against Jews who had converted to Christianity to armed revolt against Roman authorities.

Despite their marginal position in the empire, Jews did retain some security because most emperors honored traditional obligations to protect all their subjects. Roman emperors repeatedly issued laws forbidding the destruction of synagogues. They permitted Jews to worship on the sabbath and excused them from performing public or private business on that day, as Jewish law required. Zealous bishops often objected to such treatment of Jews, and some bishops goaded Christians into attacking synagogues. For example, in 388 the bishop of Callinicum, a town on the Euphrates River, destroyed the local synagogue with the assistance of his Christian congregation. When the emperor Theodosius I tried to punish the guilty citizens, Bishop Ambrose of Milan wrote a long letter stiffly rebuking the emperor: "Will you give the Jews this triumph over the Church of God, this victory over the people of Christ?" The emperor backed down, and the Christians of Callinicum went unpunished.

In 429, Roman officials abolished the office of Jewish Patriarch, the head of the Jewish community who enjoyed high official rank in the empire. The Roman emperors had long recognized the Patriarch as leader of the many Jews who were dispersed throughout the empire, and had given the Patriarch certain legal and administrative duties. With the office abolished, the Roman treasury now collected for itself the special taxes that had been paid by Jews for the Patriarch's administration. The end of the Patriarchate shows that Jews had lost their status as a legally recognized religious community in the eyes of the empire.

Individual Jewish communities continued to administer their own affairs under the leadership of rabbis—men who served as teachers and interpreters of Jewish law. With the completion of the Mishnah°, the final organization and transcription of Jewish oral law, by the end of the third century and the production of the Jerusalem and Babylonian Talmuds°, or commentaries on the law, by the end of the fourth and fifth centuries, rabbis and their courts now dominated Jewish communities. These learned men established academies of legal study in Roman Palestine and Persian Babylonia, where they produced authoritative interpretations of law that guided everyday Jewish life.

Although some Jewish women served as leaders of synagogues in late antiquity, in general rabbinic Judaism subordinated women in Jewish society. For example, Jewish women did not receive an education at the Jewish academies. Excluded from the formal process of interpreting the Bible, Jewish women did not acquire highly prized religious knowledge. Instead, men expected them to conform to submissive roles as daughters, wives, and mothers, much as women in other religious communities were expected to do.

A Greek Zodiac in a Synagogue

In late antiquity, Jews living in Palestine sometimes decorated their synagogues with mosaic floors depicting the zodiac. Although these mosaics appeared in synagogues and often contained Hebrew writing, the scenes and style of the mosaics were typical of Greek and Roman art. This blending demonstrates that members of the Jewish congregation also participated in the general non-Jewish culture of the province.

Access to Holiness: Christian Pilgrimage

Christianity not only created new communities and condemned others, it also offered new avenues of participation in religious culture. In late antiquity, Christians of all social ranks began to make religious journeys, or pilgrimages°. Their goal was to visit sacred places, especially places where holy objects, known as relics°, were housed. They believed these relics were inherently holy because they were physical objects associated with saints and martyrs, or with Jesus himself. The most highly valued relics were bones from the venerated person. Christians believed that contact with such relics could cure them of an illness, heighten their spiritual awareness, or improve their lives.

The mortal remains of Christian martyrs provided the first relics and the first objects of veneration for pilgrims, but after persecution of Christians ceased in 312, believers resorted to the bodies of great bishops and ascetic monks and nuns. From the fourth century onward, Christians regularly dug up saintly skeletons, chopped them up, and distributed the pieces to churches. The more important the holy person, the fiercer the competition for the bones and other objects associated with him or her. Churches in the largest cities of the empire, such as Rome, Constantinople, Alexandria, and Jerusalem, acquired fine collections. For example, the robe of the Virgin Mary, the mother of Jesus, was kept in a church in Constantinople. Residents of the city believed that the Virgin's robe drove away enemies when it was carried in procession along the city's battlements.

Emperors and important bishops acquired the greatest and most powerful relics of all—those that had reportedly touched Jesus himself. These included the crown of thorns he wore when crucified, the cross on which he died, and the nails that fastened him to the wood. Relics reminded Christians that Jesus' own death was symbolically repeated in the martyrdom of his followers. For this reason church altars where followers celebrated the Eucharist, the rite in which bread and wine are offered as Jesus' body and blood in memory of his death, were built over the graves or relics of martyrs.

Traveling to touch a relic was the primary motive for going on a pilgrimage. Palestine became a frequent destination of Christian pilgrims because it contained the greatest number of sacred sites and relics associated with events described in the Bible and particularly with Jesus' life and death. Between the fourth and seventh centuries, thousands of earnest Christian pilgrims flocked to Palestine to visit holy sites and pray for divine assistance and forgiveness for their sins. Helena, the mother of Emperor Constantine, made pilgrimage fashionable. In the early fourth century she visited Jerusalem, where she reportedly found remnants of the cross on which Jesus was crucified, as well as many of the sites pertaining to Jesus' life.

Inspired by his mother's journey, Constantine funded the construction of lavish shrines and monasteries at these sites, as well as guest houses for pilgrims. Practically overnight Palestine was transformed from a provincial backwater to the spiritual focus of the Christian world. Religious men and women—rich and poor, old and young, sick and healthy—streamed to Palestine and Jerusalem. There they joined processions that made their way from holy place to holy place. At each site clergymen permitted them to view and sometimes kiss or touch holy relics. On the most important holidays, such as Easter, priests held special ceremonies at the different sites of Jesus' last day on Earth—at the Mount of Olives where he was arrested by Roman soldiers, at the place of his trial, at the hill of his crucifixion, and at his tomb, called the Holy Sepulchre.

Palestine did not have a monopoly on holy places, however. Pilgrims traveled to places throughout the Roman world wherever saints had lived and died and where their relics rested. Their pilgrimages contributed to the growth of a Christian view of the world in several ways. Because pilgrimage was a holy enterprise, Christian communities gave hospitality and lodging to religious travelers. This fostered a shared sense of Christian community among people from many lands. Christians envisioned a Christian "map" dominated by spiritually significant places. Travel guides that explained this "spiritual geography" became popular among pilgrims. Most of all, pilgrims who returned home enriched in their faith and perhaps cured in mind or spirit inspired their home communities with news of a growing Christian world directly linked to the biblical lands they heard about in church.

Christian Intellectual Life

During the first three centuries after Jesus' death, when Christians were marginalized and at times persecuted in Roman society, many church leaders strongly criticized classical learning. Churchmen argued that the learning of pagan intellectuals was false wisdom, that it distracted the Christian from what was truly important—contemplation of Jesus Christ and the eternal salvation he offered—and therefore that it corrupted young Christians. However, after the persecutions ceased, many Christian thinkers began to participate actively in the empire's intellectual life. Highly educated in Christian learning as well as the traditional studies of the Roman elite, these writers examined the meaning of Christianity in the context of classical history and philosophy. In so doing they profoundly influenced every aspect of Christian thought, making Christian intellectual life compatible with classical learning at the highest level.

The Reconciliation of Christianity and the Classics

In Roman schools, the sons of wealthy families, as well as some poor boys with ambition and talent, studied the poets, dramatists, philosophers, and rhetoricians of the classi-

DOCUMENT

Bring Me the Head of Saint Paul!

Pope Gregory the Great (r. 590–604) tactfully responded to the request of Constantina, the empress in Constantinople, for the head of Saint Paul. He points to some differences between the cult of relics in the eastern and western Mediterranean, evidence of the growing cultural differences between the Latin West and the Greek East:

The Serenity of your Piety [the empress], conspicuous for religious zeal and love of holiness has charged me to send to you the head of Saint Paul, or some other part of his body, for the church which is being built in his honor in the palace in Constantinople. . . . [but] I neither can nor dare to do what you want. For the bodies of the apostles Saint Peter and Saint Paul glitter with so great miracles and terror in their churches that one cannot even go to pray there without great fear. . . . In the Roman and all the western parts [of the empire] it is unendurable and sacrilegious for any one by any chance to desire to touch the bodies of saints: and if one should presume to do this, it is certain that this temerity will by no means remain unpunished. For this reason we greatly wonder at the custom of the Greeks, who say that they pick up the bones of saints; and we scarcely believe it. . . . But since so religious a desire of my most serene lady ought not be wholly unsatisfied, I will make haste to transmit to you some portions of the chains which Saint Peter the Apostle himself bore on his neck and his hand, from which many miracles are displayed among the people, if at least I should succeed in removing it by filing. . . .

Source: With some changes from: Gregory the Great, *Selected Epistles*, Trans. James Barmby, in *Nicene and Post-Nicene Fathers*, vol. 12, ed. P. Schaff and H. Wace, 1895/1995, pp. 154–156.

cal Greek, Hellenistic, and Roman periods. By late antiquity this curriculum had become formalized into seven liberal arts: grammar, logical argument, and rhetoric (collectively called the Trivium); and geometry, arithmetic, astronomy, and music (the Quadrivium). Law and medicine were taught separately for those who aspired to those professions. This education prepared students for careers in the imperial bureaucracy and various other fields. Equally important, it provided aristocratic men with a common cultural bond—a shared version of history, a value system that legitimized their exercise of power, an appreciation of the benefits of civilized life, and a common understanding of how the universe functioned. No other institution before the rise of Christianity, not even the army, exerted such a powerful influence on the minds of the men who controlled Rome's destiny.

Classical learning and the educational system that kept it alive posed a challenge to Christian educators. Specifically, how should Christians reconcile classical teachings with the doctrines of their faith, particularly when the two conflicted? Did the classics of Greek and Roman philosophy constitute a threat to Christianity? Could Christians learn anything of value from non-Christian cultures? Should educated men turn their backs on classical learning in order to avoid being corrupted by it?

After Constantine's conversion in 312, influential voices in the Church began to answer these questions. To them classical learning no longer seemed as threatening to Christianity has it had before. Many church leaders now came from the empire's urban elite, where they had benefited from classical learning. Christian officials grudgingly approved secular education as they recognized that the traditional curriculum still had practical value because it was useful for the administration of the Church and for the law. Training in classical rhetoric, grammar, and literature became an integral part of upper-class Christian life. By the fifth century traditional schooling for Christians was accepted as a useful if risky enterprise. As Basil the Great (ca. 330–379), bishop of Caesarea in Cappadocia (in modern Turkey), explained to young men about to embark on their studies, classical learning had both benefits and dangers. Although pagan learning, he advised, had some spiritual value, the charm of words can be dangerous and poison the Christian's heart.

Writing in Greek and Latin, churchmen now drew freely from classical texts and methods of discussion, even though they considered the Christian scriptures the sole source of truth. In the process both how they understood classical learning and Christianity itself changed. For example, Christianity reshaped how Romans understood the empire's place in human history. Eusebius, the bishop of Caesarea in Palestine from 313 to 339 and an adviser to Constantine, developed a theory of history that linked the development of the Roman Empire to a divine plan for humanity's salvation. Like other Christians before him, Eusebius believed that the Bible described the main events of human history, such as the creation of the first man and woman, God's revelation of his law to the Hebrews, and the great flood. Events still to come, according to Eusebius, included the appearance of the Antichrist, who would inaugurate a brutal reign of evil on Earth, the return of Jesus, the overthrow of the Antichrist, and the End of Days, when God would judge all human beings, reward the pious, and punish the wicked.

Eusebius added the Roman Empire to this historical plan. He argued that God had sent Jesus to Earth at a divinely appointed place and time—during the reign of the emperor Augustus and thus at a time when much of the known world had been united under imperial rule. The *Pax Romana*, according to Eusebius, provided the perfect, indeed the divinely ordained, conditions for the rapid spread of Christian teaching and the rapid growth of the Christian Church. In Eusebius's view, Constantine's conversion to Christianity marked the next step in God's plan. With one world empire now united under the one true religion, it would be the emperor's job to bring this religion to all of humankind. This triumphal vision of history struck a powerful chord among the empire's Christian elite. It gave Rome a crucial role to play in human destiny. It also enabled aristocrats to justify their traditional roles as political leaders.

By the fifth century, many Romans especially in the western provinces found Eusebius's triumphalism less satisfying as troubling questions surfaced. As we saw in the chapter introduction, in 410 the Visigoths plundered the city of Rome itself. This disastrous event challenged Christians' confidence in Eusebius's vision. Did Rome really have a special role in God's divine plan for humanity? If God favored Rome, as Eusebius explained, why had he allowed Visigoths to humiliate the great city? Was God punishing Romans because they had not eradicated paganism?

Questions such as these prompted Augustine of Hippo (354–430) to reexamine conventional notions about Rome's place in the world. By examining the most troubling philosophical and historical questions in light of the scriptures, Augustine became the most influential Latin Father of the Church, a term reserved for the early Christian writers who sought to reconcile Christianity with classical learning.

Born to parents of modest means, Augustine attended traditional Roman schools as a youth, an education that made him thoroughly familiar with the classics. His talent and schooling had prepared him for a high position in public life. After his conversion to Christianity, Augustine became the influential bishop of the city of Hippo Regius in North Africa. He recounted his spiritual experiences and conversion in the *Confessions* (397), an autobiography written in his middle age. Drawing on the ideas of the Greek philosopher Plato and Christian scriptures, Augustine in the *Confessions* meditated on the meaning of life, especially on sin and redemption. To modern readers his sins may seem petty things, but for him the real message was the power of redemption that made possible eternal life. Augustine showed that intellect alone was incapable of bringing about the spiritual growth that he desired. God's intervention was necessary to achieve his spiritual goals. For a spiritual conversion to be complete he had to cleanse himself of the desires of the flesh, which led him to renounce sexuality completely. Using his episcopal office as a platform from which to defend Christianity from polytheist philosophers and to define all aspects of the Christian life, Augustine displayed a sincere respect for certain aspects of Roman cultural and intellectual accomplishments—especially rhetoric and history. But he always believed Christianity was superior. For Augustine, the most dangerous enemy of all true Christians was "antiquity, mother of all evils"—the source of false beliefs.

In his book *The City of God,* completed in 423, Augustine developed a new interpretation of history. Though Augustine admired the Romans for their many virtues, he disagreed with Eusebius, concluding that Rome played no significant role in salvation history. Even the sack of Rome in 410 had no special meaning for Christians. Augustine's historical theory disconnected Christian ideas of human destiny from the fate of the Roman Empire. In his view, the Roman Empire was just one among many that had existed and that would exist before Jesus' return. According to Augustine, the only dates humanity should view as spiritually significant were Jesus' time on Earth and the End of Days sometime in the future. The significance of all events in between remained known only to God.

Augustine's theory proved quite timely. Within a few years of his death the Vandals seized North Africa and the Roman Empire lost control of all of its provinces in western Europe. Augustine thus gave Roman Christians a new perspective with which to view this loss: Rome had contributed to world civilization and to the growth of the Christian Church, but now Christianity would grow on its own without the support of Roman emperors.

Other churchmen explained the collapse of Roman power in western Europe differently. Salvian, a clergyman from the south of France who found himself living in a new Germanic kingdom of the visigoths in the first half of the fifth century, believed that the Romans deserved to lose their empire in the West because of their sinful lives and oppressive social order. The Visigoths, while less sophisticated than Romans, were nevertheless purer at heart—better Christians despite their heretical Arian views. Salvian's views demonstrate that for many devout Christians, Roman civilization had come to the end of the road. In their eyes, it was time to build a new, Christian world.

After the collapse of the Roman Empire in the western provinces, the challenge for Christian thinkers came less from reconciling Christianity with the power of classical learning than from keeping classical learning alive at all. Like Augustine, Cassiodorus (ca. 490–ca. 585), an Italian statesman in the court of Ostrogothic rulers of Italy, regarded classical learning as an intellectual inheritance of high value. Cassiodorus was appalled by the waning of the traditional classical educational system in the chaotic final days of the Roman Empire in the West. In response, he founded a monastery at Vivarium in the south of Italy, to which he retired at the end of his political career. Eager to preserve the liberal arts, Cassiodorus instructed his monks to copy classical literature in the monastery's library. "Let the task of the ancients be our task,"[2] he told them.

Outside the monasteries traditional schooling in the classics survived only as long as cities could afford to pay for teachers. In most of the towns of the western provinces of the empire, schools gradually disappeared in the course of the fifth century as a result of the Germanic invasions. With the exception of a few major urban centers, such as Carthage in North Africa, where traditional Roman schooling continued after the establishment of the Vandal kingdom, cities no longer had the funds to pay for teachers.

In contrast in the eastern half of the empire, classical learning lasted well into the sixth century as a basic part of elite education. Traditional education declined in the eastern empire not because of invasions or poverty as in the west but because of the growing influence of Christianity on daily life. After the emperor Justinian (r. 527–565) forbade non-Christians to teach, the number of schools decreased. By the end of the seventh century, traditional schools of grammar and rhetoric had disappeared. The Psalter (the collection of Psalms in the Bible) became the primer for reading, and religious literature supplanted classical works.

Neoplatonism and Christianity

Greek and Roman philosophy continued to be enormously influential. One branch of this tradition, called Neoplatonism°, originated with Plotinus (205–270), a non-Christian philosopher. His teachings greatly influenced Christianity, an example of how classical and Christian thought intertwined in late antiquity. Plotinus, who taught in the city of Rome, traced his intellectual roots primarily to the works of Plato (ca. 429–327 B.C.E.). He also drew ideas from Aristotle (384–322 B.C.E.) and various Stoic philosophers (third century B.C.E.), as well as the writings of their followers. In a series of essays called the *Enneads,* Plotinus applied Plato's views to the issues addressed in ancient philosophy, but Plotinus's greatest influence came from interpreting Neoplatonism in religious terms. He argued that all things that exist, whether intangible ideas or tangible matter, originate in a single force called the One.

According to Neoplatonists, the One has no physical existence; it is eternal and unchanging. The One is separated from the world of matter and physical change in which humans live by three descending grades of reality: the World Mind, the World Soul, and finally Nature. The World Mind contains the Forms that Plato described (see Chapter 3). The Forms are eternal, unchanging absolutes such as Truth, Justice, and Beauty that represent true reality, as opposed to the approximations of reality that humans encounter in everyday life. The Neoplatonists argued that the World Mind holds these Forms together as pure knowledge. The World Soul produces time and space, the dimensions that humans experience as history, Earth, and the planetary bodies. Nature is the lowest of these creative principles, consisting of things that come into being, change, and go out of existence, including living things. In Neoplatonic thinking, the human soul is a microcosm of these three levels of reality. The human soul "fell" from the One through the World Mind, the World Soul, and Nature into the human body, thereby losing its connection with the One. Yet the human soul can be redeemed. Humans have the potential to reunite their souls

CHRONOLOGY

Christianity, Polytheism, and Judaism

ca. 280	Antony goes into the Egyptian desert
ca. 300	Armenia becomes the first Christian kingdom
303	Great Persecution of Christians
312	Constantine converts to Christianity
325	Council of Nicaea writes the Nicene Creed
391	Polytheist worship forbidden by Roman law
396–430	Augustine is Bishop of Hippo
ca. 400	Jerusalem Talmud completed
410	Jerome completes Latin translation of Hebrew Bible (Vulgate)
429	End of Jewish Patriarchate
451	Council of Chalcedon
ca. 500	Babylonian Talmud finished
529	Academy in Athens closed; non-Christians forbidden to teach; Benedict founds monastery at Monte Cassino in Italy
534	Benedict writes *Rule* for monastic life

with the One by overcoming their passions and physical desires that are governed by the body. Many Neoplatonists believed that by gaining the help of the gods through magical rites (called theurgy) and by studying divine revelations, the human soul can reconnect with the One and fulfill its fullest potential.

With its emphasis on the fall and return of the soul to the One, Neoplatonism appealed to many Christians. For them, the One was God, and the Bible provided the divine revelations that could lead to the salvation of the human soul and reunification with God. The churchmen Gregory of Nyssa in the Greek East and Augustine in the Latin West were only two of the many churchmen who incorporated Neoplatonism into their own works in the later fourth century. Yet Christian and non-Christian Neoplatonists soon argued over such issues as whether the identity of "the One" could be equated with the Christian God and whether the use of theurgy constituted a pagan practice. In 529 the emperor Justinian closed Plato's Academy in Athens and forbade non-Christians to teach philosophy.

Nevertheless, the impact of Neoplatonism on Christian theology remained profound. Neoplatonic thought helped shape the Christian doctrine of the immortality of the human soul. It also reinforced the ascetic ideal practiced by

monks and nuns. Thus contempt for the material, temporal world and the physical body took deep root in Christian culture.

The Breakup of the Roman Empire

■ How and why did the Roman Empire in the West disintegrate?

During the fifth century, the Roman Empire split into two parts: the Latin-speaking provinces in western Europe, and the largely Greek- and Syriac-speaking provinces in the east. As the Roman government lost control of its western domains, independent Germanic kingdoms emerged. The eastern provinces remained under the control of the Roman emperor, whose capital city was not Rome, but Constantinople. The definitive split of the Roman Empire marked the end of late antiquity. In future centuries the legacy of the Roman Empire survived in the West through Latin culture and Latin Christianity. In the East it survived as a political reality until its final collapse a thousand years later in 1453.

The Fall of Rome's Western Provinces

Why did Roman rule remain strong in the eastern Mediterranean while collapsing in western Europe? This is one of the most hotly debated subjects in all of history.

Most Christians of the time attributed the collapse of Roman rule to God's anger at the stubborn persistence of polytheist worship. Polytheists, for their part, blamed Christians for destroying the temples of the gods who had protected Rome so well in the past. In later centuries, the explanations varied. Edward Gibbon, an eighteenth-century writer whose *Decline and Fall of the Roman Empire* has influenced all historians of Rome and remains one of the most widely read history books of all time, criticized the Catholic Church for diverting able men away from public service and into religious life. Other historians attributed Rome's collapse in the West to enormous waves of savage barbarian invasions. The reason the Romans lost their western provinces is, however, more complicated and less dramatic than any of these one-dimensional explanations.

Loss of Imperial Power in the West

The end of Roman rule in western Europe came in a haphazard and gradual fashion as the cumulative result of unwise decisions, weak leadership, and military failure. During the first century, the Romans established the northern limits of their empire on the European continent along the Rhine and Danube Rivers. From that time forward, Roman generals and emperors withstood invasions of many different northern tribes looking for plunder and new lands. The Roman legions parried their attacks, maintaining a relatively stable northern frontier through not only military might and but also diplomacy. Since the time of Augustus, Roman emperors had made treaties with newcomers, permitting them to settle on Roman lands. The empire had always been able to absorb the settlers until the situation changed in the fourth century.

In the fourth century, the sudden appearance in southern Russia of the Huns, a fierce nomadic people from central Asia, set in motion a series of events that helped bring about the eventual collapse of Roman rule in western Europe. Unlike the settled farmers who lived in Europe, the Huns were nomads who herded their flocks over the plains (or *steppes*) that stretched from southern Russia to central Asia. Able to travel vast distances very quickly on their rugged horses, the highly mobile Huns consistently overran adversaries from settled agricultural communities who were attempting to protect their farms and families. They also earned a reputation for ferocity in battle. Always living under the specter of starvation, they lusted after the great riches and easy lifestyles they observed in the urbanized empires of Rome and Persia.

In 376, in what is now south Russia, an army of Huns drove a group of Visigoths from their farmlands. The refugees gained permission from the Roman emperor Valens to cross the Danube and settle in the Balkans in return for supplying troops to the Roman army. In the past, Roman rulers had frequently made this sort of arrangement with newcomers eager to settle in the empire. The Roman officials in charge of this resettlement, however, flagrantly exploited the refugees by charging

them exorbitant fees for food and supplies. The situation grew so intolerable that in 378 the Visigoths revolted. At the battle of Adrianople in Thrace they killed Valens and destroyed an entire Roman army and the emperor who led it.

The Visigoths' successful rebellion wounded the empire, but not fatally. Rome's response to the disaster, however, sowed the seeds for a serious loss of imperial power in the west. Necessity forced the new emperor, Theodosius the Great (r. 379–395), to permit Visigothic soldiers to serve in the Roman army under their own Visigothic commanders. But this precedent of allowing independent military forces of dubious loyalty operate freely within the empire was a terrible mistake. The consequences of Theodosius's decision to allow the Visigoths their own commanders became all too clear in the mid-390s when Alaric, the new Visigothic king, adopted a new policy toward the empire and began to attack and plunder Roman cities in the Balkans and Greece. In 401 Alaric invaded Italy, but was driven out by Roman soldiers under the leadership of Stilicho, Rome's most powerful general in the West. Stilicho served Rome loyally, defending it against Alaric and other menacing barbarians. The Roman Senate turned on him in 408, however, because he could not eliminate Alaric's forces. Rather than plunge

Stilicho and His Family

Between 395 and 408 the general Stilicho ruled the western half of the empire as the regent for Honorius, the son of Theodosius I. Though his father was a Vandal, Stilicho was completely loyal to Rome. Carved in traditional Roman style, these ivory panels show Stilicho dressed in Vandal clothing, accompanied by his wife and son.

Italy into civil war, Stilicho bravely accepted a death sentence. Two years later Alaric reappeared at the walls of Rome, demanding a huge payment of gold and pepper, a precious spice. Without Stilicho to protect them, the powerless senators yielded to Alaric's extortion.

Alaric's success at extortion only expanded his ambitions. For two years following this success, Alaric became involved in a long series of negotiations with the Senate in Rome and the emperor of the west, who now lived in Ravenna. He wanted to be appointed to the highest military rank in the western empire, but the emperor refused. Finally a new emperor granted his request. In 410, however, when the Roman senate denied him parts of northern Italy and the western coast of the Balkans, and when imperial forces attacked him, Alaric and his troops sacked Rome for three days. Disbelieving senators and citizens alike could only watch as the Visigoths rampaged through their streets. Because Alaric died soon after his triumph, he was unable to follow up on his great victory. To keep his burial place secret, his followers diverted the Busento River in Italy, buried their fallen leader and all his loot, and then executed the grave diggers. Finally, they returned the river to its original course. The exact location of Alaric's grave remains a mystery to this day, awaiting an archaeologist's spade.

The Visigoths' sack of Rome not only dealt a psychological blow to the empire's inhabitants, it also led indirectly to the loss of many of Rome's western provinces. To fight Alaric, Rome's armies withdrew from the empire's northwestern defenses, leaving the frontier in Britain and along the Rhine vulnerable.

In Britain, Rome abandoned its control entirely after an ambitious general, styling himself Constantine III, led Britain's last legions across the English Channel in an unsuccessful attempt to grab the imperial throne. This action left Britain defenseless, vulnerable to groups of Germanic tribesmen known as the Saxons already settled on British soil. Originally from the shores of the North Sea near modern Denmark, the Saxons had been fighting in Britain as allies of Roman forces. Now they turned on their former partners and attacked Roman-held Britain. The desperate inhabitants begged for help from the emperor Honorius. According to one contemporary, in 410 the beleaguered ruler merely told the Britons to fend for themselves.

Elsewhere the chaos spread. In December 406, the Rhine River froze, enabling an array of migrating Germanic tribes to enter the empire with little opposition from Roman forces. Small bands of these marauding tribes such as Alans, Burgundians, and Sueves roamed through Gaul, while the Vandals and their allies raided their way through Spain. For more than a decade, the various invaders tried to secure territory for themselves within the imperial borders by force. Vastly outnumbered by the provincial populations, they survived by plundering the farms of the Romans.

Although the invading bands were small, the imperial government in the west no longer possessed the administrative capacity to marshal its military resources and push the invaders out. Instead, it turned to diplomacy, offering the invaders a place within the Roman Empire. In Gaul, for example, the treaty of 418 granted the Visigoths a home in Aquitania (a region of southwestern Gaul). According to the treaty, the Visigoths received lands on which to settle permanently, something they had sought for nearly two generations. In return they would pay taxes and fight under Rome's banner to combat peasant rebels and other invading tribes. Within a generation, however, the Visigoths shook off their subordinate status to Rome. Refusing to pay taxes to Roman officials or send troops to fight in Roman armies, they established a kingdom of their own in Gaul by 450. A similar process of encroachment and settlement took place elsewhere in the western provinces. In 429 the Vandals moved from Spain to North Africa, where they soon established an independent kingdom. In 439 they seized Carthage and made it their capital.

Thus, encroaching bands of Germanic peoples established independent kingdoms in the regions of Britain, Gaul, Spain, and North Africa through a gradual process (see Map 6.2). The empire was not invaded by overwhelming numbers of savage invaders. In fact, their numbers were puny compared to the millions of Roman provincials against whom they pitted themselves. And although the Germans plundered and pillaged, they could not hold on to imperial lands and settle there without the active cooperation of Roman administrators who thought they could bargain with the tribesmen. Once they put down roots, however, they steadily consolidated their strength and established rule on their own. By then, Roman authorities lacked both the organization and the strength to defeat them.

DOCUMENT

Excerpt from Salvian: *The Governance of God*

Even though most of the western provinces had fallen to invaders by 450, the Romans managed to hold on to Italy for a short while longer. The city of Rome remained the home of the Senate, while the emperor of the western provinces resided in Ravenna, a town on Italy's northeast coast. Warlords, however, held the real power in Italy, although they were formally subordinate to the emperor. These soldiers were usually not Romans by birth, but they adopted Roman culture and fought for Rome's advantage. In 476 one of these warlords, a Germanic general named Odovacar, ended the charade of obedience to the emperor. He deposed the last emperor in the west, a boy named Romulus Augustulus. Odovacar then assumed full power over the Italian peninsula, naming himself king of Italy. For many historians the year 476 used to symbolize the end of the Roman Empire in the west. In actuality, however, 476 is a date of little significance. The Romans' control of their western provinces had all but slipped away decades earlier.

The Empire of Attila

The Huns, who had driven the Visigoths into the Balkans and sparked the series of events that led to Rome's loss of

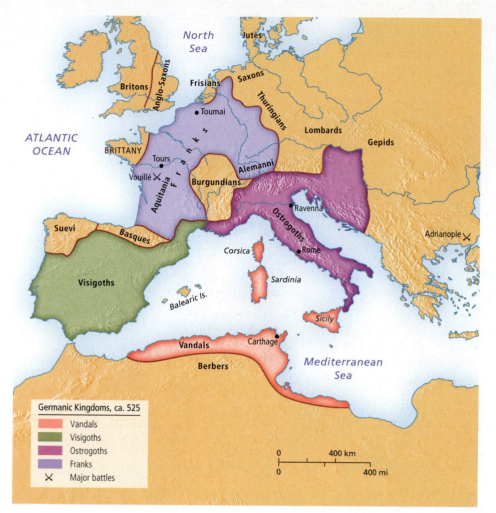

North Sea

Jutes

Britons

Anglo-Saxons

Frisians

Saxons

Thuringians

Lombards

Gepids

ATLANTIC OCEAN

BRITTANY

Toumai

F r a n k s

Tours

Vouillé

Aquitania

Alemanni

Burgundians

Ravenna

Ostrogoths

Adrianople

Suevi

Basques

Corsica

Rome

Sardinia

Visigoths

Balearic Is.

Sicily

Vandals

Carthage

Berbers

Mediterranean Sea

Germanic Kingdoms, ca. 525
- Vandals
- Visigoths
- Ostrogoths
- Franks
- ✕ Major battles

0 — 400 km
0 — 400 mi

Map 6.2 Germanic Kingdoms, ca. 525

In little more than a century after their entry into the Roman Empire, different Germanic peoples had established several powerful kingdoms in western Europe.

its western provinces, continued to advance on Europe. By 400 they had carved out a powerful kingdom on the great plain of Hungary, where they could graze their horses and flocks. Throughout the first half of the fifth century the Huns remained a violent and disruptive presence on the European continent, relentlessly raiding the Balkans and western Europe.

By 445, the charismatic and ruthless king Attila (r. 434–453) emerged as the sole leader of the Hunnic tribes and their allies. Attila expanded the Huns' empire to extend from southern Russia to France. His aggression brought him face to face with the Roman Empire in the east. To their surprise, Roman diplomats from Constantinople who visited Attila's court found the Hunnic king to be a sophisticated bargainer as well as an able administrator. Attila, they discovered, included chieftains of subject peoples among his trusted assistants. The diplomats also found Roman merchants and craftsmen who had been attracted to Attila's camp, where they enjoyed freedom from oppressive Roman taxation and corrupt Roman officials.

Yet the Hunnic ruler had a shockingly brutal side as well. From his base of operations on the Hungarian plain, Attila

hammered the Balkan provinces and forced the Roman emperor in Constantinople to pay him tribute in gold every year. In 450, when a new emperor refused to submit any longer to Attila's extortion, the Hun turned westward and invaded Gaul with an immense army. The savagery of his attack and the fear he inspired earned him the title "the Scourge of God."

The next year, the tide began to turn against Attila. A force of Visigoths (who still hated the Huns for having driven them from their homelands in south Russia nearly a century earlier) joined with Romans and other allies from the Germanic kingdoms in western Europe. This allied force stopped Attila's advance in a battle at the Catalaunian Fields in central Gaul in 451. The following year the tenacious warrior launched a new attack on Italy but failed to take the city of Rome, perhaps because his army was weakened by disease.

Soon after the ill-fated invasion of Italy, Attila died while in bed with a young bride. His sons divided the Hunnic Empire among themselves, but the realm could not endure without its great leader. Soon the Huns' subject peoples rebelled against their oppressors and reclaimed

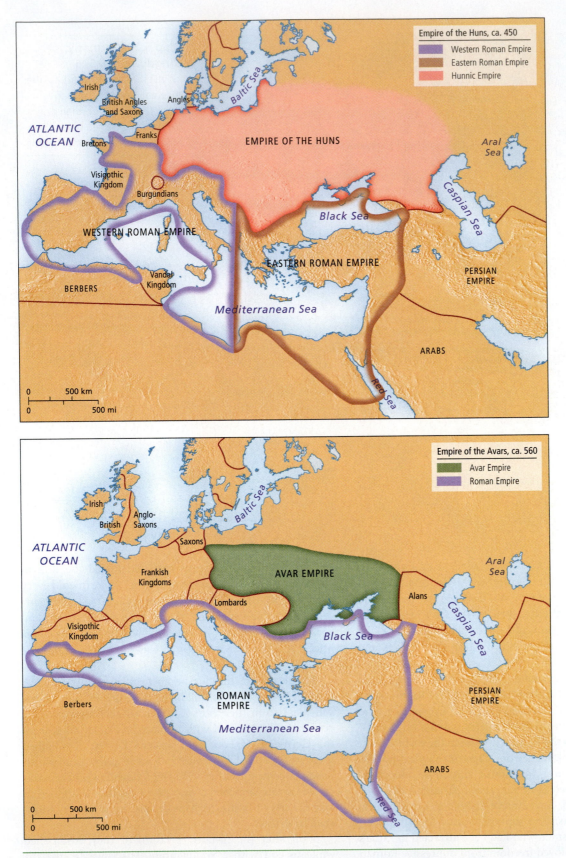

Map 6.3 Nomad Empires

During late antiquity, the Huns and later the Avars established powerful empires based on the Hungarian plain. These fierce horsemen terrified the settled peoples of the Roman world.

their independence. The mighty empire of the Huns fragmented and disappeared. Within a century another nomadic people, the Avars, replaced the Huns as the biggest menace to the Roman Empire and its successor kingdoms (see Map 6.3). The Huns seem to have made no material or intellectual contribution to Western civilization. But they did leave a chilling cultural legacy. As a common enemy of the peoples of the settled Mediterranean world, they embedded in Western culture a frightening memory of bloodthirsty steppe peoples who attacked from the east.

Cultural Encounters After the End of Roman Rule

By the mid-fifth century, when the fighting between Germanic invaders and the Romans ended, the two sides had to learn to live with one another. The rulers of Germanic tribes of Vandals, Ostrogoths, and Visigoths possessed military power but were vastly outnumbered by the Romans. For example, only 40,000 Vandals controlled North Africa, which had a population of several million Romans. Although the Romans had no military power, they dominated urban life and agricultural production. The Romans continued to enjoy urban life and education but were ruled by Germanic masters who maintained separate churches because they were Arian Christians. Their law courts were separate from the Romans' as well so that the two communities could live by their own legal traditions. Both sides faced challenges in adapting to the new situation.

In Britain the Germanic invaders were polytheists who snuffed out the Roman Christians. Yet legends hint at a fierce resistance against the invaders. The stories about King Arthur that have captivated English-speaking audiences since the Middle Ages are based on memories of valiant resistance to the Saxon invaders in the mid-fifth century. In Gaul, North Africa, Italy, and Spain, the new settlers were Christian, but followed Arian Christianity, a creed that viewed Jesus Christ as subordinate to God the Father. The Romans, on the other hand, followed Chalcedonian (Catholic) Christianity and thus saw the invaders as heretics. Although this religious difference caused considerable friction between the two peoples, it also worked to their mutual advantage. Roman law forbade marriage with Arian Christians, so the conquerors remained a distinctive minority in their new domains. This enabled them to maintain a separate Arian clergy and separate churches and hence a distinct identity in the midst of the vastly larger numbers of Roman provincials they ruled.

Confident in their position of power, the newcomers easily slipped into the role of military protectors of the Roman provincials they now ruled. For example, Vandal forces fought against Berber nomads from the foothills of the Atlas Mountains who tried to raid North Africa's fertile farmlands. To many Roman peasants, the new masters provided a welcome alternative to the callous imperial officials who had exploited them for so long.

Of all the former empire's western provinces, Italy prospered the most under Germanic rule, particularly under the long reign of Theodoric the Ostrogoth (r. 493–526). In 493 Theodoric left the Balkans for Italy at the instigation of the Roman emperor in Constantinople. The emperor told Theodoric that he could rule Italy if he was able to capture it from Odovacar, who was currently ruling there. The crafty emperor calculated that if Odovacar defeated Theodoric, the situation in Italy would remain unchanged, but the menace Theodoric presented would be gone from the Balkans. If Theodoric won, the Balkans would still be safe and there would be another barbarian ruling Italy, which was less of a threat to Constantinople. Either way he had little to lose and much to gain. Theodoric accepted the challenge and murdered Odovacar in Italy. Once on the

---

DOCUMENT

Romans Deserve Their Fate

Salvian, a priest at Marseilles, believed that the Arian Christian "barbarians," even though they were not orthodox Christians, had seized Rome's western provinces because the Romans had sinned and were being punished by God. He condemned Roman oppression of the poor as a sin:

Almost all barbarians . . . love one another; almost all Romans persecute each other. . . . The Roman poor are despoiled, the widows groan, the orphans are tread underfoot, so much so that many of them, and they are not of obscure birth and have received a liberal education, flee to the enemy lest they die from the pain of public persecution. They seek among the barbarians the dignity of the Roman because they cannot bear barbarous indignity among the Romans. Although these Romans differ in religion and language from the barbarians to whom they flee, and differ from them in respect to filthiness of body and clothing, nevertheless, they prefer to bear among the barbarians a worship unlike their own rather than rampant injustice among the Romans. Thus far and wide they migrate to the barbarians everywhere in power. . . . They prefer to live as free men under an outward form of captivity than as captives under an appearance of liberty. Therefore, the name of Roman citizens, at one time not only greatly valued but acquired with great effort, is now repudiated and fled from, and it is almost considered not only base but even deserving of abhorrence.

Source: Salvian, *On the Governance of God* 5.4-7. Trans. Jeremiah O'Sullivan. *Fathers of the Church. The Writings of Salvian the Presbyter.* NY: CIMA, 1947, 131–137, with some changes.

CHRONOLOGY

Roman Empire, East and West

235–284	Crisis in Roman government
284	Diocletian begins imperial reforms
293	Tetrarchy established
312	Constantine wins control of western empire
324	Constantinople founded
378	Battle of Adrianople; Visigoths invade empire
406	Vandals and other tribes cross the Rhine
410	Romans withdraw from Britain; Visigoths plunder Rome
418	Visigoths settle in Gaul
429–439	Vandals take North Africa
445–453	Attila rules the Hunnic Empire
476	Romulus Augustulus, last western emperor, deposed
493–526	Theodoric the Ostrogoth rules Italy

gave way to oaths of loyalty to local chieftains. Over time, new warrior-based aristocracies took shape in which landowning noblemen forged ties of personal loyalty to their local king.

Roman culture did not abruptly come to an end with the last vestiges of Roman rule. It remained a vital presence in most regions, but it took different forms in the various lands now ruled by Germanic leaders. In Britain, Roman culture perhaps fared the worst and little of it survived into later ages. There the Germanic language the Saxon invaders and their Angle allies spoke took hold and began developing into the English spoken today. In Gaul, Italy, and Spain, the Germanic settlers quickly learned the tongues of the Romans they ruled. Within several centuries these Latin-based "Romance" (based on the Roman speech) languages grew into the early versions of French, Italian, Spanish, and Portuguese. Latin continued as the language of literacy, and the settlers borrowed heavily from Roman literary forms. Writing in Latin, they produced histories of their tribal kingdoms in imitation of Roman historians. They also developed law codes composed in Latin influenced by Roman models.

throne of Italy, Theodoric took care to acknowledge the emperor's superior status. In politics, Theodoric sought to create an atmosphere of mutual respect between Ostrogoths and Romans by maintaining two separate administrations—one for his Ostrogoths, the other for the Romans—so that both communities could manage their own affairs under his supervision. He also included aristocratic Romans among his closest advisers and most trusted administrators. Even in his religious policies Theodoric pursued mutual tolerance. As an Arian Christian, Theodoric supported the separate Arian clergy, but he also maintained excellent ties with the pope, leader of the Roman Christians. Theodoric united Visigothic kingdoms in Spain and Gaul with his own in Italy, ultimately wielding great influence throughout western Europe. Italy prospered under his rule, and the communities of Ostrogoths and Romans lived together amicably.

Throughout the western provinces links to the Roman Empire in the east began to weaken. Most of the invaders had brought their traditional practice of pledging fidelity and obedience to a local chieftain, and this tradition began to erode loyalty to the far-off Roman emperor in Constantinople. By pledging themselves to a Germanic king, men gained a place in the "tribe" of their new chieftain. Many of these men had been soldiers who served in units of the Roman army under their own Germanic officers, but now they looked to their king—not to the emperor—to provide gifts and the opportunities to win prestige, honor, and land. Thus service to the empire gradually

The Survival of Rome's Eastern Provinces

Despite the profound alterations wrought by Christianity and Rome's loss of the western provinces, the Roman Empire endured in the eastern Mediterranean without interruption. Constantinople, the imperial city founded by Constantine in 324, became the center of a remodeled empire that over several centuries merged Christian and Roman characteristics. Inhabitants of the realm continued to think of themselves as citizens of the Roman Empire for another thousand years. The remodeled Roman Empire in the east is referred to as the Byzantine Empire.

Christianity and Law Under Justinian

The most important amalgamation of Christian and Roman traditions took place during the reign of the emperor Justinian (r. 527–565). Born in the Balkans, Justinian was the last emperor to speak Latin as his native language. He combined a powerful intellect, an unshakable Christian faith, and a driving ambition to reform the empire. He defied convention by marrying Theodora, a strong-willed former actress, and included her in imperial decision making once he became emperor in 527.

Emperor Justinian

Justinian inaugurated a number of changes that highlighted his role as a Christian emperor. First of all, he emphasized the position of the emperor at the center of society

Consular Diptych?

This ivory panel celebrates a consul at Constantinople in the early sixth century. He holds the mappa, a ceremonial cloth that symbolizes his office, in his right hand. Behind him stand personifications of Rome (on his left) and Constantinople (on his right). Such panels were given as gifts when consuls took office; this one demonstrates Roman traditions continuing in the new world of Byzantium.

reached an agreement with the Anti-Chalcedonian communities in Syria and Egypt. After these regions were conquered by the armies of Islam in the following century, the Christian churches there fell out of imperial control (see Chapter 7). In the west the bishops of North Africa and Italy deeply resented Justinian's attempts to meddle in ecclesiastical affairs by determining doctrine. As a result a bitter division arose between Christian churches in the eastern and western Mediterranean over the rights of bishops to resist imperial authority on religious matters.

Justinian attempted to create a Christian society by using Roman law coupled with military force. Unlike rulers of Rome's early empire, who permitted subject peoples to maintain their own customary laws, Justinian suppressed local laws throughout his realm. He envisioned all of his subjects obeying only Roman law—law that he defined and that God approved. (Justinian was sure that if God did not approve of his legislative changes, God would not allow him to continue as emperor.)

Thus, in his God-given mission as emperor-legislator, Justinian reformed Roman law. In an effort to simplify the vast body of civil law, he ordered his lawyers to sort through all the laws that had accumulated over the centuries and determine which of them should still be enforced. This monumental effort, which was completed in 534, is known as the *Code of Justinian*. His lawyers also prepared a handbook of basic Roman law for law students, called the *Institutes*, as well as the *Digest*, a collection and summary of several centuries' worth of commentary on Roman law by legal experts. Justinian then banned any additional commentary on the law, naming himself as the only interpreter of existing laws and the sole source of new laws. While the *Code, Digest*, and *Institutes* were composed in Latin, the traditional legal language of Rome, Justinian's new legislation, called the *Novels*, was issued in Greek, the common language of the eastern empire. Collectively, this legal work is now called the *Corpus of Civil Law°*. The body of Roman law passed down to later generations primarily through this compilation. At the end of the eleventh century, scholars in Italy discovered manuscripts of Justinian's legal works in church libraries, and interest in Roman law began to revive. The *Digest* became the most influential

in explicitly Christian terms. He was the first emperor to use the title "Beloved of Christ" and he amplified the emperor's role in Church affairs. Justinian considered it his duty as emperor to impose uniform religious belief throughout the empire by enforcing the decrees of the Council of Chalcedon as he interpreted them. In the east this meant stamping out the survivals of polytheist worship and struggling to find a common ground with the Anti-Chalcedonians. After he reconquered some of the western domains of the empire it meant dealing with the Arian Christian Vandals and Ostrogoths living there. In the east he succeeded in suppressing polytheism, but he never

Two Martyrdoms: Culture and Religion on Trial

Justice in History

Between the reigns of Diocletian (r. 284–305) and Justinian (r. 527–565), the status of Christians changed dramatically. Christians went from being a religious minority persecuted by the imperial government to a majority that persecuted non-Christians with the Roman government's backing. One thing did not change during this period, however. Whether polytheist or Christian, emperors used force to compel their subjects to believe and worship in prescribed ways, hoping to keep the empire in the gods' good graces. To ensure religious conformity, emperors used the Roman judicial system. A comparison of the trials of a Christian soldier named Julius in 303, and Phocas, an aristocrat in Constantinople accused of paganism in 529 and 545, illustrates the objectives and methods of the Roman government's religious prosecution.

In 303 officials arrested a veteran soldier named Julius and brought him before the prefect Maximus. The following excerpt comes from a description of the trial:

"Who is this?" asked Maximus. One of the staff replied: "This is a Christian who will not obey the laws." "What is your name?" asked the prefect. "Julius," was the reply. "Well, what say you, Julius?" asked the prefect. "Are these allegations true?" "Yes, they are," said Julius. "I am indeed a Christian. I do not deny that I am precisely what I am." "You are surely aware," said the prefect, "of the emperors' edicts which order you to sacrifice to the gods?" "I am aware of them," answered Julius. "I am indeed a Christian and cannot do what you want; for I must not lose sight of my living and true God." . . . "If you think it a sin," answered the prefect Maximus, "let me take the blame. I am the one who is forcing you, so that you may not give impression of having consented voluntarily. Afterwards you can go home in peace, you will pick up your ten-year bonus, and no one will ever trouble you again. . . . If you do not respect the imperial decrees and offer sacrifice, I am going to cut your head off." "That is a good plan," answered Julius, "Only I beg . . . that you execute your plan and pass sentence on me so that my prayers may be answered. . . . I have chosen death for now so that I might live with the saints forever." The prefect Maximus then delivered the sentence as follows: "Whereas Julius has refused to obey the imperial edicts, he is sentenced to death."[3]

After Constantine's conversion to Christianity in 312, persecution of Christians stopped, and Christian officials began to attack polytheism with the government's support. The emperor Justinian severely enforced laws against polytheists, executing anyone who sacrificed animals to non-Christian gods. During Justinian's reign, the imperial government launched three major persecutions of polytheists. In the first episode of persecution in 528–529, one year after Justinian ascended to the throne, a handful of government officials were charged with the crime of worshiping pagan gods.

One of these men was Phocas the Patrician, an aristocratic lawyer with an illustrious career in the emperor's service. After serving as the chief of protocol at court, he was sent to Antioch with funds to rebuild the city after a ruinous earthquake in 526. Cleared of charges of practicing paganism in 529, he continued to enjoy Justinian's trust and earn further promotions. In 532 he served for a year as Praetorian Prefect, the most powerful position in the realm after that of emperor. During this time, Phocas was responsible for raising revenues and administering the empire. He assisted in the construction of the new Cathedral of Holy Wisdom (see Haghia Sophia illustration in Chapter 7) in Constantinople by raising revenues. He also spent his personal funds in supporting smaller churches and ransoming hostages captured by Byzantium's enemies. Justinian next made him a judge and sent him on a mission to investigate the murder of a bishop. Then, in 545–546, during the second wave of persecution, despite his publicly recognized activities in support of the church and his faithful service to Justinian, Phocas was arrested again. He was among the doctors, teachers, and government officials suddenly charged with being pagans. A contemporary historian described a time of terror in Constantinople, when officials accused of worshiping the old gods in secret were driven from public office, had their property confiscated by the emperor, and were executed. In a panic, some of the accused men took their own lives. Phocas was one of them. Rather than undergo the humiliation of public execution, Phocas committed suicide. The furious emperor ordered that Phocas's body be buried in a ditch like an animal, without prayer or ceremony of any sort.

Phocas thus missed the third purge of 562, when polytheists were arrested throughout the empire, paraded in public, imprisoned, tried, and sentenced. Zealous crowds threw thousands of non-Christian books into bonfires in the empire's cities.

198

`198`

A representation of Jesus holding a cross and making a gesture of blessing.

An angel of victory hovers next to the emperor, another supports his foot. An attendant carries a statue adorned with wreath of victory.

Subject barbarians in native clothing bring offerings of gold and ivory.

Justinian
This mid-sixth-century ivory panel depicts the emperor Justinian in a standard pose of Roman emperors. The panel sends the message that Justinian rules the world with the approval and support of God.

The official reason for persecuting Christians, such as Maximus, was relatively simple: Christians broke the law by refusing to make sacrifices to the Roman gods. But why did the later Christian governments use such a heavy hand in persecuting polytheists? Men like Phocas who were attacked as pagans were highly educated in the traditional learning of the Greco-Roman world. Indeed, it was this learning that was really on trial. Phocas and other victims had a deep commitment to traditional Roman culture; their "paganism" was not the furtive worship of old gods like Zeus or Apollo. Rather, Phocas was considered a pagan because he was loyal to classical philosophy, literature, and rhetoric, without any Christian overlay or interpretation. In Justinian's eyes, this sort of classical learning had no place in a Christian empire.

Question of Justice

1. Why did both polytheist and Christian governments of Rome think it was necessary to persecute adherents of non-official religions?

Taking It Further

Helgeland, John. *Christians in the Military: The Early Experience.* 1985. An introduction to the persecutions of Christians in the Roman army and their depiction in Christian literature.

Maas, Michael. *John Lydus and the Roman Past: Antiquarianism and Politics in the Age of Justinian.* 1992. This book explains how Justinian's policies about religion also involved an encounter with the empire's classical heritage.

legal text in medieval Europe. Thus the *Corpus of Civil Law* became a pillar of Latin-speaking European civilization.

Reconquering the Provinces in the West

Once he had reorganized Byzantium's legal system, Justinian turned his attention to Rome's fallen western provinces. He wanted to reestablish imperial control over these territories, now ruled by Germanic kings. Once the empire was restored to its former glory, Justinian's plan was to impose his version of Christian orthodoxy upon the Arian Christian Vandals and Ostrogoths still living in his western domains. He would also force them to live under his version of Roman law and government.

In 533, Justinian sent a fleet of 10,000 men and 5,000 cavalry under the command of his general Belisarius to attack the Vandal kingdom in North Africa. The Vandal kingdom fell quickly, and within a year Belisarius celebrated a triumph in Constantinople. Encouraged by this easy victory, Justinian set his sights on Italy, where the Ostrogothic ruling family was embroiled in political infighting. This time Justinian had underestimated his opponents. The Ostrogoths, who had won the support of the Roman population in Italy, mounted a fierce resistance to Belisarius's invasion in 536. Justinian, for his part, did not trust his own general and failed to support him with adequate funds and soldiers. Bitter fighting between Justinian's troops and the Ostrogothic armies dragged on for two decades. Justinian's armies eventually wrestled Italy back under imperial control, but the long-term effects of the protracted reconquest had disastrous consequences for Justinian's empire. The many years of fighting devastated Italy's cities and countryside. Between pouring precious financial resources into the Italy campaign and maintaining his grip on North Africa, Justinian was draining his empire's resources dry.

One of the reasons Justinian's reconquest of Italy took decades was the visitation of a lethal plague. The plague struck the empire in 542 and spread throughout Justinian's realm, migrating swiftly to Italy, North Africa, and Gaul. The first onslaught took the lives of about a quarter of a million people, which was half the population of Constantinople. An estimated one-third of the entire population of the empire's inhabitants succumbed to the dreaded disease. With the population devastated by the plague, Justinian's army could not recruit the large number of soldiers it needed to fight on several fronts; the protracted battle for Italy was the result. The plague also weakened the economy. In many provinces farms lay deserted and city populations shriveled. Commercial ties between the eastern and western Mediterranean declined, and in the western provinces economies became more "local" and self-sufficient (see Map 6.4).

The Struggle with Persia

Although Justinian's greatest military successes were in the western Mediterranean, his most dangerous enemy was the Persian Empire on his eastern flank. This huge, multiethnic empire, under the rule of the Sasanian dynasty (ca. 220–633), had been Rome's main rival throughout late antiquity (see Map 6.5). The tension stemmed chiefly from competition over Armenia, which was a rich source of troops, and Syria, which possessed enormous wealth. From the time that Emperor Julian died in combat against Persia in 363, emperors at Constantinople kept up their guard against this eastern threat. Though wars were frequent, neither side could win permanent superiority over the other.

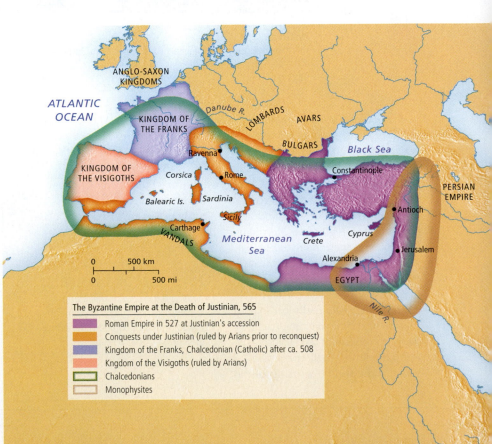

Map 6.4 The Byzantine Empire at the Death of Justinian

When Justinian died in 565, the territories of Italy, North Africa, and part of Spain that had been lost in the fifth century were restored, temporarily, to imperial rule.

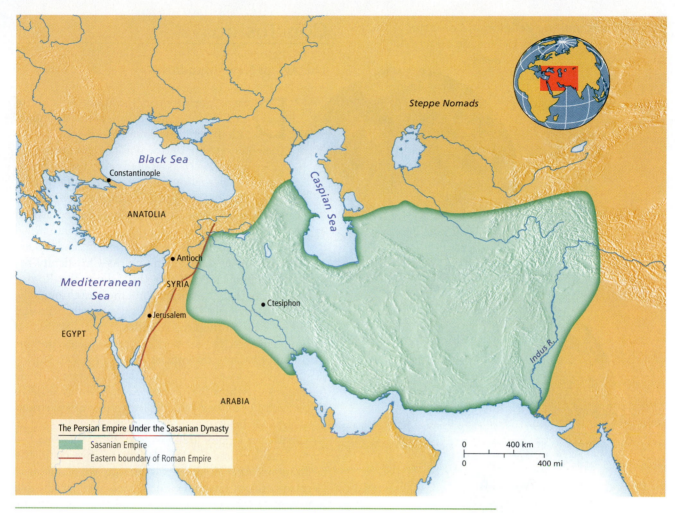

Map 6.5 The Persian Empire Under the Sasanian Dynasty

Under the dynamic Sasanian dynasty, the Persian Empire fought many wars with the Roman Empire. Neither empire had an advantage because they were roughly the same size and possessed equivalent resources of wealth and manpower.

Justinian fought several brutal wars with Persia. The emperor gave top priority to the struggle on his eastern frontier by supplying more than half of his troops, led by his best generals. He also provided more financial resources to the struggle in the east than to the wars of reconquest in the west. Chosroes I, the aggressive and ambitious Great King of Persia, proved to be a worthy adversary for Justinian. Chosroes repeatedly invaded the Roman Empire, causing great damage. In 540, for example, he sacked Antioch, the wealthiest city in Syria. Because war with Persia was extraordinarily expensive, Justinian made peace by paying thousands of pounds of gold to the Persian monarch in order to bring the fighting to a close. Even this great cost was less than continuing to fight every year.

By the time of Justinian's death, the two superpowers had established an uneasy coexistence, but the basic animosity between them remained unresolved. For the next half century, Justinian's successors engaged in intermittent bitter warfare with the Persian rulers. This protracted struggle between Constantinople and Persia demonstrates how the most important enemies lay to the east. Fighting to regain provinces in the west brought glory, but war with Persia was a matter of life and death for the eastern Roman Empire.

By fighting expensive wars on the eastern and western flanks of his empire, Justinian hastened the disintegration of imperial rule beyond the eastern provinces. The overextension of resources ensured that Constantinople could not maintain lasting control of the western Mediterranean region. When new invaders descended on Italy and the Balkans in the late sixth century, the empire would not have the strength to resist them. The drain of resources on

Persian Coins and the Religion of Zoroaster
This silver Persian coin depicts the Sasanian Great King Ohrmazd II (r. 302–309). He wears an elaborate crown. On the coin's other side two Zoroastrian priests tend a fire altar. Zoroastrianism was the state religion of the Persian Empire in late antiquity.

the Persian front also helped weaken the empire, and in the seventh century the remaining Roman provinces in North Africa, Egypt, and Syria were lost. Nevertheless, in what remained of the Roman Empire Justinian succeeded in creating a Christian-Roman society, united under one God, one emperor, and one law.

CHRONOLOGY

The Reign of Justinian

527–565	Reign of Justinian
529	Plato's Academy in Athens closed
529–532	War with Persia
527–533	Law Code of Justinian
534	Reconquest of North Africa
542	Plague strikes empire

Conclusion

The Age of New Boundaries

During late antiquity the transformation of the Roman world into new political configurations with new boundaries helped create a new conception of the West. Henceforth, the West was closely associated with the legacy of Roman civilization filtered through the lens of Christianity. The most lasting development of the period came from the encounter between Christianity, which before the fourth century had been the faith of a persecuted minority, and the civilization of the Roman Empire. As Christianity became the dominant religion throughout the Roman Empire, it was itself transformed, not the least through the attempts to reconcile Christian revelation with classical learning. Christian thinkers assimilated much of classical culture, and with the support of the Roman emperors Christianity became the official religion by 400. During this process of assimilation, Christians disagreed among themselves over how they explained the divinity of Jesus Christ, and these disagreements led to distinctive strains of Christian belief that have survived to this day.

The Roman Empire itself was irreparably split into two parts, which became the foundations for two distinctive civilizations. After Roman rule in the west collapsed, Germanic rulers established new kingdoms in the old Roman provinces. Some of these kingdoms spoke Romance languages derived from Latin, and all of them used Latin for religious worship. Latin remained the language of learning and the law, even in places such as Britain where the spoken language derived from a Germanic language. Through the spread of the Latin Christianity that developed in the western provinces of the Roman Empire during late antiquity, Latin civilization spread to parts of central, eastern, and northern Europe that had never been part of the Roman Empire. In the eastern Mediterranean, the Roman Empire survived as the Byzantine Empire (discussed in the next chapter) and became the home of Greek Orthodox Christianity. In Byzantium Greek remained the dominant tongue of daily life, learning, and Christian worship.

When Islam emerged as a powerful religious and political entity at the end of the late antique period, as we will discuss in the next chapter, its adherents were also influenced by classical learning and Roman institutions. But the Muslim and Christian Empires became enemies, a tendency that created the most lasting borders among the peoples who had once been citizens of the Roman Empire. The North African and Middle Eastern lands that Islamic conquerors seized from the Byzantine Empire lost their place in the roster of "Western" communities, while those lands not conquered by Islam became the bastion of a medieval civilization that defined itself primarily as European and Christian.

Suggestions for Further Reading

For a comprehensive listing of suggested readings, please go to www.ablongman.com/levack2e/chapter6

Bowersock, G. W. *Hellenism in Late Antiquity.* 1990. Explains the important role of traditional Greek culture in shaping late antiquity.

Bowersock, G. W., Peter Brown, and Oleg Grabar, eds. *Late Antiquity: A Guide to the Postclassical World.* 1999. An indispensable handbook containing synthetic essays and shorter encyclopedia entries.

Brown, Peter. *The Cult of the Saints: Its Rise and Function in Late Antiquity.* 1981. A brilliant and highly influential study.

Brown, Peter. *The Rise of Western Christendom: Triumph and Diversity.* 1996. An influential and highly accessible survey.

Brown, Peter. *The World of Late Antiquity.* 1971. A classic treatment of the period.

Cameron, Averil. *The Later Roman Empire.* 1993. *The Mediterranean World in Late Antiquity.* 1997. Excellent textbooks with bibliography and maps.

Clark, Gillian. *Women in Late Antiquity: Pagan and Christian Life-Styles.* 1993. The starting point of modern discussion; lucid and reliable.

Harries, Jill. *Law and Empire in Late Antiquity.* 1999. Explores the presence and practice of law in Roman society.

Lee, A. D. *Information and Frontiers: Roman Foreign Relations in Late Antiquity.* 1993. An exciting and original investigation.

Maas, Michael. *The Cambridge Companion to the Age of Justinian.* 2005. A collection of twenty chapters by different experts on all aspects of the Mediterranean world in the sixth century.

Maas, Michael. *Readings in Late Antiquity: A Sourcebook.* 2000. Hundreds of ancient sources in translation illustrating all aspects of late antiquity.

Markus, Robert. *The End of Ancient Christianity.* 1995. Excellent introduction to the transformation of Christianity in late antiquity.

Rich, John, ed. *The City in Late Antiquity.* 1992. Important studies of changes in late antique urbanism.

Thompson, E. A. *The Huns,* rev. Peter Heather. 1996. The best introduction to major issues.

Notes

1. Libanius, *On the Temples,* in A. F. Norman, *Libanius: Selected Works* (1977), 107–109.

2. Marcia L. Colish, *Medieval Foundations of the Western Intellectual Tradition* (1997), 49.

3. John Helgeland, *Christians in the Military: The Early Experience* (1985), 64–65.

Medieval Empires and Borderlands: Byzantium and Islam

N 860 FIERCE RUS TRIBESMEN ABOARD A FLEET OF SLEEK DRAGON SHIPS RAIDED the villages along the shores of the Black Sea and then stomped up to the gates of Constantinople, ready for pillage and rape. Taken by surprise, the inhabitants were gripped with panic. The Patriarch of Constantinople, Photius, called upon the people to repent of their sins to avoid God's wrath, and when the Rus unexpectedly broke camp and departed, it was interpreted as an act of divine intervention.

Strategically located where the Black Sea meets the Mediterranean, Constantinople was the shining remnant of the Roman Empire. The western provinces of the empire, including Rome itself, had been lost during the fifth century to Germanic tribes. Historians call the vestige of the Roman Empire in the east with its capital at Constantinople the Byzantine Empire because Constantinople was founded on the site of the ancient Greek city of Byzantium. Roman rule continued uninterrupted in the Byzantine Empire for a thousand years after the collapse of Roman rule in the west, and its citizens continued to call themselves the Romans.

Constantinople was the largest and richest city in the western world. Its Greek-speaking inhabitants clearly considered the Rus merchants as little more than savages, prone to the worst kinds of violence, and tried to keep them under control by signing treaties. The treaties stipulated that no more than fifty Rus could enter the city at one time, all must be unarmed, and they all had to leave by autumn. In exchange for civilized behavior, however, the Rus received during their stay free baths, food, provisions for a month, and equipment for their return. By the ninth century the Rus had established a regular pattern. Each spring after spending the winters along the river valleys of the north collecting tribute from the Slavic tribes, the Rus set off in their boats, risking dangerous rapids and waterfalls on the Dnieper River and ambush from hostile tribes, to reach the Black Sea and the splendid emporium

CHAPTER OUTLINE

- Byzantium: The Survival of the Roman Empire

- The New World of Islam

The Cathedral of Holy Wisdom (Haghia Sophia) When Justinian entered his newly completed cathedral of Holy Wisdom (Haghia Sophia) in Constantinople, he boasted, "Solomon, I have outdone you!" He meant that his church was bigger than the Jerusalem Temple built by the biblical King Solomon. For centuries Haghia Sophia was the largest building in Europe. In 1453 the church became a mosque. Today it is a public museum.

VIDEO
Haghia Sophia

of the world, Constantinople, which they called simply the "Great City."

Accustomed to the rough life of long winter treks, grubby little villages, and constant danger, they were dazzled by the sight of the Great City, with its half a million inhabitants, the gilded cupolas of its churches, the marble palaces of the aristocrats and emperor, the cavernous wharves and warehouses of its merchants, and the twelve miles of fortifications and walls that protected the city. The people of Constantinople were equally astonished by the sight of the Rus merchants—sun-worn, fur-clad, and armed to the teeth—whom they met with fascination and fear. To them the Rus seemed like so many other barbarian peoples: They could not speak Greek, were not Christians, and did not recognize the authority of the Byzantine Emperor, which the Greeks believed came directly from God. Despite constant threats to their borders by barbarian raiders and the armies of other civilized empires, Byzantium managed to thrive for many centuries and to survive for many more.

The usual purpose of these repeated barbarian visits was trade. The merchants of Constantinople traded Byzantine and Chinese silks, Persian glass, Arabic silver coins (highly prized by the Rus), and Indian spices for honey, wax, slaves, and musty bales of furs from Scandinavia and what is now northern Russia. Despite their sense of superiority, the Byzantines needed the barbarians. In the merchant stalls of Constantinople, traders from many cultures met, haggled, and came to know something of one another. None perhaps were more unlike each other than the rough Rus and the refined Byzantines, but their mutual desires for profit kept them in a persistent, if tentative, embrace. These repeated interactions among very different peoples who traded, competed, and fought with one another offer clues for understanding the medieval world, also known as the Middle Ages.

The term *Middle Ages* refers to the period between the ancient and modern civilizations from about the fifth to fifteenth centuries. Medieval culture rested on the foundations of three great civilizations: the Greek Christianity of Byzantium; the Arabic-speaking Islamic caliphates of the Middle East, North Africa, and Spain; and the Latin Christian kingdoms of western Europe. The dynamic interactions among these three civilizations, distinguished by religion and language, lay at the heart of medieval culture. From the seventh to eleventh centuries, the most energetic and creative of these three civilizations was Islam, which threatened militarily both Byzantium and the Latin Christian kingdoms. In the century after the death of its founder, the prophet Muhammad, in 632, Islam's followers burst from their home in Arabia to conquer an empire stretching from Spain to central Asia. Especially during the tenth and eleventh centuries, the Islamic empire supported important philosophical and scientific work, and produced a thriving economy.

These civilizations build empires. From the interaction and competition among them, the West created new borders that were both political and cultural. All the empires drew from Rome's legacy. The very concept of a universal empire derived from Roman political theory. The Byzantines thought of themselves as Romans and their empire as the Roman Empire. Although Muslims tended to create distinctively new forms of government and did not accept Roman law, in the cities that had once been part of the Roman Empire Muslim rulers adapted Roman administrative traditions for their own use. As we shall see in Chapter 8, the Latin rulers of the West attempted to revive the Roman Empire as a means of unifying their territories. The most distinctive feature of the medieval period was that all these civilizations were based on monotheistic religions that shared basic beliefs about God and the origin of their faiths. All struggled to eliminate either by persuasion or force vestiges of polytheism. However, because each of these medieval civilizations defined itself as an exclusive community of faith, cultural boundaries developed between them that are still visible today. The most important question raised by these encounters is, "how did the competition among the great medieval empires transform the idea of the West?"

- How did the Roman Empire's eastern provinces evolve into the Byzantine Empire?
- How did Islam develop in Arabia, and how did its followers create a vast empire so quickly?

Byzantium: The Survival of the Roman Empire

- How did the Roman Empire's eastern provinces evolve into the Byzantine Empire?

The emperor Justinian (r. 527–565) tried to restore the glory of the Roman Empire by reconquering Roman provinces in North Africa, Italy, and parts of Spain from Germanic rulers who had established kingdoms in these territories in the fifth century. When Justinian died, his realm extended from southern Spain to the Persian frontier. As we saw in Chapter 6, it was an empire in which many of the institutions and traditions of the late antique Roman state, such as the imperial bureaucracy and provincial organization, still functioned. Despite these continuities with the Roman Empire of earlier centuries, Justinian brought profound changes. By insisting that his subjects follow Orthodox Christianity, eradicating the last traces of polytheist worship, and emphasizing the role of Christian faith in every aspect of government and education, he integrated classical culture and Christianity to a new degree. But he failed in his goal to unify the empire through Orthodox Christianity and completely alienated the bishops who disagreed with him.

Justinian's rule also represented a watershed in the military fortunes of the empire. After Justinian's death in 565, the Byzantine Empire still faced powerful enemies who surrounded it on all sides. To thwart its many adversaries, emperors reorganized Byzantium for military purposes. Byzantine institutions remained principally defensive, but they were effective in helping the empire survive formidable challenges.

In late antiquity Constantinople and Rome symbolized the two halves of the Roman Empire. Once joined in a common Christian culture, eastern and western Christians began to grow apart so that by the late ninth century they began to constitute separate civilizations. There were still cultural exchanges among them as merchants, pilgrims, and scholars crossed back and forth, but the two civilizations had ceased to understand one another. They held different opinions about religious matters, such as the dating of Easter, the rituals of the liturgy, the role of images in worship, and the extent of the authority of the bishop in Rome, the pope. The East and West also spoke different languages. In the East, Greek was the language of most of the population, and Latin had been largely forgotten by the end of the sixth century. In the West, Latin or local dialects of Latin prevailed; except in southern Italy and Sicily, only a tiny few knew some Greek.

As an extension of the great Eurasian steppes inhabited by polytheist farmers and nomads, eastern Europe became an unstable borderland on the flanks of Byzantium. In eastern Europe rival missionaries practicing Greek and Latin forms of Christianity competed for converts and allies to their respective sides, and the struggle between the two has left permanent scars in the cultural divisions of the region. One of the most long-lasting achievements of Byzantium was the conversion of many of the Slavic peoples to Orthodox Christianity, a faith that survived even after the collapse of Byzantium itself.

An Embattled Empire

After Justinian the Byzantine Empire was gradually reduced to a much smaller regional power struggling for survival against many enemies. Some of the threats came from nomadic tribes from the Eurasian steppes, such as the Avars, Slavs, and Bulgars, who migrated into the Balkans and permanently settled within the borders of the empire. These peoples became the ancestors of some of the current inhabitants of the region. In the west the Byzantines faced the Germanic kingdom of the Lombards who eroded the imperial rule over northern Italy that Justinian had reestablished. To the east the Byzantines confronted their old rival,

the Persian Empire. And from the south an entirely new threat arose out of the Arabian peninsula from the armies of Islam. The encounters between these diverse enemies and Byzantium were usually hostile, and their encirclement of Byzantium forced important changes in Byzantine administration and military policy.

Out of the Steppes: Borderlands in Eastern Europe

Like so many others before and after them, raiders and migrants poured out of the Eurasian steppes, a band of grasslands that spread some 5,000 miles from what is now Hungary and the Ukraine in Europe into Central Asia. Nomads could easily cross the grasslands on horseback. In much of the Balkan peninsula from the late sixth through ninth centuries, the weakness of Byzantium created a power vacuum that made the settled inhabitants who were Christians and still considered themselves subjects of the Roman Empire vulnerable to polytheist invaders from the steppes. The nomadic Avars, who first appeared on the steppes north of the Black Sea in the sixth century, had a bone-chilling reputation for cruelty and ferocity in warfare. They suddenly and violently arrived in the plains of present-day Hungary, from which they extended their territory into central Europe and the Balkans. These tenacious warriors dominated the region until the early ninth century and posed a constant menace to Byzantium and the new kingdoms taking shape in Italy and France (see Map 7.1).

The Avars created an empire by forcing conquered peoples to serve in their armies. Some of the peoples were Slavs. Between about 400 and 600, Slavic societies had formed from a blending of many cultures and ethnic groups. The Slavic communities that developed in eastern Europe between the Baltic Sea and the Balkans lay outside Byzantium's borders. Their Avar conquerors ruled by brute force, and most Slavs could not win back their independence. However, a few Slavic communities managed to overthrow Avar rule. In the middle of the seventh century, for example, in the territory of the modern Czech Republic, the Slavic king Samo led a successful revolt against the Avars and ruled a small, independent kingdom for nearly forty years.

In the second half of the sixth century, bands of Slavs began to migrate south across the Danube River into the Balkans, searching for new homes. Collaborating with groups of marauding Avars, the Slavs settled in sparsely populated frontier lands in the northern Balkans in what is now Croatia and Serbia. As the Slavs pushed south, many Byzantines fled their cities, abandoning them to the invaders.

By 600, Slavic and Avar groups had seized most Byzantine lands from the Danube to Greece. In 626, Slav and Avar forces attacked Constantinople from the northwest, while their Persian allies approached from the east.

The capital city survived their combined assault, but it took the Byzantines nearly four hundred years to reassert control over the Balkans.

By the ninth century, however, most of these tribes began to convert to one or another form of Christianity, and the patterns of those conversions have had lasting consequences to this day. The religious dividing line between those who adhered to Roman Catholicism and those who followed Orthodox rites cut directly through eastern Europe. The various tribes in eastern Europe were extremely fragmented politically, which mirrored the intricate distribution of ethnic and linguistic groups. State building was especially complicated in eastern Europe because most of the region had never been under Roman rule and lacked the legacies of Roman cities, institutions, and law that made the survival of Byzantium possible and the Germanic kingdoms of western Europe viable.

Fast on the heels of the Avars and Slavs from the steppes came the nomadic peoples called the Bulgars who established rule over the largely Slavic inhabitants of the Balkans by the eighth century. The Bulgars destroyed the surviving old Roman cities there, expelled what Christians remained, and attacked the Byzantine Empire. In 811, after annihilating the Byzantine army, the Bulgarian khan (the head of a confederation of clans) Krum (r. 808–814) had the Byzantine emperor murdered and lined his skull with silver in order to turn the rival's head into a drinking cup. With this symbolic act of debasement, the Bulgarians gained a fierce reputation as enemies of Christianity and Byzantium.

In 865, however, Khan Boris I (r. 852–889) dramatically changed course by accepting the Orthodox Christianity of his former enemies in Byzantium. His conversion illustrates the politics of the period. During the ninth century Christianity began to acquire a powerful allure among the

Map 7.1 The Byzantine Empire, ca. 600

By 600 the Byzantine Empire consisted of Anatolia, Greece, part of the Balkans, Syria, Egypt, and some territories in North Africa and Spain. Until the rise of Islam, the Persian Empire remained its greatest enemy.

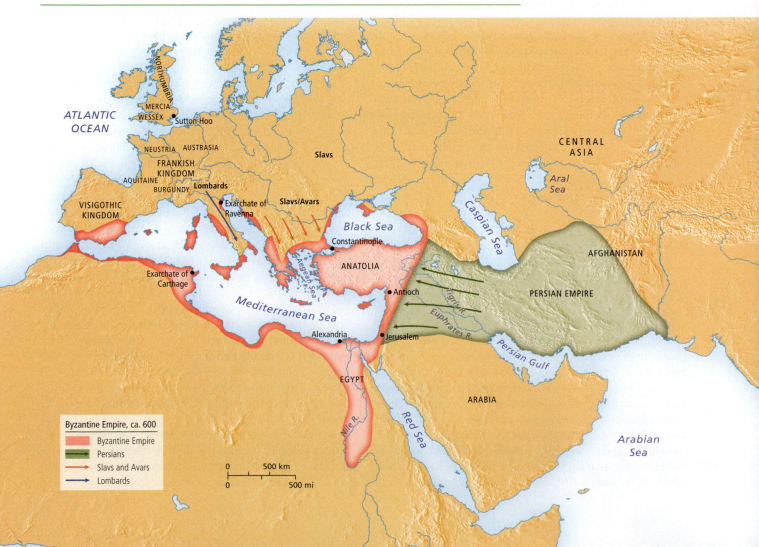

Avar Stirrups and Saber
Originally a nomadic people from central Asia, the Avars settled in Hungary and created an empire in central Europe. They depended on their heavily armed cavalry in battle. Byzantine military writers carefully studied Avar cavalry tactics and maneuvers. This pair of iron stirrups supported the weight of heavily armed cavalry and gave an Avar rider extra striking power with a slashing saber.

polytheistic tribes, not the least because Christian rulers considered so-called pagans legitimate objects of aggression, and their acceptance of Christianity opened the possibility for diplomatic ties and alliances. For Boris, therefore, conversion was a way to ward off Byzantine aggression and to make peace. For four years, Boris brilliantly negotiated with Rome, Constantinople, and German missionaries, all of whom sought to convert the Bulgars. In the end Boris got what he wanted—a Bulgarian Church that recognized the ultimate authority of the patriarch of Constantinople but was essentially autonomous.

The autonomy of the Bulgarian Church was further guaranteed later in the ninth century by the adoption of a Slavic rather than Latin or Greek liturgy. This was made possible by the missionary work in neighboring Moravia of Cyril (ca. 826–869) and his brother Methodius (815–885), who had invented an alphabet to write the Slavic language. They translated a Greek church liturgy into a version of the Slavic language now known as Old Church Slavonic. The acceptance of the Slavonic liturgy gradually led the ethnically and linguistically mixed peoples of Bulgaria to identify

with Slavic culture and language. From a string of monasteries established by the Bulgarians, the Old Church Slavonic liturgy spread among the Serbs, the Romanians, and eventually the Russians, creating cultural ties among these widespread peoples that have survived to the present.

Despite their conversion to Orthodox Christianity, the Bulgarians remained military rivals of Byzantium. A foolhardy Bulgarian attempt to capture impregnable Constantinople, safe behind its massive circuit of walls, provoked a formidable military reaction. By 1018 Bulgaria had lost its independence and was reincorporated into the Byzantine Empire.

Unlike the Bulgarians, the Rus did not represent an organized military threat to Byzantium even if their annual visits to Constantinople seemed vaguely threatening to the inhabitants of the city. From their trade with Constantinople, the Rus came to admire Byzantine culture. They established a headquarters at Kiev on the Dnieper River and gradually extended their domination over the local Slav tribes. From among the merchant-warriors of the Rus arose the forebears of the princes of Kiev, who by the end

DOCUMENT

Constantinople and the Avars: A Change in Tactics

After the death of Justinian in 565, the new emperor Justin II (565–578), confronted by an empty treasury, changed his policy toward the Avars. He refused to pay them their annual subsidies of gold to maintain peace with them, and so in 566 a delegation of Avars came to the palace to demand their gold. When the Avars were brought into the palace to meet the emperor, everything possible was done to impress them with the wealth and power of Constantinople and so subtly threaten them. A poet at court named Corippus described the Avar embassy's visit to the huge and gleaming palace:

The imperial throne ennobles the inmost sanctum, girded with four marvelous columns over which in the middle a canopy shining with liquid gold, like the vault of the curving sky, shades over the immortal head and throne of the emperor as he sits there. . . . Guards stood at the high entrance and kept out the unworthy. . . . When the officials had filled the decorated palace with their groups arranged in order, a glorious light shone from the inner chamber and filled all the meeting place. The emperor came forth surrounded by the great senate. . . . When the happy emperor had ascended the lofty throne and settled his limbs high up with his purple robes, the master of offices ordered the Avars to enter and announced that they were before the first doors of the imperial hall begging to see the holy feet of the merciful emperor. . . . The barbarian warriors marveled as they crossed the first threshold and at the great hall. They saw the tall men standing there, the golden shields, and looked up at their gold javelins as they glittered with their long iron tips and at the gilded helmet tops and red crosses. They shuddered at the sight of the lances and cruel axes and saw the other wonders of the noble procession. And they believed that the Roman palace was another heaven. But when the curtain was drawn aside and the inner part was revealed, and when the hall of the gilded building glittered and Tregazis the Avar looked up at the head of the emperor shining with the holy diadem, he lay down three times in adoration and remained fixed to the ground. The other Avars followed him in similar fear and fell on their faces, and brushed the carpets with their foreheads. . . .

Source: Corippus, *In Laudem Justini Minoris,* ed. Averil Cameron (London: 1976), 3.190–270 (pp. 106–107).

of the tenth century ruled a vast steppe and forest domain through a loose collective of principalities. The term *Rus* (later *Russian*) came to be applied to all the lands ruled by the princes of Kiev.

The zenith of Kievan Rus was under Vladimir the Great (r. 980–1015) and his son Iaroslav the Wise (r. 1019–1054). A ruthless fighter, Vladimir consolidated into a single state the provinces of Kiev and Novgorod, a city in the far north that had grown rich from the fur trade. A polytheist by birth, Vladimir had seven wives and took part in human sacrifices. However, when offered a military alliance with Byzantium in 987, he abandoned his other wives, married the Byzantine emperor's sister, and accepted conversion to Orthodox Christianity. He then forced the inhabitants of Kiev and Novgorod to be baptized and had their idols cast into the rivers. The Byzantine Church established administrative control over the Rus Church by appointing an Orthodox archbishop for Kiev. The liturgy was in Old Church Slavonic, which provided a written language and the stimulus for the literature, art, and music at the foundations of Russian culture.

The religious and political connection between the Rus and Byzantium influenced the course of Russian history, and it limited the eastward spread of Latin Christianity or Roman Catholicism. Iaroslav helped establish a bulwark of Orthodox culture throughout the Kievan state by collecting books, employing scribes to translate Greek religious books into Old Slavonic, and founding new churches and monasteries (see Map 7.2).

The Loss of the Western Provinces

Justinian reconquered the western provinces of the Roman Empire in North Africa, parts of Spain, and Italy. The Byzantine emperors after Justinian tried to hold on to the western provinces by reorganizing the administration of North Africa and Italy into two new units called *exarchates*—the Exarchate of Carthage and the Exarchate of Ravenna. Because of their long distance from Constantinople and the immediate press of the local problems they confronted, the two exarchates had a certain autonomy from the rest of the Byzantine Empire. The exarchs (or governors) ruled the exarchates, holding authority over civilian as well as military affairs—a break from Roman tradition that had kept these two spheres separate. This joint command augmented the exarch's authority and independence, but the unity of civil administration and the army under one command was a sign of how grave were the problems the exarchs faced. The Exarchate of Carthage administered southern Spain and North Africa, but it failed to resist the onslaught of enemies. Southern Spain fell to the Visigoths in the 630s, and North Africa lasted until 698 when it was lost to Muslim armies.

In Italy, the exarchate was based in Ravenna, a city located in an easily defensible marshy area on the northeastern coast. The Exarchate of Ravenna administered the Byzantine possessions in Italy and Sicily, including the city of Rome, where because of his prestige the support of the pope was important for implementing Byzantine policies. But in 751 the Germanic Lombards captured Ravenna, put an end to the exarchate, and eliminated forever the tenuous vestiges of authority the Byzantines had managed to preserve in Italy since the conquests of Justinian.

The Old Enemy: Persia

On the southeastern front, Persia, ruled by the Sasanian dynasty (224–651), continued to threaten Byzantium after Justinian's death. The two powers fought intermittently for the rest of the sixth century. In 602 the struggle entered a new and final phase when the Persian ruler Chosroes II launched a series of devastating attacks against Byzantium. In 614 Chosroes seized Antioch, the richest Byzantine city in Syria. Then he captured Jerusalem, the holiest Christian city in the Byzantine Empire, and stole the holiest relic in the Christian world: a fragment of the cross on which Jesus reportedly had been crucified, known as the True Cross.

Motivated by a desire to avenge these losses and regain the holy relics, the Byzantine emperor Heraclius (r. 610–641) devoted his life to crushing the Persians once and for all. This resourceful and tenacious emperor spent most of his reign locked in a life-and-death struggle against Persia. In 622 Heraclius took a huge gamble. Leaving Constantinople in the hands of its capable patriarch Sergius, he led the Byzantine army deep into Persian territory, where he campaigned for years. Believing that Constantinople now lay vulnerable due to the emperor's absence, the Persians made an alliance with the Avars in 626 and attacked the Byzantine capital. The city's massive walls, however, thwarted their assault. After two more years of desperate fighting, Heraclius finally defeated Chosroes on Persian territory.

When Heraclius defeated the Persian emperor, he recovered the fragment of Jesus' cross that had been stolen from Jerusalem. When the Byzantine emperor returned the cherished relic to Jerusalem, he won a spiritual as well as a military and political triumph. Writers of the day described his struggle with Persia as a victory of Christianity. Heraclius announced his victory to the inhabitants of Constantinople with these words: "Let all the earth raise a cry to God . . . and let all we Christians, praising and glorifying, give thanks to the one God, rejoicing with great joy in his holy name, for fallen is the arrogant Chosroes, opponent of God." Heraclius's victory over Persia, however, had exacted a huge toll. It left the Byzantines (and the Persians) too

---

Map 7.2 The Expanding States of Eastern and Northern Europe

Eastern Europe during the Early Middle Ages was home to a very diverse population of tribes and fledgling states. Within this diversity the states of Bulgaria, Kievan Rus, and Poland emerged by the beginning of the eleventh century.

The Expanding States of Eastern and Northern Europe

Relics and International Diplomacy: Constantinople and the West

Emperors in Constantinople distributed relics in order to maintain relations with the rulers of the Latin kingdoms of western Europe. Queen Radegund of Poitiers (520–587), after several years of childless marriage to King Clothar (d. 561), left the royal court to found a nunnery in the city of Poitiers, where she devoted her life to charity and the ascetic life. Because of her piety she eventually was made a saint, the first female ruler ever to be honored in this way. Even while in the nunnery she played a role in domestic and international politics. The following excerpt, taken from her biography, describes how she obtained a fragment of what was believed to be the True Cross, on which Jesus had been crucified, as well as other gifts, from the reigning Byzantine emperor, Justin II, about the year 570. The passage illustrates the Mediterranean-wide scope of diplomacy and the importance of Constantinople as a source of prestige. Justin II sent the gifts to demonstrate his influence in the West.

. . . Because [Radegund] did not wish to do anything without counsel as long as she lived, she sent letters to the most excellent lord king Sigibert (her stepson), under whose power our land of Gaul is ruled, that he might permit her, for the safety of the whole land and the stability of his kingdom, to see the wood of the Lord's (Jesus's) cross from the emperor in Constantinople. Sigibert gave his consent most graciously to the petition of the holy queen. She, full of devotion, on fire with longing, sent no gifts to the emperor, since she had made herself poor for the sake of God, but with prayer prevailing, and with the presence of the saints, whom she invoked ceaselessly, she sent her messengers. And she obtained that which her vows had requested, namely that she, remaining in one place, gloried in the possession of the blessed wood of the Lord's cross, adorned with gold and gems, and many relics of the saints, which the East used to have. In response to the petition of the holy woman, the emperor sent representatives with the Gospels adorned in gold and gems.

Source: Based on the translation of the *Life of Radegund* II.16, by Martha Jenks, in *From Queen to Bishop, A Political Biography of Radegund of Poitiers* (Diss. U.C. Berkeley, 1999), p. 181.

exhausted to resist the sudden onslaught of a new enemy, the Muslim Arab armies.

The New Enemy: Islam

After the defeat of the Persian emperor, a ferocious new enemy challenged Byzantium: the armies of Islam. The military vigor of the Muslim Arab armies derived from the new religion of Islam that appeared in the Arabian peninsula in the seventh century. Islam is discussed in detail later in this chapter, but for the Byzantines the Muslim armies represented a new and what would prove to be a persistent threat. After the 630s, Islamic armies attacked the Byzantine Empire continually from the east, raiding deep into Anatolia (modern Turkey) and sometimes threatening Constantinople itself. In 636, the formidable Arab enemy crushed a Byzantine army at the battle of the Yarmuk River, forcing the Byzantines to abandon the wealthy province of Syria. A few years later Arab troops seized Egypt from Byzantine hands. Encouraged by their victories, an enormous Arab force of more than 100,000 men and 1,800 ships besieged Constantinople itself between 716 and 718. The attack failed because of the strength of Constantinople's walls, the courage of the defenders, and logistical problems among the Arabs. However, the Byzantines were certain their salvation was a miracle, a sign of God's favor. They claimed that the Virgin Mary had personally helped defend their capital.

Unfazed by their failure to capture Constantinople, Arab troops soon resumed their annual raids into Byzantine territory, defeating every Byzantine army that opposed them. Finally, in 740, Emperor Leo III (r. 717–741) won the Byzantine Empire's first important victory over the Muslim armies at the battle of Akroinon in western Asia Minor. Exhausted Byzantine troops could not go on the offensive, but they had slowed Arab momentum against their empire. The Byzantines were no more often at war with Muslim armies than with others, but the Muslims came to represent a singular threat in the eyes of Byzantine Christians largely because Muslim armies were so persistently successful against them. The Muslims quickly conquered all of North Africa, the Middle East, southern Spain, and Sicily, chipping away huge parts of what had once been Byzantine territory.

One of the lasting fruits of these conflicts were legends of great heroes. These legends began as stories recited in verse to entertain Byzantine aristocrats whose ancestors had fought the Arabs, and several of these oral legends were eventually refashioned into epic poems that became extremely popular and much imitated. The epic tenth-century Greek poem *Digenes Akritas* describes the heroic feats of soldiers during the late eighth century on the eastern

King David Plate

Nine silver plates made in Constantinople about 630 illustrate scenes from the career of the biblical King David. The largest plate (about 20 inches in diameter) shows David battling the giant Goliath. Though the subject matter is biblical, the style of representing clothing, human bodies, and spatial relationships comes directly from the classical tradition. The artist may have intended to show a connection between the warrior king of the Bible and the emperor Heraclius, who defeated the mighty Persian emperor Chosroes II.

which provided spiritual guidance and resolved the religious controversies. Each of these institutions contributed to stability in a world of turmoil. The Byzantine system was perhaps most successful in reorganizing its military institutions, which made it possible to respond to armed threats on the frontiers without direct authorization from Constantinople. Despite terrible losses Byzantium endured.

Imperial Administration and Economy

Based in the capital city of Constantinople, the emperor stood at the very center of Byzantine society. His authority, which his people believed had been granted by God, reached to every corner of the empire. This supreme ruler governed with the assistance of a large bureaucracy that he tightly controlled. In this hierarchical bureaucracy different clothing indicated different levels of importance. Only the emperor or members of his household, for example, could wear the color purple, a symbol of royalty. High dignitaries wore silk garments of distinctive colors encrusted with jewels; the higher the official, the more gems he was permitted to display. Bureaucrats and courtiers (members of the emperor's personal retinue) lined up in elaborate processions in order of their importance, as indicated by the color of their clothing and shoes. Through these ceremonial processions the emperor displayed the government to the people. Such processions were not just a form of political propaganda. They made the constitution of the empire evident through the hierarchic order of the procession, and they provided an indicator of the politics of the court as favored courtiers moved to a higher-ranked position in the procession and those out of favor moved to a lower-ranked place or disappeared from the procession altogether.

Men fortunate enough to obtain an office in the imperial government acquired considerable wealth and influence. For this reason leading provincial families sent their sons to Constantinople in search of positions in the imperial hierarchy. Through this method of recruitment Constantinople remained in close touch with the outlying regions of the

frontier of the empire, where Byzantine and Arab populations both fought and cooperated in a complex symbiosis. The father of the hero of the poem was an Arab soldier who abducted the daughter of a Byzantine general, married her, and converted to Christianity. The son of this mixed marriage was Digenes ("two-blooded"), a man of two peoples and two religions, who became a border fighter. This greatest Byzantine hero, who lived between two cultures, was the poetic embodiment of the engagement between Byzantium and Islam at a time when the former seemed clearly in the ascendant. The legends surrounding *Digenes Akritas* had a profound influence on Greek literature. Later writers referred to it and retold its stories again and again.

Byzantine Civilization

In addition to assaults from so many directions, the Byzantine Empire faced turmoil from within. The loss of territories caused economic suffering, and doctrinal controversies during the eighth century severely divided the Orthodox Christian Church. It seems remarkable that the Byzantine Empire survived at all, but it did. Its survival points to the strength of three institutions that held the empire together: the emperor, who set policies and safeguarded his subjects' welfare; the army that defended the realm's frontiers; and the Orthodox Christian Church, empire. This aspect of the system was a strength because it gave both provincial families a stake in the success of the imperial system and the provinces a voice in the capital. However, the governmental system was also vulnerable to corruption. Many men obtained their positions by bribing court officials who worked for the emperor. Many office-holders probably owed their jobs to family influence or bribes rather than talent, but even a corrupt system can be an effective form of government because official corruption made loyalty to the emperor more rewarding than opposition to him.

From his position at the head of this elaborate hierarchy, the emperor controlled Byzantium's economy. The Byzantine economy was monopolistic in that official monopolies controlled the production and distribution of specific commodities. These monopolies were designed to protect the interests of the emperor and those he rewarded by stifling all forms of competition. As long as the monopolies flourished the government had a source of revenue through taxation. When Justinian died, the imperial taxation system that Constantine had established in the early fourth century still generated sufficient funds to keep the imperial system working. Trade within the empire was stimulated by the ready availability of imperial coinage, which spurred a flourishing cash-based economy.

By the end of the seventh century, however, when the rich provinces of Egypt and Syria and the wealthy cities of Alexandria, Antioch, Jerusalem, and many others had fallen to the Arabs, the Byzantine economy stumbled. Thousands of refugees from lands conquered by Muslims streamed into the empire and strained its dwindling resources. In conquered provinces, Muslim rulers monopolized Middle Eastern trade revenues and prevented Byzantine merchants from participating in long-distance commerce, which badly hurt the official monopolies. Cut off from foreign markets, Byzantines stopped manufacturing goods for export. As the economy shriveled, Byzantines stopped building new homes and churches. By 750, the standard of living in most Byzantine cities steeply declined.

The Military System of the Themes

In response to the many external threats, Byzantine society was reorganized for constant preparation for war. Emperors relied on their armies to protect Constantinople, the nerve center of the shrinking Byzantine state, and to defend the borders against invaders. By about 650 in Anatolia, emperors abandoned the late antique system of relying on the provincial governors to protect the frontiers. In place of the Anatolian provinces the emperors created buffer territories against Muslim armies—the four military districts called *themes*. Each of the themes had its own army and administration commanded by a general chosen by the emperor. The themes' armies developed strong traditions of local identity and prided themselves on their expert military skills, a legacy the Byzantine Empire had inherited from the Roman legions. These military forces remained effective enough to keep the empire from collapsing in spite of devastating losses to Islamic armies throughout the seventh century.

By 750 the themes developed considerable independence from Constantinople and were the basis of further reorganization of the agricultural economy and procedures for recruitment. Soldiers and sailors who were once paid in cash from the emperor's tax revenues now were granted land on which to support themselves. Fighting men had to provide their own weapons from their income as farmers, and the theme system enabled the various parts of the empire to function without direct support from the imperial treasury. The theme system created some measure of defensive flexibility for the empire. While it could no longer launch large-scale offensive conquests, as was possible in the time of Justinian, Byzantium could at least make an attempt at defending its shrinking borders.

Over time the four original themes were subdivided and new ones added in other regions until by the end of the eleventh century there were thirty-eight themes. The military strength of the empire came to depend on the theme system in which free, tax-paying soldier-farmers lived in villages under the supervision of a military commander who was also civil administrator. These soldier-farmers usually fought in their own districts, which meant they were defending their homes and families, and they provided a formidable bulwark against invaders. Because of their strong local roots the themes were more effective for defending against aggressors than conducting offensive campaigns.

Even with reorganized territorial defenses in the themes, Constantinople could not be protected without naval power. During the seventh and eighth centuries, the Byzantine fleet successfully kept Arab forces at bay through the use of "Greek Fire," a kind of napalm hurled against enemy ships to ignite them. Muslims soon learned how to use "Greek Fire," but the Byzantines used it more effectively in battle. Byzantine naval policy was also primarily defensive. Byzantium did not attempt great naval expeditions that landed troops abroad, but the navy was capable of maintaining a fleet that kept the capital safe from Muslim fleets.

The Byzantine borders were especially harassed by Muslim enemies, but from the first thrust of Muslim armies against Byzantium's frontier in the seventh century until its final collapse more than eight hundred years later, Constantinople held on. While Persia and other territories fell to Arab armies, Byzantium survived. That fact is perhaps the most important measure of the success of its military reorganization and defensive strategy.

The Church and Religious Life

Most Byzantines identified themselves as Orthodox Christians, meaning that like the emperor they accepted the doctrines established by the first seven church councils, especially the Council of Chalcedon in 451. That important council defined Christ's human and divine natures as being united in one divine "person" without any separation, division, or change. This distinguished Byzantine Christians from other Christian communities that interpreted the nature of Christ differently, as discussed in Chapter 6.

Constantinople boasted so many churches and sacred relics that by 600 Byzantines had begun to think of it as a holy city, protected by God and under the special care of the Virgin Mary, Jesus' human mother. Churchmen taught that Constantinople was a "New Jerusalem" that would be at the center of events at the end of days when God would bring history to an end and judge humanity.

One of the institutional pillars of the Orthodox Church was that the clergy were organized hierarchically like the imperial bureaucracy. The Patriarch, or chief bishop, of Constantinople led the Orthodox Church, administering several thousand clergymen in the capital and directing church affairs throughout the empire. Emperors generally controlled the appointment of new Patriarchs, and often they worked closely together, serving Byzantium's spiritual needs. The Patriarch helped impose religious unity throughout the empire by controlling the network of bishops based in cities. As the leader of urban religious life, a city's bishop supervised the veneration of the saints' relics housed in its churches. Byzantines believed that relics protected their communities, as the polytheist gods had done in the pre-Christian past. Because bishops usually came from the city's elite, they were influential local leaders, responsible for many kinds of decisions for the public good, not just religious ones.

Many cities were also home to monasteries, which played a significant role in the empire's daily life. Men and women

IMAGE

Monastery of the Holy Trinity in Meteora, Greece

went to separate monasteries to live a spiritual life, praying for their salvation and that of other people. People in need of assistance, such as orphans, the elderly, battered wives, and the physically and mentally ill, found refuge and assistance in monasteries. Monks and nuns regularly distributed food and clothing to the needy outside the monastery walls. Generous donors gave lavishly to monasteries to fund these activities, and many monasteries grew extremely wealthy through these gifts.

During the seventh and eighth centuries, Christian instruction under the supervision of the Church replaced the traditional Roman educational system. By about 600, financially strapped city leaders had stopped paying schoolmasters to offer traditional instruction. Learning so declined that most Byzantines could neither read nor write. Pious Christians also developed a deep suspicion of classical

learning, with its references to ancient gods and customs frowned on by the Church. Those few who learned how to read did so by studying the Bible, not the classics of Greek antiquity. As a result of this general decline in learning, the Church monopolized all culture and thought. Knowledge of classical literature, history, and science disappeared everywhere except in Constantinople, and even there the academic community was tiny. Many Byzantines, for example, had no memory of the polytheist religions and thought that the marble statues from earlier centuries adorning their cities were sinister demons.

Icons and the Iconoclastic Controversy

The Orthodox Church created unity of faith and culture, but that unity was broken in the eighth century by controversy within the church itself. As enemies tore at the borders of the empire, Byzantines wondered why God was punishing them so severely. Their answer was that somehow they were failing God. Convinced that only appeasing God could save them, Emperor Leo III (r. 717–741) took action. In order to make Byzantium a completely Christian empire, he forcibly converted communities of Jews. His most important move was to challenge the use of icons°, the images of Christ and saints found everywhere in Byzantine worship.

In contrast to Byzantine practice, the first Christians had refused to make images of Christ and other holy individuals. They had two reasons for banning such representations. First, the Hebrew Bible forbids creating any representations of God, and they considered this aspect of the old law of the Hebrews still in effect for Christians. Second, they thought that Christians might start to worship their images in the same way that polytheists worshiped statues in their temples. "When images are put up, the customs of the pagans do the rest," wrote one church leader in the fourth century.

Despite such warnings, many Christians responded aesthetically to the beautiful polytheist statues and images that filled the cities in which they lived. Christian sculptors and painters started to create a distinctive Christian art that combined religious images with the styles and techniques of classical art. After Constantine converted to Christianity in 312 and put an end to the persecutions of Christians, this new art flourished. Artists routinely portrayed Christ and the saints in churches. During the sixth and seventh centuries Byzantines used religious images with greater zeal than ever before. By 600, for example, the emperor placed a large image of Christ above the Bronze Gate, the main entrance to the imperial palace in Constantinople. Smaller paintings became intensely popular in churches and in people's homes.

Byzantine theologians defended icons as doorways through which the divine presence could make itself accessible to believers. Churchmen cautioned that God or saints do not actually reside within the icons, and so believers should not worship the images themselves. Rather, they should consider icons as openings to a spiritual world, enabling believers to encounter a holy presence. Thus Byzantines treated icons with great love and respect.

However, by the eighth century some Byzantine religious thinkers thought matters had gone too far and sought to revive the early Christian prohibitions against religious images. They advised Emperor Leo that icon veneration should be halted because too many uneducated people believed icons were divine themselves. These simple believers confused the image of the icon with what it represented and worshiped icons as polytheists had worshiped statues in their temples. Besides following the advice of these theologians, Leo decided to act after a volcanic eruption destroyed the island of Santorini, proving in his mind that God had

been angered by icon veneration. Leo prohibited the veneration and ordered the destruction of holy images (except for crucifixes) throughout the empire, but public resistance forced him to move very carefully. For example, when he ordered workers to remove the image of Christ from the Bronze Gate at the imperial palace in 726, the people of Constantinople rioted. Four years later, Leo renewed the general prohibition. The destruction of icons, known as iconoclasm° (image breaking), sparked a bitter controversy that divided Byzantine society until 842.

Epitome of the Iconoclastic 7th Synod (754)

Leo's iconoclasm backfired because the veneration of icons was such a vital part of popular religious life. He found it difficult to enforce iconoclasm outside Constantinople. Revolts broke out in Greece and southern Italy when imperial messengers arrived with orders to destroy images. The iconoclastic controversy affected international politics as well. Outraged by the Byzantine emperor's prohibition of icons, the Roman pope, by then the dominant religious and political figure in the West, excommunicated Leo. In retaliation Leo deprived the pope of political authority over southern Italy, Sicily, and Illyricum (the Balkan coast of the Adriatic Sea), a political authority the popes claimed they had inherited from long-gone Roman emperors of the west. The Roman popes never forgave the emperor for this slight. This conflict contributed to a growing rift between Greek Orthodox and Latin Christianity.

After years of turmoil, two Byzantine empresses who sympathized with their subjects' religious convictions restored icons to churches. In 787, the empress Irene called a general church council that reversed Leo's ruling. After a brief renewal of iconoclasm, in 843 the empress Theodora introduced a religious ceremony for commemorating images, which Orthodox Christians still celebrate annually. Icons remain an integral part of Orthodox worship today. The iconoclastic controversy may have widened the gap between Greek Orthodoxy and Latin Christianity, but its resolution created even greater religious unity within the Byzantine world. A common religious culture not only unified the Byzantines, but also provided solace and a spiritual connection to Byzantium for many Christians who found themselves in the former Byzantine territories that had been conquered by Islamic rulers.

The Macedonian Renaissance

Byzantium's losses to external enemies were reversed during the Macedonian dynasty (867–1056), the term for a line of emperors from the Makedonikon Theme that lasted six generations. Before the Macedonians there was always the potential for instability when an emperor died because powerful families struggled over who would become the new emperor. But after Basil I (r. 867–886) murdered his way to the throne, he kept his family in power by naming

Byzantine Manuscript

In this ninth-century Byzantine manuscript the figure with a pole is shown whiting out an image of Christ.

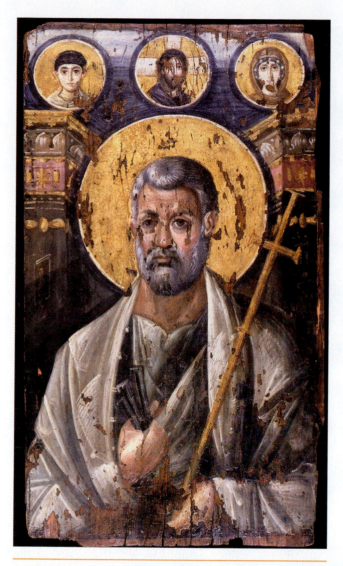

An Icon that Survived Iconoclasm:
St. Peter in the Monastery at Mount Sinai
This image of St. Peter, painted sometime during the sixth century, is in the Monastery of St. Catherine on Mount Sinai in Egypt. Because Egypt was in Muslim hands when the iconoclastic controversy broke out, this image survived.

his sons co-emperors and encouraging the principle of dynastic succession.

Byzantium and Islam had been engaged in a life-and-death struggle since the seventh century. Under the Macedonian emperors from the middle of the ninth century to the late tenth century, Byzantine armies and fleets fought Muslim armies on several fronts. In the East the Byzantines pushed into Syria and Palestine almost to Jerusalem. A large portion of the Mesopotamian river valley fell into their hands. They annexed the kingdom of Georgia and part of Armenia. In the Mediterranean the Byzantines retook the island of Cyprus and kept the Muslims from southern Italy, although they were unable to prevent Muslim conquests of Crete and Sicily, which became thriving centers of Muslim culture.

Whereas on the eastern borders the only option against the Muslims was a military one, in the polytheistic Balkans missionary efforts helped create new alliances. As discussed previously, the conversion of the southern Slavs and the Bulgars was well underway before the Macedonian Renaissance, which enhanced the cultural allure of Byzantium for these newly converted peoples. The Bulgars were incorporated into the Byzantine sphere of influence, but they proved inconstant allies. Perhaps the greatest achievement in the spread of Christianity under the Macedonians was the conversion of the Rus, which made them less isolated and more open to Byzantine influence.

The Byzantine success at converting the Slavs, Bulgars, and Rus magnified a growing bitterness with the Latin or Catholic Christians in western Europe. For their part, the Byzantines under the Macedonian dynasty took heart from their military successes and assumed it was only a matter of time before the West returned to obedience to the one true emperor in Constantinople. Needless to say, Latin Christians did not accept the Byzantine vision of an empire in which they played a subordinate role, and relations between East and West soured during the tenth and eleventh centuries. Especially after the Saxon king Otto I was crowned Roman emperor in 962, the Macedonian dynasty was hostile to the Latins. Visiting western ambassadors were treated with scorn and a superior attitude that precluded cooperation between Orthodox and Catholic Christians, especially against their common Muslim foes.

Under the Macedonian dynasty, the economy of Constantinople thrived. Home to more than half a million people by the tenth century, the city became a great marketplace where goods from as far away as China and the British Isles were exchanged. It was also a center for the production of luxury goods, especially silk cloth and brocades, which were traded throughout Europe, Asia, and northern Africa. During this period aristocratic families, the Church, and monasteries became immensely rich, and devoted themselves to embellishing the city with magnificent buildings, mosaics, and icons, creating the Macedonian Renaissance°.

The settlement of the iconoclastic controversy in 842 by Empress Theodora released great creative energies by defining the religious beliefs of Orthodoxy and creating unity within the Orthodox Church. Some of those energies went into missionary work, but the educated classes of courtiers, churchmen, monks, and scholars also produced a remarkable body of work. The most original work was spiritual in nature, embodied in sermons, theological scholarship, and especially hymns, but thanks to generous imperial patronage Constantinople also became a center for philosophical study. The accumulation of ancient manuscripts and the compilations of ancient philosophy created an important cultural link between the ancient and medieval worlds.

The Patriarch Photius (ca. 810–ca. 893) became the most eminent scholar in the history of Byzantium. Photius maintained a huge library, which became a major center for the study of ancient Greek literature based on the rare manuscripts he had collected. Photius was the author of several important works, including the *Library,* an encyclopedic compendium of classical, late antique, and early Byzantine writers in both theology and secular literatures. Photius's summaries and analyses of these writers remain especially vital to this day because many of these books have been lost since his time. In addition to writing, Photius was deeply involved in church politics. Photius's election as Patriarch while still a layman was strongly opposed by the Roman pope. Photius was twice deposed from office due to the shifts of political winds in Constantinople. A bitter critic of the Latin Christians on matters of religious doctrine, Photius is often blamed for widening the gap, called the Photian Schism, between the two main branches of Christianity.

The quasi-sacred office of the emperor came to be magnified in elaborate court ceremonies under the Macedonian dynasty. The historian Emperor Constantine VII Porphyrogenetus (r. 912–959) wrote *On the Administration of the Empire,* an important source for Byzantine history. He also wrote the *Book of Ceremonies,* which became a model for royal ceremony throughout the Christian world and was adapted in kingdoms across Europe from Spain to Russia. The *Book of Ceremonies* disseminated Byzantine concepts of rulership, which suggested that the emperor, like Christ, had two natures. One of these natures was human and fallible, but the other was derived from God, which gave the properly consecrated ruler divine authority over his subjects. In fact, Byzantine emperors were anointed with holy oil in a ceremony that was very similar to the ordination of priests. The divine authority of emperors represented by their anointment became a central feature of political thought during the Middle Ages.

The Byzantine Portrait
This ivory plaque shows the emperor Constantine VII Porphyrogenetus being crowned by Christ. It was probably made in 944 to commemorate his becoming the sole ruler of the Byzantine Empire. Under the emperor's left hand the inscription reads "Emperor of the Romans."

Despite the achievements of the Macedonians, new threats loomed on the horizon. Under the Macedonian emperors, Byzantium had never been completely free from the external threat of invasions. The extent to which the empire succeeded in meeting these threats had depended on two factors—the political stability guaranteed by the Macedonian dynasty, and the organization and recruitment of the army through the military districts of the themes.

Emperor Basil II died in 1025 and left no direct heirs. But members of his family continued to rule until 1056, largely because of the general assumption that the peace and prosperity of the empire depended on the dynasty. Basil's successors, however, were not the strong leaders that had distinguished the earlier Macedonian dynasty. Administration of the empire was highly centralized, with a tangled bureaucracy that supervised everything from diplomatic ceremony to the training of lowly artisans. Without energetic leadership, the Byzantine bureaucracy quickly degenerated into routine and failed to respond to new challenges.

The early Macedonian emperors' success in checking invasions had been largely the result of Byzantium's superior military capacities, guaranteed by the systematic organization of the army in the themes, the steady support of the navy, and the strength of the economy. As discussed earlier, the success of the themes depended on a system in which free, tax-paying soldier-farmers fought in their own districts, defending their homes and families. However, by the eleventh century the independence of these soldier-farmers was threatened by deteriorating economic conditions. Every time a crop failed or a drought or famine struck, starving soldier-farmers in the themes were forced to surrender their land and their independence to one of the prosperous aristocrats who offered them food. As the great landowners acquired more land, the small farmers who were the backbone of the army began to disappear or lose their freedom. Because only free landholders could perform military service, the concentration of land in the hands of a few was disastrous for the army. Qualified soldiers with the land to support them became rare. The late Macedonian emperors lacked the will to initiate reforms that would have arrested this dangerous trend in which the land-grabbing of the aristocrats led to the decay of the army. These emperors found themselves in a difficult bind. Their income largely depended on their control of virtually all industry and trade, but that control meant that the only profitable alternative form of investment for the aristocrats was the acquisition of land. Because economic reforms that opened up the economy might have hurt their own incomes, the emperors failed to do what was necessary to protect the empire.

To make matters worse, after 1025 Byzantium faced formidable new enemies. In the west the Normans advanced on southern Italy and Sicily, crushing Byzantine power in Italy forever. The Normans, however, preserved a great deal of Byzantine culture in these regions, even as the Byzantine Empire became a distant memory. Official documents were issued in Latin, Greek, and Arabic, and the Norman princes acted as patrons of the Greek monasteries. Greek continued to be spoken in southern Italy for many centuries as remnants of Byzantine civilization survived alongside other languages and cultures.

In the east Byzantium faced an even more dangerous enemy. In 1071, the Seljuk Turks, who had converted to Sunni Islam in the previous century, captured the Byzantine emperor himself at the battle of Manzikert in Armenia. After their victory the Seljuks advanced across Asia Minor and threatened the very survival of Byzantium. The situation looked bleak indeed, and over the succeeding centuries, western European armies and the Turks ate away at Byzantium until its final collapse in 1453.

The New World of Islam

■ How did Islam develop in Arabia, and how did its followers create a vast empire so quickly?

The Muslim armies that battered Byzantium created a thriving civilization that transformed the Mediterranean world. Today more than one billion Muslims around the globe adhere to Islam, playing a significant role in world affairs. This rapidly growing faith has left an indelible stamp not only on the West but also on the rest of the world.

CHRONOLOGY

The Byzantine Empire

527–565	Reign of Justinian I
614–616	Persians take Jerusalem and Egypt
626	Avars and Persians besiege Constantinople
630	Heraclius defeats Persian king and restores True Cross to Jerusalem
636	Byzantines lose Battle of Yarmuk, Arabs take Syria and Jerusalem
642	Muslims take Egypt
698	Muslims take Carthage
716–718	Muslims besiege Constantinople
740	Byzantines defeat Arabs at Akroinon
751	Lombards conquer Ravenna and end the Exarchate of Italy
ca. 810–ca. 893	Life of Photius, Patriarch of Constantinople
867–1056	Macedonian dynasty
1071	Seljuk Turks defeat Byzantine army at the Battle of Manzikert

Islam originated in the early seventh century among the inhabitants of the Arabian peninsula. Through conquest and expansion, Muslims created a single Islamic Empire stretching from Spain to central Asia by 750 (see Map 7.3).

Arabs Before Islam

Before the emergence of Islam, Arabs were tribal people from the Arabian peninsula and the Middle East who spoke Arabic, a semitic language related to Hebrew (the ancient language of the Jews), Aramaic (the language spoken by Jews and other peoples at the time of Jesus), and Akkadian. Despite their shared language, Arab communities varied from nomadic bands to sophisticated cities. Those living in the interior of the Arabian peninsula led a nomadic life herding camels. On the edges of the desert they raised goats and sheep. In south Arabia, they farmed, lived in towns, and developed extensive commercial networks. During the late Roman Empire some Arabs had lived within the empire while others traded there, an experience that gave them considerable knowledge of both Roman civilization and Christianity. The communities of Arabia and the Middle East, however, were not unified into a single state.

Arabs have a long history in the Middle East. They were first mentioned in the Hebrew Bible about 1000 B.C.E., and

Ships of the Desert:
Camels from Morocco to Central Asia

A remarkable thing happened when the Arab followers of the dynamic new religion of Islam encountered the humble beast of burden the camel. The camel helped make Arab armies lethal in battle, which meant that the message of Islam spread rapidly through conquest. In addition the caravan trade that transported goods on the backs of camels brought the Arabs into contact with a vast stretch of the world from Spain to China. In the exchanges that took place along the caravan routes, Islamic religious ideas were widely disseminated, and Arab merchants gained access to a lucrative trade that enriched Muslim cities. The success of the caravan trade changed the very appearance of large parts of the West by making obsolete the old Roman roads and the shipping lanes that had unified the Mediterranean, Europe, and North Africa in the ancient world. Narrow camel tracks replaced roads; oases and cities along the caravan routes supplanted ports in economic significance.

Before Muhammad began to recite, the camel had already transformed the life of Arabia. Camels were highly efficient beasts of burden, especially in arid regions, because of their bodies' capacity to conserve water. Able to drink as much as twenty-eight gallons at a time, camels can last four to nine days without water and travel great distances in this period. The fat in their humps allows camels to survive for even longer without food. As pack animals, camels are more efficient than carts pulled by animals because they can traverse roadless rough terrain and cross rivers without bridges. They require fewer people to manage them on a journey than do wheeled vehicles.

Arab fighters were especially menacing because they developed the "North Arabian saddle" that let them ride the one-humped Arabian camel with comfort in battle. The new saddle required only one rider who could grasp the camel's reins with one hand while slashing downward at enemy troops with a sword in his other hand. Warriors on camels could attack infantry with speed and crushing force. By 300 C.E., camel-breeding Arab tribesmen, empowered by their new military technology, inaugurated the "Caravan Age." The Arabs seized control of the lucrative spice trade routes and became an economic, military, and political force by exploiting and guarding the wealth of the caravans.

After Muhammad established his community in Mecca, Islam literally "took off" on camelback. Tribesmen on camels proved an unstoppable force as they spread Islam first throughout Arabia and the Middle East, and then with lightning speed across North Africa into Spain and Central Asia. Camels played a significant role in the expanding Islamic economy because they made long-distance trade extremely profitable. The transformations the camel brought were most evident in the former Roman provinces where the famous Roman roads had been a primary conduit of land trade. Thousands of miles of roads connected the provinces of the Roman Empire and let troops march easily from one front to another. However, camels changed all of that. Because these "ships of the desert" do not need paved roads, caravan routes did not have to stick to Roman road systems, and merchants bypassed them altogether. New trade routes across the desert and other harsh terrains well suited to camels quickly developed from Morocco to Central Asia, with the astonishing consequence that after 700 paved roads started to disappear. Because camels can easily walk on narrow paths, the broad streets and wide markets suited to carts and wagons that typified Greek and Roman cities fell out of use. Bazaars with narrow, winding lanes appropriate to camel traffic sprung up to replace them; carts and wheeled vehicles all but disappeared in these lands. It was not just roads and the shape of cities that changed. There were cultural consequences as well. In particular, caravan traffic reached as far as China, bringing Chinese goods and Chinese ideas to the West.

Question for Discussion

How might the history of the West have differed had not camel caravans replaced the system of Roman roads?

The Camel Caravan
This modern photograph shows a string of camels crossing sand dunes in the desert, carrying heavy loads, just as camel caravans would have in antiquity.

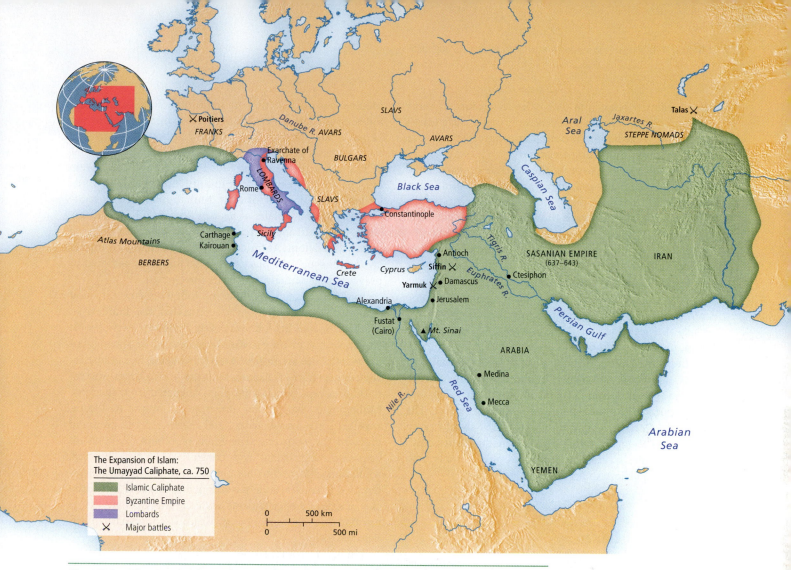

Map 7.3 The Expansion of Islam: The Umayyad Caliphate, ca. 750

By about 750 the Umayyad caliphate had reached its greatest extent. It provided political unity to territories stretching from central Asia to Spain. Islam became the dominant religion in this vast empire.

Middle Eastern, Greek, and Roman historical records continued to describe them for 1,500 years as raiders of settled communities but never as serious military threats. The Arabs became more threatening to their enemies after 300 B.C.E. because of an innovation in military technology that allowed them to fight effectively from the backs of camels. Military strength combined with trade in luxury goods made some Arab communities wealthy and powerful. By the first century B.C.E. Arabs had seized control of Petra, a merchant city in modern Jordan that controlled the incense trade. Merchants brought this precious, fragrant spice used in religious rituals across the Arabian peninsula from ports on the Red Sea and the Persian Gulf to Petra, where it was sold to other merchants from throughout the Middle East and the Mediterranean region. Petra also received merchandise such as ivory and gold from Egyptian traders. Other Arab cities such as Medina, located on the western coast of the Arabian peninsula, also flourished due to long-

distance caravan trade. Their merchants traded throughout the Middle East, sailed to India, and had extensive contacts with eastern Africa. At the same time, Arabs in north Arabia bred sturdier camels that could endure the harsh, arid terrain of central Asia. This enabled Arab merchants to travel to China along the silk route.

Most Arab communities organized themselves into tribes, each of which claimed descent from a common male ancestor. There was no formal government holding each tribe together. The chiefs who led their tribes did so by personal prestige and by the common consent of the tribesmen. Arab tribes, however, performed many of the functions of a state, which included protecting the lives and property of all their members. Arab tribesmen frequently feuded with one another, killing the men and stealing the herds and women of other tribes. Honor required retribution for every grievance, and so cycles of violence often lasted for generations. An injury to any member of a tribe obliged fellow tribesmen to seek either vengeance or compensation. Some feuding men chose to settle their grievances through mediation. If both parties agreed, mediators would set fair terms of compensation.

Before the rise of Islam in the seventh century, most Arabs worshiped many gods, including natural objects such as the sun and certain rocks or trees. Unlike their Egyptian and Greco-Roman neighbors, however, they did not erect huge temples to these deities. While most Arabs were probably polytheists, there was a strain of monotheism within Arab culture, which was reinforced through encounters with Jews, Christians, and Zoroastrians in Syria, Palestine, Mesopotamia, and Arabia. From these encounters some Arabs learned about different versions of monotheism, especially as revealed in sacred texts such as the Bible and the Avesta, the sacred text of Zoroastrians. Large Jewish communities existed in the cities of western Arabia as well as in Yemen, the southwest corner of the Arabian peninsula. Christianity had spread on Arabia's southern coast, and small groups of Zoroastrians lived in eastern Arabia. The Jewish and Christian Arabs developed ideas about heaven and hell and about the judgment of individuals after death that opened the way to the teachings of a prophet who many came to believe spoke directly for God.

The Rise of Islam

Islam is based on the Qur'an and the sayings of the prophet Muhammad (ca. 570–632). Muhammad was born in 570 to the powerful Hashimite clan of the Quraysh tribe in the cosmopolitan and wealthy west Arabian trading city of Mecca. This city was the site of the Kaaba, a sacred stone where polytheist Arabs worshiped various deities. As a young man Muhammad married a widowed businesswoman, Khadija, and worked as a caravan merchant. In this profession he earned a reputation as a skilled arbitrator of disputes among feuding tribes. At about age 40, Muhammad reported that while he was meditating in solitude an angel appeared before him, saying, "Muhammad, I am Gabriel and you are the Messenger of God. Recite!" According to Muhammad's account the angel gave him a message to convey to the people of Mecca. Muhammad's message was a call to all Arabs to

DOCUMENT

The Holy
Qur'an
7th C. C.E.

worship the one true God (the god of Abraham) and to warn of the fires of hell if they failed to answer that call. Muhammad continued to report what he considered revelations for the rest of his life. They were written down as the Qur'an (meaning "recitation"), the holy book of Islam. Though Muhammad won some followers among friends and family, the people of Mecca initially did not accept his monotheist message and some were openly hostile to him.

In 622, Muhammad and his followers moved from Mecca to Medina, a city 200 miles to the north. Aware of Muhammad's skill as a mediator, several feuding tribes in Medina had invited him to settle their long-lasting disputes. Muhammad's emigration to Medina, known as the *Hijra,* is the starting date of the Muslim calendar. The event marks a historical turning point in the development of Islam. For the first time Muhammad and his followers lived as an independent community. Accepted by his followers as the prophet of God, Muhammad strictly regulated the internal affairs of his new community and its relations with outsiders, creating a society that was political as well as religious. At the center of this Islamic community lay the mosque°, the place where his followers gathered to pray and hear Muhammad recite the Qur'an.

Initially, Muhammad and his followers enjoyed good relations with the Jews who controlled the markets in Medina. He and his followers even abided by some Jewish rituals, such as turning toward Jerusalem while praying. But as his influence among the Arab tribes grew, he became involved in a series of disputes with the Jewish tribes who refused to accept him as a prophet. Alienated from the Jews, Muhammad changed the direction of prayer to Mecca, expelled some Jewish tribes, and massacred the men and enslaved the women and children of others. With Jewish opposition eliminated and control of Medina secured, Muhammad turned to his old enemies in Mecca and attempted to convince them of his divine mission. After a series of military engagements with the Meccans, he led an army of his followers against Mecca itself, which surrendered in 630.

Using a combination of force and negotiation, Muhammad drew many Arab tribes into his new religious community. His authority rested both on his ability as a military leader who was successful at raiding caravans and defeating enemy tribes and his reputation as a prophet. By the time of his death in 632 he had unified most of Arabia under Islam. Muhammad created a tightly controlled community that was inspired by his teachings.

Muhammad's Teachings

Islam teaches that Allah (which means "God" in Arabic) revealed his message to Muhammad, the last in a line of prophets. Such prophets included Abraham, Moses, and David, all pivotal biblical figures in the Jewish tradition who transmitted divine instruction to humanity, and Jesus Christ, whom Muslims accept as a prophet but not the son of God. Muslims claimed Abraham as their ancestor because he was the father of Ishmael, whom they consider to be the father of the Arab peoples. Thus, Islam shares some of the fundamental religious beliefs of Judaism and Christianity.

Muhammad taught his followers basic principles that eventually came to be called the five Pillars of Islam°. *Islam* means "submission," and by performing these acts of faith Muslims demonstrate submission to the will of God. First, all Muslims must acknowledge that there is only one God and that Muhammad is his prophet. Second, they must state this belief in prayer five times a day. On Fridays, the noon prayers must be recited in the company of other believers. Muslims may say their prayers anywhere. Third, Muslims must fast between sunrise and sunset during Ramadan, the ninth month of the Muslim calendar. Fourth, Muslims must give generous donations of money and food to the needy in their community. Islam expects its followers to be kind to one another, especially to orphans and widows, and to work for the good of the entire Islamic community. Fifth, Muslims must make a pilgrimage to Mecca at least once in their lives if it is possible. As the focus of prayer and pilgrimage, Mecca quickly became the center of the Muslim world. The Qur'an affirmed Mecca's special role in Islam with these words:

> *Announce the Pilgrimage to the people. They will come to you on foot and riding along distant roads on lean and slender beasts, in order to reach the place of advantage (the Kaaba) for them, and to pronounce the name of God on appointed days over cattle he has given them as food; then eat the food and feed the needy and the poor. (Qur'an 22:26)*

With the spread of Islam to Persia, Asia, and parts of Europe in the seventh century, Muslims from many different lands encountered one another in Mecca, developing a shared Islamic identity.

While the Qur'an contains many examples of proper behavior for the community to follow, Muslims also looked to the prophet Muhammad's example as a guide. Muhammad taught his followers to struggle for the good of the Muslim community. This struggle is called *jihad*. Islam teaches that the duty of *jihad* should be fulfilled by the heart, the tongue, the hand, and the sword. The *jihad* of the heart consists of a spiritual purification by doing battle with the Devil and avoiding temptations to do evil. *Jihad* of the tongue requires believers to propagate the faith and of the hand to correct moral wrongs. The fourth way to fulfill one's duty is to employ the sword by waging war against unbelievers and enemies of Islam. They could either convert to Islam or submit to Islamic political rule by paying special taxes. If they rejected both options, they became subject to *jihad* of the sword. Most modern Muslim scholars understand *jihad* as waging war with one's inner self, but some Muslims have revived the concept of *jihad* of the sword in support of military engagements.

The Succession Crisis After Muhammad: Sunnis and Shi'ites

Muhammad had demonstrated a remarkable talent for leadership during his lifetime, but he did not choose anyone to succeed him. His death in 632 caused a profound crisis among his followers. Would the Islamic community stay united under a single new leader or break up into smaller groups? After many deliberations, Muslim elders chose the prophet's father-in-law, Abu Bakr, to lead them. Abu Bakr (r. 632–634) became the first caliph, or successor to Muhammad. The form of Islamic government that evolved under his leadership is called the caliphate°.

Most Muslims supported Abu Bakr, but some opposed him. One group claimed that Muhammad's son-in-law and cousin, Ali, should have become the first caliph instead. Other Arab tribes rejected not only Abu Bakr's succession, but Islam itself. They rebelled, claiming that their membership in the Islamic community had been valid only when Muhammad was alive. Abu Bakr crushed these forces in a struggle called the Wars of Apostasy (a word meaning renunciation of a previous faith). By the time of his death in 634, Abu Bakr had brought most of Arabia back under his

The Kaaba in Mecca

In pre-Islamic times, Arabs worshiped a large, black stone at the Kaaba shrine in the center of Mecca. When Muhammad established Islam in Mecca in 629, he rejected the polytheist past and transformed the Kaaba into the holiest place in the Islamic world, revered as the House of God. Muslim teachers interpreted polytheist rituals that continued under Islam, such as walking around the Kaaba seven times, as symbols of the Muslim believer's entry into God's presence. Muslims from all over the world make pilgrimages to the Kaaba. These journeys foster a sense of shared religious identity among them, no matter where their homelands lie.

"Judgment Belongs to God Alone": The Battle and Arbitration at Siffin

On a spring day in 657, two Muslim armies confronted each other at Siffin, a village on the Euphrates River in Mesopotamia. The armies were commanded by men who had been longtime rivals, the caliph Ali (r. 656–661) and Muawiya, the governor of Syria. Their rivalry stemmed from Muawiya's refusal to accept Ali's authority as caliph. The Battle of Siffin became a defining moment in the development of the Islamic state. Basic Islamic ideas about divine judgment were put to the test, leading to passionate debate about how God makes his judgment known to Muslims.

Ali had taken power after the assassination of his predecessor, Caliph Uthman, in 656. The murder went unpunished, but many people considered Ali responsible because when he became caliph he appointed officials known to have taken part in the murder and because he had never disavowed the crime. Uthman belonged to the influential Umayyad clan, and his supporters and family felt an obligation to avenge their kinsman's death. Chief among Ali's opponents was Muawiya, a leading member of the Umayyad clan. Muawiya maintained a strong army and powerful support in Syria.

The immediate provocation of the confrontation between Muawiya and Ali was Uthman's murder, but the men's quarrel also stemmed from tensions about status and membership in the Muslim community. The earliest converts to Islam and their descendants believed that their association with Muhammad entitled them to greater status than the many new non-Arab converts to the religion, most of whom supported Ali. Resenting Ali's popularity among the newer members of the Islamic community, the early converts supported Muawiya. Further support for Muawiya came from many tribal leaders who opposed the caliph's growing authority.

The new converts to Islam also had complaints. In their view, the earliest Muslims, including the Umayyad clan, unfairly enjoyed a privileged position in the Islamic community even though all Muslims were supposed to be treated equally.

When Ali and Muawiya confronted each other at Siffin, they hesitated to fight because many of their soldiers felt strongly that Muslims should not shed the blood of other Muslims. As one of Ali's followers said,

> It is one of the worst wrongs and most terrible trials that we should be sent against our own people and they against us. . . . Yet, if we do not assist our community and act faithfully toward our leader, we deny our faith, and if we do that, we abandon our honor and extinguish our fire.[1]

So for three months, the armies engaged in only occasional skirmishes.

Finally, in July 657, real fighting broke out. Ali encouraged his men with these words: "Be steadfast! May God's spirit descend on you, and may God make you firm with conviction so that he who is put to flight knows that he displeases his God. . . . "

The furious battle came to a sudden halt in July when Muawiya's soldiers held up pages of the Qur'an on the ends of their spears and appealed for arbitration. When Ali's men saw this symbolic gesture, they stopped fighting and demanded that their leader settle his differences with Muawiya peacefully through arbitration.

Mediation of conflicts by third-party arbitrators frequently occurred among Arab tribes. Muhammad himself had earned renown as a skilled mediator before Islam was revealed to him. However, the arbitration between Ali and Muawiya failed to resolve the conflict. The two men and their armies separated without having reached an agreement. Ali continued to rule as caliph for six more years, but his authority declined rapidly because many Arabs interpreted his willingness to go to arbitration as a sign of weakness. In 661 Ali was assassinated.

In contrast, Muawiya's power grew after the Battle of Siffin. He openly claimed the caliphate for himself and began making deals with the tribal leaders for their support in order to form his own coalition. After Ali's assassination, Muawiya became caliph.

The fact that the arbitration at Siffin occurred at all had long-lasting consequences. Most important, a small but influential Muslim faction emerged when the two leaders first confronted one another. They objected to Ali's initial agreement to arbitration, arguing that God was the only true arbitrator. They believed that Ali should pull out of the arbitration and submit to God's judgment, which they believed could be known only through battle. These Muslims wanted to fight Muawiya in order to find out what God wanted. This splinter group became known as the Kharijites or "seceders." The Kharijites expressed their view in the phrase "Judgment belongs to God alone."

The Qur'an
Muslim artists devised elaborate Arabic scripts to enhance the beauty of the Qur'an, the holiest text of their faith. This page of the Qur'an, dating to the Umayyad caliphate, is written in the elegant and highly decorative Kufic script.

The Kharijites went one step further in their beliefs. They declared not only that Ali was wrong to accept human arbitration, but that he and his supporters should no longer be considered Muslims. In their view, Ali and his supporters had committed an unpardonable grave sin by accepting arbitration. The Kharijites claimed that they were the only true Muslims. Small in numbers, they established several independent communities in the Islamic Empire and turned their backs on Islamic society. They lived as bandits until the tenth century, when they disappeared from the historical record.

Other Muslims who disagreed with the Kharijites proclaimed that neither the Kharijites nor any other human being could know whether sinners were still Muslims in the eyes of God. In their opinion, believers would discover God's judgment on these matters only at the End of Days, when God will judge all humanity.

Question of Justice

During this early period of the Islamic Empire, how did different Arab beliefs about how God makes his judgment known influence the Arabic sense of the proper forms of human justice?

Taking It Further

W. M. Watt. *The Formative Period of Islamic Thought.* 1973. This account discusses the formation of sects and political groups in early Islamic history.

control, but disputes between the followers of Ali and those of Abu Bakr led to a permanent split within Islam between the minority Shi'ites, who followed Ali, and the majority Sunnis, who followed Abu Bakr. While the Shi'ites and Sunnis both considered the caliphate a hereditary office restricted to members of Muhammad's Hashimite clan of the Quraysh tribe, the Shi'ites believed that only direct descendants of Muhammad through his daughter Fatima and son-in-law Ali should rule the Islamic community. The Sunnis, in contrast, devised a more flexible theory of succession that allowed them later to accept the Abbasid caliphs and even foreign caliphs. The caliphate developed into an office that combined some governmental and some religious responsibilities.

In the course of the wars among Muslims after the death of Muhammad, Abu Bakr created a highly trained Muslim army eager to spread the faith and gain additional wealth and power. The rich Persian and Byzantine Empires became irresistible targets. Under the leadership of the second caliph, Umar (r. 634–644), Muslim forces moved north from the Arabian peninsula and invaded the rich territories of the Byzantine and Persian Empires. As discussed earlier, they seized Syria in 636. The next year they crushed the main Persian army and captured the Persian capital city, Ctesiphon. Within just a decade Islamic troops had conquered Egypt and all of Persia as far east as India. Meanwhile, Muslim navies, manned by subject Egyptian and Syrian sailors and Arab troops, seized Cyprus, raided in the eastern Mediterranean, and defeated a large Byzantine fleet. Muslim armies were racing across North Africa without serious opposition when civil war broke out in 655 and temporarily halted their advance.

Two groups struggled for control of the caliphate during this six-year civil war. On one side were Muhammad's son-in-law Ali, who had become caliph in 656, and his supporters, the Shi'ites. On the other side was the wealthy Umayyad family, who opposed him and whose supporters were Sunnis. The lasting cracks in the unity of Islam broke open over the proper succession to the caliphate, represented in the two parties of Shi'ites and the Sunnis. In 661 the Umayyads arranged Ali's assassination and took control of the caliphate, creating a new dynasty that would last until 750. The Umayyads established Damascus in Syria as their new capital city, which shifted Islam's power center away from Mecca.

The Umayyad Caliphate

The Umayyad dynasty produced brilliant administrators and generals. At the end of the civil war in 661, these talented leaders consolidated their control of conquered territories and established peaceful conditions in the empire. Then they resumed wars of conquest to enhance the Islamic state's power and to gain wealth.

The "House of War"

As we saw in Chapter 5, the Romans distinguished themselves from uncivilized "barbarians" who had not yet come under Roman rule. In a similar fashion, the Umayyads viewed the world as consisting of two parts: the "House of Islam," which contained the territories under their political control, and the "House of War," which included all non-Muslim lands, which they hoped to conquer. By 700, Muslim armies had rolled west across North Africa as far as the Atlantic Ocean in order to conquer non-Muslim lands.

Eleven years later, they invaded much of Spain and overthrew the Visigothic kingdom in just one battle. From Spain they attacked France, but in 732, Charles Martel "the Hammer," leading a Frankish army, stopped their advance into Europe at the Battle of Poitiers. After their defeat, the Umayyad armies retreated to their territories in Spain.

Umayyad caliphs attempted to conquer the Christian kingdom of Nubia south of Egypt to obtain its gold and spread Islam. The Nubians successfully repelled the Muslim invaders, however, and in 661 a lasting peace treaty was signed between the Umayyad caliphate and Nubian kingdoms. This treaty was unique, because the Nubians belonged to the "House of War," which meant that they were enemies still to be conquered. While struggling with the Nubians, Umayyad armies continued to strike at the Byzantine Empire. After seizing Egypt and Syria, they made regular attacks on the Byzantine territories, sometimes reaching as far as Constantinople, which remained protected by its formidable walls.

Umayyad armies moved eastward with equal speed and success. They reached the territories of modern Pakistan and India and even penetrated central Asia, where they captured the caravan city of Samarkand. During the Umayyad caliphate, this city served as a commercial hub on the trade route to China. In 751, just after the death of the last Umayyad caliph, Muslim armies defeated Chinese troops of the expansionist Chinese Tang dynasty at the Battle of Talas in central Asia. Despite their victory, the Muslims decided to halt their expansion and did not advance further into Chinese-controlled areas in central Asia. One consequence of this encounter was the introduction of paper from China into the Islamic world, from where it spread into Europe 500 years later.

Like the battle of Poitiers, which marked the limit of the Umayyads' expansion into western Europe, the battle of Talas marked the limit of Muslim military expansion into central Asia. For the next four centuries, these borders would define the Islamic world.

Governing the Islamic Empire

In less than a century the Umayyads had built an empire that reached from southern Spain to central Asia and India.

The Umayyads developed a highly centralized regime that changed the political character of the Muslim community. The first Umayyad caliph, Muawiya (r. 661–680), established a hereditary monarchy to ensure orderly succession of power. This was a major change in the caliphate. Unlike the first four caliphs, who ruled by virtue of their prestige (as did Arab tribal chiefs) and more importantly by the consent of the community, the Umayyads made the caliphate an authoritarian institution. Because of this, the soldiers protested that the Umayyads had turned "God's servants into slaves," corrupted the faith, and seized the property of God. A second civil war broke out (683–692) between these protestors and the Umayyads, but the Umayyads emerged victorious.

To control their vast empire, Umayyad rulers were obliged to create a new administrative system that both borrowed from and supplanted Byzantine and Persian institutions. The Umayyads designed new provinces that replaced old Byzantine and Persian administrative units. In addition, the Umayyads created a professional bureaucracy based in the capital of Damascus to meet their expanding financial needs and to ensure that the taxes collected in the provinces came to the central treasury. Most of the administrators were local officials who had served the Byzantine or Persian Empire. Many of them were non-Muslims, but a large number converted to Islam with Umayyad encouragement. These officials provided significant administrative continuity between the conquered empires and the caliphate.

After the Umayyads made Arabic the official language of their empire, Arabic gradually replaced the languages of the conquered peoples. Only in Iran did Persian survive as a widely spoken language, and even there Arabic served as the language of government. In the Umayyad caliphate, the Arabic language functioned as Latin had done in the ancient Roman Empire: It provided a common language for diverse subject peoples. By 800 Arabic had become the essential language of administration and international commerce in lands from Morocco to central Asia.

The rapid expansion of Islam created problems for Umayyad rulers eager to consolidate their power. Arab armies had conquered enormous territories, but Arabs were only a small minority among the huge non-Muslim populations. Umayyad policy was to establish garrison cities in conquered lands to hold down the more numerous local populations. Just as Greek colonists followed in the footsteps of Alexander the Great in the fourth century B.C.E., Arab settlers from the Arabian peninsula migrated to newly conquered lands in great numbers. They established themselves first in the garrison towns where government officials were based and then became a significant presence in major cities, such as Alexandria, Jerusalem, and Antioch. Some immigrants were nomadic tribes that adopted a settled way of life for the first time. Others were farmers from the highlands of Yemen, who brought sophisticated irrigation systems and agricultural traditions to their new homes. Arab migrations to cities ended many old Arab traditions of nomadic life.

DOCUMENT

The Rules of War According to the Muslim Conquerors

In 632, Abu Bakr composed a book called the Rules of War that makes clear how the warriors of Islam were to conduct themselves in battle:

O people! I charge you with ten rules; learn them well!

Do not betray or misappropriate any part of the booty; do not practice treachery or mutilation. Do not kill a young child, an old man, or a woman. Do not uproot or burn palms or cut down fruitful trees. Do not slaughter a sheep or a cow or a camel, except for food. You will meet people who have set themselves apart in hermitages; leave them to accomplish the purpose for which they have done this. You will come upon people who will bring you dishes with various kinds of foods. If you partake of them, pronounce God's name over what you eat. You will meet people who have shaved the crown of their heads, leaving a band of hair around it (monks). Strike them with the sword.

Go in God's name, and may God protect you from sword and pestilence.

Source: Al-Tabari, *The History of the Prophets and Kings* I.1850, in Bernard Lewis, ed., *Islam from the Prophet Muhammad to the Capture of Constantinople, vol. 1: Politics and War* (New York: Walker and Company, 1974), p. 213.

In addition to settling in existing cities, Arabs founded many new ones. In Egypt they built Fustat, which would later become Cairo. In North Africa, they established Kairouan in Tunisia. In Mesopotamia they created Basra, an important port city, as well as Kufa on the Euphrates River. Though built on a smaller scale than the major urban centers of the Roman and Persian Empires, most new Arab cities drew from Hellenistic town planning. They had a square shape, walls with gates on all four sides, towers, and a central plaza. In the heart of all of these cities, Umayyad caliphs built a mosque to emphasize the central role of Islam in community life and to celebrate their own authority. The magnificent mosques in Damascus, Jerusalem, and other cities were intended to surpass the grand Christian churches in prestige.

Interior of the Blue Mosque in Istanbul, Turkey

In formerly Byzantine cities such as Jerusalem, Antioch, and Alexandria, Muslim officials introduced or permitted significant structural changes, especially in urban street patterns. Winding, narrow alleys in which camels could easily maneuver replaced the long, straight, wide streets

The Dome of the Rock in Jerusalem
The Dome of the Rock, an eight-sided building with a gilded dome, dominates Jerusalem's skyline. Completed in 692 on the Temple Mount (the site of the Jewish Temple destroyed by the Romans in 69 C.E.), the building encloses a rock projecting from the floor. Scholars disagree about the structure's original purpose. A Muslim of the tenth century thought it had been built as a statement of Islam's triumph at the heart of the holiest Christian city. During the sixteenth century the story began to circulate that when Muhammad ascended to heaven at night, his winged horse took one leap from Mecca to the rock and then sprang skyward. The artists who completed the dome's interior mosaics probably came from Constantinople, the only place where art of such high quality was being produced. The mosaic patterns also draw from contemporary styles in the Mediterranean world and Persia.

appropriate for wagons that typified Hellenistic and Roman cities. Wheeled vehicles gradually disappeared from use in cities where alleys predominated. Especially in markets, the old, wide streets and sidewalks filled up with small shops, and pedestrians walked through narrow alleys behind the shops. In many of these cities, tightly packed bazaars connected by narrow alleys persist to this day.

Patterns of daily activity also changed under Muslim rule. With Islam now dominating public life, cities ceased to celebrate Greco-Roman culture. Theaters fell out of use because there was no Arabic tradition of publicly performed drama and comedy. The exercise fields, sports buildings, libraries, schools, and gymnasiums surviving from the Classical Age were also abandoned or adapted for other purposes. Revenues once earmarked for gymnasiums and public buildings now went to local mosques. These centers of Islamic urban culture replaced the forums and agoras of the Roman and Greek world as the chief public space for men. Mosque schools provided education for the community. Muslims gathered at mosques for public festivals and,

of course, for religious worship. In their capacity as administrative centers, mosques provided courtrooms, assembly halls, and treasuries for the community. Judges, tax collectors, bureaucrats, and emissaries from the caliph conducted their affairs in the mosque precinct.

During the Umayyad caliphate, the majority of Muslims were farmers and artisans who lived in prosperous villages. Many of these small communities stood on the vast estates of rich landowners who controlled the workers' labor. The caliphate also sponsored huge land reclamation projects on the edges of the desert in Syria and Mesopotamia. Officials of the imperial government drew revenues directly from the villages that sprang up in these new farmlands.

Becoming Muslims

Islam sharply defined the differences between Muslims and their non-Muslim subjects. The conquerors understood themselves as a community of faith. Only individuals who converted to Islam could gain full participation in the Islamic community. Their ethnicity did not matter. Therefore Muslims defined their new subjects by their religions, something Egyptians, Assyrians, Persians, Greeks, or Romans before Constantine had never done. The Qur'an states that "there is no compulsion in religion," meaning that monotheists (Jews, Christians, and Zoroastrians) cannot be forced to convert to Islam. These monotheists were required to accept Islamic political authority, pay a special tax, and accept some other restrictions. However, Muslims viewed polytheists differently. Polytheists could not be tolerated and had the choice of conversion to the Muslim faith or death.

Throughout the Umayyad period, the number of Muslims grew slowly, reaching perhaps only 10 percent of the total population. Perhaps most of the first converts had been Christians, Jews, and Zoroastrians who willingly accepted the new religion. Other converts were slaves in the households of their Muslim owners whose willingness to convert is less easy to determine. Still others were villagers who migrated to garrison cities and converted in the hope of sharing in the spoils of conquest—and avoiding the taxes demanded of non-Muslims. Their eagerness to convert so threatened the tax base that some Muslim officials refused to acknowledge their conversion and sent them back to their villages.

Conversion to Islam increased as Muslim armies fought their way across North Africa. In the huge area that stretches from Egypt to the Atlantic Ocean, the Muslims conquered many distinct polytheist ethnic groups whom the Arab conquerors collectively called Berbers. Faced with the choice of conversion or death, huge numbers of Berbers joined the victorious Muslim armies. Islam unified the Berber populations and brought them into a wider Islamic world. With the aid of these troops, Islamic power spread even more quickly across North Africa and into Spain.

Peoples of the Book

How do empires govern subject peoples? Do they have the same privileges and obligations as their rulers? Can they freely enter into the society of their masters? Previous chapters show how the Assyrians, Persians, Hellenistic Greeks, and Romans answered these questions. Though their solutions differed, none of these great empires considered the religions of their subjects when deciding their place in society.

By distinguishing their subjects on religious, not ethnic grounds, the Umayyad caliphate took a different approach to governing their subject peoples. Jews, Christians, and Zoroastrians constituted the main religions among conquered peoples. Islamic law called them "Peoples of the Book" because each of these religious communities had a sacred book. They had lower status than Muslims, but they were free to practice their religion. Islamic law forbade their persecution or forcible conversion. For this reason, large communities of Jews, Christians, and Zoroastrians lived peacefully under Muslim rule.

Several Christian communities, separated by old controversies about doctrinal issues, coexisted within the Islamic Empire because the caliphate was indifferent to which Christian doctrine they followed. Followers of the Chalcedonian Orthodox church changed the language of prayer from Greek to Syriac and then to Arabic. Though these Christians had no direct ties with Constantinople, they followed the Byzantine emperors' Chalcedonian Orthodoxy. Thus their church was called the Melkite, or Royal, church. The Melkite church continues to be the largest Christian community in Muslim lands in the Middle East today. Another Christian church, called the Jacobite church, was formed by Anti-Chalcedonian (Monophysite) Christians in the late sixth century, as discussed in Chapter 6. The Jacobite Bible and prayers are in Syriac. The Nestorian church, comprising Christians who emphasized Jesus' humanity rather than the combination of his humanity and divinity, also flourished under Muslim rule in Persia, Syria, and northern Arabia. Nestorians established communities in India, central Asia, and China. The variety of Christian communities in the caliphate was greater than in Byzantium and the Latin Christian kingdoms where conformity to the dogmas of one particular Church, Orthodox or Catholic, was enforced by law.

Jewish communities also flourished throughout Umayyad lands, notably in southern Spain and Mesopotamia. Jews found their subordinate but protected status under Islam preferable to the open persecution they suffered in many Christian kingdoms. In Persia, Zoroastrian communities fared less well under Islamic rule. As they were slowly forced into remote regions of central Iran, their numbers gradually dwindled. In the tenth century, many Zoroastrians migrated to India, where they are known today as Farsis, a word that means "Persians."

Commercial Encounters

The Umayyads managed to transform the economic system of the empire to strengthen their hand as rulers. From the time of the first conquests, revenues were derived primarily from the huge amounts of gold and silver taken in war, taxes, and contributions made by Muslims to support widows and orphans. To increase their revenues further, Umayyad rulers introduced a land tax for Muslim landowners, in imitation of Byzantine and Persian systems of taxation. Even the proud Arab tribesmen, for whom paying taxes was a humiliation because it implied subordination to a greater authority, had to pay taxes, though not as much as non-Muslims. With land tax revenues Umayyad caliphs could afford to establish a standing professional army. This further reduced the fighting role of individual Arab tribes, enabling caliphs to cement their authority more firmly.

Long-distance overland trade rapidly expanded due to the peaceful conditions achieved after years of fighting. Although merchants could travel safely from Morocco to central Asia and earn great sums, such long-distance expeditions were expensive. The Qur'an approves of mercantile trading, and Islamic law permitted letters of credit, loans, and other financial instruments that made commerce over huge distances possible long before they were known in Christian Europe.

Umayyad rulers further stimulated international commerce by creating a new currency that imitated Persian and Byzantine coinage. The Persian silver *drahm* (a word derived from the Greek *drachma*) inspired the Umayyad *dirham,* which became the standard coin throughout the caliphate by the 780s. Muslim merchants, as well as businessmen as far away as western Europe, Scandinavia, and Russia, used silver dirhams to pay for goods. For gold coinage the Umayyads minted the *dinar* (a word derived from a Roman coin, the *denarius*). Like the dirham, the dinar also became a standard coin in the caliphate as well as in distant lands. Merchants could depend on the value of this currency wherever they did business.

In addition to supporting long-distance overland trade by camel caravans, Umayyad caliphs also developed maritime trade. The Egyptian city of Alexandria became the chief Mediterranean naval base for Arab commercial shipping. The Syrian port cities of Acre and Tyre also contributed to maritime shipping in the eastern Mediterranean region. The Umayyads maintained peaceful conditions in the Persian Gulf and the Indian Ocean. Arab merchants

Designing Muslim Coins: The Encounter with Byzantine Prototypes

In the early years of the Umayyad state, caliphs experimented with the design of Islamic coins. Because Arabs had no tradition of minting coins, they borrowed freely from the images they saw on Persian and Byzantine coins. Then they made the necessary adjustments to change Christian or Persian symbols to Islamic ones. On a dinar of Abd al-Malik (r. 685–705) (top), the artist changed the Byzantine emperor Heraclius and his heirs, who carry globes with small crosses (shown on the back of a Byzantine coin at bottom left), to the caliph and his heirs, holding globes without crosses. On the Islamic coin's reverse side, Muhammad's scepter replaced the Christian cross (shown bottom right, on the back of another Byzantine coin). By the end of his reign, Abd al-Malik did away with images altogether and decorated his coins entirely with written quotations from the Qur'an.

Islamic coin

(front)   (back)

Byzantine prototypes

(back)   (back)

sailed past Zanzibar and India to Canton in southern China, following sea routes established by Persian navigators. Arab traders also sailed down the coast of East Africa to obtain slaves and natural resources brought from the interior. In later centuries Muslim navigators reached Malaysia, Indochina, and eventually Indonesia and the Philippines.

By 850, Muslims in cities throughout the caliphate could buy many exotic luxuries. These goods included panther skins, rubies, and coconuts from India; paper, silk, fine ceramics, eunuchs (castrated men), slaves, and marble workers from China; hawks from North Africa; Egyptian papyrus; and furs and sugar cane from central Asia. People could also buy less-expensive fabrics and manufactured items crafted locally.

Arab traders also brought back valuable ideas and scientific knowledge from the peoples encountered through trade in the East. Many Arabic nautical terms, which were picked up by sailors, derive from Persian. By late in the eighth century Arabic intellectual life became much more

sophisticated as scholars translated Persian and Indian astronomical works into Arabic, the beginning of an explosion of scientific knowledge in the Islamic world.

Throughout the formative period of Islam and the Umayyad caliphate, Muslims took firm hold of territories stretching from North Africa to central Asia, creating a single political realm there for the first time in history. The inhabitants of the entire Arabian peninsula, with their trade connections to Africa and Asia, joined the peoples of the Middle East and the Mediterranean in an intricate system of commerce and government.

The principal reason for the rapid spread of the religion of the prophet Muhammad was the capacity of his message to unify many diverse communities in Arabia. Especially during its early centuries, Islam disseminated Muhammad's message by both force and persuasion.

The Breakup of the Umayyad Caliphate

The Umayyad clan, who governed a vast Islamic Empire between 661 and 750, were never firmly in control of the entire Islamic world and faced a series of rebellions, especially from the Shi'ites and the Abbasid clan, who were descendants of Muhammad's uncle. These two groups—the Shi'ites and the Abbasids—were briefly allied in mutual hostility to the Umayyads. However, after the last Umayyad caliph died in a battle in 750, the Abbasids seized the caliphate and Shi'ite support for the Abbasids collapsed.

Once they had secured the caliphate, the Abbasids engaged in a campaign to exterminate the entire Umayyad family. The only Umayyad to escape the death order, Abd al-Rahman I (r. 756–788), fled to Spain where he founded what would later become the Umayyad caliphate of Córdoba. In the tenth century the Fatimids established the Shi'ite caliphate in North Africa, which claimed direct succession from Muhammad's daughter, Fatima, and opposed both the Abbasids and the Umayyads of Spain. From this time on, the Muslim world split apart into rival caliphates.

The Abbasid Caliphate

The Abbasid caliphate (750–945) quickly altered the character of the Muslim world. In 762–763 a new capital was established in Baghdad. In this new location, the Abbasids were exposed to the ceremonial and administrative traditions of Persia, which helped expand the intellectual horizons of the caliphs, their courtiers, and bureaucrats. The Abbasid caliphate continued to be dominated by Arabs, and Arabic remained the language of the court. Nevertheless, the Abbasids considered all Muslims equals, whether Arabs or not. This belief fostered a distinctive Islamic civilization that fused ideas and practices derived from Arabic, Persian, Byzantine, and Syrian cultures. Despite opposition from purists, the Abbasids married non-Arabs and recruited Turks, Slavs, and other non-Muslims to serve as palace guards.

The Abbasid caliphs expanded their control over society, but they were far from despots. The caliph was first and foremost an emir—that is, the commander of a professional army. He was also responsible for internal security, which meant suppressing rebellions, supervising officials, and making sure taxes were honestly collected. But the caliph did not become involved in other public institutions, such as the mosques, hospitals, and schools. The principal exception was the office of market inspector, through which the caliph guaranteed fair business practices. In this commitment to the integrity of markets and trade, the Islamic caliphate was considerably more advanced than either Byzantium, where privileged monopolies dominated the economy, or the Latin states where a market economy hardly existed.

Trade Routes in the Medieval Islamic World

The period of Abbasid greatness lasted about a century (754–861), and its eclectic nature is reflected in its literature. The famous *Arabian Nights*, stories written down for the caliph Harun al-Rashid (r. 786–809), were based on Hellenistic, Jewish, Indian, and Arab legends. The *Arabian Nights* and the rich tradition of Arabic poetry, which often recounted tales of thwarted love, in turn influenced the western Christian poetry of romantic love. Caliph Harun al-Rashid began the grand project of translating into Arabic the literature of ancient Greece, as well as texts from Syria, India, and Persia.

Philosophical and scientific inquiry thrived under Caliph al-Mamun (r. 813–833), who had an astronomical observatory built in Baghdad and who appreciated the work of al-Kindi (who died sometime after 870), the first outstanding Islamic philosopher. Al-Kindi grappled with questions specific to Islam but also with the works of Aristotle and problems in astrology, medicine, optics, arithmetic, cooking, and metallurgy—topics that made him well known outside the Islamic world. The work of the Arabic translators in the ninth and tenth centuries created a crucial cultural link between the ancient and medieval worlds. The Muslims supplied Arabic translations of ancient Greek and Syriac texts to a later generation of Jews and Christians in Spain, who translated them into Latin. These second- and third-hand Latin translations of ancient philosophy and science became the core of the university curriculum in western Europe during the twelfth century.

Abbasid political power ceased in 945 when a clan of rough tribesmen from northwestern Iran seized Baghdad. The Abbasid caliphs remained figureheads, and there were occasional attempts to reinvigorate the caliphate, but its greatness as a ruling institution had ceased. However, the caliphate remained a vital symbol of Islamic unity and survived as formal institution, at least, for another 300 years.

Islamic Civilization in Europe

During the eighth and ninth centuries the Muslim armies chipped away at Christian territories in Europe. Unlike their fellow Muslims in the Middle East and North Africa, most of the Muslims in Europe conducted themselves more as raiders than conquerors. They plundered and pillaged but did not stay long and did not attempt a mass conversion of Christians to Islam. The effects of these raids, however, cannot be underestimated. The populations of many Mediterranean cities were vulnerable and diminished almost to the point of disappearing as urban life became impossible. The only hope for survival was to disperse into the countryside, where families could live off the land and find protection with one of the many local lords who built castles for defense.

The significant exceptions to the pattern of raiding were in Sicily and Spain. Between 703 and 1060, Arab farmers and merchants migrated to Sicily from North Africa, and Islam spread among the general population even though pockets of Greek and Latin Christianity remained. In Spain,

Muslim conquests in the early eighth century brought the peninsula into the orbit of Islam except for the mountains and coastal regions of the extreme north.

Sicily and Spain became the principal borderlands through which Arabic learning and science filtered into Catholic Europe. These borderlands became zones of particularly intense cultural interaction, where several languages were spoken and where in accord with Muslim toleration for other monotheist religions Christians and Jews were allowed to observe their own faiths. Although small, Muslim Sicily and Spain were among the most dynamic places in Europe during the eighth to early eleventh centuries. No Christian city in western Europe could rival Córdoba in size and prosperity. Even within the Muslim world, which enjoyed many splendid cities, the only city comparable to Baghdad was Córdoba. A German nun visiting Córdoba in Muslim Spain during the tenth century thought the city embodied "the majesty and adornment of the world, the wondrous capital . . . radiating in affluence of all earthly blessings."[2] During the tenth century the Umayyad caliphate of Córdoba became the most important intellectual capital in western Europe, renowned for the learning of both its Muslim and Jewish scholars.

Córdoba's fame derived from the extensive authority and magnificent building projects encouraged by the caliph Abd al-Rahman III (r. 912–961) and his three successors.

With an ethnically mixed population of more than 100,000, Córdoba boasted 700 mosques, 3,000 public baths, 5,000 silk looms, and 70 libraries. The caliph alone possessed a library housing more than 400,000 volumes. The streets of the city were paved and illuminated at night, the best houses enjoyed indoor plumbing, and the rich enjoyed country villas as vacation retreats. (In contrast, the city of Rome did not erect streetlamps for another thousand years.) Besides the great mosque, which was one of the most famous religious monuments in Islam, the architectural centerpiece of the city was Madinat az-Zahra, a colossal 400-room palace that Abd al-Rahman III built for his favorite concubine, Zahra. Adorned with marble and semiprecious stones from Constantinople, the palace took twenty years to build and housed 13,000 household servants in addition to the diplomats and courtiers who attended the caliph.

The lasting influence of the golden age of Córdoba can be found in the legacy of the poets, scientists, physicians, astronomers, and architects who thrived under the caliphs'

DOCUMENT

A Humble Christian Monk Meets the Caliph of Córdoba

In 953 the German emperor Otto I sent the abbot John of Gorze on a diplomatic mission to the court of Abd al-Rahman III, the caliph of Córdoba, in order to enlist his help in stamping out piracy in the western Mediterranean. Unfortunately for John, because the letters he carried from the emperor were overtly hostile to Islam, he was put under house arrest for three years. The caliph also could not understand the commitment to poverty and filth required of a Christian monk and interpreted John's refusal to dress elegantly as a calculated slight. However, John's pious sincerity eventually changed the caliph's mind. In recognition of the power of John's convictions, the caliph extended him a sign of exceptional respect by allowing him to kiss the royal hand.

John, released from almost three years of cloistered seclusion, was ordered to appear in the royal presence. When he was told by the messengers to make himself presentable to royalty by cutting his hair, washing his body, and putting on clean clothes, he refused, lest they should tell the caliph that he had changed in his essential being beneath a mere change of clothes. The caliph then sent John ten pounds in coin, so that he might purchase clothing to put on and be decent in the royal eyes, for it was not right for people to be presented in slovenly dress. John could not at first decide whether to accept the money, but eventually he reasoned that it would be better spent for the relief of the poor, and sent thanks for the caliph's generosity and for the solicitude he had deigned to show him. The monk added in his reply: "I do not despise royal gifts, but it is not permitted for a monk to wear anything other than his usual habit, nor indeed could I put on any garment of a color other than black." When this was reported to the caliph, he remarked: "In this reply I perceive his unyielding firmness of mind. Even if he comes dressed in a sack, I will most gladly receive him." . . .

When John arrived at the dais where the caliph was seated alone—almost like a godhead accessible to none or to very few—he saw everything draped with rare coverings, and floor-tiles stretching evenly to the walls. The caliph himself reclined upon a most richly ornate couch. As John came into his presence, the caliph stretched out a hand to be kissed. The hand-kissing not being customarily granted to any of his own people or to foreigners, and never to persons of low and middling mark, the caliph none the less gave John his hand to kiss.

Source: From Colin Smith, *Christians and Moors in Spain, Volume 1* (Aris and Phillips, 1988).

Mosque of Córdoba
The great mosque was one of the wonders of the world during the tenth century. Because Islam prohibited the depiction of the human body, mosques were embellished with geometrical forms and quotations from the Qur'an. The repetition of multiple arches creates an intricate pattern that changes as the viewer moves about in the space.

patronage. Despite some tensions among Muslims and Jews, many of the prominent intellectuals in the caliphs' court were Arabized Jews. Typical of the many non-Muslims who served Arab rulers, Hasdai ibn Shaprut (915–970), who was probably a Jew, became famous for his medical skills, in particular his antidotes for poisons. In the caliphs' court the demand for his cures was strong, because several princes had fallen victim to conspiracies hatched in the palace harem or had been poisoned by a lover. The trust that Hasdai gained from his medical skills led to political appointments to deal with sensitive customs and diplomatic disputes. Both Muslim and Christian rulers considered Jews like Hasdai politically neutral, making them prized as diplomatic envoys. The Jew Samuel ibn Nagrela (993–1055) astonishingly rose to the position of vizier (minister) of the neighboring Muslim kingdom of

Granada. An able Hebrew poet, biblical commentator, and philosopher, Samuel ibn Nagrela was also an effective commander of Muslim armies. His brilliant career reflected the value Muslims placed on learning and skill.

During the early eleventh century after a series of succession disputes that led to the murder of several caliphs, the caliphate of Córdoba splintered into numerous small states. The disunity of Muslim Spain provided opportunities for the stubborn little Christian states to push against the frontiers of their opulent Muslim neighbors. The kingdom of Navarre under Sancho I (r. 1000–1035) was the first to achieve dramatic success against Muslims. After Sancho's death the division of his conquests created the three kingdoms of Navarre, Aragon, and Castile. During the reign of Alfonso VI (r. 1072–1109), Castile became the dominant military power on the peninsula. Forcing Muslims to pay tribute to him to finance further wars and gathering assistance from French knights eager for plunder and French monks ardent for converts, Alfonso launched a massive campaign known as the Spanish Reconquest° that led to the capture of Toledo in 1085. The center of Spanish Christianity before the Muslim conquests, Toledo provided Alfonso with a glorious prize that made him famous throughout Christian Europe (see Map 7.4).

The loss of Toledo so shocked the Muslim states that they invited into Spain a sect of warriors called the Almoravids from northern Africa. The Almoravids defeated Alfonso VI and temporarily halted the Spanish Reconquest in 1086.

CHRONOLOGY

The New World of Islam

ca. 570	Muhammad born in Mecca
622	Muhammad flees to Medina (the *Hijra*)
632	Muhammad dies in Medina
640–642	Byzantines abandon Alexandria; Muslims conquer Egypt
651	Muslims conquer Persia
661	Caliph Ali is assassinated
661–750	Umayyad caliphate
703–1060	Arab occupation of Sicily
713	Muslims conquer most of Spain
750–945	Abbasid caliphate
756–1031	Umayyad dynasty of Córdoba
After 870	Death of al-Kindi
1085	Christian capture of Toledo from Muslims

Map 7.4 Christian Reconquest of Muslim Spain
The Spanish Reconquest refers to the numerous military campaigns by the Christian kingdoms of northern Spain to capture the Muslim-controlled cities and kingdoms of southern Spain. This long, intermittent struggle began with the capture of Toledo in 1085 and lasted until Granada fell to Christian armies in 1492.

Christian Reconquest of Muslim Spain
Reconquered:
- Before 914
- 914–1080
- 1080–1130
- 1130–1210
- 1210–1250
- 1250–1480
- After 1480
- ✕ Major battles

The halt of active warfare against the Muslims provided the young Christian kingdoms time to mature by establishing the basic institutions of government. After the time of Alfonso VI, the Reconquest lost steam, and a few surviving remnants of Muslim power managed to hang on in Spain for another 400 years.

Conclusion

Three Cultural Realms

The death of the Byzantine emperor Justinian I in 565 marked the last time all the territory spanning from Spain to North Africa to Asia Minor would be united under one imperial ruler. The Persian Empire still menaced Byzantium's eastern frontier, and except for Italy and some coastal areas of Spain, western Europe was now ruled by Germanic kings. During the next two centuries western Europe, the Mediterranean world, and the Middle East as far as India and central Asia were utterly reconfigured politically and culturally. Part of that reconfiguration came about as new peoples migrated into central Europe and the Balkans from the steppe frontiers. As threatening as they were these new arrivals were eventually absorbed into the civilizations of the West through conversions to Christianity. By ca. 750, three new realms had come into sharp focus: the Christian Byzantine Empire based at Constantinople; the vast Umayyad caliphate created by Muhammad's Islamic followers; and, as the next chapter examines, Latin Christendom in western Europe, which was fragmented politically but united culturally by Christianity. Each of these regions was constituted as a community of religious faith, each of which had, at best, a limited toleration of other faiths. The cultural foundations they established as well as the divisions that emerged among them are still shaping the West today.

These three cultural realms of the West each borrowed from the heritage of ancient Rome, especially its network of cities, which survived most completely in the Mediterranean and the Middle East in the Byzantine and Islamic Empires. The three realms were each influenced by the reli-

gious traditions of antiquity, especially the emphasis on monotheism in Judaism. They each adapted parts of Roman law but reshaped it to suit changing needs and new cultural influences. The heritage of Rome remained strongest in Byzantium. Indeed, the Byzantines continued to call themselves Romans. But between the sixth and eleventh centuries these three cultural realms came to be distinguished by the language that dominated intellectual and religious life and by the forms of monotheism practiced. In Byzantium the Greek language and Orthodox Christianity with its distinctively elaborate ceremonies defined the culture. By the end of the Umayyad caliphate, the Arabic language was becoming widespread and many Islamic beliefs and practices were becoming standard over a wide area. In western Europe, many languages were spoken but Latin became the universal language of the Church and government.

The year 750 saw the end of the Umayyad caliphate and the limit of Muslim expansion in western Europe and central Asia. After that the Byzantine Empire struggled for survival. In the next chapter we will see how the kingdom of the Franks arrested Muslim incursions into western Europe. However, the very survival of many western European kingdoms was put to the test during the ninth and tenth centuries by yet more invasions and migrations from the Eurasian steppes and Scandinavia. By the end of the eleventh century the Latin kingdoms of western Europe had gathered sufficient cohesion and military strength to launch a vast counterstroke against Islam in the form of the Crusades.

Suggestions for Further Reading

For a comprehensive listing of suggested readings, please go to www.ablongman.com/levack2e/chapter7

Bowersock, Glen, Peter Brown, and Oleg Grabar, eds. *Late Antiquity: A Guide to the Post-Classical World.* 1999. Interpretive essays combined with encyclopedia entries make this a starting point for discussion.

Brown, Thomas S. *Gentlemen and Officers: Imperial Administration and Aristocratic Power in Byzantine Italy,* A.D. *554–800.* 1984. The basic study of Byzantine rule in Italy between Justinian and Charlemagne.

Bulliet, Richard W. *The Camel and the Wheel.* 1990. A fascinating investigation of the importance of the camel in history.

Cook, Michael. *Muhammad.* 1996. A short, incisive account of Muhammad's life that questions the traditional picture.

Cormack, Robin. *Writing in Gold: Byzantine Society and Its Icons.* 1985. An expert discussion of icons in the Byzantine world.

Donner, Fred M. *The Early Islamic Conquests.* 1981. Discusses the first phases of Islamic expansion.

Fletcher, Richard. *Moorish Spain.* 1992. Highly readable.

Franklin, Simon, and Jonathan Shepard. *The Emergence of Rus: 750–1200.* 1996. The standard text for this period.

Herrin, Judith. *The Formation of Christendom.* 2001. An exceptionally learned and lucid book; Herrin sees Byzantium as crucial both for the development of Christianity and Islam.

Hourani, George. *Arab Seafaring in the Indian Ocean in Ancient and Early Medieval Times.* 1995. The standard discussion of Arab maritime activity.

King, Charles. *The Black Sea: A History.* 2004. A comprehensive history of the Black Sea region from antiquity to the present. It is especially useful for anyone interested in this borderland among cultures.

Moorhead, John. *The Roman Empire Divided, 400–700.* 2001. A reliable and up-to-date survey of the period.

Robinson, Francis, ed. *The Cambridge Illustrated History of the Islamic World.* 1977. Many excellent and well-illustrated articles that will be useful for beginners.

Treadgold, Warren T. *A Concise History of Byzantium.* 2001. A reliable and insightful short survey.

Treadgold, Warren. *A History of the Byzantine State and Society.* 1997. A reliable narrative of Byzantine history.

Notes

1. Al-Tabari, *The History of Al-Tabari,* Vol. 17: *The First Civil War,* trans. and annotated by G. R. Hawting (1985), 50.

2. Quoted in Jane S. Gerber, *The Jews of Spain: A History of the Sephardic Experience* (1992), 28.

Medieval Empires and Borderlands: The Latin West

8

ONE GRAY DAY IN CENTRAL GERMANY IN 740, AN ENGLISH MONK named Boniface swung his axe at an enormous oak tree. This was the sacred Oak of Thor, where German men and women had prayed for centuries to one of their mightiest gods. Some local Christians cheered and applauded the monk. But an angry crowd of men and women gathered as well, cursing Boniface for attacking their sacred tree. Then something extraordinary occurred. Though Boniface had only taken one small chop, the entire tree came crashing down, split neatly into four parts. Boniface's biographer, a monk named Willibald, explained the strange event as God's judgment against "pagan" worshipers. In Willibald's account of the incident, the hostile crowd was so impressed by the miracle that they immediately embraced Christianity. As the news spread, more and more Germans accepted the faith, and Boniface's fame grew. According to Willibald, "The sound of Boniface's name was heard through the greater part of Europe. From the land of Britain, a great host of monks came to him—readers, and writers, and men trained in other skills."[1]

Whether or not the miracle at the Oak of Thor actually occurred, Boniface, a missionary who worked closely with the pope in Rome, played a leading role in spreading Christianity among the peoples of northern Europe. The Christian missionaries who traveled to lands far beyond the Mediterranean world brought Latin books and established monasteries. Through Christianity and the literacy that spread from these monastic centers, the monks established cultural ties among the new Germanic converts to Roman learning and the late antique world.

But Boniface was not Roman. He was English, a descendant of the Germanic settlers, called the Anglo-Saxons, who took control of much of

CHAPTER OUTLINE

The Image of a Man (Imago Hominis) In Christian iconography, the image of a man symbolizes the Evangelist Matthew. The other three evangelists, Mark, Luke, and John, were symbolized by a lion, bull, and eagle. These Christian symbols were related to the fixed signs of the zodiac, created by ancient polytheist astronomers. The adaptation of Christianity to pagan symbolism conveyed the message that Christianity represented the fulfillment of ancient wisdom. This page introducing the Gospel of St. Matthew comes from an illuminated manuscript, the Echternach Gospel Book, made in Anglo-Saxon England in the first half of the eighth century.

Britain after the Roman legions abandoned it in the early fourth century. Boniface's England (as southern Britain is called after the Anglo-Saxon settlements) was just one of the former Roman provinces in western Europe that had been settled and eventually ruled by Germanic tribes. In England Roman culture had been overwhelmed and was reintroduced only indirectly through Christianity. In Spain, Italy, and France, in contrast, the Germanic settlers grafted their societies onto a still-living Roman stalk. The intermingling of these cultures produced Christian kingdoms on a Roman foundation. Historians refer to these continental kingdoms plus Britain as Latin Christendom° because they celebrated the Christian liturgy in Latin and accepted the authority of the pope in Rome.

Historians use the term *Latin Christianity* for this early period rather than *Roman Catholicism* because people at the time did not use *Catholicism* with the same meaning as today. Then they usually described themselves as "Christians" to distinguish themselves from polytheists, Jews, and Muslims, or as "Latins" to distinguish themselves from the Greek Orthodox. Now Roman Catholicism identifies itself as in the Latin Christian tradition, which for many Christians makes the terms interchangeable. Even though they no longer celebrate the liturgy in Latin as they did in the Middle Ages, Catholics today continue to accept the authority of the pope in Rome and the traditions of medieval Latin Christianity.

As discussed in Chapter 7, Latin Christianity and Orthodox Christianity gradually grew apart during the Middle Ages, primarily over theological differences and disputes about who held the ultimate authority in the Church. For most Christians, however, the crucial differences were over liturgy and language. The liturgy° consists of the forms of worship—prayers, chants, and rituals. In the Middle Ages there was a great deal of variety in the Christian liturgy, and a number of languages were used, but followers of the Roman church gradually came to identify themselves with the Latin liturgy and the Latin language. As a result, the diverse peoples of medieval western Europe began to be called the "Latin people," although they spoke many different languages. The term *Latin* came to represent more than a liturgy or language; during the Middle Ages it became a religious and even cultural identity.

The Latin Christendom that came to dominate western Europe was only one of three major civilizations that emerged on the ruins of the late antique Roman world and that constituted the West during this period. During the Middle Ages, the Latin Christian, Greek Orthodox, and Arabic Muslim kingdoms and empires began to form a distinctively Western civilization. However, recurrently pressing across the frontiers of these civilizations were barbarian peoples coming from the Eurasian steppes and Scandinavia. Like the Avars, Slavs, Rus, and Bulgars who threatened Byzantium, the raiders and invaders from the steppes and the North—the Germanic tribes, the Magyars, and the

Vikings—who entered the western half of the Roman Empire eventually became Christians. Their conversions took place through missionary efforts, the profession of tribal leaders and kings who brought entire peoples with them, and military expeditions that forced the conquered to convert. By the end of the eleventh century few polytheists could still be found in Europe. With the exception of the Muslim pockets in Spain and Sicily and isolated communities of Jews, Christianity had become the dominant faith. Unlike most of the earlier invaders from the steppes who were converted to Orthodox Christianity, those who invaded western Europe eventually accepted the Latin form of Christianity.

In this crucial phase in forming Western civilization from about 350 to 1100, new political formations in western Europe made possible greater political cohesion that brought together ethnically and linguistically diverse peoples under obedience to an emperor or king. As in Byzantium and the Islamic caliphates the empires and kingdoms of the Latin West enforced or encouraged uniformity of religion, spread a common language among the ruling elite, and instituted systematic principles for governing. The Carolingian Empire, which lasted from 800 to 843 and controlled much of western Europe, reestablished the Roman Empire in the West for the first time in more than 300 years and sponsored a revival of interest in antiquity called the Carolingian Renaissance. The Carolingian Empire's collapse was followed by a period of anarchy as Europe faced wave after wave of hostile invaders. During the eleventh century, however, the Latin West recovered in dramatic fashion. By the end of the century the Latin kingdoms were strong enough to engage in a massive counterassault against Islam, in part in defense of fellow Christians in Byzantium. These wars with Islam, known as the Crusades, produced a series of wars in the Middle East and North Africa that continued throughout the Middle Ages. But the ideals of the Crusaders lasted well into modern times, long after active fighting ceased. The transformations in this period raise the question, how did Latin Christianity help strengthen the new kingdoms of the Latin West so that they were eventually able to deal effectively with both barbarian invaders and Muslim rivals?

- **How did Latin Christendom—the new kingdoms of western Europe—build on Rome's legal and governmental legacies and how did Christianity spread in these new kingdoms?**
- **How did the Carolingian Empire contribute to establishing a distinctive western European culture?**
- **After the collapse of the Carolingian Empire, how did the western kingdoms consolidate in the core of the European continent and how did Latin Christianity spread to its periphery?**
- **What were the causes and consequences of the Crusades?**

The Birth of Latin Christendom

■ How did Latin Christendom—the new kingdoms of western Europe—build on Rome's legal and governmental legacies and how did Christianity spread in these new kingdoms?

By the time the Roman Empire collapsed in the West during the fifth century, numerous Germanic tribes had settled in the lands of the former empire. These tribes became the nucleus for new kingdoms as Germanic chiefs transformed themselves into kings. By 750, several of these new kingdoms had emerged. Various Anglo-Saxon kings controlled most of England. The Franks ruled over the territories that constitute modern France, Germany, and the Netherlands; the Visigoths Spain; and the Lombards Italy. These territories were not politically united as they had been under the Roman Empire (see Map 8.1). Though their populations were quite diverse ethnically and linguistically, they shared certain social and religious characteristics. They had enough in common that historians refer to these kingdoms collectively as Latin Christendom.

Germanic Kingdoms on Roman Foundations

These new Germanic kingdoms of Christendom borrowed from Roman law while establishing government institutions; they developed their own cultural identity and they

Map 8.1 Europe, ca. 750

By about 750 the kingdom of the Franks had become the dominant power in western Europe. The Umayyad caliphate controlled Spain, and the Lombard kingdom governed most of Italy. The Byzantine Empire held power in Greece, as well as its core lands in Asia Minor.

relied on their own methods of rule. Thus, they were able to unify the kingdoms in three ways. First, in the Germanic kingdoms personal loyalty rather than legal rights unified society. Kinship obligations to a particular clan of blood relatives rather than citizenship, as in the Roman Empire, defined a person's place in society and his or her relationship to rulers. Second, Christianity became the dominant religion in the kingdoms. The common faith linked rulers with their subjects. A third unifying force was Latin. Latin served as the language of worship, learning, and diplomacy in these kingdoms.

Anglo-Saxon England

Roman civilization collapsed more completely in Britain during the fifth century than it did on the European continent, largely because of Britain's long distance from Rome and the small number of Romans who had settled there. About 400, the Roman economic and administrative infrastructure of Britain fell apart, and the last Roman legions left the island to fight on the continent. Raiders from the coast of the North Sea called Angles and Saxons (historians refer to them as Anglo-Saxons) took advantage of Britain's weakened defenses and launched invasions. They began to probe the island's southeast coast, pillaging the small villages they found there and establishing permanent settlements of their own.

The economic situation in Britain continued to deteriorate. By 420 coinage had fallen out of use on the island, and barter became the sole means of exchange. By 450, cities either shrank to very small villages or lay abandoned. A century later, fortified villas in the countryside—the last vestige of Roman life—had disappeared.

Christian worship was threatened but survived in all the areas held by the Roman Britons, Wales, Cornwall, and southern Scotland. Due to the efforts of missionaries from Italy, Gaul, and Ireland, by 750 Christianity was reinvigorated and become deeply embedded in Anglo-Saxon culture.

Because the small bands of Anglo-Saxon settlers fought as often among themselves as they did against the Roman Britons, the island remained fragmented politically during the first few centuries of the invaders' rule. But by 750, three warring kingdoms managed to seize enough land to coalesce and dominate Britain: Mercia, Wessex, and Northumbria.

Because Roman culture had virtually disappeared in these areas, Roman legal traditions had to be reintroduced through the spread of Christianity. The English language derives primarily from the Germanic languages spoken by the Anglo-Saxon settlers of Britain. In contrast, the Romance (or Roman-based) languages of Spanish, Italian, and French developed from Latin spoken in Rome's former provinces on the Continent, where Roman civilization was more deeply rooted. In Wales, which the Anglo-Saxons did not conquer, the Welsh language shows a combination of Latin and the region's older Celtic tongues.

The Franks: A Dual Heritage

The encounter between Roman and Frankish cultures from the third to the seventh century produced the largest and most powerful kingdom on the continent of western Europe, that of the Franks. Yet the Franks had modest origins. In the third century a number of small tribes living in what is now the Netherlands and the northwestern part of Germany organized themselves into a loose confederation. According to Roman records, Frankish warbands launched destructive attacks on northern Gaul (now northern France) and raided Spain and North Africa during the second half of the third century. The armies of the Roman emperor Constantine finally brought the Franks under control in the early fourth century. After that the Franks who lived beyond Roman borders did not dare to attack Rome, and Franks living within the empire served faithfully as soldiers in the Roman army. These men retained dual identities, remaining both Frankish and Roman. As a third century soldier's gravestone proudly states: "I am a Frank, a Roman citizen, and an armed soldier."[2] Several Franks even became important Roman generals.

But in the course of the fifth century, as Roman imperial control of western Europe disintegrated, Frankish power grew. One group among the Franks, called Salians, gradually gained preeminence among the Frankish people. The Salians' leading family were the Merovingians. A crafty Merovingian war chief named Childeric ruled a powerful band of Salian Franks from about 460 until his death in 481.

During his long reign, Childeric set the stage for the rapid consolidation and expansion of Frankish power. Childeric gave his warriors the opportunity to participate in campaigns to seize lands in Roman Gaul, rewarding them handsomely with loot. But the complex political situation in Gaul posed a problem for the Merovingian leader. After Roman imperial government collapsed throughout most of Gaul by the 450s, some independent groups of Romans continued to fight for control of territory against Huns, Visigoths, and other peoples who had settled there. In a few places Roman churchmen and aristocrats managed to hold on to some authority. Although Childeric was not Christian, he cooperated with these Romans in an effort to win their support against their common enemies.

With the support of loyal Frankish soldiers, Childeric laid the foundation for the Merovingian kingdom. His energetic and ruthless son Clovis (r. 481–511) made the Franks one of the leading powers in the western provinces of the old Roman Empire. Clovis aggressively expanded his father's power base through conquest of northern Gaul and neighboring territories. He also murdered many of his relatives and other Frankish chieftains whom he considered rivals. In 486 he overcame the last Roman stronghold in northern Gaul.

Clovis's wife, Clotild, followed Latin Christianity, the religion of most of the inhabitants of the former Roman Empire in western Europe. Historians refer to this version of Christianity as Latin Christianity because its followers used a Latin Bible, performed church services in Latin, and at least formally accepted the authority of the pope in Rome. Latin Christianity, like the Greek-based Orthodox Christianity in the Byzantine Empire, teaches the full equality of the Father, the Son, and the Holy Spirit in the Trinity. In contrast to Latin Christianity in the western provinces was the Arian Christianity practiced by the Germanic kings, who had established new kingdoms in western Europe during the fifth century. Arians believed that Christ was divine, but inferior to God the Father in rank, authority, and glory.

DOCUMENT

History of the Franks

The theological distinction between Latin and Arian Christians in western Europe was a crucial political issue that divided the Roman subjects from their Germanic rulers, who were usually Arians. Around 500, perhaps influenced by his wife's beliefs, the polytheist Clovis converted to Latin Christianity. About 3,000 warriors, the core of his army, joined their king in this change to the new faith. Clovis had practical reasons to convert as well. He intended to attack the Visigothic kingdom in southern Gaul. The Visigoths followed Arian Christianity, but their subjects, the Roman inhabitants of the region, followed Latin Christianity. By converting to Latin Christianity, Clovis won the support of many of the Visigoths' subjects. With their help Clovis and his Frankish army crushed the Visigothic king Alaric II, who died at the battle of Vouillé in the summer of 507. Clovis now controlled almost all of Gaul as far as Spain, but the Visigoths in Spain continued to resist and to maintain the independence of their territories.

Clovis went on to conquer other Germanic peoples. His armies overran the kingdom of the Thuringians to the east of his homeland. They also defeated the Alemanni, who lived in what are now Switzerland and southwest Germany. In order to consolidate his authority in these varied lands, Clovis needed recognition from both the emperor in Constantinople and the Roman Church in Gaul. He shrewdly achieved both. After defeating Alaric II, the Merovingian ruler won the support of Gaul's clergy by donating much of the booty from his victory to the church of the most important saint in Gaul, Martin of Tours. Clovis then earned the recognition of the Byzantine emperor by formally acknowledging his authority. At the pageant when Clovis brought the treasure to Martin's church, ambassadors of the Byzantine emperor may have made him an honorary consul. Wearing a Roman military uniform, Clovis celebrated a Roman-style victory parade in which he scattered gold coins to the crowd. For the next three centuries, Merovingian kings followed Latin Christianity and received similar honors from Byzantine emperors.

The Frankish kingdom thrived under several able monarchs in the sixth and seventh centuries. Continuing their father's expansionist policies, Clovis's sons conquered the Burgundian kingdom in 534 and acquired Provence on the southeastern coast of Gaul two years later.

Despite these successes, the Merovingian dynasty gradually grew weak as a result of conflicts among kings, their quarrelsome sons, and independent-minded aristocrats. As a result of these squabbles, Clovis's kingdom split into four separate realms: Neustria in the west; Austrasia, which included lands east of the Rhine River as well as in Gaul; Aquitaine in the southwest; and Burgundy in the southeast. These realms later reunified and separated several additional times, which is a measure of the instability of the Merovingian system. Rulers of these independent kingdoms issued their own law codes, collected taxes from their subjects—and quarreled bitterly with one another. As they went their separate ways politically, striking linguistic differences emerged. For example, in Neustria, the people spoke an early form of French, while in Austrasia they spoke a German language. While the political divisions of Merovingian Gaul were never made permanent, the cultural distinctions have had lasting effects.

Though Merovingian kings still ruled Gaul, they had become so ineffectual that real power passed to the official in charge of the royal household called the "Mayor of the Palace." One of these mayors, Charles Martel "the Hammer" (r. 719–741), established his personal power by regaining control over regions that had slipped away from Merovingian rule and by defeating an invading Muslim army at Poitiers in 732. Martel's son, Pepin the Short (r. 741–768), succeeded his father as Mayor of the Palace, but dethroned the last of the Merovingian monarchs and in 751 made himself king of the Franks.

Visigoths in Spain

In contrast to the Frankish kings who after Clovis accepted Latin Christianity, during the sixth century the Visigothic kings, who controlled southern Gaul and most of Spain, adhered to Arian Christianity. By favoring Arianism these kings generated animosity among the subject population, most of whom were Latin Christians. When the Frankish king, Clovis, invaded southern Gaul in 507, many Latin Christians welcomed him and provided the invaders with military assistance. As a consequence of defeat, the Visigoth kings retreated to Spain, where they concentrated on unifying the people through the spread of Arianism and the acceptance of Roman law, which influenced the Visigoth law codes.

By 600, Visigoth kings ruled over most of the Spanish peninsula and had even managed to drive the last Byzantine forces from its southern coast. Under the Visigoths Spain thrived. From its vast, rich estates, surpluses of grain, olive oil, and leather were exported by international merchants, including a substantial community of Jews as well as Greeks and even Syrians. By taxing this trade the Visigoth kings filled their treasuries with gold and became the envy of their neighbors.

The Visigoth kings failed to spread Arianism among the population, and when King Reccared (r. 586–601) converted to Latin Christianity most of the remaining Arians followed. The kings began to imitate the Byzantine emperors with the elaborate court ceremonies of Constantinople and used frequent church councils as assemblies that enforced their will. Thus the key to their success was the ability to employ the spiritual authority of the Church to enhance the secular authority of the king. However, the autocratic instincts of the Visigoth kings alienated many of the substantial landowners who were easily lured by the promises of invaders to treat them more favorably.

In 711 invading armies of Muslims from North Africa vanquished the last Visigothic king. As a result, Spain became part of the Umayyad caliphate. The Jews, in particular, welcomed the Muslim conquerors because Islam granted them a measure of religious toleration they had not experienced under the Christian Visigoths. Many Christians from the upper classes converted to Islam to preserve the property and offices of authority. Some survivors of the Visigoth kingdoms held on in the northwest of Spain, where they managed to keep Christianity alive.

Lombards in Italy

Between 568 and 774, a Germanic people known as the Lombards controlled most of northern and central Italy. They were called *Langobardi*, or "Long Beards," from which the name *Lombard* derives. In the first part of the sixth century under their ruler Waccho, Lombards established a kingdom in the area of modern Hungary. As we have seen, Justinian's wars and a devastating plague drained the Byzantine Empire's strength. Without imperial troops to defend Italy, the peninsula became vulnerable to invasion. The Lombard king Alboin (r. ca. 565–572) took advantage of the situation and invaded Italy in 568. Alboin's army contained soldiers of different ethnic backgrounds. In addition to Lombards, his forces included smaller bands of Goths, Avars, Saxons, and other non-Romans. Some were Arian Christians; others were Latin Christians. Still others practiced polytheism. Alboin's highly diverse army indicated his ability to attract followers but also implied a lack of common purpose among them other than taking the opportunity to pillage. That lack of unity made it impossible for Alboin to build a strong, lasting kingdom.

The Romans living in Italy put up a feeble resistance. Within three years Alboin controlled all of northern Italy, Tuscany, and parts of southern Italy in the region of Spoleto, near Naples. Yet until 700, the Lombard kings proved weak rulers. Throughout their lands real power lay in the hands of semi-independent dukes based in the most populated urban centers such as Benevento and Spoleto. These dukes gradually expanded their possessions within Italy, jockeying among themselves for land and power. After 700, the Lombard kings reasserted their authority by developing a royal bureaucracy of judges and legal officials, compensating somewhat for the weaknesses of the Lombard system evident in the initial conquest. The new infrastructure enabled them to overshadow the dukes' local authority.

Despite the Lombard kings' newfound strength, they still faced two formidable external enemies. The most dangerous of these were the Byzantine forces who remained in the Exarchate of Ravenna. These soldiers hoped to crush the Lombards and regain control of Italy in the name of the Byzantine emperors. Again and again they battled with Lombards, but their efforts proved futile. In 751 the Lombard ruler Aistulf defeated the Exarchate of Ravenna, leading to its abandonment as the Byzantine capital in the West.

The Franks posed the second threat to the Lombards. These hardy warriors marched into Italy several times during the seventh century, trying to crush the Lombards and seize their lands. Sometimes they joined with Byzantine forces from the Exarchate of Ravenna. During other attacks, the Franks had the backing of the popes in Rome, who resented the Lombards' power. Despite their diplomatic and military efforts, however, the Franks failed to achieve their goals of conquest.

The tide of battle soon turned against the Lombards. In the middle of the eighth century, internal political disputes once again tore at the kingdom. The Lombards' diplomatic relations with the papacy and their uneasy standoff with the Franks deteriorated. As will be discussed shortly, the Frankish king Charlemagne, responding to a call for assistance from Pope Leo III, invaded Italy and crushed the Lombards in 774.

Different Kingdoms, Shared Traditions

With the exception of England, where Anglo-Saxon invaders overwhelmed the Roman population, the leaders of the new Germanic kingdoms faced a common problem: how should the Germanic minority govern subject peoples who vastly outnumbered them? These rulers found a solution to this problem by blending Roman and Germanic traditions. For example, the kings served as administrators of the civil order in the style of the Roman emperor, issuing laws and managing a bureaucracy. They also served as war leaders in the Germanic tradition, leading their men into battle in search of glory and loot. As the Germanic kings defined new roles for themselves, they discovered that Christianity could bind all their subjects together into one community of believers. The merging of Roman and Germanic traditions could also be traced in the law, which eventually erased the distinctions between Romans and Germans, and in the ability of women to own property, a right far more common among the Romans than the Germans.

Civil Authority: The Roman Legacy

In imitation of Roman practice, the monarchs of Latin Christendom designated themselves the source of all law and believed that they ruled with God's approval. Kings controlled all appointments to civil, military, and religious office. Accompanied by troops and administrative assistants, they also traveled throughout their lands to dispense justice, collect taxes, and enforce royal authority.

Frankish Gaul provides an apt example of how these monarchs adopted preexisting Roman institutions. When Clovis conquered the Visigoths in Gaul, he inherited the nearly intact Roman infrastructure and administrative system that had survived the collapse of Roman imperial authority. Merovingian kings (as well as Visigoth and Lombard rulers in Spain and Italy) found it useful to maintain parts of the preexisting system and kept the officials who ran them. For instance, Frankish kings relied on the bishops and counts in each region to deal with local problems. Because Roman aristocrats were literate and had experience in Roman administration on the local level, they often served as counts. Based in cities, these officials presided in local law courts, collected revenues, and raised troops for the king's army. Most bishops also stemmed from the Roman aristocracy. In addition to performing their religious responsibilities, bishops aided their king by providing for the poor, ransoming hostages who had been captured by enemy warriors from other kingdoms, and bringing social and legal injustices to the monarch's attention. Finally, the kings used dukes, most of whom were Franks, to serve as local military commanders, which made them important patrons of the community. Thus, the civil and religious administration tended to remain the responsibility of the Roman counts and bishops, but military command fell to the Franks.

War Leaders and *Wergild*: The Germanic Legacy

The kingdoms of Latin Christendom developed from war bands led by Germanic chieftains. By rewarding brave warriors with land and loot taken in war, as well as with revenues skimmed from subject peoples, chieftains created political communities of loyal men and their families, called clans° or kin groups°. Though these followers sometimes came from diverse backgrounds, they all owed military service to the clan chiefs. Because leadership in Germanic society was hereditary, networks of loyalty and kinship expanded through the generations.

Though the principle of loyalty to a superior defined life in these Germanic communities, many men ignored this principle in the pursuit of their own interests. Rivalries among warriors unwilling to follow their chieftain and among power-hungry men who competed for the kingship within the royal families often led to bloody struggles that weakened the political fabric of the kingdoms. Frankish leaders proved particularly vicious in their quest for power, thinking nothing of betrayal and assassination of their rivals, including members of their own families. Despite the bloodshed and brutal competition for power, the various political communities gradually evolved into distinct ethnic groups led by a king, such as the Lombards and the Franks.

These ethnic groups developed a sense of shared history, kinship, and culture. The coalescence of these kingdoms resulted from the Germanic settlers' pride in their new homelands as well as from their allegiance to their monarchs who governed them fairly at home and who protected them from foreign enemies.

The new Germanic kingdoms had highly hierarchic societies geared for warfare. Kinship-based clans stood as the most basic unit of Germanic society. The clan consisted of all the households and blood relations loyal to the clan chief, and a warrior who protected them and spoke on their behalf before the king on matters of justice. Clan chieftains in turn swore oaths of loyalty to their kings and agreed to fight for him in wars against other kingdoms. The clan leaders formed an aristocracy among the Germanic peoples. Like the Roman elites before them, the royal house and the clan-based aristocracy consisted of rich men and women who controlled huge estates. The new Germanic aristocrats intermarried with the preexisting Roman elites of wealthy landholders, thus maintaining control of most of the land. These people stood at the very top of the social order, winning the loyalty of their followers by giving them gifts and parcels of land. Under the weight of this new upper class, the majority of the population, the ordinary farmers and artisans, slipped into a deepening dependence on these nobles. Eventually, ordinary farmers merged with the Roman peasantry. Most peasants could not enter into legal transactions in their own name, and they had few protections and privileges under the law. Even so, they were better off than the slaves who toiled at society's very lowest depths. Valued simply as property, these men, women, and children had virtually no rights in the eyes of the law.

Though this social hierarchy showed some similarities to societies in earlier Roman times, the new kingdoms' various social groups were defined by law in a fundamentally different way. Unlike Roman law, which defined people by citizenship rights and obligations, the laws of the new kingdoms defined people by their wergild°. A Germanic concept, *wergild* referred to what an individual was worth in case he or she suffered some grievance at the hands of another. If someone injured or murdered someone else, wergild was the amount of compensation in gold that the wrongdoer's family had to pay to the victim's family.

In the wergild system, every person had a price that depended on social status and perceived usefulness to the community. For example, among the Lombards service to the king increased a free man's worth—his wergild was higher than that of a peasant. In the Frankish kingdom, if a freeborn woman of childbearing age was murdered, the killer's family had to pay 600 pieces of gold. Two-thirds of that sum went to the victim's family. The king received the rest. Noble women and men had higher wergild than peasants, while slaves and women past childbearing age were worth very little.

If proper wergild was not paid, the injured party's kin group felt obligated to gain vengeance for their loss. The desire for revenge and compensation frequently led to vicious feuding. In order to minimize the bloodletting that could sometimes drag on for generations after a crime had been committed, representatives of the king or a local aristocrat urged families to accept wergild.

Unity Through Law and Christianity

Within the kingdoms of Latin Christendom, rulers tried to achieve unity by merging Germanic and Roman legal principles and by accepting the cultural influence of the Church. Religious diversity among the peoples in their kingdoms made this unity difficult to establish. As discussed in Chapter 6, many of the tribes that invaded the Roman Empire during the fifth century practiced Arian Christianity. They kept themselves apart from the Latin Christians by force of law. For example, they declared marriage between Arian and Latin Christians illegal.

These barriers began to collapse when some Germanic kings converted to the Latin Christianity of their Roman subjects. Some converted for reasons of personal belief, or because their wives were Latin Christians. Others decided to become Latin Christians to gain wider political support. For instance, when Clovis converted about 500, laws against intermarriage between Arians and Latin Christians in Gaul disappeared. More and more Franks and Romans began to marry one another, blending the two formerly separate communities into one and reinforcing the strength of the Latin Church. Similarly in 587, when the Visigothic king Reccared converted from Arianism to Latin Christianity, he made it the official religion of Spain. Soon Visigoths and Romans began to intermarry legally. Many of the Lombards had already converted to Latin Christianity when they entered Italy so they, too, began to marry Romans. By 750 most of the western European kingdoms had officially become Latin Christian, even if substantial pockets of polytheist practice survived and communities of Jews were allowed to practice their faith.

Germanic kings adopted Latin Christianity, but they had no intention of abandoning their own Germanic law, which differed from Roman law on many issues, especially relating to the family and property. Instead, they offered their Roman subjects the opportunity to live under the Germanic law that governed the king. Clovis's *Law Code* or *Salic Law,* published sometime between 508 and 511, illustrates this development. The *Law Code* applied to Franks and to any other non-Roman peoples in his realm who chose to live according to Frankish law. Because the Romans dwelling in the Frankish kingdom technically still followed the laws of Byzantium, Clovis did not presume to legislate for them. Romans could follow their own law if they wished, or they could follow his laws and become Franks.

Permitting his subjects to switch to Frankish law helped Clovis strengthen his kingdom. It fostered a shared sense of Frankish identity throughout his kingdom. Eventually the Frankish king's policies eroded distinctions among Romans, Franks, and other ethnic groups within his realm. By 750, most Romans had chosen to abandon their legal identity as Romans and live according to Frankish law, and the distinction between Roman and Frank lost all meaning.

A similar process occurred in other Germanic kingdoms. The Lombards slowly mixed with the Romans living in Italy. By 750 their law, which originally protected only Lombards, now applied to all the Latin Christian inhabitants of Italy. In Spain, the Roman and Visigothic populations merged once the religious barriers came down. In 654 the Visigothic king Recceswinth abolished the separate Roman law entirely and brought his entire population under Visigothic law. As in the Frankish and Lombard kingdoms, this unification of two peoples under one law happened without protest, a sign that various groups had blended politically, religiously, and culturally.

Women and Property

Roman law influenced more than just local administration in Latin Christendom. It also prompted Germanic rulers to reconsider the question of a woman's right to inherit land. In the Roman Empire, women had inherited land without difficulty. Indeed, perhaps as much as 25 percent of the land in the entire realm had been owned by women. In many Germanic societies, however, men could inherit land and property far more easily than women. Attitudes about female inheritance began to shift when the Germanic settlers established their homes in previously Roman provinces—and began to marry Roman women who owned property.

By comparing the law codes of the new kingdoms over time, historians have detected the impact of Roman customs on Germanic inheritance laws. By the late eighth century women in Frankish Gaul, Lombard Italy, and Visigothic Spain could inherit land, though often under the restriction that they must eventually pass it on to their sons. Germanic rulers adopted the custom of female inheritance because it enabled the new settlers to keep within their own families the property that their Roman wives had inherited and brought to the marriage. Despite these limitations, the new laws transformed women's lives. A woman who received an inheritance of land could live more independently, support herself if her husband died, and have a say in the community's decisions.

The Spread of Latin Christianity in the New Kingdoms of Western Europe

As Latin Christianity spread as the official religion through the new kingdoms, churchmen decided that they had a moral responsibility to convert all the people of these kingdoms and beyond to their faith. They sent out missionaries to explain the religion to nonbelievers and challenge the worship of polytheist gods.

Meanwhile, bishops based in cities directed people's spiritual lives, instilling the moral and social conventions of Christianity through sermons delivered in church. Monks such as Boniface, who introduced this chapter, traveled from their home monasteries in Ireland, England, and Gaul to spread the faith to Germanic tribes east of the Rhine. Monasteries became centers of intellectual life, and monks replaced urban aristocrats as the keepers of books and learning.

The Growth of the Papacy

In theory, the Byzantine emperors still had political authority over the city of Rome and its surrounding lands during this violent time. However, strapped for cash and troops, these distant rulers proved unequal to the task of defending the city from internal or external threats. In the resulting power vacuum, the popes stepped in to manage local affairs and became, in effect, princes who ruled over a significant part of Italy.

Gregory the Great (r. 590–604) stands out as the most powerful of these popes. The pragmatic Gregory wrote repeatedly to Constantinople, pleading for military assistance that never came. Without any succor from the Byzantines, Gregory had to look elsewhere for help. Through clever diplomacy, Gregory successfully cultivated the goodwill of the Christian communities of western Europe by offering religious sanction to the authority of friendly kings. He negotiated skillfully with his Lombard, Frankish, and Byzantine neighbors to gain their support and establish the authority of the Roman church. He also encouraged Christian missionaries to spread the faith in England and Germany. In addition, he took steps to train educated clergymen for future generations, in this way securing Christianity's future in western Europe.

Gregory had set the stage for a dramatic increase in papal power. As his successors' authority expanded over the next few centuries, relations between Rome and the Byzantine emperors slowly soured, especially during the Iconoclastic Controversy discussed in Chapter 7. By the early eighth century the popes abandoned the fiction that they were still subject to the Byzantines and sought protection from the Frankish kings. The popes established political independence during the period but remained dependent on the Franks for military assistance when necessary.

Converting the Irish

Though the Romans had conquered most of Britain during the imperial period, they never attempted to bring Ireland into their empire. Thus the island off Britain's west coast had had only minimal contact with Christianity. Little is known for certain of how Christianity came to Ireland. There were probably missionaries who traveled with traders from the Roman Empire, but the earliest firm date is 431 when Palladius was supposedly sent to administer to those in Ireland who were already Christians. Subsequent missionary history in Ireland is dominated by the figure of Patrick (died ca. 492 or 493), whose later biographers improbably gave him credit for converting all the Irish to Christianity. A ninth-century record describes his capture from a Roman villa in Britain by Irish raiders, who sold him into slavery in Ireland. Patrick learned Irish during his years in captivity. He managed to escape to Britain, where he was ordained into the priesthood and sent back to Ireland as a missionary. A great deal of confusion exists regarding Patrick's life, and some scholars argue that tradition merged the experiences of the two missionaries Palladius and Patrick. However, by the end of the fifth century Christianity had a firm foothold in Ireland.

But Ireland was still a rural place. The early missionaries wondered how to Christianize the Irish without a Roman urban foundation to build on. Elsewhere in the West Christianity spread out into the countryside from cities, with bishops administering the local church from their city cathedrals. However, the island lacked cities in which to build churches and housing for bishops. No one living in Ireland knew Latin, Greek, or any of the other languages into which the Bible had been translated. And no schools existed where churchmen might teach the Gospel to new converts.

Irish churchmen found solutions to these problems in monasteries, places where priests could receive training and men and women from the surrounding communities could learn to read Latin and absorb the basics of Christian education. By 750, the Irish scholars produced by these monasteries gained a high reputation for their learning in their own lands as well as across western Europe. Irish monasteries sent out dozens of missionaries, who in turn founded new monasteries in England, France, and Germany. Irish scholars produced magnificently illustrated manuscripts in their libraries. These books brought Irish art to all the lands where the missionaries traveled.

Irish monasteries sometimes grew rich from the gifts of money and property provided by kings and other pious folk. Such centers, especially those that became bishops' headquarters, acquired substantial economic and political influence in their local communities by settling disputes, caring for the sick, and employing local laborers. Having proved its value in Ireland, the monastery system spread from the island to England and then to the European continent.

Converting the Anglo-Saxons

By 600, numerous Irish missionaries had begun to travel to England and the European continent to establish new monasteries. Columbanus (543–615), for example, founded several monasteries on the Irish model in the kingdom of Burgundy. The most notable among these were the monastery of Luxeuil in the Rhône River valley, and Bobbio in northern Italy. These centers inspired the founding of many additional nunneries and monasteries in northern Gaul. From there Latin Christianity spread east of the Rhine River, into lands where the religion had not yet penetrated.

Irish missionaries also expanded their monastic network in their own land. Columba (521–597), for instance, founded several new monasteries in Ireland as well as one on the island of Iona, off Scotland's western coast. From this thriving community missionaries began to bring Christianity to the peoples of Scotland. The offshoot monastery of Lindisfarne in northern England also became a dynamic center of learning and missionary activity. During the seventh century, missionaries based there carried Christianity to many other parts of England. They also began converting the people of Frisia on the North Sea, in the area of the modern Netherlands.

Besides the Irish monks who went to Anglo-Saxon England, Pope Gregory the Great (r. 590–604) and his successors sent other missionary monks from Rome. Through missionary efforts Gregory hoped to save souls and in so doing forged a Christian community not just in England but throughout Europe. Gregory understood that the first step in creating the new community was to convert as many people as possible to the faith; deep learning about the religion could come later. To that end he instructed missionaries to permit local variations in worship and to accommodate harmless vestiges of pre-Christian worship practices. "Don't tear down their temples," Gregory advised; "put a cross on the roofs!"

Following Gregory's pragmatic suggestion, missionaries in England accepted certain Anglo-Saxon calendar conventions that stemmed from polytheist worship. For example, in the Anglo-Saxon calendar, the weekdays took their names from old gods: Tuesday derived from Tiw, a war god; Wednesday from Woden, king of the gods; Thursday from Thor, god of thunder; and Friday from Freya, goddess of agriculture. Anglo-Saxon deities eventually found their way into the Christian calendar as well. Eostre, for example, a goddess whose festival came in April, gave her name to the Christian holiday Easter.

Despite their common commitment to Latin Christianity, the Irish and Roman monks working throughout England disagreed strongly about proper Christian practice. For instance, they argued over how to perform baptism, the ritual of anointing someone with water to admit him or her into the Christian community. They bickered about how monks should shave the tops of their heads to show their religious dedication, and they squabbled about the correct means of calculating the date of Easter. These disputes threatened to create deep divisions among England's Christians. The overall conflict finally found resolution in 664 in the Anglo-Saxon kingdom of Northumbria, where monastic life flourished. At a council of monks and royal advisers called the Synod of Whitby, the Northumbrian monarch commanded that the Roman version of Christianity would prevail in his kingdom. His decision eventually was accepted throughout England.

Monastic Intellectual Life

The missionaries from Rome were members of the vigorous monastic movement initiated by Benedict of Nursia (ca. 480–547) from his monastery at Monte Cassino in Italy (see Chapter 6). These monks followed Benedict's *Rule,* a guidebook for the management of monastic life and spirituality. In the *Rule* Benedict had written that individual monks should live temperate lives devoted to spiritual contemplation, communal prayer, and manual labor. So that their contemplations might not depart from the path of truth, Benedict had encouraged monks to seek guidance in the Bible, in the writings of the renowned theologians, and in works of spiritual edification. For Benedict, contemplative reading constituted a fundamental part of monastic life. Thus monks had to be literate in Latin. They needed training in the Latin classics, which required books.

Medieval monasteries set aside at least two rooms—the scriptorium° and the library—to meet the growing demand for books. In the scriptorium, scribes laboriously copied Latin and Greek manuscripts as an act of religious devotion. Monastery libraries were small in comparison to the public libraries of classical Rome, but the volumes were cherished and carefully controlled. Because books were precious possessions, these libraries set forth strict rules for their use. Some librarians chained books to tables to prevent theft. Others pronounced a curse against anyone who failed to return a borrowed book. Nevertheless, librarians also generously lent books to other monasteries to copy.

Monks preferred to read Christian texts with a spiritual message, so these books were the most frequently copied. In many monasteries, however, monks preserved non-Christian texts. By doing so, they helped to keep knowledge of Latin and classical learning alive. Indeed, many of the surviving works by authors of the Classical Age were copied and passed on by monks in the sixth and seventh centuries. In addition to Christian works, monks also studied the writings of Latin poets such as Virgil and Juvenal, scientists such as Pliny the Elder, and philosophers such as Boethius and Cicero, as well as the works of grammarians, mathematicians, scientists, and physicians from the ancient world. Without the monasteries and scriptoria, knowledge today of the literature of the classical world would be greatly reduced.

Sometimes classical works survived merely by accident. Because parchment, the specially prepared sheepskin on which writers copied their manuscripts, was expensive, many monks scrubbed old manuscripts clean and reused them to copy religious texts. By studying these reused parchment sheets, called palimpsests°, modern scholars have succeeded in reclaiming vital classical texts or portions of them that otherwise would have been lost forever. Cicero's treatise *On the Republic,* which has influenced many political thinkers including the writers of the U.S. Constitution, is one example. Although other parts had survived since antiquity and the whole is still not known, sections of this work survived only because in the seventh century, at the monastery of Bobbio in northern Italy, a monk erased Cicero's text and copied an interpretation of the Psalms by Augustine onto the parchment. Modern scholars can read Cicero's words below Augustine's.

Monks did far more than merely copy ancient texts, however. Some wrote original books of their own. At the English monastery at Jarrow, for example, Bede (d. 735) became the most distinguished scholar in eighth-century Europe. He wrote many books, including the *History of the English Church and People.* This work provides an invaluable source of information about the early Anglo-Saxon kingdoms.

Monks carried books with them when they embarked on missionary journeys. They also acquired new books during their travels. For instance, Benedict Biscop, the founder of the monasteries of Wearmouth (674) and Jarrow (682) in England, made six trips to Italy. Each time he brought back crates of books on all subjects, including works written by classical authors whom monks studied with interest. Other Anglo-Saxon missionaries transported this literary heritage to the monasteries they founded in Germany during the eighth century. As monks avidly read, copied, wrote, and transported books of all sorts, knowledge and intellectual discourse flourished in the monasteries.

Monks shared their expanding knowledge with Christians outside the monastery walls. They established schools at monasteries where boys (and in some places girls) could learn to read and write. In Italy some public schools survived from antiquity, but elsewhere most of the very few literate people who lived between 550 and 750 gained their education at monastery schools. The men trained in these schools played an important role in society as officials and bureaucrats. Their skills in reading and writing were necessary for keeping records and writing business and diplomatic letters.

Jews in a Christian World

For Jews during this era, quality of life varied in the different western European kingdoms. Jews continued to work in every profession, own land, serve in the army, and engage in trade. The vast majority of monarchs protected the Jewish minorities living in their kingdoms. Thus many Jews prospered in the Frankish, Visigothic, and Lombard realms (no Jews lived in England during this period). At times, theological curiosity led to intellectual encounters between Jews and Christians. In Lombard Italy, for example, Jews and Christians sometimes engaged in public debates about their religious beliefs.

Christian churchmen still blamed Jews collectively for Jesus' death and especially feared that Christians might be tempted to convert to Judaism. Some bishops advocated persecuting Jews, but only a few rulers were willing to follow their advice. Leading churchmen in the western kingdoms also developed theological reasons for wanting Jews to convert to Christianity. Pope Gregory urged conversion

CHRONOLOGY	
The Birth of Latin Christendom	
481–511	Clovis reigns; Frankish kingdom divided at his death
ca. 525	Benedict founds monastery at Monte Cassino
568	Lombards invade Italy
587	Visigothic king of Spain converts to Latin Christianity; Columbanus travels to Gaul from Ireland
ca. 700	Lombards accept Latin Christianity
732	Charles Martel defeats Muslims at Poitiers
751	Pepin overthrows last Merovingian king; Exarchate of Ravenna falls to Lombards

because he believed that Christ would return to Earth only when Jews embraced Christianity. Nevertheless, Gregory advocated the use of persuasion and kindness to encourage conversion, rather than force or terror. On numerous occasions he intervened to stop Christians from committing violence against Jews. Other Christian writers, such as Isidore of Seville (in Spain), further developed the idea that Jews had a place in Christian society because of their role in bringing about Christ's return and then the Day of Judgment. Highly ambivalent about the Jews, Christians both persecuted and protected them.

The Carolingians

■ **How did the Carolingian Empire contribute to establishing a distinctive western European culture?**

Among the successor kingdoms to the Roman Empire in the West, discussed in the previous section, none was more powerful militarily than the Merovingian kingdom of the Salian Franks, which ruled the northern part of the ancient Roman province of Gaul and at various periods most of the rest of Gaul from the late fifth through the middle of the eighth centuries. The Merovingian dynasty was plagued by factions, royal assassinations, and do-nothing kings. When Pepin the Short deposed the last of the Merovingian kings in 751, he made himself king of the Franks and inaugurated the Carolingian dynasty.

Both the weak Merovingians and the strong Carolingians illustrated how the problem of succession from one king to another destabilized early medieval monarchies. The kingdom was considered the private property of the royal family, and according to Frankish custom, a father was obliged to divide his estates among his legitimate sons. As a result, whenever a king of the Franks died, the kingdom was divided up as happened numerous times under the Merovingians. When Pepin died in 768, the kingdom was divided between his sons, Charlemagne and Carloman. When Carloman died suddenly in 771, Charlemagne ignored the inheritance rights of Carloman's sons and may even have had them killed, making himself the sole ruler of the Franks.

The Leadership of Charlemagne

Charlemagne's (r. 768–814) ruthlessness with his own nephews epitomized the crafty leadership that made him the mightiest ruler in western Europe and gave him the nickname of Charles the Great. One of his court poets labeled him "The King Father of Europe"; no monarch in European history has enjoyed such posthumous fame.

An unusually tall and imposing figure, Charlemagne was a superb athlete and swimmer, a lover of jokes and high living, but also a deeply pious Christian. As Pepin's eldest son, he had frequently accompanied the army during his father's campaigns, and these youthful experiences gave him an unbending will and a fighting spirit.

During his reign, Charlemagne engaged in almost constant warfare, especially against polytheistic tribes that when defeated were usually compelled to accept Christianity. He went to war eighteen times against the Germanic tribe the Saxons, whose forced conversion only encouraged subsequent rebellions. The causes for Charlemagne's persistent warfare were complex. He believed he had an obligation to spread Christianity. He also needed to protect his borders

Map 8.2   Carolingian Empire

Charlemagne's conquests were the greatest military achievement of the Early Middle Ages. The Carolingian armies successfully reunified all western European territories of the ancient Roman Empire except for southern Italy, Spain, and Britain. However, the empire was fragile due to Frankish inheritance laws that required all legitimate sons to inherit lands from their father. By the time of Charlemagne's grandsons the empire began to fragment.

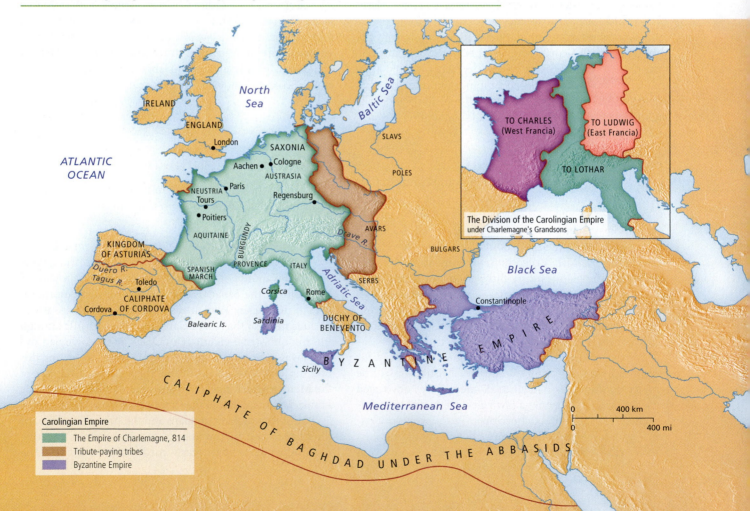

The Coronation of Charlemagne

Previous rulers of the Franks had styled themselves kings and none had challenged the Byzantine Emperor's claim to be the sole heir to the emperors of ancient Rome. However, in 800 when the pope crowned Charlemagne emperor, the Byzantines took it as an attempt to usurp the throne. Charlemagne's biographer, Einhard, described Charlemagne's support of the pope and the controversial circumstances of his imperial coronation. Einhard's Life of Charlemagne *is an example of how Carolingian Renaissance literature imitated ancient literary models, in this case to show that Charlemagne acted like an ancient emperor.*

Beyond all other sacred and venerable places he loved the church of the holy Apostle Peter at Rome, and he poured into its treasury great wealth in silver and gold and precious stones. He sent innumerable gifts to the Pope; and during the whole course of his reign he strove with all his might (and, indeed, no object was nearer to his heart than this) to restore to the city of Rome her ancient authority, and not merely to defend the church of Saint Peter but to decorate and enrich it out of his resources above all other churches. But although he valued Rome so much, still, during all the forty-seven years that he reigned, he only went there four times to pay his vows and offer up his prayers.

But such were not the only objects of his last visit; for the Romans had grievously outraged Pope Leo, had torn out his eyes and cut off his tongue, and thus forced him to throw himself upon the protection of the King. He, therefore, came to Rome to restore the condition of the church, which was terribly disturbed, and spent the whole of the winter there. It was then that he received the title of Emperor and Augustus, which he so disliked at first that he affirmed that he would not have entered the church on that day—though it was the chief festival of the church—if he could have foreseen the design of the Pope. But when he had taken the title he bore very quietly the hostility that it caused and the indignation of the Roman emperors [in Byzantium]. He conquered their ill-feeling by his magnanimity, in which doubtless, he far excelled them, and sent frequent embassies to them, and called them his brothers.

Source: *Early Lives of Charlemagne* by Einhard and the Monk of St. Gall, trans. A. J. Grant (1922): 43–44.

---

from incursions by hostile tribes. Perhaps most important, however, was his need to satisfy his followers, especially the members of the aristocracy, by providing them with opportunities for plunder and new lands. As a result of these wars, he established a network of subservient kingdoms that owed tribute to the Carolingian Empire (see Map 8.2).

The extraordinary expansion of the Carolingian Empire represented a significant departure from the small, loosely governed kingdoms that had prevailed in the wake of the collapse of the Roman Empire. Charlemagne's empire covered all of western Europe except for southern Italy, Spain, and the British Isles. His military ambitions had brought the Franks into direct confrontation with other cultures—the polytheistic German tribes, Scandinavians, and Slavs; the Orthodox Christians of Byzantium; and the Muslims in Spain. These confrontations were usually hostile and violent, characterized as they were by the imposition of Frankish rule and Latin Christian faith.

Coronation of Charlemagne as Emperor

Charlemagne's coronation as Roman emperor at the hands of Pope Leo III (r. 795–816) conferred extraordinary authority on the Frankish kingdom. In 799 Pope Leo found himself embroiled in a vicious dispute with a faction of Roman nobles who accused him of adultery and lying. Kidnapped on the streets of Rome, the pope was beaten and perhaps maimed before he was rescued by some of his attendants. Charlemagne put together a commission of prominent churchmen and nobles to conduct a judicial inquiry into the charges against the pope, and then in the autumn of 800 the king himself set out for Rome to restore order to the Church. After Leo was cleared of the accusations against him, on Christmas Day 800 in front of a large crowd at St. Peter's Basilica, the pope presided over a ceremony in which Charlemagne was crowned emperor. Historians have debated exactly what happened, but according to the most widely accepted account, the assembled throng acclaimed Charlemagne as Augustus and emperor, and the pope prostrated himself before the new emperor in a public demonstration of submission. Charlemagne's biographer Einhard later stated that the coronation came as a surprise to the king. Certainly there were dangers in accepting the imperial crown because the coronation was certain to antagonize Constantinople, where there already was a Roman emperor. Nevertheless, Charlemagne became the first Roman emperor in the West since the fifth century.

The coronation exemplified two of the most prominent characteristics of the Carolingians. The first was the conscious imitation of the ancient Roman Empire, especially the Christian empire of Constantine. Charlemagne's conquests acquired much of the former territory of the western Roman Empire, and the churches built during his reign were modeled after the fourth- and fifth-century basilicas of Rome. The second characteristic of Carolingian rule was the obligation of the Frankish kings to protect the Roman popes, an obligation that began under Charlemagne's father Pepin. In exchange for this protection, the popes offered the Carolingian monarchs the legitimacy of divine sanction.

The imperial title bestowed on Charlemagne tremendous prestige and tremendous risk. With the imperial crown came the rulership of northern Italy and theoretical superiority over all other rulers in the West. But it made dangerous enemies of the Byzantine emperors. They had been calling themselves Roman emperors since the fourth century and justly claimed to be the true heirs of the legal authority of the ancient Roman Empire. To them Charlemagne was nothing more than a barbarian usurper of the imperial crown. In their minds the pope had no right to crown anyone emperor. Instead of reuniting the eastern and western halves of the ancient Roman Empire, the coronation of Charlemagne drove them further apart.

Carolingian Rulership

Even under the discerning and strong rulership of Charlemagne, the Carolingian Empire never enjoyed the assets that had united the ancient Roman Empire for so many centuries. The Carolingians lacked a standing army and navy, professional civil servants, properly maintained roads, regular communications, and a money economy, a stark contrast with Byzantium and the Muslim caliphates, which could also boast splendid capital cities of Constantinople, Damascus, Baghdad, and Córdoba. However, Charlemagne governed very effectively without a capital, spending much of his time ruling from the saddle. From Christmas to Easter and sometimes longer, Charlemagne wintered in one of the imperial palaces, usually in the Frankish heartland. In the summer he and his court traveled about, camping out or living as guests in the castles of friendly lords, where he dispensed justice, decided disputes, and enforced obedience to his rule. During these summer travels he frequently conducted campaigns against the Saxon tribes.

Such a system of government depended more on personal than institutional forms of rule. Personal loyalty to the Carolingian monarch, expressed in an oath of allegiance, provided the strongest bonds unifying the realm, but betrayals were frequent. The Carolingian system required a monarch with outstanding personal abilities and unflagging energy, such as Charlemagne possessed, but a weak monarch threatened the collapse of the entire empire. Until the reign of Charlemagne, royal commands had been delivered orally, and there were few written records of what decisions had been made. Charlemagne's decrees (capitularies) gradually came to be written out. The written capitularies began to strengthen and institutionalize governmental procedures through written aids to memory. In addition, Charlemagne's leading adviser, Alcuin, insisted that all official communications be stated in the appropriate Latin form, which would help prevent falsification be-

cause only the educated members of Charlemagne's court were well enough educated to know the proper forms.

One of the weaknesses of the Merovingian dynasty had been the decentralization of power, as local dukes appropriated royal resources and public functions for themselves. To combat this weakness, Charlemagne followed his father's lead in reorganizing government around territorial units called counties°, each administered by a count. The counts were rewarded with lands from the king and sent to areas where they had no family ties to serve as a combined provincial governor, judge, military commander, and representative of the king. To check on the counts, traveling circuit inspectors reviewed the counts' activities on a regular basis and remedied abuses of office. On the frontiers of their sprawling kingdom, the Franks established special territories called marches°, which were ruled by margraves with extended powers necessary to defend vulnerable borders.

In many respects, however, the Church provided the most vital foundations for the Carolingian system of rulership. As discussed in Chapter 6, during the last years of the ancient Roman Empire the administration of the Church was organized around the office of the bishop. By the late seventh century this system had almost completely collapsed, as many bishoprics were left vacant or were occupied by royal favorites and relatives who lacked qualifications for church office. Because Carolingian monarchs considered themselves responsible for the welfare of Christianity, they took charge of the appointment of bishops and reorganized church administration into a strict hierarchy of archbishops who supervised bishops who, in turn, supervised parish priests. Pepin and Charlemagne also revitalized the monasteries and endowed new ones, which provided the royal court with trained personnel—scribes, advisers, and spiritual assistants. Most laymen of the time were illiterate, so monks and priests wrote the emperor's letters for him, kept government records, composed histories, and promoted education—all essential for Carolingian rule.

The Carolingian Renaissance

In addition to organizing efficient political administration, Charlemagne sought to make the royal court an intellectual center. He gathered around him prominent scholars from throughout the realm and other countries. Under Charlemagne's patronage, these scholars were responsible for the flowering of culture that is called the Carolingian Renaissance.

The Carolingian Renaissance° ("rebirth") was one of a series of revivals of interest in ancient Greek and Latin literature. Charlemagne understood that both governmental efficiency and the propagation of the Christian faith required the intensive study of Latin, which was the language of the law, learning, and the Church. The Latin of everyday speech had evolved considerably since antiquity. During Charlemagne's time, spoken Latin had already been transformed into early versions of the Romance languages of Spanish, Italian, Portuguese, and French. Distressed that the poor Latin of many clergymen meant they misunderstood the Bible, Charlemagne ordered that all prospective priests undergo a rigorous education and recommended the liberal application of physical punishment if a pupil was slow in his lessons. However, due to the lack of properly educated teachers the Carolingian reforms did not penetrate very far into the lower levels of the clergy, who taught by rote the rudiments of Christianity to the nonliterate peasants.

Charlemagne's patronage was crucial for the Carolingian Renaissance, which took place in the monasteries and the imperial court. Many of the heads of the monastic writing rooms wrote literary works of their own, including poetry and theology. The Carolingian scholars developed a beautiful new style of handwriting called the Carolingian minuscule, in which each letter was carefully and clearly formed. Texts collected by Carolingian librarians provided the foundation for the laws of the Church (called *canon law*) and codified the liturgy, which consisted of the prayers offered, texts read, and chants sung on each day of the year.

During the Carolingian period, the copying and studying of ancient Latin texts intensified. The works of some seventy ancient authors were preserved by Carolingian scribes. Some 8,000 Carolingian manuscripts still exist, a small portion of the total number known to have been produced.

The brighter young clerics and some promising laymen required instruction more advanced than the typical monastery could provide; to meet this need, Charlemagne established a school in his palace in Aachen. To staff his school and to serve as advisers, Charlemagne sought the best talent from within and outside the empire. Grammarians, historians, geographers, and astronomers from Ireland, England, Italy, Germany, and Spain flocked to Charlemagne's call.

The man most fully responsible for the Carolingian Renaissance was the English poet and cleric Alcuin of York (ca. 732–804), whom Charlemagne invited to head the palace school. Charlemagne himself joined his sons, his friends, and his friends' sons as a student, and under Alcuin's guidance the court became a lively center of discussion and exchange of knowledge. They debated issues such as the existence or nonexistence of Hell, the meaning of solar eclipses, and the nature of the Holy Trinity. After fifteen years at court, Alcuin became the abbot of the monastery of St. Martin at Tours, where he expanded the library and produced a number of works on education, theology, and philosophy.

A brilliant young monk named Einhard (ca. 770–840), who studied in the palace school, quickly became a trusted friend and adviser to Charlemagne. Based on twenty-three years of service to Charlemagne and research in royal documents, Einhard wrote the *Life of Charlemagne* (830–833), which describes Charlemagne's family, foreign policy, con-

The Palatine Chapel of Charlemagne

The Palatine Chapel, which is now a component of the cathedral of Aachen, Germany, is the most significant surviving example of Carolingian architecture. Consecrated in 805, it served as Charlemagne's imperial chapel and his resting place. The intricate design of the octagonal core was modeled after the Byzantine church of San Vitale in Ravenna, Italy.

quests, administration, and personal attributes. In Einhard's vivid Latin prose, Charlemagne comes alive as a great leader, a lover of hunting and fighting, who unlike his rough companions possessed a towering sense of responsibility for the welfare of his subjects and the salvation of their souls. In Einhard's biography, Charlemagne appears as an idealist, the first Christian prince in medieval Europe to imagine that his role was not just to acquire more possessions but to better humankind.

DOCUMENT

Einhard, *Life of Charlemagne*

Charlemagne's rule and reputation have had lasting significance for western Europe. Around 776 an Anglo-Saxon monk referred to the vast new kingdom of the Franks as the

Carolingian Renaissance Art
This exquisitely carved bookcover for the Psalter of Dagulf was made for Pope Hadrian (d. 795) in the workshops of Charlemagne's palace. In the upper left side panel, King David orders the psalms be written down. In the lower left he sings them. In the upper right the pope orders Saint Jerome to edit the psalms for inclusion in the Bible, which he does in the lower right.

Kingdom of Europe, reviving the Roman geographical term *Europa*. Thanks to the Carolingians, Europe became more than a geographical expression. It became the geographical center of a new civilization that supplanted the Roman civilization of the Mediterranean and transformed the culture of the West.

The Division of Western Europe

None of Charlemagne's successors possessed his personal skills, and without a permanent institutional basis for administration, the empire was vulnerable to fragmentation and disorder. When Charlemagne died in 814, the imperial crown passed to his only surviving son, Louis the Pious (r. 814–840). Louis's most serious problem was dividing the empire among his own three sons, as required by Frankish inheritance laws. Disputes among Louis's sons led to civil war, even before the death of their father, and while they were fighting the administration of the empire was neglected.

CHRONOLOGY

The Carolingian Dynasty

751	Pepin the Short deposes last Merovingian king
800	Charlemagne crowned emperor in Rome
843	Treaty of Verdun divides Frankish kingdom
987	Death of the last Carolingian king

After years of fighting, the three sons—Charles the Bald (d. 877), Lothair (d. 855), and Louis the German (d. 876)—negotiated the Treaty of Verdun, which divided the Frankish kingdom. Charles the Bald received the western part of the territories, the kingdom of West Francia. Louis the German received the eastern portion, the kingdom of East Francia. Lothair obtained the imperial title as well as the central portion of the kingdom, the "Middle Kingdom," which extended from Rome to the North Sea (see Map 8.2). In succeeding generations, the laws of inheritance created further fragmentation of these kingdoms, and during the ninth and tenth centuries the descendants of Charlemagne died out or lost control of their lands. By 987 none were left.

The Carolingian Empire lasted only a few generations. Carolingian military power, however, had been formidable, providing within the Frankish lands an unusual period of security from hostile enemies, measured by the fact that few settlements were fortified. After the empire's collapse virtually every surviving community in western Europe required fortifications, represented by castles and town walls. Post-Carolingian Europe became fragmented as local aristocrats stepped into the vacuum created by the demise of the Carolingians—and it became vulnerable, as a new wave of raiders from the steppes and the North plundered and carved out land for themselves.

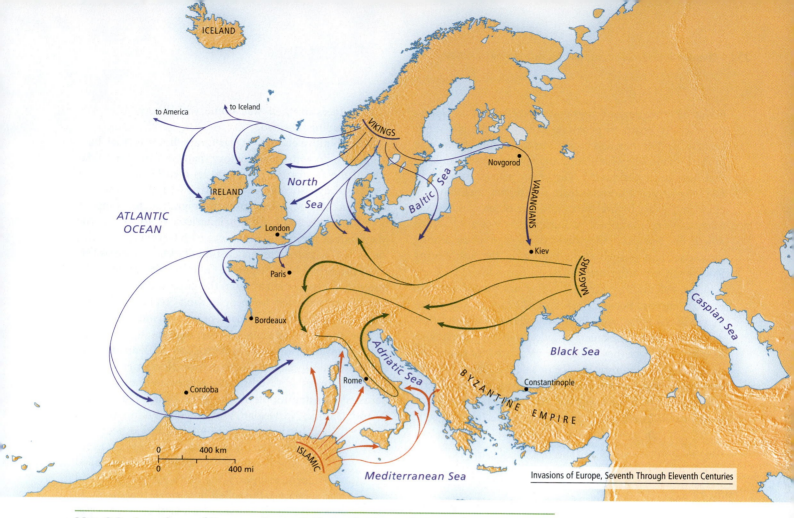

Invasions of Europe, Seventh Through Eleventh Centuries

Map 8.3 Invasions of Europe, Seventh Through Eleventh Centuries

Especially after the division of the Carolingian empire, Europe came under severe pressure from invading Viking bands from Scandinavia. The effects of the Viking invasions were felt most gravely in the British Isles and northern France. From the east came the Magyars, who eventually settled in the vast Hungarian plain. From the south there were persistent raids and conquests from various Islamic states, some of which established a rich Muslim civilization in Europe.

Invasions and Recovery in the Latin West

■ After the collapse of the Carolingian Empire, how did the western kingdoms consolidate in the core of the European continent and how did Latin Christianity spread to its periphery?

Despite Charlemagne's campaigns of conquest and conversion, the spread of Christianity throughout western Europe remained uneven and incomplete. By 900, Latin Christianity was limited to a few regions that constituted the heartland of western Europe—the Frankish lands, Italy, parts of Germany that had been under Carolingian rule, the British Isles, and a fringe in Spain. During the ninth and tenth centuries, hostile polytheistic tribes raided deep into the tightly packed Christian core of western Europe (see Map 8.3). Despite these attacks

Christianity survived, and the polytheist tribes eventually accepted the Christian faith. These conversions were not always the consequence of Christian victories in battle, as had often been the case during late antiquity and the Carolingian period. More frequently they resulted from organized missionary efforts by monks and bishops.

The Polytheist Invaders of the Latin West

Some of the raiders during the eighth to eleventh centuries plundered what they could from the Christian settlements of the West and returned home. Others seized lands, settled down, and established new principalities. The two groups who took advantage of the weakness of the Latin West most often during this period were the Magyars and Vikings.

The original homeland of the Magyars, later known as the Hungarians, was in the central Asian steppes. Gradually driven by other nomads to the western edge of the steppes, the Magyars began to penetrate Europe in the late ninth century. By 896 they had crossed en masse into the middle of the Danube River basin, occupying sparsely settled lands that were easily conquered. The grassy plains of this basin had long attracted nomads from the steppes, including the Huns and Avars before them, and like other nomads, the Magyars were accomplished horsemen. Once they settled down, the Magyar tribes divided the vast plain among themselves and pushed at the borders of the neighboring Slavic and German principalities.

Mounted raiding parties of Magyars ranged far into western Europe. Between 898 and 920 they sacked settlements in the prosperous Po River valley of Italy and then descended on the remnant kingdoms of the Carolingian Empire. Wherever they went they plundered for booty and took slaves for domestic service or sale. The kings of western and central Europe were powerless against these fierce raiders, who were unstoppable until 955 when the Saxon king Otto I (who later became emperor) destroyed a band of marauders on their way home with booty. After 955, Magyar raiding subsided.

The definitive end of Magyar forays, however, may have had less to do with Otto's victory than with the consolidation of the Hungarian plain into its own kingdom under the Árpád dynasty, named after Árpád (d. 907), who had led seven Magyar tribes in their migration to Hungary. Both Orthodox and Latin missionaries vied to convert the Magyars, but because of an alliance with German monarchs, the Árpáds accepted Roman Christianity. On Christmas Day 1000, the Árpád king Stephen I (r. 997–1038) received the insignia of royalty directly from the pope and was crowned king. To help convert his people, King Stephen laid out a network of bishoprics and lavishly endowed monasteries.

The most devastating of the eighth- to eleventh-century invaders of western European settlements were the Vikings, also called Norsemen or Northmen. (These Viking warriors were ethnically related to the Rus who harassed Constantinople at the same time.) During this period, Danish, Norwegian, and Swedish Viking warriors sailed on long-distance raiding expeditions from their homes in Scandinavia. Every spring the long Viking dragon ships sailed forth, each carrying 50 to 100 warriors avid for loot. Propelled by a single square sail or by oarsmen when the winds failed or were blowing in the wrong direction, Viking ships were unmatched for seaworthiness and regularly sailed into the wild seas of the North Atlantic. The shallow-draft vessels could also be rowed up the lazy rivers of Europe to plunder monasteries and villages far into the interior.

VIDEO

The Viking Ship Museum in Oslo

The causes for the enormous Viking onslaught were complex. Higher annual temperatures in the North may have stimulated a spurt in population that encouraged raiding and eventually emigration. But the primary motive seems to have been an insatiable thirst for silver, which was deemed the essential standard of social distinction in Scandinavian society. As a result, monasteries and cathedrals with their silver liturgical vessels were especially prized sources of plunder for Viking raiding parties. In 793, for example, the great English monastery at Lindisfarne was pillaged for silver and largely destroyed in the process.

By the middle of the ninth century, the Vikings began to maintain winter quarters in the British Isles and on the shores of the weak Carolingian kingdoms—locations that enabled them to house and feed ever-larger raiding parties. These raiders soon became

Viking Ship

This reconstructed Viking ship, discovered at Oseberg, Norway, dates from ca. 800. It would have been propelled by a single square sail or rowed by oarsmen. Horses and warriors crowded into the ship. The tiller was mounted on the starboard side toward the stern. Stern-mounted rudders, which gave the helmsman much greater control of the direction of the ship, were gradually introduced during the twelfth century.

Viking Treasure Hoard
The Vikings were engaged in long-distance trading and raiding. One of the principal motives for their long treks was the accumulation of silver. This hoard from an eleventh century site is mainly made up of Byzantine and Islamic silver coins.

invading armies that took land and settled their families on it. As a result, the Vikings moved from disruptive pillaging to permanent occupation, which created a lasting mark on Europe. Amid the ruins of the Carolingian Empire, Viking settlements on the Seine River formed the beginnings of the duchy of Normandy ("Northman land"), whose soldiers would conquer during the eleventh century England, Sicily, and much of southern Italy.

The most long-lasting influence of the Vikings outside Scandinavia was in the British Isles and North Atlantic. In 865 a great Viking army conquered large parts of northeastern England, creating a loosely organized network of territories known as the Danelaw. The Danish and Norse conquests in the British Isles left deep cultural residues in local dialects, geographical names, personal names, social structure, and literature. The most enduring example in Old English, the earliest form of spoken and written English, remains the epic of *Beowulf*, which recounts the exploits of a great Scandinavian adventurer in combat with the monster Grendel, Grendel's mother, and a fiery dragon.

In the North Atlantic, Vikings undertook long voyages into the unknown across cold rough seas. Beginning about 870, settlers poured into unsettled Iceland. Using Iceland as a base, they ventured farther and established new colonies in Greenland. In Iceland the adventures of these Viking warriors, explorers, and settlers were celebrated in poetry and sagas. The sagas of Erik the Red and the Greenlanders recount hazardous voyages to the coasts of Canada. These Europeans arrived in America 500 years before Christopher Columbus. In 930 the fiercely independent Icelanders founded a national parliament, the *althing*, an institution at which disputes were adjudicated through legal procedures rather than combat.

After the mid-ninth century, the kings of Scandinavia (Norway, Denmark, and Sweden) began to assert control over the bands of raiders who had constituted the vanguard of the Viking invasions. By the end of the tenth century, the great age of Viking raiding by small parties ended. The Scandinavian kings established firm hold over the settled population and converted to Christianity, bringing their subjects with them into the new faith. Henceforth, the descendants of the Viking raiders settled down to become peaceable farmers and shepherds.

The Rulers in the Latin West

As a consequence of the disintegration of the Carolingian order and the subsequent invasions, people during the ninth and tenth centuries began to seek protection from local warlords who assumed responsibilities once invested in royal authorities.

Lords and Vassals

The society of warlords derived from Germanic military traditions in which a great chief attracted followers who fought alongside him. The relationship was voluntary and egalitarian. By the eighth century, however, the chief had become a lord° who dominated others, and his dependents were known as vassals°.

The bond of loyalty between lord and vassal was formalized by an oath. In the Carolingian period the vassal proved his loyalty to the lord by performing an act of homage, which made the vassal the "man" of the lord. The act of homage was a ritual in which the kneeling vassal placed his clasped hands between the hands of the lord and made a verbal declaration of intent, usually something such as, "Sir, I become your man." In return for the vassal's homage or fealty, as it came to be called, the lord swore to protect the vassal. The oath established a personal relationship in which the lord reciprocated the vassal's loyalty and willingness to obey the lord with protection and in some cases with a land grant called a fief°. Lords frequently called on their vassals for military assistance to resist invaders or to fight with other lords. The fief supplied the vassal with an income to cover the expenses of armor and weapons and of raising and feeding horses, all of which were necessary to be an effective mounted soldier, known by the twelfth century as a knight°. This connection between lord-vassal relations and the holding of a fief is called feudalism°.

Revealing the Truth: Oaths and Ordeals

No participant in a lawsuit or criminal trial today would dream of entering the courtroom without an accompanying pile of documents to prove the case. In modern society we trust written over oral evidence because we are aware of how easily memories can be distorted. In an early medieval court, however, the participants usually arrived with nothing more than their own sworn testimony and personal reputations to support their cause. Papers alleging to prove one thing or another meant little in a largely illiterate society. Unable to read and perhaps aware that the few who could read might deceive them, most people trusted what they had personally seen and heard. Count Berthold of Hamm expressed the opinion of many when, after being presented with documents opposing his claim to a piece of land, he "laughed at the documents, saying that since anyone's pen could write what they liked, he ought not to lose his rights over it."

To settle disputes, medieval courts put much more faith in confession or in eyewitness testimony than in documents. In 1124 Pope Calixtus II pronounced that "we put greater faith in the oral testimony of living witnesses than in the written word."

Under normal trial procedures, a man would give his oath that what he was saying was true. If he was an established and respected member of the community, he would also have a number of "oath-witnesses" testify for his reliability, although not to the truth or falsehood of his evidence. The court would also hear from witnesses in the case. This system worked well enough when two local men, known in the community, were at odds. But what happened when there was a trial involving a person who had a bad reputation, was a known liar, or was a stranger? What would happen in a case with no witnesses?

In these instances, medieval courts sometimes turned to trial by ordeal to settle the matter. The judicial ordeal was used only as a last resort, as a German law code of 1220 declared: "It is not right to use the ordeal in any case, except that the truth may be known in no other way." The wide range of situations and people handed over to the ordeal makes clear that in the eyes of the medieval courts, the ordeal was a fallback method when all else failed to reveal the truth.

What was a trial by ordeal? There were several types. The most common was trial by fire. The accused would plunge his or her arm into a cauldron of boiling water to retrieve a coin or a jewel, or alternately would pick up a red-hot iron and walk nine paces. A variation of this method was to walk over hot coals or red-hot plowshares. After the accused suffered this ordeal, his or her hand or foot would be bound for three days and then examined. If the wound was healing "cleanly," meaning without infection, the accused was declared innocent. If not, he or she was adjudged guilty. Another common form of the ordeal was immersion in cold water, or "swimming," made famous in later centuries by its use in witch trials. The accused would be thrown into a river or lake. If the water "rejected" her and she floated, then she was guilty. If the water "embraced" her and she sank, then she was innocent. The obvious complication that a sinking person, even though innocent, may have also been a drowning person did not seem to deter use of trial by water.

The ordeal was especially widespread in judging crimes such as heresy and adultery and in assigning paternity. In 1218, Inga of Varteig carried the hot iron to prove that her son, born out of wedlock, was the son of deceased King Hakon III, which if true would change the line of succession in Norway. The ordeal was also used to decide much more pedestrian matters. In 1090, Gautier of Meigné claimed a plot of land from the monks of Saint Auban at Angers, arguing that he had traded a horse in return for the property. He too carried a hot iron to prove his claim.

The belief that an ordeal could effectively reveal guilt or innocence in a judicial matter was based on the widespread conviction that God constantly and actively intervened in earthly affairs and that his judgment could be seen immediately. To focus God's attention on a specific issue, the participants performed the ordeal in a ritual manner. A priest was usually present to invoke God's power and to bless the implements employed in the ordeal. In one typical formula, the priest asked God "to bless and sanctify this fiery iron, which is used in the just examination of doubtful issues." Priests would also inform the accused, "If you are innocent of this charge . . . you may confidently receive this iron in your hand and the Lord, the just judge, will free you." The ritual element of the judicial ordeal emphasized the judgment of God over the judgment of men.

During the eleventh and twelfth centuries, the use of the ordeal waned. The recovery of Roman law, the rise of literacy and written documents in society at large, and a greater confidence in the power of courts to settle disputes all con-

Trial by Ordeal
This fifteenth-century painting by Dieric Bouts (c. 1415–1475), was commissioned by the city of Louvain in 1468 for a large project on the theme of the Last Judgment.

This panel illustrates an episode from the legend of the Holy Roman emperor Otto III (980–1002) who presided over the trial.

The woman, accused of murdering her husband, embraces his head with her right arm and holds a red-hot iron in her left hand in a trial by ordeal.

tributed to the gradual replacement of the ordeal with the jury trial or the use of torture to elicit a confession from the accused. In England the common law began to entrust the determination of the truth to a jury of peers who listened to and evaluated all the testimony. The jury system valued the opinions of members of the community over the reliability of the ordeal to reveal God's judgment. These changes mark a shift in medieval society toward a growing belief in the power of secular society to organize and police itself, leaving divine justice to the afterlife. But the most crucial shift came from within the Church itself, which felt its spiritual mission compromised by the involvement of priests in supervising ordeals. In 1215 the Fourth Lateran Council forbade priests from participating, and their absence made it impossible for the ordeal to continue as a formal legal procedure.

Questions of Justice

1. Why was someone's reputation in the community so significant for determining the truth in a medieval trial? How do reputations play a role in trials today?
2. What do oaths and the trial by ordeal reveal about the relationship between human and divine justice during the Middle Ages?

Taking It Further

Bartlett, Robert. *Trial by Fire and Water: The Medieval Judicial Ordeal.* 1986. Associates the spread of the trial by ordeal with the expansion of Christianity. The best study of the ordeal.

van Caenegen, R. C. *An Historical Introduction to Private Law.* 1992. A basic narrative from late antiquity to the nineteenth century that traces the evolution of early medieval trial procedures.

During the ninth and tenth centuries, the lords often became the only effective rulers in a particular locality. After the collapse of public authority during the invasions and the dissolution of the Carolingian Empire, lordship implied political and legal jurisdiction over the inhabitants of the land. These lords came to exercise many of the powers of the state, such as adjudicating disputes over property or inheritance and punishing thieves and murderers. The rendering of justice represented the most elementary attribute of government, and in the absence of a formal legal system and systematic record keeping, local lords rendered a rough and ready justice. The personal loyalties of those involved in a dispute were crucial for determining the outcome. Those well-connected to the lord, especially those who were his vassals, were always better off than those who were outsiders or had fallen into his disfavor. In a society in which personal ties meant everything, the truth of conflicting testimonies was often determined by the public reputations and personal connections of those who testified. When the reputations of disputants or an alleged criminal could not determine whom to believe, lords acting as judges relied on oaths and ordeals to determine the truth.

The mixture of personal lord-vassal obligations, property rights conveyed by the fief, and legal jurisdiction over communities caused endless complications. The king's vassals were also lords of their own vassals, who in turn were lords over lesser vassals down to the level of simple knight. In theory such a system created a hierarchy of authority that descended down from the king, but reality was never that simple. In France, for example, many of the great lords enjoyed as much land as the king, which made it very difficult for the king to force them to enact his will. Many vassals held different fiefs from different lords, which created a confusion of loyalties, especially when two lords of the same vassal went to war against one another.

Women could inherit fiefs and own property of their own, although they could not perform military services. They often managed royal and aristocratic property when men were absent or dead, decided how property would be divided up among heirs, and functioned as lords when receiving the homage of male vassals. The lineage and accomplishments of prominent ladies enhanced their husbands' social prestige. A number of aristocratic families traced their descent from the female line, if it was more prestigious than the male line, and named their children after the wife's illustrious ancestors.

Lord-vassal relationships infiltrated many medieval social institutions and practices. Since most vassals owed military service to their lords, medieval armies were at least partially composed of vassal-knights who were obliged to fight for their lord for a certain number of days (often forty) per year. Vassals were required to provide their lord with other kinds of support as well. When summoned, they had to appear at the lord's court to offer advice or sit in judgment of other vassals who were their peers. When the

DOCUMENT

An Oath of Voluntary Submission to a Lord

Many men who found themselves in desperate circumstances became vassals in order to feed themselves and to find protection from someone richer and stronger. This voluntary oath of obedience reflects the origins of the relationship of dominance and submission between lords and vassals. In the eighth century according to the prescribed formula a destitute man was supposed to address his "magnificent lord" as follows:

Inasmuch as it is known to all and sundry that I lack the wherewithal to feed and clothe myself, I have asked of your pity, and your goodwill has granted to me permission to deliver and commend myself into your authority and protection . . . in return you have undertaken to aid and sustain me in food and clothing, while I have undertaken to serve you and deserve well of you as far as lies in my power. And for as long as I shall live, I am bound to serve you and respect you as a free man ought, and during my lifetime I have not the right to withdraw from your authority and protection, but must, on the contrary for the remainder of my days remain under it.

And in virtue of this action, if one of us wishes to alter the terms of the agreement, he can do so after paying a fine of ten solidi to the other. But the agreement itself shall remain in force. Whence it has seemed good to us that we should both draw up and confirm two documents of the same tenor, and this they have done.

Source: This example of a voluntary oath of obedience comes from Tours, in the eighth century.

lord traveled, his vassal was obliged to provide food and shelter in the vassal's castle, sometimes for a large entourage of family and retainers who accompanied the lord. Vassals were obliged to pay their lord certain fees on special occasions, such as the marriage of the lord's daughter. If the lord was captured in battle, his vassals had to pay the ransom.

The Western European Kingdoms After the Carolingians

At a time when the bonds of loyalty and support between lords and vassals were the only form of protection from invaders and marauders, lordship was a stronger social institution than the vague obligations all subjects owed to their kings. To rule effectively, a king was obliged to be a strong lord, in effect to become the lord of all the other lords, who in turn would discipline their own vassals. Achieving this difficult goal took several steps. First, the king had to establish a firm hand over his own lands, the royal domain. With the domain supplying food, materiel, and fighting men, the king could attempt the second step—establishing control over lords who lived outside the royal domain. To hold sway over these independent-minded lords, kings sometimes employed force but frequently offered lucrative rewards by giving out royal prerogatives to loyal lords. These prerogatives included the rights to receive fines in courts of law, to collect taxes, and to perform other governmental functions. As a result, some medieval kingdoms, such as France and England, began to combine in the hands of the same people the personal authority of lordship with the legal authority of the king, creating feudal kingship.

The final step in the process of establishing royal authority was to emphasize the sacred character of kingship. With the assistance of the clergy, kings emulated the great Christian emperors of Rome, Constantine and Justinian. Medieval kings became quasi priests who received obedience from their subjects because they believed kings represented the majesty of God on Earth. The institution of sacred kingship gave kings an additional weapon for persuading the nobles to recognize the king's superiority over them.

Under the influence of ancient Roman ideas of rulership, some kings began to envision their kingdoms as something grander than private property. As the Germanic king and later emperor Conrad II (r. 1024–1039) put it, "If the king is dead the kingdom remains, just as the ship remains even if the helmsman falls overboard."[3] The idea slowly began to take hold that the kingdom had an eternal existence separate from the mortal person of the king and that it was superior to its component parts—its provinces, tribes, lords, families, bishoprics, and cities. This profound idea reached its fullest theoretical expression many centuries later. Promoting the sacred and eternal character of kingship required monarchs to patronize priests, monks, writers, and artists who could formulate and express these ideas.

The kingdoms of East and West Francia, which arose out of the remnants of the Carolingian Empire, produced kings who attempted to expand the power of the monarchy and enhance the idea of kingship. East Francia largely consisted of Germanic tribes, each governed by a Frankish official called a duke. During the tenth century, several of these dukes became powerful lords, but they had to rule from the saddle, constantly on the

road—being seen, making judgments, suppressing revolts, punishing disloyal vassals, and rewarding loyal ones.

After 919 the dukes of Saxony were elected the kings of East Francia, establishing the foundations for the Saxon dynasty. With few lands of their own, the Saxon kings maintained their power by acquiring other duchies and controlling appointments to high church offices, which went to family members or loyal followers. The greatest of the Saxon kings, Otto I the Great (936–973), combined deep Christian piety with formidable military ability. More than any other tenth-century king, he supported the foundation of missionary bishoprics in polytheist Slavic and Scandinavian lands, thereby pushing the boundaries of Christianity beyond what they had been under Charlemagne. Otto launched a major expedition to Italy, where he reestablished order in anarchic Rome, deposed one pope, and nominated another. As a consequence of his intervention in Italy, the new pope crowned him emperor in 962, reviving the Roman Empire in the West, as Charlemagne had done earlier. Otto and his successors in the Saxon dynasty attempted to rule a more restricted version of the western empire than had Charlemagne. By the 1030s the German Empire consisted of most of the Germanic duchies, north-central Italy, and Burgundy. In later centuries these regions collectively came to be called the Holy Roman Empire.

As had been the case under Charlemagne, effective rulership in the new German Empire included the patronage of learned men and

Otto III

The Emperor Otto III is represented here in a form usually reserved for Christ. The emperor sits on a throne, is surrounded by a mandorla (lines surrounding his body in the shape of an almond), and reaches out to the four evangelists—Matthew, Mark, Luke, and John—who are signified by the winged figures of an eagle, lion, bull, and man. The hand of God reaches down from the heavens to crown Otto. The idea of divine sanction of kingship could not be more graphic.

women who enhanced the reputation of the monarch. Otto and his able brother Bruno, the archbishop of Cologne, initiated a cultural revival, the Ottonian Renaissance°, which centered on the imperial court. Learned Irish and English monks, Greek philosophers from Byzantium, and Italian scholars found positions there. Among the many intellectuals patronized by Otto, the most notable was Liutprand of Cremona (ca. 920–ca. 972), a vivid writer whose unabashed histories reflected the passions of the troubled times. For example, his history of contemporary Europe vilified his enemies and was aptly titled *Revenge*.

Like East Francia, West Francia included many groups with separate ethnic and linguistic identities, but the kingdom had been Christianized much longer because it had been part of the Roman Empire. Thus West Francia, although highly fragmented, possessed the potential for greater unity by using fully established Christianity to champion the authority of the king.

Strengthening the monarchy became the crucial goal of the Capetian dynasty, which succeeded the last of the Carolingian kings. Hugh Capet (r. 987–996) was elevated king of West Francia in an elaborate coronation ceremony in which the prayers of the archbishop of Reims offered divine sanction to the new dynasty. The involvement of the archbishop established an important precedent for the French monarchy: From this point on, the monarchy and the church hierarchy were closely entwined. From this mutually beneficial relationship, the king received ecclesiastical and spiritual support while the upper clergy gained royal protection and patronage. The term *France* at first applied only to Capet's feudal domain, a small but rich region around Paris, but through the persistence of the Capetians West Francia became so unified that the name France came to refer to the entire kingdom.

The Capetians were especially successful in soliciting homage and services from the great lords of the land—despite some initial resistance. Hugh and his successors distinguished themselves by emphasizing that unlike other lords, kings were appointed by God. Shortly after his own coronation, Hugh had his son crowned—a strategy that ensured the succession of the Capetian family. Hugh's son, Robert II, the Pious (r. 996–1031), was apparently the first to perform the king's touch, the reputed power of the king to cure certain skin diseases. The royal coronation cult and the king's touch established the reputation of French kings as miracle workers.

Anglo-Saxon England had never been part of the Carolingian Empire, but because it was Christian, England shared in the culture of the Latin West. England suffered extensive damage at the hands of the Vikings. After England was almost overwhelmed by a Danish invasion during the winter of 878–879, Alfred the Great (r. 871–899) finally defeated the Danes as spring approached. As king of only Wessex (not of all England), Alfred consolidated his authority and issued a new law code. Alfred's able successors

cooperated with the nobility more effectively than the monarchs in either East or West Francia and built a broad base of support in the local units of government, the hundreds and shires. The Anglo-Saxon monarchy also enjoyed the support of the Church, which provided it with skilled servants and spiritual authorization.

During the late ninth and tenth centuries, Anglo-Saxon England experienced a cultural revival under royal patronage. King Alfred proclaimed that the Viking invasions had been God's punishment for the neglect of learning, without which God's will could not be known. Alfred accordingly promoted the study of Latin. He also desired that all men of wealth learn to read the language of the English people. Under Alfred a highly sophisticated literature appeared in Old English. This literature included poems, sermons, commentaries on the Bible, and translations of important Latin works. The masterpiece of this era was a history called the *Anglo-Saxon Chronicle*. It was begun during Alfred's reign but maintained over several generations.

During the late tenth and early eleventh centuries, England was weakened by another series of Viking raids and a succession of feeble kings. In 1066 William, the duke of Normandy and a descendant of Vikings who had settled in the north of France, defeated King Harold, the last Anglo-Saxon king. William seized the English throne. William the Conqueror opened a new era in which English affairs became deeply intertwined with those of the duchy of Normandy and the kingdom of France.

DOCUMENT

Battle of Hastings (1066)

The Conversion of the Last Polytheists

As the core of the Latin West became politically stronger and economically more prosperous during the tenth and eleventh centuries, Christians made concerted attempts to convert the invaders, especially the polytheistic tribes in northern and eastern Europe. Through conversion, Latin Christianity dominated northern Europe up to the Russian border where Orthodox Christianity adopted from Byzantium held sway.

Among the polytheistic tribes in Scandinavia, the Baltic Sea region, and parts of eastern Europe, the first Christian conversions usually took place when a king or chieftain accepted Christianity. His subjects were expected to follow. Teaching Christian principles and forms of worship required much more time and effort, of course. Missionary monks usually arrived after a king's conversion, but these monks tended to take a tolerant attitude about variations in the liturgy. Because most Christians were isolated from one another, new converts tended to practice their own local forms of worship and belief. Missionaries and Christian princes discovered that the most effective way to combat this localizing tendency was to found bishoprics. The bishopric was a territorial unit (called the *diocese*), presided

Christian Church Imitates Polytheist Temple
The stave church was a type of wooden church built in northern Europe during the Middle Ages. Most of the surviving examples in Scandinavia are generally assumed to be modeled on polytheist temples. The Borgund church in Norway pictured here dates from about 1150.

over by an official (called the *bishop*), who was responsible for enforcing correct worship, combating the vestiges of polytheism and false Christian beliefs (known as *heresy*), and disciplining immorality. Especially among the nonliterate, formerly polytheist tribes in northern and eastern Europe, the foundation of bishoprics created cultural centers of considerable prestige that attracted members of the upper classes. Those educated under the supervision of these new bishops became influential servants to the ruling families, further enhancing the stature of Christian culture.

From the middle of the tenth century along the eastern frontiers of Germany, a line of newly established Catholic bishoprics became the base for the conversion of the polytheist Slavic tribes. Over a period of about sixty years, these German bishoprics pushed the Latin form of Christianity deep into east-central Europe. This effort ensured that the Poles, Bohemians (Czechs), and Magyars (Hungarians) looked to the West and the pope for their cultural models and religious leadership. These peoples remain overwhelmingly Catholic to this day.

The first bishoprics in Scandinavia were also established in the last half of the tenth century. Whereas Germans were primarily responsible for the spread of Latin Christianity among the Slavs, it was English missionaries who evangelized Scandinavia. Denmark had the first completely organized church in Scandinavia, represented by the establishment of nine bishoprics by 1060. The diffusion into Sweden, Norway, and Iceland came later after the strong kingdoms developed in those countries and a pro-Christian dynasty could assist the spread of the new religion. Christian conversion especially benefited women through the abandonment of polygamous marriages, common among the polytheist peoples. As a result, aristocratic women played an important role in helping convert their peoples to Christianity. That role gave them a lasting influence in the churches of the newly converted lands, both as founders and patrons of convents and as writers on religious subjects. By the end of the fourteenth century organized polytheistic worship had disappeared.

Unlike Bulgaria and Kievan Rus, Poland favored Latin Christianity, an association that helped create strong political and cultural ties to western Europe. The Slavic Poles inhabited a flat plain of forested land with small clearings for farming. First exposed to missionaries tied to Saint Methodius, Poland resisted Christianity until Prince Mieszko (ca. 960–992) created the most powerful of the Slav states and accepted Latin Christianity in 966 in an attempt to build political alliances with Christian princes. A new bishopric was established at Poznan with the design of coordinating missionary activities throughout the country. However, German dukes interfered with the administration of the Polish church in an attempt to expand their influence at Poland's expense. To gain outside assistance to counter the German threat, Mieszko formally subordinated his country to the Roman pope with the Donation of Poland (ca. 991). Thus began Poland's long and special relationship with the

CHRONOLOGY

The Western European Kingdoms Emerge

843–911	Carolingian dynasty in East Francia
843–987	Carolingian dynasty in West Francia
919–1024	Saxon or Ottonian dynasty
955	Otto I defeats Magyars
962	Otto crowned emperor in Rome
987–1328	Capetian dynasty in France
1066	William the Conqueror defeats last Anglo-Saxon king

papacy. At Mieszko's death, the territory of Poland approximated what it was at the end of World War II.

Mieszko's successor, Boleslaw the Brave (992–1025), expanded his territories through conquest, making Poland one of the largest European kingdoms. He guaranteed the independence of the Polish church from German ecclesiastical control by obtaining the pope's approval for a Polish archdiocese, and within a few years a string of bishoprics were set up across Poland. In 1000 the German emperor recognized the independence of Poland. In 1025 the pope gave Boleslaw a royal crown, making him the equal of any monarch in Europe. Boleslaw's immediate successors, however, allowed the central authority of the government to slip away into the hands of the local nobility and even lost the title of king.

The West in the East: The Crusades

■ What were the causes and consequences of the Crusades?

On a chilly November day in 1095 in a bare field outside Clermont, France, Pope Urban II (r. 1088–1099) delivered a landmark sermon to the assembled French clergy and laypeople eager to hear the pope. In stirring words Urban recalled that Muslims in the East were persecuting Christians and that the holy places in Palestine had been ransacked. He called upon the knights "to take up the cross" to defend their fellow Christians in distress.

Urban's appeal for a Crusade was stunningly successful. When he finished speaking, the crowd chanted back, "God wills it." The news of Urban's call for a holy war in the East spread like wildfire, and all across France and the western part of the German Empire knights prepared for the journey to Jerusalem. Unexpectedly and probably contrary to the pope's intentions, the poor and dispossessed also became enthused about an armed pilgrimage to the Holy Land. The zealous Peter the Hermit (ca. 1050–1115) preached the Crusade among the poor and homeless and gathered a huge unequipped, undisciplined army, which left for Jerusalem well in advance of the knights. The army was annihilated along the way.

Urban's call for a Crusade gave powerful religious sanction to the western Christian military expeditions against Islam. From 1095 until well into the thirteenth century, there were recurrent, large-scale Crusading expeditions as Christian knights from the Latin West attempted to take, retake, and protect Christian Jerusalem (see Map 8.4). But the ideal of going on a Crusade lasted long after the thirteenth century into modern times.

IMAGE

Crusaders Besieging a Medieval Castle

DOCUMENT

Pope Urban II Calls for the Crusades

Robert the Monk recorded what Pope Urban said to the assembly at the Council of Clermont in 1095. He addressed the crowd as the "race of Franks, race from across the mountains, race beloved and chosen by God." He went on to describe the situation in Jerusalem.

From the confines of Jerusalem and from the city of Constantinople a grievous report has gone forth and has repeatedly been brought to our ears; namely, that a race from the kingdom of the Persians, an accursed race, a race wholly alienated from God, "a generation that set not their heart aright, and whose spirit was not steadfast with God," has violently invaded the lands of those Christians and has depopulated them by pillage and fire. They have led away a part of the captives into their own country, and a part they have killed by cruel tortures. They have either destroyed the churches of God or appropriated them for the rites of their own religion. They destroy the altars, after having defiled them with their uncleanness. . . .

Let hatred therefore depart from among you, let your quarrels end, let wars cease, and let all dissensions and controversies slumber. Enter upon the road to the Holy Sepulcher; wrest that land from the wicked race, and subject it to yourselves. That land which, as the Scripture says, "floweth with milk and honey" was given by God into the power of the children of Israel. Jerusalem is the center of the earth; the land is fruitful above all others, like another paradise of delights. This spot the Redeemer of mankind has made illustrious by his advent, has beautified by his sojourn, has consecrated by his passion, has redeemed by his death, has glorified by his burial.

This royal city, however, situated at the center of the earth, is now held captive by the enemies of Christ and is subjected, by those who do not know God, to the worship of the heathen. She seeks, therefore, and desires to be liberated and ceases not to implore you to come to her aid. . . . Accordingly, undertake this journey eagerly for the remission of your sins, with the assurance of the reward of imperishable glory in the kingdom of heaven.

Source: Dennis Sherman, A. Tom Grunfeld, Gerald Markowitz, David Rosner, and Linda Heywood, eds. *World Civilizations: Sources, Images, and Interpretations,* 3rd ed. Copyright 2002, 1998, vol. 1, pp. 201–202.

The Origins of Holy War

The original impulse for the Crusades° was the threat that Muslim armies posed to Christian peoples, pilgrims, and holy places in the eastern Mediterranean. By the middle of the eleventh century the Seljuk Turks, who had converted to Islam, were putting pressure on the Byzantine empire. In 1071 the Seljuks defeated the Byzantine army at Manzikert; their victory opened all of Asia Minor to Muslim occupation. Pope Urban's appeal for a Crusade in 1095 came in response to a request for military assistance from the Byzantine emperor Alexius Comnenus, who probably thought he would get yet another band of Western mercenaries to help him reconquer Byzantine territory lost to the Seljuks. Instead, he got something utterly unprecedented, a massive volunteer army of perhaps 100,000 soldiers devoted less to cooperating with their Byzantine Christian brethren than to wresting Jerusalem from Muslim hands.

To people in the eleventh century, the very idea of Jerusalem had a mystical allure. Enhancing this allure was a widespread confusion between the actual earthly city of Jerusalem in Palestine, where Jesus had been crucified more than a millennium before, and the fantastic heavenly city of Jerusalem with walls of dazzling precious stones as promised in the Bible (Revelation 21:10ff). Many of the crusaders probably could not distinguish between the earthly and the heavenly cities and thought that when they abandoned their homes for Jerusalem, they were marching directly to Paradise. The promise of an eternal reward was reinforced by a special offer Pope Urban made in his famous sermon at Clermont to remit all penance for sin for those who went on the Crusade. Moreover, a penitential pilgrimage to a holy site such as Jerusalem provided a sinner with a pardon for capital crimes such as murder.

There was a significant difference between a pilgrim and a crusader, however. A pilgrim was always unarmed. A crusader carried weapons and was willing not just to

Map 8.4 The Major Crusades

During the first three Crusades, Christian armies and fleets from western Europe attacked Muslim strongholds and fortresses in the Middle East in an attempt to capture and hold Jerusalem. The Fourth Crusade never arrived in the Middle East, as it was diverted to besiege Constantinople.

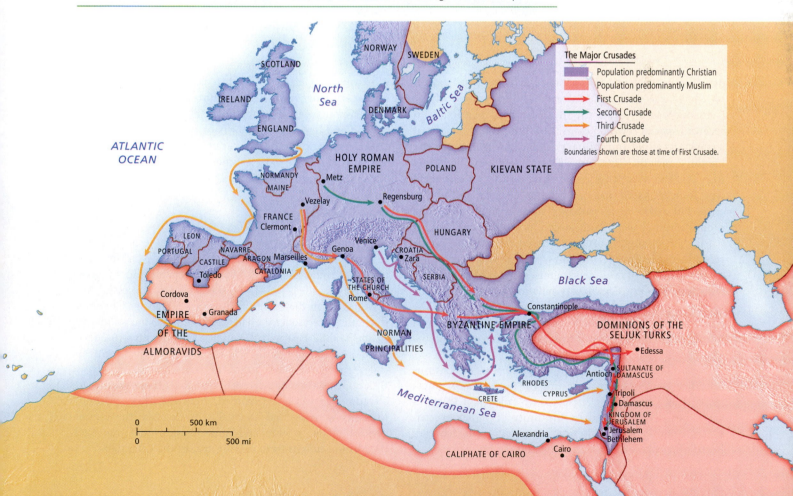

Jesus Christ Leading the Crusaders

The rider on the white horse is Jesus, who holds the Gospels in his right hand and the sword of righteousness in his teeth. The crusading knights bearing banners and shields emblazoned with the cross follow him. The figure in the upper left-hand corner represents St. John the Evangelist, whose writings were understood to prophesy the Crusades. This manuscript illumination dates from ca. 1310–1325.

defend other pilgrims from attack but to launch an assault on those he considered heathens. The innovation of the Crusades was to create the idea of armed pilgrims who received special rewards from the Church. The merger of a spiritual calling and military action was strongest in the knightly orders—Templars, Hospitallers, and Teutonic Knights. The men who joined these orders were soldiers who took monastic vows of poverty, chastity, and obedience. But rather than isolating themselves to pray in a monastery, they went forth, sword in hand, to conquer for Christ. These knightly orders exercised considerable political influence in Europe and amassed great wealth.

In the minds of crusader-knights, greed probably jostled with fervent piety. Growing population pressures and the spread of primogeniture (passing landed estates on to the eldest male heir) left younger sons with little to anticipate at home and much to hope for by seeking their fortunes in the Crusades.

Nevertheless, crusaders testified to the sense of community they enjoyed by participating in "the common enterprise of all Christians." The crusader Fulcher of Chartres was especially captivated by the unity displayed by crusaders from so many different countries: "Who has ever heard of speakers of so many languages in one army . . . If a Breton or a German wished to ask me something, I was utterly without words to reply. But although we were divided by language, we seemed to be like brothers in the love of God and like near neighbors of one mind."[4] For many crusaders the exhilarating experience of brotherhood in the love of God seemed to be a sufficient motive.

Crusading Warfare

The crusaders' enthusiasm for getting to Jerusalem impelled them to capture the holy city from the Muslims soon after they landed in the Middle East. In achieving this goal, the First Crusade (1095–1099) was strikingly successful, but it was as much the result of Muslim weakness as Christian strength. Several factors had weakened Muslim solidarity in the Middle East and the ability to resist the crusaders. First, the onslaught of the Seljuk Turks threatened the Arab states that controlled access to Jerusalem as much as Byzantium. When the crusaders arrived, these states had already been weakened from fighting the Turks. Second, Muslims were divided internally. There were theological divisions between Sunni and Shi'ite Muslims that prevented the Muslim caliphs from uniting against the Christians.

In 1099, after a little more than a month's siege, the crusaders scaled the walls of Jerusalem and took possession of the city, which was also holy to Muslims and Jews and previously largely inhabited by them. The Christian triumph led to the establishment of the Latin principalities, which were devoted to maintaining a Western foothold in the Holy Land. The Latin principalities included all of the territory in contemporary Lebanon, Israel, and Palestine.

The subsequent crusades never achieved the success of the first. In 1144 Muslims captured the northernmost Latin principality, the county of Edessa—a warning to westerners of the fragility of a defensive system that relied on a few scattered fortresses strung along a thin strip of coastline. In response to the loss of Edessa, Christians launched the Second Crusade (1147–1149). The ambitious offensive on several fronts failed disastrously. In 1187, the sultan of Egypt and Syria, Saladin (1137–1193), recaptured Jerusalem for Islam. In response to this dispiriting loss, the Third Crusade (1189–1192) assembled the most spectacular army of European chivalry ever seen, led by Europe's three most powerful kings: German emperor Frederick Barbarossa, Philip Augustus of France, and Richard the Lion-Heart of England. After Frederick drowned wading in a river en route and Philip went home, Richard the Lion-Heart negotiated a truce with Saladin.

The Fourth Crusade proved a particular disaster, at least for the integrity of the Crusading ideal. In 1199, Pope Innocent III called for yet another Crusade to recapture Jerusalem, but the Frankish knights and Venetian fleet were diverted to intervene in a disputed imperial succession in Byzantium. In 1204 they besieged and captured Constantinople. After the conquest the Westerners divided up among themselves the Byzantine Empire, set up a Latin regime that lasted until 1261, and neglected their oaths to reconquer Jerusalem. The Fourth Crusade dangerously weakened the Byzantine Empire by making it a prize for Western adventurers. None of the subsequent Crusades achieved lasting success in the Middle East, but the idea of

DOCUMENT

A Muslim Appeal for Jihad Against the Crusaders

After the Second Crusade (1147–1149) failed to conquer Damascus, Syria, an important Muslim city inland from the crusader states established in what is now Lebanon, an anonymous Muslim author called on all Muslims to resist another attack. In this appeal he calls for a defensive jihad. The passage begins with a quotation from Abu Hamid Al Ghazali (1058–1128), a prominent Muslim scholar.

All Muslims who were free, responsible for their acts and capable of bearing arms must march against [the unbelievers] until they form a force large enough to smite them. This war is to glorify the Word of God and to make His religion victorious over its enemies. . . . If the enemy attacks a town [in Syria] that is incapable of self-defense, all the towns in Syria must raise an army that could drive him back. . . . If, however, the soldiers in Syria are insufficient for the task, the inhabitants of the nearer surrounding countries have the duty to assist them, while those of the more remote lands are free from this obligation.

Apply yourself to carry out the precept of jihad! Help one another in order to protect your religion and your brothers! Seize this opportunity and march forth against the unbelievers, for it does not require too great an effort and God has prepared you for it! . . . Commit jihad to make combat in your soul before committing jihad against your enemies because your souls are worse enemies for you than your foes. Turn your soul away from disobedience to its creator so that you would achieve the much desired victory. . . . Forsake the sins that you insist on committing and then begin to do good deeds. . . . Fight for God as He deserves it!

Source: Richard Lim and David Kammerling Smith, eds. *The West in the Wider World: Sources and Perspectives*, vol. 1 (2003): 278.

Krak des Chevaliers
This crusader castle survives in northern Syria in what was once the County of Edessa, a Latin Christian principality constructed to defend the Holy Land. The word *krak* derives from an Arabic word meaning "strong fort."

Legends of the Borderlands: Roland and El Cid

From the eighth to the fifteenth centuries, Muslim and Latin Christian armies grappled with one another in the borderlands between their two civilizations in the Iberian peninsula, the territory now called Spain. The borderlands, however, were more than just places of conflict. During times of peace, Christians and Muslims traded with and even married one another, and in the confused loyalties typical of the times, soldiers and generals from both faiths frequently switched sides. These borderland clashes produced legends of great heroes, which once refashioned into epic poems created a lasting memory of Muslim and Christian animosity.

The Song of Roland, an Old French epic poem that dates from around 1100, tells a story about the Battle of Roncesvalles, which took place in 778. The actual historical battle had been a minor skirmish between Charlemagne's armies and some local inhabitants in Spain who were not Muslims at all, but *The Song of Roland* transforms this sordid episode into a great epic of Christian-Muslim conflict. In the climax of the poem, the Christian hero Roland, seeking renown for his valor, rejects his companion Oliver's advice to blow a horn to alert Charlemagne of a Muslim attack. The battle is hopeless, and when the horn is finally sounded it is too late to save Roland or Oliver. Roland's recklessness made him the model of a brave Christian knight.

In the subsequent Spanish border wars, the most renowned soldier was Rodrigo Díaz de Vivar (ca. 1043–1099), known to history as El Cid (from the Arabic word for "lord"). He is remembered in legend as a heroic knight fight-ing for the Christian Reconquest of the peninsula, but the real story of El Cid was much more self-serving. El Cid repeatedly switched allegiances to the Muslims. Even when a major Muslim invasion from North Africa threatened the very existence of Christian Spain, El Cid did not come to the rescue and instead undertook a private adventure to carve out a kingdom for himself in Muslim Valencia.

Soon after El Cid's death and despite his inconstant loyalty to Castile and Christianity, he was elevated to the status of the great hero of Christian Spain. The popularity of the twelfth-century epic poem *The Poem of My Cid* transformed this cruel, vindictive, and utterly self-interested man into a model of Christian virtue and self-sacrificing loyalty.

The medieval borderlands created legends of heroism and epic struggles that often stretched the truth. The borderlands were a wild frontier, not unlike the American frontier, into which desperate men fled to hide or to make opportunities for themselves. However, the lasting significance of the violent encounters that took place in these borderlands is not the nasty realities but the heroic models they produced. Poetry transformed reality into a higher truth that emphasized courage and faithfulness. Because these poems were memorized and recited in the vernacular languages of Old French and Castilian (now Spanish), they became a model of aristocratic values in medieval society and over the centuries a source for a national literary culture. Thus, becoming French or Spanish meant, in some respects, rejecting Islam, which has created a lasting anti-Muslim strain in western European culture.

Question for Discussion

How did transforming the accounts of battles between Christian and Muslims into heroic poems change how these events would be remembered among Christians?

The Death of Roland
No legend from the borderlands between Christianity and Islam had a greater influence on European Christian society than that of Roland.

He hands his glove, symbolizing a knight's honor, to God the Father. The gesture captures the concept that God accepted Roland's sacrifice for Christianity.

With his horn he slays a Muslim warrior.

In this fourteenth-century illuminated chronicle of the reign of Charlemagne, Roland is shown mortally wounded.

the Crusade continued to spark the imagination of Latin Christians for centuries.

The Significance of the Crusades

Despite the capture of Jerusalem during the First Crusade, the crusaders could not maintain control of the city and for more than two centuries wasted enormous efforts on what proved to be a futile enterprise. Neither did any of the Latin principalities in the Middle East survive for very long. The crusaders who resided in these principalities were obliged to learn how to live and trade with their Muslim neighbors, but few of them learned Arabic or took seriously Muslim learning. The strongest Islamic cultural and intellectual influences on Christian Europe came through Sicily and Spain rather than via returning crusaders.

The most important immediate consequence of the Crusades was not the tenuous Western possession of the Holy Land but the expansion of trade and economic contacts the expeditions facilitated. No one profited more from the Crusades than the Italian cities that provided transportation and supplies to the crusading armies. During the Crusades, Genoa, Pisa, and Venice were transformed from small ports of regional significance into hubs of international trade. Genoa and Venice established their own colonial outposts in the eastern Mediterranean, and both vied to monopolize the rich commerce of Byzantium. The new trade controlled by these cities included luxury goods, such as silk, Persian carpets, medicine, and spices, all expensive, exotic consumer goods found in the bazaars of the Middle East. Profits from this trade helped galvanize the economy of western Europe, leading to an era of exuberant economic growth during the twelfth and thirteenth centuries.

During the Crusades Muslims and Christians mixed mutual curiosity with militant hostility. Their tentative appreciation of each other was undermined by grotesque misunderstandings. The complexity of the relationship became especially clear in spiritual centers such as the mosques and churches of Jerusalem. While Jerusalem was occupied by Christian crusaders, an Arab nobleman named Ousama made a business trip to Jerusalem. To fulfill the obligation of his Muslim faith to pray daily, Ousama went to the Al-Aksa mosque, the oldest Muslim shrine in Jerusalem. He was struck by the contrast between the crusaders who had resided in Jerusalem for some time and had an understanding of Islam and those who had just arrived and "show themselves more inhuman." Some of the old-timers had even befriended him and made certain he had a place to pray. But the newcomers were far less friendly. Ousama reported, "One day I went into [the mosque] and glorified

DOCUMENT

An Arab-Syrian Gentleman Discusses the Franks

Allah. I was engrossed in my praying when one of the Franks [as Muslims called all western Europeans] rushed at me, seized me and turned my face to the East, saying, 'That is how to pray!'" At that time Christians were supposed to pray facing the rising sun in the East. Muslims pray facing Mecca to the south of Jerusalem. On two occasions the Templars, members of the Christian military order who guarded the mosque, had to expel the zealous Frank from the mosque so Ousama could return to his prayers. The Templars apologized to Ousama, saying, "He is a stranger who has only recently arrived from Frankish lands. He has never seen anyone praying without turning to the East."

An uneasy familiarity developed among the Christians and Muslims in Jerusalem during this period. It was possible for an Arab such as Ousama to describe the Templars as his "friends," and they in turn protected him from the intolerance of the newly arrived Europeans. This peculiar mixture of friendliness and intolerance cut both ways. Ousama recounted another scene he witnessed at the Dome of the Rock, the place from which it was believed that Muhammad had ascended to heaven but which the crusaders had transformed into a Christian church. A Templar approached a Muslim and asked if he would like to see God as a child. When the Muslim answered "yes," the Templar displayed a painting of the Virgin Mary with the Christ child on her lap. The Muslims were shocked at the Christian's idolatry of referring to an image as God. Ousama exclaimed, "May Allah raise himself high above those who speak such impious things!"[5]

CHRONOLOGY	
The Crusades	
1071	Battle of Manzikert; Seljuk Turks defeat the Byzantine emperor
1095	Council of Clermont; Urban II calls First Crusade
1095–1099	First Crusade
1099	Christians capture Jerusalem
1147–1149	Second Crusade
1189–1192	Third Crusade, led by Emperor Frederick Barbarossa (who drowned), King Richard the Lion-Heart of England, and King Philip II of France
1202–1204	Fourth Crusade, culminates in capture of Constantinople by Western crusaders

Conclusion

An Emerging Unity in the Latin West

The most lasting legacy of the Early Middle Ages was the distinction between western and eastern Europe, established by the patterns of conversion to Christianity. Slavs in eastern Europe, such as the Poles, who were converted to Latin Christianity looked to Rome as a source for inspiration and eventually considered themselves part of the West. Those who converted to Orthodox Christianity, such as the Bulgarians and Russians, remained Europeans certainly but came to see themselves as culturally distinct from their Western counterparts. The southern border of Christian Europe was defined by the presence of the Islamic caliphates, which, despite recurrent border wars with Christian kingdoms, greatly contributed to the cultural vitality of the West during this period.

During this same period, however, a tentative unity began to emerge among western European Christians, just as Byzantium fell into decline and Islam divided among competing caliphates. That ephemeral unity was born in the hero worship of Charlemagne and the resurrection of the Roman Empire in the West, symbolized by his coronation in Rome. The collapse of the Carolingian Empire created the basis for the European kingdoms that dominated the political order of Europe for most of the subsequent millennium. These new kingdoms were each quite distinctive, and yet they shared a heritage from ancient Rome and the Carolingians that emphasized the power of the law on the one hand and the intimate relationship between royal and ecclesiastical authority on the other. The most distinguishing mark of western Europe became the practice of Latin Christianity, a distinctive form of Christianity identifiable by the use of the Latin language and the celebration of the church liturgy in Latin.

In the wake of the Carolingian Empire, a system of personal loyalties associated with lordship and vassalage came to dominate the military and political life of Latin Christendom. All medieval kings were obliged to build their monarchies on the social foundations of lordship, which provided cohesion in kingdoms that lacked bureaucracies and sufficient numbers of trained officials. In addition to the lords and vassals the Latin kingdoms relied on the support of the Church to provide unity and often to provide the services of local government. By the end of the eleventh century, emerging western Europe had recovered sufficiently from the many destructive invaders and had built new political and ecclesiastical institutions that enabled it to assert itself on a broader stage. The first move was sensational: The leaders of the Latin Church declared their intention to achieve what the Byzantines had failed to do—recapture Jerusalem from Islam. With the Crusades, western Europeans began an aggressive engagement outside their own continent.

Suggestions for Further Reading

For a comprehensive listing of suggested readings, please go to www.ablongman.com/levack2e/chapter8

Bachrach, Bernard S. *Early Medieval Jewish Policy in Western Europe.* 1977. A significant revisionist view of the history of the Jews in Latin Christian Europe.

Bartlett, Robert. *The Making of Europe: Conquest, Colonization and Cultural Change: 950–1350.* 1993. The best, and often greatly stimulating, analysis of how Latin Christianity spread in post-Carolingian Europe.

Brown, Peter. *The Rise of Western Christendom: Triumph and Diversity* A.D. *200–1000.* 2001. A brilliant interpretation of the development of Christianity in its social context.

Cohen, Jeremy. *Living Letters of the Law: Ideas of the Jew in Medieval Christianity.* 1999. A masterful investigation of early medieval Judaism.

Geary, Patrick J. *The Peoples of Europe in the Early Middle Ages.* 2002. Discusses the emergence of the new kingdoms of Europe, stressing the incorporation of Roman elements.

Hollister, C. Warren. *Medieval Europe: A Short History.* 1997. This concise, crisply written text presents the development of Europe during the Middle Ages by charting its progression from a primitive rural society, sparsely settled and impoverished, to a powerful and distinctive civilization.

Jones, Gwyn. *A History of the Vikings.* 2001. A comprehensive, highly readable analysis.

Keen, Maurice, ed. *Medieval Warfare: A History.* 1999. Lucid specialist studies of aspects of medieval warfare.

Lawrence, C. H. *Medieval Monasticism.* 2001. A fine introduction to the phenomenon of Christian monasticism.

Mayr-Harting, Henry. *The Coming of Christianity to Anglo-Saxon England.* 1991. How a Germanic people were converted to Christianity.

McKitterick, Rosamond. *The Early Middle Ages.* 2001. The best up-to-date survey for the period 400–1000. It is composed of separate essays by leading specialists.

Moorhead, John. *The Roman Empire Divided, 400–700.* 2001. The best recent survey of the period.

Reuter, Timothy. *Germany in the Early Middle Ages, c. 800–1056.* 1991. A lucid explanation of the complexities of German history in this period.

Reynolds, Susan. *Fiefs and Vassals: The Medieval Evidence Reinterpreted.* 1994. The most important reexamination of the feudalism problem.

Riché, Pierre. *The Carolingians: A Family Who Forged Europe.* 1993. Translated from the 1983 French edition, this book traces the rise, fall, and revival of the Carolingian dynasty, and shows how it molded the shape of a post-Roman Europe that still prevails today. This is basically a family history, but the family dominated Europe for more than two centuries.

Riché, Pierre. *Education and Culture in the Barbarian West, Sixth Through Eighth Centuries,* translated from the 3rd French ed.

by John J. Contreni. 1975. Demonstrates the rich complexity of learning during this period, once thought to be the Dark Ages of education.

Riley-Smith, Jonathan Simon Christopher. *The Crusades: A Short History.* 1987. Exactly what the title says.

Riley-Smith, Jonathan Simon Christopher. *The Oxford Illustrated History of the Crusades.* 2001. An utterly engaging, comprehensive study.

Stenton, Frank M. *Anglo-Saxon England.* 2001. This classic history covers the period ca. 550–1087 and traces the development of English society from the oldest Anglo-Saxon laws and kings to the extension of private lordship.

Strayer, Joseph B., ed. *Dictionary of the Middle Ages.* 1986. An indispensable reference work.

Webster, Leslie, and Michelle Brown, eds. *The Transformation of the Roman World, A.D. 400–900.* 1997. A well-illustrated synthesis with maps and bibliography.

Wickham, Chris. *Early Medieval Italy: Central Government and Local Society, 400–1000.* 1981. Examines the economic and social transformation of Italy.

Notes

1. Willibald, *The Life of Boniface,* in Clinton Albertson, trans., *Anglo-Saxon Saints and Heroes* (1967), 308–310.

2. Kent Rigsby, *Zeitschrift für Papyrologie and Epigraphik,* 126 (1999), 175–176.

3. Quoted in Edward Peters, *Europe and the Middle Ages* (1989), 158.

4. Fulcher of Chartres, *Historia Hierosolymitana,* ed. Heinrich Hagenmeyer (1913), 202–203.

5. *The Autobiography of Ousama* (1995–1188), trans. G. R. Potter, in Brian Tierney, ed., *The Middle Ages,* Vol. 1: *Sources of Medieval History,* 3rd ed. (1978), 162.

Medieval Civilization: The Rise of Western Europe

FRANCIS OF ASSISI (CA. 1182–1226) WAS THE SON OF A PROSPEROUS MER-chant in a modest-sized town in central Italy. As a young man of 20, Francis joined his friends and neighbors as a member of the Assisi forces in a war with the nearby town of Perugia. Taken prisoner, he spent nearly a year in captivity; on his release he became seriously ill, the first of many painful illnesses that afflicted him periodically throughout his life. During a journey to join another army, he had the first of his many visions or dreams that led him to give up fighting and to convert to a life of spiritu-ality and service to others. Initially he searched about for what to do. He went on a pilgrimage to Rome as a beggar, and although lepers personally disgusted him he not only gave alms to a leper but kissed his hand. Then, according to his earliest biographer, while praying in the dilapidated chapel of San Damiano outside the gates of Assisi, he received a direct command from the crucifix above the altar: "Go Francis, and repair my house which, as you see, is nearly in ruins."

At first, Francis understood this command literally and began to repair churches and chapels. To raise money he took some of the best cloth from his father's shop and rode off to a nearby town where he sold the cloth and the horse. When the priest of San Damiano rejected the funds, Francis threw the money out the window. Angered by the theft of cloth, his father de-nounced him to the town's authorities, and when Francis refused the sum-mons to court, his father had him brought to be interrogated by the bishop of Assisi. Before his father could say anything to the bishop, Francis "without a word stripped off his clothing even removing his pants and gave them back to his father." Stark naked, Francis announced that he was switching his obe-dience from his earthly to his heavenly father. The astonished bishop gave him a cloak, but Francis renounced all family ties and worldly goods to live a life of complete poverty. Henceforth, he seemed to understand the com-mand to "repair my house" as a metaphor for the entire Church, which he intended to serve in a new way.

Interior of a Gothic Cathedral The narrow columns and pointed arches of the Gothic style drew the worshipers' eyes upward toward Heaven. The play of light from the stained-glass windows created mysterious visual effects.

Dressed in rags, he went about town begging for food, preaching repentance in the streets, and ministering to outcasts and lepers. Without training as a priest or license as a preacher, Francis at first seemed like a devout eccentric or even a dangerous heretic, but his rigorous imitation of Jesus began to attract like-minded followers. In 1210 Francis and twelve of his ragged brothers showed up in the opulent papal court of Pope Innocent III seeking approval of Francis's rule for a new religious order. A less discerning man than Innocent would have sent the strange band packing or thrown them in prison as a danger to established society, but Innocent was impressed by Francis's sincerity and his willingness to profess obedience to the pope. Innocent's provisional approval of the Franciscans was a brilliant stroke, in that it gave the papacy a way to manage the widespread enthusiasm for a life of spirituality and purity.

The life of Francis of Assisi and the religious order he founded, the Friars Minor (Lesser Brothers), known as the Franciscans, epitomized the strengths and tensions of medieval Europe. Francis was a product of the newly prosperous towns of Europe, which began to grow at an unprecedented rate after about 1050. In the streets of the towns like Assisi that thrived on profits from the international cloth trade, the extremes of wealth and poverty were always on display. Rich merchants such as Francis's father lived in splendid comfort and financed an urban building boom that had not been seen in the West for more than a thousand years. The most lasting manifestations of that building boom were the vast new cathedrals, the pride of every medieval city. At the same time wretchedly poor people, many of them immigrants from the overpopulated countryside, starving, and homeless, lined the steps into the great churches begging for alms. Francis abhorred the immorality of this contrast between wealth and poverty. His reaction was to reject all forms of wealth, to give away all his possessions, and to distain money as if it were some kind of poison. He and his followers devoted themselves to the poor and abandoned. They became traveling street preachers who relied entirely on the charity of others for food and shelter. Francis's rejection of the material world was not just a protest against the materialist values of his times. It was a total denial of the self, or to put it in modern terms, a rejection of all forms of egotism.

In a period that placed great emphasis on hierarchic authority and on the privileges of rank in both society and the Church, Francis insisted on absolute equality within his order. Unlike other orders in which the educated, aristocratic monks prayed and sang while the uneducated lay brothers performed physical labor, the Franciscans made no distinctions on the basis of learning or social rank among its members. Francis's commitment to equality was stunningly revolutionary for his times. Just as revolutionary was his brave commitment to convert the Muslims through persuasion rather than force. During Francis's lifetime, crusaders from western Europe had been fighting Muslims on and off for more than a century. After several attempts to travel to Muslim lands, Francis went to Egypt, where crusaders were besieging Damietta. He managed to enter the Muslim camp and preached to the sultan himself, who was reportedly so impressed that he gave Francis permission to travel to the Holy Land.

Based on the efforts of the knights who fought in the Crusades, European merchants, and Latin Christian preachers and thinkers, the Catholic West began to assert itself militarily, economically, and intellectually both in Byzantium and against the Muslim world. As a result, western Europeans more sharply distinguished themselves from the Orthodox and Muslim worlds. The West became more exclusively Latin and Catholic.

St. Francis of Assisi Asks Pope Innocent III for a License to Preach
The drama of the meeting between the simple brothers shown kneeling, presenting their rule to the pope, and the sumptuous prelates of the curia is captured by the greatest of all medieval painters, Giotto. This fresco was painted in the Franciscan church in Assisi shortly before 1300.

The consolidation of a distinctive Western identity and the projection of Western power outside Europe were made possible by internal developments within Europe. The agricultural revolution of the eleventh century stimulated population growth and urbanization. Fed by more productive farms, the expanding cities began to produce industrial goods, such as woolen cloth, that could be sold abroad in exchange for luxury goods from the Middle East and Asia. A number of vigorous kings created political stability in the West by consolidating their authority through financial and judicial bureaucracies. The most effective of these kings used a variety of strategies to force the most dangerous element in society, the landed aristocrats, to serve the royal interest. At the same time, the West experienced a period of creative ferment unequaled since antiquity. The Roman Catholic Church played a central role in encouraging intellectual and artistic activity, but there was also a flourishing literature in the vernacular languages such as French, German, and Italian. All these developments lead to the question, how did western European civilization mature during the eleventh through thirteenth centuries?

■ How was medieval western European economy and society organized around manors and cities?
■ How did the Catholic Church consolidate its hold over the Latin West?
■ How did the western European monarchies strengthen themselves?
■ What made western European culture distinctive?

Two Worlds: Manors and Cities

■ How was medieval western European economy and society organized around manors and cities?

After the end of the destructive Magyar and Viking invasions of the ninth and tenth centuries, the population of western Europe recovered dramatically. Technological innovations created the agricultural revolution° that increased the supply of food. With more food available, people were better nourished than they had been in more than 500 years. As a result of more and better food, the population began to grow. In the seventh century all of Europe was home to only 14 million inhabitants. Much of the land cultivated in the ancient world had reverted to wild forests, simply because there were not enough people left to farm it due to the deaths from plague and the Germanic invasions. By 1300 the population had exploded to 74 million. From the seventh to the fourteenth centuries, then, the population grew many times over, perhaps as much as 500 percent. The most dramatic signs of population growth began after the year 1000.

The Medieval Agricultural Revolution

At the beginning of the eleventh century, the vast majority of people lived in small villages or isolated farmsteads. Peasants literally scratched out a living from a small area of cleared land around the village by employing a light scratch plow that barely turned over the soil. The farms produced mostly grain, which was consumed as bread, porridge, and ale or beer. Vegetables were rare, meat and fish uncommon. Over the course of the century, the productivity of the land was greatly enhanced by a number of innovations that came into widespread use.

Technological Innovations

The invention of new labor-saving devices ushered in the power revolution. This development, which occurred in the

A Scratch Plow
This illumination, dated 1028 from the Abbey of Montecassino in Italy, depicts the labor of the four seasons. The plowman on the right uses a light, unwheeled scratch plow that could not dig deeply into the soil, providing less efficient aeration than the heavy *carruca* plow, which was introduced later in the eleventh century.

tenth to twelfth centuries, harnessed the first new sources of power since the domestication of oxen and the invention of the ship in the ancient world. There would not be a technological discovery of similar magnitude until the development of steam power in the eighteenth century. Perhaps the most notable innovation was the exploitation of non-animal sources of power from water and wind. The water mill was invented in late Roman times, but it came into widespread use only in the tenth and eleventh centuries. Water mills were first used to grind grain but were gradually adapted to a wide variety of tasks, including turning saws to mill timber. By the end of the twelfth century windmills also began to appear, which were used for similar purposes.

As important as the harnessing of water and wind power was the enhanced ability to use animal power. Knights began to breed large, powerful war-horses. They equipped their horses with metal armor and stirrups, which kept knights on their horses, and metal horseshoes (until then, horses' hooves had been bound in cloth), which gave horses better footing and traction. The exploitation of power of animals also became more efficient with the introduction of a new type of horse collar, which increased the animal's pulling power. Earlier collars fit tightly around a horse's neck, which choked the animal if it pulled too great a weight. The new collar transferred the pressure points from the throat to the shoulders. Originally devised to make horses more effective at fighting, the collar was adapted to make both horses and oxen more efficient farm draft animals. With enhanced animal pulling power, farmers could plow the damp, heavy clay soils of northern Europe much more efficiently.

The centerpiece of the agricultural revolution was the heavy plow, which replaced the widely used Mediterranean scratch plow. Developed for light, sandy soils that were easily broken up, the scratch plow was barely able to dig into the poorly drained soils of the northern European plain.

The heavy plow had several distinctive advantages. It cut through and lifted the soil, aerating it and bringing to the surface minerals vital for plant growth. It created a furrow that channeled drainage, preventing the fields from being flooded by the frequent rains of northern Europe. The heavy plow was very cumbersome, however. It required six or eight horses or oxen to pull it, and no single peasant family in the tenth or eleventh century was able to afford that many draft animals. Farmers had to pool their animals to create plow teams, a practice that required mutual planning and cooperation. A two-wheeled heavy plow pulled by a team of eight oxen was difficult to turn, which meant it was best to continue plowing in a straight line for as long as possible. Thus, the heavy plow required peasants to cooperate further in redesigning their fields—from compact square fields, which had been cross-plowed with the older scratch plow, to long narrow fields that minimized the number of turns and provided a headland at the end to permit the draft team to make a wide turn. The new plow created the elongated fields that were distinctive to northern Europe.

The necessity to replenish the soil meant that half the arable land lay fallow while the other half was planted with crops. The fields would be reversed in the following year. In northern Europe farm animals were allowed to graze in the fallow field, what was called the open field, leaving their manure to recondition its soil. This practice, the two-field system, was gradually supplanted by the three-field system. In the three-field system one field was planted in the fall with grain; one was planted in the spring with beans, peas, or lentils; and one lay fallow. Both fall and spring plantings were harvested in the summer, after which all the fields shifted. The open three-field system produced extraordinary advantages: the amount of land under cultivation was increased from one-half to two-thirds; beans planted in the spring rotation returned nitrogen to the soil; and the crop

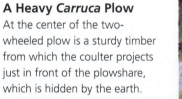

A Heavy *Carruca* Plow
At the center of the two-wheeled plow is a sturdy timber from which the coulter projects just in front of the plowshare, which is hidden by the earth.

rotation combined with animal manure reduced soil exhaustion from excessive grain planting.

The agricultural revolution had a significant effect on society. First, villagers learned to cooperate—by pooling draft animals for plow teams, redesigning and elongating their fields, coordinating the three-field rotation of crops, and timing the harvest schedule. To accomplish these cooperative ventures, they created village councils and developed habits of collective decision making that were essential for stable community life. Second, the system produced not only more food, but better food. Beans and other vegetables grown in the spring planting were rich in proteins. Slaughtering cattle for meat was still out of the question for peasants, but a plate of beans had a nutritional value similar to that of beef.

Manors and Peasants

The medieval agricultural economy bound landlords and peasants together in a unit of management called the manor. A manor referred to the holding of a single lord and the community of farmers who worked it. A single village might be divided up to serve several small manors, or a large manor might draw from several villages. Some lords possessed several manors and traveled from one to another throughout the year. The lord of the manor usually had his own large house or stone castle and served as the presiding judge of the community. However, most lords probably did not dictate what happened at the sessions of the manor court, which probably functioned as a kind of village meeting in most cases. Although the lord was clearly the social superior of the peasants on his manor, he could not rule effectively without their cooperation. The lord typically appointed the priest of the parish church and was responsible for enforcing church attendance and maintaining the church buildings. The parish priest worked land loaned to him by the lord in exchange for his religious services to the village and manor.

Unlike in the ancient world, in which slaves performed most of the heavy farm work, slaves seldom worked on farms during the Middle Ages. A much more common status for a farm worker or peasant was that of serf. Unlike slaves, serfs° were not owned, but they were tied to a specific manor, which they could not leave. They had certain legal rights denied slaves, such as the right to a certain portion of what they produced, but they were obliged to subject themselves to the lord's will. In theory, at least, the relationship between the lord and his serfs was reciprocal. The lord supplied the land, sometimes tools and seed, and protection from invaders and bandits. In return serfs supplied the labor necessary to work the land. Serfs were most common in England and northern France.

There were also peasants, known as freeholders, who worked as independent farmers and owned their land outright. Freeholders appeared in Scandinavia, northern Germany, southern France, Switzerland, and northern Italy. In many villages of Europe freeholders could be found scattered among larger communities of serfs.

At the bottom of rural peasant society were the numerous impoverished cottagers who farmed smaller plots of land than serfs or free peasants but who did not have the right to pass the land down to succeeding generations as serfs and free peasants did. Even serfdom, which was onerous, was preferable to being a cottager or completely landless; at least serfdom provided peasants with the means to feed themselves and their families.

The most important social units on a medieval manor were families who worked the land together, each member performing tasks suitable to their abilities, strength, and age. The rigors of medieval farm labor did not permit a fastidious division of labor between women and men. Women did not usually drive the heavy plow, but they toiled at other physically demanding tasks. The life of one young girl—documented because she later achieved sainthood as Saint Alpaix—was probably typical. From age 12, Alpaix

Twelfth-Century Manor Made Possible by the Heavy Plow

Aerial photograph of the manor of West Whelpington North (England), which was settled in the twelfth century but whose inhabitants died out during the Black Death of the fourteenth century (see Chapter 10). Outlines of the individual families' farm gardens can be seen in the left center. On the lower right are the ridges and furrows of the elongated fields required by the use of the heavy plow.

worked with her father in the fields, carrying heavy baskets of manure and sheep dung to fertilize the garden. When her arms became exhausted, she was harnessed to a sledge by a rope so that she could drag manure to the fields. During the critical harvest times, women and children worked alongside men from dawn to dusk. Young girls typically worked as gleaners, picking up the stalks and kernels that the male harvesters dropped or left behind, and girls were responsible for weeding and cleaning the fields. Before the use of water mills and windmills, women ground the grain by hand.

The Great Migrations and the Hunger for Land

During the Middle Ages most peasant families, whether serfs or freeholders, were considerably better off than had been their ancestors before the new technological innovations. After the agricultural revolution nutritional levels improved so dramatically that the condition of permanent famine that had plagued Europe for centuries was over. At first the population seems to have grown through a decrease in death rates but after 1100 a "baby boom" led to even greater increases in the population.

The effect of the baby boom meant that the amount of land available to farm was insufficient to support the expanding population of the manors. As more and more young people entered the workforce, they either sought opportunities in the cities or sought land of their own. Both options meant that many young people and whole families had to migrate. On the rutted old Roman roads and the paths that had sprung up where the roads did not go was a continuous traffic of travelers—the younger sons of nobles, demobilized soldiers, merchants, monks, pilgrims, and innumerable peasants—all moving from village to village, from village to town, and even to distant lands. For example, in an English village in 1247 there were forty-seven heads of families, three of whom were recent immigrants. Among their sons twelve boys went away to join the Church, seven sought jobs in town, twenty-four wandered off to places unknown in search of their fortunes, and only twenty-three were still there. In other words, two-thirds of the boys left home. Among the daughters twenty-seven, a little less than half, married outside the village.

Where did all these people go? At first, many invaded the "common lands." Surrounding every cultivated manor were common lands consisting of pastures, wetlands, scrub, and forests, reserved to common use. Cattle grazed in the pastures, anyone could gather reeds or berries in the wetlands or scrub, and the forests supplied wood for fuel and building materials as well as forage for pigs. The common lands, especially the scrub and forests, were the first to be cleared and put under the plow to grow more grain. Some of these lands had been plowed in ancient times but allowed to revert to the forest during the centuries of declining and stagnant population before 1000. Other clearings pushed into virgin forests and mountain slopes that had been avoided

because of the difficulty of farming them. But another solution was also at hand: invading someone else's land.

Migrants seeking to clear new lands for agriculture moved in three directions: Germans into the Slavic lands to the east, Scandinavians to the far north and north Atlantic islands, and Christian Spaniards to the south into previously Muslim territories. In east-central Europe Germanic and Slavic-speaking peoples had fought for centuries for control of the productive farm lands. Up until about 1100 the struggle had been fairly balanced, especially after Poland unified and became Christian. During the twelfth and thirteenth centuries, however, the balance decisively shifted in favor of the Germans, who launched a concerted assault on Polish lands. The German invasion of Poland involved the most dramatic example of racism found in the Middle Ages as the Poles, despite their conversion to Christianity, were described in propaganda as "pagans" and "repulsive beasts." The German peasants who migrated had military support and were encouraged by ambitious princes with names such as Albert the Bear and Henry the Lion. The German movement eastward was steady and relentless, especially after the crusading knights of the Teutonic Order spread fire and sword across northern Poland into Estonia until they completely cut off the rest of Poland from access to the sea. To attract immigrants in these newly acquired lands, peasants were offered lower feudal dues than in Germany and granted very large plots. Scattered across Poland and Bohemia, German-speaking villages sprung up that were autonomous enough to ignore the laws of the host country.

In the north Vikings in the ninth, tenth, and early eleventh centuries had raided and invaded deep into northern Europe and the British Isles and had established settlements as far as Normandy in France and Sicily, where they had taken over already occupied lands. When Vikings arrived in Iceland there was not a single living soul there and in Greenland only a few Eskimos from Baffin Island. After 1100 their descendants in Scandinavia launched a new phase of expansion as they cleared lands for farming on the Scandinavian peninsula, which except for Denmark was barely settled at all. During the twelfth and thirteenth centuries, families hungry for land pushed into the inland forests of Scandinavia and up the coast of Norway. Because of the difficulties of living in the far north, these villages were almost completely independent from obligations to the king and created strong collective obligations, unknown elsewhere in the West.

Whereas the Germans killed off or drove away the Poles, and the Scandinavians cleared uninhabited lands, in Spain a very different kind of process took place. Chapters 7 and 8 discussed the Spanish Reconquest, the military efforts of the Christian kings of northern Spain to reconquer the parts of southern and central Spain under Muslim caliphates. The Reconquest was a military and ideological enterprise that lasted from the eleventh to fifteenth centuries, but in the van of the soldiers followed a much more peaceful process of settlement and assimilation. Once the caliphs were defeated, massacres and expulsions of Muslims ceased as Christian settlers moved into the newly reconquered lands. The population was regrouped into separate Muslim and Christian neighborhoods and villages, and with much less violence than the Germans in Poland, Christian Spaniards migrated into formerly Muslim lands in large numbers.

Between 1100 and 1300, while the population was growing enormously, between 15 and 40 percent more land was brought under cultivation in Europe. The new land either had been untouched for farming as in northern Scandinavia or was taken from peoples who had lived on the borders of Latin Christendom, especially in the East. As Chapter 10 discusses, by about 1300 all the new lands potentially available for cultivation were gone. At that point the ability of Europe to sustain its population growth was compromised and a massive demographic catastrophe followed in the fourteenth century. However, the vibrant civilization discussed in the rest of this chapter was the direct consequence of the European demographic success of the eleventh through thirteenth centuries.

The Growth of Cities

Before the eleventh century the vast majority of people in Europe lived on manors, in rural villages, or perhaps in small market towns of a few thousand people. The cities that survived from the ancient world remained small, except in the Mediterranean. Constantinople was by far the largest city, with a population in the hundreds of thousands. The vibrant Islamic cities of Spain were the largest in western Europe, and it was said that more people could fit into the mosque of Córdoba than lived in Rome. When the population began to grow as a consequence of the agricultural revolution, migrants from the manors and villages swelled the small market towns into cities and repopulated the few cities that had survived from antiquity.

The Challenge of Free Cities

The newly thriving cities proved to be troublesome for the lords, bishops, and kings who usually had legal authority over them. As the population grew and urban merchants, such as Francis of Assisi's father, became increasingly rich, the cities in which they lived enjoyed even greater resources in people and money than those available to the rural lords. In many places the citizens of the new enlarged towns attempted to rid themselves of their lords to establish self-rule or, at least, substantial autonomy for their city. In the cities of north-central Italy, for example, the prominent townsmen began to chafe at the violent authority the rural lords held over them. The lords taxed or even stole the wealth that the townsmen earned through manufacturing

and trade. The lords made life unsafe and unbearable, fighting among themselves and abusing the unarmed townsmen. To counter the power of the lords, townsmen formed sworn defensive associations called communes°, which quickly became the effective government of the towns. The communes evolved into city-states, which were self-governing cities that became small states by seizing control of the surrounding countryside. Perhaps as many as a hundred or more cities in north-central Italy formed communes after 1070.

The Italian communes created the institutions and culture of self-rule. They were not fully democratic, but in many of them a significant percentage of the male population, including artisans, could vote for public officials, hold office themselves, and have a voice in important decisions such as going to war or raising new taxes. They also developed a new ethic that emphasized the civic responsibilities of citizens to protect the weakest members of the community, to beautify the city with public buildings and monuments, and to defend it by serving in the militia and paying taxes. These cities created vital and lasting community institutions, some of which survive to this day.

Outside Italy the movement for urban liberty was strongest in southern France, the Christian parts of Spain, and the Netherlands. Kings fiercely resisted attempts to establish urban autonomy. Especially in northern Europe, urban liberty was often extracted at a high price. Townsmen bought their freedom by agreeing to pay higher taxes to kings, who were always desperate for cash. London, an ancient Roman city that revived by the end of the eleventh century, bartered with several kings for civic autonomy, which it never entirely achieved.

In the wake of the Crusades several north Italian cities, especially Venice, Genoa, and Pisa, became ports of international significance. Sailors from these cities had transported the Crusading knights to the Holy Land, Egypt, Syria, and Byzantium. Even after the Latin kingdoms of the Levant collapsed, these cities kept footholds in the eastern Mediterranean, some of which evolved into colonies. Through these trading cities western Europe became integrated into the international luxury trade, which they carried out with ships crisscrossing the Mediterranean. By the thirteenth century the Italian shipping merchants began to challenge the domination of the Muslim caravan trade.

The Economic Boom Years

The cities of the medieval West thrived on an economic base of unprecedented prosperity. What made possible the twelfth- and thirteenth-century economic boom? Besides the agricultural revolution of the eleventh century that enabled population growth, three other factors proved crucial.

First, there were advances in transportation networks. Trade in grain, woolen cloth, and other bulk goods depended on the use of relatively cheap water transportation for hauling goods. Where there were neither seaports nor

A Medieval Town

Painted on the wall of the city council chambers in Siena, Italy, this fresco from 1338–1339 depicts what a well-governed medieval town should look like. Workers repair buildings, merchants bring goods into the bustling city, students quietly study, and the streets are so safe that young women dance in the streets on their way to a wedding.

navigable rivers, goods had to be hauled cross-country by pack train, a very expensive enterprise. In western Europe there were no land transportation routes or pack animals that rivaled the efficiency of the camel in the deserts of North Africa and the steppes of Asia. To address the problem and to facilitate transportation and trade, new roads and bridges were built, and old Roman roads that had been neglected for a thousand years were repaired. These improvements, however, were unevenly distributed, leaving large parts of Europe without any effective form of transportation. Many roads were little more than rutted tracks, blocked in places by bogs of mud or fallen trees. Few lords or cities were willing to make the investment to repair the roads and clear the blockages. Without a cheap way to move grain to places of scarcity, one village could be suffering from famine while another nearby enjoyed a surplus.

The most lucrative trade was the international commerce in luxury goods. Because these goods were lightweight and high-priced, they could sustain the cost of long-distance transportation across land. Italian merchants virtually monopolized the European luxury trade. The Genoese distributed rare alum—the fixing agent for dyeing cloth—from the west coast of Asia Minor to the entire European cloth industry. Venetians and Genoese imported cotton from the Middle East. Raw silk, transported aboard camel caravans from China and Turkestan, was sold at trading posts on the shores of the Black Sea and in Constantinople to Italian merchants who shipped the goods across the Mediterranean and then earned enormous profits selling shimmering silk fabric to the ladies and gentlemen of the western European aristocracy. The silk trade was quite small in quantity, but it was of great value to international commerce because silk was so highly prized. One ounce of fine Chinese black silk sold on the London market for as much as a highly skilled mason would earn in a week's labor.

Rubies, pearls, coral, and diamonds were also easily transported for fantastic profits. Marco Polo of Venice, for example, specialized in trading jewels, which he sewed into the linings of his clothing for safety when he trekked across Asia from Venice to China and back. During the thirteenth century, he was one of countless European merchants who crisscrossed the caravan routes of Asia and North Africa. Italian merchant fleets sailed the Mediterranean, but transportation from the European ports in the Mediterranean to northern Europe still employed costly pack trains traversing the Alpine passes north. By the end of the thirteenth century, however, first Genoese and then other Italian fleets regularly ventured beyond the Straits of Gibraltar into the stormy Atlantic, dramatically improving transportation between northern and southern Europe.

Even the bulk commodities the Italians brought from the East were valuable enough to sustain the high transportation costs. Known by the generic term "spices," these included hundreds of exotic items: True spices such as pepper, sugar, cloves, nutmeg, ginger, saffron, mace, and cinnamon were used to enhance the otherwise boring, bland cuisine; for dyeing cloth indigo was used for blue and madder root for red; and medicinal herbs including opiates were used as pain relievers. The profits from spices generated most of the capital in European financial markets.

The second factor responsible for the economic boom of the twelfth and thirteenth centuries was the creation of new business techniques that long-distance trade necessitated. For example, the expansion of trade and new markets required a moneyed economy. Coins had almost disappeared in the West for nearly 400 years during the Early Middle Ages, when most people lived self-sufficiently on manors and bartered for what they could not produce for themselves. The few coins that circulated came from Byzantium or the Muslim caliphates. By the thirteenth century Venice and Florence were minting their own gold coins, which became the medium for exchange across much of Europe.

Merchants who engaged in long-distance trade began to develop the essential business tools of capitalism during this period. They created business partnerships, uniform accounting practices, merchants' courts to enforce contracts and resolve disputes, letters of credit (used like modern traveler's checks), bank deposits and loans, and even insurance policies. The Italian cities established primary schools to train merchants' sons to write business letters and keep accounts—a sign of the growing professional character of business. Two centuries earlier an international merchant had been an itinerant peddler who led pack trains over dusty and muddy tracks to customers in small villages and castles. But by the end of the thirteenth century an international merchant could stay at home behind a desk, writing letters to business partners and ship captains and enjoying the profits from his labors in the bustling atmosphere of a thriving city.

At the center of the European market were the Champagne fairs in France, where merchants from northern and southern Europe met every summer to bargain and haggle (see Map 9.1). The Italians exchanged their spices for English raw wool, Dutch woolen cloth, German furs and linens, and Spanish leather. From the Champagne fairs, prosperity spread into previously wild parts of Europe. Cities along the German rivers and the Baltic coast thrived through the trade of raw materials such as timber and iron, livestock, salt fish, and hides. The most prominent of the North German towns was Lübeck, which became the center of a loose trade association of cities in Germany and the Baltic coast known as the Hanseatic League. Never achieving the level of a unified government, the league nonetheless provided its members mutual security and trading monopolies—necessary because of the weakness of the German imperial government.

The third factor in the economic prosperity of the period was the cities themselves. Cities both facilitated the commercial boom and were the primary beneficiaries of it. All across Europe, especially in Flanders, the Netherlands, and north-central Italy, cities exploded in size from what they had been. Exact population figures are difficult to determine, and by contemporary standards most of these cities were modest in size—numbering in the tens of thousands rather than hundreds of thousands—but there is ample evidence of stunning growth. Between 1160 and 1300 Ghent had to expand its city walls five times to accommodate all its inhabitants. During the thirteenth century the population of Florence grew by an estimated 640 percent.

Urban civilization, one of the major achievements of the Middle Ages, was an outgrowth of commerce. From urban civilization came other achievements. All the cities built a large new cathedral to flaunt their accumulated wealth and to honor God. New educational institutions, especially universities, trained the sons of the urban, commercial elite in

Map 9.1 European Fairs and Trade Routes

Trade routes crisscrossed the Mediterranean Sea and hugged the Atlantic Ocean, North Sea, and Baltic Sea coastlines. Land routes converged in central France at the Champagne fairs. Other trade routes led to the large market cities in Germany and Flanders.

the professions. However, these merchants who commanded the booming urban economy were not necessarily society's heroes. The populace at large viewed them with deep ambivalence, despite the immeasurable ways in which they enriched society. The landed aristocrats treated merchants with withering disdain even when forced to borrow money from them and to tax them to finance grandiose expenditures. Many merchants themselves were ambivalent about trade and aspired to retire as soon as they could afford to buy land and take up life as a country gentleman.

Churchmen worried about the morality of making profits. Church councils condemned usury—the lending of money for interest—even though papal finances depended on it. Theologians promulgated the idea of a "just price," the idea that there should be a fixed price for any particular commodity. The just price was anathema to hardheaded merchants who were committed to the laws of supply and demand. Part of the ambivalence toward trade and merchants came from the inequities created in all market-based economies—the rewards of the market were unevenly distributed, both socially and geographically. The prosperous merchants were the most visible signs of puzzling social changes, but they were also the dynamic force that made possible the intellectual and artistic flowering of the High Middle Ages.

The Consolidation of Roman Catholicism

■ How did the Catholic Church consolidate its hold over the Latin West?

The late eleventh through thirteenth centuries witnessed one of the greatest periods of religious vitality in the history of Roman Catholicism. Manifest by the rise of new religious orders, remarkable intellectual creativity, and the final triumphant battle with the surviving polytheistic tribes of northern and eastern Europe, the religious vitality of the era was due in no small part to the effective leadership of a series of able popes. They gave the Church the benefits of the most advanced, centralized government in Europe. However, the papacy's successful intervention in worldly affairs helped undermine its spiritual authority, opening the way to the degradation of the papacy in the fourteenth century.

The Task of Church Reform

As the bishops of the Church accepted many of the administrative responsibilities that in the ancient world had been performed by secular authorities, their spiritual mission sometimes suffered. They become overly involved in the business of the world. In addition, over the centuries many wealthy and pious people had made large donations of land to the Church, making many monasteries, in particular, immensely wealthy. Such wealth tempted the less pious to corruption, and some of the Roman popes who had benefited from the wealth of the Church were reluctant to promote reforms that would have reduced corruption. Even those who wanted to eliminate the temptations of wealth were slow to assemble the administrative machinery necessary to enforce their will across the unruly lands of Latin Christianity.

As discussed in Chapter 8, Pope Gregory the Great (r. 590–604) became the moral guidepost of the western Church and the model for a strong papacy. But after Gregory the papacy gradually fell into a degraded moral state. Popes were caught in a web of scandal spun by the ambitious aristocratic families of Rome that involved the theft of church property, sexual intrigue, and even murder. During the tenth century the Crescentii family became the virtual dictators of papal administration, were rumored to have murdered popes who got in their way, and set members of their own clan on the papal throne. The slow but determined progress of the popes from the eleventh to thirteenth centuries to regain prominence as moral reformers is one of the most remarkable achievements of the medieval papacy.

The movement for reform, however, did not begin with the popes. The idea and energy for the reform of the Church came out of the monasteries. Monks thought the best way to clean up corruption in the Church would be to improve the morals of individuals. If men and women conducted themselves with a sense of moral responsibility, the whole institution of the Church could be purified. The model for self-improvement was that provided by monks and nuns themselves, who set an example for the rest of the Church and for society at large. The most influential of the reform-minded monasteries was that of Cluny° in Burgundy, which was established in 910. Cluny itself became the center of a far-reaching reform movement that was sustained in more than 1,500 Cluniac monasteries.

From the very beginning Cluny was exceptional, for several reasons. First, its aristocratic founder offered the monastery as a gift to the pope. As a result, it was directly connected to Rome and completely independent from local political pressures, which so often caused corruption. The Rome connection positioned Cluniacs to assist in reforming the papacy itself. Second, the various abbots who headed Cluny over the years closely coordinated reform activities of the various monasteries in the Cluniac system. Some of these abbots were men of exceptional ability and learning who had a European-wide reputation for their moral stature. Third, Cluny regulated the life of monks much more closely than did other monasteries, so the monks there were models of devotion. To the Cluniacs moral purity required as complete a renunciation of the benefits of the material world as possible and a commitment to stimulating spiritual experiences. Cluniac purity was symbolized by the elegantly simple liturgy in which the monks themselves sung the text of the mass and other prayers. The beauty of the music enhanced the spiritual experience, and its simplicity clarified rather than obscured the meaning of the words. The Cluniac liturgy spread to the far corners of Europe.

The success of Cluny and other reformed monasteries provided the base from which reform ideas spread beyond the isolated world of monks to the rest of the Church. The first candidates for reform were parish priests and bishops. Called the *secular clergy* (in Latin *saeculum,* meaning "secular") because they lived in the secular world, they differed from the regular clergy (in Latin *regula,* those who followed a "rule") who lived in monasteries apart from the world. The lives of many secular clergy differed little from their lay neighbors. (*Laypeople* or *the laity* referred to all Christians who had not taken religious vows to become a priest, monk, or nun.) In contrast to celibate monks, who were sexually chaste, many priests kept concubines or were married and tried to bequeath church property to their children. In contrast to the Orthodox Church, in which priests were allowed to marry, the Roman Church had repeatedly forbidden married priests, but the prohibitions had been ineffective until Cluniac reform stressed the ideal of the sexually pure priest. During the eleventh century Roman bishops, church councils, and reformist popes began to insist on a celibate clergy.

The other objective of the clerical reform movement was the elimination of the corrupt practices of simony and lay investiture. Simony° was the practice of buying and selling church offices. Lay investiture° took place when nobles, kings, or emperors actually installed churchmen and gave them their symbols of office ("invested" them). Through this practice, the powerful laity dominated the clergy and usurped the property of the Church for their own use. Many nobles conceived of church offices as a form of vassalage and expected to be able to name their own candidates as priests and bishops in exchange for protecting the Church. The reformers saw as sinful any form of lay authority over the Church—whether that of the local lord or the emperor himself. The reformers wanted the emperor and all other lords to keep their hands off. As a result of this controversy, the most troublesome issue of the eleventh century became establishing the boundaries between temporal and spiritual authorities.

The Pope Becomes a Monarch

Religious reform and vitality required unity within the Church. The most important step in building unity was to define what it meant to be a Catholic. Catholics began to define themselves in two ways. First, the Church insisted on conformity in rites. Rites consisted of the forms of public worship called the liturgy, which included certain prescribed prayers and chants, usually in Latin. Uniform rites meant that Catholics could hear the Mass celebrated in essentially the same way everywhere from Poland to Portugal, Iceland to Croatia. Conformity of worship created a cultural unity that transcended differences in language and ethnicity. When Catholics from far-flung locales encountered one another, they shared something meaningful to them all because of the uniformity of the rites. The second thing that defined a Catholic was obedience to the pope. Ritual uniformity and obedience to the pope were closely interrelated because both the ritual and the pope were Roman. There were many bishops in Christianity, but as one monk put it, "Rome is . . . the head of the world."

The task of the medieval popes was to make this theoretical claim to authority real—in short, to make the papacy a religious monarchy. In the last half of the eleventh century under a series of dynamic reformers, the papacy firmly reasserted itself as the head of the Roman Catholic world. Among the reformers who gathered in Rome was Hildebrand (ca. 1020–1085), one of the most remarkable figures in the history of the Church, a man beloved as saintly by his admirers and considered an ambitious, self-serving megalomaniac by many others. From 1055 to 1073 during the pontificates of some four popes, Hildebrand became the power behind the throne, helping enact wide-ranging reforms that enforced uniformity of worship and establishing the rules for electing new popes by the college of cardinals. In 1073 Hildebrand was himself elected pope and took the name Gregory VII (r. 1073–1085).

Gregory's greatness lay in his leadership over the internal reform of the Church. Every year he held a Church council in Rome where he decreed against simony (the buying and selling of church offices) and priests who married and attempted to bequeath church property to their children. Gregory centralized authority over the Church itself by sending out papal legates, representatives who delivered orders to local bishops, and attempted to free it from external influence by asserting the superiority of the pope over all other authorities. Gregory's theory of papal supremacy led him into direct conflict with the German emperor Henry IV (r. 1056–1106). The issue was lay investiture, the power of kings and emperors to pick their own candidates for ecclesiastical offices, especially bishoprics. During the eighth and ninth centuries weak popes relied on the Carolingian kings and emperors to name suitable candidates for these offices in order to keep them out of the hands of local aristocrats. At stake was not only power and authority, but also the income from the enormous amount of property controlled by the Church, which the emperor was in the best position to protect. During the eleventh century, Gregory VII and other reform-minded popes sought to regain control of this property. Without the ability to name his own candidates as bishops, Gregory recognized that his whole campaign for church reform would falter.

When Pope Gregory tried to negotiate with the emperor over the appointment of the bishop of Milan, Henry was defiant, ordering Gregory to resign the papacy in a letter with the notorious salutation, "Henry, King not by usurpation, but by the pious ordination of God to Hildebrand now not Pope but false monk."

Gregory struck back in an escalating confrontation now known as the Investiture Controversy°. He deposed Henry from the imperial throne and excommunicated him. Excommunication° prohibited the sinner from participating in the sacraments and forbade any social contact whatsoever with the surrounding community. People caught talking to an excommunicated person or writing a letter or even offering a drink of water could themselves be excommunicated. Excommunication was a form of social death, a dire punishment indeed, especially if the excommunicated person was a king. Both sides marshaled arguments from

The Investiture Controversy

When Pope Gregory VII sought refuge at Canossa in 1177, his host was his strong supporter, Countess Matilda of Tuscany. In this illumination in a chronicle of the life of Matilda, Emperor Henry IV kneels at her feet asking her to intercede for him with Pope Gregory. Another of the pope's supporters, Abbot Hugo of Cluny, sits behind the emperor holding a staff. The image of an emperor humbling himself before a mere countess conveyed the idea to medieval viewers of the complete subordination of the imperial authority to that of the pope and his allies.

Scripture and history, but the excommunication was effective. Henry's friends started to abandon him, rebellion broke out in Germany, and the most powerful German lords called for a meeting to elect a new emperor. Backed into a corner, Henry plotted a clever counterstroke.

Early in the winter of 1077 Pope Gregory set out to cross the Alps to meet with the German lords. When Gregory reached the Alpine passes, however, he learned that Emperor Henry was on his way to Italy. In fear of what the emperor would do, Gregory retreated to the castle of Canossa, where he expected to be attacked. Henry surprised Gregory, however, by arriving not with an army but as a supplicant asking the pope to hear his confession. As a priest Gregory could hardly refuse to hear the confession of a penitent sinner, but he nevertheless attempted to humiliate Henry by making him wait for three days, kneeling in the snow outside the castle. Henry's presentation of himself as a penitent sinner posed a dilemma for Gregory. The German lords were waiting for Gregory to appear in his capacity as the chief justice of Christendom to judge Henry, but Henry himself was asking the pope to act in his capacity as priest to grant absolution for sin. The priest in Gregory won out over the judge, and he absolved Henry.

Even after the deaths of Gregory and Henry, the Investiture Controversy continued to poison relations between the popes and emperors until the Concordat of Worms in 1122 resolved the issue in a formal treaty. The emperor retained the right to nominate high churchmen, but in a concession to the papacy, the emperor lost the ceremonial privileges of investiture that conveyed spiritual authority. Without the ceremony of investiture, no bishop could exercise his office. By refusing to invest unsuitable nominees, the popes had the last word. Gregory VII's vision of papal supremacy over all kings and emperors persevered.

How the Popes Ruled

The most lasting accomplishment of the popes during the twelfth and thirteenth centuries derived less from dramatic confrontations with emperors than from the humdrum routine of the law. Beginning with Gregory VII, the papacy became the supreme court of the Catholic world by claiming authority over a vast range of issues. To justify these claims, Gregory and his assistants conducted massive research among old laws and treatises. These were organized into a body of legal texts called canon law°.

Canon law came to encompass many kinds of cases, including all those involving the clergy, disputes about church property, and donations to the Church. The law of the Church also touched on many of the most vital concerns of the laity—all those who were not priests, monks, or nuns—including annulling marriages, legitimating bastards, prosecuting bigamy, protecting widows and orphans, and resolving inheritance disputes. Most of the cases originated in the courts of the bishops, but the bishops' decisions could be appealed to the pope and cardinals sitting together in the papal consistory. The consistory could make exceptions from the letter of the law, called dispensations, giving it considerable power over kings and aristocrats who wanted to marry a cousin, divorce a wife, legitimate a bastard, or annul a will. By the middle of the twelfth century, Rome was awash with legal business. The functions of the canon law courts became so important that those who were elected popes were no longer monks but trained canon lawyers, men very capable in the ways of the world.

The pope also presided over the curia°, the administrative bureaucracy of the Church. The cardinals served as ministers in the papal administration and were sent off to foreign princes and cities as ambassadors, or legates. Because large amounts of revenue were flowing into the coffers of the Church, Rome became the financial capital of the West.

In addition to its legal, administrative, and financial authority, the papacy also made use of two powerful spiritual weapons against the disobedient. Any Christian who refused to repent of a sin could be excommunicated, as the Emperor Henry IV had been. The second spiritual weapon was the interdict°, which usually applied to a whole city or kingdom whose ruler had displeased the pope. During an interdict, the sacraments were not celebrated and the churches closed their doors, creating panic among the faithful who could not baptize their children or bury their dead. The interdict, which encouraged a public outcry, could be a very effective weapon for undermining the political support of any monarch who ran afoul of the pope.

Map 9.2   Universal Monarchy of Pope Innocent III
Besides his direct control of the Papal States in central Italy, Pope Innocent III made vassals of many of the kings of Catholic Europe. These feudal ties provided a legal foundation for his claim to be the highest authority in Christian Europe.

The Pinnacle of the Medieval Papacy: Pope Innocent III

The most capable of the medieval popes was Innocent III (r. 1198–1216). Only 37 when elected, Innocent was tough-minded and the ideal candidate to bolster the papal monarchy, because of both his extensive family connections in Italy and Germany and his training in theology and canon law. Innocent possessed a clear-sighted concept of the papal monarchy. To him the pope was the overlord and moral guide of the Christian community, with authority over the entire world. He recognized the right of kings to rule over the secular sphere, but he considered it his duty to prevent and punish sin, a duty that gave him wide latitude to meddle in the affairs of kings and princes. The indefatigable pope pummeled the world with commands and advice, which were not to be taken lightly. Under Innocent, the

sheer volume of correspondence to Spain, for example, increased by some twenty-five times over what it had been under the hyperactive Pope Gregory VII.

Innocent's first task was to provide the papacy with a strong territorial base of support so that the popes could act with the same freedom as kings and princes. Innocent is generally considered to be the founder of the Papal State in central Italy, an independent state that lasted until 1870 and survives today in a tiny fragment as Vatican City.

Innocent's second task was keeping alive the Crusading ideal. He called the Fourth Crusade, which went awry when the crusaders attacked Constantinople. He also expanded the definition of Crusading by calling for a Crusade to eliminate heresy within Christian Europe. Innocent was deeply concerned about the spread of new heresies, which attracted enormous numbers of converts, especially in the growing cities of southern Europe. By Crusading against Christian heretics, the Cathars and Waldensians, Innocent authorized the use of military methods to enforce uniformity of belief.

The third objective of this ambitious and energetic pope was to assert the power of the papacy over political affairs. Innocent managed the election of Emperor Frederick II; he also assumed the right to veto imperial elections. He excommunicated King Philip II of France to force him to take back an unwanted wife. And he placed England under the interdict to compel King John to cede his kingdom to the papacy and receive it back as a fief, a transaction that made the king of England the vassal of the pope. Using whatever means necessary, he made papal vassals of the rulers of Aragon, Bulgaria, Denmark, Hungary, Poland, Portugal, and Serbia. Through the use of the feudal law of vassalage, Innocent brought the papacy to its closest approximation of a universal Christian monarchy (see Map 9.2).

Innocent's fourth and greatest accomplishment was to codify the rites of the liturgy and to define the dogmas of the faith. This monumental task was the achievement of the Fourth Lateran Council, held in Rome in 1215. This council, attended by more than 400 bishops, 800 abbots, and the ambassadors of the monarchs of Catholic Europe, issued decrees that reinforced the celebration of the sacraments as the centerpiece of Christian life. They included rules to educate the clergy, define their qualifications, and govern elections of bishops. The council condemned heretical beliefs, and it called yet another Crusade. It became the guidepost that has governed many aspects of Catholic practice, especially with regard to the sacraments. It did more than any other council to fulfill the goal of uniformity of rites in Catholicism, and its influence survives to this day.

The Troubled Legacy of the Papal Monarchy

Innocent was a crafty, intelligent man who in single-minded fashion pursued the greater good of the Church as he saw it. His policies, however, had ruinous results in the hands of his less able successors. Their blunders undermined the pope's spiritual mission, especially when they attempted to influence the fate of the kingdom of Sicily, which lay on the southern border of the Papal State. Innocent's successors went beyond defending the Papal

State and embroiled all Italy in a series of bloody civil wars between the Guelfs, who supported the popes, and the Ghibellines, who opposed them. The pope's position as a monarch superior to all others collapsed under the weight of immense folly and hypocrisy during the pontificate of Boniface VIII (r. 1294–1303). His personal faults, which included breathtaking vanity and rudeness, did little to help the papacy's blemished reputation. Widely believed to be a religious skeptic addicted to amulets and magic, Boniface enjoyed the company of riotous companions and loved to dress up in the regalia of an emperor.

In 1302 Boniface promulgated the most extreme theoretical assertion of papal superiority over lay rulers. Behind the statement was a specific dispute with King Philip IV of France (r. 1285–1314), who was attempting to try a French bishop for treason. The larger issue behind the dispute was similar to the Investiture Controversy of the eleventh century, but this time no one paid much attention to the pope. The loss of papal moral authority had taken its toll. In the heat of the confrontation, King Philip accused Pope Boniface of heresy, one of the few sins of which he was not guilty, and sent his agents to arrest the pope. They forced their way into his rooms at the papal palace of Anagni in 1303, where they found the 70-year-old Boniface in bed. Traumatized by the arrest and the threats of violence against him, the old man died shortly after he was released. With Boniface the papal monarchy died as well. It took more than a century for the popes to recover their complete independence from French influence and longer still to recapture their dignity.

DOCUMENT

Pope Boniface VIII, Unam Sanctum (1302)

Discovering God in the World

Even before the First Crusade, Catholic Europe began to experience an unprecedented spiritual awakening. The eleventh-century papal campaign to reform the morals of the clergy helped make priests both more respectable and better educated. At the same time, many laypeople who had previously been Christians in name only began to show genuine enthusiasm for the Church. A better-educated clergy educated the laity more effectively, and the teachings of Christianity became less a matter of public conformity, manifest by attendance at Mass, than of personal devotion. In large numbers Latin Christians began to internalize the teachings of the Church. The most devout were drawn to dedicating their lives to religion. In England, for example, the number of monks increased tenfold from the late eleventh century to 1200. The newly expanding cities built loyalty and encouraged peaceable behavior through the veneration of civic patron saints. The most vital indication of spiritual renewal was the success of new religious orders, which satisfied a widespread yearning to discover the hand of God in the world.

CHRONOLOGY

The Papal Monarchy

1073–1085	Reign of Pope Gregory VII
1075–1122	The Investiture Controversy
1198–1216	Reign of Pope Innocent III
1215	Fourth Lateran Council
1294–1303	Reign of Pope Boniface VIII

The Patron Saints

Saints are holy people whose moral perfection gives them a special relationship with the sacred. Ordinary Christians venerated saints to gain access to supernatural powers, protection, and intercession with God. A saintly intercessor was someone who could be trusted to obtain God's favor. In many places the newly converted simply transformed polytheistic deities into saints, a process that greatly facilitated the adoption of Christianity.

The relationship between Christian believers and the saints was profoundly intimate and intertwined with many aspects of life: Christian children were named after saints who became their special protectors; every church was dedicated to a saint; every town and city adopted a patron saint. And even entire peoples cherished a patron saint; for example, the Irish adopted Saint Patrick, who supposedly brought Christianity to the island.

A city gained protection from a patron saint by obtaining the saint's corpse or skeleton or part of the skeleton or some object associated with the saint. These body parts and material objects, called relics, served as contacts between Earth and Heaven and were said to have been verified by miracles. The belief in the miraculous powers of relics created an enormous demand for them in the thriving medieval cities. But because the remains of the martyrs and early saints of the church were spread across the Middle East and Mediterranean from Jerusalem to Rome, relics first had to be discovered and transferred from where they were buried to new homes in the churches of the growing western European cities. The demand created a thriving market in saints' bones and body parts. They were bought or stolen, and there was ample room for fraud in passing off unauthentic bones to gullible buyers. During the Crusades the supply of relics greatly increased, both because the Crusading knights had access to the tombs of early Christian saints and martyrs and because the thriving cities of the West produced a great demand for them.

Possessing relics was also important for establishing the legitimacy of political authority. For example, the ruler of the city of Venice, the doge, claimed to possess the relics of St. Mark, one of the four evangelists who wrote the gospels of the New Testament. Based on their possession of these prestigious relics, the Venetians argued that God had authorized the city's liberty from outside interference. They used this argument against their one-time imperial masters in Constantinople, against the Carolingians who attempted to conquer the thriving city, against bishops from the mainland who claimed authority over Venice's churches, and eventually even against the pope when he attempted to control the Venetian church. The great basilica of St. Mark in Venice became a pilgrimage shrine visited by Christians from all over Europe on their way to the Holy Land. Each pilgrim learned of Venice's intimate association with St. Mark from the magnificent mosaics that adorned the basilica's ceilings and walls.

During the twelfth and thirteenth centuries, public veneration of saints also began to undergo a subtle shift of emphasis, away from the cults of the local patron saints toward more universal figures such as Jesus and the Virgin Mary. The patron saints had functioned almost like the family deities of antiquity who served the particular interests of individuals and communities, but the papal monarchy

Mosaics in the Basilica of St. Mark in Venice

Pilgrims learned of Venice's intimate association with St. Mark from the magnificent mosaics that adorned the basilica's ceilings and walls. This scene shows a miracle that occurred after St. Mark's body was lost during a fire in the basilica. After the leaders of Venice spent days in prayer, shown on the left, St. Mark opened a door in a column shown at the far right to reveal the place where his body was hidden. In between these two scenes, those who witnessed the miracle turn to one another in amazement.

A Tale of Two Marys

Medieval thinking about women began with the fundamental dichotomy between Eve, the symbol of women as they are, and Mary, the ideal to which all women strived. Eve brought sin and sex into the world through her disobedience to God. Mary, the Virgin Mother, kept her body inviolate.

Into the gap between the two natures of women emerged Mary Magdalen, a repentant prostitute whose veneration reached a pinnacle in the twelfth century. In contrast to the perpetually virginal ideal of Mary, the mother of Christ, Magdalen offered the possibility of redemption to all women. The clerical discussion of the natures of these two Marys—the Virgin Mary and Mary Magdalen—reveals a complex and changing medieval discussion about the nature of women. This discussion was pursued through a theoretical examination of women's bodies and their sexuality.

The precise significance of Mary's virginity long preoccupied Christian thinkers. Two of the Gospels simply assert that Mary had not known a man before she became pregnant with the Christ child. Later Christian thinkers extended this idea to assert that she remained a virgin after the birth of Jesus and even that she miraculously managed to preserve her virginity "before, during, and after delivery" of the infant. By discussing her as a virgin who gave birth and still remained a virgin, these Christian thinkers relegated Mary to a heavenly realm where the physical facts of real women's lives did not apply.

Geoffroy of Vendôme (d. 1132), a cleric educated in a cathedral

school, drew an astonishing conclusion from these speculations about Mary's reproductive anatomy:

Virtuous Mary gave birth to Christ, and in Christ she gave birth to Christians. Hence the mother of Christ is the mother of all Christians. If the mother of Christ is the mother of all Christians, then clearly Christ and Christians are brothers. Not only is Christ the brother of all Christians, he is also the father of all men and primarily of Christians. From which it follows that Christ is the Virgin's father and husband as well as her son.[1]

Geoffroy collapsed all male family relationships into one: the lineage of father, husband, and son merges with the equality of brotherhood among all Christians. What is most remarkable about Geoffroy's way of thinking is that this great Christian drama takes place within the confines of a mother's womb, invisible to sight yet so mysteriously open to speculative examination. The problem with this way of thinking was that its implications were not merely theoretical. Geoffroy and other priests were pastors who offered practical advice to real women. The model of the Virgin Mary left them with only one avenue for giving advice: They recommended

that women remain lifelong virgins, which was rather impractical advice for the vast majority of women who were married.

Mary Magdalen's life provided an alternative, more practical model to follow. Known in the early Church, her veneration spread after the abbey at Vézelay, Burgundy, changed its dedication from the Virgin Mary to Mary Magdalen in 1095 and began to flourish as a pilgrimage site. Throughout France, "Madeleine" became a popular name for girls. In 1105 Geoffroy of Vendôme assembled most of the known and presumed information about her in a sermon, "In Honor of the Blessed Mary Magdalen." All writers agreed she had been a prostitute. But she had redeemed herself. By confessing her sins, she saved herself, and Christ forgave her. Thus, a woman whose body had once been corrupted saved not only herself but through her example brought others to repentance. If Magdalen could achieve redemption from her degraded state, did she not offer hope to all women?

For Discussion

What did the medieval depiction of the two Marys reveal about the way people thought about women, sexuality, and moral worth?

Mary Magdalen represented the possibility of redemption for all sinners.

The Virgin Mary suckles the baby Jesus, an image of the Christian ideal of selfless Charity.

Saint Anthony of Padua holds a lily, symbolizing purity and innocence.

The Two Marys: The Mother of God and the Repentant Prostitute

The Human Body in History

encouraged uniform rites that were universal throughout Catholicism.

Christians had always honored the Virgin Mary, but beginning in the twelfth century her immense popularity provided Catholics with a positive female image that contradicted the traditional misogyny and mistrust associated with Eve. Clerics and monks had long depicted women as deceitful and lustful in luring men to their moral ruin. In contrast, the veneration of the Virgin Mary promoted the image of a loving mother who would intervene with her son on behalf of sinners at the Last Judgment. Theologians still taught that the woman Eve had brought sin into the world, but the woman Mary offered help in escaping the consequences of sin.

The popularity of Mary was evident everywhere. Most of the new cathedrals in the burgeoning cities of Europe were dedicated to her. She became the favorite example of preachers as a model for women, and numerous miracles were attributed to her. Part of her appeal derived from her image as the ideal mother with the bouncing Christ child on her knee. Countless paintings and sculptures of the Madonna and child adorned the churches of Europe, and Mary's tender humanity stimulated artists to find new ways to evoke human emotions. Mary became the center of a renewed interest in the family and the Christian value of love within the family.

Mary became a model with whom women could identify, presenting a positive image of femininity. In images of her suckling the Christ child, she became the perfect embodiment of the virtue of charity, the willingness to give without any expectation of reward. Through the image of the nursing Virgin Mary, the ability to nurture became associated not just with Mary but with Christ himself. In contrast to the early Christian saints who were predominantly martyrs and missionaries, during the twelfth and thirteenth centuries saints exhibited sanctity more through nurturing others, especially by feeding the poor and healing the sick. Nurturing was associated with women, and many more women became saints during this period than during the entire first millennium of Christianity. In 1100 fewer than 10 percent of all the saints were female. By 1300 the percentage had increased to 24 percent. During the fifteenth century about 30 percent were women. Far from a feminist religion, Catholicism nevertheless developed a sacred female principle and offered an ideal woman for veneration much more prominently than did Judaism or Islam.

The New Religious Orders

By the eleventh century many men attracted to the religious life found the Benedictines too lax in their discipline and the Cluniacs too worldly with their elaborate liturgy and decorated churches. In 1098 a small group of Benedictine monks removed themselves to an isolated wasteland to establish the Cistercian Order. The Cistercians practiced a very strict discipline. They ate only enough to stay alive.

DOCUMENT

The Position of Women in the Eyes of the Medieval Church

In the view of the medieval Church, women were spiritually equal to men but legally and socially inferior. Women were to be subject to male control. The Decretum, *written by the jurist Gratian in about 1140, codified the canon law. In this passage Gratian defines the legal status of women in Christian society.*

Women should be subject to their men. The natural order for mankind is that women should serve men and children their parents, for it is just that the lesser serve the greater.

The image of God is in man and it is one. Women were drawn from man, who has God's jurisdiction as if he were God's vicar, because he has the image of the one God. Therefore woman is not made in God's image.

Woman's authority is nil; let her in all things be subject to the rule of man. . . . And neither can she teach, nor be a witness, nor give a guarantee, nor sit in judgment.

Adam was beguiled by Eve, not she by him. It is right then that he whom woman led into wrongdoing should have her under his direction, so that he may not fail a second time through female levity.

Source: From Julia O'Faolain and Lauro Martines, *Not in God's Image* (1973).

Each monk possessed only one robe. Unlike other orders that required monks to attend frequent and lengthy services, the Cistercians spent more time in private prayer and manual labor. Their churches were bare of all decoration. Under the brilliant leadership of Bernard of Clairvaux (1090–1153), the Cistercians grew rapidly, as many men disillusioned with the sinful and materialistic society around them joined the new order. Bernard's asceticism led him to seek refuge from the affairs of the world, but he was also a religious reformer and activist, engaged with the important issues of his time. He even helped settle a disputed papal election and preached a crusade.

The Cistercians established their new monasteries in isolated, uninhabited places where they cleared forests and worked the land so that they could live in complete isolation from the troubled affairs of the world. Their hard work had an ironic result. By bringing new lands under the plow and by employing the latest technological innovations, such as water mills, many of the Cistercian monasteries produced more than was needed for the monks, and the sale of excess produce made the Cistercians very rich. The economic success of the Cistercians helped them expand even more rapidly. In their first century, the Cistercians built more than 500 new monasteries, many in places previously untouched by Western monasticism. Numerous colonies of Cistercian monks moved into northeastern Europe in areas recently converted to Latin Christianity. English Cistercians moved into the newly settled parts of Norway, Germans into the confiscated lands of Poland. There were also foundations in Greece and Syria, both bastions of Eastern Orthodoxy. The rapid Cistercian push beyond the frontiers of Latin Europe helped disseminate the culture of Catholic Christianity through educating the local elites and attracting members of the aristocracy to join the Cistercians. By recruiting lay brothers, known as *converse*, the Cistercians made important connections with the peasants.

More than a century after the foundation of the Cistercians in France, the Spaniard Dominic and the Italian Francis formulated a new kind of religious order composed of mendicant friars°. From the very beginning the friars wanted to distinguish themselves from monks. As the opening of this chapter indicated, instead of working in a monastery to feed themselves as did the Cistercians, friars ("brothers") wandered from city to city and throughout the countryside begging for alms (*mendicare* means "to beg," hence *mendicant*). Unlike monks who remained in a cloister, friars tried to help ordinary laypeople with their problems by preaching and administering to the sick and poor.

The Spaniard Dominic (1170–1221) founded the Dominican Order to convert Muslims and Jews and to combat heresy among Christians against whom he began his preaching mission while traveling through southern France. The ever-perceptive Pope Innocent III recognized Dominic's talents while he was visiting Rome and gave his new order provisional approval. Dominic believed the task of conversion could be achieved through persuasion and argument. To hone the Dominicans' persuasive skills, they created the first multigrade, comprehensive educational system. It connected schools located in individual friaries with more advanced regional schools that offered specialized training in languages, philosophy, and especially theology. Most Dominican friars never studied at a university but enjoyed, nevertheless, a highly sophisticated education that made them exceptionally influential in European intellectual life. Famed for their preaching skills, Dominicans were equally successful in moving the illiterate masses and debating sophisticated opponents.

From the beginning, the Dominican Order synthesized the contemplative life of the monastery and the active ministry of preaching to laypeople. In contrast to traditional monastic orders, the Dominican Order was organized like an army. Each province was under the supervision of a master general, and each Dominican was ready to travel wherever needed to preach and convert.

The Franciscan Order enjoyed a similar success. Francis of Assisi (1182–1226), whose story opened this chapter, deeply influenced Clare of Assisi (1194–1253), who founded a parallel order for women, the Poor Clares. Like the Franciscans, she and her followers enjoyed the "privilege of perfect poverty," which forbade the ownership of any property even by the community itself. Clare devoted herself to penitential prayer, which was said to have twice saved the town of Assisi from besieging armies.

Both the Dominican and Franciscan Orders spread rapidly. Whereas the successful Cistercians had founded 500 new houses in their first century, the Franciscans established more than 1,400 in their first hundred years. Liberated from the obligation to live in a monastery, the mendicant friars traveled wherever the pope ordered them, making them effective agents of the papal monarchy. They preached Crusades. They pacified the poor. They converted heretics and non-Christians through their inspiring preaching revivals. Even more effectively than the Cistercians before them, they established Catholic colonies along the frontiers of the West and beyond. They became missionary scouts looking for opportunities to disseminate Christian culture. In 1254 the Great Khan in Mongolia sponsored a debate on the principal religions of the world. There, many

DOCUMENT

The Song of Brother Sun

Francis of Assisi is known as a nature mystic, which means he celebrated God's Creation through a love of nature. In one of the most renowned celebrations of nature ever written, "The Song of Brother Sun," Francis transforms the inanimate forces of nature into his spiritual brothers and sisters.

Be praised, my Lord, with all Your creatures,
Especially Sir Brother Sun,
By whom You give us the light of day!
And he is beautiful and radiant with great splendor.
Of You, Most High, he is a symbol!
Be praised, my Lord, for Sister Moon and the Stars!
In the sky You formed them bright and lovely and fair.
Be praised, my Lord, for Brother Wind
And for the Air and cloudy and clear and all Weather,
By which You give sustenance to Your creatures!
Be praised, my Lord, for Sister Water,
Who is very useful and humble and lovely and chaste!
Be praised, my Lord, for Brother Fire,
By whom You give us light at night,
And he is beautiful and merry and mighty and strong!
Be praised, my Lord, for our Sister Mother Earth,
Who sustains and governs us,
And produces fruits with colorful flowers and leaves!

Source: From *The Little Flowers of St. Francis* by St. Francis of Assisi, translated by Raphael Brown, copyright © 1958 by Beverly Brown. Used by permission of Doubleday, a division of Random House, Inc.

thousands of miles from Catholic Europe, was a Franciscan friar ready to debate the learned men representing Islam, Buddhism, and Confucianism.

The Flowering of Religious Sensibilities

During the twelfth and thirteenth centuries the widespread enthusiasm for religion exalted spiritual creativity. Experimentation pushed Christian piety in new directions, not just for aristocratic men, who dominated the Church hierarchy and the monasteries, but for women and laypeople from all social levels.

Catholic worship concentrated on the celebration of the Eucharist°. The Eucharist, which was the crucial ritual moment during the Mass, celebrated Jesus' last meal with his apostles. The Eucharistic rite consecrated wafers of bread and wine as the body and blood of Christ. After the consecration, the celebrating priest distributed to the congregation the bread, called the host. Drinking from the chalice of wine, however, was a special privilege of the priesthood. More than anything else, belief in the miraculous change from bread to flesh and wine to blood, along with the sacrament of baptism, distinguished Christian believers from others. The Fourth Lateran Council in 1215 obligated all Christians to partake of the Eucharist:

> All the faithful of both sexes shall after they have reached the age of discretion faithfully confess all their sins at least once a year to their own priest, and perform to the best of their ability the penance imposed, receiving reverently, at least at Easter, the sacrament of the Eucharist, unless perchance at the advice of their own priest they may for a good reason abstain for a time from its reception; otherwise they shall be cut off from the Church during life, and deprived of Christian burial in death.[2]

This statement in its stark simplicity defined the core obligation of all medieval Catholics. As simple as it was as a ritual observance, belief in the Eucharistic miracle presented a vexing and complex theological problem—why the host still looked, tasted, and smelled like bread rather than flesh, and why the blood in the chalice still seemed to be wine rather than blood. After the Fourth Lateran Council, Catholics solved this problem with the doctrine of transubstantiation°. The doctrine rested on a distinction between the outward appearances of the object, which the five senses can perceive, and the substance of an object, which they cannot perceive. When the priest spoke the words of consecration during the Mass, the bread and wine were changed into the flesh and blood of Christ in substance ("transubstantiated") but not in outward appearances. Thus, the substance of the Eucharist literally became God's body, but the senses of taste, smell, and sight perceived it as bread.

Veneration of the Eucharist enabled the faithful to identify with Christ because believers considered the consecrated Eucharistic wafer to be Christ himself. By eating the host, they had literally ingested Christ, making his body

part of their bodies. Eucharistic veneration became enormously popular in the thirteenth century and the climax of dazzling ritual performance. Priests enhanced the effect of the miracle by dramatically elevating the host at the moment of consecration, holding it in upraised hands. Altar screens had special peepholes so that many people could adore the host at the elevation, and the faithful would rush from altar to altar or church to church to witness a succession of host elevations.

Many Christians became attracted to mysticism, the attempt to achieve union of the self with God. To the mystic, complete understanding of the divine was spiritual, not intellectual, an understanding best achieved through asceticism, the repudiation of material and bodily comforts. Both men and women were mystics, but women concentrated on the more extreme forms of asceticism. For example, some women allowed themselves to be walled up in dark chambers to achieve perfect seclusion from the world and avoid distractions from their mystical pursuits. Others had themselves whipped, wore painful scratching clothing, starved themselves in a form of holy anorexia, or claimed to survive with the Eucharist as their only food. Female mystics, such as Juliana of Norwich (1342–ca. 1416), envisioned a holy family in which God the Father was almighty but the Mother was all wisdom. Some female mystics believed that Christ had a female body because he was the perfect nurturer, and they ecstatically contemplated spiritual union with him.

Mystics, however, were exceptional people. Most Christians contented themselves with the sacraments, especially baptism, penance, and the Eucharist; perhaps a pilgrimage to a saint's shrine; and a final attempt at salvation by making a pious gift to the Church on their deathbed. The benevolent process of discovering God also stimulated a related malevolent process of attempting to detect the influence of the Devil in the world. To eradicate the Devil's influence, Christians made some people the outcasts of Western society.

Creating the Outcasts of Europe

As churchmen and kings sought to enforce religious unity and moral reform during the twelfth and thirteenth centuries, they were disturbed by peoples who did not seem to fit into official notions of Christian society. Some of these people, such as lepers and male homosexuals, were physically or socially different; others, such as heretics and Jews, actively rejected church authority. The papacy began a dramatic wave of military expeditions against heretical lords in order to deprive them of their lands and to inquire into the beliefs that they had allowed to flourish in their territories. Follow-up campaigns attempted to convert, control, or suppress these religious minorities, who were made social outcasts.

The Heretics: Cathars and Waldensians

In its efforts to defend the faith, the Church during the first half of the thirteenth century began to authorize bishops and other clerics to conduct inquisitions (formal inquiries) into specific instances of heresy or perceived heresy. The so-called heretics tended to be faithful people who sought a form of religion purer than what the Church provided. During the thirteenth and early fourteenth centuries, inquisitions and systematic persecutions targeted the Cathars and Waldensians, who at first had lived peacefully with their Catholic neighbors and shared many of the same beliefs with them.

The Cathars were especially strong in northern Italy and southern France. The name *Cathar* derives from the Greek word for purity. Heavily concentrated around the French town of Albi, the Cathars were also known as Albigensians. They departed from Catholic doctrine, which held that God created the Earth, because they believed that an evil force had created all matter. To purify themselves, an elite few—known as "perfects"—rejected their own bodies as corrupt matter, refused to marry and procreate, and in extreme cases gradually starved themselves. These purified perfects provided a dramatic contrast to the more worldly Catholic clergy. For many, Catharism became a form of protest against the wealth and power of the Church. By the 1150s the Cathars had organized their own churches, performed their own rituals, and even elected their own bishops. Where they became deeply rooted, as in the south of France, they practiced their faith openly until Pope Innocent III authorized a Crusade against them.

The Waldensians were the followers of Peter Waldo (d. ca. 1184), a merchant of Lyons, France, who like Francis of Assisi had abandoned all his possessions and taken a vow of poverty. Desiring to imitate the life of Jesus and live in simple purity, the Waldensians preached and translated the Gospels into their own language so that laypeople who did not know Latin could understand them. At first the Waldensians' seemed similar to the Franciscans, but because of the Waldensians' failure to obtain licenses to preach as the Franciscans had done, they came to be depicted by Church authorities as heretics. In response the Waldensians created an alternative church that became widespread in southern France, Rhineland Germany, and northern Italy.

Catholic authorities, who were often the objects of strong criticisms from the Cathars and Waldensians, grew ever more hostile to them. Bishops declared heretics liable to the same legal penalties as those guilty of treason, which authorized the political authorities to proceed against them. In 1208 Pope Innocent III called the Albigensian Crusade, the first of several holy wars launched against heretics in the south of France. The king of France was only too happy to fight the Albigensian Crusade because he saw it as a means of expanding royal power in a region of France where his authority was weak. To eradicate the remaining Cathars and Waldensians, several kings and popes initiated inquisitions. By the middle of the thirteenth century the Cathars had been converted or exterminated except for a few isolated pockets in the mountains, which were stamped out by later inquisitors. The Waldensians were nearly wiped out by inquisitorial campaigns, but a few scattered groups have managed to survive to this day, mostly by retreating to the relative safety of the high Alps and later to the Americas.

Systematic Persecution of the Jews

Before the Crusades, Christians and Jews had lived in relative harmony in Europe. In fact, during the Carolingian period the Frankish kings and emperors had protected Jewish communities from the occasional hostility of bishops who sought to expel them. The Crusades, however, fomented increased violence against Jews. Discrimination and assaults against Jews soon became far more common than ever before. In 1182 Jews were expelled from France and allowed to return only under dire financial penalties. In England the monarchy discriminated against the Jews, opening the way for the massacre and mass suicide of the entire Jewish community of York in 1190. The 1215 decrees of the Fourth Lateran Council, which were the centerpiece of Innocent III's pontificate, attempted to regulate the activities of the Jews of Europe. These decrees prohibited Jews from holding public offices and required them to wear distinctive dress.

Christians justified their persecution of Jews during the twelfth and thirteenth centuries in two ways. First, they depicted Jews as the enemies of Christ. This bias was based on the belief that Jews were members of a conspiratorial organization devoted to the destruction of Christianity. Second, jurists began to consider Jews as royal serfs because they lived in a Christian kingdom at the king's sufferance. By classifying Jews as serfs, the law deprived them of the rights of private property. As the jurist Bracton put it, "The Jew can have nothing of his own, for whatever he acquires he acquires not for himself but for the king; for the Jews live not for themselves but for others and so they acquire not for themselves but for others."[3] This precept, which was promulgated in Spain, England, and the German Empire, justified the repeated royal confiscations of Jewish property. Especially when faced with a fiscal shortfall, kings were inclined to solve their financial problems by expropriating the property of the Jewish community. As a result of these policies most Jews were desperately poor. Because they were prohibited from owning land or joining craft guilds, Jews were forced to seek other means of support. Because Christians were barred from loaning money at interest, running pawn shops and banking were some of the few economic activities open to European Jews.

The Church's Policy Toward the Jews

At the Fourth Lateran Council of 1215, Pope Innocent III presided over a number of decrees that regulated the lives of Jews. Many of the decrees of the council were based on earlier laws, but by bringing all these laws together the council attempted to separate the Jews entirely from Christians. The first passage treats the issue of usury, the taking of interest payments on loans. The second orders Jews and Muslims to wear distinctive clothing in order to prevent sexual relations among adherents to different faiths.

The more the Christian religion is restrained in the exaction of interest so much more does the knavery of the Jews in this matter increase, so that in a short time they exhaust the wealth of Christians. Wishing therefore to provide for Christians in this matter lest they be burdened excessively by the Jews, we ordain through synodal decree that if they hereafter extort heavy and unrestrained interest, no matter what the pretext be, Christians shall be withdrawn from association with them until the Jews give adequate satisfaction for their unmitigated oppression. Also the Christians shall be compelled, if necessary, through Church punishment from which an appeal will be disregarded, to abstain from business relations with the Jews. . . .

In some provinces a difference in dress distinguishes the Jews or Saracens [Muslims] from the Christians, but in certain others such a confusion has grown up that they cannot be distinguished by any difference. Thus it happens at times that through error Christians have relations with the women of Jews or Saracens, and Jews or Saracens with Christian women. Therefore, that they may not, under pretext of error of this sort excuse themselves in the future for the excesses of such prohibited intercourse, we decree that such Jews and Saracens of both sexes in every Christian province and at all time shall be marked off in the eyes of the public from other peoples through the character of their dress.

Source: From Richard Lim and David Kammerling Smith, eds. *The West in the Wider World: Sources and Perspectives,* vol. 1 (2003): 298.

"The Living Dead": Lepers

The widespread presence of lepers produced dramatically conflicting emotions in medieval Europe. Leprosy (Hansen's disease), which destroys the blood vessels, skin tissues, and ligaments of those who have it, creating grotesque disfigurements and bone deformations, was greatly feared. The exact means of transmission of leprosy is still unclear, and it can probably be contracted from another person only after long physical contact. Even though it was not particularly contagious, lepers were shunned. Leviticus 13:45–46 says of the leper, "he is unclean: he shall dwell alone." Following these biblical precepts, many communities during the twelfth century established leper houses to segregate people with leprosy and other disfiguring or repellent diseases. Lepers' separation from the world made them objects of admiration for some pious Christians. To wash the sores and kiss the lesions of lepers constituted a charitable act of special merit, especially for pious women.

Some medieval thinkers equated lepers with heretics and Jews. A monk was reported to have shouted to a heretical preacher, "you too are a leper, scarred by heresy, excluded from communion by the judgment of the priest, according to the law, bare-headed, with ragged clothing, your body covered by an infected and filthy garment." In 1321 rumors alleged that a conspiracy between lepers and Jews had poisoned the wells in France. Heretics, lepers, and Jews became interchangeable co-conspirators in league with the Devil to destroy Christianity. As the assumed common enemy, they all became subject to persecution.

The Creation of Sexual Crimes

The Christian disapproval of men who engaged in sexual relations with other men derived from a medieval interpretation of the biblical condemnation of the Sodomites, the people of the city of Sodom and its sister cities. Ezekiel 16:49 states, "This was the guilt of your sister Sodom: she and her daughters had pride, excess of food, and prosperous ease, but did not aid the poor and needy." According to this passage, the sin of the people of Sodom was the failure to be charitable; sexual behavior was not mentioned. In fact, during the first thousand years of Christianity, there was no particular concern about homosexuality. Christian theologians advocated chastity for everyone and did not consider homosexual relations between men to be any more sinful than any other form of sexual behavior.

During the eleventh century, however, the sin of Sodom came to be associated with homosexual relations, prompted perhaps by reports of forced child prostitution in Muslim lands. The first church legislation against the practice came in 1179. The reasons for this dramatic shift of opinion—from treating such behavior as sinful but tolerable to treating it as criminal—are obscure, but the language of the time paired sodomy with leprosy. Male sodomites began to be persecuted, and by 1300 most governments had made male sodomy punishable by death, in many statutes death

Inquiring into Heresy:
The Inquisition in Montaillou

In 1208 Pope Innocent III issued a call for a Crusade against the Cathars or Albigensians. Fighting on behalf of French King Philip II, Simon de Montfort decisively defeated the pro-Cathar barons of southern France at Muret in 1213. Catharism retreated to the mountains, where it was kept alive by a clandestine network of adherents. The obliteration of these stubborn remnants required methods more subtle than the blunt instrument of a Crusade. It required the techniques of inquisitors adept at interrogation and investigation.

Against the Cathar underground, the inquisition conducted its business through a combination of denunciations, exhaustive interrogations of witnesses and suspects, and confessions. Because its avowed purpose was to root out doctrinal error and to reconcile heretics to the Church, eliciting confessions was the preferred technique. But confessed heretics could not receive absolution until they informed on their friends and associates.

One of the last and most extensively documented inquisition cases against Catharism took place in Montaillou, a village in the Pyrenees Mountains, near the border of modern France and Spain. The Montaillou inquisition began in 1308, a century after the launch of the Albigensian Crusade and long after the heyday of Catharism.

However, the detailed records of the inquisitors provide a revealing glimpse into Catharism and its suppression as well as the procedures of the inquisition. The first to investigate Montaillou was Geoffrey d'Ablis, the inquisitor of Carcassone. In 1308 he had every resident over age 12 seized and imprisoned. After the investigation, the villagers suffered the full range of inquisitorial penalties for their Cathar faith. Some were burned at the stake or sentenced to life in prison. Many who were allowed to return to Montaillou were forced to wear a yellow cross, the symbol of a heretic, sewn to the outside of their garments.

Unfortunately for these survivors, Montaillou was investigated again from 1318 to 1325 by the most fearsome inquisitor of the age, Jacques Fournier, who was later elected Pope Benedict XII. Known as an efficient, rigorous opponent of heresy, Fournier forced virtually all the surviving adults in Montaillou to appear before his tribunal. When the scrupulous Fournier took up a case, his inquiries were notoriously lengthy and rigorous. Both witnesses and defendants spoke of his tenacity, skill, and close attention to detail in conducting interrogations. If Fournier and his assistants could not uncover evidence through interrogation and confession, they did not hesitate to employ informers and spies to obtain the necessary information. When Pierre Maury, a shepherd who had been sought by the inquisitors for many years, returned to the village for a visit, an old friend received him with caution: "When we saw you again we felt both joy and fear. Joy, because it was a long time since we had seen you. Fear, because I was afraid lest the Inquisition had captured you up there: if they had they would have made you confess everything and come back among us as a spy in order to bring about my capture."[4]

Fournier's success in Montaillou depended on his ability to play local factions against each other by encouraging members of one clan to denounce the members of another. Fournier's persistence even turned family members against one another. The clearest example of this convoluted play of local alliances and animosities, family ties, religious belief, and self-interest is the case of Montaillou's wealthiest family, the Clergues.

Bernard Clergue was the count's local representative, which made him a kind of sheriff, and his brother Pierre was the parish priest. Together they represented both the secular and religious arms of the inquisition in Montaillou. In his youth, Pierre had Cathar sympathies, and he reportedly had kept a heretical book or calendar in his home. Nevertheless, at some time before 1308, he and Bernard betrayed the local Cathars to the inquisition. In the proceedings that followed, they had the power to either protect or expose their neighbors and family members. When one of his relatives was summoned to appear before the inquisition, Bernard warned her to "say you fell off the ladder in your house; pretend you have broken bones everywhere. Otherwise it's prison for you."[5] Pierre relentlessly used his influence for his own and his family's benefit. A notorious womanizer, Pierre frightened women into sleeping with him by threatening to denounce them to the inquisition. Those he personally testified against were primarily from other prominent Montaillou families who represented a challenge to the Clergues' power. As one resident bitterly testified, "the priest himself cause[s] many inhabitants of Montaillou to be summoned by the Lord Inquisitor of Carcassone.

Burning of the Heretical Books of the Cathars
In this fifteenth-century painting, St. Dominic presides over the burning of the heretical books of the Cathars.

A Catholic book, which contains the truth, miraculously floats above the flames.

St. Dominic is depicted with a halo.

It is high time the people of the priest's house were thrust as deep in prison as the other inhabitants of Montaillou."[6]

Despite the Clergues' attempted misuse of the inquisitorial investigation for their own purposes, the inquisitor Fournier persevered according to his own standards of evidence. In 1320 he finally had Pierre Clergue arrested as a heretic. The sly priest died in prison.

Questions of Justice

1. How did the methods of the inquisition help create outcasts from Catholic society? How did these methods help consolidate Catholic identity?
2. The primary function of the inquisition was to investigate what people believed. What do you think the inquisitors thought justice to be?

Taking It Further

Lambert, Malcolm. *The Cathars*. 1998. The best place to investigate the Cathar movement in the full sweep of its troubled history.

Le Roy Ladurie, Emmanuel. *Montaillou: The Promised Land of Error,* trans. Barbara Bray. 1978. The best-selling and fascinating account of life in a Cathar village based on the records of Fournier's inquisition.

Moore, R. I. *The Formation of a Persecuting Society: Power and Deviance in Western Europe, 950–1250*. 1987. Places the harassment of heretics in the broader context of medieval persecutions.

CHRONOLOGY

Medieval Religious Developments	
1098	Founding of Cistercian Order
1221	Death of Dominic
1226	Death of Francis of Assisi
1208–1213	Albigensian Crusade
1215	Fourth Lateran Council promulgates dogma of transubstantiation

by burning. In the process of creating new outcasts, however, female homosexuals were never mentioned. It appears that the male authors of penal legislation could not imagine that erotic relationships between women were even possible.

By the thirteenth century, heretics, Jews, lepers, and male sodomites were identified as outcasts and subjected to legal discrimination, persecution, and violence. The so-called cleansing of Christian Europe of its outcasts was a particularly violent example of the use of power by the dominant society over certain minority groups within it. One of the ways medieval Christian society became more uniform was by ostracizing certain groups of people from within its midst.

Strengthening the Center of the West

■ How did the western European monarchies strengthen themselves?

During the twelfth and thirteenth centuries, Catholic western Europe became the supreme political and economic power in the Christian world, eclipsing Byzantium—an achievement that made it a potent rival to the Islamic states. One reason was stronger political unity.

The three forms of government during the Middle Ages were empires, city-states, and monarchies. The best example of an empire was Byzantium, a potentially formidable military power, but too diverse and far-flung to maintain the loyalty of its subjects. It remained on the defensive, especially against the powerful Islamic caliphates, which also were empires. The other Christian empire was the German Empire, which boasted some impressive monarchs but lacked unity and thus never achieved its potential as the dominant power in Europe. Italian city-states, such as Venice, Milan, Florence, Pisa, and Genoa, thrived as the engines of economic innovation and vitality, but they were vulnerable to foreign conquest and frequently enfeebled by

internal rivalries and feuds. In contrast to overextended empires and underdefended city-states, the western European monarchies gathered the military resources and created the bureaucratic structures necessary to surpass all other forms of government. These kingdoms created the foundations of the modern nation-states, which remain to this day the dominant forms of government around the globe. What happened in France and England during the twelfth and thirteenth centuries, therefore, represents one of the most important and lasting contributions of the West to world history.

The Monarchies of Western Europe

During the High Middle Ages, France and England began to exhibit the fundamental characteristics of unified kingdoms. Several developments explain how these kingdoms strengthened themselves. First, they formed political units that persisted. These units had borders that survived despite changes in rulers and dynasties. Second, these kingdoms developed lasting, impersonal institutions that managed finances and administration. We can blame this period for the rise of bureaucracies. Third, they established a system for resolving disputes and rendering justice in which the final authority was the king—the principle of sovereignty. Fourth, the medieval monarchies resolved that the fundamental loyalty of subjects should be to the laws of the state, a loyalty greater than the obligations of a vassal to a lord or even a son to a father. Stable borders, permanent bureaucracies, sovereignty, and the rule of law were the foundations on which France and England became the most powerful kingdoms in Europe during the twelfth and thirteenth centuries (see Map 9.3).

Expansion of Power: France

For the French kings, the pressing task was to unify their hodge-podge kingdom. Through most of the twelfth century the only part of France the kings ruled directly was the royal domain, the Ile-de-France, an area roughly the size of Vermont but with the fertile soil of Illinois. Over the rest of the kingdom, the king of France was merely the overlord with vague obligations from his vassals, one of whom, the king of England, directly controlled more French territory than he did. On these unpromising foundations, the twelfth- and thirteenth-century French monarchs built the most powerful kingdom in Europe and one of the most unified. The kings of France achieved unity through military conquests and shrewd administrative reforms.

France enjoyed a continuous succession of kings who ruled for long periods of time, produced male heirs, and avoided succession disputes. In the turbulent Middle Ages, dynastic continuity was a key ingredient in building loyalty and avoiding chaos. The vigorous Philip I (r. 1060–1108) initiated a succession of extremely effective kings.

Unpopular with the clergy because of his alleged adultery, Philip took charge of his own domain, where he countermanded the arbitrary justice of local lords by extending royal justice. By focusing his attention on establishing himself as the undisputed lord of his own domain, Philip provided his descendants with a powerful lordship on which they built the French monarchy.

Louis VI, the Fat (r. 1108–1137), secured complete control of the Ile-de-France, thus providing the dynasty with a dependable income from the region's abundant farms and the thriving trade of Paris. He shoved aside the great barons who had dominated the royal administration and replaced them with career bureaucrats who were loyal only to the king. The most prominent of these was the highly talented Suger, a lower-class priest who had been Louis's tutor and served the king as a statesman of vision.

Louis's grandson, Philip II Augustus (r. 1180–1223), proved himself a shrewd realist who outmaneuvered his vassal, the English king John, to recover much of western France for himself. To administer his domain and newly ac-quired lands, Philip introduced new royal officials, the *baillis*, who were paid professionals; some were trained in Roman law. Directly responsible to the king, they had full administrative, judicial, and military powers in their districts. Philip tolerated considerable regional diversity, but the *baillis* laid the foundation for a bureaucracy that centralized French government. Many historians consider Philip Augustus the most important figure in establishing the unity of the French state.

The medieval French king who came closest to exemplifying the moral ideals of kingship was Louis IX (r. 1226–1270), who was canonized St. Louis in 1297 for his exemplary piety and reputation for justice. A tall imposing figure, Louis was blessed with impeccable manners and a chivalrous nature. Prompted by an ardent desire to lead a Crusade to the Holy Land, he sought to strengthen the kingdom so that it could operate and survive in his absence. He introduced a system of judicial appeals that expanded royal justice and investigated the honesty of the *baillis*.

Map 9.3   Western European Kingdoms in the Late Twelfth Century

The kings of England occupied Ireland as well as much of western France. France itself was consolidated around the Ile-de-France, the area around Paris. The kingdoms of Germany, Bohemia, Burgundy, and Italy were ruled by the German emperors.

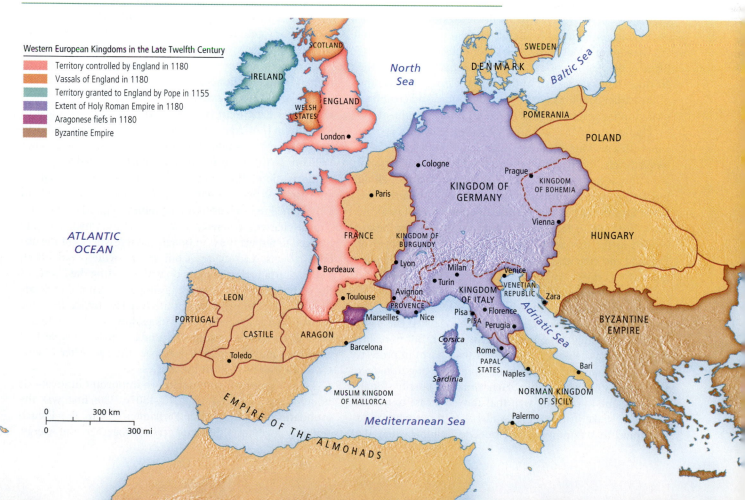

The reputation of the monarchy so carefully burnished by Louis IX suffered during the reign of his grandson, Philip IV, the Fair (r. 1285–1314)—known for his ruthless use of power. Philip greatly expanded the king's authority and also managed to bring the Church under his personal control, making the French clergy largely exempt from papal supervision. To pay for his frequent wars, Philip expelled the Jews after stripping them of their lands and goods, and then turned against the rich Order of the Knights Templar, a crusader order that had amassed a fortune as the papal banker and creditor of Philip. He confiscated the Templars' lands and tortured the knights to extort confessions to various crimes in a perverse campaign to discredit them. Philip was perhaps most effective in finding new ways to increase taxation. Under Philip, royal revenues grew tenfold from what they had been in the saintly reign of Louis IX.

Lord of All Lords: The King of England

When William I, the Conqueror (r. 1066–1087), seized England in 1066, he claimed all the land for himself. The new king kept about one-fifth of the land under his personal rule and parceled out the rest to the loyal nobles, monasteries, and the churches. This policy ensured that every bit of England was held as a fief, directly or indirectly, from the king, a principle of lordship enforced by an oath of loyalty to the crown required of all vassals. About 180 great lords from among the Norman aristocracy held land directly from the king, and hundreds of lesser nobles were vassals of these great lords. William accomplished what other kings only dreamed about: He had truly made himself the lord of all lords. William's hierarchy of nobles transformed the nature of the English monarchy, giving the Norman kings far greater authority over England than any of the earlier Anglo-Saxon kings had enjoyed and creating a more unified realm than any kingdom on the continent.

The legacy of the conquest provided William's successors with a decided advantage in centralizing the monarchy. Nevertheless, the system required the king's close personal attention. King Henry II (r. 1154–1189) proved himself an indefatigable administrator and calculating realist who made England the best-governed kingdom in Europe at the time. Reacting to the anarchy that prevailed when he ascended to the throne, he strengthened the government of England and extended English authority—with varying degrees of success—over Ireland, Wales, and Scotland.

The greatest innovations of Henry's rule were judicial. His use of sheriffs to enforce the royal will produced the legends of Robin Hood, the bandit who resisted the nasty sheriff of Nottingham on behalf of the poor. But in reality the sheriffs probably did more good than harm in protecting the weak against the powerful. In attempting to reduce the jurisdiction of the nobles, Henry made it possible for almost anyone to obtain a writ that moved a case to a royal court. To make justice more available to those who could not travel to Westminster, just outside London where the royal court usually sat, Henry introduced a system of itinerant circuit court° judges who visited every shire in the land four times a year. When this judge arrived, the sheriff was required to assemble a group of men familiar with local affairs to report the major crimes that had been committed since the judge's last visit. These assemblies were the origins of the grand jury° system, which persists to this day as the means for indicting someone for a crime.

For disputes over the possession of land, sheriffs assembled a group of twelve local men who testified under oath about the claims of the disputants, and the judge made his decision on the basis of their testimony. These assemblies were the beginning of trial by jury°. The system was later extended to criminal cases and remains the basis for rendering legal verdicts in common-law countries, including Britain, the United States, and Canada.

With his usual directness, Henry tackled the special legal privileges of the clergy, the thorn in the side of medieval kings everywhere. According to canon law, priests could be tried only in church courts, which were notoriously easygoing in punishing even murderers with a simple penance. Moreover, these verdicts—however trivial—could be appealed to Rome, a process that could delay justice for years. Henry wanted to subject priests who had committed crimes to the jurisdiction of the royal courts in order to establish a universal justice that applied to everyone in the realm, a principle fiercely opposed by Thomas Becket, the archbishop of Canterbury. When four knights—believing they were acting on the king's wishes—murdered Becket before the altar of Canterbury cathedral, the public was outraged, and Henry's attempts to subject the Church to royal justice were ruined. Becket was soon canonized and revered as England's most famous saint.

The royal powers assembled by Henry met strong reaction under King John (r. 1199–1216). In 1204 John lost to King Philip II of France the duchy of Normandy, which had been one of the foundations of English royal power since William the Conqueror. After the French defeated King John at the Battle of Bouvines in 1214, the barons of England grew tired of being asked to pay for wars the king lost. In 1215 some English barons forced John to sign Magna Carta° ("great charter," in reference to its size), in which the king pledged to respect the traditional feudal privileges of the nobility, towns, and clergy. Contrary to widespread belief, Magna Carta had nothing to do with asserting the liberty of the common people or guaranteeing universal rights. It addressed only the privileges of a select few rather than the rights of the many. Subsequent kings, however, swore to uphold it, thereby accepting the fundamental principle that even the king was obliged to respect the law. After Magna Carta the lord of all lords became less so.

English government boasted two important innovations under King Edward I (r. 1272–1307). The first was the foundation of the English Parliament (from the French "talking together"). Edward called together the clergy, barons, knights, and townsmen in Parliament in order to raise large sums of money for his foreign wars. The members of Parliament had little choice but to comply with the king's demands, and all they received in return was Edward's explanation of what he was going to do with their money. The English Parliament differed from similar assemblies on the Continent in that it more often included representatives of the "commons." The commons consisted of townsmen and prosperous farmers who lacked titles of nobility but whom the king summoned because he needed their money. The second governmental innovation during Edward's reign consisted of an extensive body of legal reforms. Edward curtailed the power of the local courts, which were dominated by rural landlords and aristocrats. He began to issue statutes that applied to the entire kingdom. Under Edward, lawyers began to practice at the Inns of Court in London, where they transformed customary legal practices into the common law that still survives as the foundation of Anglo-American law.

A Divided Regime: The German Empire

Heir to the old Carolingian kingdom of East Francia, the German Empire suffered from the division between its principal component parts in Germany and northern Italy. Germany itself was an ill-defined region, subdivided by deep ethnic diversity and powerful dukes who ruled their lands with a spirit of fierce independence. As a result, emperors could not rule Germany directly but only by demanding homage from the dukes who became imperial vassals. These feudal bonds were fragile substitutes for the kinds of monarchic institutions that evolved in France and England. An effective emperor could call on the dukes to help him crush rivals, but he could neither dictate to his vassals nor claim vacant fiefs for the crown, as in France and England. The emperor's best asset was the force of his personality and his willingness to engage in a perpetual show of force to prevent rebellion. In northern Italy, the other part of the emperor's dominion, he did not even enjoy these extensive ties of vassalage and could rely only on vague legal rights granted by the imperial title and his ability to keep an army on the scene.

The century between the election of Frederick I (r. 1152–1190), known as Barbarossa or "red-beard," and the death of his grandson Frederick II (r. 1212–1250) represented the great age of the medieval German Empire, a period of relative stability preceded and followed by disastrous phases of anarchy and civil war. Both of these Hohenstaufen emperors, however, faced hostility from the popes whose own monarchic pretensions clashed with imperial rule in Italy.

Barbarossa projected enormous personal charisma that helped him awe recalcitrant vassals. He became a careful student of the imperial dignities encoded in Roman law, surrounded himself with experts in that law, and considered himself the heir of the great emperors Constantine, Justinian, and Charlemagne. He even managed to have Charlemagne canonized a saint.

Barbarossa's lofty ambitions contrasted with the flimsy base of his support. His own ancestral lands were in Swabia, an impoverished region barely capable of subsistence let alone supporting Frederick's imperial adventures. To set himself on a firmer financial footing, Frederick launched a series of expeditions across the Alps to subdue the enormously wealthy Italian cities that were technically part of his realm, even though they acted as if they were independent. The campaign proved a disaster. It galvanized papal opposition to him and forced the Italian city-states to put aside their rivalries to form an anti-imperial coalition, the Lombard League. At the Battle of Legnano in 1176 the League decisively defeated the German imperial army, forcing Barbarossa to recognize the autonomy of the city-states.

Barbarossa's young grandson, Frederick II, turned the traditional policy of the German emperors upside down. Instead of residing in Germany and attempting to influence Italian affairs from afar, Frederick, who loved the warm climate and engaging society of the South, lived in Sicily and left Germany alone.

Frederick has long enjoyed a remarkable historical reputation as the "wonder of the world," the most cosmopolitan monarch of the Middle Ages, who laid out grand plans for a united Italy embodied in the Constitutions of Melfi, which he put forth in 1231 (see Map 9.4). Through them, he proposed to rule through a professional imperial bureaucracy, to employ itinerant inspectors to check corruption, and to introduce uniform statutes based on Roman law. In effect, he sought a level of uniformity similar to what France and England had achieved during this period, and he was probably subject to similar influences derived from ancient Roman political theory and law. However, the popes' enduring antagonism to these plans and Frederick's own despotic tendencies undermined these ambitious and potentially fruitful reforms. He cut himself off from honest advice by declaring it an act of sacrilege even to discuss, let

---

CHRONOLOGY

Strengthening the Center of the West

1170	Murder of Thomas Becket
1176	Battle of Legnano; Lombard League defeats Emperor Frederick I (Barbarossa)
1214	Battle of Bouvines; Philip II of France, allied to Emperor Frederick II, defeats John of England and his allies
1215	Magna Carta
1231	Constitutions of Melfi

alone question, any of his decisions. He so overtaxed southern Italy and Sicily that these lands, which were once the richest in Italy, became an economic backwater. His abandonment of Germany to its feuding princes prevented the centralization and implementation of legal reforms that took place in France and England.

After Frederick II's death, his successors lost their hold on both Italy and Germany. During the nearly constant warfare and turmoil of the late thirteenth century, the exceedingly inappropriate name of "Holy Roman Empire" came into general use for the German Empire. The term suggested a universal empire ordained by God and descended from ancient Rome, but the lofty claims embedded in the name found no basis in the crude reality of the rebellious, disunited lands of Germany and Italy.

Map 9.4   The Empire and the Papacy in Italy
During the reign of Emperor Frederick II, the kingdom of Sicily became the most potent power in Italy and presented a challenge to the papacy. After Frederick's death, the peninsula suffered from a long series of wars as rival claimants attempted to replace him in Sicily and the popes attempted to control events.

Medieval Culture: The Search for Understanding

- ■ What made western European culture distinctive?

Cultural encounters during the High Middle Ages took many forms. Some were direct exchanges, as when Christians and Muslims in crusader Jerusalem discovered their different ways of praying. Other encounters were more indirect, as when medieval thinkers read the books of ancient philosophers and so were confronted with challenging ideas that did not fit easily into their view of the world. During the twelfth and thirteenth centuries, this second kind of encounter, based on the renewed availability of works of classical Greek philosophy, opened creative possibilities, especially in theology. The Greek philosophers had been dead for nearly 1,500 years, but the medieval thinkers who rediscovered ancient philosophy experienced a profound cultural shock. First Muslim and then Jewish and Christian writers struggled to reconcile the rational approach of Aristotle and other Greek philosophers with the faith demanded by Islam, Judaism, and Christianity. Some suffered from a crisis of faith. Others confronted the challenge presented by ancient philosophy and attempted to reconcile reason and faith by creating new philosophical systems.

The medieval intellectual engagement with new ideas spread in many directions. Lawyers began to look back to ancient Roman law for guidance about how to settle disputes, adjudicate crimes, and create governmental institutions. Muslim influences reinvigorated the Christian understanding of the sciences. Themes found in Persian love poetry, which were echoed in Arabic poems, found their way into the Christian notion of courtly love. Catholic western Europe experienced a cultural flowering through the spread of education, the growing power of Latin learning, and the invention of the university. Distinctively Western forms developed in literature, music, drama, and above all the Romanesque and Gothic architecture of Europe's great cathedrals.

The city of Paris was the breeding ground for much creative activity. The dynamism of Paris attracted thinkers and artists from all over Europe. Thirteenth-century Paris represented the cultural pinnacle of the High Middle Ages, comparable to Athens in the fifth century B.C.E. or Florence in the fifteenth century.

Revival of Learning

The magnitude of the educational revolution in medieval western Europe is clear from simple statistics. In 1050 less than 1 percent of the population of Latin Christian Europe could read, and most of these literate people were priests who knew just enough Latin to recite the offices of the liturgy. Four hundred years later, as much as 40 percent of men and a smaller percentage of women were literate in the cities of western Europe. Europeans had embraced learning on a massive scale even before inexpensive printed books became available in the late fifteenth century. In fact, the printing revolution of the fifteenth century was not so much the stimulus for new learning as a response to the escalating demand for more books. How did this demand come about?

In 1050 education was available only in monasteries and cathedral schools, and the curriculum was very basic, usually only reading and writing. These two kinds of schools had different educational missions. Monastic education trained monks to read the books available in their libraries as an aid to contemplating the mysteries of the next world. In contrast, the cathedral schools, which trained members of the ecclesiastical hierarchy, emphasized the practical skills of rational analysis that would help future priests, bishops, and royal advisers solve the problems of this world.

By 1100 the number of cathedral schools had grown significantly and the curriculum expanded to include the study of the ancient Roman masters, Cicero and Virgil, who became models for clear Latin composition. These schools met the demand for trained officials from various sources—the thriving cities, the growing church bureaucracy, and the infant bureaucracies of the Western kingdoms. As the number of schools expanded, they became less exclusively devoted to religious training and began to provide a practical education for laypeople. But the Church was still the dominant force.

Scholasticism: A Christian Philosophy

In addition to teaching Latin grammar, cathedral schools recognized a growing need for training in logic as well. Refuting heresies required precise logical arguments. Anselm of Canterbury (ca. 1033–1109), for example, employed strict logic in an attempt to prove the existence of God. He began with the question of how the mind conceived ideas. He could not imagine ideas coming from

nothing, arguing that they must have some basis in reality. Did not the very presence of the idea of God in the mind, Anselm concluded, demonstrate that God must exist? Intrigued by such arguments, students began to seek more advanced instruction than that provided by the standard curriculum. They tended to gather around popular lecturers in the cathedral schools, where they were trained in scholasticism, which emphasized the critical methods of reasoning, pioneered by Anselm.

Scholasticism° literally means "of the schools," but the term also refers to a broad philosophical and theological movement that dominated medieval thought. In this broader sense, scholasticism refers to the use of logic learned from Aristotle to interpret the meaning of the Bible and the writings of the Church Fathers, who created Christian theology in its first centuries. Books were scarce in the cathedral schools because the only means of duplication before the invention of the printing press was hand copying onto expensive sheepskin parchment. So the principal method of teaching and learning was the lecture. Teachers read Latin texts out loud, and students were obliged to memorize what they heard. In the classroom the lecturer would recite a short passage, present the comments of other authorities on it, and draw his own conclusions. He would then move on to another brief passage and repeat the process. Students heard the same lectures over and over again until they had thoroughly memorized the text under discussion. In addition to lectures, scholastics engaged in disputations. Participants in a disputation presented oral arguments for or against a particular thesis, a process called dialectical reasoning. Disputants were evaluated on their ability to investigate through logic the truth of a thesis. Disputations required several skills—verbal facility, a prodigious memory so that apt citations could be made, and the ability to think quickly. The process we know today as debate originated with these medieval disputations. Lectures and disputations became the core activities of the scholastics, who considered all subjects, however sacred, as appropriate for reasoned examination.

None of the scholastic teachers was more popular than the acerbic, witty, and daring Peter Abelard (1079–1142). Students from all over Europe flocked to hear Abelard's lectures at the cathedral school of Paris. Abelard's clever criticisms of the ideas of other thinkers delighted students. In *Sic et Non* ("Yes and No"), Abelard boldly examined some of the foundations of Christian truth. Employing the dialectical reasoning of a disputation, he presented both sides of 150 theological problems discussed by the Church Fathers. He left the conclusions open in order to challenge his students and readers to think further, but his intention seems to have been less to undermine accepted biblical truths than to point out how apparent disagreements among the experts masked a deeper level of agreement about Christian truth.

Universities: Organizing Learning

From the cathedral schools arose the first universities. The University of Paris evolved from the cathedral school where Abelard once taught. Initially the universities were little more than guilds (trade associations), organized by either students or teachers to protect their interests. As members of a guild, students bargained with their professors and townspeople, as would other tradesmen, over costs and established minimum standards of instruction. The guild of the law students at Bologna received a charter in 1158, which probably made it the first university. Some of the early universities were professional schools, such as the medical faculty at Salerno, but true to their origins as cathedral schools, most emphasized theology over other subjects.

The medieval universities formulated the basic educational practices that are still in place today. They established a curriculum, examined students, conferred degrees, and conducted graduation ceremonies. Students and teachers wore distinctive robes, which are still worn at graduation ceremonies. Teachers were clergymen—that is, they "professed" religion; hence the title of *professor* for a university instructor. In their first years students pursued the liberal arts curriculum, which consisted of the *trivium* (grammar, rhetoric, and logic) and the *quadrivium* (arithmetic, geometry, astronomy, and music). This curriculum is forerunner of the arts and sciences faculties and distribution requirements in modern universities. Medieval university students devoted many years to rigorous study and rote memoriza-

tion. Completion of a professional doctorate in law, medicine, or theology typically required more than ten years.

Medieval universities did not admit women, in part because women were barred from the priesthood and most university students were training to become priests. (Women did not attend universities in significant numbers until the nineteenth century.) There was also a widespread fear of learned women who might think on their own. The few women who did receive advanced educations had to rely on a private tutor.

The Ancients: Renaissance of the Twelfth Century

The scholastics' integration of Greek philosophy with Christian theology represents a key facet of the Twelfth-Century Renaissance°, a revival of interest in the ancients comparable in importance to the Carolingian Renaissance of the ninth century and the Italian Renaissance of the fifteenth. During Peter Abelard's lifetime, very few western Europeans knew Greek, the language of ancient philosophy, and only a few works of the Greeks were available in Latin translations. Between about 1140 and 1260 this cultural isolation dramatically changed.

A flood of new Latin translations of the Greek classics came from Sicily and Spain, where Christians had close contacts with Muslims and Jews. Muslim philosophers had translated into Arabic the Greek philosophical and scientific classics, which were readily available in the Middle East and North Africa. These Arabic translations were then translated into Latin, often by Jewish scholars who knew both languages. Later a few Catholic scholars traveled to Byzantium, where they learned enough Greek to make even better translations from the originals.

As they encountered the philosophy of the ancients, Muslim, Jewish, and Christian thinkers faced profoundly disturbing problems. The principles of faith revealed in the Qur'an of Islam and the Hebrew and Christian Bibles were not easily reconciled with the philosophical method of reasoning found in Greek works, especially those by Aristotle. These religious thinkers recognized the superiority of Greek thought over their own. They worried that the power of philosophical reasoning undermined religious truth. As men of faith they challenged themselves to demonstrate that philosophy did not contradict religious teaching, and some of them went even further to employ philosophical reasoning to demonstrate the truth of religion. They always faced opposition within their own religious faiths, how-

A Lecture in a Medieval University
Some of the students are sleeping and others are chatting with their neighbors. The most earnest students are sitting in the front row. Some things never change.

ever, especially from people who thought philosophical reason was an impediment to religious faith.

Avicenna (980–1037) was the first Muslim thinker to confront the questions raised by Greek philosophy, such as how to prove the existence of God or account for the creation of the world. An Iranian physician, Avicenna's commentaries on Aristotle deeply influenced the Catholic scholastics, who quoted him extensively. Avicenna attempted a rational proof of the existence of God based on the "necessary existent." Without God nothing exists; therefore, if we exist, so must God.

Following Avicenna's lead, Al-Ghazali (1058–1111) taught the ancient Greek philosophers to Muslim students. But from the daunting task of reconciling philosophy and religion he suffered a nervous breakdown, which forced him to abandon lecturing temporarily and turn to religious mysticism. After this experience, he wrote *The Incoherence of the Philosophers,* in which he argued that religious truth was more accessible through mystical experience than through rational and systematic analysis.

The most powerful answer to Al-Ghazali's critique of philosophy came from Averroës (1126–1198), who rose to become the chief judge of Córdoba, Spain, and an adviser to the caliph. In *The Incoherence of the Incoherence* (1179–1180), Averroës argued that the aim of philosophy is to explain the true, inner meaning of religious revelations. This inner meaning, however, should not be disclosed to the unlettered masses, which must be told only the simple, literal stories and metaphors of Scripture. Although lively and persuasive, Averroës's defense of philosophy failed to revive philosophical speculation within Islam. Once far superior to that of the Latin Christian world, Islamic philosophy and science declined as Muslim thinkers turned to mysticism and rote learning over rational debate. Averroës received a more sympathetic hearing among Jews and Catholics than among Muslims.

DOCUMENT

Ibn Rushd
(Averroës)
(12th c.)

Within Judaism, many had attempted unsuccessfully to reconcile Greek philosophy with Hebrew law and scripture. Success was achieved by a contemporary of Averroës, also from Córdoba—the Jewish philosopher, jurist, and physician Moses Maimonides (1135–1204). His most important work in religious philosophy was *The Guide for the Perplexed* (ca. 1191), which synthesized Greek philosophy, science, and Judaism. Widely read in Arabic, Hebrew, and Latin versions, the book stimulated both Jewish and Christian philosophy. Maimonides's efforts, like those of Averroës, distressed many of his fellow Jews, some of whom desecrated his tomb, but as controversy abated he came to be recognized as a pillar of Jewish thought.

For medieval Catholic philosophers, one of the most difficult tasks was reconciling the biblical account of the divine creation with Aristotle's teaching that the universe was eternal. Even in this early clash between science and religion, creationism was the sticking point. Following the lead

established by Avicenna, Averroës, and Maimonides, the great project of the scholastics became to demonstrate the fundamental harmony between Christian faith and the philosophical knowledge of the ancients.

The most effective resolution of the apparent conflict between faith and philosophy was found in the work of Thomas Aquinas (1225–1274), whose philosophy is called Thomism°. A Dominican friar, Aquinas spent most of his career developing a school system for the Dominicans in Italy, but he also spent two short periods teaching at the University of Paris. Aquinas avoided distracting controversies and academic disputes to concentrate on his two great summaries of human knowledge—the *Summary of the Catholic Faith Against the Gentiles* (1261) and the *Summary of Theology* (1265–1274). In both of these massive scholastic works, reason fully confirmed Christian faith. Encyclopedias of knowledge, they rigorously examined whole fields through dialectical reasoning. Aquinas's method was to pose a question derived from the Bible—such as "Whether woman was made from man?"—and then draw on the accumulated thought of the past to suggest answers, raise critical objections to the answers, refute the objections, and reach a conclusion. Then he proceeded to the next question, "Whether [woman was made] of man's rib?"

Building on the works of Averroës, Aquinas solved the problem of reconciling philosophy and religion by drawing a distinction between *natural truth* and *revealed truth.* For Aquinas, natural truth meant the kinds of things anyone can know through the operation of human reason; revealed truth referred to the things that can be known only through revelation, such as the Trinity and the incarnation of Christ. Aquinas argued that these two kinds of truths could not possibly contradict one another because both came from God. Apparent contradictions could be accommodated by an understanding of a higher truth. On the issue of Creation, for example, Aquinas argued that Aristotle's understanding of the eternal universe was inferior to the higher revealed truth of the Bible that God created the universe in seven days.

The most influential of the scholastic thinkers, Aquinas asserted that to achieve religious truth one should start with faith and then use reason to reach conclusions. He was the first to understand theology systematically in this way, and in doing so he raised a storm of opposition among Christians who were threatened by philosophical reason. Like the work of Avicenna and Maimonides before him, Aquinas's writings were at first prohibited by the theological faculties in universities. Nevertheless, his method remains crucial for Catholic theology to this day.

Just as scholastic theologians looked to ancient Greek philosophy as a guide to reason, jurists revived ancient Roman law, especially at the universities of Bologna and Pavia in Italy. In the law faculties, students were required to learn the legal work of the Emperor Justinian—the text of the *Body of the Civil Law,* together with the commentaries on it. The systematic approach of Roman law provided a way to make the legal system less arbitrary for judges, lawyers, bureaucrats, and advisers to kings and popes. Laws had long consisted of a contradictory mess of municipal regulations, Germanic customs, and feudal precepts. Under Roman law, judges were obliged to justify their verdicts according to prescribed standards of evidence and procedure. The revival of Roman law in the twelfth century made possible the legal system that still guides most of continental Europe.

Epic Violence and Courtly Love

In addition to the developments in philosophy, theology, and the law, the Twelfth-Century Renaissance included a remarkable literary output in the vernacular languages, the tongues spoken in everyday life. The great heroic epics, most of which were adapted from oral tradition or composed between 1050 and 1150, were in English, German, Celtic, Slavonic, Nordic, Icelandic, French, and Spanish. These epics, often repeated from memory as popular entertainment, recounted adventure stories about medieval warriors. They were manly stories that celebrated the beauty and terror of battle and glorified cracked skulls and brutal death: "Now Roland feels that he is at death's door; Out of his ears the brain is running forth." Women hardly appear at all in these epics, except as backdrops to the battles among men or as battered wives.

By the end of the twelfth century, however, a new vernacular literature appeared, created by poets called troubadours°. Unlike the creators of vernacular epics, the troubadour poets included women as well as men, and their literature reflected an entirely new sensibility about the relationships between men and women. The troubadours wrote poems of love, meant to be sung to music; their literary movement is called courtly love°. They composed in Provençal, one of the languages of southern France, and the first audience for their poems was in the courts of southern France. These graciously elegant poems clearly show influences from Arabic love poetry and especially from Muslim mystical literature in which the soul, depicted as feminine, seeks her masculine God/lover. The troubadours secularized this theme of religious union by portraying the ennobling possibilities of the love between a woman and a man. In so doing, they popularized the idea of romantic love, one of the most powerful concepts in all of Western history, an ideal that still dominates popular culture to this day.

An innovative aspect of the courtly love poems of the troubadours was their idealization of women. The male troubadours, such as Chrétien de Troyes (1135–1183), placed women on a pedestal and treated men as the "love vassals" of beloved women to whom they owed loyalty and service. Female troubadours, such as Marie de France (dates unknown), did not place women on a pedestal but idealized emotionally honest and open relationships between lovers. Unlike the epics in which women were brutalized, the troubadours typically saw women as holding power over men or acting as their equals. From southern France, courtly love spread to Germany and elsewhere throughout Europe. Based on a now lost version in Old French, Gottfried von Strassburg recomposed in German the romance of Tristan and Iseult. At first the two lovers struggle to resist temptation and to doubt the other's love, but they find themselves unable to keep away from one another. His resistance is motivated by a sense of honor and hers by "maiden shame," but the power of love triumphs over prudence and the two consummate the relationship. Many of the German poems were romances that reinterpreted the stories of the epics to conform to the values of courtly love. The courtly love ideal has persisted across the centuries in innumerable popular revivals.

The Center of Medieval Culture: The Great Cathedrals

When tourists visit a European city today, they usually want to see its cathedral. Most of these imposing structures were built between 1050 and 1300 and symbolize the soaring ambitions and imaginations of their largely unknown builders. During the great medieval building boom, old churches, which were often perfectly adequate but out of style, were ripped down. In their place hundreds of new cathedrals and thousands of other churches were erected, sparing no expense and reflecting the latest experimental techniques in architectural engineering and artistic fashion. These buildings became multimedia centers for the arts— incorporating architecture, sculpture, stained glass, and painting in their structure and providing a setting for the performance of music and drama. The medieval cathedrals took decades, sometimes centuries, to build at great cost and sacrifice. They are magnificent examples of the pious devotion to God of the people who built them.

Architecture: The Romanesque and Gothic Styles

The Romanesque° style spread throughout western Europe during the eleventh century and the first half of the twelfth century because the master masons who understood sophisticated stone construction techniques traveled from one building site to another, bringing with them a uniform style. The principal innovation of the Romanesque was the arched stone roofs, which were more aesthetically pleasing and less vulnerable to fire than the flat roofs they replaced. The rounded arches of these stone roofs were called barrel vaults because they looked like the inside of a barrel.

Romanesque Cathedral Architecture

The rounded arches, the massive columns, the barrel vaults in the ceilings, and the small windows were characteristic of the Romanesque style. Compare the massiveness of this interior with the Gothic style of the Abbey Church of St. Denis in the next illustration. This Romanesque church in Vezelay, France, was dedicated to Mary Magdalen and became a center for her veneration during the Middle Ages.

Romanesque churches employed transepts, which fashioned the church into the shape of a cross if viewed from above, the vantage point of God. The intersection of the transept with the nave of the church required a cross vault, a construction that demanded considerable expertise. The high stone vaults of Romanesque churches and cathedrals required the support of massive stone pillars and thick walls. As a result, windows were small slits that imitated the slit windows of castles. Romanesque churches had a dark, yet cozy appearance, which was sometimes enlivened by painted walls or sculpture.

The religious experience of worshiping in a Romanesque cathedral had an intimate, almost familiar quality to it. The worshiper was enveloped by a comforting space, surrounded by family and neighbors, and close to deceased relatives buried beneath the pavement or in tombs that lined the walls. Romanesque churches and cathedrals were the first architectural expression of the new and growing medieval cities, proud and wealthy places. In such a building, God became a fellow townsman, an associate in the grand new project of making cities habitable and comfortable.

More than a century after the urban revival began, the Gothic° style replaced the Romanesque during the late twelfth and thirteenth centuries. The innovation of this style was the ribbed vault and pointed arches, which superseded the barrel vault of the Romanesque. These narrow pointed arches drew the viewer's eye upward toward God and gave the building the appearance of weightlessness that symbolized the Christian's uplifting reach for heaven. The neighborly solidity of the Romanesque style was abandoned for an effect that stimulated a mystical appreciation of God's utter otherness, the supreme divinity far above mortal men and women. The Gothic style also introduced the innovation of the flying buttress, an arched construction on the outside of the walls that redistributed the weight of the roof. This innovation allowed for thin walls, which were pierced by windows much bigger than was possible with Romanesque construction techniques.

Notre-Dame, Paris

The result was stunning. The stonework of a Gothic cathedral became a skeleton to support massive expanses of stained glass, transforming the interior spaces into a mystical haven from the outside world. At different times of the day, the multicolored windows converted sunlight into an ever-changing light show that offered sparkling hints of the secret truths of God's Creation. See, for example, the image on page 304. The light that passed through these windows symbolized the light of God. The windows themselves contained scenes that were an encyclopedia of medieval knowledge and lore. In addition to Bible stories and the lives of saints, these windows depicted common people at their trades, animals, plants, and natural wonders. These windows celebrated not only the promise of salvation but all the wonders of God's creation. They drew worshipers out of the busy city in which they lived and worked toward the perfect realm of the divine.

The first Gothic church was built at the abbey of St. Denis, outside Paris, under the direction of the abbot Suger. From northern France the style spread all across Europe. In France, Germany, Italy, Spain, and England, cities made enormous financial sacrifices to construct new Gothic cathedrals during the economic boom years of the thirteenth century. Gothic cathedrals expressed civic pride as well as Christian piety, and cities vied to build taller and taller cathedrals with ever more daringly thin walls. The French city of Beauvais pushed beyond reasonable limits by building its cathedral so high that it collapsed. Because costs were so high, many cathedrals, such as the one in Siena, Italy, remained unfinished, but even the incomplete ones became vital symbols of local identity.

Gothic Vaults
The delicately ribbed ceiling vaults and vast expanses of stained glass in the Abbey Church of St. Denis, France, contrast with the heavy barrel vaults of the Romanesque Cathedral in Vezelay.

Flying Buttresses of Chartres Cathedral
The flying buttress did more than hold up the thin walls of Gothic cathedrals. The buttress created an almost lacelike appearance on the outside of the building, magnifying the sense of mystery evoked by the style.

Music and Drama: Reaching God's Ear and the Christian's Soul

The churches and cathedrals were devoted to the celebration of the Latin liturgy, which at the time was a chanted form of prayer. Because the function of chant was worship, music was one of the most exquisite expressions of medieval religious life. The liturgical chant that survives from the Middle Ages can still be sung today because the Benedictine monk Guido of Arezzo (ca. 990–1050) devised a system of musical notation, which forms the basis for modern Western musical notation. In Guido's time, chant was primarily plainchant°, a straightforward melody sung with simple harmony by a choir to accompany the recitation of the text of the liturgy. The simple clarity of plainchant matched the solid familiarity of the Romanesque style in church architecture.

In the Paris cathedral around 1170, however, musical experiments led to an important new breakthrough. Instead of using a simple plainchant melody to sing the liturgy, the simultaneous singing of two melodies was employed. This new form was called polyphony°, the singing of two or more independent melodies at the same time. Polyphony represented a major innovation in music by creating an enchanting sound to echo throughout the vast stone chambers of Gothic cathedrals, a musical form of praise that enhanced the mystical experience of worship.

In addition to its advances in architecture and music, Paris became the center for innovation in liturgical drama. Some time during the twelfth century, portions of the liturgy began to be acted out in short Latin plays, usually inside the church. These rudimentary plays were soon translated into the vernacular language so that everyone in the congregation could understand them. As they became more popular, the performances moved outside in front of the church. The function of these liturgical dramas was to educate as well as to worship. The priests who put on the plays wanted to teach Christian stories and provide moral examples to the young and to the uneducated laity. From these early liturgical plays arose the Western dramatic tradition that evolved into the secular theater of Shakespeare and the ubiquitous dramas of modern television and film.

Conclusion

Asserting Western Culture

During the twelfth and thirteenth centuries, western Europe matured into its own self-confident identity. Through penal laws and discrimination heretical groups within Europe were systematically transformed into outcasts or eliminated altogether. The processes of creating outcasts within Europe and defining what it meant to be a Catholic accompanied the external assertion of Latin power. The West looked both inward and outward as it measured itself, defined itself, and promoted itself, especially through the Crusades.

Less a semibarbarian backwater than it had been even in the time of Charlemagne, western Europe cultivated modes of thought that revealed an almost limitless capacity for creative renewal and critical self-examination. That capacity, first evident during the Twelfth-Century Renaissance, is what has most distinguished the West ever since. Part of the reason for this creative capacity rested in the cultivation of critical methods of thinking based on applying the logic of ancient Greek philosophy to the Bible and on defending the conclusions drawn through disputations. These methods were codified in scholasticism. No medieval thinker followed these critical methods consistently, and they repeatedly caused alarm among some believers. However, this tendency to question basic assumptions is among the greatest achievements of Western civilization. The western European university system, which was based on teaching methods of critical inquiry, differed from the educational institutions in other cultures, such as Byzantium or Islam, that were devoted to passing on received knowledge. This distinctive critical spirit connects the cultures of the ancient, medieval, and modern West.

Suggestions for Further Reading

For a comprehensive listing of suggested readings, please go to www.ablongman.com/levack2e/chapter9

Bony, Jean. *French Gothic Architecture of the Twelfth and Thirteenth Centuries.* 1983. With many beautiful illustrations, this is a good way to begin an investigation of these magnificent buildings.

Colish, Marcia L. *Medieval Foundations of the Western Intellectual Tradition, 400–1400.* 1997. The best general study.

Gimpel, Jean. *The Medieval Machine: The Industrial Revolution of the Middle Ages.* 1976. A short, lucid account of the power and agricultural revolutions.

Keen, Maurice. *Chivalry.* 1984. Readable and balanced in its coverage of this sometimes misunderstood phenomenon.

Lambert, Malcolm. *Medieval Heresy: Popular Movements from the Gregorian Reform to the Reformation.* 2nd ed. 1992. The best general study of heresy.

Lawrence, C. H. *The Friars: The Impact of the Early Mendicant Movement on Western Society.* 1994. The best general study of the influence of Dominicans and Franciscans.

Moore, R. I. *The Formation of a Persecuting Society: Power and Deviance in Western Europe, 950–1250.* 1987. A brilliant analysis of how Europe became a persecuting society.

Morris, Colin. *The Papal Monarchy: The Western Church from 1050 to 1250.* 1989. A thorough study that should be the beginning point for further investigation of the many fascinating figures in the medieval Church.

Mundy, John H. *Europe in the High Middle Ages, 1150–1309.* 3rd ed. 1999. A comprehensive introduction to the period.

Peters, Edward. *Europe and the Middle Ages.* 1989. An excellent general survey.

Strayer, Joseph R. *On the Medieval Origins of the Modern State.* 1970. Still the best short analysis.

Notes

1. Cited in Jacques Dalarun, "The Clerical Gaze," in Christiane Klapisch-Zuber, ed., *A History of Women in the West,* Vol. 2: *Silences of the Middle Ages* (1992), 27.

2. Edward Peters, *Heresy and Authority in the Middle Ages* (1980), 177.

3. A. F. Pollock and F. W. Maitland, *The History of English Law,* Vol. 1 (1895), 468.

4. Cited in Emmanuel Le Roy Ladurie, *Montaillou: Promised Land of Error,* trans. Barbara Bray (1978), 130.

5. Ibid., 56.

6. Ibid., 63.

The Medieval West in Crisis

THE FOURTEENTH CENTURY DAWNED WITH A CHILL. IN 1303 AND THEN again during 1306–1307, the Baltic Sea froze over. No one had ever heard of that happening before, and the freezings foretold worse disasters. The cold spread beyond its normal winter season, arriving earlier in the autumn and staying later into the summer. Then it started to rain and did not let up. The Caspian Sea began to rise, flooding villages along its shores. In the summer of 1314 all across Europe, crops rotted in sodden fields. The meager harvest came late, precipitating a surge in prices for farm produce and forcing King Edward II of England to impose price controls. But capping prices did not grow more food.

In 1315 the situation got worse. In England during that year, the price of wheat rose 800 percent. Preachers compared the ceaseless rains to the great flood in the Bible, and floods did come, overwhelming dikes in the Netherlands and England, washing away entire towns in Germany, turning fields into lakes in France. Everywhere crops failed.

Things got much worse. Torrential rains fell again in 1316, and for the third straight year the crops failed, creating the most severe famine in recorded European history. The effects were most dramatic in the far north. In Scandinavia agriculture almost disappeared, in Iceland peasants abandoned farming and turned to fishing and herding sheep, and in Greenland the European settlers began to die out. Already malnourished, the people of Europe became susceptible to disease and starvation. Desperate people resorted to desperate options. They ate cats, rats, insects, reptiles, animal dung, and tree leaves. Stories spread that some ate their own children. In Poland the starving were said to cut down criminals from the gallows for food.

By the 1340s, nearly all of Europe was gripped by a seemingly endless cycle of disease and famine. Then came the deadliest epidemic in European history, the Black Death, which killed at least one-third of the total population.

The Mongol Threat This detail from the "Martyrdom of the Franciscans at Ceuta" shows a stereotypical Mongol, the man in the middle with a tall peaked hat. Ceuta is in North Africa, far from Mongol lands, but the depiction of a Mongol among the Muslims who executed Franciscan missionaries illustrates how Christians felt as threatened by the distant Mongols as by the nearby Muslims. The fresco is in the Franciscan church in Siena, Italy.

The economy collapsed. Trade disappeared. Industry shriveled. Hopeless peasants and urban workers revolted against their masters, demanding relief for their families. Neither state nor church could provide it. The two great medieval kingdoms of France and England became locked in a struggle that depleted royal treasuries and wasted the aristocracy in a series of clashes that historians call the Hundred Years' War. The popes left the dangerous streets of Rome for Avignon, France, where they were obliged to extort money to survive. After the pope returned to Rome, a group of French cardinals refused to go and elected a second pope, leading to the Great Schism when Europe was divided by allegiances to two different popes.

Of all the frightening elements of these disasters, perhaps most frightening was that their causes were hidden or completely unknowable given the technology and medical understanding that became available only a century ago. In many respects, the West was held captive by the climate, economic forces that no one completely understood, and microbes that would not be identified for another 550 years. During the twelfth and thirteenth centuries the West had asserted itself against Islam through the Crusades and spread Catholic Christianity to the far corners of Europe. During the fourteenth and early fifteenth centuries, however, the West drew into itself due to war, epidemics, and conflicts with the Mongol and Ottoman Empires. Western European contact with Russia became more intermittent, and the Byzantine Empire, once the bastion of Orthodox Christianity, fell to the Muslim armies of the Ottomans. The contact during the fourteenth and fifteenth centuries between Europe and the powerful Asian empires and between Europe and epidemic diseases raises the question of how such encounters could so profoundly transform the identity of the West.

- What caused the deaths of so many Europeans?
- How did forces outside Europe, in particular the Mongol and Ottoman Empires, influence conditions in the West?
- How did disturbances in the rudimentary global economy of the Middle Ages precipitate almost complete financial collapse and widespread social discontent in Europe?
- How did incessant warfare transform the most powerful medieval states?
- Why did the church fail to provide leadership and spiritual guidance during these difficult times?
- How did European culture offer explanations and solace for the otherwise inexplicable calamities of the times?

A Time of Death

- What caused the deaths of so many Europeans?

Because of demographic research, we know a great deal about life and death during the fourteenth century. The magnitude of Europe's demographic crisis is evident from the raw numbers. In 1300 the population of Europe was about 74 million—roughly 15 percent of its current population. Population size can be an elementary measure of the success of a subsistence economy to keep people alive, and by this measure Europe had been very successful up to about 1300. It had approximately doubled its population over the previous 300 years. After the 1340s, however, Europe's ability to sustain its population evaporated. Population fell to just 52 million.

The raw numbers, however, hardly touch the magnitude of human suffering, which fell disproportionately on the poor, the very young, and the old. Death by starvation and disease became the fate of uncomprehending millions. The demographic crisis of the fourteenth century was the greatest natural disaster in Western civilization since the epidemics of antiquity. How did it happen?

Mass Starvation

Widespread famine began during the decade of 1310–1320. During the famines in 1315 and 1316 alone, more than 10 percent of Europe's population probably died. One eyewitness described bands of people as thin as skeletons in 1315:

We saw a large number of both sexes, not only from nearby places but from places as much as five leagues away, barefooted, and many even, except the women, in a completely nude condition, with their priests coming together in procession at the church of the holy martyrs, and they devoutly carried bodies of the saints and other relics to be adored.[1]

A crisis in agriculture produced the Great Famine.

The agricultural revolution of the eleventh century had made available more food and more nutritious food, triggering the growth of the population during the Middle Ages. During the twelfth and thirteenth centuries, vast tracks of virgin forests were cleared for farming, especially in eastern Europe. By the thirteenth century this region resembled the American frontier during the nineteenth century, as settlers flocked in, staked out farms, and established new towns. The additional land under the plow created an escape valve for population growth by preventing large numbers of people from going hungry. But by the fourteenth century no more virgin land was available for clearing, which meant that an ever-growing population tried to survive on a fixed amount of farming land. Because of the limitations of medieval agriculture, the ability of farmers to produce food could not keep up with unchecked population growth.

At the same time there was probably a change in climate, known as the "Little Ice Age." The mean annual temperatures dropped just enough to make it impossible to grow crops in the more northerly parts of Europe and at high elevations such as the Alps. Before the fourteenth century, for example, grapes were grown in England to produce wine, but with the decline in temperatures, the grape vineyards ceased to produce. Growing grapes in England became possible again only with global warming in the late twentieth century. The result of the Little Ice Age was twofold. First, there was less land available for cultivation as it became impossible to grow crops in marginal areas. Second, a harsher climate shortened the growing season, which meant that even where crops could still grow they were less abundant.

The imbalance between food production and population set off a dreadful cycle of famine and disease. Insufficient food resulted in either malnutrition or starvation. Those who suffered from prolonged malnutrition were particularly susceptible to epidemic diseases, such as typhus, cholera, and dysentery. By 1300, children of the poor faced the probability of extreme hunger once or twice during the course of their childhood. In Pistoia, Italy, priests kept the *Book of the Dead,* which recorded the pattern: famine in 1313, famine in 1328–1329, famine and epidemic in 1339–1340 that killed one-quarter of the population, famine in 1346, famine and epidemic in 1347, and then the killing hammer blow—the Black Death in 1348 (see Map 10.1).

The Black Death

Following on the heels of the Great Famine, the Black Death arrived in Europe in the spring of 1348 with brutal force. In the lovely hilltop city of Siena, Italy, all industry stopped, carters refused to bring produce and cooking oil in from the countryside, and on June 2 the daily records of the

Map 10.1 Spread of the Black Death

After the Black Death first appeared in the ports of Italy in 1348, it spread relentlessly throughout most of Europe, killing at least 20 million people in Europe alone.

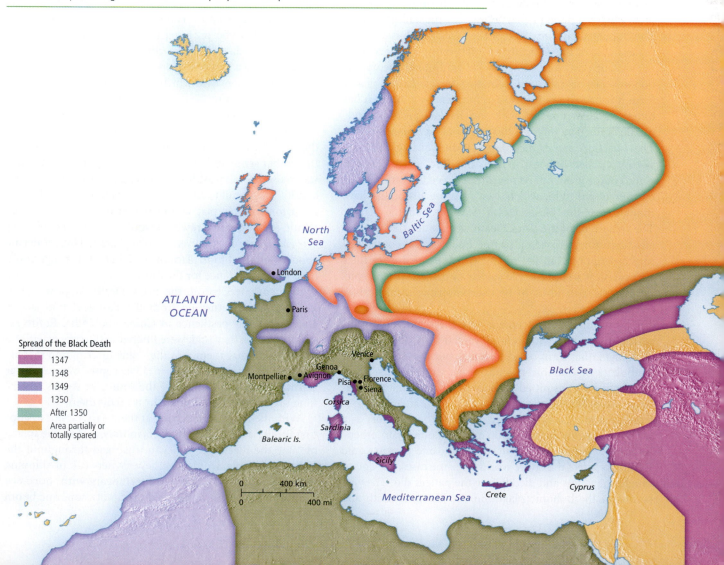

city council and civil courts abruptly ended, as if the city fathers and judges had all died or rushed home in panic. A local chronicler, Agnolo di Tura, wrote down his memories of those terrible days:

> Father abandoned child, wife husband, one brother another; for this illness seemed to strike through the breath and sight. And so they died. And none could be found to bury the dead for money or friendship. Members of a household brought their dead to a ditch as best they could, without priest, without divine offices. Nor did the [death] bell sound. And in many places in Siena great pits were dug and piled deep with the multitude of dead. . . . And I, Agnolo di Tura, called the Fat, buried my five children with my own hands. And there were also those who were so sparsely covered with earth that the dogs dragged them forth and devoured many bodies throughout the city.[2]

During the summer of 1348 more than half of the Sienese died. The construction of Siena's great cathedral, planned to be the largest in the world, stopped and was never resumed due to a lack of workers. In fact, Siena, once among the most prosperous cities in Europe, never fully recovered and lost its economic preeminence to other cities.

Experts still dispute the cause of the Black Death, but there is growing doubt about the validity of the traditional theory that the bubonic plague° was the most likely culprit. The dispute about the cause of the Black Death is a revealing example of the difficulty of interpreting evidence from the distant past. According to the traditional theory the bubonic plague can appear in two forms. In the classic form it is usually transmitted to humans by a flea that has bitten a rodent infected with the *Yersinia pestis* bacillus, usually a rat. The infected flea then bites a human victim. The infection enters the bloodstream, causing inflamed swellings called buboes (hence, "bubonic" plague) in the glands of the groin or armpit, internal bleeding, and discoloration of the skin, which is why some historians have thought that the "Black Death" was the bubonic plague. The symptoms of the Black Death were, indeed, exceptionally disgusting, according to one quite typical contemporary description: "all the matter which exuded from their bodies let off an unbearable stench; sweat, excrement, spittle, breath, so fetid as to be overpowering; urine turbid, thick, black or red. . . ."[3]

The second form of plague was the pneumonic type, which infected the lungs and spread by coughing and sneezing. Either form could be lethal, but the complex epidemiology of bubonic plague meant that the first form could not be transmitted directly from one person to another. According to the traditional theory, after being infected, many victims probably developed pneumonia as a secondary symptom, which then spread quickly to others. As one contemporary physician put it, one person could seemingly infect the entire world. In some cases, the doctor caught the illness and died before the patient did. The visitations of the bubonic plague in the late nineteenth and twentieth centuries, which have been observed by physicians trained in modern medicine, formed that basis for this theory. Alexandre Yersin discovered the bubonic plague bacillus in Hong Kong in 1894 and traced its spread through rats and fleas. For more than a century most historians and epidemiologists have thought that something similar to this must have happened in 1348.

However, there are problems with the traditional theory that the Black Death was caused by bubonic plague. The Black Death spread much more rapidly from person to person and place to place than the bubonic plague does in modern epidemics. For example, rats do not travel very fast, and in modern examples the bubonic plague has rarely spread more than twelve miles per year. In 1348, however, the Black Death traveled as far in a day as rat-borne bubonic plague does in a year. Many of the reported symptoms from the fourteenth century do not match the symptoms observed in modern plague victims. Moreover, the Black Death, unlike the bubonic plague, seems to have had a long incubation period before the first symptoms appeared. Because of the long incubation, those who had the disease transmitted it to others before they knew they were sick, which helps explain why the disease was so lethal despite attempts to quarantine those afflicted with it. The most recent revisionist research suggests that the Black Death may have been caused by an unidentified virus that produced bleeding similar to the Ebola virus that has appeared in Africa in recent years.

Why does it matter which theory for the cause of the Black Death is correct—the traditional one about bubonic plague or the revisionist one about a bleeding virus? In one sense it does not matter because it is clear that the effects of the Black Death were devastating no matter what the cause. In another sense, it does matter because if the Black Death was caused by a virus, it could reappear again at any time and kill many millions again. There is now medical treatment for bubonic plague, but if a virus caused the Black Death, then extensive research would need to take place to provide a cure in the event it reappeared. Thus, a debate about events that took place more than 650 years ago could have vital importance for the future.

Two summers before the Black Death's appearance in Europe, sailors returning from the East had told stories about a terrible pestilence in China and India. Entire regions of India, they said, were littered with corpses with no survivors to bury them. But the vague information that arrived in European seaports in 1346 caused no particular alarm. Asia was far away and the source of stories so baffling that most people could hardly credit them.

With the galley slaves dying at their oars, Genoese ships first brought the disease to ports in Italy, and by the spring of 1348 the Black Death began to spread throughout the Italian peninsula. Ironically, the very network of shipping that had connected the Mediterranean with northern European waters and propelled the great economic boom of the Middle Ages spread the deadly disease. By summer the pestilence had traveled as far north as Paris; by the end of the year it had crossed the English Channel, following William the Conqueror's old route from Normandy to England. From Italy the Black Death passed through the rugged Alpine passes into Switzerland and Hungary. In 1349 the relentless surge continued, passing from France into the Netherlands and from England to Scotland, Ireland, and Norway, where a ghost ship of dead men ran aground near Bergen. From Norway the deadly disease migrated to Sweden, Denmark, Prussia, Iceland, and Greenland. By 1351 it had arrived in Russia.

Modern estimates indicate that during the late 1340s and early 1350s from India to Iceland, about one-third of the population perished. In Europe this would have meant that about 20 million people died, with the deaths usually clustered in a matter of a few weeks or months after the disease first appeared in a particular locale. The death toll, however, varied erratically from place to place, ranging from about 20 to 90 percent. So great was the toll that entire villages were depopulated or abandoned. In Avignon 400 died daily, in Pisa 500, in Paris 800. Paris lost half its population, Florence as much as four-fifths, and Venice two-thirds. In the seaport of Trapani, Italy, everyone apparently died or left. Living in enclosed spaces, monks and nuns were especially hard hit. All the Franciscans of Carcassonne and Marseille in France died. In Montpellier, France, only 7 of the 140 Dominicans survived. In isolated Kilkenny,

Ireland, Brother John Clyn found himself left alone among his dead brothers, and he began to write a diary of what he had witnessed because he was afraid he might be the last person left alive in the world.

Civic and religious leaders had neither the knowledge nor the power to prevent or contain the disease. Following the biblical passages that prescribed ostracizing lepers, governments began to treat Black Death victims as temporary lepers and quarantined them for forty days. Because such measures were ineffective, the Black Death kept coming back. In the Mediterranean basin where the many port cities formed a network of contagion, the plague reappeared between 1348 and 1721 in one port or another about every fifteen to twenty years. Some of the later outbreaks were just as lethal as the initial 1348 catastrophe. Florence lost half its population in 1400; Venice lost a third in 1575–1577 and a third again in 1630–1631. Half a million people died in northern Spain from an epidemic in 1596–1602. Less exposed than the Mediterranean, northern Europe suffered less and saw the last of the dread disease in the Great Plague of London of 1665–1666.

No matter which theory of the cause of the Black Death is correct, both demonstrate how the fate of the West was largely in the hands of unknown forces that ensnared Eurasia and Africa in a unified biological web. If the revisionist theory is correct, then the disease came out of Africa, afflicting Europe via Italy, which had regular contacts with North Africa and where the disease first appeared. If the

Flagellants

During the Black Death many people believed God was punishing them for their sins. In order to expiate those sins some young men practiced flagellation, a practice once reserved for monks who whipped themselves as a form of penance. In order to control the practice among laymen, confraternities were formed in which collective flagellation was organized and carried out under the supervision of a priest. These confraternities took on a variety of charitable obligations, including succoring the sick, building hospitals and orphanages, and burying the dead.

The Black Death: The Signs of Disease

Infectious diseases are invisible. They are carried by viruses or bacteria that infect the body, but until the invention of the microscope in the seventeenth century and the development of epidemiology in the nineteenth the disease itself could not be directly observed. Diseases manifest themselves indirectly through symptoms: fevers, cold sweats, pain, coughing, vomiting, diarrhea, paleness, glandular swellings, skin lesions, and rashes. Through these symptoms, the disease leaves a distinctive sign on the body.

No disease left more distinctive and disturbing signs on the body than the Black Death. In the introduction to *The Decameron,* Giovanni Boccaccio described what he had witnessed of the symptoms:

> In the year 1348 after the fruitful incarnation of the Son of God, that most beautiful of Italian cities, noble Florence, was attacked by deadly plague. . . . The symptoms . . . began both in men and women with certain swellings in the groin or under the armpit. They grew to the size of a small apple or an egg, more or less, and were vulgarly called tumors. In a short space of time these tumors spread from the two parts named [to] all over the body. Soon after this the symptoms changed and black or purple spots appeared on the arms or thighs or any other part of the body, sometimes a few large ones, sometimes many little ones. These spots were a certain sign of death, just as the original tumor had been and still remained.[4]

The fear of the Black Death and the inability to discern its causes focused the attention of contemporaries on the bodies of the sick, and when someone fell ill there was intense concern to determine whether the signs of the Black Death were present. As a result, almost any discoloration of the skin or glandular swellings could be interpreted as a sign of its presence, and other diseases, such as smallpox, could be diagnosed as the Black Death. Physicians and surgeons, of course, were the experts in reading the signs of the body for disease. As victims and their distraught families soon discovered, however, physicians did not really know what the glandular swellings and discolorations of the skin meant. Boccaccio reported that "No doctor's advice, no medicine could overcome or alleviate this disease. . . . Either the disease was such that no treatment was possible or the doctors were so ignorant that they did not know what caused it, and consequently could not administer the proper remedy."[5]

On the advice of physicians, governmental authorities tried to stop the contagion by placing the houses of the sick and sometimes entire neighborhoods under quarantine when plague was suspected. Within the councils of city governments, greater attention began to be paid to the poor, largely because their bodies were more likely to manifest deformities and skin problems because of malnutrition and poor living conditions. The bodies of the poor became subject to systematic regulation. In general, the poor were much more likely to be quarantined than the rich. The deformed might even be driven out of town. Cities established hospitals to segregate the most wretched of the poor, and health officials set up border guards to prevent poor vagabonds from entering towns. To maintain quarantines and bury the dead, a public health bureaucracy was created, complete with its own staff physicians, grave diggers, and police force. The extraordinary powers granted to the public health authorities helped expand the authority of the state over its citizens in the name of pursuing the common good. The expansion of governmental bureaucracy that distinguished modern from medieval states was partly the result of the need to keep human bodies under surveillance and control—a need that began with the Black Death.

For Discussion

How did the government's need to control the Black Death contribute to the expansion of the state? How did it reveal the limits of the power of the state?

The Triumph of Death
A detail from Francesco Traini's fresco *The Triumph of Death,* in the Camposanto, Pisa, ca. 1350. Frescoes such as this reflect the horror of the Black Death.

traditional theory is correct then Europe was victimized by a disease from Asia. Modern research has suggested that the homeland of the *Yersinia pestis* bacillus is an extremely isolated area in Central Asia, from which the plague could have spread during the fourteenth century. The strongest strands in that web were those of merchant traders and armies who were responsible for accidentally disseminating microbes. Whether or not they were the means for transmitting the Black Death, no armies were as important for the fate of Europe as the mounted warriors of the distant Mongol tribes, whose relentless conquests drove them from Outer Mongolia across central Asia toward Europe.

A Cold Wind from the East

■ How did forces outside Europe, in particular the Mongol and Ottoman Empires, influence conditions in the West?

The Mongols and Turks were nomadic peoples from central Asia. Closely related culturally but speaking different languages, these peoples exerted an extraordinary influence on world history despite a rather small population. Map 10.2 shows the place of origin of the

Map 10.2   The Mongol Empire, 1206–1405

The Mongols and Turks were nomadic peoples who spread out across Asia and Europe from their homeland in the region of Mongolia. The Mongol armies eventually conquered vast territories from Korea to the borders of Hungary and from the Arctic Ocean to the Arabian Sea.

Mongols and Turks and where they spread across a wide belt of open, relatively flat steppe land stretching from the Yellow Sea between China and the Korean peninsula to the Baltic Sea and the Danube River basin in Europe. Virtually unwooded and interrupted only by a few easily traversed mountain ranges, the broad Eurasian steppes have been the great migration highway of world history from prehistoric times to the medieval caravans and the modern trans-Siberian railway.

As the Mongols and Turks charged westward out of central Asia on their fast ponies, they put pressure on the kingdoms of the West. Mongol armies hobbled Russia, and Turks conquered Constantinople. As a consequence the potential Orthodox allies in the East of the Catholic Christian West were weakened or eliminated. Under the Ottomans, adherents to Islam were reinserted into the West, this time in the Balkans. In contrast to the era of the twelfth-century Crusades, Catholic Europe found itself on the defensive against a powerful Muslim foe.

The Mongol Invasions

Whereas the Europeans became successful sailors because of their extensive coastlines and close proximity to the sea, the Mongols became roving horsemen because they needed to migrate several times a year in search of grass and water for their ponies and livestock. They also became highly skilled warriors because they competed persistently with other tribes for access to the grasslands.

Between 1206 and 1258, the Mongols transformed themselves from a collection of disunited tribes with a vague ethnic affinity to create the most extensive empire in the history of the world. The epic rise of the previously obscure Mongols was the work of a Mongol chief who succeeded in uniting the various quarreling tribes and transforming them into a world power. In 1206 he was proclaimed Genghis Khan (ca. 1162–1227) ("Very Mighty King"), the supreme ruler over all the Mongols. Genghis broke through the Great Wall of China, destroyed the Jin (Chin) empire in northern China, and occupied Beijing. His cavalry swept across Asia as far as Azerbaijan, Georgia, northern Persia, and Russia. Eventually, Mongol armies conquered territories that stretched from Korea to Hungary and from the Arctic Ocean to the Arabian Sea. They even attempted seaborne expeditions to overpower Japan, which ended in disaster, and Java, which they were able to hold only temporarily. These failures indicated that Mongol strength was in their army rather than their navy.

The Mongol success was accomplished through a highly disciplined military organization, tactics that relied on extremely mobile cavalry forces, and a sophisticated intelligence network. During the Russian campaign in the winter of 1223, the Mongol cavalry moved with lightning speed

Mongol Horseman
Unlike the fourteenth-century European representations of the Mongols, this contemporary Chinese illustration of a Mongol archer on horseback accurately depicts their appearance, dress, and equipment.

across frozen rivers to accomplish the only successful winter invasion of Russia in history. Although the Russian forces outnumbered the Mongol armies and had superior armor, they were crushed in every encounter with the Mongols.

The Mongol armies employed clever tactics. First they unnerved enemy soldiers with a hail of arrows. Then the Mongols would appear to retreat, only to draw the enemy into false confidence before the Mongol horsemen delivered a deadly final blow. European chroniclers at the time tried to explain their many defeats at the hands of the Mongols by reporting that the Mongol "hordes" had overwhelming numbers, but evidence clearly shows that their victories were the result not of superior numbers but of superior discipline and the sophistication of the Mongol intelligence network.

The Mongol invasions completely altered the composition of Asia and much of eastern Europe—economically, politically, and ethnically. Once they had conquered new territories, they established the Mongol Peace by reopening the caravan routes across the Asian steppes, making trans-Eurasian trade possible and merchants safe from robbers. The most famous of the many merchants who traversed this route were the Venetians from the Polo family, including Marco Polo, who arrived at the court of the Great Khan in China in 1275. Marco Polo's book about his travels offers a vivid and often remarkably perceptive account of the Mongol Empire during the Mongol Peace. It also illustrates better than any other source the cultural engagement of the Christian West with the Mongol East during the late thirteenth century, an encounter in which both sides demonstrated an abiding fascination with the other's religion and social mores.

Mongol power climaxed in 1260. In that year the Mongols suffered a crushing defeat in Syria at the hands of the Mamluk rulers of Egypt, an event that ended the Mongol reputation for invincibility. Conflicts and succession disputes among the various Mongol tribes made them vulnerable to rivals and to rebellion from their unhappy subjects. The Mongol Empire did not disappear overnight, but its various successor kingdoms never recaptured the dynamic unity forged by Genghis Khan. During the fourteenth century the Mongol Peace fitfully sputtered to an end.

In the wake of these upheavals, a warrior of Mongol descent known as Tamerlane (r. 1369–1405) created an army composed of Mongols, Turks, and Persians, which challenged the established Mongol khanates. Tamerlane's conquests rivaled those of Genghis Khan, but with very different results. His armies pillaged the rich cities that supplied the caravan routes. Thus, in his attempt to monopolize the lucrative trans-Eurasian trade, Tamerlane largely destroyed it. The collapse of the Mongol Peace broke the thread of commerce across Eurasia and stimulated the European search for alternative routes to China that ultimately resulted in the voyages of Christopher Columbus in 1492.

CHRONOLOGY

The Mongols

1206–1227	Reign of Genghis Khan
1206–1258	Mongol armies advance undefeated across Eurasia
1260	Defeat in Syria of Mongols by Mamluks of Egypt
1369–1405	Reign of Tamerlane

The Rise of the Ottoman Turks

The Mongol armies were never very large, so the Mongols had always augmented their numbers with Turkish tribes. The result was that outside Mongolia, Turks gradually absorbed the Mongols. Turkish replaced Mongolian as the dominant language, and the Turks took over the government of the central Asian empires that had been scraped together by the Mongol conquests. In contrast to the Mongols, many of whom remained Buddhists, the Turks became Muslims and created an exceptionally dynamic, expansionist society of their own (see Map 10.3).

Among the Turkish peoples, the most successful state builders were the Ottomans. Named for Osman I (r. 1281–1326), who brought it to prominence, the Ottoman dynasty endured for more than 600 years, until 1924. The nucleus of the Ottoman state was a small principality in Anatolia (a portion of present-day Turkey), which in the early fourteenth century began to expand at the expense of its weaker neighbors, including the Byzantine Empire. The Ottoman state was built not on national, linguistic, or ethnic unity, but on a purely dynastic network of personal and military loyalties to the Ottoman prince, called the sultan. Thus the vitality of the empire depended on the energy of the individual sultans. The Ottomans thought of themselves as *ghazis,* warriors for Islam devoted to destroying polytheists, including Christians. (To some Muslims in this period the Christian belief in the Trinity and veneration of numerous saints demonstrated that Christians were not true monotheists.) During the fourteenth century, incessant Ottoman guerilla actions gradually chipped away at the Byzantine frontier.

The Byzantine Empire in the middle of the thirteenth century was emerging from a period of domination by Frankish knights and Venetian merchants who had conquered Constantinople during the Fourth Crusade in 1204. In 1261, the Byzantine emperor Michael VIII Palaeologus (r. 1260–1282) recaptured the great city. The revived Byzantine Empire, however, was a pale vestige of what it once had been, and the Palaeologi emperors desperately sought military assistance from western Europe to defend themselves from the Ottomans. Dependent on mercenary armies and divided by civil wars, the Byzantines offered only pathetic resistance to the all-conquering Ottomans.

Map 10.3   The Ottoman Empire
The Ottoman state expanded from a small principality in Anatolia, which is south of the Black Sea. From there the Ottomans spread eastward into Kurdistan and Armenia. In the West they captured all of Greece and much of the Balkan peninsula.

From their base in Anatolia, the Ottomans raided far and wide, launching pirate fleets into the Aegean and gradually encircling Constantinople after they crossed over into Europe in 1308. By 1402 Ottoman territory had grown to forty times its size a century earlier. During that century of conquests, the frontier between Christianity and Islam shifted. The former subjects of the Byzantines in the Balkans fell to the Ottoman Turks. Fragile Serbia, a bastion of Orthodox Christianity in the Balkans, broke under Ottoman pressure. First unified in the late twelfth century, Serbia established political independence from Byzantium and autonomy for the Serbian church. Although the Serbs had taken control over a number of former Byzantine provinces, they fell to the invincible Ottomans at the Battle of Kosovo in 1389. Lamenting the Battle of Kosovo has remained the bedrock of Serbian national identity to this day.

Serbia's western neighbors, the kingdoms of Bosnia and Herzegovina, deflated under Ottoman pressure during the late fifteenth century. Unlike Serbia, where most of the population remained loyal to the Serbian Orthodox Church, Bosnia and Herzegovina had long been divided by religious schisms. The dominant, educated classes were Serbian-speaking Muslims; the subjugated peasants, also Serbian-speaking, were Orthodox Christians who turned over one-third of everything they raised to their Muslim lords. The parallel divisions along religious and class lines long enfeebled Bosnian unity.

When Mehmed II, "The Conqueror" (r. 1451–1481), became the Ottoman sultan, he began to obliterate the last remnants of the Byzantine Empire. During the winter of 1451–1452, the sultan ordered the encirclement of Constantinople, a city that had

DOCUMENT

Mehmed II

once been the largest in the world but now was reduced from perhaps a million people to fewer than 50,000. The Ottoman siege strategy was to bombard Constantinople into submission with daily rounds from enormous cannons. The largest was a monster cannon, twenty-nine feet long, that could shoot 1,200-pound stones. It required a crew of 200 soldiers and sixty oxen to handle it, and each firing generated so much heat that it took hours to cool off before it could be fired again. The siege was a gargantuan task because the walls of Constantinople, which had been built, repaired, and improved over a period of a thousand years, were formidable. However, the new weapon of gunpowder artillery had rendered city walls a military anachronism. Brought from China by the Mongols, gunpowder had gradually revolutionized warfare, and breaching city walls in sieges was merely a matter of time as long as the heavy metal cannons could be dragged into position. Quarrels among the Christians also hampered the defense of the walls. Toward the end, the Byzantine emperor was forced to melt down church treasures so "that from them coins should be struck and given to the soldiers, the sappers and

the builders, who selfishly cared so little for the public welfare that they were refusing to go to their work unless they were first paid."[6]

The final assault came in May 1453 and lasted less than a day. When the city fell, the Ottoman army spent the day plundering, raping, and enslaving the populace. The last Byzantine emperor, Constantine XI, was never found amid the multitude of the dead. The fall of Constantinople ended the Christian Byzantine Empire, the continuous remnant of the ancient Roman Empire. But the idea of Rome was not so easily snuffed out. The first Ottoman sultans residing in Constantinople continued to be called "Roman emperors."

Nestor-Iskander on the Fall of Constantinople

Although the western European princes had done little to save Byzantium, its demise was a profound shock, rendering them vulnerable to the Ottoman onslaught. For the next 200 years the Ottomans used Constantinople as a base to threaten Christian Europe. Hungary and the eastern Mediterranean empire of Venice remained the last lines of defense for the West, and at various times in succeeding

---

DOCUMENT

The Ottoman Conquest of Constantinople

The Turkish sultan Mehmed II led the Ottoman army and navy in the final siege of Constantinople. A brilliant leader and strategist, he succeeded in taking the capital of Byzantium, which had been unsuccessfully attacked so many times before. This account of what he said to inspire his troops before the final assault on the walls on Constantinople is by a Greek named Kritovoulos who began to work for Mehmed shortly after the conquest. He gathered this account from many eyewitnesses. Notice how Mehmed emphasizes the various rewards promised by the conquest of the city.

My friends and my comrades in the present struggle! I have called you together here . . . to show you how many and how great [are the rewards] and what great glory and honor accompany the winning. And I also wish that you may know well how to carry on the struggle for the very highest rewards.

First, then, there is a great wealth of all sorts in this city, some in the royal palaces and some in the houses of the mighty, some in the homes of the common people and still other, finer and more abundant, laid up in the churches as votive offerings and treasures of all sorts, constructed of gold and silver and precious stones and costly pearls.

Then too, there are very many noble and distinguished men, some of whom will be your slaves, and the rest will be

put up for sale; also very many and very beautiful women, young and good-looking, and virgins lovely for marriage, noble, and of noble families, and even till now unseen by masculine eyes, some of them, evidently intended for the weddings of great men. . . .

And you will have boys, too, very many and very beautiful and of noble families.

Further, you will enjoy the beauty of the churches and public buildings and splendid houses and gardens, and many such things, suited to look at and enjoy and take pleasure in and profit by.

And the greatest of all is this, that you will capture a city whose renown has gone out to all parts of the world. It is evident that to whatever extent the leadership and glory of this city has spread, to a like extent the renown of your valor and bravery will spread for having captured by assault a city such as this. . . .

And, best of all, we shall demolish a city that has been hostile to use from the beginning and is constantly growing at our expense and in every way plotting against our rule. . . .

I myself will be in the van of the attack [applause by all the gathering]. Yes, I myself will lead the attack, and will be fighting by your side and will watch to see what each one of you does."

Source: From Kritovoulos, *History of Mehmed the Conqueror,* translated by Charles T. Riggs (Westport, Conn.: Greenwood Press, 1970), 61–64.

centuries the Ottomans launched expeditions against Europe, including two sieges of Vienna (1529 and 1683) and several invasions of Italy.

Hundreds of years of attacks by the Mongol and Ottoman Empires redrew the map of the West. Events in western Europe did not and could not take place in isolation from the eastern pressures and influences. For more than 200 years Christian Russia was isolated from cultural influences in the rest of the Christian world. The experience made the Russians much more aware of their eastern neighbors, and when they did recover from the Mongol conquests in the fifteenth century, much of their energy and military might was directed toward expanding eastward into the void left by the collapse of the Mongol Empire. The Ottoman conquests also created a lasting Muslim presence within the borders of Europe, especially in Bosnia and Albania. In succeeding centuries Christian Europe and the Muslim Ottoman Empire would be locked in a deadly competitive embrace, but they also benefited from innumerable cultural exchanges and regular trade. Hostility between the two sides was recurrent but never inevitable and was broken by long periods of peaceful engagement. In fact, the Christian kingdoms of western Europe went to war far more often with one another than with the Turks.

Economic Depression and Social Turmoil

■ **How did disturbances in the rudimentary global economy of the Middle Ages precipitate almost complete financial collapse and widespread social discontent in Europe?**

Adding insult to injury in this time of famine, plague, and conquest, the West began to suffer a major economic depression during the fourteenth century. The economic boom fueled by the agricultural revolution and the revitalization of European cities during the eleventh century and the commercial prosperity of the twelfth and thirteenth centuries petered out in the fourteenth. The causes of this economic catastrophe were complex, but the consequences were obvious. Businesses went bust, banks collapsed, guilds were in turmoil, and workers rebelled.

At the same time, the effects of the depression were unevenly felt. The economic conditions for many peasants actually improved because there was a labor shortage in the countryside due to the loss of population. Forced to pay their peasants more for their labor and crops, landlords saw their own fortunes decline. Finding it harder to pay the higher prices for food, urban workers probably suffered the most because their wages did not keep up with the cost of living.

The Collapse of International Trade and Banking

The Mongol Peace during the thirteenth century had stimulated vast, lucrative trade in exotic luxury items between Europe and Asia. When the Mongol Empire began to break up in the fourteenth century, the trade routes were cut off or displaced. Later in the century, Tamerlane's forcible channeling of the caravan trade through his own territory created a narrow trade corridor with outlets on the coast of the Middle East. Rulers along this path, such as the Mamluks in Egypt, took advantage of the situation to levy heavy tolls on trade, raising the price of goods beyond what the market could bear. As a result, trade dwindled. Alternative routes would have taken merchants through Constantinople, but Ottoman pressure on Byzantium endangered these routes.

The financial infrastructure of medieval Europe was tied to international trade in luxury goods. The successful, entrepreneurial Italian merchants who dominated the luxury trade deposited their enormous profits in Italian banks. The Italian bankers lent money to the aristocracy and royalty of northern Europe to finance the purchases of exotic luxuries and to fight wars. The whole system was mutually reinforcing, but it was very fragile. With the disruption of supply sources for luxury goods, the financial networks of Europe collapsed, precipitating a major depression.

For most of the thirteenth century the Italian city of Siena had been one of the principal banking centers of the world, the equivalent of New York or Tokyo today. In 1298, however, panic caused a run on its largest bank, which failed. Soon the lesser Sienese banks were forced to close, and the entire city fell into a deep economic depression. Siena never recovered its economic stature and is a major tourist attraction today simply because it is largely unchanged from the time when the banks went broke.

In nearby Florence, several local banks took advantage of Siena's collapse and became even bigger than the Sienese banks had been. Through these banks, the coinage of Florence, the florin, became the common currency of Europe. By 1346, however, all of these banks crashed due to a series of bad loans to several kings of Europe. With the bank crash, virtually all sources of credit dried up all across Europe. At the same time, wars between France and England deprived their aristocracies of the money to buy luxuries from the Italian merchants whose deposits had been the principal source of capital for the banks. With disruptions in the supply of Asian luxury goods, a catastrophic loss of capital by Italian bankers, and a decline in demand for luxuries in France and England, Europe entered a major depression.

Rebellions from Below

The luxury trade that brought exotic items from Asia to Europe represented only half of the economic equation. The other half was the raw materials and manufactured goods that Europeans sold in exchange, principally woolen cloth. The production of woolen cloth depended on a highly sophisticated economic system that connected shepherds in England, the Netherlands, and Spain with woolen cloth manufacturers in cities. The manufacture of cloth and other commodities was organized by guilds. The collapse of the luxury trade reduced the demand for the goods produced by the guilds, depriving guildsmen and urban workers of employment at a time when the cost of food to feed their children was rising. The situation must have seemed ironic. Workers knew that the population decline from famine and pestilence had created a labor shortage, which according to the elementary laws of supply and demand should have produced higher wages for the workers who survived. However, wages stagnated because of the decline in business. Royal and local governments made matters worse by trying to control wages and raise taxes in a period of declining revenues. Frustrated and enraged, workers rebelled.

An Economy of Monopolies: Guilds

Central to the political and economic control of medieval cities were the guilds°. Guilds were professional associations devoted to protecting the special interests of a particular trade or craft and to monopolizing production and trade in the goods the guild produced. There were two dominant types of guilds. The first type, merchant guilds, attempted to monopolize the local market for a particular commodity. There were spice guilds, fruit and vegetable guilds, and apothecary guilds. The second type, craft guilds, regulated the manufacturing processes of artisans, such as carpenters, bricklayers, woolen-cloth manufacturers, glass blowers, and painters. These guilds were dominated by master craftsmen, who ran their own shops. Working for wages in these shops

were the journeymen, who knew the craft but could not yet afford to open their own shops. Under the masters and journeymen were apprentices, who worked usually without pay for a specific number of years to learn the trade.

Guild regulations governed virtually all aspects of guildsmen's lives. In fact, until a youth passed from apprenticeship to become a journeyman, he could not marry or own property. Craft guilds functioned like a modern professional association by guaranteeing that producers met certain standards of training and competence before they could practice a trade. Like merchant guilds, they also regulated competition and prices in an attempt to protect the masters' local monopoly in the craft.

In many cities the guilds expanded far beyond the economic regulation of trade and manufacturing to become the backbone of urban society and politics. The masters of the guilds constituted part of the urban elite, and guild membership was often a prerequisite for holding public office. One of the obligations of city government was to protect the interests of the guildsmen, who in turn helped stabilize the economy through their influence in city hall. The guilds were often at the center of a city's social life as well, countering the anonymity of city life by offering fellowship and a sense of belonging. Medieval festivals were often organized by the guilds, whose members engaged in sports competitions with other guilds. In Nuremberg, for example, the butchers' guild organized and financed the elaborate carnival festivities that absorbed the energies of the entire city for days on end. In many places guilds supplied the actors for the Corpus Christi plays that acted out stories from the Bible or the lives of the saints for the entertainment and edification of their fellow citizens. In Florence the church of the guildsmen became a display case for works of sculpture by the city's most prominent artists, each work sponsored by a specific guild. The guilds endowed magnificent chapels and provided funeral insurance for their members and welfare for the injured and widows of masters.

When the economy declined during the fourteenth century, the urban guilds became lightning rods for mounting social tension. Guild monopolies produced considerable conflict, provoking anger among those who were blocked from joining guilds, young journeymen who earned low wages, and those who found themselves unemployed due to the depression. These tensions exploded into dangerous revolts.

"Long Live the People, Long Live Liberty"

Economic pressures erupted into rebellion most dramatically among woolen-cloth workers in the urban centers in Italy, the Netherlands, and France. The most famous revolt involved the Ciompi, the laborers in the woolen-cloth industry of Florence, Italy, where guilds were the most powerful force in city government. The Ciompi, who performed the heaviest jobs such as carting and the most noxious tasks such as dyeing, had not been allowed to have their own guild and were therefore deprived of the political and economic rights of guild membership.

Fueling the Ciompi's frustration was the fact that by the middle of the fourteenth century woolen-cloth production in Florence dropped by two-thirds, leaving many workers unemployed. In 1378 the desperate Ciompi rebelled. A crowd chanting, "Long live the people, long live liberty," broke into the houses of prominent citizens, released political prisoners from the city jails, and sacked the rich convents that housed the pampered daughters of the wealthy. Over the course of a few months, the rebels managed to force their way onto the city council, where they demanded tax and economic reforms and the right to form their own guild. The Ciompi revolt is one of the earliest cases of workers demanding political rights. The disenfranchised workers did not want to eliminate the guilds' monopoly on political power; they merely wanted a guild of their own so that they could join the regime. That was not to be, however. After a few weeks of success, the Ciompi were divided and defeated.

Shortly after the Ciompi revolt faded, troubles broke out in the woolen-cloth centers of Ghent and Bruges in Flanders and in Paris and Rouen in France. In these cases, however, the revolt spread beyond woolen-cloth workers to voice the more generalized grievances of urban workers. In Ghent and Bruges the weavers attempted to wrest control of their cities from the local leaders who dominated politics and the economy. In Paris and Rouen in 1380, social unrest erupted in resistance to high taxes and attacks by the poor on the rich. The pinnacle of the violence involved the *Maillotins* ("people who fight with mallets") in Paris during March 1382, when the houses of tax collectors were sacked and the inhabitants murdered. Although the violence in Flanders and France was precipitated by local issues, such as control of the town council and taxes, both cases were symptomatic of the widespread social conflicts that followed in the wake of the great depression of the fourteenth century that profoundly affected the crucial woolen-cloth industry.

Like urban workers, many rural peasants also rebelled during the troubled fourteenth century. In France in 1358 a peasant revolt broke out that came to be called the *Jacquerie,* a term derived from "Jacques Bonhomme" ("James Goodfellow"), the traditional name for the typical peasant. Jacquerie became synonymous with extreme, seemingly mindless violence. Filled with hatred for the aristocracy, the peasants indulged in pillaging, murder, and rape, but they offered no plan for an alternative social system or even for their own participation in the political order, so their movement had no lasting effects. They were quickly defeated by a force of nobles.

Unlike the French Jacquerie, the peasants who revolted in England in 1381 had a clear political vision for an alternative society, a fact that makes their revolt far more significant. In England the rebels' motives stemmed from the frustration of rising expectations that were never realized.

Worker Rebellions in Flanders and France

A Florentine businessman, Buonaccorso Pitti, who had witnessed the Ciompi revolt in Florence in 1378, found himself in Paris when the Maillotins *revolt broke out. Like his contemporaries, he concluded that the violence in Bruges and Ghent was somehow connected to the outbreak of violence in Rouen and Paris. This was a reasonable assumption, because the count of Flanders and the French royal court had many intimate ties. Thus, rebellion in one place had political implications elsewhere. Here is what Pitti reported.*

In 1381 the people of Ghent rebelled against their overlord, the count of Flanders, who was the father of the duchess of Burgundy. They marched in great numbers to Bruges, took the city, deposed the Count, robbed and killed all his officers, and dealt in the same way with all the other Flemish towns which fell into their hands. Their leader was Philip van Artevelde. As the number of Flemings rebelling against their overlords increased, they sent secret embassies to the populace of Paris and Rouen, urging them to do the like with their own lords, and promising them aid and succor in this undertaking. Accordingly, these two cities rebelled against the King of France. The first insurrection was that of the Paris mob, and was sparked off by a costermonger [someone who sells produce from a cart] who, when an official tried to levy a tax on the fruit and vegetables he was selling, began to roar "Down with the *gabelle* [a food tax]." At this cry the whole populace rose, ran to the tax-collectors' houses and robbed and murdered them. Then, since the mob was unarmed, one of their number led them to the Chatelet where Bertrand du Guesclin, a former High Constable, had stored 3000 lead-tipped cudgels in preparation for a battle which was to have been fought against the English. The rabble used axes to break their way into the tower where these cudgels or mallets (in French, *maillets*) were kept and, arming themselves, set forth in all directions to rob the houses of the King's representatives and in many cases to murder them. The . . . men of substance who in French are called *bourgeois,* fearing lest the mob (who were later called *Maillotins* and were of much the same kidney [nature] as the *Ciompi* in Florence) might rob them too, took arms and managed to subdue them. They then proceeded to take government into their own hands, and together with the *Maillotins,* continued the war against their royal lords.

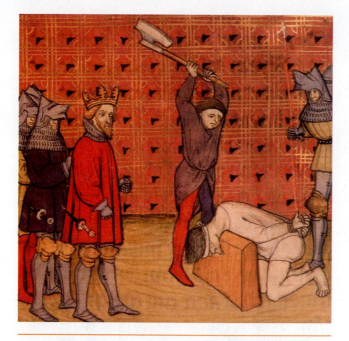

Jacquerie
A leader of the Jacquerie is beheaded while the king looks on.

The peasants believed that the labor shortage caused by the Black Death should have improved their condition, but the exact opposite was happening. Landlords clung to the old system that defined peasants as serfs who were tied to the land and unable to bargain for the price of their labor. Although the English peasants were probably better off than their fathers and grandfathers had been, their expectations of an even better life were blocked by the land-holding aristocracy. The clashing interests of the peasants and the aristocrats needed only a spark to ignite a conflagration. That spark came from the Poll Tax controversy.

The traditional means of raising revenue in England had been a levy on the more well-to-do landowners, who were taxed according to the size and value of their holdings. In 1381, however, the crown attempted to levy a Poll Tax, which taxed with little concern for the ability of each person to pay. The Poll Tax, in effect, shifted the burden of taxation to a lower social level, and the peasants bitterly resented it. As agents came to collect the Poll Tax in June 1381, riots broke out throughout eastern England, and rioters burned local tax records. The rebels briefly occupied London, where they lynched the lord chancellor and treasurer of the kingdom. The rebels demanded lower rents, higher wages, and the abolition of serfdom—all typical peasant demands—but to these they added a class-based argument against the aristocracy. They had been influenced by popular preachers who told them that in the Garden of Eden there had been no aristocracy. Following these preachers, the English rebels imagined a classless society, a utopian vision of an alternative to medieval society that was entirely structured around distinctive classes.

The 15-year-old English king, Richard II (r. 1377–1399), promised the rebels that their demands would be met. Satisfied that they had gotten what they wanted, including the abolition of serfdom, the peasants disbanded. The king then rescinded his promises and ordered that the peasant leaders be hunted down and executed. Thus, the greatest peasant rebellion in medieval English history ended with broken promises and no tangible achievements.

None of the worker or peasant revolts of the fourteenth century met with lasting success. The universal failure of lower-class rebellion was due, in part, to the lack of any clear alternative to the existing economic and political system. The Ciompi wanted to join the existing guild system. The weavers of Ghent and Bruges were as much competing with one another as rebelling against the Flanders establishment. The extreme violence of the Jacquerie frightened away potential allies. Only the English rebels had precise revolutionary demands, but they were betrayed by King Richard. However, the rebellions revealed for the first time in the West a widespread impulse among the lower classes to question and protest the existing social and economic order. The tradition of worker protest became common and recurrent during subsequent centuries.

An Age of Warfare

■ How did incessant warfare transform the most powerful medieval states?

Western Europe was further weakened during the fourteenth century by prolonged war between its two largest and previously most stable kingdoms, England and France. The Hundred Years' War° (1337–1453) was a struggle over England's attempts to assert its claims to territories in France. The prolonged conflict drained resources from the aristocracies of both kingdoms, deepening and lengthening the economic depression. The Hundred Years' War sowed the seeds of a military revolution that by the sixteenth century transformed the kingdoms of western Europe. In that transformation monarchies, ruled by relatively weak kings and strong aristocracies, evolved into modern states, ruled by strong monarchs who usurped many of the traditional privileges of the aristocracy in order to centralize authority and strengthen military prowess.

The Fragility of Monarchies

The most dangerous threat to the kings of France and England during the fourteenth and fifteenth centuries came less from worker and peasant rebellions than from members of the aristocracy, who were fiercely protective of their jurisdictional privileges over their lands. The privilege of jurisdiction allowed aristocrats to act as judges for crimes committed in their territories, a privilege that was a crucial source of their power. In both kingdoms, royal officials asserted the legal principle that aristocratic jurisdictions originated with the crown and were subordinate to it. The problem in enforcing this principle, however, was that there were overlapping, conflicting, and sometimes contradictory jurisdictions and loyalties, which were produced by many generations of inheritance. The system bred strife and limited the power of the monarch. Thus the Hundred Years' War was both a conflict between two kingdoms and a series of civil wars between aristocratic factions and imperiled monarchs.

Medieval monarchies depended on the king to maintain stability. Despite the remarkable legal reforms and bureaucratic centralization of monarchies in England and France during the twelfth and thirteenth centuries (see Chapter 9), weak or incompetent kings were all too common during the fourteenth. Weak kings created a perilous situation made worse by disputed successions. The career of Edward II (r. 1307–1327) of England illustrates the peril. Edward was unable to control the vital judicial and financial sinews of royal power. He continued the policy of his father, Edward I, by introducing resident justices of the peace who had replaced the inadequate system of itinerant judges who traveled from village to village to hear cases. In theory, these justices of the peace should have prevented the abuses of justice typical of aristocratic jurisdictions, but even though they were royal officials who answered to the king, most of those appointed were also local landowners who were deeply implicated in many of the disputes that came before them. As a result, justice in England became notoriously corrupt and the cause of discontent. Edward II was so incompetent to deal with the consequences of corrupted justice that he provoked a civil war in which his own queen joined his aristocratic enemies to depose him.

The French monarchy was no better. In fact, the French king was in an even weaker constitutional position than the

Royal Justice
English kings were preoccupied with extending their prerogatives over the judiciary as a way to express royal power. Despite the corruption of the many lower courts, the Court of the King's Bench attempted to assert a level of uniform procedures and royal control of justice.

English monarch. In France the king had effective jurisdiction over only a small part of his realm. Many of the duchies and counties of France were quasi-independent principalities, paying only nominal allegiance to the king, whose will was ignored with impunity. In these regions the administration of justice, the collection of taxes, and the recruitment of soldiers all remained in the hands of local lords. To explain why he needed to raise taxes, Philip IV, "The Fair" (r. 1285–1314), created a representative assembly, the Estates General, which met for the first time in 1302, but he still had to negotiate with each region and town individually to collect the taxes. Given the difficulty of raising taxes, the French kings resorted to makeshift solutions that hurt the economy, such as confiscating the property of vulnerable Jewish and Italian merchants and debasing the coinage to increase the value of scarce silver. Such a system made the finances of the kingdom of France especially shaky because the king lacked a dependable flow of revenue.

The Hundred Years' War

The Hundred Years' War revealed the fragility of the medieval monarchies. The initial cause of the war involved disputes over the duchy of Aquitaine. The king of England also held the title of duke of Aquitaine, who was a vassal of the French crown, which meant that the English kings technically owed military assistance to the French kings whenever they asked for it. A long succession of English kings had reluctantly paid homage as dukes of Aquitaine to the king of France, but the unusual status of the duchy was a continuing source of contention.

The second cause of the war derived from a dispute over the succession to the French crown. When King Charles IV died in 1328, his closest surviving relative was none other than the archenemy of France, Edward III (r. 1327–1377), king of England. To the barons of France, the possibility of Edward's succession to the throne was unthinkable, and they excluded him because his relation to the French royal family was through his mother. Instead the barons elected to the throne a member of the Valois family, King Philip VI (r. 1328–1350), and at first Edward reluctantly accepted the decision. However, when Philip started to hear judicial appeals from the duchy of Aquitaine, Edward changed his mind. He claimed the title of king of France for himself, sparking the beginning of more than a century of warfare (see Map 10.4).

The Hundred Years' War (1337–1453) was not a continuous formal war but a series of occasional pitched battles, punctuated by long truces and periods of general exhaustion. The term *Hundred Years' War* was invented by nineteenth-century historians to describe the prolonged time of troubles between the two countries. In terms of its potential for warfare, France, far richer and with three times the population, held the advantage over sparsely populated England. In nearly every battle the French outnumbered the English, but the English were usually victorious because of superior discipline and the ability of their longbows to break up cavalry charges. As a rule, the English avoided open battle, preferring raids, sieges of isolated castles, and capturing French knights for ransom. For many Englishmen the objective of fighting in France was to get rich by looting. Because all the fighting took place on French soil, France suffered extensive destruction and significant civilian casualties from repeated English raids.

From English Victories to French Salvation

In the early phases of the war, the English enjoyed a stunning series of victories. At the Battle of Sluys in 1340, a

Siege Warfare
English soldiers pillaging and burning a French town.

small English fleet of 150 ships carrying the English invasion forces ran into a French blockade of more than 200 ships. In the heavy hand-to-hand combat, the English captured 166 French ships and killed some 20,000 men, so many that it was later said, "If fish could talk, they would speak French." At Crécy in 1346, the English longbowmen shot thousands of arrows "like thunderbolts" into the flanks of the charging French knights, killing men and horses in shocking numbers. The French knights mounted one disorderly, hopeless charge after another, until the piles of dead blocked further charges. Though wounded, King Philip escaped, leaving 3,000 of his men dead on the field, including 1,500 knights. The aristocracy of France was decimated. At Poitiers in 1356, King John of France (r. 1350–1364) encircled 6,000 English with a vastly superior royal army of 15,000, but—as at Crécy—the English archers broke up the overly hasty French cavalry charge, and the English counterassault crushed the French. Two thousand French knights died and another 2,000 were captured, including King John himself. With its king imprisoned in England, France was forced to pay a huge ransom and grant formal sovereignty over a third of France to the king of England.

At Agincourt in 1415, King Henry V (r. 1413–1422) and England's disease-racked army of 6,000 were cut off by a French force of about 20,000. In the ensuing battle the English archers repelled a hasty French cavalry charge and

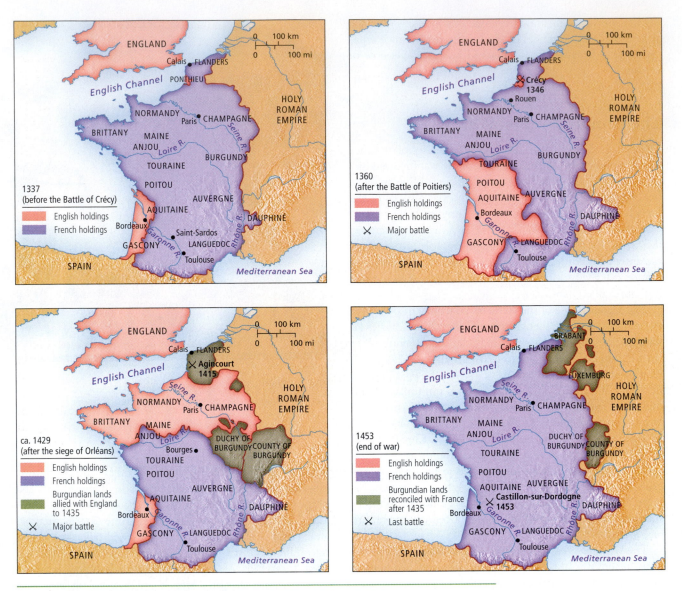

Map 10.4 The Hundred Years' War

This map illustrates four phases of the Hundred Years' War. In the first phase (1337), England maintained a small foothold in the southwest of France. In the second phase (1360), England considerably expanded the territory around Aquitaine and gained a vital base in the north of France. In the third phase (ca. 1429), England occupied much of the north of France, and England's ally Burgundy established effective independence from French authority. In the fourth phase at the end of the war (1453), England had been driven from French soil except at Calais, and Burgundy maintained control over its scattered territories.

the fleeing, terrified horses trampled the French men-at-arms as they advanced. The English lost only a few hundred, but the French suffered nearly 10,000 casualties. After Agincourt, the French never again dared challenge King Henry in open battle, and were forced to recognize him as the heir to the French throne. By 1420 the English victory appeared complete. Now with the responsibility of ruling rather than conquering France, the English could no longer

rely on their old strategy of mounted raiding and had to hold the French cities, which proved exceedingly difficult. By 1422, however, Henry V was dead, leaving two claimants to the French throne. The English asserted the rights of the infant King Henry VI of England, son of King Henry V, the victor at Agincourt. Most of the French defended the claim of the Dauphin (the title of the heir to the throne) Charles, the only surviving son of the late King Charles VI of France.

English Archers
English archers practicing the longbow. Note that the unpulled bows are the height of a man.

The Hundred Years' War entered a new phase with factions of the French aristocracy supporting the two rivals in a bloody series of engagements.

By 1429 the English were on the verge of final victory. They occupied Paris and Rheims, and their army was besieging Orleans. The Dauphin Charles was penniless and indecisive. Even his own mother denied his legitimacy as the future king. At this point a 17-year-old illiterate peasant from Burgundy, Joan of Arc (Jeanne d'Arc, ca. 1412–1431), following "divine voices," went to Orleans to lead the French armies. Under her inspiration Orleans was relieved, French forces began to defeat the English, much of the occupied territory was regained, and the Dauphin was crowned King Charles VII (r. 1429–1461) in the cathedral of Rheims. After Joan failed to recapture Paris, however, her successes ceased. The final success of the French came from the leadership of King Charles and the general exhaustion of the English forces.

Charles VII reorganized the French army and gradually chipped away at the English holdings in France, eventually taking away Aquitaine in 1453. The English lost all their possessions in France except Calais, which was finally surrendered in 1558. There was no peace treaty, just a fading away of war in France, especially after England stumbled into civil war—the War of the Roses (1455–1485).

The Hundred Years' War in Perspective

The Hundred Years' War had broad consequences. First, nearly continuous warfare between the two most powerful kingdoms in the West exacerbated other conflicts as well. Scotland, the German princes, Aragon, Castile, and most importantly Burgundy were drawn into the conflict, making the English-French brawl a European-wide war at certain stages. The squabble between France and England made it much more difficult to settle the Great Schism that split the Church during the same period. Second, the war devastated France, which eventually regained control of most of its territory but still suffered the most from the fighting. During the century of the war, the population dropped by half, due to the ravages of combat, pillage, and plague. Agriculture languished after the English repeatedly mounted raids that destroyed crops and sacked peasant villages. Third, the deaths of so many nobles and destruction of their fortunes diminished the international luxury trade; merchants and banks as far away as Italy went broke; and the Flemish woolen industry was disrupted, causing further economic damage. Finally, the war helped make England more English. Before the war the Plantagenet dynasty in England was more French than English. The monarchs possessed extensive territories in France and were embroiled in French affairs. English aristocrats also had business in France, spoke French, and married their French cousins. After 1450 the English abandoned the many French connections that had stretched across the English Channel since William the Conqueror sailed from Normandy to England in 1066. Henceforth, the English upper classes cultivated English rather than French language and culture.

CHRONOLOGY

An Age of Warfare

1285–1314	Reign of Philip IV, "The Fair," of France
1307–1327	Reign of Edward II of England
1327–1377	Reign of Edward III of England
1328–1350	Reign of Philip VI of France
1337–1453	Hundred Years' War
1340	Battle of Sluys
1346	Battle of Crécy
1356	Battle of Poitiers
1377–1399	Reign of Richard II of England
ca. 1412–1431	Life of Joan of Arc
1413–1422	Reign of Henry V of England
1415	Battle of Agincourt
1429–1461	Reign of Charles VII of France
1455–1485	War of the Roses in England

The Trial of Joan of Arc

After only fifteen months as the inspiration of the French army, Joan of Arc fell into the hands of the English, who brought her to trial for witchcraft. The English needed to stage a kind of show trial to demonstrate to their own demoralized forces that Joan's remarkable victories had been the result not of military superiority but rather of witchcraft. In the English trial, conducted at Rouen in 1431, Joan testified that her mission to save France was in response to voices she heard that commanded her to wear men's clothing. On the basis of this evidence of a confused or double gender identity, the ecclesiastical tribunal declared her a witch and a relapsed heretic. The court sentenced her to be burned at the stake.

Political motivations governed the 1431 English trial for witchcraft, but Joan's testimony provides some clues to her own identity conflicts. The two pieces of evidence against Joan ultimately resulted in her condemnation: the spiritual "voices" she claimed to hear and her cross-dressing in men's clothing.

From the beginning of her emergence onto the political scene, Joan's voices intrigued all who came into contact with her. Joan claimed that she was guided by the voices of St. Catherine, St. Margaret, and the Archangel Michael. To Joan, these voices had the authority of divine commands. The problem the English judges faced was to demonstrate that the voices came not from God but from the Devil. If they could prove that, then they had evidence of witchcraft and sorcery. Following standard inquisitorial guidelines, the judges knew that authentic messages from God would always conform to church dogma. Any deviation from official doctrines would constitute evidence of demonic influence. Thus, during Joan's trial the judges demanded that she make theological distinctions that were alien to her. When they wanted to know if the voices were those of angels or saints, Joan seemed perplexed and responded, "This voice comes from God . . . I am more afraid of failing the voices by saying what is displeasing to them than answering you."[7] The judges kept pushing, asking if the saints or angels had heads, eyes, and hair. Exasperated, Joan simply replied, "I have told you often enough, believe me if you will."

The judges reformulated Joan's words to reflect their own rigid scholastic categories and concluded that her "veneration of the saints seems to partake of idolatry and to proceed from a pact made with devils. These are less divine revelations than lies invented by Joan, suggested or shown to her by the demon in illusive apparitions, in order to mock at her imagination while she meddled with things that are beyond her and superior to the faculty of her condition."[8] In other words, Joan was just too naive and uneducated to have authentic visions. But the English judges were on dangerous ground because during the previous fifty years there had been a number of notable female mystics, including St. Catherine of Siena and St. Bridget of Sweden, whose visions had been accepted as authentic by the pope. The English could not take the chance that they were executing a real saint. They had to prove Joan was a witch by showing that her visions were theologically unsound. But that they could not do.

If they could not convict her for bad theology, the English needed evidence for superstitious practices. In an attempt to do that, they drew up seventy charges against her. Many of these consisted of allegations of performing magic, such as chanting spells, visiting a magical tree at night, and invoking demons. They attempted to prove bad behavior by insinuating that a young man had refused to marry her on account of her immoral life. They asserted that her godmother was a notorious witch who had taught her sorcery. None of these ploys worked, however, because Joan consistently denied these charges. She did, however, admit to one allegation: she cross-dressed as a man.

Some of the charges against her and many of the questions she was asked concerned how she dressed:

> *The said Joan put off and entirely abandoned women's clothes, with her hair cropped short and round in the fashion of young men, she wore shirt, breeches, doublet, with hose joined together, long and fastened to the said doublet by twenty points, long leggings laced on the outside, a short mantle reaching to the knee, or thereabouts, a close-cut cap, tight-fitting boots or buskins, long spurs, sword, dagger, breastplate, lance and other arms in the style of a man-at-arms.*[9]

The judges explained to her that "according to canon law and the Holy Scriptures" a woman dressing as a man or a man as a woman is "an abomination before God."[10] She replied simply and consistently that "everything that I have done, I did by command of the voices" and that wearing male dress "would be for the great good of France."[11] When they asked her to put on a woman's dress in order to take the Eucharist on Easter Sunday, she refused, saying the miracle of the Eucharist did not depend on whether she wore a man's or a woman's clothing. On many occasions she had been asked to put on a woman's dress and refused. "And as for womanly duties, she said there were enough other women to do them."[12]

After a long imprisonment and psychological pressure from her in-

The Execution of Joan of Arc
There are no contemporary portraits of Joan, and this image is clearly a generalized one of a young woman rather than a portrait taken from the real Joan.

The bundle of stakes will be used for the fire that will consume her.

Joan of Arc is tied to the stake before her execution.

These onlookers are holding sticks for the fire.

quisitors, Joan confessed to charges of witchcraft, signed a recantation of her heresy, and agreed to put on a dress. She was sentenced to life imprisonment on bread and water. Why did she confess? Some historians have argued that she was tricked into confessing because the inquisitors really wanted to execute her but could not do so unless she was a *relapsed* heretic. To be relapsed she had to confess and then somehow return to her heretical ways. If that was the inquisitors' intention, Joan soon obliged them. After a few days in prison, Joan threw off the women's clothes she had been given and resumed dressing as a man. As a witness put it, "The said Catherine and Margaret [instructed] this woman in the name of God to take and wear a man's clothes, and she had worn them and still wears them, stubbornly obeying the said command, to such an extent that this woman had declared she would rather die than relinquish these clothes."[13]

Joan was willing to be burned at the stake rather than disobey her voices. Why? Historians will never know for sure, but dressing as a man may have been necessary for her to fulfill her role as a military leader. The men who followed her into battle and trusted her voices accepted the necessity of this mutation of gender. In her military career, Joan had adopted the masculine qualities of chivalry: bravery, steadfastness, loyalty, and a willingness to accept pain and death. She made herself believable by dressing as a knight. A number

of soldiers who had served with her testified that although they knew Joan was a woman, they had never felt any sexual desire for her, which suggests that she seemed androgynous to them. It was precisely Joan's gender ambiguity that the inquisitors found a dangerous sign of Satan's hand. And it was Joan's refusal to abandon her ambiguous gender identity that provided the inquisitors with the evidence they needed.

Joan's condemnation was much more than another example of men's attempt to control women. The inquisitors needed evidence of demonic influence, which to their minds Joan's transgressive gender behavior supplied. Joan's confused gender identity threatened the whole system of neat hierarchical distinctions upon which scholastic theology rested. To the theologians, everything in God's Creation had its own proper place and anyone who changed his or her divinely ordained position in society presented a direct affront to God.

The English verdict and Joan's tragic fate greatly wounded French pride. In 1456 at her mother's instigation the French clergy reopened her case in a posthumous trial that sought to rehabilitate her

in the eyes of the church. To these churchmen, she was an authentic visionary and a saint who listened to a direct command from God. To the French people ever since, she has become a national symbol of pride and of French unity against a foreign invader. In our own time, Joan has been characterized as many things—a saint, a madwoman, a female warrior, a woman exercising power in a male world, and a woman openly transgressing gender categories by dressing in men's clothes.

Questions of Justice

1. In medieval ecclesiastical trials such as this one, what kinds of evidence were presented and what kind of justice was sought?
2. What did Joan's claim that she heard voices reveal about her understanding of what constituted the proper authority over her life?

Taking It Further

Joan of Arc. *In Her Own Words,* trans. Willard Trask. 1996. The record of what Joan reputedly said at her trials.

Warner, Marina. *Joan of Arc: The Image of Female Heroism.* 1981. A highly readable feminist reading of the Joan of Arc story.

The Military Revolution

The "military revolution," whose effects first became evident during the Hundred Years' War, refers to changes in warfare that marked the transition from the late medieval to the early modern state. The heavily armored mounted knights, who had dominated European warfare and society since the Carolingian period, were gradually supplanted by foot soldiers as the most effective fighting unit in battle. Infantry units were composed of men who fought on foot in disciplined ranks, which allowed them to break up cavalry charges by concentrating firepower in deadly volleys. Infantry soldiers could fight on a greater variety of terrains than mounted knights, who needed even ground and plenty of space for their horses to maneuver. The effectiveness of infantry units made battles more ferocious but also more decisive, which was why governments favored them. Infantry, however, put new requirements on the governments that recruited them. Armies now demanded large numbers of well-drilled foot soldiers who could move in disciplined ranks around a battlefield. Recruiting, training, and drilling soldiers made armies much more complex organizations than they had been, and officers needed to possess a wide range of management skills. Governments faced added expenses as they needed to arrange and pay for the logistical support necessary to feed and transport those large numbers. The creation of the highly centralized modern state resulted in part from the necessity to maintain a large army in which infantry played the crucial role.

Infantry used a variety of weapons. The English demonstrated the effectiveness of longbowmen during the Hundred Years' War. Capable of shooting at a much more rapid rate than the French crossbowmen, the English longbowmen at Agincourt protected themselves behind a hurriedly erected stockade of stakes and rained a shower of deadly arrows on the French cavalry to break up charges. In the narrow battlefield, which was wedged between two forests, the French cavalry had insufficient room to maneuver, and when some of them dismounted to create more room, their heavy armor made them easy to topple over and spear through the underarm seam in their armor. Some English infantry units deployed ranks of pikemen who created an impenetrable wall of sharp spikes.

The military revolution of the fourteenth and fifteenth centuries also introduced gunpowder to European warfare. Arriving from China with the Mongol invasions, gunpowder was first used in the West in artillery. Beginning in the 1320s huge wrought-iron cannons were used to shoot stone or iron against fortifications during sieges. By the early sixteenth century bronze muzzle-loading cannons were used in field battles. With the introduction during the late fifteenth century of the first handgun and the harquebus (a matchlock shoulder gun), properly drilled and disciplined infantrymen could deliver very destructive firepower. Gunshot pierced plate armor, whereas arrows bounced off. The slow rate of fire of these guns, however, necessitated carefully planned battle tactics. Around 1500 the Spanish introduced mixed infantry formations that pursued "shock" and "shot" tactics. Spanish pikemen provided the shock, which was quickly followed up by gunshot or missile fire. Spanish infantry formations were capable of defeating cavalry even in the open field without defensive fortifications, an unprecedented feat. By the end of the fifteenth century, trained infantry were necessary in every army.

The chivalric aristocrats, who made up the heavily armored cavalry forces and whose fighting ability justified their social privileges, tried to adapt to the changes by improving plate armor, employing longer lances, and drilling their horses for greater maneuverability. They were successful enough and retained enough political influence that heavy cavalry remained necessary in the professional armies that began to appear in the fifteenth century. However, the military revolution precipitated a major shift in European society as well as in battlefield tactics. The successful states were those that created the financial base and bureaucratic structures necessary to put into the field a well-trained professional army composed of infantry units and artillery. Armies now required officers who were capable of drilling infantry or understanding the science of warfare in order to serve as an artillery officer. The traditional landed aristocrats, accustomed to commanding armored knights, found that noble lineage was not as important as technical skills and talents.

A Troubled Church and the Demand for Religious Comfort

■ Why did the church fail to provide leadership and spiritual guidance during these difficult times?

In reaction to the suffering and widespread death during the fourteenth century, many people naturally turned to religion for spiritual consolation and for explanations of what had gone wrong. But the spiritual authority of the Church was so dangerously weakened during this period that it failed to satisfy the popular craving for solace. The moral leadership that had made the papacy such a powerful force for reform during the eleventh through thirteenth centuries was completely lacking in the fourteenth. Many laypeople gave up looking to the pope for guidance and found their own means of religious expression, making the Later Middle Ages one of the most religiously creative epochs in Christian history. Some of the new religious movements, especially in England and Bohemia, veered onto the dangerous shoals of heresy, breaking the fragile unity of the Church.

The Babylonian Captivity of the Church and the Great Schism

Faced with anarchy in the streets of Rome as local aristocrats engaged in incessant feuding, a succession of seven consecutive popes chose to reside in the relative calm of Avignon, France. This period of voluntary papal exile is known as the Babylonian Captivity of the Church° (1305–1378), a biblical reference recalling the captivity of the Jews in Babylonia (587–539 B.C.E.). The popes' presumed subservience to the kings of France during this period dangerously politicized the papacy, destroying its ability to rise above the petty squabbles of the European princes. Even though these popes were never the French kings' lackeys, the enemies of the kings of France did not trust popes who were residing in France and who were themselves French. The loss of revenues from papal lands in Italy lured several popes into questionable financial schemes, which included accepting kickbacks from appointees to church offices, taking bribes for judicial decisions, and selling indulgences°. Indulgences were certificates that allowed penitents to atone for their sins and reduce their time in Purgatory.

When Pope Urban VI (r. 1378–1389) was elevated to the papacy in 1378 and announced his intention to reside in Rome, a group of disgruntled French cardinals returned to Avignon and elected a rival French pope. The Church was then divided over allegiance to Italian and French claimants to the papal throne, a period called the Great Schism° (1378–1417). Toward the end of the schism there were actually four rival popes. Some of these antipopes completely lacked spiritual qualities. The most infamous was Baldassare Cossa, whom a faction of cardinals elected Pope

John XXIII (r. 1410–1415) because he had been an effective commander of the papal troops. The cardinals who supported rival popes charged Pope John with the crimes of piracy, murder, rape, sodomy, and incest—charges without much substance—but the publication of the allegations further undermined the moral reputation of the papacy. During the Great Schism the kings, princes, and cities of Europe divided their allegiances between the rival candidates. The Church was split not because of doctrinal differences but because competing systems of political alliances sustained the schism. The French king and the allies of France supported the French pope. The enemies of France gave aid and comfort to the Italian pope.

Urban VI's decision to return the papacy to Rome and attempt to end the Babylonian Captivity of the Church resulted from an intense demand for his presence in Italy. Part of the reason was the growing influence of a young woman mystic. Catherine Benincasa (1347–1380), now known as St. Catherine of Siena, demonstrated her mystic tendencies at an early age by locking herself in a room of her parents' house for a year to devote herself to prayer and fasting. She soon became famous for her holiness and severe asceticism, which during the troubled times of the Babylonian Captivity gave her a powerful moral authority. She went to Avignon, and although the pope ignored her, she attracted the attention of others in the papal court. Catherine became the most important advocate for encouraging the return of the pope from Avignon to Rome and launching a new crusade against the Muslims. She helped Pope Urban VI reorganize the Church after he returned to Rome, and she sent out letters and pleas to the kings and queens of Europe to gain support for him during the schism. Catherine dictated an influential body of letters,

The Babylonian Captivity of the Church
From 1303 to 1378 the popes lived in exile from Rome in this fortress-like Palace of the Popes in Avignon, France. The French claimants to the papal throne continued to live here during the Great Schism until 1417.

prayers, and treatises that attempted to remind the popes and kings of Europe of their religious responsibilities.

The Great Schism created the need for a mechanism to sort out the competing claims of rival popes. That need led to the Conciliar Movement°. The conciliarists argued that a general meeting or council of the bishops of the Church had authority over the pope, it could be called to order by a king, and it could pass judgment on a standing pope or order a conclave to elect a new one. Several general councils were held during the early fifteenth century to resolve the schism and initiate reforms, but solutions were difficult to achieve because politics and the affairs of the Church were so closely intertwined. The Council of Constance (1414–1417) finally succeeded in restoring unity to the Church and also in formally asserting the principle that a general council is superior to the pope and should be called frequently. The Council of Basel (1431–1449) approved a series of necessary reforms, although these were never implemented due to the hostility to conciliarism by Pope Eugene IV (r. 1431–1447). The failure of even the timid reforms of the Council of Basel opened the way for the more radical rejection of papal authority during the Protestant Reformation of the sixteenth century. The Conciliar Movement, however, was not a complete failure because it provided a model for how reform could take place. This model would later become central to the Catholic Reformation and the foundation of modern Catholicism (see Chapter 13).

The Search for Religious Alternatives

The popes' loss of moral authority during the Babylonian Captivity and the Great Schism opened the way for a remarkable variety of reformers, mystics, and preachers, who appealed to lay believers crying out for a direct experience of God and a return to the message of the original apostles of Christ. Most of these movements were quite traditional in their doctrines, but some were heretical, and the weakened papacy was unable to control them, as it had successfully done during the thirteenth-century crusade against the Albigensians.

Protests Against the Papacy: New Heresies

For most Catholic Christians during the fourteenth century, religious life consisted of witnessing or participating in the seven sacraments, which were formal rituals celebrated by duly consecrated priests usually within the confines of churches. After baptism, which was universally performed on infants, the most common sacraments for lay adults were penance and communion. Both of these sacraments emphasized the authority of the clergy over the laity and therefore were potential sources for resentment. The sacrament of penance required the layperson to confess his or her sins to a priest, who then prescribed certain penalties to satisfy

the sin. At communion, it was believed, the priest changed the substance of an unleavened wafer of bread, called the Eucharist, into the body of Christ and a chalice of wine into his blood, a miraculous process called transubstantiation. Priests and lay recipients of communion both ate the wafer, but the chalice was reserved for the priest alone. More than anything else, the reservation of the chalice for priests profoundly symbolized the privileges of the clergy. Because medieval Catholicism was primarily a sacramental religion, reformers and heretics tended to concentrate their criticism on sacramental rituals, especially of their spiritual value compared to other kinds of worship such as prayer.

The most serious discontent about the authority of the popes, the privileges of the clergy, and the efficacy of the sacraments appeared in England and Bohemia (a region in the modern Czech Republic). An Oxford professor, John Wycliffe (1320–1384), criticized the power and wealth of the clergy, played down the value of the sacraments for encouraging ethical behavior, and exalted the benefits of preaching, which promoted a sense of personal responsibility. During the Great Schism, Wycliffe rejected the authority of the rival popes and asserted instead the absolute authority of the Bible, which he wanted to make available to the laity in English rather than in Latin, which most laypeople could not understand.

The Execution of Jan Hus
Despite a safe-conduct from the emperor, Jan Hus was arrested and convicted as a heretic at the Council of Constance in 1415. This miniature from later in the fifteenth century depicts his burning.

Outside England Wycliffe's ideas found their most sympathetic audience among a group of reformist professors at the University of Prague in Bohemia, where Jan Hus (1369–1415) regularly preached to a large popular following. Hus's most revolutionary act was to offer the chalice of consecrated communion wine to the laity, thus symbolically diminishing the special status of the clergy. When Hus also preached against indulgences, which he said converted the sacrament of penance into a cash transaction, Pope John XXIII excommunicated him. Hus attended the Council of Constance to defend his ideas. Despite the promise of a safe-conduct from the Holy Roman emperor (whose jurisdiction included Bohemia and Constance) that would have made him immune from arrest, Hus was imprisoned, his writings were condemned, and he was burned alive as a heretic.

Imitating Christ: The Modern Devotion

In the climate of religious turmoil of the fourteenth and fifteenth centuries, many Christians sought deeper spiritual solace than the institutionalized Church could provide. Most of these people pursued deeply traditional forms of piety, exhibiting how medieval spirituality was capable of seemingly infinite renewal and vitality. By stressing individual piety, ethical behavior, and intense religious education, a movement called the Modern Devotion° built on the existing traditions of spirituality and became highly influential. Promoted by the Brothers of the Common Life, a religious order established in the Netherlands, the Modern Devotion was especially popular throughout northern Europe. In the houses for the Brothers, clerics and laity lived together without monastic vows, shared household tasks, joined in regular prayers, and engaged in religious studies. (A similar structure was devised for women.) The lay brothers continued their occupations in the outside world, thus influencing their neighbors through their pious example. The houses established schools that prepared boys for church careers through constant prayer and rigorous training in Latin. Many of the leading figures behind the Protestant Reformation in the sixteenth century had attended schools run by the Brothers of the Common Life.

The Modern Devotion was also spread by the best-seller of the late fifteenth century, the *Imitation of Christ*, written about 1441 by a Common Life brother, probably Thomas à Kempis. By emphasizing frequent private prayer and moral introspection, the *Imitation* provided a manual to guide laypeople in the path toward spiritual renewal that had traditionally been reserved for monks and nuns. There was nothing especially reformist or antisacramental about the *Imitation of Christ*, which emphasized the need for regular confession and communion. However, its popularity helped prepare the way for a broad-based reform of the Church by turning the walls of the monastery inside out, spilling out a large number of lay believers who were dedicated to becoming living examples of moral purity for their neighbors.

CHRONOLOGY	
Troubles in the Church	
1305–1378	Babylonian Captivity of the Church; popes reside in Avignon
1320–1384	John Wycliffe
1347–1380	Catherine of Siena
1369–1415	Jan Hus
1378–1417	Great Schism; more than one pope
1414–1417	Council of Constance
1431–1449	Council of Basel
ca. 1441	*Imitation of Christ*

The moral and financial degradation of the papacy during the fourteenth and early fifteenth centuries was countered by the persistent spirituality of the laity, manifest in the Modern Devotion. As a result, throughout Europe laypeople took responsibility not only for their own behavior but for the spiritual and material welfare of their entire community and of the Church itself. Lay spirituality remained deeply traditional rather than innovative. These pious people founded hospitals for the sick and dying, orphanages for abandoned children, and confraternities that engaged in a wide range of charitable good works—from providing dowries for poor women to accompanying condemned criminals to the gallows.

The Culture of Loss

■ How did European culture offer explanations and solace for the otherwise inexplicable calamities of the times?

During the fourteenth and early fifteenth centuries, the omnipresence of violence and death made suffering a common theme in the arts and strangely the subject matter for jokes, fancy-dress masquerades, and wild dances. The preoccupation with death revealed an anxious attachment to fleeting life.

This widespread anxiety had many manifestations. Some aristocrats sought escape from the terror by indulging in a beautiful fantasy life of gallant knights and beautiful ladies. Others went on long penitential pilgrimages to the shrines of saints or to the Holy Land. During the fourteenth century the tribulations of the pilgrim's travels became a metaphor for the journey of life itself, stimulating creative literature. Still others tried to find someone to blame for calamities. When no other explanation could be found, alleged witches became handy scapegoats. The search for scapegoats also focused on minority groups, especially Jews and Muslims.

Reminders of Death

In no other period of Western civilization has the idea of death constituted such a pervasive cultural force as during the fourteenth and fifteenth centuries. The religious justification for this preoccupation was the Reminder of Death, a theme found in religious books, literary works, and the visual arts. A contemporary book of moral guidance advised the reader that "when he goes to bed, he should imagine not that he is putting himself to bed, but that others are laying him in his grave."[14] Reminders of Death became the everyday theme of preachers, and popular woodcuts represented death in simple but disturbing images. These representations emphasized the transitory nature of life, admonishing that every created thing perishes. The Reminder of Death tried to encourage ethical behavior in this life by showing that in everyone's future was neither riches, nor fame, nor love, nor pleasure, but only the decay of death.

The most famous Reminder of Death was the Dance of Death. First appearing in a poem of 1376, the Dance of Death evolved into a street play, performed to illustrate sermons that called for repentance. It also appeared in church murals, depicting a procession led by a skeleton that included representatives of the social orders, from children and peasants to pope and emperor. All were being led to their inevitable deaths. At the Church of the Innocents in Paris, the mural depicting the Dance of Death is accompanied by an inscription that reads:

Tomb Effigy of a Knight
This effigy above the tomb of Jean d'Alluy shows the deceased as if he were serenely sleeping, still dressed in the armor of his worldly profession.

Advance, see yourselves in us, dead, naked, rotten and stinking. So will you be. . . . To live without thinking of this risks damnation. . . . Power, honor, riches are nothing; at the hour of death only good works count. . . . Everyone should think at least once a day of his loathsome end [in order to escape] the dreadful pain of hell without end which is unspeakable.[15]

In earlier centuries, tombs had depicted death as serene: On top of the tomb was an effigy of the deceased, dressed in the finest clothes with hands piously folded and eyes open to the promise of eternal life. In contrast, during the fourteenth century tomb effigies began to depict putrefying bodies or naked skeletons, symbols of the futility of human status and achievements. These tombs were disturbingly graphic Reminders of Death. Likewise, poems spoke of the disgusting smell of rotting flesh, the livid color of plague victims, the cold touch of the dead. Preachers loved to personalize death. They would point to the most beautiful young woman in the congregation and describe how she would look while rotting in the grave, how worms would crawl through the empty sockets that once held her alluring eyes.

In reminding people of the need to repent their sins in the face of their inevitable deaths, no sin was more condemned than pride, the high opinion

Decomposing Cadaver
The tomb effigy of Jean de Lagrange.

The Art of Dying

In this death scene, the dying man receives extreme unction (last rites) from a priest. A friar holds a crucifixion for him to contemplate. Above his head an devil and angel compete for his soul while behind him Death lurks waiting for his moment.

of one's own qualities and conduct. In contrast to modern times, when pride is often understood as a virtue, late medieval moralists saw pride as an affront to God, a rejection of God's will that humanity should concentrate on spiritual rather than worldly things. Pride, in fact, was often discussed as the ultimate source of all the other deadly sins: lust, gluttony, avarice, sloth, wrath, and covetousness. The theme was encapsulated by the inscription on the tomb of a cardinal who died in 1402: "So, miserable one, what cause for pride?"[16]

Late medieval society was completely frank about the unpleasant process of dying, unlike modern societies that hide the dying in hospitals and segregate mourning to funeral homes. Dying was a public event, almost a theatrical performance. The last rites of the Catholic Church and the Art of Dying served to assist souls in their final test before God and to separate the departed from their kin. According to the Art of Dying, which was prescribed in numerous advice books and illustrations, the sick or injured person should die in bed, surrounded by a room full of people, including children. It was believed that a dying person watched a supernatural spectacle visible to him or her alone as the heavenly host fought with Satan and his demon minions for the soul. The Art of Dying compared the deathbed contest to a horrific game of chess in which the Devil did all he could to trap the dying person into a checkmate just at the moment of death. In the best of circumstances, a priest arrived in time to hear a confession, offer words of consolation, encourage the dying individual to forgive his or her enemies and redress any wrongs, and perform the last rites.

Illusions of a Noble Life

Eventually death arrived for everyone, peasant and noble alike, a fact that the Reminders of Death were designed to

keep foremost in the minds of all Christians. Some people, especially among the nobility, sought to ignore this fundamental truth through escapist fantasies. These fantasies shielded nobles not only from the inevitability of death but also from all the other perils of the age—the worker and peasant rebellions, the economic depression that depleted their wealth, and the military revolution that challenged their monopoly on soldierly valor. During the Later Middle Ages, many nobles indulged in chivalric escapism and idealized their class as the remedy for evil times. They thought God had placed them on Earth to purify the world.

Much of the attraction of chivalry derived from its fanciful vision of the virtues of the ascetic life, the life that practices severe self-discipline and abstains from physical pleasures. The ideal medieval knight was as much a self-denying ascetic as the ideal medieval monk. The highest expression of the chivalric ideal was the knight-errant, a warrior who roamed in search of adventure. He was poor and free of ties to home and family, a man who lived a life of perfect freedom but whose virtue led him to do the right thing. In reality most knights were hardly ascetics but rich, propertied men who were completely involved in the world and who indulged in all of its pleasures.

The ideal of the ascetic knight-errant was pursued in an elaborately developed fantasy culture that occupied much of the time and cultural energy of the aristocracy. The French nobleman Philippe de Mézières (ca. 1327–1405), whose chivalric imagination knew no bounds, dreamed of establishing a new order of knights, the Order of the Passion, whose members would be spiritually removed from worldly affairs and devoted to reconquering the Holy Land. He drew up a plan for the order, but it never became a reality. He imagined that the knights in the Order of the Passion would peacefully end all wars among Christians and bind themselves together in a great Crusade against the Mongols, Jews, Turks, and other Muslims. Several kings actually did establish new crusading orders, which aristocrats joined with unbridled enthusiasm—the Order of the Garter in England, the Order of the Stars and Order of St. Michael in France, and the most fantastic of all, the Order of the Golden Fleece in Burgundy. Members of these orders indulged in extravagant acts of self-deprivation—for example, wearing fur coats in summer but refusing to wear a

A Sumptuous Aristocratic Banquet

An aristocratic banquet with scenes of fighting in the background. Dining was the principal occasion at which nobles displayed refined manners showing their commitment to the beautiful life.

coat, hat, or gloves in freezing temperatures. They loved to take vows: One knight swore he would not sleep in a bed on Sundays until he had fought the Muslims; another took an oath that he would keep his right arm bare of any armor during battle with the Turks. None of these would-be crusaders came close to fighting Turks.

Many vows were taken in the name of ladies, revealing that the chivalric ideal also included a heavy dose of erotic desire. Besides ascetic self-denial, the most persistent chivalric fantasy was the motif of the young hero who liberates a virgin, either from a dragon or from a rioting mob of peasants. The myth of the noble knight suffering to save his beloved was the product of the male imagination, revealing how men wished to be admired in the eyes of women, but the myth has had a profound and lasting influence on Western culture.

The fantasy world of the noble life especially animated the duchy of Burgundy, a quasi-independent principality that paid nominal allegiance to the French king. Burgundy set the chivalric standards for all of Europe during the fifteenth century. Famous for his lavish lifestyle, Duke Philip the Good (r. 1419–1467) was a notorious rake who seduced numerous noble ladies and produced many illegitimate children, but he also epitomized the ideals of chivalry in his love of horses, hunting, and court ceremonies. He was an extravagant patron of the arts, which made him famous throughout Europe. Musicians, manuscript illuminators, painters, tapestry makers, and historians thrived with his support and made Burgundy the center of European aristocratic fashion.

The dukes of Burgundy sustained their power through their personal ties to the nobility and elites of the cities of their dominions. They were constantly on the move, visiting palaces, castles, and towns. They created a kind of theater state, staging elaborate entry ceremonies to the towns they visited; celebrating with fantastic splendor every event in the ducal family, such as marriages and births; entertaining the nobles with tournaments and the people with elaborate processions; and guaranteeing the loyalty of the nobles by inviting them to join the Order of the Golden Fleece, which occupied its members by training for a crusade.

Pilgrims of the Imagination

During the Middle Ages, a pilgrimage offered a religiously sanctioned form of escape from the omnipresent suffering and peril. Pious Christians could go on a pilgrimage to the Holy Land, Rome, or the shrine of a saint, such as Santiago de Compostela in Spain or Canterbury in England. The usual motive for a pilgrimage was to fulfill a vow or promise made to God, or to obtain an indulgence, which exempted the pilgrim from some of the time spent in punishment in Purgatory after death. The pilgrimage became the instrument for spiritual liberation and escape from difficulties. As a result, going on a pilgrimage became a compelling model for creative literature, especially during the fourteenth century. Not all of these great works of literature were fictional pilgrimages, but many evoked the pilgrim's impulse to find a refuge from the difficulties of daily life or to find solace in the promise of a better life to come.

Dante Alighieri and *The Divine Comedy*

In *The Divine Comedy* an Italian poet from Florence, Dante Alighieri (1265–1321), imagined the most fantastic pilgrimage ever attempted, a journey through Hell, Purgatory, and Paradise. A work of astounding originality, *The Divine Comedy* remains the greatest masterpiece of medieval literature. Little is known about Dante's early life except that somehow he acquired an encyclopedic education that gave him

DOCUMENT

Dante, *Divine Comedy* (1321)

Dante and the Plague Victims
The ancient poet Virgil and Dante come across victims of the plague in their journey through Hell. This depiction, which comes from a sixteenth-century manuscript, is anachronistic because the Black Death arrived after Dante wrote *The Divine Comedy,* but he does describe victims of epidemic diseases in his poem.

expertise in Greek philosophy, scholastic theology (the application of logic to the understanding of Christianity), Latin literature, and the newly fashionable poetic forms in Provençal, the language of southern France. Dante was involved in the dangerous politics of Florence, which led to his exile under pain of death if he ever returned. During his exile Dante wandered for years, suffering grievously the loss of his home: "bitter is the taste of another man's bread and . . . heavy the way up and down another man's stair" (*Paradiso,* canto 17). While in exile, Dante sustained himself by writing his great poetic vision of human destiny and God's plan for redemption.

In the poem Dante himself travels into the Christian version of the afterlife, but the poetic journey displays numerous non-Christian influences. The passage through Hell, for example, derived from a long Muslim poem reconstructing Muhammad's *miraj,* a night journey to Jerusalem and ascent to heaven. Dante's poem can be read on many levels—personal, historical, spiritual, moral, theological— as it recounts an allegorical pilgrimage to visit the souls of the departed. Dante connects his personal suffering with the historical problems of Italy, the warnings of the dead who had sinned in life, and the promise of rewards to those who had been virtuous. Dante's trip, initially guided by the Latin poet Virgil, the epitome of ancient wisdom, starts in Hell. While traveling deeper into its harsh depths, Dante is

DOCUMENT

Dante Describes Hell

In The Divine Comedy, *Dante imagined a series of circles in Hell into which were cast those guilty of a certain class of sin. In the eighth circle Dante and his guide Virgil came upon those guilty of fraud. They suffered for all eternity in the depths of stinking, filthy caverns in the ground. Dante and Virgil followed a path through Hell, and at this point the path led to a series of arches that spanned over the caverns.*

Here we heard people whine in the next chasm,
and knock and thump themselves with open palms, and
blubber through their snouts as if in a spasm.

Steaming from that pit, a vapor rose
over the banks, crusting them with a slime
that sickened my eyes and hammered at my nose.

That chasm sinks so deep we could not sight
its bottom anywhere until we climbed
along the rock arch to its greatest height.

Once there, I peered down; and I saw long lines
of people in a river of excrement
that seemed the overflow of the world's latrines.

I saw among the felons of that pit
one wraith who might or might not have been tonsured—
one could not tell, he was so smeared with shit.

He bellowed: "You there, why do you stare at me
more than at all the others in this stew?"
And I to him: "Because if memory

serves me, I knew you when your hair was dry.
You are Alessio Interminelli da Lucca.
That's why I pick you from this filthy fry."

And he then, beating himself on his clown's head:
"Down to this have the flatteries I sold
the living sunk me here among the dead."

And my Guide prompted then: "Lean forward a bit
and look beyond them, there—do you see that one
scratching herself with dungy nails, the strumpet

who fidgets to her feet, then to a crouch?
It is the whore Thais . . ."

Source: From *The Divine Comedy* by Dante Alighieri, translated by John Ciardi. Copyright 1954, 1957, 1960, 1961, 1965, 1967, 1970 by the Ciardi Family Publishing Trust. Used by permission of W. W. Norton & Company, Inc.

warned of the harmful values of this world by meeting a cast of sinful characters who inhabit the world of the damned. In Purgatory his guide becomes Beatrice, Dante's deceased beloved, who stands for the Christian virtues. In this section of the poem, he begins the painful process of spiritual rehabilitation in which he comes to accept the Christian image of life as a pilgrimage. In Paradise he achieves spiritual fulfillment by speaking with figures from the past who have defied death.

The lasting appeal of this long, complex, and difficult poem is a wonder. Underlying the appeal of *The Divine Comedy* is perhaps its optimism, which expresses Dante's own cure to his depressing condition as an exile. The power of Dante's poetry established the form of the modern Italian language. Even in translation the images and stories can intrigue and fascinate.

Giovanni Boccaccio and *The Decameron*

Like Dante, Giovanni Boccaccio (1313–1375) was a Florentine. He grew up in a prosperous merchant banking family that was bankrupted during the Florentine financial crisis of the 1340s. Losing the shelter of economic and social privilege, Boccaccio's life became one of poverty and endless adversity. In the freedom from business responsibilities created by enforced poverty, Boccaccio turned to writing tales of chivalry and love, which were immediately very popular and had lasting influence on other writers.

After witnessing the ravages of the Black Death in Florence in 1348 and 1349, Boccaccio turned to polishing his masterpiece, *The Decameron,* a collection of 100 humorous, satirical, majestic, and sometimes pornographic stories. The book begins with a somber description of the social chaos created by the plague and tells how ten young people (seven women and three men) escaped the plague in Florence for a refuge in the country. *The Decameron* is less a story of a pilgrimage than the depiction of a refuge, but it is no less an escape from the cruel realities of the world. In their luxurious fantasy world of the country, each of the ten tells a story every night for ten nights. Displaying an open-minded attitude toward human weaknesses, *The Decameron* represents Boccaccio's initial response to the Black Death. Believing there was no future other than death, Boccaccio responded with a celebration of life in stories full of heroism, romance, unhappy love, wit, trickery, sexual license, and laughter. Although *The Decameron* was often read as escapist fantasy literature designed to lift the gloom of events, it was also a literary masterpiece that created a vivid, swift moving narrative.

Geoffrey Chaucer and *The Canterbury Tales*

Boccaccio profoundly influenced Geoffrey Chaucer (ca. 1342–1400), the most outstanding English poet prior to William Shakespeare. As a courtier and diplomat, Chaucer was a trusted adviser to three successive English kings. But he is best known for his literary output, including *The Canterbury Tales,* which exhibit some of the same earthy humor and tolerance for human folly as *The Decameron.*

In *The Canterbury Tales* a group of thirty pilgrims tell stories as they travel on horseback to the shrine at Canterbury. By employing the pilgrimage as a framing device for telling the stories, Chaucer was able to bring together a collection of people from across the social spectrum, including a wife, indulgence hawker, miller, town magistrate, clerk, landowner, lawyer, merchant, knight, abbess, and monk. The variety of characters who told the tales allowed Chaucer to experiment with many kinds of literary forms, from a chivalric romance to a sermon. The pilgrimage combined the considerations of religious morality with the fun of a spring vacation more concerned with the pleasures of this world than preparing for the next, which was the avowed purpose of going on a pilgrimage. In this intertwining of the worldly and the spiritual, Chaucer brought the abstract principles of Christian morality down to a level of common understanding.

Margery Kempe and the Autobiographical Pilgrimage

As the daughter of a town mayor, Margery Kempe (1373–1440) was destined for a comfortable life as a middle-class wife in provincial England. After her first child was born, however, she experienced a bout of depression during which she had a vision of Christ. She began to experience more visions and felt a calling to lead a more spiritual life. As a married woman she could not become a nun, which would have been the normal course for a woman with her spiritual inclinations. Instead, she accepted her marital duties and bore fourteen children.

At the age of about 40 she persuaded her husband to join her in a mutual vow of chastity and embarked on her own religious vocation. Always a bit of an eccentric, Kempe became a fervent vegetarian at a time when meat was scarce but highly desired. She also developed an insatiable wanderlust, undertaking a series of pilgrimages to Jerusalem, Rome, Germany, Norway, Spain, and numerous places in England. On these pilgrimages she sought out mystics and recluses for their spiritual advice. Her own devotions took the form of loud weeping and crying, which alienated many people who feared she might be a heretic or a madwoman. Toward the end of her life she dictated an account of her difficult dealings with her husband, her spells of madness, her ecstatic visions, and her widespread travels as a pilgrim. For Kempe the actual experience of undertaking pilgrimages made it possible for her to examine the course of her own life, which she understood as a spiritual pilgrimage. Her *Book* (1436) was the earliest autobiography in English.

Christine de Pisan and the Defense of Female Virtue

The work of the poet Christine de Pisan (1364–1430) was neither escapist like Giovanni Boccaccio's nor a spiritual pilgrimage like Dante's, Chaucer's, or Kempe's but was a thoughtful and passionate commentary on the tumultuous issues of her day. At age 15 Pisan married a notary of King Charles V of France, but by age 25 she was a widow with three young children. In order to support her family, she turned to writing and relied on the patronage of the royalty and wealthy aristocrats of France, Burgundy, Germany, and England.

Christine de Pisan championed the cause of women in a male-dominated society that was often overtly hostile to them. Following the fashion of the times, she invented a new chivalric order, the Order of the Rose, whose members took a vow to defend the honor of women. She wrote a defense of women for a male readership and an allegorical autobiography. But she is most famous for the two books she wrote for women readers, *The Book of the City of Ladies* and *The Book of Three Virtues* (both about 1407). In these she recounted tales of the heroism and virtue of women and offered moral instruction for women in different social roles. In 1415 she retired to a convent where in the last year of her life she wrote a masterpiece of ecstatic lyricism that celebrated the early victories of Joan of Arc. Pisan's book turned the martyred Joan into the heroine of France.

Defining Cultural Boundaries

During the Later Middle Ages, systematic discrimination against certain ethnic and religious groups increased markedly in Europe. As European society enforced ever-higher levels of religious uniformity, intolerance spread in the ethnically mixed societies of the European periphery. Intolerance was marked in three especially troubled areas: Spain with its mixture of Muslim, Jewish, and Christian cultures; the German borderlands in east-central Europe, where Germans mingled with Slavs; and Ireland and Wales, where Celts came under the domination of the English. Within the heartland of Europe were other areas of clashing cultures—for example, Switzerland where the folk culture of peasants and shepherds living in the isolated mountains collided with the intense Christian religiosity of the cities.

During the eleventh and twelfth centuries, ethnic diversity had been more widely accepted. A Hungarian cleric wrote in an undated work from this period, "As immigrants come from various lands, so they bring with them various languages and customs, various skills and forms of armament, which adorn and glorify the royal household and quell the pride of external powers. A kingdom of one race and custom is weak and fragile."[17] By the fourteenth and fifteenth centuries, however, this optimistic celebration of

---

DOCUMENT

Why Women Deserve an Education as Much as Men

In the Book of the City of the Ladies *Christine de Pisan addresses the reasons offered by some men who opposed the education of women. These men did not want their daughters, wives, or sisters to receive an education because it would compromise their morals. Christine forcefully answers that objection.*

Here you can clearly see that not all opinions of men are based on reason and that these men are wrong. For it must not be presumed that mores necessarily grow worse from knowing the moral sciences, which teach the virtues, indeed, there is not the slightest doubt that moral education amends and ennobles them. How could anyone think or believe that whoever follows good teaching or doctrine is the worse for it? Such an opinion cannot be expressed or maintained. . . .

Thus, not all men (and especially the wisest) share the opinion that is it bad for women to be educated. But it is very true that many foolish men have claimed this because it displeased them that women knew more than they did. . . .

If it were customary to send little girls to school and to teach them the same subjects as are taught to boys, they would learn just as fully and would understand the subtleties of all arts and sciences. Indeed maybe they would understand them better . . . for just as women's bodies are more soft than men's, so too their understanding is more sharp. . . . If they understand less it is because they do not go out and see so many different places and things but stay home and mind their own work. For there is nothing which teaches a reasonable creature so much as the experience of many different things.

Source: Christine de Pisan, *The Book of the City of Ladies*, translated by Earl Jeffrey Richards. Copyright © 1982 by Persea Books, Inc.

---

diversity had faded. Ethnic discrimination and residential segregation created the first ghettos for ethnic and religious minorities.

Spain: Religious Communities in Tension

The Iberian peninsula was home to thriving communities of Muslims, Jews, and Christians. Since the eleventh century the aggressive northern Christian kingdoms of Castile and Aragon had engaged in a protracted program of Reconquest (*Reconquista*) against the Muslim states of the peninsula. By 1248 the Reconquest was largely completed, with only a small Muslim enclave in Granada holding out until 1492. The Spanish Reconquest placed former enemies in close proximity to one another. Hostilities between Christians and Muslims ranged from active warfare to tense stalemate, with Jews working as cultural intermediaries between the two larger communities.

During the twelfth and thirteenth centuries Muslims, called the Mudejars, who capitulated to the conquering Christians, received guarantees that they could continue to practice their own religion and laws. During the fourteenth century, however, Christian kings gradually reneged on these promises. In 1301 the king of Castile decreed that the testimony of any two Christian witnesses could convict a Jew or Muslim, notwithstanding any previously granted privileges that allowed them to be tried in their own courts. The Arabic language began to disappear in Spain as the Mudejars suffered discrimination on many levels. By the sixteenth century, the practice of Islam became illegal, and the Spanish state adopted a systematic policy to destroy Mudejar culture by prohibiting Muslim dress, customs, and marriage practices.

The Jews also began to feel the pain of organized, official discrimination. Christian preachers accused Jews of poisonings, stealing Christian babies, and cannibalism. When the Black Death arrived in 1348, the Jews of Aragon were accused of having poisoned the wells, even though Jews were dying just like Christians. Beginning in 1378, a Catholic prelate in Seville, Ferrant Martínez, commenced an anti-Jewish preaching campaign by calling for the destruction of all twenty-three of the city's synagogues, the confinement of Jews to a ghetto, the dislodging of all Jews from public positions, and the prohibition of any social contact between Christians and Jews. His campaign led to an attack on the Jews of Seville in 1391. Violence spread to other cities throughout the peninsula and the nearby Balearic Islands. Jews were given a stark choice: conversion or death. After a year of mob violence, about 100,000 Jews had been murdered and an equal number had gone into hiding or fled to more tolerant Muslim countries. The 1391 pogroms led to the first significant forced conversions of Jews in Spain. A century later in 1492, on the heels of the final Christian victory of the Reconquest, all remaining Jews in Spain were compelled to either leave or convert.

German and Celtic Borderlands: Ethnic Communities in Tension

Other regions with diverse populations also witnessed discrimination and its brutal consequences. During the population boom of the twelfth and thirteenth centuries, German-speaking immigrants had established colonial towns in the Baltic and penetrated eastward, creating isolated pockets of German culture in Bohemia, Poland, and Hungary. During the fourteenth and fifteenth centuries, the bias of native populations against the colonizing Germans was manifest in various ways. One Czech prince offered 100 silver marks to anyone who brought him 100 German noses. The German settlers exhibited a similar intolerance

of the natives. The Teutonic Knights, who had been the vanguard of the German migrations in the Baltic, began to require German ancestry for membership. In German-speaking towns along the colonized borderlands of east-central Europe, city councils and guilds began to restrict by ethnicity the qualification for holding certain offices or joining a guild. The most famous example was the "German Paragraph" in guild statutes, which required candidates for admission to a guild to prove German descent. As the statutes of a bakers' guild put it, "Whoever wishes to be a member must bring proof to the councilors and the guildsmen that he is born of legitimate, upright German folk." Others required members to be "of German blood and tongue," as if language were a matter of biological inheritance.[18] German guildsmen were also forbidden to marry non-Germans.

A similar process of exclusion occurred in the Celtic fringe of the British Isles. In Ireland the ruling English promulgated laws that attempted to protect the cultural identity of the English colonists. The English prohibited native Irish from citizenship in town or guild membership. The Statutes of Kilkenny of 1366 attempted to legislate ethnic purity: They prohibited intermarriage between English and Irish; they required English colonists to speak English, use English names, wear English clothes, and ride horses in the English way; and they forbade the English to play Irish games or listen to Irish music. The aggressive legislation of the English in Ireland was essentially defensive. The tiny English community was attempting to prevent its absorption into the majority culture. A similar pattern appeared in Wales, where the lines dividing the Welsh and English communities hardened during the fourteenth century.

Enemies Within

The Black Death and its aftermath transformed many segments of Europe into a persecuting society. The year 1348 represented a watershed; in the period that followed, vague biases and dislikes sharpened into systematic violence against minorities. The plague sparked assaults against lepers, people with handicaps and physical deformities, beggars, vagabonds, foreigners, priests, pilgrims, Muslims, and Jews. Anyone who looked strange, dressed differently, spoke with an accent, practiced a minority religion, or did not fit in was vulnerable to becoming a scapegoat for the miseries of others. Minorities took the blame for calamities that could not be otherwise explained.

Violence against minorities occurred in many places, but it was most systematic in German-speaking lands. Between November 1348 and August 1350, violence against Jews occurred in more than eighty German towns. Like the allegations in Aragon, the fear that Jews poisoned the wells led to massacres in German lands even *before* plague had arrived in these communities. The frequent occurrence of violence on Sundays or feast days suggests that preachers consciously or unconsciously encouraged the rioting mobs.

The troubles caused by the Great Schism (1378–1417, when there was more than one pope) also contributed to a heightened sensitivity to cultural differences. During the Council of Basel (1431–1449), German bishops and theologians in attendance began to exchange information about cases of alleged witchcraft they had heard about in the nearby Swiss Alps. What these learned priests and friars thought of as witchcraft was probably nothing more than harmless folk magic, but to them the strange details of peasant behavior seemed evidence of a vast Satanic conspiracy to destroy Christianity. For most of its history, the Catholic Church had denied that witchcraft existed, but the terrible events of the fourteenth century cried out for explanation. In 1484 Pope Innocent VIII changed official Catholic policy by calling on two Dominican professors of theology to examine the alleged spread of witchcraft in Germany. As a guide to witch hunters, they wrote a detailed handbook on witchcraft, *The Hammer of Witches,* which went through twenty-eight editions between 1486 and 1600, evidence of its enormous success and influence.

The Hammer of Witches codified the folklore of the Alpine peasants as the basis for witchcraft practices. The book condemned as heretics those who disbelieved in the power of witches and established legal procedures for the prosecution of witches. It sanctioned torture as the most effective means for obtaining confessions, and it established much lower standards of evidence than in other kinds of cases. As an anthology of mythical stories about the activities of supposed witches, *The Hammer* summed up the worst of prevailing attitudes about women: "all witchcraft comes from carnal lust, which in women is insatiable." Most witchcraft persecutions came later in the sixteenth and seventeenth centuries, but the publication of *The Hammer of Witches* represented the culmination of the frenzied search to find enemies within European society, which was quickened by the events of the fourteenth and fifteenth centuries. With the dissemination of the idea of the reality of witchcraft, virtually anyone could be hauled before a court on charges of maintaining a secret liaison with Satan.

Conclusion

Looking Inward

Unlike the more dynamic, outward-looking thirteenth century, Europeans during the fourteenth and early fifteenth centuries turned their attention inward to their own communities and their own problems. Europe faced one calamity after another, each crisis compounding the misery. In the process the identity of the West became more defensive and the fragility of Christianity itself was laid bare. The process of changing Western identities can be seen in two ways. First, as a result of the Western encounters with the Mongol and Ottoman Empires, the political and religious frontiers of the West shifted. These two empires redrew the map of the West by ending the Christian Byzantine Empire and by leaving Christian Russia on the margins of the West. With the Mongol invasions, the eastward spread of Christianity into Asia ended. The Ottoman conquests left a lasting Muslim influence inside eastern Europe, particularly in Bosnia and Albania. Peoples who were predominantly Christian and whose political institutions were a heritage of the ancient Roman Empire now survived under the domination of Asian or Muslim empires and in a tenuous relationship with the rest of the Christian West. Most of the new subjects of these empires remained Christian, but their Mongol and Ottoman masters destroyed their political autonomy. The Ottoman Empire remained hostile to and frequently at war with the Christian West for more than 200 years.

Second, most Europeans reinforced their identity as Christians and became more self-conscious of the country in which they lived. At the same time Christian civilization was becoming eclipsed in parts of eastern Europe, it revived in the Iberian peninsula, where the Muslim population, once the most extensive in the West, suffered discrimination and defeat. The northern Spanish kingdoms, for example, began to unify their subjects around a militant form of Christianity that was overtly hostile to Muslims and Jews. In many places in the West, religious and ethnic discrimination against minorities increased. A stronger sense of self-identification by country can be most dramatically seen in France and England as a consequence of the Hundred Years' War. The French rallied around a saintly national heroine, Joan of Arc. After dropping claims to France after the Hundred Years' War, the English aristocracy stopped speaking French and adopting the customs of the French court. They became less international and more English. The Western countries became more self-consciously characterized by an attitude of "us versus them."

Except for the very visible military conquests of the Mongols and the Ottomans, the causes of most of the calamities of the fourteenth century were invisible or unknown. No one recognized a climate change or understood the dynamics of the population crisis. No one understood the cause of the epidemics. No one grasped the role of the Mongol Empire in the world economy or the causes for the collapse of banking and trade. Unable to distinguish how these forces were changing their lives, western Europeans only witnessed their consequences. In the face of these calamities, European culture became obsessed with death and with finding scapegoats to blame for events that could not be otherwise explained. However, calamity also bred creativity. The search for answers to the question, "Why did this happen to us?" produced a new spiritual sensibility and a rich literature. Following the travails of the fourteenth century, moreover, there arose in the fifteenth a new, more optimistic cultural movement—the Renaissance. Gloom and doom was not the only response to troubles. During the Renaissance some people began to search for new answers to human problems in a fashion that would transform the West anew.

Suggestions for Further Reading

For a comprehensive listing of suggested readings, please go to www.ablongman.com/levack2e/chapter10

Carmichael, Ann G. *Plague and the Poor in Renaissance Florence.* 1986. An innovative study that both questions the traditional theory of the bubonic plague as the cause of the Black Death and examines how fear of the disease led to regulation of the poor.

Cohn, Samuel. *The Black Death Transformed: Disease and Culture in Early Renaissance Europe.* 2003. A well-argued case that the Black Death was not caused by the bubonic plague.

Duby, Georges. *France in the Middle Ages, 987–1460: From Hugh Capet to Joan of Arc.* 1991. Traces the emergence of the French state.

Gordon, Bruce, and Peter Marshall, eds. *The Place of the Dead: Death and Remembrance in Late Medieval and Early Modern Europe.* 2000. A collection of essays that shows how the placing of the dead in society was an important activity that engendered considerable conflict and negotiation.

Herlihy, David. *The Black Death and the Transformation of the West.* 1997. A pithy, readable analysis of the epidemiological and historical issues surrounding the Black Death.

Holmes, George. *Europe: Hierarchy and Revolt, 1320–1450.* 1975. Excellent examination of rebellions.

Huizinga, Johan. *The Autumn of the Middle Ages,* trans. Rodney J. Payton and Urlich Mammitzsch. 1996. A new translation of the classic study of France and the Low Countries during the fourteenth and fifteenth centuries. Dated and perhaps too pessimistic, Huizinga's lucid prose and broad vision still make this an engaging reading experience.

Imber, Colin. *The Ottoman Empire, 1300–1481.* 1990. The basic work that establishes a chronology for the early Ottomans.

Jordan, William C. *The Great Famine: Northern Europe in the Early Fourteenth Century.* 1996. The most comprehensive book on the famine.

Lambert, Malcolm. *Medieval Heresy: Popular Movements from the Gregorian Reform to the Reformation.* 1992. Excellent general study of the Hussite and Lollard movements.

Le Roy Ladurie, Emmanuel. *Times of Feast, Times of Famine: A History of Climate Since the Year 1000,* trans. Barbara Bray. 1971. The book that introduced the idea of the Little Ice Age and promoted the study of the influence of climate on history.

Lynch, Joseph H. *The Medieval Church: A Brief History.* 1992. A pithy, elegant survey of ecclesiastical institutions and developments.

Morgan, David O. *The Mongols.* 1986. Best introduction to Mongol history.

Nirenberg, David. *Communities of Violence: Persecution of Minorities in the Middle Ages.* 1996. An important analysis of the persecution of minorities that is deeply rooted in Spanish evidence.

Scott, Susan, and Christopher Duncan. *Biology of Plagues: Evidence from Historical Populations.* 2001. An analysis by two epidemiologists who argue that the Black Death was not the bubonic plague but probably a virus similar to Ebola.

Sumption, Jonathan. *The Hundred Years' War: Trial by Battle.* 1991. First volume goes only to 1347. When it is completed, it will be the best comprehensive study.

Swanson, R. N. *Religion and Devotion in Europe, c. 1215–c. 1515.* 1995. The best up-to-date textbook account of late medieval religious practice.

Notes

1. Quoted in Emmanuel Le Roy Ladurie, *Times of Feast, Times of Famine: A History of Climate Since the Year 1000,* trans. Barbara Bray (1971), 47.

2. Quoted in William Bowsky, "The Impact of the Black Death," in Anthony Molho, ed., *Social and Economic Foundations of the Italian Renaissance* (1969), 92.

3. Cited in Philip Ziegler, *The Black Death* (1969), 20.

4. Giovanni Boccaccio, *The Decameron,* trans. Richard Aldington (1962), 30.

5. Ibid.

6. Quoted in Mark C. Bartusis, *The Late Byzantine Army: Arms and Society, 1204–1453* (1992), 133.

7. Trial record as quoted in Marina Warner, *Joan of Arc* (1981), 122.

8. Ibid., 127.

9. Ibid., 143.

10. *The Trial of Joan of Arc,* trans. W. S. Scott (1956), 134.

11. Ibid., 106.

12. Ibid., 135.

13. Warner, *Joan of Arc,* 145.

14. Johan Huizinga, *The Autumn of the Middle Ages,* trans. Rodney J. Payton and Ulrich Mammitzsch (1996), 156.

15. Quoted in Barbara W. Tuchman, *A Distant Mirror: The Calamitous 14th Century* (1978), 505–506. Translation has been slightly modified by the authors.

16. Ibid., 506.

17. *Libellus de institutione morum,* ed. J. Balogh, *Scriptores rerum Hungaricarum 2* (1938), 625. Quoted in Robert Bartlett, *The Making of Europe: Conquest, Colonization and Cultural Change 950–1350* (1993), 239.

18. *Codex diplomaticus Brandenburgensis,* ed. Adolph Friedrich Riedel (41 vols., 1838–1869), 365–367. Cited in Bartlett, *The Making of Europe,* 238.

The Italian Renaissance and Beyond: The Politics of Culture

For fifteen years Niccolò Machiavelli worked as a diplomat and political adviser, a man always at the center of the action in his hometown of Florence. But in 1512 there was a change of regimes in the city-state of Florence. Distrusted by the new rulers and suspected of involvement in an assassination plot, he was abruptly fired from his job, imprisoned, tortured, and finally ordered to stay out of town. Exiled to his suburban farm, impoverished, and utterly miserable, Machiavelli survived by selling lumber from his woodlot to his former colleagues, who regularly cheated him. To help feed his family he snared birds; to entertain himself he played cards in a local inn with the innkeeper, a butcher, a miller, and two bakers. As he put it, "caught this way among these lice I wipe the mold from my brain [by playing cards] and release my feeling of being ill-treated by Fate."

In the evenings, however, Machiavelli transformed himself into an entirely different person. He entered his study, removed his mud-splattered clothes, and put on the elegant robes he had once worn as a government official. And then, "dressed in a more appropriate manner I enter into the ancient courts of ancient men and am welcomed by them kindly." Machiavelli was actually reading the works of the ancient Greek and Latin historians, but he described his evening reading as a conversation: He asked the ancients about the reasons for their actions, and in reading their books he found answers. For four hours, "I feel no boredom, I dismiss every affliction, I no longer fear poverty nor do I tremble at the thought of death: I become completely part of them."[1]

Machiavelli's evening conversations with the long-dead ancients perfectly expressed the sensibility of the Italian Renaissance. This wretched man, disillusioned with his own times and bored by his empty-headed neighbors, found in the ancients the stimulating companions he could not find in life. For him the ancient past was more alive than the present. In this sense Machiavelli was very much a Renaissance man, because feeling part of antiquity is what the Renaissance is all about. For those who were captivated

The Mona Lisa Leonardo da Vinci's portrait of a Florentine woman with her enigmatic smile testifies to the Renaissance fascination with portraits of individuals who appear completely natural.

by it, the ancient past and the examples of leadership and beauty it offered seemed to be a cure for the ills of a decidedly troubled time.

As discussed in Chapter 10, during the fourteenth and fifteenth centuries Europeans experienced a prevailing sense of loss, a morbid preoccupation with death, and a widespread pessimism about the human capacity for good. Yet in Florence during this same period a cultural movement began to express a different view of life that emphasized the responsibilities of humans to better their communities through social welfare, to beautify their cities, and to devote themselves to the duties of citizenship. We now call that movement the Renaissance. The movement emerged from the desire to improve the human condition during times of trouble, and that desire was first manifest in the intellectually free environment of the independent city-states of Italy. Machiavelli—despite the bleak circumstances of his later life—was one of the Renaissance thinkers who thought the world could be set right through concerted political action. Like the medieval thinkers he was pessimistic about the frailties of human nature, but he firmly believed that the weakness of most humans could be counteracted by strong leadership and strong laws. In this respect he differed from the medieval writers who thought the contemplative life of the monk was the highest calling to which a man could aspire. The Renaissance was born and developed because the political structures of the Italian city-states encouraged cultural experimentation and fostered the idea that society could be reengineered according to the principles that made ancient Greece and Rome great.

The word Renaissance°, which means "rebirth," is a term historians invented to describe a movement that sought to imitate and understand the culture of antiquity. The fundamental Renaissance principle was the need to keep everything in balance and proportion, an aesthetic ideal derived from ancient literature. In political theory, this meant building a stable society upon the foundations of well-balanced individuals who conformed to a rigorous code of conduct. In the arts it meant searching for the underlying harmonies in nature, which typically meant employing geometry and the mathematics of proportion in drawing, painting, sculpting, and designing buildings. Renaissance artists thought geometry unlocked the secrets of nature and revealed the hidden hand of God in creation.

The Italian Renaissance was not the first time the West experienced a revival of ancient learning and thought. In the Carolingian Renaissance of the ninth century, members of the emperor Charlemagne's court reinvigorated education in Latin. And the European-wide Renaissance of the twelfth century led to the foundation of the universities, the reintroduction of Roman law, and the spread of scholastic philosophy and theology. The Renaissance considered in this chapter refers to a diffuse cultural movement that occurred at different times in different regions, and as a result its dates are very approximate. Most historians date the Italian Renaissance from about 1350 to 1550. By 1500 the

cultural movement that began in Italy had spread to much of western Europe.

The Renaissance helped refashion the concept of Western civilization. From the fifth to the fourteenth centuries, the West identified itself primarily through conformity to Latin Christianity or Roman Catholicism, which meant the celebration of uniform religious rituals in Latin and obedience to the pope. The Renaissance added a new element to this identity. Although by no means anti-Christian, Renaissance thinkers began to think of themselves as the heirs of pre-Christian cultures—Hebrew, Greek, and Roman. In this sense, they began to imagine a Western civilization that was more than just Christianity but as the history of a common culture dating back to Antiquity. Through reading the texts and viewing the works of art of the long-dead ancients, people during the Italian Renaissance gained historical and visual perspective on their own world and cultivated a critical attitude about both the past and their own culture. How then did the cultural encounter during the Renaissance with the philosophy, literature, and art of the Ancient world transform the way Europeans thought?

- In what ways did the political and social climate peculiar to the Italian city-states help create Renaissance culture?
- How did Renaissance thinkers create historical perspective and devise methods of criticism for interpreting texts?
- How did various attempts to imitate antiquity in the arts alter perceptions of nature?
- How did the monarchies of western Europe gather the strength to become more assertive and more effective during the last half of the fifteenth and early sixteenth centuries?

The Cradle of the Renaissance: The Italian City-States

- In what ways did the political and social climate peculiar to the Italian city-states help create Renaissance culture?

In comparison with the rest of Europe and other world civilizations, Renaissance Italy was distinguished by the large number and political autonomy of its thriving city-states. The Netherlands and parts of the Rhine Valley were as thoroughly urbanized, but only in Italy did cities have so much political power. The evolution of the Italian city-states can be encapsulated into two distinct phases.

The first phase in the evolution of the Italian city-states occurred during the eleventh and twelfth centuries.

During this period about one hundred Italian towns became independent republics, also known as communes, and developed the laws and institutions of self-government. The male citizens of these tiny republics gathered on a regular basis in the town square to debate important issues such as assessing new taxes, improving the city walls, or going to war. To conduct the day-to-day business of government, they elected city officials from among themselves.

The governmental practices of these city-states produced the political theory of republicanism°, which described a state in which government officials were elected by the people or a portion of the people. The theory of republicanism was first articulated by Marsilius of Padua (1270–1342) in *The Defender of the Peace*, a book that relied on the precedents established by the ancient Roman republic. Marsilius recognized two kinds of government—principalities and republics. Principalities relied upon the descending principle that political authority came directly from God and trickled down through kings and princes to the rest of humanity. According to this principle, the responsibility of government was to enforce God's laws. Marsilius, however, rejected the idea that the task of the political world was to express the will of God. His ascending principle of republicanism suggested that laws derive not from God but from the will of the people, who freely choose their own form of government and who are equally free to change it. In Marsilius's theory, citizens regularly expressed their will through voting. The first phase in the evolution of the Italian city-states established the institutions of self-government, the procedures for electing officials, and the theory of republicanism.

In the second phase of evolution, which occurred during the fourteenth century, most city-states abandoned or lost their republican institutions and came to be ruled by princes. The reasons for the transformation of these republics into principalities were related to the economic and demographic turmoil created by the international economic collapse and the Black Death. Two of the largest republics, however, did not go through this second phase and survived without losing their liberty to a prince. The Renaissance began in these two city-states, Florence and Venice (see Map 11.1). Their survival as republics, which made them exceptions to the rule by the fifteenth century, helps explain the origins of the Renaissance.

The Renaissance Republics: Florence and Venice

In an age of despotic princes, Florence and Venice were keenly aware of how different they were from other cities, and they feared they might suffer the same fate as their neighbors if they did not defend their republican institutions and liberty. In keeping alive the traditions of republican self-government, these two cities created an environment of competition and freedom that stimulated creative ingenuity. Although neither of these cities were democracies, nor were they particularly egalitarian, they were certainly more open to new ideas than cities ruled by princes. In both Florence and Venice, citizens prized discussion and debate, the skills necessary for success in business and politics. By contrast, in the principalities all cultural activity tended to revolve around and express the tastes of the prince, who monopolized much of the wealth. In Florence and Venice a few great families called the *patriciate* controlled most of the property, but these patricians competed among themselves to gain recognition

Map 11.1 Northern Italy in the Mid-Fifteenth Century

During the Renaissance the largest city-states, such as Milan, Venice, and Florence, gained control of the surrounding countryside and smaller cities in the vicinity, establishing regional territorial states. Only Venice and Florence remained republics. Milan and Savoy were ruled by dukes. The Gonzaga family ruled Mantua and the Este family Modena and Ferrara. The states of the Church were ruled by the pope in Rome.

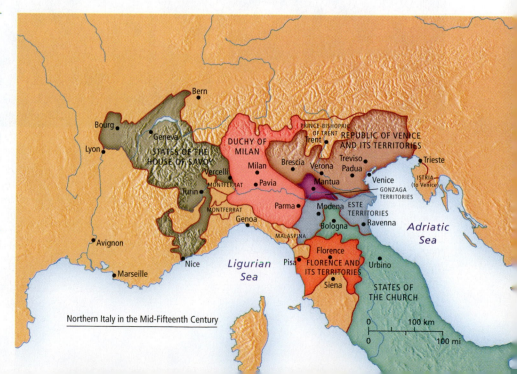

and fame by patronizing great artists and scholars. This patronage by wealthy men and women made the Renaissance possible. Because the tastes of these patricians dictated what writers and artists could do, understanding who they were helps explain Renaissance culture.

Florence Under the Medici

The greatest patron during the early Renaissance was the fabulously rich Florentine banker Cosimo de' Medici (1389–1464). Based on his financial power, Cosimo effectively took control of the Florentine republic in 1434, ushering in a period of unprecedented domestic peace and artistic splendor called the Medicean Age (1434–1494). Cosimo's style of rule was exceedingly clever. Instead of making himself a prince, which the citizens of Florence would have opposed, he managed the policies of the republic from behind the scenes. He seldom held public office, but he made himself the center of Florentine affairs through shrewd negotiating, quiet fixing of elections, and generous distribution of bribes, gifts, and jobs. Cosimo's behind-the-scenes rule illustrated a fundamental value of Renaissance culture—the desire to maintain appearances. In this case, the appearance of the Florentine republic was saved, even as the reality of Florentine liberty was subverted.

Cosimo's brilliant patronage of intellectuals and artists mirrored a similar ambition to maintain appearances. It helped make Cosimo appear a pious, generous man who modeled himself after the great statesmen of the ancient Roman republic. Cosimo appreciated intelligence and merit wherever he found it. He frequented the discussions of prominent scholars, some of whom became his lasting friends. Intrigued by what he learned from them, he personally financed the search for and acquisition of manuscripts of ancient Latin and Greek literature and philosophy for new libraries he helped establish. In return for his financial support, many Florentine scholars dedicated their works to Cosimo. He took particular interest in the revival of the ancient Greek philosopher Plato, and he set up the

The Medici as Magi

During the fifteenth century the Medici had the power but lacked the legitimacy to rule Florence because they neither had been elected nor were the princes of the city. To compensate for their lack of legal authority, they created the image of themselves as "wise men" similar to the three wise men or magi who first recognized the divinity of Christ. In this fresco in the Medici Palace, the artist Benozzo Gozzoli depicted Lorenzo the Magnificent as one of the magi. He is the young man wearing a crown and gold robe riding on a white horse. His father, grandfather, and other senior members of the Medici family follow, wearing the red hats of common Florentine citizens.

neo-Platonic philosopher Marsilio Ficino (1433–1499) with a house and steady income.

Cosimo's most significant patronage of the arts clustered in the neighborhood where he lived. He rebuilt the nearby monastery of San Marco. He personally selected Fra Angelico, a monk, to paint the austere yet deeply emotive frescoes throughout the monastery. As the centerpiece of his neighborhood beautification plans, Cosimo built for his own family a magnificent new palace, which he filled with innumerable objects of beauty and exquisite paintings.

Cosimo's artistic patronage helped create the image of a man who was an open-handed and benevolent godfather for his community. Because Cosimo had not been elected to rule Florence, his political influence was illegitimate and he needed to find a way to create a proper image that would justify his power. To do that he decorated the private chapel in his palace with frescoes that depicted him accompanying the magi, the wise men or kings who brought gifts to the baby Jesus. Thus Cosimo made himself appear similar to those ancient kings who first recognized the divinity of Christ. By having himself depicted with the magi, Cosimo created an image that helped justify the fact that he controlled elections and dictated policies.

Cosimo's grandson Lorenzo the Magnificent (r. 1469–1492) expanded the family's dominance in Florentine politics through what has been called "veiled lordship." Lorenzo never took the title of prince but behaved very much like one by intervening publicly in the affairs of the state. In contrast to his grandfather's commitment to public patronage, Lorenzo's interest in the arts concentrated on building private villas, collecting precious gems, and commissioning small bronze statues, the kinds of things that gave him private pleasure rather than a public reputation. A fine poet and an intellectual companion of the most renowned scholars of his age, Lorenzo created a lasting reputation as a well-rounded, accomplished Renaissance man, but his princely style of rule, which ignored the republican sensibilities of the Florentines, created discontent and undermined public support for the Medicis. There were several conspiracies against him; during an attempted assassination of Lorenzo, his brother Giuliano was killed.

During the fifteenth century Florence became the first society that dedicated itself to the production and appreciation of what we now call Renaissance culture. As a republic on the perilous edge of financial survival, Florence had surrendered to the behind-the-scenes rule of the Medici family, who supported a movement in philosophy and the arts that, as we shall see, imitated and celebrated the heritage of pre-Christian antiquity, especially the culture of Greece and Rome.

Venice, the Cosmopolitan Republic

Venice resembled Florence in that it survived into the Renaissance period with its republican institutions intact,

Map 11.2   Venetian Colonial Empire

The Venetian colonies included the Greek-speaking islands in the Adriatic and a number of important islands in the Aegean. Between the fifteenth and seventeenth centuries these colonies were repeatedly threatened by the Ottoman Empire, with its capital in Constantinople.

but it was far more politically stable. Situated in the midst of a vast lagoon, Venice's streets consisted of broad channels in which great seagoing merchant ships were moored and small canals choked with private gondolas for local transportation. To protect their fragile city from flooding, the Venetians recognized that they had to cooperate among themselves, and thus the imperative for survival helped create a republic that became a model of stability and ecological awareness. The Venetians, for example, created the world's first environmental regulatory agencies, which were responsible for hydrological projects, such as building dikes and dredging canals, and for forestry management to prevent soil erosion and the consequent silting up of the lagoon.

Venice was among the first European powers to have colonies abroad. To guarantee its merchant ships access to the eastern Mediterranean and Constantinople, Venice conquered a series of ports, including a significant number in Greece (see Map 11.2). Its involvement in international trade and governing distant colonies made Venice unusually cosmopolitan. Many Venetian merchants spent years living abroad and some settled in the colonies. Moreover, people from all over Europe flocked to the city of Venice— Germans, Turks, Armenians, Albanians, Greeks, Slovenes,

Croats, and Jews—each creating their own neighborhood communities and institutions. Venetian households owned Russian, Asian, Turkish, and African slaves, all of whom contributed to the remarkable diversity of the city.

Of the many foreign groups in Venice, the most influential were the Greeks. Venice had long maintained close commercial and cultural ties with the Greek world. Its churches were modeled after the huge basilicas of Constantinople, and many Venetian merchants spoke Greek. After the fall of the Byzantine Empire to the Ottoman Turks in 1453, many Greek Christian refugees found a new home in Venice and other Italian cities, including influential scholars who helped reintroduce Greek philosophy and literature to an eager Italian readership. One of these scholars was John Bessarion (1403–1472), a Byzantine archbishop who compiled a magnificent library of Greek manuscripts that he bequeathed to the republic of Venice. Venice also became the leading center in western Europe for the publication of Greek books, printing the important texts in Greek philosophy and science, and making them widely available for the first time in western Europe.

The defining characteristic of Venetian government was its social stability, a trait that made it the envy of other more troubled cities and the source of imitation by republican-minded reformers throughout Europe. Whereas the Florentine republic was notoriously unstable and subject to quiet subversion by the Medicis, Venice boasted a largely unchanging republican constitution that lasted from 1297 to 1797. Thus Venice is the longest-surviving republic in history. It was, however, a very exclusive republic. Out of a total population of nearly 150,000, only a small political elite consisting of 2,500 nobles enjoyed voting privileges. From this elite and from Venice's many wealthy religious institutions came the resources to patronize Renaissance artists.

At the top of Venetian society was the *doge,* a member of the nobility who was elected to the job for life. The most notable Renaissance doge was Andrea Gritti (r. 1523–1538), whose reputation derived from his brilliant early career as a military administrator and diplomat. Gritti sometimes bent the laws in his favor, but he never manipulated elections or managed Venice's affairs as completely as Cosimo de' Medici did in Florence a century before. Like the Medicis, however, he used his own financial resources and his personal influence to transform his city into a major center of Renaissance culture.

Gritti hired some of the most prominent European artists, musicians, and poets to come to Venice. These included Pietro Aretino (1492–1556), the greatest master of satire of the sixteenth century, and the architect and sculptor Jacopo Sansovino (1486–1570). As official architect of the city, Sansovino transformed its appearance with his sculptures, palaces, and churches that imitated the styles of classical Greece and Rome. One of his most notable buildings is the Marciana Library, which was begun in 1537 to house Bessarion's collection of Greek manuscripts.

Artistic and scholarly creativity in Florence and Venice thrived on the competition among many different patrons. Neither the Medicis in Florence nor Gritti in Venice entirely dominated the cultural scene. Artistic patronage in these republics mirrored the dynamic political life that engaged many people. The diversity of patronage gave extensive employment to painters, sculptors, and architects, thereby attracting the best artists to these two cities. Later sections of the chapter will examine the works they produced.

Princes and Courtiers

Although the Renaissance began in the relative freedom of republics, such as Florence, it soon spread to principalities, those states ruled by one man, the prince. In contrast to the multiple sources of support for the arts and learning in the republics, patronage in the principalities was more constricted, confined to the prince and members of his court. The terms *lord* and *prince* refer to rulers who possessed formal aristocratic titles, such as the Marquis of Mantua, the Duke of Milan, or the King of Naples. Most Renaissance princes came from local aristocratic families who seized control of the government by force. Some, however, had been soldiers of fortune who had held on to a city as a spoil of war or had even overthrown a government that had once employed them to defend the city. Regardless of how a prince originally obtained power, his goal was to establish a dynasty, that is, to guarantee the rights of his descendants to continue to rule the city. Some dynasties—such as that of the D'Este family, which ruled Ferrara from 1240 to 1597—were well established and quite popular.

The Ideal Prince, the Ideal Princess

Federico II da Montefeltro (1422–1482), Duke of Urbino, succeeded in achieving the lasting fame and glorious reputation that so many princes craved. Although he was illegitimate, his father gave him the best possible education by sending him to study at the most fashionable school in Italy and to apprentice as a soldier under a renowned mercenary captain. In Renaissance Italy, an illegitimate boy could not inherit his father's property. Thus he usually had two career options: He could become a priest to obtain a living from the church, or he could become a mercenary and take his chances at war. Federico became a mercenary. From among the peasants of the duchy he recruited an army, which he hired out to the highest bidder. He soon earned a European-wide reputation for his many victories and enriched the duchy with the income from mercenary contracts and plunder. When his half-brother was assassinated in 1444, Federico became the ruler of Urbino, and by 1474 he obtained from the pope the title of duke. Federico epitomized the ideal Renaissance prince—a father figure to his subjects, astute diplomat, brilliant soldier, generous patron, avid collector, and man of learning. He was a prince who combined the insights of contempla-

Federico da Montefeltro as the Ideal Prince
The papal tiara in the upper left alludes to the pope's authorization of his title as duke. Federico is shown studying a book while dressed in armor, reflecting his two sides as scholar and soldier. His dynastic ambitions are represented by the presence of his son and potential successor standing at his feet.

tive study with active involvement in the affairs of the world.

Federico's rule was paternalistic. He was concerned for the welfare of his subjects and personally listened to their complaints and adjudicated their disputes. His military adventures tripled the size of his duchy. Conquests brought the prosperity that financed his expensive building projects and his collection of Latin manuscripts. Federico's personal library surpassed that of any contemporary university library in Europe, and his wide-ranging reading interests

showed his openness to the latest developments in learning. Federico's greatest achievement, however, was the building of a vast palace. At one stage the project was supervised by the architect Luciano Laurana (ca. 1420–1479), but it was Federico who clearly deserves most of the credit for what remains the single best example of Renaissance architectural ideals in a palace. Because of Federico, the small mountainous duchy of Urbino acquired a cultural importance far greater than its size warranted.

The best candidate for the ideal princess was Isabella d'Este (1474–1539), the Marchioness of Mantua. Such was her fame as a patron that she was known during her lifetime as "the first lady of the world." Enjoying an education that was exceptional for a girl in the fifteenth century, she grew up in the court at Ferrara, where she was surrounded by famous painters and poets and where she cultivated foreign ambassadors and leading intellectuals of the time. But her influence went far beyond that. When her husband was absent and after his death, she ruled Mantua by herself, earning a reputation for her just decisions and witty charm. She gained renown for her ability as a tenacious negotiator and behind-the-scenes diplomat. An avid reader and collector, she personally knew virtually all the great artists and writers of her age. Her influence spread far beyond Mantua, in part through her voluminous correspondence, which is estimated to include 12,000 letters.

The Ideal Courtier

The Renaissance republics developed a code of conduct for the ideal citizen. The code encouraged citizens to devote their time and energies to public service. The code insisted that the most valuable services of the citizen were to hold public office, to pay taxes honestly, and to help beautify the city through patronage of the arts. In similar fashion the Renaissance principalities created a code for the ideal courtier. A courtier was a man or woman who lived in or regularly visited the palace of a prince. Courtiers helped the prince's household function by performing all kinds of services, such as taking care of the family's wardrobe, managing servants, educating children, providing entertainment, keeping accounts, administering estates, going on diplomatic missions, and fighting battles. To best serve the princely family in whatever was needed, a courtier needed to cultivate a wide range of skills. Men trained in horsemanship, swordplay, and all kinds of sports, which were useful for keeping in shape for war. Women learned to draw, dance, play musical instruments, and engage in witty conversation. Both men and women needed to be adept at foreign languages so that they could converse with visitors and diplomats. According to the ideal, men should also know Latin and Greek, which were the foundations of a formal education. Some of the women in the courts also learned these ancient languages.

The stability and efficiency of the princely states depended on the abilities of the courtiers, who performed many of the functions that elected officials did in the republics. It was also extremely important to prevent conflicts among the courtiers; otherwise the peace of the state would be compromised. The most influential guide to how a courtier should behave was *The Book of the Courtier* (composed between 1508 and 1528) by the cultivated diplomat Baldassare Castiglione (1478–1529). Underlying the behavior and conversation of the ideal courtier described in this book were two general principles that governed all courtly manners—nonchalance and ease:

> *I have found quite a universal rule which . . . seems to me valid above all others, and in all human affairs whether in word or deed: and that is to avoid affectation in every way possible as though it were some very rough and dangerous reef; and (to pronounce a new word perhaps) to practice in all things a certain nonchalance, so as to conceal all art and make whatever is done or said appear to be without effort and almost without any thought about it. . . .*
>
> *Therefore we may call that art true art which does not seem to be art; nor must one be more careful of anything than of concealing it, because if it is discovered, this robs a man of all credit and causes him to be held in slight esteem.[2]*

In other words, nonchalance is the ability to do something that requires considerable training and effort while making it appear to be natural and without effort. The need to maintain appearances, which we first saw in the disguised rulership of Cosimo de' Medici in Florence, became one of the distinguishing traits of Italian Renaissance culture. According to Castiglione, all human action and communication should be moderate and balanced, creating the effect of ease. In effect, *The Book of the Courtier* translated the ideals of harmony and proportion so admired in Renaissance culture into a plan for human comportment. By using courtly manners, human beings governed the movements of the body according to an almost mathematical ideal of proportion.

Through *The Book of the Courtier* and its many imitators, the Renaissance ideal of courtly manners began to be widely disseminated during the sixteenth century due to the capacity of the newly invented printing press to produce inexpensive copies of the same text. Written in a lucid Italian that made for lively reading, the book was translated into Latin, English, French, and Spanish and absorbed into the literature of Europe. By studying these books, any young man or woman of talent and ambition could aspire to act and speak like a great aristocrat. The courtly ideal was completely accessible to anyone who could read, and many of its precepts were incorporated into the educational curriculum of schools, where it has survived to the present in the institution of the prom.

The Papal Prince

The Renaissance popes were the heads of the Church; they also had jurisdiction over the Papal State in central Italy. Thus they combined the roles of priest and prince. The Papal State was supposed to supply the pope with the in-

Courtiers Waiting on a Princely Family
Male courtiers pose while waiting around in the court of the Gonzaga in Mantua. These elegant gentlemen epitomized the nonchalance and ease idealized in Baldassare Castiglione's *The Book of the Courtier.*

come to run the affairs of the Church, but during the period when the popes left Rome and resided in Avignon (France) and during the Great Schism of 1305–1417, the popes lost control of the Papal State. After 1418 the popes saw that they had two main tasks—regain the revenues of the Papal State and rebuild the city of Rome, which had become a neglected ruin. To collect the taxes and revenues due them, many popes were obliged to use military force to bring the rebellious lords and cities into obedience. The popes also squabbled with the neighboring states that had taken advantage of the weakness of the papacy during the schism.

These military and diplomatic adventures thrust the popes into some very nasty quarrels—a situation that undermined the popes' ability to provide moral leadership. Pope Alexander VI (r. 1492–1503) financed his son Cesare Borgia's attempts to carve out a principality for himself along the northern fringe of the Papal State. He also married off his daughter, Lucrezia Borgia, in succession to several different Italian princes who were useful allies in the pope's military ambitions. The members of the Borgia family made many enemies who accused them of all kinds of evil deeds, including the poisoning of one of Lucrezia's husbands, brother-sister and father-daughter incest, and conducting orgies in the Vatican. Even though many of these allegations were false or exaggerated, the reputation of the papacy suffered. Alexander's successor, Pope Julius II (r. 1503–1513), continued to pursue a military strategy for regaining control of the Papal State. He took his princely role so seriously that he donned armor, personally led troops during the siege of Bologna, and rather presumptuously rewarded himself with a triumphal procession, an honor that had been granted in ancient Rome to victorious generals such as Julius Caesar.

Many of the Renaissance popes were embarrassed by the squalor of the city of Rome, an unfit place to serve as the capital of the Church. A number of popes sought to create a capital they felt worthy for Christendom. The most clear-sighted of the builders of Rome was Pope Leo X (r. 1513–1521), the second son of Lorenzo the Magnificent. Educated by the circle of scholars who surrounded the Medicis, Leo was destined for a clerical career at a young age. He received a doctorate in canon law and was made a cardinal at age 17. During Leo's pontificate, Rome was transformed into one of the centers of Renaissance culture. Leo made the University of Rome a distinguished institution through the appointment of famous professors. For his own private secretaries he chose intellectuals who had already gained an international reputation for their scholarship and learning. Leo's ambition can best be measured in his project to rebuild St. Peter's Basilica as the largest church in the world. He tore down the old basilica, which had been a major pilgrimage destination for more than a thousand years, and planned the great church that still dominates Rome today.

The Contradictions of the Patriarchal Family

The contradiction between the theory of the patriarchal family and realities of family life produced much of the creative energy of the Italian Renaissance. When theory dramatically departed from actual experience, many people began to distrust the theory and seek alternative ways of looking at society and the world. That is what happened in Renaissance Italy.

DOCUMENT

Juan Luis Vives, *The Office and Dutie of an Husband* (1529)

Advice books on family management, such as Leon Battista Alberti's *Four Books on the Family* (written in the 1430s), provide evidence for the widespread concern for better understanding the family. Such books propounded the theory that husbands and fathers ruled. These patriarchs were the sources of social order and discipline, and not just within the family but of all of society. Groups of male relatives

were responsible for rectifying injuries and especially for avenging any assault on a family member. Nearly all marriages were arranged by fathers or male guardians who sought beneficial financial and political alliances with other families, a situation that gave older men an advantage in the marriage market, as they were usually better off financially than younger ones. As a result, husbands tended to be much older than wives. In Florence in 1427, for example, the typical first marriage was between a 30-year-old man and an 18-year-old woman. Husbands were encouraged to treat their spouses with a kindly but distant paternalism. All women were supposed to be kept under strict male supervision, and the only honorable role for an unmarried woman was as a nun.

However, the reality of family life often departed from theory. A number of factors explain the disparity. First, a variety of circumstances made family life insecure and the very survival of families tenuous—death from epidemic diseases, especially the Black Death, and separations due to marital strife, which were common enough even though divorce was not possible. Second, the wide age gap between husbands and wives meant that husbands were likely to die long before their wives, and thus many women became widows at a relatively young age with children still to raise. Third, many men, especially international merchants and migrant workers, were away from their families for long periods of time. Regardless of the patriarchal assertion that

Vendetta as Private Justice

During the fourteenth and fifteenth centuries, the official justice provided by the law courts competed with the private justice of revenge. Private justice was based on the principle of retaliation. When someone was murdered or assaulted, it became the obligation of the victim's closest male relatives to avenge the injury by harming the perpetrator or one of his relatives to a similar degree. A son was obliged to avenge the death of his father, a brother the injury of his brother. Given the weakness of most governments, the only effective justice was often private justice or, as the Italians called it, *vendetta*. As the most significant source of disorder during the Renaissance, vendetta was a practice that all governments struggled to eradicate.

One of the attributes that distinguished an act of private justice from a simple violent crime was that avengers committed their acts openly and even bragged about what they had done. A criminal covered his tracks. An avenger did not. Therefore, the violence of an act of revenge was carried out in public so there would be witnesses, and often it was performed in a highly symbolic way in order to humiliate the victim as much as possible.

In Renaissance Italy private justice took many forms, but always such acts sought to do more than create another victim. They sought to deliver a message. After a period of disorder in 1342, the Florentines granted extraordinary judicial powers to a soldier of fortune, Walter of Brienne, known as the Duke of Athens. But Walter offended many Florentines by arresting and executing members of prominent families. In September of that year a crowd led by these families besieged the government palace and captured the duke's most hated henchmen, the "conservator" and his son.

Even though the conservator had been the highest judge of Florence, the Florentines repudiated his authority by obtaining revenge. An eyewitness reported what happened next:

The son was pushed out in front, and they cut him up and dismembered him. This done, they shoved out the conservator himself and did the same to him. Some carried a piece of him on a lance or sword throughout the city, and there were those so cruel, so bestial in their anger, and full of such hatred that they ate the raw flesh.[3]

This story of revenge in the most sophisticated city in Europe on the eve of the Renaissance illustrates the brutality of private justice, especially the need to make a public example of the victim.

Another account from nearly 200 years later tells of the murder of Antonio Savorgnan, a nobleman from Friuli who had killed a number of his enemies the previous year. Rather than attempting to have Antonio arrested as they could have, the murderers avenged their dead relatives through private justice. One eyewitness recounted that Antonio was attacked while leaving church, and then, "It was by divine miracle that Antonio Savorgnan was wounded: his head opened, he fell down, and he never spoke another word. But before he died, a giant dog came there and ate all his brains, and one cannot possibly deny that his brains were eaten."[4] This time a dog did the avengers' work for them. Perhaps the strangest detail in both of these accounts is that the writers wanted readers to believe that the victim had been eaten, either by humans or by a dog. Why was this an important message to get across?

The eating of a victim was one way avengers signaled that they were killing as an act of private justice. In both of the killings just described, the killers were retaliating for the murder of one of their close relatives and symbolically announcing to others that the attack was not an unjustifiable crime but a legitimate act of revenge. To convey that message, avengers could not ambush their opponent in the dark of night but were obliged to confront him openly in broad daylight before witnesses. There had to be the appearance, at least, of a fair fight. Murderers symbolized their revenge in several ways: They butchered the corpse as if it were the prey of a hunt or fed the remains to hunting dogs or even ate it themselves in what appeared to be a frenzy of revenge.

One of the major objectives of any government, whether a tiny city-state or a great monarchy, was to substitute public justice for private justice; but the persistence of tradition was strong. During the sixteenth century as governments sought to control violence and as the Renaissance values of moderation spread, a different kind of private justice appeared—the duel. Traditionally, the duel had been a means of solving disputes among medieval knights, but during the sixteenth century duels became much more common, even among men who had never been soldiers. Dueling required potential combatants to conform to an elaborate set of rules: The legitimate causes for a challenge to a duel were few, the combatants had to recognize each other as honorable men, the actual fight took place only after extensive preparations, judges who were experts on honor had to serve as witnesses, and the combatants had to swear to accept the outcome and abstain from fighting one another in the future.

The very complexity of the rules of dueling limited the vio-

Private Justice
In Titian's painting *The Bravo* (ca. 1515/1520), a man wearing a breastplate and hiding a drawn sword behind his back grabs the collar of his enemy before assaulting him. To enact honorable revenge the attacker could not stab his enemy in the back but had to give him a chance in a fair fight.

lence of private justice, and that meant that fewer fights actually took place. Dueling, in effect, civilized private justice. Although dueling was always against the law, princes tended to wink at duels because they kept conflicts among their own courtiers under control. At the same time, governments became far less tolerant of other forms of private justice, especially among the lower classes. They at-tempted to abolish feuds and vendettas and insisted that all disputes be submitted to the courts.

Questions of Justice

1. How did the persistence of private justice present a challenge to the emerging states of the Renaissance?
2. In what ways did private justice reflect Renaissance values, such as the value of keeping appearances?

Taking It Further

Muir, Edward. *Mad Blood Stirring: Vendetta in Renaissance Italy.* 1998. A study of the most extensive and long-lasting vendetta in Renaissance Italy. It traces the evolution of vendetta violence into dueling.

Weinstein, Donald. *The Captain's Concubine: Love, Honor, and Violence in Renaissance Tuscany.* 2000. A delightfully engaging account of an ambush and fight among two nobles over a woman who was the concubine of the father of one of the fighters and the lover of the other. It reveals the disturbing relationship between love and violence in Renaissance society.

The Age Gap Between Husbands and Wives

In Renaissance Italy older men typically married much younger women. In the middle of this fresco, *Marriage of the Virgin* by Fra Angelico, the young Mary holds out her hands to a rabbi who joins her in marriage to the gray-bearded Joseph. Behind Joseph young men hold up their fists as if to strike him. Fra Angelico dramatically conveys the anger of the young men about a marriage system that made it impossible for them to compete for brides with the older men.

fathers should be in control, in reality they were often absent or dead.

The contradiction between the theory of patriarchy and the fragile reality of family life had far-reaching consequences. Instead of wielding a strong hand over their families, most fathers were remote figures who had little direct influence. Mothers who were supposed to be modest, obedient to their husbands, and invisible to the outside world not only had to raise children alone but often had to manage their dead or absent husband's business and political affairs. By necessity, many resilient, strong, and active women were deeply involved in the management of worldly affairs, and mothers had much more direct influence on children than fathers. Despite the theory of patriarchy, the families of Renaissance Italy were in fact matriarchies in which mothers ruled.

The contradictions of family life became one of the most discussed problems in the Renaissance. Making fun of impotent old husbands married to beautiful but unfulfilled young wives became a major theme in comic drama. Given the demographic ravages of the Black Death, concern for the care of babies preoccupied preachers, while the many Renaissance paintings in which little cherubs seem to fall from the sky manifested a widespread craving for healthy children. A deep anxiety produced by the contradictions of family life and by the tenuous hold many families had on survival stimulated the distinctive family theme in the culture of Renaissance Italy.

The Influence of Ancient Culture

■ How did Renaissance thinkers create historical perspective and devise methods of criticism for interpreting texts?

The need in Renaissance Italy to provide effective models for how citizens, courtiers, and families should behave stimulated a reexamination of ancient culture. The civilizations of ancient Greece and Rome had long fascinated the educated classes in the West. In Italy, where most cities were built around or on top of the ruins of the ancient past, the seduction of antiquity was particularly pronounced. During the fourteenth and fifteenth centuries many Italian thinkers and artists attempted to foster a rebirth of ancient cultures. At first they merely attempted to imitate the Latin style of the best Roman writers. Then scholars tried to do the same thing with Greek, stimulated in part by direct contact with Greek-speaking refugees from Byzantium. Artists trekked to Rome to fill their notebooks with sketches of ancient ruins, sculptures, and medallions. Wealthy collectors hoarded manuscripts of ancient philosophy, built libraries to house them, bought up every piece of ancient sculpture they could find, and dug up ruins to find more antiquities to adorn their palaces. Patrons demanded that artists produce new works that imitated the styles of the ancients and that displayed a similar concern for rendering natural forms. Especially prized were lifelike representations of the human body.

Patrons, artists, and scholars during the Renaissance not only appreciated the achievements of the past but began to understand the enormous cultural distance between themselves and the ancients. That insight made their perspective historical. They also developed techniques of literary analysis to determine when a particular text had been written and to differentiate authentic texts from ones that had been corrupted by the mistakes of copyists. That ability made their perspective critical.

Petrarch and the Illustrious Ancients

The founder of the historical critical perspective that characterized the Renaissance was Francesco Petrarca (1304–1374), known in English as Petrarch. In contrast to the medieval thinkers who admired the ancients and treated their words as repositories of eternal wisdom, Petrarch discovered that the ancients were mere men much like himself. More than anything else, that insight might distinguish what was new about the Italian Renaissance, and Petrarch was the first to explore its implications.

Petrarch's early fame came from his poetry, in both his native Italian and Latin. In an attempt to improve his Latin style, Petrarch engaged in a detailed study of the best ancient Roman writers and searched to find old manuscripts that were the least corrupted by copyists. In that search he was always watching for anything by the Roman orator Cicero (106–43 B.C.E.), who was the Latinist most revered for literary style. In 1345 Petrarch briefly visited Verona to see what he could find in the library of a local monastery. While thumbing through the dusty volumes, he excitedly happened upon a previously unknown collection of letters Cicero had written to his friend Atticus.

As Petrarch began to read the letters, however, he suffered a profound shock. Cicero had a reputation as the greatest sage of the Romans, a model of good Latin style, of philosophical sophistication, and most of all of high ethical standards. But in the letters Petrarch found not sage moral advice but gossip, rumors, and crude political calculations. Cicero looked like a scheming politician, a man of crass ambition rather than grand philosophical wisdom. Although Petrarch could never forgive Cicero for being less than what he had avowed in his philosophical writings, he had discovered the human Cicero rather than just the idealized Cicero, a man so human you could imagine having a conversation with him.

And having a conversation was precisely what Petrarch set out to do. Cicero, however, had been dead for 1,388 years. So Petrarch wrote a letter to Cicero's ghost. Adopting Cicero's own elegant Latin style, Petrarch lambasted the Roman for going against the moral advice he had given others. Petrarch quoted Cicero back to Cicero, asking him how he could be such a hypocrite:

DOCUMENT

Petrarch, Letters to Cicero (14th c.)

> *Your letters I sought for long and diligently; and finally, where I least expected it, I found them. At once I read them, over and over, with the utmost eagerness. And as I read I seemed to hear your bodily voice, O Marcus Tullius [Cicero's given names], saying many things, uttering many lamentations, ranging through many phases of thought and feeling. I long had known how excellent a guide you have proved for others; at last I was to learn what sort of guidance you gave yourself. . . . Now it is your turn to be the listener.[5]*

Petrarch went on to lecture Cicero for his false dealings, his corruption, and his moral failures. The point of the exercise of writing a letter to a dead man was to compare the ideals Cicero had avowed in his philosophical work and the reality he seemed to have lived. Making comparisons is one of the elementary techniques of a critical method, and it became the hallmark of Petrarch's mode of analysis. Petrarch's letter reduced the stature of the ancients a bit, making them less like gods and more like other men who made mistakes and told lies. Petrarch ended this remarkable, unprecedented letter with a specific date, given in both the Roman and Christian ways, and a description of Verona's location in a way an ancient Roman would understand—as if he were making it possible for Cicero to find and answer him. This concern for historical precision typified the aspect that was most revolutionary about Petrarch's approach. No longer a repository of timeless truths, the ancient world became a specific time and place that Petrarch perceived to be at a great distance from himself. The ancients had ceased to be godlike; they had become historical figures. After his letter to Cicero, Petrarch wrote a series of letters to other illustrious ancients in which he revealed the human qualities and shortcomings of each.

Petrarch and his follower Lorenzo Valla (1407–1457) developed critical methods by editing classical texts, including parts of Livy's history of Rome, which was written about the time of Jesus. Petrarch compared different manuscript versions of Livy's work in an attempt to establish exactly the original words, a method very different from the medieval scribe's temptation to alter or improve a text as he saw fit. Petrarch strived to get the words right because he wanted to understand exactly what Livy had meant, a method now called the philological approach. Philology° is the comparative study of language, devoted to understanding the meaning of a word in a particular historical context. Valla elaborated on Petrarch's insights into philology to demonstrate that words do not have fixed meanings but take on different meanings depending on who is using them and when they were written. It was obvious, for example, that the word *virtue* had meant something quite different to the polytheist Livy than it did to readers in the fourteenth and fifteenth centuries, who understood virtue in Christian terms. A concern for philology gave Petrarch and his followers access to the individuality of a writer. In the particularity of words, Petrarch discovered the particularity of actual individuals who lived and wrote many centuries before.

An interest in the meaning of words led Petrarch to study the rhetoric° of language. Rhetoric refers to the art of persuasive or emotive speaking and writing. From his studies of rhetoric, Petrarch became less confident about the ability of language to represent truth than he was about its capacity to motivate readers and listeners to action. He came to think that rhetoric was superior to philosophy because he preferred a good man over a wise one, and rhetoric offered examples worthy of emulation rather than abstract principles subject to debate. Petrarch wanted people to behave morally, not just talk or write about morality. And he believed that the most efficient way to inspire his readers to do the right thing was to write moving rhetoric.

The Humanists: The Latin Point of View

Those who followed Petrarch's approach to the classical authors were the Renaissance humanists°. The Renaissance humanists studied Latin and sometimes Greek texts on grammar, rhetoric, poetry, history, and ethics. (The term *humanist* in the Renaissance meant something very different from what it means today—someone concerned with human welfare and dignity.) The humanists sought to resurrect a form of Latin that had been dead for more than a thousand years and was distinct from the living Latin used by the Church, law courts, and universities—which they thought was mediocre compared to ancient Latin. In this effort, humanists acquired a difficult but functional skill that opened a wide variety of employment opportunities to them and gave them great public influence. They worked as schoolmasters, secretaries, bureaucrats, official court or civic historians, and ambassadors. Many other humanists were wealthy men who did not need a job but were fascinated with the rhetorical capabilities of the new learning to persuade other people to do what they wanted them to do.

Because humanists could be found on different sides of almost all important questions of the day, the significance of their work lies less in what they said than in how they said it. They wrote about practically everything: painting pictures, designing buildings, planting crops, draining swamps, raising children, managing a household, and educating women. They debated the nature of human liberty, the virtues of famous men, the vices of infamous ones, the meaning of Egyptian hieroglyphics, and the cosmology of the universe.

How did the humanists' use of Latin words and grammar influence the understanding of this vast range of subjects? Their approach was entirely literary. When they wanted to design a building, they read ancient books on architecture instead of consulting masons and builders. By studying the ancients, humanists organized experience into new categories that changed people's perceptions of themselves, the society they lived in, and the universe they inhabited. Humanist writing revealed what might be called the *Latin point of view*. Each language organizes experience according to the needs of the people who speak it, and all languages make arbitrary distinctions, dividing up the world into different categories. People who study a foreign language run across these arbitrary distinctions when they learn that some expressions can never be translated exactly.

The humanists' recovery of the Latin point of view contributed new words, new sentence patterns, and new rhetorical models that often altered their own perceptions in very subtle ways. For example, when a fifteenth-century humanist examined what the ancient Romans had written about painting, he found the phrase *ars et ingenium. Ars* referred to skills that can be learned by following established rules and adhering to models provided by the best painters. Thus, the ability of a painter to draw a straight line, to mix colors properly, and to identify a saint with the correct symbol are examples of *ars* or what we would call craftsmanship. The meaning of *ingenium* was more difficult to pin down, however. It referred to the inventive capacity of the painter, to his or her ingenuity. The humanists discovered that the ancients had made a distinction between the craftsmanship and the ingenuity of a painter. As a result, when humanists and their pupils looked at paintings, they began to make the same distinction and began to admire the genius of artists whose work showed ingenuity as well as craftsmanship. Ingenuity came to refer to the ability of the painter to arrange figures in a novel way, to employ unusual colors, or to create emotionally exciting effects that conveyed piety, sorrow, or joy as the subject demanded. So widespread was the influence of the humanists that the most ingenious artists demanded higher prices and became the most sought after. In this way, creative innovation was encouraged in the arts, but it all started very simply with the introduction of new words into the Latin vocabulary of the people who paid for paintings. A similar process of establishing new categories altered every subject the humanists touched.

The humanist movement spread rapidly during the fifteenth century. Leonardo Bruni (ca. 1370–1444), who became the chancellor of Florence (the head of the government's bureaucracy), employed humanist techniques to defend the republican institutions and values of the city. Bruni's defense of republican government is called civic humanism°. He argued that the truly ethical man should devote himself to active service to his city rather than to passive contemplation in scholarly retreat or monastic seclusion. Thus Bruni formulated the ethic of responsible citizenship that remains today as necessary to sustain a free society. Given the supreme value Christianity had long placed on the passive contemplation of divine truth, Bruni's assertion that active public service constituted an even higher vocation was radical indeed.

Lorenzo Valla employed philological criticism to undermine papal claims to authority over secular rulers, such as

DOCUMENT

A Humanist Laments the Ruins of Rome

In 1430 the distinguished humanist Poggio Bracciolini (1380–1459) was working in Rome as a papal secretary. In this account he describes his and a friend's response to seeing the ruins of the once-great city of Rome. Poggio's lament and those of other humanists stimulated popes to commit themselves to the rebuilding of the city, but the enthusiasm to return Rome to its ancient splendor had some unfortunate side effects. Many of the building materials for the new Rome were pillaged from the ruins of the old Rome. As a result, much of the destruction of the ancient city of Rome occurred during the Renaissance.

Not long ago, after Pope Martin left Rome shortly before his death for a farewell visit to the Tuscan countryside, and when Antonio Lusco, a very distinguished man, and I were free of business and public duties, we used to contemplate the desert places of the city with wonder in our hearts as we reflected on the former greatness of the broken buildings and the vast ruins of the ancient city, and again on the truly prodigious and astounding fall of its great empire and the deplorable inconstancy of fortune. And once when we had climbed the Capitoline hill, and Antonio, who was a little weary from riding, wanted to rest, we dismounted from our horses and sat down together within the very enclosures of the Tarpeian ruins, behind the great marble threshold of its very doors, as I believe, and the numerous broken columns lying here and there, whence a view of a large part of the city opens out.

Here, after he had looked about for some time, sighing and as if struck dumb, Antonio declared, "Oh, Poggio, how remote are these ruins from the Capitol that our Vergil celebrated: 'Golden now, once bristling with thorn bushes.' How justly one can transpose this verse and say: 'Golden once, now rough with thorns and overgrown with briars.'"

Source: "The Ruins of Rome" by Poggio Bracciolini, translated by Mary Martin McLaughlin, from *The Portable Renaissance Reader* by James B. Ross and Mary Martin McLaughlin, editors, copyright 1953, renewed © 1981 by Viking Penguin Inc. Used by permission of Viking Penguin, a division of Penguin Group (USA) Inc.

---

the princes and republics of Italy. He did so by proving that a famous document, the Donation of Constantine, was a forgery. The Donation recorded that during the fourth century the emperor Constantine had transferred his imperial authority in Italy to the pope, and although Renaissance popes could not get what they wanted just by citing this document, it was part of the legal arsenal popes used against secular rulers. Valla demonstrated that the Donation had actually been forged in the ninth century, a work of detection that showed how the historical analysis of documents could be immensely useful for resolving contemporary political disputes. The controversy between defenders and enemies of the papacy that followed Valla's discovery stimulated the demand for humanist learning because it became clear that humanist methods were necessary for political debate and propaganda.

The intellectual curiosity of the humanists led them to master many fields of endeavor. This breadth of accomplishment contributed to the ideal of the "Renaissance Man," a person who sought excellence in everything he did. No one came closer to this ideal than Leon Battista Alberti (1404–1472). As a young man, Alberti wrote Latin comedies and satirical works that drew on Greek and Roman models, but as he matured he tackled more serious subjects. Although he was a bachelor and thus knew nothing firsthand about marriage, he drew upon the ancient writers to create the most influential Renaissance book on the family, which included sections on relations between husbands and wives, raising children, and estate management. He composed the first grammar of the Italian language. He dabbled in mathematics and wrote on painting, law, the duties of bishops, love, horsemanship, dogs, agriculture, and flies. He mapped the city of Rome and wrote the most important fifteenth-century work on the theory and practice of architecture. His interest in architecture, moreover, was not just theoretical. In the last decades of his life, he dedicated much of his spare time to architectural projects that included restoring an ancient church in Rome, designing Renaissance façades for medieval churches, and building a palace for his most important patron. One of his last projects was the first significant work for making and deciphering secret codes in the West.

The humanists guaranteed their lasting influence through their innovations in the educational curriculum. The objective of humanist education was to create well-rounded male pupils (girls were not usually accepted in humanist schools) who were not specialists or professionals, such as the theologians, lawyers, and physicians trained in universities, but critical thinkers who could tackle any problems that life presented. It was a curriculum well suited for the active life of civic leaders, courtiers, princes, and churchmen. The influence of the humanist curriculum persists in the general-education requirements of modern universities, which require students, now of both sexes, to obtain intellectual breadth before they specialize in narrow professional training.

Historians have identified a few female humanists from the Renaissance. Because they were so unusual, learned humanist women were often ridiculed. Jealous men accused the humanist Isotta Nogarola (1418–1466) of promiscuity and incest, and other women insulted her in public. A famous male schoolmaster said that Isotta was too feminine in her writings and should learn how to find "a man within the woman."[6] Laura Cereta (1475–1506), who knew Greek as well as Latin and was adept at mathematics, answered the scorn of a male critic with rhetorical insult worthy of Petrarch himself:

> *I would have been silent, believe me, if that savage old enmity of yours had attacked me alone. . . . But I cannot tolerate your having attacked my entire sex. For this reason my thirsty soul seeks revenge, my sleeping pen is aroused to literary struggle, raging anger stirs mental passions long chained by silence. With just cause I am moved to demonstrate how great a reputation for learning and virtue women have won by their inborn excellence, manifested in every age as knowledge, the [purveyor] of honor. Certain, indeed, and legitimate is our possession of this inheritance, come to us from a long eternity of ages past.[7]*

These few humanist women can be seen as among the first feminists. They advocated female equality and female education but also urged women to take control of their own lives. Nogarola answered her critics in a typical humanist fashion by reinterpreting the past. Thinking at this time suggested that all women were the daughters of Eve, who in her weakness had submitted to the temptation of the serpent, which led to the exile of humanity from the Garden of Eden. Nogarola pointed out that Eve had been no weaker than Adam, who also ate of the forbidden fruit, and therefore women should not be blamed for the Fall from God's grace. Cereta was the most optimistic of the female humanists. She maintained that if women paid as much attention to learning as they did to their appearances, they would achieve equality. Despite the efforts of Cereta and other female humanists, progress in women's education was extremely slow. The universities remained closed to talented women. The first woman to earn a degree from a university did so in 1678, and it took another 200 years before very many others could follow her example.

Through the influence of the humanists, the Latin point of view permeated Renaissance culture. They educated generations of wealthy young gentlemen whose appreciation of antiquity led them to pay to collect manuscripts of ancient literature, philosophy, and science. These patrons were also responsible for encouraging artists to imitate the ancients. What began as a narrow literary movement became the stimulus to see human society and nature through entirely new eyes. Some humanists, especially in northern Europe, applied these techniques with revolutionary results to the study of the Bible and the sources of Christianity.

Understanding Nature: Moving Beyond the Science of the Ancients

The humanists' initial concern was to emulate the language of the ancients. Most of them preferred to spend time reading a book rather than observing the world around them. In fact, their methods were ill-suited to understanding nature, and when they wanted to explain some natural phenomenon such as the movement of blood through the body or the apparent movements of the planets and stars, they looked to ancient authorities for answers rather than to nature itself. The Renaissance humanists' most prominent contributions to science consisted of recovering classical texts and translating the work of ancient Greek scientists into the more widely understood Latin. This is in contrast to the scientific method of today, in which scientists form a hypothesis and then determine whether it is correct by observing the natural world as directly as possible. In contrast, Renaissance scientists searched for ancient texts about nature, and then debated about which ancient author had been correct.

These translated texts broadened the discussion of two subjects crucial to the scientific revolution of the late sixteenth and seventeenth centuries—astronomy and anatomy. In 1543 the Polish humanist Nicolaus Copernicus (1473–1543) resolved the complications in the cosmological system of the second-century astronomer Ptolemy. Whereas Ptolemy's writings had placed Earth at the center of the universe, Copernicus cited other ancient writers who put the sun in the center. Thus the first breakthrough in theoretical astronomy was achieved not by making new observations but by comparing ancient texts. Nothing was proven, however, until Galileo Galilei (1564–1642) turned his telescope to the heavens in 1610 to observe the stars through his own eyes rather than through an ancient text.

Andreas Vesalius (1514–1564) built upon recently published studies in anatomy from ancient Greece to write a survey of human anatomy, *On the Fabric of the Human Body* (1543), a book that encouraged dissection and anatomical observations. With Vesalius, anatomy moved away from relying exclusively on the authority of ancient books to encouraging medical students and physicians to examine the human body with their own eyes. Building upon Vesalius's work, Gabriele Falloppio (ca. 1523–1562) made many original observations of muscles, nerves, kidneys, bones, and most famously the "Fallopian tubes," which he described for the first time. By the late sixteenth century, astronomy and anatomy had surpassed what the ancients had known.

Besides recovering ancient scientific texts, the most important Renaissance contributions to science came secondhand from developments in the visual arts and technology. A number of Florentine artists experimented during the early fifteenth century with the application of mathematics to the preliminary design of paintings. The goal was to make paintings more accurately represent reality by creating the visual illusion of the third dimension of depth on a two-dimensional rectangular surface, a technique known as linear perspective (see next section). These artists contributed to a more refined understanding of how the eye perceives objects, and their understanding of how the eye worked led to experiments with glass lenses. A more thorough knowledge of optics made possible the invention of the telescope and microscope.

Of all the developments in the fifteenth century, however, none matched the long-term significance of a pair of rather simple inventions—cheap manufactured paper and the printing press. Paper made from rags created an inexpensive alternative to sheepskins, which had been the preferred medium for medieval scribes. And just as paper replaced sheepskin, the printing press replaced the scribe. Several Dutch and German craftsmen had experimented with printing during the 1440s, but credit for the essential innovation of movable metal type has traditionally been accredited to Johannes Gutenberg (ca. 1398–1468) of Mainz in the 1450s. German immigrants brought printing to Italy, which rapidly became the publishing center of Europe, largely because it boasted a large, literate urban population who bought books.

Scientific books accounted for only about 10 percent of the titles of the first printed books, but the significance of printing for science was greater than the sales figures would indicate. In addition to making ancient scientific texts more readily available, print meant that new discoveries and new ideas reached a wider audience, duplication of scientific investigation could be avoided, illustrations were standardized, and scientists built upon each other's work. With the invention of the printing press, scientific work became closely intertwined with publishing, so that published scientific work advanced science, and scientific work that was not published went largely unnoticed. It is revealing that Leonardo da Vinci (1452–1519), the greatest Renaissance observer of nature, contributed nothing to science because he failed to publish his findings. The fundamental principle of modern science and, in fact, of all modern scholarship is that research must be made available to everyone through publication.

Antiquity and Nature in the Arts

■ How did various attempts to imitate antiquity in the arts alter perceptions of nature?

More than any other age in Western history, the Italian Renaissance is identified with the visual arts. The unprecedented clusters of brilliant artists active in a handful of Italian cities during the fifteenth and sixteenth centuries overshadow any other contribution of Renaissance culture. Under the influence of the humanists, Renaissance artists began to imitate the sculpture, architecture, and painting of the ancients. At first they concerned themselves with merely copying ancient styles and poses. But soon they attempted a more sophisticated form of imitation. They wanted to understand the principles that made

CHRONOLOGY

The Influence of Ancient Culture

106–43 B.C.E.	Marcus Tullius Cicero, Latin rhetorician
1304–1374	Francesco Petrarca (Petrarch), first humanist
ca. 1370–1444	Leonardo Bruni, chancellor of Florence
1404–1472	Leon Battista Alberti, humanist and architect
1407–1457	Lorenzo Valla, humanist
1418–1466	Isotta Nogarola, first female humanist
ca. 1454	Johannes Gutenberg begins printing books
1473–1543	Nicolaus Copernicus, humanist and cosmological theorist
1475–1506	Laura Cereta, humanist
1514–1564	Andreas Vesalius, writer on anatomy
ca. 1523–1562	Gabriele Falloppio, conducted anatomical dissections
1564–1642	Galileo Galilei, astronomer

it possible for the artists from classical Greece and Rome to make their figures so lifelike. That led them to observe more directly nature itself, especially the anatomy of the human body. Renaissance art was driven by the passionate desire of artists and their patrons both to imitate ancient models and to imitate nature. These twin desires produced a certain creative tension in their work because the ancients, whose works of art often depicted gods and goddesses, had idealized and improved on what they observed in nature. Renaissance artists sought to depict simultaneously the ideal and the real—an impossible goal, but one that sparked remarkable creativity.

All of the Renaissance arts displayed the mark of patrons, the discriminating and wealthy people who controlled the city-states and who had been educated in humanist schools. Until the end of the sixteenth century, all painters, sculptors, and even poets worked for a patron. An individual patron would commission a particular work of art, such as an altar painting, portrait bust, or palace. The patron and artist would agree to the terms of the work through a contract, which might spell out in considerable detail exactly what the artist was to do, what kinds of materials he was to use, how much they could cost, how much he was allowed to rely on assistants, how much he had to do himself, and even how he was to arrange figures. The same sort of contract was used when work was commissioned by a group—for example, a guild, lay religious society (called a confraternity), convent, or government. Michelangelo Buonarroti (1475–1564) sculpted *David*, which has become the most famous work of Renaissance art, to fulfill a contract that had been debated in a committee meeting. Regardless of their talent or ingenuity, artists were never free agents who could do whatever they wanted.

Another kind of patron supported the career of an artist for an extended period of time. Princes, in particular, liked to take on an artist—give him a regular salary and perhaps even some official title—in exchange for having him perform whatever duties the prince deemed necessary. In this kind of an arrangement, Duke Lodovico Sforza (1451–1508) brought Leonardo da Vinci to Milan, where Leonardo painted a portrait of the duke's mistress, devised plans for a giant equestrian statue of the duke's father, designed stage sets and carnival pageants, painted the interior decorations of the castle, and did engineering work. The artist Cosmè Tura (active ca. 1450–1495) probably spent more time painting furniture than canvases for the Duke of Ferrara.

Most patrons supported the arts in order to enhance their own prestige and power. Some, such as Pope Julius II, had exceptional influence on the work of artists. He persuaded the very reluctant Michelangelo, who saw himself as a sculptor, to become a painter in order to decorate the ceiling of the Sistine Chapel.

Sculpture, Architecture, and Painting: The Natural and the Ideal

Just as humanists recaptured antiquity by collecting, translating, and analyzing the writings of classical authors, so Renaissance artists made drawings of surviving classical medals, sculpture, and architecture. Collected in sketch books, these drawings often served as pattern books from which the apprentices in artists' workshops learned how to draw. Because artists believed that the classical world enjoyed an artistic tradition vastly superior to their own, these sketches became valuable models from which other artists could learn. Two of the most influential Florentine artists, the architect Filippo Brunelleschi (1377–1446) and the sculptor Donatello (1386–1466), may have gone to Rome together as young men to sketch the ancient monuments. No Roman paintings survived into the fifteenth century (Pompeii, which proved to have a treasure trove of Roman art buried under layers of volcanic ash, had not yet been excavated), and no Renaissance artist ever saw a Greek building, so the only examples of ancient art to copy were the ruins of Roman buildings and a few surviving Roman

The Competition Panels of the Sacrifice of Isaac

These two panels were the finalists in a competition to design the cast bronze doors on the north side of the Baptistery in Florence. Each demonstrates a bold new design that attempted to capture the emotional trauma of the exact moment when an angel arrests Abraham's arm from sacrificing his son Isaac (Genesis 22:1–12). Both artists went on to be closely associated with the new style of the Renaissance. The panel on the left, by Filippo Brunelleschi, lost to the one on the right, by Lorenzo Ghiberti. Notice how the Ghiberti relief better conveys the drama of the scene by projecting the elbow of Abraham's upraised arm outward toward the viewer. As a result the viewer's line of sight follows the line of the arm and knife directly toward Isaac's throat.

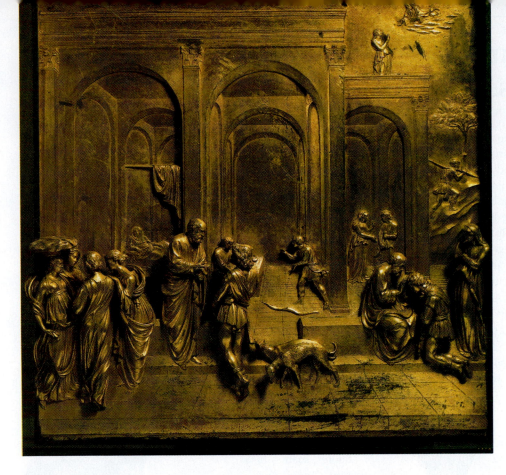

Linear Perspective

In these panels Ghiberti broke out of the Gothic frame that had inhibited him in the panels on the north doors. Now he was free to explore the full potential of the newly discovered principles of linear perspective.

statues. As a result, architecture and sculpture led the way in the imitation of ancient art, but Renaissance artists imposed their own sensibilities on the ancients as much as they imitated them.

The Renaissance style evolved in Florence during the first few decades of the fifteenth century. In 1401 the 24-year-old Brunelleschi entered a competition to design bronze relief panels for the north doors of the Baptistery. He narrowly lost to the even younger Lorenzo Ghiberti (1378–1455). Look at the illustrations on page 360. The rules of the competition required both artists to fit their relief panels within a fancy decorative frame in the Gothic style, which had been in fashion for nearly 300 years. However, both competition relief panels seem constrained by the curves and angles of the frame. For example, some of the figures in the Brunelleschi panel project outside it as if trying to escape the restraints of the style. Ghiberti's relief shows the two characteristic elements of the early Renaissance style: The head of Isaac is modeled after a classical Roman sculpture, and the figures and horse on the left are depicted as realistically as possible. In these elements, Ghiberti was imitating both antiquity and nature.

Ghiberti worked on the north doors for twenty-one years and won such renown as a result that when he finished he was immediately offered a new commission to complete panels for the east portal. These doors, begun in 1425, took twenty-seven years to finish. In the east doors, Ghiberti substituted a simple square frame for the Gothic frame of the north doors, thereby liberating his composi-

tion. In the illustration above, which depicts the biblical story of Jacob and Esau, the squares in the pavement set up an underlying geometry to the scene. The background architecture of rounded arches and crisp-angled columns in the classical style creates the illusion of depth in the relief. This illusion is achieved through linear perspective°, that is, the use of geometrical principles to depict a three-dimensional space on a flat, two-dimensional surface. The rigorous geometry of the composition provided the additional benefit of allowing Ghiberti to divide up the space to depict several different scenes within one panel. In the panels of the east doors, he created the definitive Renaissance interpretation of the ancient principles of the harmony produced by geometry. Michelangelo later remarked that the doors were fit to serve as the "gates of paradise."

After failing to win the competition for the Baptistery doors, Brunelleschi turned to architecture. In his own time, Brunelleschi was considered to have revived ancient Roman principles, but it is evident now that he was less a student of antiquity than an astutely original thinker. In his buildings he employed a proportional system of design that is best seen in his masterpiece, the Pazzi Chapel. He began with a basic geometric unit represented by each of the small rectangles clustered in groups of four on the upper third of the façade of the chapel. The height of each of these was approximately the height of an average man. All the other dimensions of the building were multiples of these basic rectangles. Thus the building was formed from the proportions of a human being. Brunelleschi employed

The Natural and the Ideal Body in Renaissance Art

During the Italian Renaissance artists depicted the human body, especially the nude body, with a greater sensitivity to anatomy than at any time since antiquity. In attempting to portray the human body, Renaissance sculptors and painters explored two possible approaches. Should they attempt to imitate nature by depicting human bodies as they really appear, or should they improve upon nature by representing human bodies in an idealized way?

The Florentine sculptor Donatello (1386–1466) was the master of the first approach, the naturalistic representation of the human body. His major achievement was solving the difficult technical problem of creating a freestanding life-size statue of a human being that looked as if the person depicted were standing in a natural way. In his solution, called *contraposto*, one leg of the human form is kept straight and the other is slightly bent, with the hips slanting in the opposite direction from the slant of the shoulders. One contemporary described Donatello's statues as so lively that they appeared to move. Following Donatello's lead, Florentine sculptors dedicated themselves to "the return to nature," the attempt to make inanimate works of art imitate not just ancient sculpture, but nature itself.

During the later Renaissance, Michelangelo Buonarroti (1475–1564) perfected the second approach by idealizing the human body. He did not want just to imitate nature, he wanted to surpass nature. His figures, such as his famous *David,* often seemed superhuman. In creating figures such as this, he brought the Renaissance preoccupation with antiquity full circle because many classical sculptors had intended to achieve the same effect. After all, most of their work was for polytheist temples, and by improving on nature they wanted to create images of the perfect bodies of the gods.

With Michelangelo, Western art entered an entirely new phase. He advanced art from the simple goal of imitating classical motifs and observing nature to a more grandiose goal of improving on the ancients and on nature. According to Michelangelo, because nature alone never achieved perfection, great art can be even more powerful than nature itself.

The Idealized Body
This larger-than-life figure of the biblical warrior King David transformed the young boy who slew the giant Goliath into a kind of superman whose physical bearing was greater than any normal man. Michelangelo altered the proportions of a natural man, making the head and hands significantly larger than normal. In its original placement on a staircase in a large open square, the statue towered above viewers.

The Naturalistic Body
In the *contraposto* pose of Donatello's David, the weight of the figure is carried on one leg of the human form, which appears straight and taut while the other seems relaxed and slightly bent.

For Discussion
How might the Renaissance humanist concerns for imitation produce both the artistic conceptions of naturalism and idealized beauty?

worked in fresco. A common form of decoration in churches, fresco was the technique of applying paint to wet plaster on a wall. In his great fresco cycle for the Brancacci chapel painted in the 1420s, Masaccio depicted street scenes from Florence complete with portraits of actual people, including himself. These were examples of naturalism. On other figures—Jesus, St. Peter, and St. John—he placed heads copied from ancient sculptures of gods. These were examples of idealized beauty, which were especially suitable for saints. In Masaccio's frescoes, both realistic and idealized figures appeared in the same work. The realistic figures helped viewers identify with the subject of the picture by allowing them to recognize people they actually knew. The idealized figures represented the saintly, whose superior moral qualities made them appear different from average people.

Masaccio developed the technical means for employing linear perspective in painting. To achieve the effect of perspective, he organized the entire composition around the position he assumed a viewer would take while looking at the picture. Once he established the point of view, he composed the picture to direct the viewer's gaze through the

The Engineering of Renaissance Architecture
Filippo Brunelleschi designed the dome for the cathedral in Florence, which became the most famous engineering achievement of the Renaissance. The dome spanned the largest space without columns to support it of any structure built since antiquity.

what he saw as the natural dimensions of humanity and transformed them into principles of architectural geometry. The result was a stunning impression of harmony in all the spaces of the building. For the dome of the Cathedral of Florence he employed innovative engineering technologies to span a huge space that had been left open for more than a century because no one knew how to build a dome over such a large expanse.

Later sculptors and architects built upon the innovations of Ghiberti and Brunelleschi. Florence became renowned for its tradition of sculpture, producing the two greatest Renaissance masters of the art, Donatello and Michelangelo. In their representations of the human form, both of these sculptors demonstrated the Renaissance preoccupation with the relationship between the ideal and the natural.

Conceptions of both the ideal and the natural are evident in the work of the most important painter of the early Florentine Renaissance, Masaccio (1401–ca. 1428), who

Portraits in Renaissance Paintings
During the fifteenth century artists idealized some figures and made others appear as natural as possible. Natural effects were created by incorporating portraits of actual people into scenes. In this example from a fresco by Masaccio depicting one of the miracles of St. Peter, the crowd witnessing the event includes portraits of notable artists. Starting from the far right are portraits of Brunelleschi, Leon Battista Alberti, Masaccio, and Masolino, who helped Masaccio paint the frescoes in the Brancacci Chapel from which this detail comes.

The Tribute Money:
Combining Natural and Idealized Representations

In this detail of a fresco of Christ and his apostles, Masaccio mixed naturalism and idealized beauty. The figure on the right with his back turned to the viewer is a tax collector, who is depicted as a normal human being. The head of the fourth figure to the left of him, who represents one of the apostles, was copied from an ancient statue that represents ancient ideals of beauty.

pictorial space. In *The Tribute Money,* he drew the spectator's eye to the head of Jesus, who is the figure in the middle pointing with his right hand. In addition, Masaccio recognized that the human eye perceives an object when light shines on it to form lighted surfaces and shadows. He used this understanding in creating a painting technique called *chiaroscuro* ("light and shade"). There is a single source of light in the painting coming from the same direction as the light in the room. That light defines figures and objects in the painting through the play of light and shadow. The strokes of Masaccio's paintbrush tried to duplicate the way natural light plays upon surfaces.

The techniques developed by Masaccio came to complete fulfillment in the career of Leonardo da Vinci (1452–1519). So compelling was Leonardo's curiosity and desire to tackle new problems that many of his paintings remained unfinished. He was a restless experimenter, never settling on simple solutions. Because of experiments Leonardo made with paint, his *Last Supper* fresco in Milan has seriously deteriorated. His mature works, such as *Mona Lisa,* completely reconciled the technical problems of representing human figures with realistic accuracy and the spiritual goal of evoking deep emotions. Unlike some of his predecessors, who grouped figures in a painting as if they were statues, Leonardo managed to make his figures appear to interact and communicate with one another.

The technique of painting with oils achieved new levels among painters in the Netherlands and in Flanders (in present-day Belgium, but at the time a province in the Duchy of Burgundy). By carefully layering numerous coats of tinted oil glazes over the surface of the painting, these painters created

DOCUMENT

Vasari on Leonardo da Vinci

IMAGE

Leonardo da Vinci, *Madonna with the Carnation,* c. 1435

Leonardo Invents an Airplane

Leonardo da Vinci's notebooks are filled with numerous examples of his unprecedented inventions. In this drawing he designed the fuselage of a flying machine. However, Leonardo had no influence at all on science or technology because he kept his inventions in his secret notebooks, and no one knew about them until they were discovered centuries later.

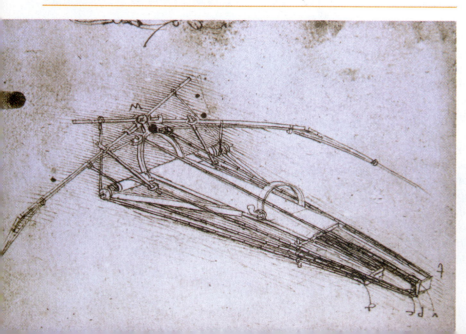

Northern Renaissance Art

In this fifteenth-century Flemish painting by Jan van Eyck, the use of oil paint and glazes made it possible to convey the shimmering surfaces of the brass chandelier and mirror hanging in the background. Shown in the mirror are the backs of the posing couple and the artist at his easel. Northern European artists delighted in using oils and glazes to create visual tricks, such as mirrored images. This is a portrait of Giovanni Arnolfini and Giovanna Cenami, who were married in 1434. Arnolfini was an Italian banker residing in the Flemish city of Bruges.

a luminous surface that gave the illusion of depth. The use of glazes enabled painters to blend brushstrokes in a way that made them virtually imperceptible. As a result Flemish and Dutch painters excelled in painting meticulous details, such as the textures of textiles, the reflections of gems, and the features of distant landscapes. Jan van Eyck (ca. 1395–1441) was the most famous Flemish painter. He worked as a court painter for the Duke of Burgundy, for whom he undertook many kinds of projects including decorating his palaces and designing stage sets and ornaments for festivals. His oil paintings were so famous that he was much praised by the Italian humanists, and numerous Italian patrons, including the Medicis, bought his works.

Most humanist theorists of painting linked artistic creativity with masculinity. By the sixteenth century, however, these theorists were proved wrong, as a number of female painters rose to prominence. The most notable was Sofonisba Anguissola (ca. 1532–1625). Born into an aristocratic family in Cremona, Italy, she received a humanist education along with her five sisters and brother. Because she was a woman, she was prohibited from studying anatomy or drawing male models. As a result she specialized in portraits, often of members of her family, and self-portraits. She developed a distinctive style of depicting animated faces. Her example inspired other aristocratic women to take up painting.

Music of the Emotions

Renaissance humanists' fascination with the visual arts of the ancients led them to assume that composers should imitate ancient music. But in attempting to turn humanist theories about music into real music, fifteenth-century composers faced a formidable problem—no one had the slightest clue what ancient Greek music actually sounded like. As a result, musical innovations lagged behind the other arts until the late sixteenth century, when a musical Renaissance finally took hold.

During the fourteenth and fifteenth centuries the principal composers came from France and the Netherlands. The greatest of them, Josquin de Prez (ca. 1440–1521), was born

and trained in the Netherlands and later found patrons in Milan, Rome, and Ferrara. His finest talent as a composer consisted of his ability to enhance musically the meaning of lyrics. In contrast to Josquin's sensitivity to matching music and lyric, most other composers relied on stereotypical rhythmic patterns and a simple melodic line that had no connection to the text. In fact, almost any lyric could be sung to the same music.

Recognizing that the music of their time did not measure up to what ancient writers had reported about the emotional intensity of their music, several prominent musician-humanists conducted extensive discussions about how to combine music and words in a way that would create a fuller aesthetic and emotional experience. The initial consequence of these discussions was the Renaissance madrigal, a type of song in which the music closely followed a poetic lyric to accentuate the shades of textual meaning. For example, when the text described a happy mood, the music would rise up the scale. A somber text would be lower-pitched. When the lyric described agitation or fear, the rhythm would quicken in imitation of the heart beating faster.

The most important consequence of the discussions about the need for a richer musical experience was the invention of opera° during the final decades of the sixteenth century. A group of humanist thinkers called the *Camerata* thought the power of ancient Greek music could be recovered by writing continuous music to accompany a full drama. The drama was performed as a kind of speech-song with the range of pitch and rhythms closely following those of natural speech. Singers were accompanied by a small ensemble of musicians. The first operas composed in this vein were by Jacopo Peri (1561–1633) and Giulio Caccini (ca. 1550–1618) and were performed in Florence

at the Grand Duke's court around 1600. These lengthy, bloated works attracted little attention among audiences, and opera likely would have sunk under its own weight had it not been for Claudio Monteverdi (1567–1643), who discovered its dramatic and lyrical potential. His sumptuous productions employed large ensembles of singers and instrumentalists, punctuated speech-song with arias (long sung solos) and dances, and included magnificent stage machines that simulated earthquakes, fires, and battles. Under Monteverdi's masterful hand, opera became the first complete multimedia art form. Arias from his productions became popular hits sung on every street corner, and opera moved from being a private amusement for princely courtiers to mass entertainment. The first public opera house opened in Venice in 1637. By the end of the seventeenth century, Venice boasted seventeen opera houses for a population of only 140,000. With the rise of opera houses and theaters for plays, the close bond between patrons and artists began to break down. Until then, artists were bound by the wishes of patrons. Now they began to serve the much larger marketplace for popular entertainment.

The Early Modern European State System

■ **How did the monarchies of western Europe gather the strength to become more assertive and more effective during the last half of the fifteenth and early sixteenth centuries?**

The civic independence that had made the Italian Renaissance possible was profoundly challenged during the Italian Wars (1494–1530). During these wars France, Spain, and the Holy Roman Empire attempted to carve up the peninsula for themselves, and the Italian city-states were thrown into turmoil. By 1530 the Italian city-states, with the exception of Venice, had lost their independence to the triumphant king of Spain. The surrender of the rich city-states of Italy was the first and most prominent sign of a major transformation in the European system of states. The age of city-states was over because they could never muster the level of materiel and manpower necessary to put and keep a large army in the field. Only the large monarchies of the West could do that. The Italian Wars revealed the outlines of the early modern European state system, which was built on the power of large countries that had been brought under control by their own kings. These kings amassed an unprecedented level of resources that not only crushed Italy but made possible the European domination of much of the globe through establishment of colonies in the Americas, Asia, and eventually Africa.

Monarchies: The Foundation of the State System

During the last half of the fifteenth century, the monarchies of western Europe began to show signs of recovery from the turmoil of the fourteenth and early fifteenth centuries, which had been marked by famine, plague, revolts, and the Hundred Years' War. France and England ended the Hundred Years' War, which had bled both kingdoms of men and resources during the century before 1453. England escaped from its civil war, the War of the Roses, in 1485. The kingdoms of Castile and Aragon joined in 1479 to create the new kingdom of Spain, which in 1492 completed the reconquest of territories from the Muslims that had been underway since the eleventh century. The Holy Roman Empire, which became allied to Spain through marriage, pursued a grand new vision for unifying the diverse principalities of Germany.

The early modern European state system was the consequence of five developments. First, governments established standing armies. As a result of the military revolution that brought large numbers of infantrymen to the field of battle and gunpowder cannons to besiege cities and castles, governments were obliged to modernize their armies or face defeat. Since the ninth century, kings had relied on feudal levies, in which soldiers were recruited to fulfill their personal obligation to a lord, but by the late fifteenth century governments began to organize standing armies. These armies enjoyed high levels of professionalism and skill, but they were very expensive to maintain because the soldiers had to be regularly paid. Moreover, the new artillery was costly, and improvements in the effectiveness of artillery bombardments necessitated extensive improvements in the walls of castles, fortresses, and cities. As a result, kings were desperate for new revenues.

The need for revenues led to the second development, the systematic expansion of taxation. Every European state struggled with the problem of taxation. The need to tax efficiently produced the beginnings of a bureaucracy of tax assessors and collectors in many states.

People naturally resisted the burden of new taxes, and monarchs naturally responded to the resistance. This tension led to the third development. Monarchs attempted to weaken the institutional seats of resistance by abolishing the tax-exempt privileges of local communities and ignoring regional assemblies and parliaments that were supposed to approve new taxes. During the twelfth and thirteenth centuries, effective government was local government, and kings seldom had the power to interfere in the affairs of towns and regions. During the fifteenth century, however,

kings everywhere attempted to eliminate or erode the independence of towns and regional parliaments in order to raise taxes more effectively and to express the royal will throughout the realm.

The fourth development, closely linked to the third, can be seen in monarchs' attempts to constrain the independence of the aristocracy and the Church. In virtually every kingdom, the most significant threats to the power of the king were the powerful aristocrats. In England a civil war among aristocrats almost tore the kingdom apart. Kings everywhere struggled to co-opt or force submission from these aristocrats. Likewise, the autonomy of the Church threatened monarchical authority, and most monarchs took measures to oblige churchmen to act as agents of government policy.

The fifth development in the evolution of the European state system was the institution of resident ambassadors. During the Italian Wars, the kings of Europe began to exchange permanent, resident ambassadors who were responsible for informing their sovereign about conditions in the host country and representing the interests of their country abroad. Resident ambassadors became the linchpins in a sophisticated information network that provided intelligence about the intentions and capabilities of other kings, princes, and cities. These ambassadors typically enjoyed a humanist education, which helped them adapt to many strange and unpredictable situations, understand foreign languages, negotiate effectively, and speak persuasively. Ambassadors cultivated courtly manners, which smoothed over personal conflicts. For the development of the new state system, gathering reliable information became just as important as maintaining armies and collecting taxes.

France: Consolidating Power and Cultivating Renaissance Values

With the largest territory in western Europe and a population of more than 16 million, France had the potential to become the most powerful state in Europe if the king could figure out how to take advantage of the kingdom's size and resources. By 1453 the Hundred Years' War between France and England had come to an end. With the inspiration of Joan of Arc and with the reform of royal finances by the merchant-banker Jacques Coeur, King Charles VII (r. 1422–1461) expelled the English and regained control of his kingdom. Under Charles, France created its first professional army. Equally important, during the Hundred Years' War the Pragmatic Sanction of Bourges° (1438) guaranteed the virtual autonomy of the French Church from papal control, giving the French king unparalleled opportunities to interfere in religious affairs and to exploit Church revenues for government purposes.

Louis XI (r. 1461–1483), called the "Spider King" because of his fondness for secret intrigue, took up the challenge of consolidating power over the great nobles of his kingdom, who thwarted his state building and threatened his throne. When Louis came to power, the Duchy of

Brittany was virtually independent; one great aristocrat, René of Anjou, controlled more territory and was richer than the king himself; and, most dangerous of all, the dukes of Burgundy had carved out their own splendid principality, which celebrated extravagant forms of courtly ritual and threatened to eclipse the prestige of France itself.

Against these powerful rivals, Louis turned to an equally powerful new weapon—the *taille*. During the final years of the Hundred Years' War, in order to support the army, the Estates General (France's parliament) granted the king the *taille*, the right to collect an annual direct tax. After the war, the tax continued and Louis turned it into a permanent source of revenue for himself and his successors. Armed with the financial resources of the *taille*, Louis took on his most rebellious vassal, Charles the Bold, the Duke of Burgundy, and in 1477 professional Swiss infantrymen in the pay of Louis defeated the plumed knights of Burgundy. Charles was killed in battle, and only his daughter Mary's hurried marriage to the Habsburg Archduke Maximilian bought the protection Burgundy needed to prevent France from seizing all of the duchy.

The monarch most responsible for the spread of Renaissance culture in France was Francis I (r. 1515–1547), a sportsman and warrior who thrilled to the frenzy of battle. Much of his early career was devoted to pursuing French interests in the Italian Wars, until he was captured in battle in 1525 in Italy. Thereafter he focused more on patronizing Italian artists and humanists at his court and importing Italian Renaissance styles. He had the first Renaissance-style chateau built in the Loire Valley and hired artists, including Leonardo da Vinci. As a result of Francis's patronage, Italy was no longer the exclusive center of Renaissance culture.

Spain: Unification by Marriage

In the early fifteenth century the Iberian peninsula was a diverse place, lacking political unity. It was home to several different kingdoms—Portugal, Castile, Navarre, and Aragon, which were all Christian, and Granada, which was Muslim. Each kingdom had its own laws, political institutions, customs, and languages. Unlike France, the Christian kingdoms of medieval Iberia were poor, underpopulated, and preoccupied with the reconquest, the attempt to drive

---

DOCUMENT

The Expulsion of the Jews from Spain

In 1492 after the conquest of Granada, the last Muslim kingdom on the Iberian peninsula, Ferdinand and Isabella ordered the expulsion of all Jews, who were given three months to leave Spain. Some sought an agreement to remain in the country in return for the payment of a large sum of money. However, the Jews soon discovered that was impossible. This account was written by a Jew living in Italy in 1495 who assembled his information from the reports of Jewish refugees.

Then they saw that there was evil determined against them by the King, and they gave up the hope of remaining. But the time had become short, and they had to hasten their exodus from Spain. They sold their houses, their landed estates, and their cattle for very small prices to save themselves. The King did not allow them to carry silver and gold out of his country, so that they were compelled to exchange their silver and gold for merchandise of cloths and skins and other things. . . .

One hundred and twenty thousand of them went to Portugal, according to a compact which a prominent man, Don Vidal bar Benveniste del Cavalleria, had made with the King of Portugal, and they paid one ducat for every soul, and the fourth part of all the merchandise they had carried thither; and he allowed them to stay in his country six months. This King acted much worse toward them than the King of Spain, and after the six months had elapsed he made

slaves of all those that remained in his country, and banished seven hundred children to a remote island to settle it, and all of them died. Some say that there were double as many. . . .

Many of the exiled Spaniards went to Mohammedan countries. . . . On account of their large numbers the Moors did not allow them into their cities, and many of them died in the fields from hunger, thirst, and lack of everything. The lions and bears, which are numerous in this country, killed some of them while they lay starving outside of the cities.

When the edict of expulsion became known in the other countries, vessels came from Genoa to the Spanish harbors to carry away the Jews. The crews of these vessels, too, acted maliciously and meanly toward the Jews, robbed them, and delivered some of them to the famous pirate of that time who was called the Corsair of Genoa. To those who escaped and arrived at Genoa the people of the city showed themselves merciless, and oppressed and robbed them, and the cruelty of their wicked hearts went so far that they took the infants from their mothers' breasts.

Many ships with Jews, especially from Sicily, went to the city of Naples on the coast. The King of this country was friendly to the Jews, received them all, and was merciful towards them, and he helped them with money. The Jews that were at Naples supplied them with food as much as they could, and sent around to the other parts of Italy to collect money to sustain them. . . . Even the Dominican Brotherhood acted mercifully toward them. . . .

Source: Jacob R. Marcus, ed., *The Jew in the Medieval World: A Source Book, 315–1791* (Cincinnati: Sinai Press, 1938), 51–55.

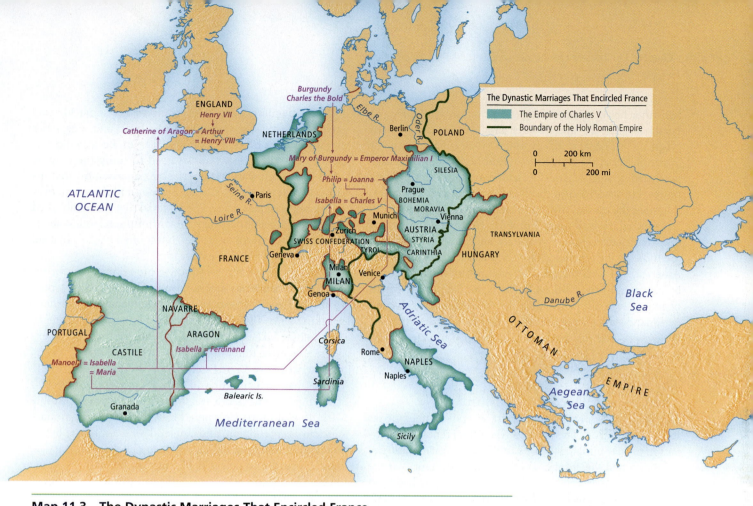

Map 11.3 The Dynastic Marriages That Encircled France

Through skillfully arranging the marriages of their sons and daughters, Ferdinand of Aragon and Isabella of Castile managed to completely surround the rival kingdom of France with a network of alliances.

the Muslims from the peninsula. There was little reason to assume that this region would become one of the greatest powers in Europe, the rival of France.

That rise to power began with a wedding. In 1469 Isabella, who later would become queen of Castile (r. 1474–1504), married Ferdinand, who later would be king of Aragon (r. 1479–1516). The objective of this arranged marriage was to solidify an alliance between the two kingdoms, not to unify them, but in 1479 Castile and Aragon were combined into the kingdom of Spain. Of the two, Castile was the larger, with a population of perhaps six million, and the richer because of the government-supported sheep-raising industry called the *Mesta*. Aragon had less than a million people and was a hybrid of three very distinct regions that had nothing in common except that they shared the same king. Together Isabella and Ferdinand, each still ruling their own kingdoms, at least partially subdued the rebellious aristocracy and built up a bureaucracy of well-educated middle-class lawyers and priests to manage the administration of the government.

The Christian kings of Iberia had long aspired to making the entire peninsula Christian. In 1492 the armies of Isabella and Ferdinand defeated the last remaining Iberian

Muslim kingdom of Granada. While celebrating the victory over Islam, the monarchs made two momentous decisions. The first was to rid Spain of Jews as well as Muslims. Isabella and Ferdinand decreed that within six months all Jews must either convert to Christianity or leave. To enforce conformity to Christianity among the converted Jews who did not leave, the king and queen authorized an ecclesiastical tribunal, the Spanish Inquisition, to investigate the sincerity of conversions. The second decision was Isabella's alone. She financed a voyage by a Genoese sea captain, Christopher Columbus, to sail west into the Atlantic in an attempt to reach India and China. Isabella's intention seems to have been to outflank the Muslim kingdoms of the Middle East and find allies in Asia. As we shall see in the next chapter, Columbus's voyage had consequences more far-reaching than Isabella's intentions, adding to the crown of Castile immense lands in the Americas.

Despite the diversity of their kingdoms, Isabella and Ferdinand made Spain a great power. The clever dynastic marriages they arranged for their children allowed Spain to encircle rival France and established the framework for the diplomatic relations among European states for the next century and a half (see Map 11.3). Their eldest daughter and, after her death, her sister were married to the king of Portugal. Their son and another daughter, Joanna, married offspring of Mary of Burgundy and the Emperor Maximilian I of the Holy Roman Empire. Joanna's marriage produced a son, Charles V, who amassed extraordinary power. He succeeded to the Habsburg lands of Burgundy, inherited the crowns of Castile and Aragon (r. 1516–1556), was elected Holy Roman Emperor (r. 1519–1558), ruled over the Spanish conquests in Italy, and was the emperor of the Indies, which included all of Spanish Central and South America. This was the greatest accumulation of territories by a European ruler since Charlemagne. The encirclement of France was completed with the wedding of Isabella and Ferdinand's daughter Catherine of Aragon to the Prince of Wales and, after his death, to his brother, King Henry VIII (r. 1509–1547) of England.

The Holy Roman Empire: The Costs of Decentralization

Like Spain, the Holy Roman Empire saw powerful France as its most dangerous enemy. And when the French king's invasion of Italy initiated the Italian Wars, it launched a struggle that pitted the empire and Spain against France for the next 200 years. Members of the Habsburg family had been elected to the throne of the Holy Roman Empire since 1438. Emperor Maximilian I (r. 1493–1519) wed Mary, the daughter of Charles the Bold of Burgundy, and although they were not able to preserve all of Burgundy from the French, they did keep substantial parts, including the extremely rich Netherlands.

In an era of coolly calculating monarchs, Maximilian cut an odd figure. Like his father-in-law, Charles the Bold, he loved chivalry and enjoyed nothing more than to play the role of a knight leading his men into battle. The problem was that he was not very good in that role. His military adventures led to a series of disasters, often at the hands of the rough Swiss mercenaries who were experts in using the pike (a long pole with a metal spearhead) to cut up aristocratic cavalrymen and who passionately hated everything about the autocratic Habsburgs who had once ruled their lands. Maximilian also came under the influence of Italian Renaissance culture and imagined himself another Caesar with a special mission to reconquer Italy for the Holy Roman Empire. The French invasion of Italy in 1494 drew him into the quagmire of Italian affairs as he attempted to counter French influence there. His erratic military policies, however, could not quite keep pace with these imperial ambitions.

Maximilian's inability to execute a consistent military policy in Italy was a consequence of the highly decentralized nature of the empire. Unlike the other European monarchs who inherited their thrones at the death of their predecessors, the emperor was selected by seven electors, who even after an election exercised considerable independent power. The German part of the Holy Roman Empire, home to 15 to 20 million people, was composed of some 300 sovereign and quasi-sovereign principalities and free cities (legally exempt from direct imperial rule). Besides the emperor, only a few institutions served to unify the empire. Most important was the imperial diet, an assembly that included the seven electors, other princes, and representatives of the imperial free cities. The imperial diet was established during the fifteenth century to control the relentless feuding among the German princes, but it often became instead a forum for resisting the emperor.

Maximilian's reign produced some limited reforms. These included a moratorium on feuds, a Supreme Court to impose ancient Roman law throughout the German-speaking portions of the empire, a graduated property and income tax, and eventually an imperial council to exercise executive functions in the absence of the emperor. In practice, however, these institutions worked only to the degree that the emperor and German princes cooperated. The empire remained a fractured, dissent-ridden jumble with no real unity. Compared to the centralizing monarchies in France, Spain, and England, or even to the better managed among the Italian city-states such as tiny Venice, which recurrently defeated Maximilian in battle, the empire under Maximilian was little more than a glorious-sounding name.

England: From Civil War to Stability Under the Tudors

At the end of the Hundred Years' War in 1453, the English crown was defeated. Thousands of disbanded mercenaries were let loose in England and enlisted with one quarreling side or the other in feuds among aristocratic families. The mercenaries brought to England the evil habits of pillage, murder, and violence they had previously practiced in the wars with France. King Henry VI (r. 1422–1461) suffered from bouts of madness that made him unfit to rule and unable to control the disorder. Under the tensions caused by defeat and revolt, the royal family fractured into the two houses of Lancaster and York, which fought a vicious civil war, now known as the Wars of the Roses (1455–1485) from the red and white roses used to identify members of the two opposing sides.

After decades of bloody conflict, the cynical but able Richard III (r. 1483–1485) usurped the throne from his 12-year-old nephew Edward V and had Edward and his brother imprisoned in the Tower of London, where they were murdered, perhaps on Richard's orders. Richard's apparent cruelty and his scandalous intent to marry Edward's young sister, now heir to the throne, precipitated open defections against him. When Henry Tudor challenged Richard, many nobles flocked to Henry's banner. At the Battle of Bosworth Field (1485), Richard was slain and his crown discovered on the field of battle. His naked corpse was dragged off and buried in an unmarked grave.

The Tower of London

When Henry Tudor became King Henry VII (r. 1485–1509), there was little reason to believe that exhausted England could again become a major force in European events. It took years of patient effort for Henry to become safe on his own throne. He revived the Court of Star Chamber as an instrument of royal will to punish unruly nobles who had long bribed and intimidated their way out of trouble with the courts. Because the king's own hand-picked councilors served as judges, Henry could guarantee that the court system became more equitable and obedient to his wishes. Henry confiscated the lands of the rebellious lords, thereby increasing his own income, and he prohibited all private armies except those that served his interests. By managing his administration efficiently, eliminating unnecessary expenses, and staying out of war, Henry governed without the need to call on Parliament for increased revenues.

England was still a backward country and, with fewer than three million people, a fraction of the size of France. By nourishing an alliance with newly unified Spain, Henry was able to bring England back into European affairs. When his son Henry VIII succeeded to the throne, the Tudor dynasty was more secure than any of its predecessors and England more stable than it had ever been before. By the reign of Henry VII's granddaughter, Elizabeth I (r. 1558–1603), England could boast of a splendid Renaissance court and a fleet that would make it a world power.

CHRONOLOGY	
The Early Modern European State System	
1422–1461	Reign of Charles VII of France
1455–1485	Wars of the Roses in England
1461–1483	Reign of Louis XI of France
1474–1504	Reign of Isabella of Castile
1479–1516	Reign of Ferdinand of Aragon
1479	Unification of Spain
1483–1485	Reign of Richard III of England
1485–1509	Reign of Henry VII of England
1492	Conquest of Granada; expulsion of the Jews from Spain; voyage of Christopher Columbus
1493–1519	Reign of Maximilian I, Holy Roman Emperor
1494–1530	The Italian Wars
1515–1547	Reign of Francis I of France
1516–1556	Reign of Charles I, king of Spain, who also became Charles V, Holy Roman Emperor (1519–1558)

The Origins of Modern Historical and Political Thought

The revival of the monarchies of western Europe and the loss of the independence of the Italian city-states forced a rethinking of politics. As in so many other fields, the Florentines led the way. In an attempt to understand their own troubled city-state, they analyzed politics by making historical comparisons between one kind of government and another and by carefully observing current events. Two crucial figures in these developments, Francesco Guicciardini and Niccolò Machiavelli, had both served Florence as diplomats, an experience that was crucial in forming their views.

History: The Search for Causes

During the fifteenth century there were two kinds of historians. The first kind consisted of chroniclers who kept records of the important events in their city or principality. The chroniclers recorded a great deal of factual information in the simple form of one-occurrence-after-another. In so doing they established chronologies, which meant they arranged history according to a sequence of dates. But they lacked any sense of how one event caused another, and they failed to interpret the meaning and consequences of the decisions leaders and other people had made.

The second kind of historians consisted of the humanists. Petrarch established that the fundamental principle for writing humanist history was to maintain historical distance—the sense that the past was past and had to be reconstructed in its own terms. The most dangerous historical error in writing history became anachronism, that is, imposing present sensibilities and understandings on the past. Before the Renaissance the most common version of anachronism was for historians to interpret pre-Christian history in the light of Christian understandings of God's plan for humanity. In contrast to that approach, humanist historians attempted to offer explanations for why things had happened in human terms. When they interpreted past events, they tried to respect the limitations people had faced. For example, they understood that the moral code of the Roman orator and senator Cicero, who died two generations before Jesus was born, derived from Greek philosophy and Roman ethics rather than a premonition of Christianity. The humanists' interest in rhetoric, however, led them to make moral judgments about the past in an attempt to encourage morality among their readers. Thus, they were prone to pull especially compelling instances of good or bad conduct out of the historical context in which it had taken place and to compare it with other cases. For example, they might compare the behavior of the citizens in fifth-century-B.C.E. Athens with the actions of citizens in fifteenth-century Florence.

The shock of the Italian Wars that began in 1494 stimulated a quest for understanding the causes of Italy's fall and prompted a new kind of history writing. The first person to write a successful history in the new vein was Francesco Guicciardini (1483–1540). Born to a well-placed Florentine family, educated in a humanist school, and experienced as a diplomat, governor, and adviser to the Medicis, Guicciardini combined literary skill and practical political experience. Besides collecting information about contemporary events, Guicciardini kept a record of how his own thoughts and values evolved in response to what he observed. One of the hallmarks of his work was that as he analyzed the motives of others, he engaged in self-scrutiny and self-criticism.

From this habit of criticizing himself and others, Guicciardini developed a strong interpretive framework for his histories. His masterpiece, *The History of Italy* (1536–1540), was the first account of events that occurred across the entire Italian peninsula. In many respects, this book originated the idea that Italy is more than just a geographical term and has had a common historical experience. Like the humanist historians, Guicciardini saw human causes for historical events rather than the hidden hand of God, but he refined the understanding of causation through his psychological insights. He suggested, for example, that emotions mattered more than rational calculation and noted that nothing ever turns out quite as anticipated.

Political Thought: Considering the End Result

Guicciardini's contemporary and Florentine compatriot Niccolò Machiavelli (1469–1527) also wrote histories, but he is best known as a political theorist. Trained as a humanist, he lacked the personal wealth and family connections that allowed Guicciardini to move as a matter of birthright in high social and political circles. As seen in the story that opened this chapter, Machiavelli had worked as a diplomat and military official but was exiled for complicity in a plot against the Medici family, who had retaken Florence in 1512. While in exile he wrote a book of advice

DOCUMENT

Machiavelli's *The Prince*

for the Medicis in the vain hope that they would give him back his job. They probably never read his little book, *The Prince* (1513), but it became a classic in political thought. In it he encouraged rulers to understand the underlying principles of political power, which differed from the personal morality expected of those who were not rulers. He thought it was important for a prince to appear to be a moral person, but Machiavelli pointed out that the successful prince might sometimes be obliged to be immoral in order to protect the interests of the state. How would the prince know when this might be the case?

Machiavelli's answer was that "necessity" forced political decisions to go against normal morality. The prince "must consider the end result," which meant that his highest obligation was preserving the very existence of the state, which had been entrusted to him and which provided security for all citizens of the state. This obligation was higher even than his obligation to religion.

Machiavelli's *The Prince* has sometimes been considered a blueprint for tyrants. However, as his more learned and serious work, *The Discourses of the First Decade of Livy* (1516–1519), makes clear, Machiavelli himself preferred a free republic over a despotic princely government. In some ways, *The Discourses* is an even more radical work than *The Prince* because it suggests that class conflict is the source of political liberty: "In every republic there are two different inclinations: that of the people and that of the upper class, and . . . all the laws which are made in favor of liberty are born of the conflict between the two."[8] In this passage,

Machiavelli suggested that political turmoil was not necessarily a bad thing, because it was by provoking conflict that the lower classes prevented the upper classes from acting like tyrants.

In all his works, Machiavelli sought to understand the dynamics behind political events. To do this, he theorized that human events were the product of the interaction between two forces. One force was fortune, a term derived from the name of the ancient Roman goddess Fortuna. Fortune stood for all things beyond human control and could be equated with luck or chance. Machiavelli depicted fortune as extremely powerful, like an irresistible flood that swept all before it or like the headstrong goddess who determined the fate of men. Fortune controlled perhaps half of all human events. The problem with fortune was its changeability and unpredictability: "since Fortune changes and men remain set in their ways, men will succeed when the two are in harmony and fail when they are not in accord." How could rulers or even simple citizens put themselves in harmony with fortune and predict its shifts? The answer could be found in the characteristics of the second force, virtue, which he understood as deriving from the Roman concept of *virtus,* literally "manliness." The best description of virtue could be found in the code expected of an ancient Roman warrior: strength, loyalty, and courage. If a man possessed these traits he was most likely to be able to confront the unpredictable. As Machiavelli put it, "I am certainly convinced of this: that it is better to be impetuous than cautious."[9] The man possessing virtue, therefore, looked for opportunities to take control of events before they took control of him. In that way he put himself in harmony with fortune.

Through Guicciardini's analysis of human motivations and Machiavelli's attempt to discover the hidden forces behind events, history and political thought moved in a new direction. The key to understanding history and politics was in the details of human events. To Guicciardini these details provided clues to the psychology of leaders. To Machiavelli they revealed the hidden mechanisms of chance and planning that governed not just political decisions but all human events.

Conclusion

The Politics of Culture

The Renaissance began simply enough as an attempt to imitate the Latin style of the best ancient Latin authors and orators. Within a generation, however, humanists and artists pushed this narrowly technical literary project into a full-scale attempt to refashion human society on the model of ancient cultures. Reading about the an-

cients and looking at their works of art provoked comparisons with contemporary Renaissance society. The result was the development of a critical approach to the past and present. The critical approach was accompanied by an enhanced historical sensibility, which transformed the idea of the West from one defined primarily by religious identification with Christianity to one forged by a common historical experience.

During the sixteenth century, western Europeans absorbed the critical-historical methods of the Renaissance and turned them in new directions. As shown in the next chapter, Spanish and Portuguese sailors encountered previously unknown cultures in the Americas and only vaguely known ones in Africa and Asia. Because of the Renaissance, those who thought and wrote about these strange new cultures did so with the perspective of antiquity in mind. As shown in Chapter 13, in northern Europe the critical historical methods of the humanists were used to better understand the historical sources of Christianity, especially the Bible. With that development, Christianity began to take on new shades of meaning, and many thoughtful Christians attempted to make the practices of the Church conform more closely to the Bible. The humanist approach to religion led down a path that permanently divided Christians into contending camps over the interpretation of Scripture, breaking apart the hard-won unity of the Roman Catholic West.

Suggestions for Further Reading

For a comprehensive listing of suggested readings, please go to www.ablongman.com/levack2e/chapter11

Baxandall, Michael. *Painting and Experience in Fifteenth Century Italy: A Primer in the Social History of Pictorial Style.* 1988. A fascinating study of how the daily social experiences of Florentine bankers and churchgoers influenced how these individuals saw Renaissance paintings and how painters responded to the viewers' experience. One of the best books on Italian painting.

Brown, Howard M. *Music in the Renaissance.* 1976. Dated but still the best general study of Renaissance music.

Brown, Patricia Fortini. *Art and Life in Renaissance Venice.* 1997. A delightful study about how art fit into the daily lives and homes of the Venetian upper classes.

Brucker, Gene. *Florence: The Golden Age, 1138–1737.* 1998. A brilliant, beautifully illustrated history by the most prominent American historian of Florence.

Burke, Peter. *The Italian Renaissance.* 1999. A concise and readable synthesis of the most recent research.

Hale, J. R. *Renaissance Europe, 1480–1520.* 2000. A witty, engaging, and enlightening study of Europe during the formation of the early modern state system. Strong on establishing the material and social limitations of Renaissance society.

King, Margaret L. *Women of the Renaissance.* 1991. The best general study of women in Renaissance Europe. It is especially strong on female intellectuals and women's education.

Kohl, Benjamin G., and Alison Andrews Smith, eds. *Major Problems in the History of the Italian Renaissance.* 1995. A useful collection of articles and short studies of major historical problems in the study of the Renaissance.

Martines, Lauro. *Power and Imagination: City-States in Renaissance Italy.* 1988. An excellent general survey that is strong on class conflicts and patronage.

Nauert, Charles G., Jr. *Humanism and the Culture of Renaissance Europe.* 1995. The best survey of humanism for students new to the subject. It is clear and comprehensive.

Skinner, Quentin. *Machiavelli: A Very Short Introduction.* 2000. This is the place to begin in the study of Machiavelli. Always clear and precise, this is a beautiful little book.

Stephens, John. *The Italian Renaissance: The Origins of Intellectual and Artistic Change Before the Reformation.* 1990. A stimulating analysis of how cultural change took place.

Vasari, Giorgio. *The Lives of the Artists.* 1998. Written by a sixteenth-century Florentine who was himself a prominent artist, this series of artistic biographies captures the spirit of Renaissance society.

Notes

1. *The Portable Machiavelli,* trans. and ed. Peter Bondanella and Mark Musa (1979), 67–69.

2. Baldesar Castiglione, *The Book of the Courtier,* trans. Charles S. Singleton (1959), 43.

3. Giovanni Villani, *Cronica,* vol. 7 (1823), p. 52. Translation by the authors.

4. Agostino di Colloredo, "Chroniche friulane, 1508–18," *Pagine friulane* 2 (1889), 6. Translation by the authors.

5. Francesco Petrarca, "Letter to the Shade of Cicero," in Kenneth R. Bartlett, ed., *The Civilization of the Italian Renaissance: A Sourcebook* (1992), 31.

6. Quoted in Margaret L. King, *Women of the Renaissance* (1991), 197.

7. "Laura Cereta to Bibulus Sempronius: Defense of the Liberal Instruction of Women," in Margaret King and Alfred Rabil, eds., *Her Immaculate Hand: Selected Words by and About the Women Humanists of Quattrocento Italy* (1983), 82.

8. *The Portable Machiavelli,* 183.

9. Ibid., 161–162.

Glossary

acropolis (p. 70) The defensible hilltop around which a polis grew. In classical Athens, the Acropolis was the site of the Parthenon (Temple of Athena).

Aeneid (p. 157) Written by Virgil (70–19 B.C.E.), this magnificent epic poem celebrates the emperor Augustus by linking him to his mythical ancestor, Aeneas, the Trojan refugee who founded the Roman people. Considered by many to be the greatest work of Latin literature, the poem has had enormous influence in the West.

agricultural revolution (p. 273) Refers to technological innovations that began to appear during the eleventh century, making possible a dramatic growth in population. The agricultural revolution came about through harnessing new sources of power with water and wind mills, improving the pulling power of animals with better collars, using heavy plows to better exploit the soils of northern Europe, and employing a three-field crop rotation system that increased the amount and quality of food available.

agricultural societies (p. 14) Settled communities in which people depend on farming and raising livestock as their sources of food.

Antonine Decree (p. 149) In 212 C.E. the emperor Aurelius Antoninus, called Caracalla, issued a decree that granted citizenship to all the free inhabitants of the Roman Empire. The decree enabled Roman law to embrace the entire population of the empire.

Apologists (p. 164) Christian writers in the second and third centuries C.E. who explained their religion to learned non-Christians. In the process they helped Christianity absorb much of Hellenistic culture.

Arians (p. 183) Christians who believe that God the Father is superior to Jesus Christ his Son. Most of the Germanic settlers in western Europe in the fifth century were Arians.

Asceticism (p. 183) The Christian practice of severely suppressing physical needs and daily desires in an effort to achieve a spiritual union with God. Asceticism is the practice that underlies the monastic movement.

Babylonian Captivity of the Church (p. 329) Between 1305 and 1378 seven consecutive popes voluntarily chose to reside in Avignon, France, in order to escape anarchy in the streets of Rome. During this period the popes became subservient to the kings of France.

Babylonian Exile (p. 64) The period of Jewish history between the destruction of Solomon's temple in Jerusalem by Babylonian armies in 587 B.C.E., and 538 B.C.E., when Cyrus of Persia permitted Jews to return to Palestine and rebuild the temple.

Battle of Kadesh (p. 42) The battle between Egyptian and Hittite armies in Syria in 1274 B.C.E. that set the territorial limits of both empires in Canaan and the Middle East for a century during the International Bronze Age.

bronze (p. 33) An alloy of tin and copper that produces a hard metal suitable for weapons, tools, ornaments, and household objects. Bronze production began about 3200 B.C.E.

bubonic plague (p. 310) An epidemic disease spread from rats to humans via flea bites. The infection enters the bloodstream, causing inflamed swellings called buboes (hence, "bubonic" plague) in the glands of the groin or armpit, internal bleeding, and discoloration. Although disputed by some, most experts consider bubonic plague the cause of the Black Death, which killed at least one-third of the population of Europe between 1348 and the early 1350s. Bubonic plague reappeared recurrently in the West between 1348 and 1721.

caliph (p. 226) After Muhammad's death in 632, the ruler of the Islamic state was called the caliph. The sectarian division within Islam between the Shi'ites and Sunni derived from a disagreement over how to determine the hereditary succession from Muhammad to the caliphate, which combined governmental and some religious responsibilities.

caliphate (p. 223) The Islamic imperial government that evolved under the leadership of Abu Bakr (r. 632–634), the successor of the prophet Muhammad.

canon law (p. 282) The collected laws of the Roman Catholic Church. Canon law applied to cases involving the clergy, disputes about church property, and donations to the Church. It also applied to the laity for annulling marriages, legitimating bastards, prosecuting bigamy, protecting widows and orphans, and resolving inheritance disputes.

Carolingian Renaissance (p. 250) The "rebirth" of interest in ancient Greek and Latin literature and language during the reign of the Frankish emperor Charlemagne (r. 768–814). Charlemagne promoted the intensive study of Latin to promote governmental efficiency and to propagate the Christian faith.

Chalcedonians (p. 181) Christians who follow the doctrinal decisions and definitions of the Council of Chalcedon in 451 C.E. stating that Christ's human and divine natures were equal, but entirely distinct and united in one person "without confusion, division, separation, or change." Chalcedonian Christianity came to be associated with the Byzantine Empire and is called Greek Orthodoxy. In western Europe it is known as Roman Catholicism.

circuit court (p. 296) Established by King Henry II (r. 1154–1189) to make royal justice available to virtually anyone in England. Circuit court judges visited every shire in England four times a year.

civic humanism (p. 356) A branch of humanism introduced by the Florentine chancellor Leonardo Bruni who defended the republican institutions and values of the city. Civic humanism promoted the ethic of responsible citizenship.

civilization (p. 12) The term used by archaeologists to describe a society differentiated by levels of wealth and power, and in which religious, economic, and political control are based in cities.

civitas (p. 143) The Roman term for a city. A city included the town itself, all the surrounding territory that it controlled, and all the people who lived in the town and the countryside.

clans or kin groups (p. 243) The basic social and political unit of Germanic society consisting of blood relatives obliged to defend one another and take vengeance for crimes against the group and its members.

Cluny (p. 280) A monastery founded in Burgundy in 910 that became the center of a far-reaching movement to reform the Church that was sustained in more than 1,500 Cluniac monasteries, modeled after the original in Cluny.

communes (p. 277) Sworn defensive associations of merchants and workers that appeared in north-central Italy after 1070 and that became the effective government of more than a hundred cities. The communes evolved into city-states by seizing control of the surrounding countryside.

Conciliar Movement (p. 330) A fifteenth-century movement that advocated ending the Great Schism and reforming church government by calling a general meeting or council of the bishops, who would exercise authority over the rival popes.

Corpus of Civil Law (p. 197) The body of Roman law compiled by the emperor Justinian in Constantinople in 534. The Corpus became a pillar of Latin-speaking European civilization.

counties (p. 250) Territorial units devised by the Carolingian dynasty during the eighth and ninth centuries for the administration of the empire. Each county was administered by a count who was rewarded with lands and sent to areas where he had no family ties to serve as a combined provincial governor, judge, military commander, and representative of the king.

courtly love (p. 302) An ethic first found in the poems of the late twelfth- and thirteenth-century troubadours that portrayed the ennobling possibilities of the love between a man and a woman. Courtly love formed the basis for the modern idea of romantic love.

Crusades (p. 263) Between 1095 and 1291, Latin Christians heeding the call of the pope launched eight major expeditions and many smaller ones against Muslim armies in an attempt to gain control of and hold Jerusalem.

culture (p. 12) The knowledge and adaptive behavior created by communities that helps them to mediate between themselves and the natural world through time.

cuneiform (p. 17) A kind of writing in which wedge-shaped symbols are pressed into clay tablets to indicate words and ideas. Cuneiform writing originated in ancient Sumer.

Curia (p. 283) The administrative bureaucracy of the Roman Catholic Church.

Cynics (p. 105) Cynics followed the teachings of Antisthenes (ca. 445–360 B.C.E.) by rejecting pleasures, possessions, and social conventions in order to find peace of mind.

Delian League (p. 76) The alliance among many Greek cities organized by Athens in 478 B.C.E. in order to fight Persian forces in the eastern Aegean Sea. The Athenians gradually turned the Delian League into the Athenian Empire.

democracy (p. 58) A form of government in which citizens devise their own governing institutions and choose their leaders; began in Athens, Greece, in the fifth century B.C.E.

Diaspora (p. 160) Literally "dispersion of population;" usually used to refer to the dispersion of the Jewish population after the Roman destruction of the Temple in Jerusalem in 70 C.E.

domestication (p. 13) Manipulating the breeding of animals over many generations in order to make them more useful to humans as sources of food, wool, and other byproducts. Domestication of animals began about 10,000 years ago.

Epicureans (p. 104) Followers of the teachings of the philosopher Epicurus (341–271 B.C.E.). Epicureans tried to gain peace of mind by choosing pleasures rationally.

Etruscans (p. 111) A people native to Italy, the Etruscans established a league of militaristic cities in central Italy that grew rich from war and trade. Etruscans had a great influence on the formation of the Roman state.

Eucharist (p. 289) Also known as Holy Communion or the Lord's Supper, the Eucharistic rite of the Mass celebrates Jesus' last meal with his apostles when the priest-celebrant consecrates wafers of bread and a chalice of wine as the body and blood of Christ. In the Middle Ages the wafers of bread were distributed for the congregation to eat, but drinking from the chalice was a special privilege of the priesthood. Protestants in the sixteenth century and Catholics in the late twentieth century began to allow the laity to drink from the chalice.

excommunication (p. 282) A decree by the pope or a bishop prohibiting a sinner from participating in the sacraments of the Church and forbidding any social contact whatsoever with the surrounding community.

Fertile Crescent (p. 14) Also known as the Levantine Corridor, this twenty-five mile wide arc of land stretching from the Jordan River to the Euphrates River was the place where food production and settled communities first appeared in Southwest Asia (the Middle East).

feudalism (p. 255) A term historians use to describe a social system common during the Middle Ages in which lords granted fiefs (tracts of land or some other form of income) to dependents, known as vassals, who owed their lords personal services in exchange. Feudalism refers to a society governed through personal ties of dependency rather than public political institutions.

fief (p. 255) During the Middle Ages a fief was a grant of land or some other form of income that a lord gave to a vassal in exchange for loyalty and certain services (usually military assistance).

First Triumvirate (p. 125) The informal political alliance made by Julius Caesar, Pompey, and Crassus in 60 B.C.E. to share power in the Roman Republic. It led directly to the collapse of the Republic.

Forms (p. 85) In the philosophical teachings of Plato, these are eternal, unchanging absolutes such as Truth, Justice, and Beauty that represent true reality, as opposed to the approximations of reality that humans encounter in everyday life.

Forum (p. 111) The political and religious center of the city of Rome throughout antiquity. All cities in the empire had a forum in imitation of the capital city.

Gothic (p. 303) A style in architecture in western Europe from the late twelfth and thirteenth centuries, characterized by ribbed vaults and pointed arches, which drew the eyes of worshipers upward toward God. Flying buttresses, which redistributed the weight of the roof, made possible thin walls pierced by large expanses of stained glass.

grand jury (p. 296) In medieval England after the judicial reforms of King Henry II (r. 1154–1189), grand juries were called when the circuit court judge arrived in a shire. The sheriff assembled a group of men familiar with local affairs who constituted the grand jury and who reported to the judge the major crimes that had been committed since the judge's last visit.

Great Persecution (p. 174) An attack on Christians in the Roman empire begun by the emperor Galerius in 303 C.E. on the grounds that their worship was endangering the empire. Several thousand Christians were executed.

Great Schism (p. 329) The division of the Catholic Church (1378–1417) between rival Italian and French claimants to the papal throne.

guilds (p. 319) Professional associations devoted to protecting the special interests of a particular trade or craft and to monopolizing production and trade in the goods the guild produced.

Hallstatt (p. 109) The first Celtic civilization in central Europe is called Halstatt. From about 750 to about 450 B.C.E., Hallstatt Celts spread throughout Europe.

helots (p. 73) The brutally oppressed subject peoples of the Spartans. Tied to the land they farmed for Spartan masters, they were treated little better than beasts of burden.

heresies (p. 181) Forms of Christian belief that are not considered Orthodox.

hetairai (p. 80) Elite courtesans in ancient Greece who provided intellectual as well as sexual companionship.

Homo sapiens sapiens (p. 13) Scientific term meaning "most intelligent people" applied to physically and intellectually modern human beings that first appeared between 200,000 and 100,000 years ago in Africa.

hoplites (p. 72) Greek soldiers in the Archaic Age who could afford their own weapons. Hoplite tactics made soldiers fighting as a group dependent on one another. This contributed to the internal cohesion of the polis and eventually to the rise of democracy.

humanists (p. 365) During the Renaissance humanists were writers and orators who studied Latin and sometimes Greek texts on grammar, rhetoric, poetry, history, and ethics.

Hundred Years' War (p. 321) Refers to a series of engagements (1337–1453) between England and France over England's attempts to assert its claims to territories in France.

Iconoclasm (p. 216) The destruction of religious images in the Byzantine empire in the eighth century.

icons (p. 215) The Christian images of God and saints found in Byzantine art.

indulgences (p. 329) Certificates that allowed penitents to atone for their sins and reduce their time in purgatory. Usually these were issued for going on a pilgrimage or performing a pious act, but during the Babylonian Captivity of the Church (1305–1378) popes began to sell them, a practice Martin Luther protested in 1517 in an act that brought on the Protestant Reformation.

interdict (p. 283) A papal decree prohibiting the celebration of the sacraments in an entire city or kingdom.

Investiture Controversy (p. 282) A dispute that began in 1076 between the popes and the German emperors over the right to invest bishops with their offices. The most famous episode was the conflict between Pope Gregory VII and Emperor Henry IV. The controversy was resolved by the Concordat of Worms in 1122.

knight (p. 255) During the Middle Ages a knight was a soldier who fought on horseback. A knight was a vassal or dependent of a lord, who usually financed the knight's expenses of armor and weapons and of raising and feeding horses with a grant of land known as a fief.

Koine (p. 101) The standard version of the Greek language spoken throughout the Hellenistic world.

La Tène (p. 109) A phase of Celtic civilization that lasted from about 450 to 200 B.C.E. La Tène culture became strong especially in the regions of the Rhine and Danube Rivers.

lapis lazuli (p. 45) A precious, deep-blue gemstone found in the Middle East that was traded widely for jewelry during the International Bronze Age.

latifundia (p. 155) These huge agricultural estates owned by wealthy Romans, including the emperor, often used large slave-gangs as labor.

Latin Christendom (pp. 181, 238) The parts of medieval Europe, including all of western Europe, united by Christianity and the use of Latin in worship and intellectual life. Latin served as an international language among the ruling elites in western Europe, even though they spoke different languages in their daily lives.

lay investiture (p. 281) The practice of nobles, kings, or emperors installing churchmen and giving them the symbols of office.

Levantine Corridor (p. 14) Also known as the Fertile Crescent, this twenty-five mile wide arc of land stretching from the Jordan River to the Euphrates River was the place where food production and settled communities first appeared in Southwest Asia (the Middle East).

linear perspective (p. 361) In the arts the use of geometrical principles to depict a three-dimensional space on a flat, two-dimensional surface.

liturgy (p. 238) The forms of Christian worship, including the prayers, chants, and rituals to be said, sung, or performed throughout the year.

lord (p. 255) During the Middle Ages a lord was someone who offered protection to dependents, known as vassals, who took an oath of loyalty to him. Most lords demanded military services from their vassals and sometimes granted them tracts of land known as fiefs.

Macedonian Renaissance (p. 217) During the Macedonian dynasty's rule of Byzantium (867–1056), aristocratic families, the Church, and monasteries devoted their immense riches to embellishing Constantinople with new buildings, mosaics, and icons. The emperors sponsored historical, philosophical, and religious writing.

Magna Carta (p. 296) In 1215 some English barons forced King John to sign the "great charter," in which the king pledged to respect the traditional feudal privileges of the nobility, towns, and clergy. Subsequent kings swore to uphold it, thereby accepting the fundamental principle that even the king was obliged to respect the law.

marches (p. 250) Territorial units of the Carolingian empire for the administration of frontier regions. Each march was ruled by a margrave who had special powers necessary to defend vulnerable borders.

mendicant friars (p. 288) Members of a religious order, such as the Dominicans or Franciscans, who wandered from city to city and throughout the countryside begging for alms rather than residing in a monastery. Mendicant friars tended to help ordinary laypeople by preaching and administering to the sick and poor.

Mishnah (p. 186) The final organization and transcription of Jewish oral law, completed by the end of the third century C.E.

Modern Devotion (p. 331) A fifteenth-century religious movement that stressed individual piety, ethical behavior, and intense religious education. The Modern Devotion was promoted by the Brothers of the Common Life, a religious order whose influence was broadly felt through its extensive network of schools.

monastic movement (p. 183) In Late Antiquity, Christian ascetics organized communities where men and women could pursue a life of spirituality through work, prayer, and asceticism. Called the monastic movement, this spiritual quest spread quickly throughout Christian lands.

Monophysites (p. 181) Christians who do not accept the Council of Chalcedon (see Chalcedonians). Monophysites believe that Jesus Christ has only one nature, equally divine and human.

monotheism (p. 39) The belief in only one god, first attributed to the ancient Hebrews. Monotheism is the foundation of Judaism, Christianity, Islam, and Zoroastrianism.

mosque (p. 222) A place of Muslim worship.

Neoplatonism (p. 189) A philosophy based on the teachings of Plato and his successors that flourished in Late Antiquity, especially in the teachings of Plotinus. Neoplatonism influenced Christianity in Late Antiquity. During the Renaissance Neoplatonism was linked to the belief that the natural world was charged with occult forces that could be used in the practice of magic.

oligarchy (p. 78) A government consisting of only a few people rather than the entire community.

opera (p. 366) A musical form invented in the final decades of the sixteenth century by a group of humanist-musicians who thought the power of ancient Greek music could be recovered by writing continuous music to accompany a full drama. The drama was performed as a kind of speech-song with the range of pitch and rhythms closely following those of natural speech.

orthodox (p. 181) In Christianity, the term indicates doctrinally correct belief. Definitions of Orthodoxy changed numerous times.

ostracism (p. 77) Developed in democratic Athens, this practice enabled citizens in the assembly to vote to expel any Athenian citizen from the city for ten years for any reason.

Ottonian Renaissance (p. 260) Under the patronage of the Saxon Emperor Otto I (936–973) and his brother Bruno, learned monks, Greek philosophers from Byzantium, and Italian scholars gathered at the imperial court, stimulating a cultural revival in literature and the arts. The writers and artists enhanced the reputation of Otto.

paganism (p. 178) The Christian term for polytheist worship (worshiping more than one god). In the course of Late Antiquity, the Christian church suppressed paganism, the traditional religions of the Roman empire.

palimpsests (p. 246) Because parchment sheets used for copying were expensive, monks often scrubbed off an old text and copied another in its place. These reused sheets of parchment often contain layers of valuable texts that can be retrieved by scientists.

panhellenic (p. 72) This word means covering all Greek communities. It applies, for example, to the Olympic Games, in which competitors came from all over the Greek world.

papacy (p. 177) The bishop of the city of Rome is called the Pope, or Father. The papacy refers to the administrative and political institutions controlled by the Pope. The papacy began to gain strength in the sixth century in the absence of Roman imperial government in Italy.

pastoralist societies (p. 14) Nomadic communities that move from place to place to find pastures for their herds of domesticated animals.

patricians (p. 113) In ancient Rome, patricians were aristocratic clans with the highest status and the most political influence.

patrons and clients (p. 119) In ancient Roman society, a powerful man (the patron) would exercise influence on behalf of a social subordinate (the client) in anticipation of future support or assistance.

Pax Romana (p. 132) Latin for "Roman Peace", this term refers to the Roman Empire established by Augustus that lasted until the early third century C.E.

personal rule (p. 500) The period from 1629 to 1640 in England when King Charles I ruled without Parliament.

phalanx (p. 72) The military formation favored by hoplite soldiers. Standing shoulder to shoulder in ranks often eight men deep, hoplites moved in unison and depended on one another for protection.

philology (p. 355) A method reintroduced by the humanists during the Italian Renaissance devoted to the comparative study of language, especially to understanding the meaning of a word in a particular historical context.

pilgrimage (p. 186) Religious journeys made to holy sites in order to encounter relics.

Pillars of Islam (p. 222) The five basic principles of Islam as taught by Muhammad.

plainchant (p. 304) A medieval form of singing based on a straightforward melody sung with simple harmony by a choir to accompany the recitation of the text of the liturgy.

plebeians (p. 113) The poorest Roman citizens.

polis (p. 70) Or city-state, developed by Greeks in the Archaic Age. A polis was a self-governing community consisting of a defensible hilltop, the town itself, and all the surrounding fields farmed by the citizens of the polis. Poleis (plural) shared similar institutions: an assembly place for men to gather and discuss community affairs, a council of elders, and an open agora, which served as a market and a place for informal discussions.

polyphony (p. 304) A form for singing the Christian liturgy developed around 1170 in which two or more independent melodies were sung at the same time.

polytheistic (p. 21) Refers to polytheism, the belief in many gods.

Raiders of the Land and Sea (p. 49) The name given by Egyptians to the diverse groups of peoples whose combined naval and land forces destroyed many cities and kingdoms in the eastern Mediterranean and Anatolia, thereby bringing the International Bronze Age to an end.

relics (p. 186) In Christian belief, relics are sacred objects that have miraculous powers. They are associated with saints, biblical figures, or some object associated with them. They served as contacts between Earth and Heaven and were verified by miracles.

Renaissance (p. 344) A term meaning "rebirth" used by historians to describe a movement that sought to imitate and understand the culture of antiquity. The Renaissance generally refers to a movement that began in Italy and then spread throughout Europe from about 1350 to 1550.

republicanism (p. 345) A political theory first developed by the ancient Greeks, especially the philosopher Plato, but elaborated by the ancient Romans and rediscovered during the Italian Renaissance. The fundamental principle of republicanism as developed during the Italian Renaissance was that government officials should be elected by the people or a portion of the people.

rhetoric (p. 356) The art of persuasive or emotive speaking and writing, which was especially valued by the Renaissance humanists.

Roman Republic (p. 110) The name given to the Roman state from about 500 B.C.E., when the last king of Rome was expelled, to 31 B.C.E., when Augustus established the Roman Empire. The Roman Republic was a militaristic oligarchy.

Romanesque (p. 302) A style in architecture that spread throughout western Europe during the eleventh and the first half of the twelfth centuries and characterized by arched stone roofs supported by rounded arches, massive stone pillars, and thick walls.

romanization (p. 149) The process by which conquered peoples absorbed aspects of Roman culture, especially the Latin language, city-life, and religion.

scholasticism (p. 299) A term referring to a broad philosophical and theological movement that dominated medieval thought and university training. Scholasticism used logic learned from Aristotle to interpret the meaning of the Bible and the writings of the Church Fathers, who created Christian theology in its first centuries.

scriptorium (p. 246) The room in a monastery where monks copied books and manuscripts.

Second Triumvirate (p. 126) In 43 B.C.E. Octavian (later called Augustus), Mark Antony, and Lepidus made an informal alliance to share power in Rome while they jockeyed for control. Octavian emerged as the sole ruler of Rome in 31 B.C.E.

Septuagint (p. 103) The Greek translation of the Hebrew Bible (Old Testament).

serfs (p. 275) During the Middle Ages serfs were agricultural laborers who worked and lived on a plot of land granted them by a lord to whom they owed a certain portion of their crops. They could not leave the land, but they had certain legal rights that were denied to slaves.

simony (p. 281) The practice of buying and selling church offices.

Sophists (p. 85) Professional educators who traveled throughout the ancient Greek world, teaching many subjects. Their goal was to teach people the best ways to lead better lives.

Spanish Reconquest (p. 233) Refers to the numerous military campaigns by the Christian kingdoms of northern Spain to capture the Muslim-controlled cities and kingdoms of southern Spain. This long, intermittent struggle began with the capture of Toledo in 1085 and lasted until Granada fell to Christian armies in 1492.

Stoicism (p. 104) The philosophy developed by Zeno of Citium (ca. 335–ca. 263 B.C.E.) that urged acceptance of fate while participating fully in everyday life.

Struggle of the Orders (p. 113) The political strife between patrician and plebeian Romans beginning in the fifth century B.C.E. The plebeians gradually won political rights and influence as a result of the struggle.

Syncretism (p. 158) The practice of equating two gods and fusing their cults was common throughout the Roman Empire and helped to unify the diverse peoples and religions under Roman rule.

Talmuds (p. 186) Commentaries on Jewish law. Rabbis completed the Babylonian Talmud and the Jerusalem Talmud by the end of the fifth century C.E.

Tetrarchy (p. 172) The government by four rulers established by the Roman emperor Diocletian in 293 C.E. that lasted until 312. During the Tetrarchy many administrative and military reforms altered the fabric of Roman society.

Thomism (p. 301) A branch of medieval philosophy associated with the work of the Dominican thinker, Thomas Aquinas (1225–1274), who wrote encyclopedic summaries of human knowledge that confirmed Christian faith.

transubstantiation (p. 289) A doctrine promulgated at the Fourth Lateran Council in 1215 that explained by distinguishing between the outward appearances and the inner substance how the Eucharistic bread and wine changed into the body and blood of Christ.

trial by jury (p. 296) When disputes about the possession of land arose after the late twelfth century in England, sheriffs assembled a group of twelve local men who testified under oath about the claims of the plaintiffs, and the circuit court judge made his decision on the basis of their testimony. The system was later extended to criminal cases.

triremes (p. 75) Greek warships with three banks of oars. Triremes manned by the poorest people of Athenian society became the backbone of the Athenian empire.

troubadours (p. 302) Poets from the late twelfth and thirteenth centuries who wrote love poems, meant to be sung to music, which reflected a new sensibility, called courtly love, about the ennobling possibilities of the love between a man and a woman.

Twelfth-Century Renaissance (p. 300) An intellectual revival of interest in ancient Greek philosophy and science and in Roman law in western Europe during the twelfth and early thirteenth centuries. The term also refers to a flowering of vernacular literature and the Romanesque and Gothic styles in architecture.

tyrants (p. 72) Political leaders from the upper classes who championed the cause of hoplites in Greek city-states during the Archaic Age. The word "tyrant" gained its negative connotation when democracies developed in Greece that gave more political voice to male citizens than permitted by tyrants.

vassals (p. 255) During the Middle Ages men voluntarily submitted themselves to a lord by taking an oath of loyalty. Vassals owed the lord certain services—usually military assistance—and sometimes received in exchange a grant of land known as a fief.

wergild (p. 243) In Germanic societies the term referred to what an individual was worth in case he or she suffered an injury. It was the amount of compensation in gold that the wrongdoer's family had to pay to the victim's family.

Zoroastrianism (p. 59) The monotheistic religion of Persia founded by Zoroaster that became the official religion of the Persian Empire.

Credits

Unless otherwise acknowledged, all photographs are the property of Pearson Education, Inc.
Page abbreviations are as follows: (T) Top, (B) Bottom, (L) Left, (R) Right, (C) Center.

What Is the West?
2 Canali Photobank **4** European Space Agency/Photo Researchers, Inc. **5** Courtesy of Adler Planetarium & Astronomy Museum, Chicago, Illinois (W-264). **8** American Museum of Natural History Library (AMNH#314372)

Chapter 1
10 Giraudon/Art Resource, NY **12** Augustin Ochsenreiter/South Tyrol Museum of Archaeology **17** Courtesy of the Trustees of the British Museum **19** Robert Harding Picture Library **21** Scala/Art Resource, NY **23** Erich Lessing/Art Resource, NY **29** Roger Ressmeyer/Corbis

Chapter 2
33 The Art Archive/National Archaeological Museum Athens/Dagli Ort **36** Dagli Orti/The Art Archive **38** The Art Archive/Egyptian Museum Cairo/Dagli Orti (A) **39** Osiride Head of Hatshepsut, originally from a statue. Provenance: Thebes, Deir el Bahri. Limestone, painted. H. 64 cm. H. with crown 124.5 cm. The Metropolitan Museum of Art, Rogers Fund, 1931, (31.3.157) Photograph © 1983 The Metropolitan Museum of Art **41** British Museum, London/Bridgeman Art Library **44** Nimatallah/Art Resource, NY **48** Hirmer Fotoarchiv **53** Erich Lessing/Art Resource, NY

Chapter 3
56 Erich Lessing/Art Resource, NY **61** SEF/Art Resource, NY **66** Israel Museum **71 (BR)** The American Numismatic Society **71 (BL)** The American Numismatic Society **71 (TR)** The American Numismatic Society **71 (TL)** The American Numismatic Society **75** Erich Lessing/Art Resource, NY **79 (T)** Foto Marburg/Art Resource, NY **79 (BR)** Pedicini/Index s.a.s. **79 (BL)** Louvre, Paris, France/Bridgeman Art Library **80** Staatliche Antikensammlungen und Glyptothek, Munich **81** Robert Harding Picture Library **84** Column krater (missing bowl) (detail), Greek, Archaic Period (Late Corinthian), about 550 B.C., Place of manufacture: Greece, Corinthia, Corinth, Ceramic, Black Figure, Height 33 cm (13 in); diameter: 41cm ($16\frac{1}{8}$ in.), Museum of Fine Arts, Boston, Helen and Alice Colburn Fund (63.420) Photograph © 2003 Museum of Fine Arts, Boston **85** British Museum, London, Great Britain/HIP/Art Resource, NY **87** Scala/Art Resource, NY **88** Scala/Art Resource, NY

Chapter 4
92 Scala/Art Resource, NY **96** Bildarchiv Prüßischer Kulturbesitz/Art Resource, NY **100** Réunion des Musées Nationaux/Art Resource, NY **101** Bildarchiv Prüßischer Kulturbesitz/Art Resource, NY **102** Réunion des Musées Nationaux/Art Resource, NY **105** Erich Lessing/Art Resource, NY **110 (T)** Erich Lessing/Art Resource, NY **110 (B)** Bildarchiv Prüßischer Kulturbesitz/Art Resource, NY **112** Robert Harding Picture Library **119** Vanni/Art Resource, NY **121** Alinari/Art Resource, NY

Chapter 5
130 Erich Lessing/Art Resource, NY **134** Erich Lessing/Art Resource, NY **137** SEF/Art Resource, NY **139** Leo C. Curran **141** Erich Lessing/Art Resource, NY **144** Yann Arthus-Bertrand/Corbis **148** Vasari/Index s.a.s. **150** Robert Harding Picture Library **152** akg-images **156** Scala/Art Resource, NY **159** Scala/Art Resource, NY **160** Scala/Art Resource, NY **161** Jewish Museum, London **162** Courtesy of the Trustees of the British Museum

Chapter 6
168 Österreichische Nationalbibliothek, Vienna **170** Scala/Art Resource, NY **171** SEF/Art Resource, NY **172** Erich Lessing/Art Resource, NY **177** Scala/Art Resource, NY **179** Victoria & Albert Museum, London/Art Resource, NY **182** Réunion des Musées Nationaux/Art Resource, NY **186** The Jewish Museum, New York, NY/Art Resource, NY **191** Alinari/Art Resource, NY **197** Réunion des Musées Nationaux/Art Resource, NY **199** Scala/Art Resource, NY **202 (T)** Courtesy of the Trustees of the British Museum **202 (B)** Courtesy of the Trustees of the British Museum

Chapter 7
204 Erich Lessing/Art Resource, NY **209 (T)** Balatoni Museum, Keszthely, Hungary **209 (B)** Balatoni Museum, Keszthely, Hungary **213** David and Goliath, Byzantine, Made in Constantinople, 629–630; Early Byzantine, Silver, D. $1\frac{1}{2}$ in. (3.8 cm); Diam. $19\frac{1}{2}$ in (49.4 cm); The Metropolitan Museum of Art, Gift of J. Pierpont Morgan, 1917 (17.190.396) Photograph © 2000 The Metropolitan Museum of Art **215** British Museum/The Art Archive **216** State Historical Museum, Moscow **217** Courtesy of His Eminence Archbishop Damianos and the Holy Council of the Fathers, Saint Catherine's Monastery. Photograph © Idryma Orous Sina, Mt. Sinai Foundation **218** Pushkin Museum, Moscow, Russia/Bridgeman Art Library **220** Werner Forman/Art Resource, NY **223** Associate Press/AP **225** Freer Gallery of Art, Smithsonian Institution, Washington, D.C.: Purchase, F1930.60a **228** Robert Harding Picture Library **230 (TR)** The Nasser D. Khalili Collection of Islamic Art **230 (TL)** The Nasser D. Khalili Collection of Islamic Art **230 (BR)** Bibliothèque Nationale de France (2001 A 83708) **230 (BL)** Bibliothèque Nationale de France (2001 A 83707) **233** Vanni/Art Resource, NY

Chapter 8
236 Art Resource, NY **251** Vanni/Art Resource, NY **252** Eric Lessing/Art Resource, NY **254** Werner Forman/Art Resource, NY **255** Werner Forman/Art Resource, NY **257** Scala/Art Resource, NY **259** akg-images **261** Werner Forman/Art Resource, NY **264** HIP/Scala/Art Resource, NY **265** Dagli Orti/The Art Archive **266** Bildarchiv Preussischer Kulturbesitz/Art Resource, NY **274** Réunion des Musées Nationaux/Art Resource, NY

Index

Aachen: school at, 251; Palatine Chapel in, 251 (illus.)

Abbasid caliphate, 231

Abbey Church (St. Denis), 303, 304 (illus.)

Abd al-Malik (caliph), 230 (illus.)

Abd al-Rahman III (caliph), 232

Abelard, Peter, 299, 300

Abraham (biblical), 62; Muslims and, 222

Abu Bakr (Muhammad's father-in-law), 223–226; *Rules of War,* 227

Abu Hamid Al Ghazali (Muslim scholar), 265

Abu Hureyra, Syria (settlement), 14

Accomplishments of Augustus, The (Augustus), 135

Achaemenid dynasty, 61–62

Achilles (Greek hero), 70

Acre, Syria, 229

Acropolis (hilltop), 70; in Athens, 81 (illus.)

Actium, Battle of, 127

A.D.: dating with, 178

Adam and Eve (Bible), 184. *See also* Eve (Bible)

Adaptation: tools for, 13

Administration: of Egypt, 21; of Hittite Empire, 42; of Babylonia, 43; of Minoan Crete, 44–45; Mycenaean, 45; of Neo-Assyrian Empire, 51–52; Roman, 126, 139–140, 142, 145, 175, 242–243; of Christian Church, 176; by Theodoric, 196; Byzantine, 213–214; of Islamic Empire, 227; Carolingian, 250. *See also* Government(s)

Adoption of successors, 134

Adrianople, Battle of, 191

Aedui (Celtic tribe), 117

Aegean region: Troy and, 47–48; Greek colonization in, 70

Aeneid (Virgil), 150, 157

Aequitas (goddess), 162 (illus.)

Aeschylus, 82–83

Afghanistan: Medes in, 58; Bactria in, 99

Africa: Brazilian culture and, 4; Western values and, 5; Egypt and, 26, 37–38; Greek trade with, 107; Roman provinces of, 117; Roman exploration of, 153; Black Death and, 311. *See also* North Africa

Afterlife: in Zoroastrianism, 60

Agamemnon (Mycenae), 48 (illus.); in *Oresteia,* 83

"Age of Pericles," 76–77

Agincourt, battle at, 323–324

Agricola (Gnaeus Julius Agricola, Rome), 142, 142 (illus.), 157

Agricultural revolution: in Middle Ages, 273–277

Agriculture: development of, 13–15; in Abu Hureyra, 14; in Ur, 18; in Roman Empire, 146 (map), 155; medieval, 273–277; famines and, 307, 308; Hundred Years' War and, 325

Ahmot I (Egypt), 35

Ahura Mazda (god), 60, 61, 108

Airplane: Leonardo's invention of, 364 (illus.)

Aistulf (Lombards), 242

Akhenaten (Egypt), 39, 46

Akkad and Akkadians, 17–18, 18 (map)

Akkadian language, 38, 42

Akroinon, Battle of, 212

Al-Aksa mosque (Jerusalem), 267

Alan people, 192

Alaric (Visigoths), 169, 191–192

Alaric II (Visigoths), 241

Albania: Muslims in, 318

Alberti, Leon Battista, 351, 357, 363 (illus.)

Albert the Bear (Germany), 276

Albigensian Crusade, 290, 292

Alboin (Lombards), 242

Alcibiades (Athens), 77

Alcuin of York, 250, 251

Alemanni: Clovis' control of, 241

Alexander VI (Pope), 350–351

Alexander the Great (Macedon), 94, 96 (illus.); cultural areas before, 95 (map); at Chaeronea, 96; conquests by, 96–98; kingdoms after, 98–100, 99 (map)

Alexandria, Egypt, 100, 214; education for women in, 103; Jews in, 108; as Christian center, 177; destruction of temple, 179; Muslims in, 227; Arab shipping in, 229

Alexandrianism, 104

Alexius Comnenus (Byzantine emperor), 263

Alfonso VI (Castile), 233, 234

Alfred the Great (Wessex), 260

Ali (caliph), 224–226

Ali (Muhammad's son-in-law), 226

Allah, 222

Alliances: Athenian, 76; Roman, 114

Allies: Roman, 122, 124–125

Alluy, Jean d', 332 (illus.)

Almagest (Ptolemy), 158

Almoravids: in Spain, 233–234

Alms, 288

Alpaix (Saint), 275–276

Alphabet: Ugaritic, 47; Phoenician, 51, 68, 69; in Greece, 68–69

Altar of Victory (Rome), 178, 179

Althing (Icelandic parliament), 255

Amarna Period: in Egypt, 39

Amazons, 79 (illus.)

Ambassadors: state system and, 367

Ambrose (bishop of Milan), 185

Amenemhet I (Egypt), 25

Amenhotep III (Egypt). *See* Akhenaten (Egypt)

America(s): in West, 5; pre-European culture of, 7–8; Vikings in, 255

Amorites, 19

Amos (Hebrew prophet), 64

Amphitheaters, 144, 144 (illus.)

Amun: temple of (Karnak), 35

Amun-Re (god), 38

Anarchy: in Akkad, 18; in Middle Ages, 238

Anatolia (Turkey), 212; food production in, 14–15; Assyrians in, 20 (map); International Bronze Age and, 34; Egypt and, 37; Hittite Empire in, 42–43; in Byzantine Empire, 208 (map); Ottomans in, 315, 316 (map). *See also* Turkey

Anatomy, 106; Vesalius and, 358; Renaissance art and, 359

Anaximander, 83

Anaximenes of Miletus, 83–84

Angelico, Fra (Guido di Pietro), 354 (illus.)

Angles (Germanic tribe): language of, 196

Anglo-Saxon Chronicle, 260

Anglo-Saxons: in Britain, 237–238; in England, 239, 240, 260; conversion to Christianity, 245–246

Angra Mainyu (god), 60, 61, 108

Anguissola, Sofonisba, 365

Animals: domestication of, 13–14; agriculture and, 274

Anselm of Canterbury, 299

Anthropology: "culture" defined by, 12

Anti-Chalcedonian (Monophysite) Christians, 181, 197, 229

Antichrist: Eusebius on, 188

Antigone (Sophocles), 83

Antigonid kings, 98, 99, 100

Antioch, Syria, 175, 214; Christianity in, 164, 177; temples of, 179; sack of, 201; Persia and, 211; Muslims in, 227

Antiochus III (Syria), 117–118

Antiochus IV Epiphanes: Jews and, 108

Antipopes, 329

Antiquity: Renaissance arts and, 359–366

Antisthenes, 105

Antonine age (Rome), 134

Antonine Decree, 149

Antoninus Pius (Rome), 134, 148

Contemporary Political Map of the World